MW01274200

"A most valuable guide to a very important subject. This book is both a fascination to read and invaluable as a work of reference."

Rupert Sheldrake, Ph.D.
author of *A New Science of Life*

"Dr. Benor's manuscript goes well beyond anything that I have seen in documenting the abundance of work in the psychic-healing field. I am personally delighted to have had an opportunity to review the manuscript prior to publication. Work such as this needs wide dissemination."

C. Norman Shealy, M.D. Ph.D.
founding president, *American Holistic Medical Association*

"I find the book to be an excellent resource on research in healing. Some of the studies quoted in his book I can find nowhere else. I refer to this book often. It is well-written and contains much valuable information."

Richard Gerber, M.D.
author of *Vibrational Medicine*

". . .truly a remarkable effort. This book makes available the literature not only on healing but also on other diagnostic and therapeutic modalities. By adopting an energy paradigm, Dr. Benor brings a coherence to what would otherwise be a confusing picture."

Bernard Grad, Ph.D.
a pioneer in healing research

"Spiritual Healing is a comprehensive overview of scientific investigations on spiritual healing. In this volume, Dr. Benor has assembled data from all over the world. His explanatory theories provide a solid base for badly needed research on these controversial phenomena. The material is clearly presented, masterfully organized and discussed in a manner that is fascinating without being sensationalized. "

Stanley Krippner, Ph.D.
authority on Shamanism

SPIRITUAL HEALING

SCIENTIFIC VALIDATION
OF A
HEALING REVOLUTION

by

DANIEL J. BENOR, M.D.

Library of Congress Card Number: 00-109788

ISBN 10 = 0-9754248-5-8
ISBN 13 = 978-0-9754248-5-8

Second Edition
Wholistic Healing Publications
PO Box 76
Bellmawr, NJ 08099

Printed in the United States of America

First Edition
Vision Publications
Southfield, MI

Parts of this book appeared in an earlier version as
Healing Research, Holistic Energy Medicine and Spirituality,
© 1992 by Helix Editions Ltd.

CONTENTS

FOREWORD

Predicting the future is generally a hazardous thing to do. We can make one prediction, however, with 100 percent certainty: Modern medicine will change dramatically in the future. Throughout history, medical theory and practice have been extraordinarily dynamic: change has been the rule.

What will "future medicine" look like? It is certain to retain its technological face. There will be further developments in immunology, genetic manipulation, and transplant science. New fields such as psycho-neuroimmunology will continue to evolve. Entirely new breakthroughs in high-tech medicine will also emerge, probably on fronts we cannot now imagine. But perhaps the most important area in which radical change will occur is our understanding of the nature of consciousness and its role in healing.

Many in the field of so-called holistic or complementary, alternative medicine believe that future developments in using "the power of consciousness" will be limited to the intrapersonal area—the purposeful use by an individual of his or her thoughts to bring about healthful effects in his or her body. There is a wealth of clinical data supporting this possibility. For example, by using mental techniques in conjunction with diet and exercise, coronary artery disease has been reversed. People who had been so severely disabled by heart disease that they were scheduled for cardiac surgery have been able to alter their own bodies to the point that they are able to exercise normally. Group dynamic therapy, in which feelings are allowed to surface freely and are then explored, has been shown to correlate with a doubling of survival time following the diagnosis of metastatic breast cancer, when used in conjunction with standard forms of therapy.

These developments, as marvelous as they are, are the tip of the iceberg of the power of consciousness to intervene in illness. We face abundant evidence that an individual's mind can affect not just his or her own body, but may affect the body of a another person, sometimes at a great distance. Much of this evidence is reviewed in Volume I of *Healing Research*. This evidence is crucial in formulating a comprehensive image of the mind, and is extended in Volumes II, III, and IV.

Healing Research asks the reader to set aside all preconceived ideas of how the mind ought to work. It asks us to venture to the frontiers of science—to go through the emerging data about the nature of consciousness, not around it.

Today, most scientists equate the mind with the chemistry and anatomy of the brain. There are, however, serious reasons to question this belief. There is compelling evidence that there is some aspect of the mind that cannot be confined to points in space, such as brains or bodies, or to points in time, such as the present moment. Such an aspect of the mind is said to be nonlocal.

The spiritual implications of a nonlocal view of the mind are rich indeed. Nonlocality, as currently conceived within science, implies infinitude in space and time (a limited nonlocality is a contradiction in terms). If something of the mind is nonlocal, therefore, it is omnipresent, eternal, and immortal. If some aspect of consciousness is nonlocal, it cannot be confined to individual brains and bodies and walled off from all other minds. At some level, nonlocal minds must merge, leading to the ancient idea of the Universal or One Mind. Then there are implications of a nonlocal mind for the concept of our relationship to the Absolute (God, Goddess, the Divine and so forth). In the West, we have traditionally assigned certain qualities to the Absolute—omnipresence, immortality, infinitude in space and time. These are precisely the qualities suggested by the empirical evidence for a nonlocal aspect of consciousness. This implies shared characteristics between human beings and the Absolute—the idea of 'the Divine within,' which has occupied a high place in so many of the world's great religious traditions.

Nonlocality of consciousness permits phenomena such as intuitive diagnosis and healing at a distance, amply evidenced in the anecdotes and research reviewed in this volume; biological energy medicine, reviewed in Volume II; and reincarnation, apparitions, out-of-body experiences, and the like, reviewed in Volume III—although it cannot confirm them. One cannot defend such robust claims in a foreword. This has been done elsewhere, and that is one of the tasks of *Healing Research*. A familiarity with the possibility of nonlocal mind allows the discussions in these volumes to feel less strange, and makes it possible for us to be more open to the evidence.

As we enter a new millennium, we are in the process of re-evaluating our fundamental ideas of the nature of human consciousness—its space/time/energy characteristics, how it manifests in the world, and its relationship to the brain and body. Current theory is being expanded so drastically that in the future it will hardly be recognizable, except by persons with a knowledge of the history of these ideas. Oddly—or perhaps predictably—the picture of consciousness coming into view within science resembles many ancient ideas of the mind: mind as infinite, mind as creative and generative, mind as a unity, mind as divine.

Because these ideas are ancient, there is a temptation to think that the emerging evidence of the mind's nonlocal nature is somehow old-fashioned or wrong. But in science it does not matter what we think about an idea; what counts is what can be demonstrated. That is why many of these ideas are likely to survive, old as they may be: they rest on empirical evidence.

If the emerging picture of the mind is old, why do we need science? Why not go with the ancient models? There are several reasons. One is that we are obliged to construct our own world view, our own "story" of our existence, although we may be guided by the prior wisdom and experience of others. If we appropriate wholesale someone else's world view, it is unlikely to serve us well because it will not be genuinely and authentically our own. Furthermore, a culture's "story" always changes: if it does not evolve, it ceases to impart life, and ossifies and dies. Also, our story cannot be like the story of earlier cultures because, for better or worse, we honor the language and methods of empirical science. This means that if our picture of consciousness is inconsistent with science, it is unlikely to prove satisfying. Science is our language, and our story of who we are needs to be anchored in it.

When the history of the exploration of the role of consciousness in healing is written, Daniel J. Benor will occupy an important place. His research and writings have been very instrumental in forming the new picture of the mind. He has glimpsed the emerging vision, and he has had the courage to attempt to share it.

Larry Dossey, M.D.

Co-chair, Panel on Mind/Body Interventions
Office of Alternative Medicine
National Institutes of Health
Bethseda, Maryland, U.S.A.
Author of *Healing Words*, and
Editor of the Journal *Alternative Therapies*.

ACKNOWLEDGMENTS

My thanks to all the authors, journals and publishers who agreed so generously to permit me to quote their works. My thanks to all the healers who have given of their time and who have shared openly of themselves, explaining to this initially skeptical scientist about their work and beliefs.

My deepest thanks to the healers who have given me healing. It is through the experience of having healing that I have come to know most about myself, about healing, and about what feels important in the world.

My special thanks to Larry Dossey, who has been an inspiration and support in my work. In his many books he has articulated wholistic and spiritual concepts and has promoted awareness of research in these areas. I am also grateful personally that Larry included an early summary of *Healing Research* in his well known book, *Healing Words*.

I am grateful to J. Warren ("Jack") Salmon for his review and helpful comments on an early edition of the MS of this book, and the Kathy .Falk for her editorial inputs in sections of the revised edition.

Acknowledgment is made to the following for permission to quote longer excerpts from copyrighted material:

Kenneth Sancier, East West Academy of Healing Arts, Menlo Park, CA, for excerpts from the Qigong Database

Excerpts from *Five Great Healers Speak Here* by Nancy and Esmond Gardner, Wheaton, IL: Quest Books 1982

INTRODUCTION

Miracles do not happen in contradiction to Nature, but only in contradiction to that which is known to us in Nature.

—St. Augustine

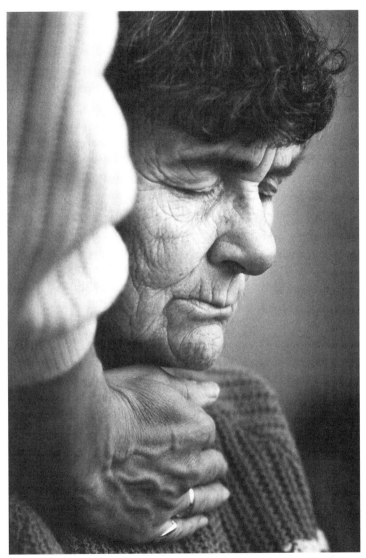

Figure 1-1. Healing brings us to a place of inner peace and harmony. *Photograph by Tony Sleep*

HEALING IN THE WORLD TODAY

Since we have come to the understanding that science is not a description of reality but a metaphysical ordering of experience, the new science does not impugn the old. It is not a question of which view is true in some ultimate sense. Rather, it is a matter of which picture is more useful in guiding human affairs.

—Willis Harman

I started out as a complete skeptic about spiritual healing. In medical school, I had learned of the vast natural curative capacities of the body, and of spontaneous waxings and wanings of diseases which could account for many healings attributed to healers. In my undergraduate training in psychology and my graduate training in psychiatry, as well as in my experience in clinical medicine, I learned many ways in which people could heal themselves of pains, anxieties, hysterical muscular and sensory problems, warts, and emotional difficulties. All of my training and experience left me certain that spiritual healing was merely a variant on the placebo—the *sugar pill* effect. I was convinced that people resorted to healing out of a wish to avoid unpleasant treatments, a reluctance to face serious illness, or a fear of death.

When a new acquaintance asked in 1980 what I thought about healing, I told him in no uncertain terms what I thought. He challenged me, asking: "Have you ever observed a healer?" Humbled, I had to admit I'd never even spoken with one, and sheepishly accepted his invitation to observe a healer at work.

Ethel Lombardi, a Reiki Master,[1] did a laying-on of hands on a young man we'll call "Joe,"[2] who had a lump under his nipple. She invited me to examine him. The lesion was 1 by 2 centimeters, rubbery firm (like an eraser), not as mobile as I'd like to see (suggesting the possibility of an invasive growth), and quite tender. Joe was a skeptic who had come only because he hoped he might avoid surgery on the lesion that was scheduled for two weeks later.

Ethel proceeded with a laying-on of hands treatment lasting half an hour, at the end of which she invited me to examine Joe again. I was astounded to find that the lesion had shrunk by a centimeter, was very soft, completely mobile, and no longer tender.

This was a healing of my skepticism as much as it was a healing of Joe's lump.[3] I knew instantly that this was something I would have to study further. I have been studying healing in every way I can ever since—

interviewing healers, gathering anecdotal reports and research literature, and consulting on setting up studies of healing.

Healers practice in every country in the world. They report they can help to improve nearly every malady known to humanity. In some instances, they facilitate miraculous cures for illnesses for which conventional medicine offers only a diagnosis and disheartening prognosis. Far more often, they provide a modest reduction of suffering and a healthier perspective.

Spiritual healing in the form of prayer, healing meditation, or the laying-on of hands has been practiced in virtually every known culture. Prayers and rituals for healing are a part of most religions. Reports of folk-healers are familiar from legend, the Bible, anthropological studies of traditional cultures, the popular press, and more recently from scientific research.

There are two broad categories of healing. In the first, prayers or meditation for the ill person's return to health are conducted either by an individual or a group. The healer(s) may be at the side of the healee[4] or may be many miles away. The second form of healing involves some variation of a laying-on of hands. Healers place their hands either on or near the body and may move them slowly or in sweeping fashion around the body.

I prefer the term *spiritual healing* or simply *healing*. Others favor such expressions as *mental healing, bio-energo-therapy*, or any of an enormous variety of other names. (See Table Intro-1.) All touch upon some part-truths in a phenomenon which this volume of *Healing Research** will explore in depth. The difficulty in choosing an appropriate term reflects our ignorance of mechanisms involved in the healing process.

A physician who is also a healer told me, "When I finish my conventional treatments I ask whether patients might let me try a little *magic* on them which might help. I rarely have anyone refuse. I am surprised myself how pains, even chronic ones, sometimes clear up rapidly with my healing touch. Sometimes a patient catches me out and says, 'Oh! You've given me a healing.' I confess at that point that they are right. But if I were to mention the word 'healing' at the beginning, I would have fifteen minutes of explaining to them about their notions on what healing isn't or shouldn't be."

A wide variety of sources was tapped for this book. I hope that the availability of the literature presented will excite interest in spiritual healing, alert more people to its benefits and facilitate further healing research. Some of the information in volumes I and II appeared in European editions in 1992-3. This revised edition includes many new research reports[5] and personal observations of healers that has doubled it's size. I include these many quotes because I feel it is essential to present the words of other explorers in the realms of healing in addition to my own. We are discussing inner experiences which are difficult to put into words. Because of the limitations of language to describe inner experiences, each is only an approximation of the truth. The more points of view we have, the greater will be the accuracy in sorting out the common denominators

---

* A description of each volume of *Healing Research* can be found in the back of this book.

between the views. I point out important features of each anecdotal and research report in my introductory remarks and summarizing discussions. I do not limit the reports to those features, because if I did so I would be imposing my own biases upon the reporters—who may have presented us with gold which I could have mistakenly taken to be dross.

For the purposes of this review, *spiritual healing* is defined as a systematic, purposeful intervention by one or more persons aiming to help another living being (person, animal, plant, or other living system) by means of focused intention, hand contact, or *passes* to improve their condition. Spiritual healing is brought about without the use of conventional energetic, mechanical, or chemical interventions. Some healers attribute spiritual healing occurences to God, Christ, other "higher powers," spirits, universal or cosmic forces or energies, biological healing energies or forces residing in the healer, psychokinesis (mind over matter), or self-healing powers or energies latent in the healee. Psychological interventions are inevitably part of healing, but spiritual healing adds many dimensions to interpersonal factors.

Healing Research addresses two broad questions: The first is, *"Does spiritual healing work?"*

The spectrum of healers' reports on what they do and how they do it is very broad. Can we believe these reports? Very few healers are trained in scientific observation or in research. Their stories of cures contradict conventional medical understandings of disease processes. Some of the cures attributed to healing might have ordinary explanations. Yet there are so many descriptions of unusual cures, some of them witnessed by medical doctors, that it seems possible some—if not all of them—may be real and true.

This book thoroughly examines research that addresses this question. I am impressed that the answer is a resounding "Yes!"

If this is so, we are led to a second question: *"How does spiritual healing work?"*

Clearly, healing does not fit within our current Western scientific explanations of health and illness. Healers seem to be able to influence the minds and bodies of healees in ways that go well beyond ordinary physical or psychological interventions.

The reports from individual healers and the research studies suggest a variety of answers to our second question.

The rest of *Healing Research,* Volumes II through IV, presents evidence to begin to answer both questions.

A wealth of research, some rigorous, some not, and a wide range of anecdotal evidence demonstrate that spiritual healing, biological energy fields, and related phenomena exist. More controlled experiments have been conducted on healing than on all the other complementary therapies (with the exception of hypnosis and psychoneuroimmunology).[6] There is significant evidence for healing effects on humans, animals, plants, yeasts, bacteria, cells in a laboratory, enzymes, and DNA. These findings challenge

Western medicine to make major adjustments in its basic understanding of health and illness and reflect more general winds of change overtaking Western science.[7]

Many scientists will dispute my interpretations of findings reported in this book. They will seek explanations within conventional science to account for unusual healings. Skeptics often argue that healing cannot be more than the effects of suggestion, which is known to promote self-healings of many physical problems. There are, for instance, endless cures for warts, such as buying them off someone, painting them with various nostrums, praying them away, burying a piece of paper under a tree during the full moon (with the wish written on the paper that the warts should be gone) and the like. Various researchers have confused these sorts of cures with spiritual healings. Such wart cures all have the common denominator of suggestion that enable people to cure themselves.

Table Intro-1.
Many names speculate on the forces or energies associated with healing.

NAME FOR ENERGIES/FORCES	SOURCE
Qi (pronounced *chee*; alt. Spelling: *chi, ki*)	Ancient Chinese, Japanese
Prana	Ancient Hindu
Atua	Maoris (New Zealand)
Mana	Pacific civilizations, parts of ancient Europe
Pneuma	Pythagoras
Vis medicatrix naturae	Hippocrates
Archaeus/Mumia	Paracelsus
Gana	South America
Astral light	Kabbalists
Vital fluid	Hermes Trismegistus
Universal fluid	Jan Baptista von Helmont; Franz Anton Mesmer
Odic force	Baron Karl von Reichenbach
Orgone energy, Od or Odyle	Wilhelm Reich
X-Force	L. E. Eeman
Life beams; Spiritus	Robert Fludd
Prephysical energy/biomagnetism	Geroge de la Warr
Eloptic energy	T. Galen Hieronymus
Reiki	Usui (Japan)
Astral Light	H. P. Blavatsky
L-fields	Harold S. Burr; Leonard Ravitz
T-fields	Edward Russell
DC fields	Robert Becker
DC fields	Robert Becker
Telergy	Brother Macedo
Paraelectricity	Ambrose Worrall
Psychotronic energy/Bioplasma	Soviet and Eastern European healers and researchers
Biothermal reaction	Alexei Sergeyev
Zoophoretic light	Gordon Turner
Non-Hertzian fields	Glenn Rein
Universal love energy	Benor
Distant mental influence on living systems	William Braud
Biological PK	Parapsychologists

The mechanical and biochemical models favored by conventional medicine cannot explain many aspects of health and illness. The mind and body are intimately linked, each influencing the other. Here is another example. Hypnotic and postanesthetic suggestion can dramatically alleviate pain and other postsurgical discomforts and complications.[8] Sadly, most surgeons are either unaware of these methods or find them too alien to study them.[9] Despite the rigorous research reviewed in this book, the revolutionary ideas associated with spiritual healing and energy medicine are so radical within Western scientific paradigms that they are often ignored or totally rejected.[10] Theories to account for spiritual healing phenomena are presented in Volume IV, Chapter 2. Many of these theories have been handed down from the earliest recorded history and are part of the customs and understanding of many other cultures but are alien to Western, Newtonian scientific thinking.

How healing works is the substance of this book, emphasizing research perspectives.

Chapter 1 presents healers' descriptions of their practices and beliefs. From innumerable sources I have selected a few which delineate particular methods or beliefs. In the selection, I strongly favored those reports which include some measure of critical analysis or discussion and tended to avoid those which preached particular approaches as gospel.

Chapter 2 surveys scientific observations on how healers may influence water, electromagnetic equipment, photographic film, and other aspects of the physical world.

Chapter 3 summarizes research in parapsychology that helps to explain aspects of spiritual healing. Healing involves alterations in the body apparently influenced by the minds of the healer and healee, and includes diagnoses by healers which appear based on telepathic or clairsentient perceptions. Chapter 3 reviews relevant research on clairsentience, telepathy, psychokinesis (mind over matter), and related subjects.

Many studies of healing have been published in journals of complementary/ alternative therapy and parapsychology. Most of the parapsychological journals have professional peer review systems.[11] Parapsychology is an accepted subsection within the American Academy for the Advancement of Science.

Some readers will view with suspicion studies published in parapsychological rather than medical journals. This is an unfair criticism. Most medical journals have refused to publish articles on spiritual healing research because it is not within the accepted realms of Western medical practice and because it has not been published previously in medical journals. An entire issue of the *Journal of the American Medical Association (JAMA)* was devoted to such problems of publication bias (March 9, 1990).

Despite this earlier awareness of publication biases, the editor of *JAMA* in 1998, George D. Lundberg, M.D., demonstrated an egregiously glaring example of publication bias. He published a study (done by a fourth grade student!) which only tested the abilities of healers to sense the energy field of the experimenter. Though the study produced negative results, it in no way assessed the subjects' healing abilities. The study is seriously flawed, and the adult authors (members of an organization which is anti-parapsychology and healing) grossly misrepresent the research evidence available in the published literature.[12] Nevertheless, Lundberg suggests that on the basis of the negative results in this study "I believe that practitioners should disclose these results to patients, third-party payers should question whether they should pay for this procedure, and patients should save their money and refuse to pay for this procedure until or unless additional honest experimentation demonstrates an actual effect." Newspapers such as the *New York Times* trumpeted the failure of healing on the basis of this article and editorial.

Another example of publication biases is the shameful response of John Maddox, editor of the prestigious journal, *Nature*, to an article on homeopathy which he had approved for publication in his own journal. Maddox published a disclaimer in the same issue, expressing doubts about the research, and hastily convened an investigation of the laboratory where the research had been done. No biologist was on the reviewing body, and his chief investigator was Randy the magician. The review was conducted in a most unprofessional manner and a damning article was published by Maddox and colleagues in the following issue.[13]

Chapter 4 reviews experiments meeting rigorous research standards, including comments on the strengths and weaknesses of each.

My favorite study of healing was done by Randall Byrd, a California cardiologist. He arranged by random selection for people to pray from afar for some of the patients on his cardiac intensive care unit but not for others. Neither the patients nor the doctors knew which were being sent healing and which not. At the end of the study, Byrd found there had been significantly fewer cardiopulmonary arrests, intubations, and less need for various medications in those who had received prayers compared to those who had not.[14]

My second favorite series of studies is on plants. Grad and others showed that healers could produce significantly greater growth when they gave healing to the water with which the plants were watered.[15]

Of the 191 controlled studies of healing, 124 show significant results (83 at a probability of $p < .01$ or less and 41 at a probability between $p < .02$ - $.05$ that they could occur by chance). This is an impressive body of research, including studies demonstrating healing effects on wounds, hypertension, pain, anxiety, depression, enhancement and retardation of growth of various organisms, and alterations in DNA.

Replications of studies reassure us that initial findings were not due to chance results. There are successful replications of studies of healing for increasing yeast growth, increasing and decreasing bacterial growth, enhancing plant growth, waking mice selectively from anesthesia, accelerating wound healing in mice, influencing human electrodermal responses, reducing post-surgical pain, and reducing anxiety and treating AIDS and patients in a cardiac intensive care unit.[16]

Chapter 5 presents less rigorous—though no less interesting—studies, followed by a brief discussion of shamanism.

Volume II in this series reviews the spectrum of self-healing and energy medicine to clarify how spiritual healing may transcend such ordinary and extraordinary mind-body interactions as charming away warts, and more. The reader is challenged to join in the criticisms and to suggest theories to explain away the findings and healing theories considered here and in later volumes.

Chapter 2 of Volume II highlights aspects of the numerous complementary therapies proliferating today. Many of these variations on the theme of energy medicine have broad overlaps with healing.

Changes in the world of matter appear to require energy. Descriptions of healing phenomena also suggest that the process of spiritual healing may involve one or more biological energies (Benor 1984). Fields and energies in and near the body are discussed in Chapters 3 and 4 of Volume II and Chapters 2 and 3 of Volume IV.

Healers find that spiritual changes often accompany treatments. Some healers report that spirits help in doing healing and that healings may include aspects of reincarnation. These, along with religious contexts for healing, are considered in Volume III. Psychic surgery, combining many aspects of energy medicine and mediumistic phenomena, is reviewed in Chapter 7 of Volume III.

Spirituality is a facet to healing that is again alien to much of Western science. Volume III considers research that begins to confirm that consciousness survives death and that our spirit appears to be a vital part of our being. Many healers consider that the spiritual effects of their treatments are more important than the physical ones. After prolonged studies, I have overcome my skepticism. I agree with them both on the basis of reason and because of the personal spiritual awarenesses which have opened within me as a result of my involvement with healing.

. . . The more we "know" about healing, the more we are simultaneously carried toward something unknowable. For this reason all healing is in essence spiritual.

—Richard Moss (in Carlson/ Shield, p.36)

My own beliefs shifted as I immersed myself in writing this book. I set out to clarify the basis for believing that spiritual healing might be effective. From extensive reading in parapsychology I was receptive to that possibility. Although I had studied medical and psychological research, placebo effects, suggestion, hypnosis, biofeedback, and other methods by which people can cure themselves, I was still skeptical of spiritual healing. Subsequent personal experiences and studies have convinced me that spiritual healing exists and is a potent therapy.

I have done my best to present the enormous complexity of healing as clearly as possible. In Chapter 1 of Volume IV, I share my personal experiences of being a healee and of learning to be a healer, my world view and biases. As it is impossible to be entirely neutral in any such presentation, I have done my best throughout the four volumes of *Healing Research* to keep summaries of research separate from discussions and speculations. Brief summaries and observations precede and follow the statements of healers and researchers. Chapter 3 of Volume IV presents broader and briefer topical summaries and discussions.

I dedicate this book to the scientists who brave their colleagues' skepticism, disapproval, and sanctions against spiritual healing. They are exploring parts of a world that Western society has not only neglected but actually shunned. I take my hat off to those who have chosen to explore and champion subjects that are at best tolerated by much of the establishment and frequently rejected out of hand. They risk their professional standing in researching methods and exploring new theoretical frontiers to help deal with physical, emotional, and spiritual suffering. These modern-day Galileos dare to question the credos of the established Newtonian scientific community; dare to suggest that mind and spirit are separable from brain but intimately integrated with the entire body; and dare to explore the implications and consequences of these beliefs. Although not threatened with burning at the stake, they risk inquisitions and ostracism by their peers, curtailment of research funds, and termination of employment.

I dedicate this book equally to the healers who have learned to trust their inner guidance and to provide a service that benefits healees, all the while braving the censure of disbelievers from scientific and healing communities.

The community of healing practitioners is divided into many houses, each with its own beliefs and practices, some separated off by thick walls or even with barbed wire. Sadly, many healers are no more tolerant than their critics when it comes to the beliefs of others. I hope that this book may serve to open the eyes and ears and hearts of healers to the many rooms in the mansions of healing. One may visit or live in any one room without rejecting the others.

EXAMINING THE EVIDENCE

Let me share a personal anecdotal report of a modest healing.

A nurse at a hospital where I worked complained of an excruciating headache. "My forehead feels like a truck ran over it!" she moaned.

Although previously she had expressed considerable skepticism about spiritual healing, in her distress she gladly accepted my offer of treatment. I passed my hands a few inches away from her body, scanning her biological energy field with my hand. As I did so, I noted a "sticky" feeling over her forehead, and a generally weak energy field around her entire body.

I then treated her head with a laying-on of hands. Within a few minutes she told me the headache was gone. I also picked up a mental image of this woman carrying a burden which was much too heavy for her. I shared this with her and she broke into tears. She told me of her struggles in supporting two children as a single parent; having to work extra hours in order to make ends meet; sorting out a relationship with a man who was having legal difficulties; and not having enough time for meeting her own needs. She was very grateful for the healing and for our discussion on reducing the stresses in her life.

Another instance was related by the late M. H. Tester, a gifted British healer. A woman nearing forty came to him for treatment of a duodenal ulcer which had caused severe pain and had not responded to drug or dietary therapy, nor to tranquilizers. Her physician recommended surgery but she feared this.

> She wanted to know if I could heal her and how she could avoid the dreaded operation. . . . I never give medical advice. It is not my function. I do not have the requisite qualifications. But I do explain the healing process and the philosophy that surrounds it. And somewhere along the line, the questions all answer themselves. . . .

The woman discussed stresses contributing to her ulcer, including being widowed three years earlier and raising three teenage children.

> I put my right hand on the top of her stomach and my left hand on her back. My conscious mind shut itself off as the power flowed through me. At these moments, I lose an appreciation of time. I had no idea if I had been "out" for a few seconds or for many minutes. Later, I realized it must have been quite a while . . . . She sat quite still, with her eyes closed. The nervousness had left her. She seemed completely relaxed.
>
> When she opened her eyes, she was almost serene. For a while, she said nothing. Then she smiled. It was the first smile I had seen. The lines of tension were gone.
>
> I asked about the pain in her chest. There was none. There was no discomfort, either. She felt fine.

She was scheduled for a barium X-ray ten days later and for a preoperative examination a week after. Tester made an appointment for the next week.

> As she left, she asked me if I thought the operation would now be necessary. I said I did not know. She asked if she should keep to her bland diet. I said it was up to her.
>
> The following Monday, she was a changed woman. She came in smiling and full of good news. She had been completely free of pain and discomfort for a week. She was sleeping right through the night and eating "like a horse." For the first time in years, she had eaten fish and chips.

The X-rays showed only scar tissue and the surgeon did not recommend any further treatment. At a final visit, Tester discussed the woman's philosophical views and recommended several books. Tester felt that changes on this level would help her to avoid a recurrence.

Science has viewed with skepticism such anecdotal reports of healers, even from physicians who, like myself, are also healers (Casdorph; Strauch). Skeptics discount our observations. Reports of healing contradict conventional beliefs too drastically. Scientists demand a theory consistent with conventional paradigms to explain healing.[17] They have a hard time acknowledging that modern science may not have arrived as yet at the final explanations for our cosmos, and that scientific theories may require serious modifications in the light of evidence presented by spiritual healing.

Figure 1-2. M.H. Tester, a healer who wrote one of the clearest books on his healing work.

Photo courtesy of Psychic News

Because our understanding of spiritual healing is embryonic, research is essential to explain it and to help it become more generally accepted. Unfortunately, little systematic research was done with humans until the last few decades. This has fed the skepticism of Western scientists, resulting in a vicious circle.

Established institutions are unwilling to invest in studies of healing, so long as respected journals hesitate to publish works on healing. Since only a few *medical* publications on the subject are available, the scientific community remains largely ignorant of the considerable evidence about the nature and efficacy of spiritual healing. This, in turn, feeds the skepticism.

The aged mathematician Clavius expressed the opinion that the satellites of Jupiter were the children of Galileo's telescope; but the honest Jesuit frankly admitted his mistake when he had himself seen them. Deterred by their backsliding, those of feebler faith declined to look, lest they should be perverted by what they saw.

—Richard A. Proctor

Scientists wish to protect the public from charlatanism. They recommend that treatments which are not sound and effective should not be used, and that explanations which are unsupported by research evidence should not be promoted.

Suggestion, hypnosis, and other mind-body mechanisms can bring about dramatic cures of many illnesses. In essence, these are methods of self-healing. Instances of alleged spiritual healings, such as that of the headache described above, may be no more than self-healings which are brought about by psychological changes or relaxation.

Healers have countless success stories like that of Tester. People often come for healing late in the course of their illnesses, often as a last resort, after many months and years of conventional treatments with less than satisfactory results. Healers argue that instances of significant improvements following spiritual healing should be convincing evidence that healing works.

However, some people experience spontaneous wanings of symptoms in the course of most illnesses. Scientists question whether or not self-healing factors may have produced the reported improvements rather than the spiritual healing.

Researchers seek to answer this question by conducting a *controlled* study of any new treatment, be it medication, surgical procedure, psychotherapy, or any other ministration for illness. This is done in the following way: Individuals with similar problems are randomly assigned to two groups. The experimental group is given the treatment while the control group is given a treatment of known effect or no treatment. All other variables (such as age, sex, severity of illness) are kept constant between the two groups as far as possible. If people in the experimental group change more than in the control group, the treatment being studied is given the credit (Benor/ Ditman).

In interpreting research results, scientists worry about two types of errors: *Type I errors* that lead us to accept as true or valid some findings that are really due only to chance; and *Type II errors* that lead us to reject as false other findings that are actually valid.

Statistical analyses indicate whether or not the differences between the groups are too great to be explainable as chance effects. Scientists generally accept that a difference that will occur by chance five times in a hundred is not due to chance, and are even happier if the statistics indicate it will occur only one time in a hundred or less—abbreviated, respectively, as "p (*probability*) less than 0.05 or 0.01" or alternatively "$p < 0.05$".

About one third of any group of people may respond readily to suggestions that they are getting an effective treatment. The power of suggestion (the *placebo effect*) could explain improvements which appear to be due to spiritual healing.

Even in a controlled study, if *experimenters* are aware of which treatment is being provided to which group, *they* may give subtle cues to members of the group receiving the experimental treatment that their condition *ought* to improve, or may unintentionally hint to the control group that they do not expect improvement (Shapiro/Morris). For these reasons it is common to run controlled experiments in *double-blind* fashion, concealing from the experimenters and experimental subjects which group is receiving the active treatment and which is the control group. Double-blind studies distribute blatant or latent suggestion effects evenly over experimental and control groups, leaving the variable under study (here a specific healing technique) as the one most likely to have caused any differences.

Some studies use a *cross-over design with sequential self-controls*. In these studies, each individual receives one form of treatment for a certain period and is then switched (if possible, without clinicians' or patients' knowledge of the timing of the switch) to an alternative treatment. Identical active drug and placebo pills can be used in coded fashion. This experimental design is especially appropriate for studies of drug efficacy in chronic illnesses where treatment alleviates symptoms but does not cure the disease. Because people serve as their own comparison, this design lessens uncertainty about whether control and experimental groups are comparable.

Western medicine, in its zeal to avoid making Type I experimental errors (of accepting as true something that is not), has sometimes gone to the extreme of a Type II research error (rejecting as being useless treatments that actually are of value). In this way it has dismissed out-of-hand even a consideration of the possibility that spiritual healing may be effective. Western medicine behaves as Petrarch admitted, "I am so afraid of error that I keep hurtling myself into the arms of doubt rather than into the arms of truth."

How we interpret the results of experiments is a matter of personal belief and preference. There is no way to know whether we are definitely making a Type I or a Type II error. For this reason, I discuss the results of studies in Chapter 4 from the vantages of more accepting and less accepting biases, leaving you, the reader, to decide which appears more appropriate.[18]

> *There is a great deal, in the most acceptable science of today, that represents a rehabilitation of supposed legends, superstitions, and folklore. Recall Voltaire's incredulity as to fossils, which according to him only a few peasants would believe in . . . Here was one of the keenest of minds; but it could not accept data, because it rejected explanations of these data.*
>
> —Charles Fort

To ensure that we do not reject valuable information as a result of this attitude, anecdotal reports and clinical observations that have not been verified by controlled studies are reviewed in Chapters 1 and 5. Chapter 5 also includes more systematic, in-depth studies of individuals' responses to healing through qualitative, *grounded theory* research.

Cost effectiveness may also be assessed by research. This is an important element in these days of concern over spending for health care. Anecdotal reports indicate that people who have had spiritual healing need less medication and fewer visits to their doctors. One study of cost-effectiveness of healing in a primary care physician's practice confirmed that considerable savings are possible.[19]

Western science distrusts personal experience and assumes that people cannot be objective in reporting what goes on inside themselves. It is assumed, however, that we can be objective in reporting observations outside ourselves. In fact, *there is no such thing as objectivity.* We all interpret our perceptions in the light of our beliefs and expectations. We must even interpret the readings on the dials of an ostensibly objective machine in order to derive meaning from them.

I believe that personal experiences of healing are every bit as valid as the most sophisticated scientific research, and often much more meaningful to us. However, in evaluating our inner experiences we have a greater danger of Type I research errors—of accepting as true something that is not. We can reduce this risk by repeating our inner explorations to see whether or not they are consistent. If they are not, then we must ask such questions as: Are we experiencing systematic variations which arise from our expectations and imagination? Can we identify random factors that contribute to or cause the variations? We may also check with others who explore their inner worlds, to learn whether their experiences are similar or different.

Wherever possible, I have inserted suggestions for the reader's personal explorations which can add the dimension of personal study to our understanding of healing. This is most relevant to the subject matter in Volumes II and III.

Let us summarize the several different ways to study healing:

- **Personal experience**—Providing individual, personal, direct, and immediate inner awarenesses.
- **Anecdotal reports**—Helpful particularly when presented by an educated observer who can explore questions of healing that those who are observed might not think to ask. As accounts of similar experiences begin to accumulate, directions for more focused research are suggested.
- **Qualitative research**—Systematic studies of subjective experiences of groups of people, shaped by the beliefs of the researcher. Here, a start is made towards systematically exploring commonalties across the experiences of groups of people.
- **Observational studies**—Surveying larger groups of people, either selected by outcome and compared for prevalence of experiences which might explain the outcome, or selected by treatment and followed for outcomes.
- **Randomized controlled trials (RCT)**—Methodically comparing several groups of subjects who are randomly assigned to receive different treatments and then observed for differences between the groups to assess the efficacy of the treatments.
- **Outcome studies**—Following subjects after treatment for longer-term outcomes, including side-effects, quality of life, and cost-effectiveness.

    The danger of Type I errors—accepting as true something which is not, due to personal biases which may not be immediately apparent—are greater at the top of this list. Danger of Type II errors—rejecting as false something which is true—are greater at the bottom of the list. Some readers will find the evidence sound but will have difficulty accepting the implications of the findings. This is a common problem when one's world view is challenged with new materials which appear to contradict "common sense."

We are biased by our materialistic society to believe that anything which is not measurable through our senses is non*sense* or im*material*. Healing suggests that intuitive information may be valid in its own right, outside the laws of the material world. We have the same situation in modern quantum physics, where explanations make no sense in terms of classical, Newtonian physics. Further analogies with modern physics and other hypotheses to explain healing are presented and discussed in Volume IV.

HISTORICAL PERSPECTIVES

The only thing new in the world is the history you don't know.

—Harry S. Truman

Three branches of healing appear across the ages.[20] The first is the natural gift of spiritual healing, which throughout history has sprung up as a wildflower bringing its healing essence, unbidden and uncontrolled by human will, to act as a balm for the ills of body, emotions, relationships (with other people and with nature) and spirit. This gift has cropped up spontaneously in the fertile soil of human diversity, sometimes in the most ordinary of laypersons, sometimes in those who choose paths of ministering to physical or spiritual needs of others, and sometimes in the well-to-do and prominent, even amongst royalty. In recent decades we have learned to cultivate this flower within ourselves, sometimes inviting it to appear in the carefully-prepared soil of our inner being, in other instances seeking to force it to grow through artificial means—with the use of psychedelic chemicals.

The second branch of healing appears in the carefully fenced off gardens of institutionalized religious environments. In religions of traditional cultures, where buds of healing gifts have been nurtured and honored, spiritual healing has benefited the entire society. In modern societies where Western medicine is available, religious spiritual healing has lost its importance and has become for the most part an empty ritual molded by the doctrinal and political dictates of religious authorities, used more for show than to bring about actual relief from suffering. Within these settings individuals with natural gifts of healing have sometimes been welcomed and honored, and at other times suppressed. However, there are shifts in recent decades with a return to favorable attitudes toward healing.

The third branch builds upon the cultivated healing of clinical therapeutic experience and scientific traditions. Its origins extend back as far as recorded history. *The Yellow Emperor's Classic of Internal Medicine*, compiled in the first century B.C. (K. Cohen; Veith) refers to schools for subtle energy healing. This branch has grown strong over the past four centuries, particularly in the latter part of the 20th century. It focuses primarily on the physical body, though recently we have seen throwbacks to awareness of connections between mind and body, and a growing awareness of personal spirituality as a component of healing.

Natural Healing

In traditional cultures (pejoratively designated as *primitive* by many members of technologically advanced cultures), spiritual healing is known and accepted as a natural part of life. In nomadic cultures, *shamans* minister to their societies' physical, social, and spiritual needs.[21]

From anthropological studies of traditional societies, and from historical evidence of written records, it appears that our early ancestors viewed themselves as intimately involved with nature. The forces of nature, the stars, the spirits, and the gods that controlled the cosmos also ruled their lives.

Western anthropologists report that in "primitive societies" shamans and medicine men use prayers, chants, talismans, herbs, and potions to pretend to influence their environment, for lack of any real means to do so. This presumes they delude themselves through wishful thinking into believing they can influence a world that is actually beyond their comprehension and control. Closer, more open scrutiny of modern shamans such as the Cherokee and Shoshone medicine man Rolling Thunder, reveals that so-called primitives may know very effective methods of spiritual healing (Boyd). Personal explorations of healing in traditional cultures lead to greater awareness of and trust in intuitive modes of knowing. Traditional peoples *know* of what they speak, while industrial society's investigators of these cultures only *know about* these intuitive and spiritual realms.

As cultures mature, they shift from nomadic herding and gathering plants in the wild to farming, which can support greater concentrations of people. In sedentary farming cultures, healers come under the influence of the religious institutions which inevitably arise in these more complex social frameworks. Priests may view healers as competitors for the good will and support (both material and political) of the populace, and may therefore promote religious rituals, often without regard for their effectiveness in alleviating illness. Priests may also redefine illness as a test of faith.

Historical Notes

As societies grow increasingly complex, so do approaches to healing. The dichotomy between the physical and psychic approaches dates back to the dawn of recorded history. The Code of Hammurabi (circa 2000 B.C.) mentions payments to surgeons for successful operations; death for failures. It also refers to incantations and treatments for demons. Egyptian papyri several centuries later talk of dual streams of treatment: one involving magical words, charms, and incantations; another using medicines and surgery (Estes). The Ebers papyrus (1550 B.C.) mentions the laying-on of hands for relief of pain. The Persians acknowledged three forms of healing: the knife, medicines, and spells.

The Greeks, unlike the Egyptians, did not dichotomize the world. Pythagoras, a physician in the the sixth century B.C., considered healing to be the noblest of his pursuits and integrated it into his considerations of ethics, mind, and soul. He called the energy associated with healing *pneuma,* and said that it originates in a fire in the center of the universe which imparts to human beings their vitality and immortal soul. "Pythagoras's central fire was a primordial force, the sparks from which gave life to man" (Coddington). His followers conceived of the pneuma as being visible in a luminous body and held that light could cure illness. They believed that everything is composed of opposites, similar to the Eastern cosmology of *yin* and *yang.* The opposites are in conflict and need to be balanced in proper proportions to ensure harmony. The condition of the conflicting forces within the individual parallels their relationship in the world.

Hippocrates hypothesized a healing energy, the *vis medicatrix naturae* (the healing power of nature), as the vital force of life. He advised that physicians must identify blocking influences both within the individual and between the individual and the cosmos in order to restore the proper flow of pneuma. Nature (not the doctor) heals the patient. However, he taught that mind and body were separate.

Writing around the turn of the fifth century B.C., he [Hippocrates] says "It is believed by experienced doctors that the heat which oozes out of the hand, on being applied to the sick, is highly salutary . . . . It has often appeared, while I have been soothing my patients, as if there was a singular property in my hands to pull and draw away from the affected parts aches and diverse impurities, by laying my hand upon the place, and by extending my fingers towards it. Thus it is known to some of the learned that health may be implanted in the sick by certain gestures, and by contact, as some diseases may be communicated from one to another."

—David Harvey, p. 35

The theory of unity of mind and body which the Pythagoreans had advanced was soon superseded by the Hippocratic beliefs that mind and body are dichotomous. Plato criticized this view: "If the head and the body are to be well, you must begin by curing the soul; that is the first thing . . . the great error of our day in the treatment of the human body (is) that physicians separate the soul from the body." The Hippocratic system, codified by Galen in the second century a.d., became the standard for medical practices for many centuries thereafter.

Many pre-Christian *incubation temples* for the sick encouraged dreaming. Priests would interpret the dreams as a form of self-diagnosis. This practice persisted into the Middle Ages, when some churches provided mattresses and baths for these purposes. Galen (circa 180 A.D.) speculated that these temples might not be intrinsically healing so much as encouraging self-healing (L. Rose).

Jesus was a great healer. The Bible and Gospels tell of numerous individual and group healings by Christ and the Apostles. They used touch, saliva, mud and cloth as vehicles for healing, and of course, words, prayers, exorcism, faith, and compassion. [22]

In the early Christian era, many priests apparently were selected for their healing gifts (Corinthians I). They healed by exhorting the diseases to leave and by the laying-on of hands. The rites for ordination of priests included a prayer for healing powers.

Relics of saints and their shrines were increasingly credited with healing powers. St. Paul was believed to be able to transmit healing through objects he touched. He believed that healing was a personal gift. Through the third century, the church was well known for providing healing to its flocks. Unfortunately, the church gradually turned away from healing for a variety of reasons. [22] It de-emphasized healing in its ministries, sometimes even denying its existence other than in metaphor or mythology. By the fourth century, St. Chrysostom observed that miracles were becoming rare, although healing was still being given. St. Augustine was noted for curing a fistula overnight through prayer.

By the seventh century, after the conversion of Constantine to Christianity, the church gave preference to theological cosmologies, religious dogmas, and political power, and neglected healing gifts. As in the general world views of the next thousand years, historical precedents were cited as explanations for natural events. The Church discouraged and persecuted healers who were outside its aegis and "looked to the practices of its past rather than to the gifts of its living members, and its rites directed greater attention to Christ's instructions to remember His last supper than to His injunction to work (or attempt to work) other miracles in His name. . . ." (L. Rose p.31). Disease was viewed as an expression of God's will, to be addressed by prayer. Healing was neglected as a deliberate and potent intervention for everyday ills.

In some instances, Church officials also discouraged physical treatments for disease, arguing that faith held the cure for all problems. In 360 A.D., a bishop condemned physicians as magicians. In the sixth century the emperor Justinian tried to close medical schools in the provinces under his influence. Monastery hospitals founded in the ninth and following centuries, under orders such as the Knights Templar, usually emphasized preparation for a church-approved and supervised death over direct efforts to cure disease. Healing was debased further as priests boosted their incomes by selling cures, a practice condemned in the Lateran Council in 1123 (L. Rose).

The Church continued to support two healing practices: the ritual of *exorcism*, institutionalized in the Council of Antioch of 341, and the *sacrament of unction* in which the dying were anointed with holy oil.[23]

Physicians were few and too expensive for most of the populace. Apothecaries, barbers, leeches, wise women, and witches provided the primary care at the village level. Physical interventions might include herbs, sweating, cupping, bleeding, and simple surgery. Magical healing powers might be sought through talismen, relics from violent deaths, healing wells, elves, and fairies, as well as the laying-on of hands by white witches and warlocks. By tradition, the latter usually did not accept direct payments.

Figure 1-3. King Charles II administering the Royal Touch.

Such folk traditions held a strong influence through the seventeenth century and persist to this day. Untested remedies such as copper bracelets, visits to shrines, and various plant and animal products are credited with curing many symptoms and illnesses.

Unusually strong healing gifts have been acknowledged occasionally by the church, as in miraculous cures of saints—either during their lives or through testimonies of people who prayed to them or posthumously held relics belonging to them and reported cures.

Many of the monarchs of England and other European countries had healing abilities. *The royal touch* was a publicly acknowledged phenomenon, made available to the public on special days when the king might see hundreds of people. Instantaneous cures of scrofula (tuberculous swelling of the lymph tissues) and other illnesses were reported by creditable observers. (See Figure 1-3.)

Theophrastus Bombastus von Hohenheim, more popularly known as Paracelsus (1493-1541), shined the first modern healing light on the fossilized system of medicine in the Middle Ages. He refocused the study of medicine on naturalistic observations and saw human beings as an integral part of nature, reflecting within themselves the larger cosmos. He apparently saw auras because he reported "a healing energy that radiates within and around man like a luminous sphere" (Coddington). He called this force *archaeus,* and believed it could be effective from a distance and could cause as well as cure disease. He also believed that magnets, stars, and other heavenly bodies could influence humans via this force. Paracelsus promoted the idea of *magnetic* or *sympathetic medicine,* later reinforced by Mesmer and other hypnotists.

Paracelsus further asserted that a human being has a second body, which he labeled the *star,* or *sidereal* or *astral body.* He taught that the lower instincts are housed in the animal body, while higher instincts such as wisdom and art are housed in the astral. He believed that the etheric body motivates the physical body via the mind and that both body and mind are integrally related and can be subject to disease. For instance, negative thoughts can block flows of archaeus and thereby lead to illness. He held that "resolute imagination can accomplish all things" (Coddington).[24] He also believed in a third body: an immortal soul or eternal spark.

Paracelsus was eccentric, irascible, and impetuous. Despite his brilliant observations and conceptualizations, he alienated people and therefore the impact of his ideas was diminished. Moreover, his ideas were competing with those of two other scientists, Francis Bacon (1561-1626) and René Descartes (1596-1650). Bacon promoted the understanding of laws of science in order to *master* nature rather than to become harmonious with nature.

Descartes revolutionized Western thinking by applying mathematical, logical analysis to the world, including humans. Modern science, applying this reasoning, has doggedly pursued the reductionistic goal of understanding the world through ever finer analyses of the physical building blocks of the material world. The ideas of Descartes so profoundly transformed Western world views that it is hard for many to recognize that systematic, quantifiable relationships between objects and parts of objects are abstract representations of reality rather than reality itself. Few recognize that the whole of any organism is often far more complex than the combination of its individual parts.

Descartes' dichotomies made possible a *modus vivendi* between the Church and science. Science addressed the body, while the church attended to the soul. In the days when Church and state were not separated, this saved the scientists from religious persecution.

Descartes drew a firm dichotomy between body (measurable) and mind (intangible), assuming body could influence mind but not the reverse. These concepts led to great progress in the physical sciences and to the quest for physical causes and cures for illness, but were detrimental in their denial of the mind as a causal influence on the body. They have led science to denigrate everything which is not measurable and explainable through scientific theories.

Science was constructed against a lot of nonsense.

—Albert Libchaber

The West was experiencing an industrial revolution at the time Descartes' ideas were spreading. Intoxicated with growing success in comprehension, manipulation, and control of the environment, the West focused more and more on a material view of the world. In medicine this extended to a nearly exclusive concentration on physical aspects of disease. This focus has been productive in the identification of causes of disease, including bacteria, parasites, viruses, vitamins, hormones, and genetic anomalies, as well as in discoveries of chemical and mechanical ways to treat diseases. However, it has been counterproductive in producing a lopsided emphasis on *physical* causes and cures of illness.

Only a few scientists dared to question the view that the mind cannot influence the body. Gottfried Wilhelm Leibniz (1646-1716), another contemporary of Descartes, proposed that centers of force, which he termed *monads,* are the organizing principles in the universe. Monads reflect in their microcosm the macrocosm of the vaster universe. They express themselves in substance as energy and consciously strive to surpass corporeal limitations. These concepts remain little recognized even today, although they foreshadow some of the more advanced contemporary ideas on the nature of the universe.

Franz Anton Mesmer (1733-1815) popularized another mode of healing. He demonstrated that he could improve numerous symptoms with *magnetic passes* of his hands around patients' bodies. At first he held magnets in his hands but soon found he was just as effective without them. He hypothesized that he channeled a *magnetic fluid* into the patient. Although he had staunch followers, the vast majority of the medical community was critical and unaccepting of his findings. A commission set up in France to study the subject produced a negative report that effectively cut off Mesmer's methods from mainstream medicine.

The Marquis de Puysegur, a student of Mesmer, introduced a form of healing similar to that of his teacher. He demonstrated he could influence patients by an act of will, without the use of magnetic passes and with no recourse to theories of fluids. His work with hypnosis reintroduced an appreciation of the impact of thought on the body.

It is fascinating to learn (M. Long 1976) that *kahuna* healers in Hawaii were aware of the unconscious mind and of principles of suggestion, akin to hypnosis, many centuries before they were discovered in the West.

Mechanistic approaches to the study of the body continued to clarify many of the biochemical and electromagnetic aspects of physiology. Luigi Galvani (1737-1798) and Alessandro Volta (1745-1847) explored the electrical stimulation of animal muscles, puzzling out the nature of the body's electrical activity. Galvani believed this was evidence for a life force in animals.

These and other approaches of modern medicine have led Western science into mechanistic approaches to health and illness. Ken Cohen (1997), an expert on Chinese *qigong* healing, observes

> As the philosophy of vitalism was eclipsed by scientific materialism, Western exercises and physical therapies began to place an almost exclusive emphasis on strength, stamina, flexibility, and coordination. These qualities are certainly important. However, they reflect the Western preoccupation with the appearance of health: a beautiful figure, well-defined muscles, clear complexion. Modern Western exercise systems can be considered symptoms of disempowerment. The individual's internal health was believed to be beyond control and, if disturbed, required the external intervention of an expert physician. The body was reduced to a machine, without

innate intelligence, no more capable of self-correcting serious malfunctions than an automobile. This assumption is incorrect. . . . It is time to reincorporate many of the insights of vitalism and of the ancient healing systems which recognized the power of qi.

Not all scientists focused exclusively on the physical body. Karl von Reichenbach, a German industrialist, in the middle of the nineteenth century explored a variety of physical properties of living beings, relating them to a universal energy which he believed permeated the body. He called this force *od* or *odyle*.[25]

Scientists who seek to study forces within the body which appear related to health and disease have had to fight against the mainstream of scientific opinion. Since Cartesian influence has reasoning and research to support its views, scientists with theories which contradict conventional beliefs are at best ignored and often ridiculed or worse. Wilhelm Reich, a psychiatrist in the first half of the twentieth century, elaborated Reichenbach's theories of orgone energy, supporting them by clinical observations and experiments. He proposed this is a distinct form of universal energy which becomes blocked in the body as a result of emotional problems. He was persecuted and jailed by U.S. government authorities in the early 1950s because of his views, and his books were publicly burned. His followers, such as Alexander Lowen, John Pierrakos, and Barbara Brennan continued to develop and promote his ideas, though they have not gained wide acceptance.

At the turn of the century, Sigmund Freud and Carl Gustav Jung clarified that the unconscious mind may cause certain symptoms. This was the birth of modern psychosomatic medicine, which addresses mind together with body. Numerous body-mind therapies now flourish in the ground first tilled by these pioneers.

Sir William Osler recommended that physicians seek to understand the patient who has the disease and not merely the disease the patient has. This element is sorely lacking in most "efficient" modern medical treatments. The most common complaint against conventional medicine is that the doctor doesn't listen to or talk with the patient.

Mechanistic thinking, however, has permeated psychology and neurophysiology in America. Behavioral psychology demonstrates that learning by reward and punishment, or conditioning of the unconscious mind, may produce illness. Mainstream medical research in neurology shows that electrodes inserted in the brain can elicit specific sensations and memories. Here is proof that mind appears to be a product of the physical brain. This idea has contributed to the mechanistic view of human beings.[26]

Further alienation from self has resulted from the explosion of medical knowledge, which produced a need for medical specialization. No single physician today can understand all there is to know about the body. People therefore have to parcel out their bodies among various specialists, who are keepers of the required esoteric knowledge for the diagnosis and treatment of those particular parts which are ailing.

Mass-production methods in our hospitals have added to the compartmentalization of mind and body. Parts of the body are treated in one section of the hospital while mind and spirit are treated elsewhere. This mechanistic, reductionistic system subtly and insidiously perpetuates itself. Young, idealistic doctors are trained mechanistically, almost exclusively within mass-production facilities, with methods stressing mechanistic efficiency. They learn to treat patients as their superiors do and as they themselves were treated. Deviations from accepted norms meet severe censure from superiors and peers. Students and recent graduates in some institutions dare not mention interest in complementary therapies, lest their careers be jeopardized.

Economic factors also militate against the acceptance of spiritual healing as a legitimate therapy. The drug industry is a major force throughout the world. Private health care is another major industry that resists competition.

Fortunately, the public is learning to appreciate the benefits of spiritual healing and other complementary therapies, voting for them with their dollars. David Eisenberg et al. (1993; 1998) published a survey which showed that about eleven billion dollars was spent annually on complementary therapies in the United States, virtually all of it directly from the pockets of consumers. (In the same year, about thirteen billion was paid for conventional medical care, mostly through insurance.) Largely in response to these articles, along with direct public pressure, many medical schools have started offering elective courses in complementary therapies for medical students.

Western medicine has embraced numerous treatments with less research evidence (Congressional Office of Technology Assessment; R. Smith) than is available to support the efficacy of spiritual healing. Furthermore, many mechanistic Western treatments have adverse side effects (Robin). For example, some treatments for cancer are toxic, noxious, and of unproven value (Oye/Shapiro).

Materialistic world views are so ingrained in our culture that to change them is very difficult.

We would rather be ruined than changed;
We would rather die in our dread
Than climb the cross of the moment
And let our illusions die.

—W.H. Auden

Spiritual healing offers at least a nontoxic adjunct to conventional therapies for many illnesses and for this reason alone may prove to be a treatment of choice. With further research, it may become a treatment of first choice.

Healing aspects of other complementary therapies, in the framework of wholistic* medicine, are discussed in Chapter 2 of Volume II.

This book challenges the reader to see the world anew. There is considerable evidence some individuals can heal themselves and others through spiritual healing. In Chapters 1, 4, and 5, I have quoted liberally from a wide spread of reports in diverse publications because I fear that if I summarize the ideas of others, sifting their concepts through my understandings of them, I would be presenting my interpretations of these phenomena and not theirs.

The annotated bibliography of research on healing permits you to arrive at your own conclusions. I hope this review will challenge your imagination and stimulate further investigations of this important frontier, which science has barely begun to explore.

The reader may still find a straight reading of these materials daunting. Skimming may suit better than plowing directly through. Studying the evidence for healing is rather like learning bridge. It is difficult to understand the suit of healing in the game of life until one has some comprehension of other parts, such as the trumps of disease of mind which may lead to disease of body. Yet other points cannot be fully understood without an appreciation of the evidence for healing. The glossary can be of help in clarifying some of the terminology.

I highly recommend that the serious reader examine the original works reviewed and the other references mentioned in the footnotes. Many more sources of material are available than could be summarized in this work, large as it is. I have tried to include as complete a sampling of relevant data as could be reasonably assembled in a single work.

If you pull at one blade of grass, you get the whole field.
—Ancient Chinese proverb

The coherence which emerges from considerations of the diverse practices and theories considered in *Healing Research* can best be appreciated after reading the entire series.

---

* Please see the glossary for a concise definition of wholistic.

CHAPTER ONE

HEALERS

> *Sit down before fact like a child, and be prepared to*
> *give up every preconceived notion.*
> *Follow humbly wherever and to whatever abysses*
> *Nature leads, or you shall learn nothing.*
> —T.H. Huxley

This chapter presents healers' descriptions of what they do to bring about healing and how, in their view, it works.

Miraculous healings are rare. Spiritual healing usually brings about gradual, marked improvements in a wide variety of disorders for which modern medicine can provide only partial treatments or the questionable solace of a known diagnosis with small hope of palliation.

There is obvious confusion in the plethora of views and opinions on spiritual healing. We simply don't know which observations of healers might be valid and which are elaborations of cultural and personal shapings of a phenomenon for which we as yet don't even have accurate descriptive words.

The body may suffer from physical tensions, pains, congenital liabilities, infections, metabolic or hormonal disorders, injuries, allergies, toxins, growths which are out of control, degenerative problems, and physical expressions of a stressed or even tortured psyche and soul.

The mind, emotions, and feelings may suffer from personal, interpersonal and environmental stresses, traumas (past and present), anxieties, obsessions, weaknesses or rigidities, and confusions.

The spirit may have experiences from past lives, relational lessons, and subtle choices it strives to express through the garments of flesh and psyche it has taken on in this lifetime.[26] It may express itself subtly or with brutal force, or may be neglected, repressed, and disconnected from awareness, or boxed into rigidities which it finds constraining.

All of these strivings for expression through the life of the individual may be helped by spiritual healing which takes effect on many levels simultaneously.

The degree to which people respond to spiritual healing varies widely and appears to be influenced by an enormous variety of internal and external variables.[1]

Joyce Goodrich (1982) lists four possible ways in which healing might work:

- Healees may heal themselves via self-healing mechanisms. The healer's function may be to suggest the possibility of a cure, or to catalyze it in some more active manner.
- Healers may supply healing energy from their own body or being, perhaps through dimensions other than those usually employed in everyday, sensory reality (LeShan 1974a, 1976).
- Healers may channel energy from outside themselves, focusing it or making it available to the healee.
- Healers may involve the assistance of sentient external agencies such as God, angels, Christ, spirits, or others to assist also in or to perform the healing.

A combination of several of the above is possible.

Though this set of distinctions is clearly discernible in the reports of healers, combinations and overlaps are frequent. This suggests that the distinctions may either be arbitrary constructs of linear language or blended manifestations of different healing modalities.

A full comprehension of what constitutes a spiritual healing may be beyond our capacities because of sensory and psychological limitations. Altered states of consciousness and extrasensory perceptions may extend our comprehension of the world of spiritual healing. We might thus be able to advance our understanding of healing, but still might have difficulty translating it into language.

The Names that can be given Are not the Absolute Names. The Nameless is the origin of Heaven and Earth; The Nameless is the Mother of All Things.

—Lao Tsu

I invite readers to join me in efforts to determine which of the above possibilities is the most likely. The evidence is here in Volume I of *Healing Research*. My speculations and those of other researchers are presented in Volumes II-IV.

First, let the healers and investigators speak for themselves. I open with some of my own observations as a healer.

HEALERS' VIEWS OF HEALING

'Tis God gives skill, But not without men's hands: He could not make Antonio Stradivari's violins Without Antonio

—George Elliot

Daniel J. Benor

Psychotherapy and spiritual healing, *Human Potential* **1996**
Spiritual healing and psychotherapy, *The Therapist* **1993**
The overlap of psychic "readings" with psychotherapy, *Psi Research* **1986**

I find myself in the peculiar position that everything I am going to tell you is inherently "wrong." Words are inadequate to describe the subtle experiences of healing. Even were they adequate, the fact that we will focus on subsections of the whole will introduce severe distortions into our understanding of healing, which is *both/and* rather than *either/or*. Healing is the ability to let out anger and negativity but at the same time to forgive and accept the inevitable frailties of others, and even more difficult, of oneself. Healing is the finding of the quiet and sublime song which lies between the notes in the harmony of existence. Healing is in the deep silence of the soul which knows that it IS and that it is loved with an infinitely compassionate, unconditional acceptance, so blissful as to be painful to the nerve ends, which ache for a bit of balm from the All to soothe the hurts of earthly existence.

Nevertheless, as linear language is our primary mode of communication, I shall do my best to outline my understanding of how healing works, counterpointing the text with poetic, humorous, and mythic perspectives touching on the fringes and encompassing the essence of that which is beyond words.

Here is how I understand many of the problems with which I deal—both in myself and in my clients—in my practice of psychotherapy combined with spiritual healing.

On the surface we present a *persona*, or *public face* to the world—how we wish to appear to ourselves and others. Underneath the persona is a layer of psychological defenses against acknowledging that we are not quite the persona we would like to be, and defenses against layers of inner feelings we haven't had the courage to confront. Below the defenses are anxieties which we shoved deep in the closet of our unconscious, starting when we were little children. The child learns early to hide away uncomfortable feelings and memories. Our unconscious child mind believes that if the contents of the closet stay out of awareness they won't hurt, so the door of the closet is kept tightly shut and a big sign is hung on the door, saying KEEP WELL AWAY, or if the experiences were intensely negative, HERE LIE TIGERS AND DINOSAURS AND MONSTERS WAITING TO GRAB YOU. The unconscious believes if we were hurt by a given experience it is probably better to stay away from similar situations. So the unconscious adds to the sign, in very small print, exactly what we ought to keep well away from—and here it gets in trouble. It must keep some awareness of *what to stay away from*, but at the same time it must hide this awareness from the conscious mind. So it starts on the paradoxical path of stashing away more and more negative feelings related to the original insult and memories into the closet, all the while working very hard to hide these and earlier ones from the conscious mind.

At deeper levels of our being, we have warm, tender feelings for others and the need to receive such feelings ourselves. This inner core is as sensitive as a snail, and peeks out only when it is safe—when it feels certain it won't get hurt and have to jerk back into its shell behind all the other layers of the conscious and unconscious mind.

At still deeper levels of our existence, even harder to put into words, I believe life is a lesson chosen before birth by the soul in consultation with very wise advisors. These advisors guide us towards spiritual growth— through the costumes of flesh and personality we don in each lifetime on the stage of earthly existence. For life is an improvisational drama we choose to create with other actors who agree to participate in the lessons we all have to learn and to teach. The choreographers for these plays are our own higher selves, in continuous consultations with more advanced spiritual advisors—on planes of awareness we can barely perceive and cannot begin to truly comprehend, while we are engaged in the performance.

Within this framework, life itself is a healing in the progress of the soul towards unity with the All. Not a single bit of life—no event or encounter, no so-called misfortune or episode of ill-health—is a chance occurrence if we are aware and awake to ponder it and to fathom its message.

Healing is the pursuit of wholeness in body, emotions, mind, relationships (with other people and with Gaia, our planet and everything in the cosmos that is a part of this wondrous stage for our play), and spirit.

Spiritual healing offers us help in dealing with all levels of our pursuit of wholeness. Often it starts with a focus on our physical selves—with symptoms such as a pain, a body malfunction or a physical disease. These are messages from our body which tell us that something is out of harmony inside. Spiritual healing may help us to identify intuitively the causes for physical problems and restore harmony and health to our bodies. Sometimes spiritual healing alone is sufficient to bring us back to a state of wholeness. At other times healing may be a complement to allopathic medical interventions, to counseling or psychotherapy, or to any of a variety of complementary therapies.

As I write this, I glance at my left ankle, elevated on two pillows on a chair, in a plaster cast, with the toes wrapped against the chill of winter. The cast protects the marvelous healing work of the surgeon who screwed the tip of my fibula back to its shaft, holding the ankle bones in place after I fell last week. Self-healing made pain medicine unnecessary in the ten hours prior to surgery.

I am grateful for the laying-on of hands healings that Ruth, my (then) wife, has been giving me, during which I felt intense warmth in the ankle and foot. This eased some of the discomforts of having to elevate the foot constantly.

Spiritual healing can help with psychological problems. Anxieties, fears, and emotions which result from current or past conflicts can be considerably relieved with healing. Healing facilitates the building of rapport between therapist and client, with immediate awareness of care and love which are a part of the experience of giving and receiving healing. The love experienced in healing is a deep, unconditional acceptance which is beyond words. Healing can quickly open both therapist and client to intuitive awarenesses of underlying psychological problems which may be buried in the unconscious, problems often brought into consciousness by the unconscious mind through physical and emotional symptoms. Healing facilitates releases of buried emotional hurts. Psychotherapy helps people to integrate the insights and emotional releases derived through healing.

My ankle fracture was the result of a slip of my bicycle, crossing an invisible patch of black ice as I came down the hill from my village in rural England. Most people would simply call this an unfortunate accident. I consider it a message from my unconscious mind and higher Self. More accurately, it is a series of messages. First, to slow down from my Type A, driven personality style of pushing to complete the updates for the publication of the revised edition of this book as I near the signing of the contract with my new publisher. Then, to ask why I haven't been spending more time meditating and communicating with my inner Self, so that it wouldn't have to shout at me and trip me up in order to slow me down long enough for me to stop and listen to it. Next, to ask why my unconscious mind would agree to such a drastic communication. This is serious business.

Spiritual healing facilitates the release of energy blocks in one part of the body to allow a flow of energy throughout the entire body. Reduction in emotional tension is accompanied by reduction in physical tension. A more relaxed body can function more normally, free of excess stress hormones. Each level of healing influences levels above and below itself. People who are more relaxed usually gain access to higher levels of awareness which facilitates self healing.

Systemic changes can extend beyond the individual. Changes in one member of a family very quickly reverberate with others in the family. In fact, if healing is consciously directed towards tensions *between* individuals, it can bring about healings in relationships as well as in individuals.[2]

I return to look at my throbbing foot (raised to a blessedly restful position again after a trip to the bathroom, when, because it is irritated from the traumas of injury and surgery, it swelled to the painful limits the cast would allow).

I ask myself, "What psychological and relational problems may have contributed to my allowing this 'accident' to happen?" This begins to touch upon deeper layers of emotional hurts I have already spent some thirty years exploring through various psychotherapies. It resonates with a broken ankle at age three when I was left alone with friends by my mother while she attended some summer courses. It reverberates with the hurts of several sprained ankles along the way—the last during a rough patch in my life when I felt lonely and abandoned and ended up swallowing many of my hurt and angry feelings. It was no coincidence this current fracture occurred on the very day Ruth and my stepdaughter, Elizabeth, flew off to a week's holiday in the Caribbean. So I have much to chew over and journal—awaiting the return of my Jungian therapist from her honeymoon holiday in India.

This raises all sorts of issues concerning my relationship with Ruth, as well as other, unresolved dependency issues from my childhood relationships with my parents. I am certain a part of my ankle's healing will involve insights into these issues.

Spiritual healing relates through the heart of the healer to the heart of the healee. It is a feeling of rapport, a profoundly intuitive connection, which fosters inner knowings of each other. The healer knows the healee on a level beyond words, senses the blocks and hangups of the healee, knows the healee's strengths, weakness, old hurts and future hopes. The healee knows the healer's unconditional love—and through it, may open to knowing the love of the Creator, which is ever present but often lost to awareness or even forgotten.

The heart opens into the very deepest essence of the *art* of healing—balancing the wisdom of the head, and, in turn, counterbalanced by that wisdom, which must always be on the alert to screen out the healer's projections and the healee's transference.

[A]ctions set in motion always have the flavor of the doorway of their birth. This makes these things have a strong leaning in this way or that way. From the heart they are in the middle. They are born of balance and joy and cannot topple themselves over or create a snowball effect of their twist into the world. Action from the heart even leaves a little gift of balance to the maker and the acceptor. So for making the most powerful ceremonies . . . it must come pure from the heart. . . .

—Kay Cordell Whitaker p. 74

Spiritual healing opens people to intuitive, mystical, and spiritual aware-ness—areas which our materialistic and reductionistic Western society have largely rejected. Scientific methodology insists on measurable phenomena and therefore has difficulty addressing subjective inner awarenesses. It is easier to reject new evidence than to question the basic axioms of conven-tional science. It is easier to distance ourselves from that which makes us uncomfortable than to delve into why we feel uncomfortable.[3]

Healers often introduce cosmologies of religion, astrology, numerol-ogy, and reincarnation. Such concepts reframe people's problems, putting them in contexts much broader than their immediate hurts and illnesses. They introduce hope through the equations of numerology and planetary positions. Religion and reincarnation help to turn disaster into the chal-lenge of spiritual growth.[4]

Reductionists may object that all these spiritual speculations are simply excuses for our inability to cure many physical illnesses. The observation of Gary Zukav (1990, p.188) seems an appropriate response: "The body is the instrument of the soul. If the piano player is sick, does it help to repair his or her piano?" This is not to say we should overlook what is going on in the body, but that the body is more than biological chemicals and organs to be manipulated into health mechanistically.

In my practice I introduce many perspectives from which clients can view their problems. I find Transactional Analysis, Parent Effectiveness Training (Gordon) and a wide variety of books (I call this *bibliotherapy*) helpful for reassessment of problems and the search for new solutions. Gestalt therapy, dream analysis, hypnotherapy, and analysis of transference and counter-transference offer necessary emotional awareness. Group, marital, and family therapies help with interpersonal relationships. Relaxation, meditation, breathing, imagery, and Eye Movement Desensi-tization and Reprocessing (Shapiro 1995) help to integrate physical, psychological, and relational difficulties. This last group, along with fur-ther selected reading, prayer, a variety of meditations, energy medicine therapy exercises such as the Tapas Acupressure Technique, Emotional Freedom Therapy,[5] and spiritual healing introduce spiritual dimensions to the therapy.

My healing is about caring more than curing. I am a great admirer of the work and writings of Carl Jung, who noted (*Collected Works*, Vol. 8, par. 771):

> The serious problems of life . . . are never fully solved. If ever they should appear to be so this is a sure sign that something has been lost. The meaning and purpose of a problem seem to lie not in its solution but in our working at it incessantly. This alone preserves us from stultification and petrifaction

Leaving theories aside and returning to my fractured ankle:

Three weeks along, about half way through the time I expect I'll have to re-main in this cast, I am getting over my frustrations at having to slow down. I am grateful for the time I now have for meditation and contemplation. I am pleased for the time it is giving me to read several remarkable books which have been beckoning to me from my "to read" shelf for several months, in-cluding The Alchemy of Healing, *by Edward Whitmont, a remarkable Jungian homeopath,[6] several excursions into the Kalahari with Laurens van der Post, and assorted books on angels for a chapter in Volume III of* Healing Research.

Most of all, I am grateful for the deeper insights into feelings of hurt from very, very early in life. I begin to touch the edges of a hurt which is be-yond words, because it started before I had words to describe or concepts to understand it. This is a hurt of knowing there was no one around who was sensitive to my needs, an ache so deep it is beyond screaming out that I AM ALONE ON THIS EARTH IN A VULNERABLE CHILD BODY, WITH NO ONE TO LISTEN TO MY WORRIES AND FEARS, NO ONE TO COMFORT ME PROPERLY.

It was the very early beginning of a determination to stand on my own. And now I have been forced for three weeks to lie helplessly in bed and to be dependent on Ruth and some kind friends and neighbors to bring me the necessities of life so that I can keep my foot up and free of swelling. At age 54, for the first prolonged time in my life, I am learning to ask others to help me—rather than be stoically independent in order to avoid any chance of disappointment, any chance of reawakening feelings of having no one there for me.

Carl Jung had the wisdom to put much of this very simply. He pointed out that all of us have aspects of ourselves that are strongly developed and more within our conscious awareness. We also have polar aspects of our-selves, less well developed and more within our unconscious. For instance, we might be strong in thinking, in which case we are likely to be weak in expressing and dealing with our feelings; or we might have highly developed intuitive senses, in which case the polar aspect of outer senses might be weaker. Our weaker, unconscious aspects exist in what Jung termed our inner *shadow*. One of the greatest challenges and lessons in life is to bring the light of conscious awareness into the shadow of our unconscious self. Because it is an unknown to us, we tend to fear and avoid it. On an individual as well as a collective basis, a deepening aware-ness of our shadow is one of the most important healings we can bring to our lives.[7] When we ignore our shadow sides, we do so at our peril (as I am learning with my ankle). Jungian approaches to this challenge are through psychoanalysis, with a focus on dreams, drawings, and sand play, which reflect not only the individual unconscious but also a person's con-nection with the collective unconscious of all creation. Marvelous as Jungian analysis can be, however, most Jungian practitioners stop short of involvement with spiritual healing.

Even if we attempt to hold everything I've said in simultaneous awareness, this description doesn't begin to touch upon the entire picture. Our individual life dramas are merely subplots in a cosmic epic of vast proportions. We are each as a single subatomic particle in an atom in a protein in a cell in an organ in a creature of which we are an intimate part but of whose life and purpose we cannot begin to have even the dimmest awareness. One of this creature's smaller subcellular organelles is the planet Earth, a concept which we are beginning to appreciate again as the living entity the Greeks named Gaia.[8] We are doing well if we simply recognize our relationship to a something which we know is vastly greater than ourselves, and seek to communicate with it through our higher Self.

I have touched on psychic and spiritual awarenesses[9] which can extend our perceptions well beyond the stage of our life into the domain of the invisible choreographers and even the Producer. We are told by psychics, healers, meditators, and mystics that the pursuit of this awareness is the most satisfying and rewarding of all human endeavors. I begin to believe this through my personal experiences, as well as from lessons taught by experienced masters of meditation, healing, prayer, and religious practices.

When we are thus engaged, we begin to feel our participation in the *All*. The feeling of this connection transcends reason. It brings us into conscious connection with something intuitively felt to be the *Self* or *higher self* or *core* or whatever other inadequate name we give to this inner aspect of ourselves connecting us to the *All*.

Edward Whitmont observed:

> The world we live in is experienced and "created" in terms of the relationship between our minds and the universal information bank of the world mind. Our position in the world is not determined only by our conscious and unconscious volition, perception, feeling, and rational understanding. It is determined also by our active relation to the cosmic "world awareness." To this "world awareness" we relate as to an a priori potential, and unconscious superconsciousness.
>
> The practical implications of this reciprocal relationship are staggering. They amount to nothing less than a new, all-encompassing ecology of everyday life, for science, for the healing arts, and for social ordering. We cannot structure our lives solely by the wishes and hopes of our rational understanding. We are cells and partial functions of that universal mind substance. We are mind interacting with Mind, cells interacting with and dependent on organism.

Therapists must be aware that they are not just healers to those who come for their help. Clients are sent by the choreographers of life's dramas to teach therapists lessons as well. If the lessons are not picked up the first time then a second and third client with a similar problem will be sent. Doctors, psychotherapists, healers, and other careers often comment on the "coincidences" of clusters of clients arriving with the same or similar problems. Such synchronicities are *cosmic itches* which invite us to scratch below the surface occurrence to get to the organic roots behind them, to bring our attention to lessons we are needing to learn ourselves, and to open our awareness to how we are part of an *All* far vaster than our little selves.

All of life is a spiritual experience, every little bit of it. The spirituality is in how we fetch the wood and carry the water, in the awareness and intentionality that we bring to each task. This spiritual awakeness may be simple to describe, but it is most difficult to learn to practice.[10] It can be earned through the disciplines of meditation and prayer, and may be a legacy from near-death and mystical experiences.[11] It comes with being a human being rather than a human doing. Laurens van der Post (1994) has captured its essence beautifully in his descriptions of the Kalahari bushmen, who in the 1950s were sadly losing it as their stone age culture was being eroded to the point of extinction by modern civilization:

> The bows he now made were just for sale; but the one I first saw was a bow not only for enabling him to feed himself and his group but also an image of his urge to procreate and create beyond himself—the badge of the hunter on the spoor of meaning which leads to the self.

Epilogue:

It is late August 1998. Again I sit with my foot elevated in order to prevent it from throbbing when it is on the floor. I had to have the metal plate and five screws removed from my ankle. They were inserted to hold the bone fragments together, and did their job well for three years. However, bony spurs started growing on the screw heads, pushing painfully against the skin if I pressed on the ankle, even in bed at night—so I had to turn to another surgeon for his healing ministrations.

Anesthetic techniques have improved in the interval since my first surgery. The first time, I was groggy for two or three days following the procedure. This time, I was fully awake and having breakfast half an hour after the last stitch was inserted. Only six days after the operation, I'm able to walk about with minimal pain and able to care for myself while my wife, Ruth, is away in England completing her MPhil thesis.

I have learned and grown a lot in this interval. I now live in America, working as an unconventional psychiatrist (largely with children). I've learned to help people release old hurts through remarkably rapid and deeply effective self-healing pressure point techniques. This allows me to add elements of psychotherapy to my brief (limited by managed care) psychiatric interventions. Even more satisfying is the fact that these techniques empower people to help themselves, so I am "teaching clients to fish rather than just giving them a fish."

As I shift my foot on its pillows on the chair adjacent to my kitchen table, I realize just how long a way I've come since I first wrote about my injury.

I've continued my personal practice of meditation and prayer. I've grown more and more comfortable including spiritual awareness in my psychotherapy. Most important, I've been using the pressure point techniques on myself, clearing away masses of old emotional debris. Working on the pains in my ankle and on the upset stomach brought on by antibiotics prescribed to prevent infection in the bone, I came upon startling emotional awarenesses about my ankle.

I fractured my ankle (I don't recall which one) at age three. I distinctly remember my awareness—as I slipped off the top step of the ladder of a playground slide—that somewhere inside me I had intentionally done this. I did not understand at the time why.

Looking back, I now understand that my mother had left me at the summer cottage of a friend while she was working in New York City. This was meant to be a treat for me and a respite from childcare for her. I missed her and felt I was not getting enough attention. Allowing myself to fracture my ankle brought me more attention.

This precedent of seeking more intense outside attention when "abandoned" by my family surfaced again when I had my original accident. This was nowhere within my conscious awareness at the time.

It is only now, as I see myself again with my foot elevated on pillows and Ruth gone that I find some of the deeper meanings behind the surgeries. I did not trust my mother or her friends to be there for me. I had never seen my father—separated from my mother during World War II—so he wasn't there for me either. I had to injure myself to assure that I'd have more intense attention.

The same feelings, totally unconscious at the time of the accident, contributed to my allowing myself to fracture my ankle in going over the black ice on my bicycle. In the deeper meaning of things, it was no accident.

In using pressure point techniques on the pain, I came to the deeper realization that it was not only the people who were close to me that I did not trust to be there for me. I also did not trust God to be there for me.

While this might seem a leap of logic, if not a leap of faith, it works for me. My experience of life is that my physical being reflects my spiritual being. Whatever occurs to me in the physical world is a reflection of my spiritual self. So the injury and surgeries and Ruth's going away these several times all combined to waken me to my distrustful childhood programming in my unconscious, automatic piloting system.

So here are more layers of the infinite onion to peel. . . .

Let us continue now with several descriptions that give us the feel of what it is like to be a healer at work.

Gordon Turner

A Time to Heal: The Autobiography of an Extraordinary Healer, 1974

The late Gordon Turner was one of this century's great English healers. Turner believed that energies flowed both through and from himself. He was one of the most astute observers and reporters on healing. He also saw spirits. He kept an open mind regarding the questions we are examining in this book.

> Before attempting to heal the patient, I would stand behind his chair, resting the palms of my hands lightly on his shoulders. I would clear my mind and try to "sense" the person I was about to treat.
>
> After a few moments, I became aware of his feelings. If he were in pain, I would sense its echo in my own body. With practice the acuteness of my sensitivity made it possible for me to rely on my feelings during these moments of attunement.
>
> I would then let my hands move lightly over the patient's body. As long as I could still my conscious mind they would be drawn to the exact spot where the treatment was needed. My slowly expanding knowledge of anatomy and physiology was a great help. I would envisage healthy organs in place of those that were diseased. If there was an adjustment of the bones to be made, it was essential that I avoided thinking about what my hands were doing—for that matter even looking at them. Healing had to be a spontaneous rather than an intellectual matter.
>
> Healing involved the transmission of energy—I was sure of that. I could feel this flowing through me. If my attunement had been made too casually, or if I became too personally involved in the healing, it would be my own energy which was drawn upon. But if the attunement was good and my mind clear, I could feel the healing power flowing through me from some apparently inexhaustible source. On such occasions I could heal for hours without tiring.

The next healer, the late Oszkar Estebany, is of interest for several reasons. He participated in several of the early scientific investigations of healing.[12] His descriptions and explanations of how he worked put flesh to the dry bones of "a healer" mentioned in these scientific studies in Chapter 4.

Oszkar Estebany

Personal communications, 1982

The late Oszkar Estebany was a healer in well-controlled studies on enzymes and animals (producing significant results[13]) and in less rigorous studies of people.

His life and work have received little attention in healing literature. In telephone discussions and correspondence I found him to be warm, compassionate, and eager to discuss his healing gifts.

He was a major in a Hungarian army artillery unit. He reports:

Figure 1-4.
Oszkar Estebany, one of the most studied early healers in the U.S. and Canada.
Photo courtesy of "Human Dimensions."

> Like my fellow soldiers, I massaged my horse when he was exhausted. After my massage my horse was frisky while the others were hardly rested. I began experiments on the garrison horses, then on dogs and cats. Next, I found that pains of people would go away when I laid my hands on them.
>
> Once I had grown convinced I could heal with my hands I turned more and more to healing. After the Second World War when I left the army I devoted myself entirely to this. During the first years I turned no one away.

Estebany states

> The term "healer" in my opinion is completely incorrect, because we healers only give energy to the patient (call it electromagnetic, spiritual, or, if you like, psychic energy), while the actual healing comes from God, or from nature, depending on the faith and spiritual disposition of the healer. I choose God because—during my long years of practice—I received so much help from above that I would not dare to credit nature. . . .
>
> You ask me what I do and how I do it? With the . . . laying-on of hands (LH) I try to help patients by relieving pain and diagnosing ailments, often ending in prompt recovery. Studying myself I have the feeling that I am like a magnet, naturally not with all the properties of a magnet. . . . I feel as if I were surrounded by a magnetic field. I do not think that I myself radiate the energy directly

or indirectly because I was able to treat at least 20 patients daily, sometimes even 40, without feeling tired or exhausted, and the last person under my hands felt the same "sensation" as the first one. So the magnetic field around me—perhaps combined with my touch—affects the patients the same as a magnet affects a piece of soft iron. The iron approached by a magnet becomes magnetic without the magnet losing any of its magnetic power. All this looks simple and easily understandable, but what happens when the healing is a distant healing, when I can't touch my patient and can't stretch my magnet to thousands of kilometers?

Estebany often used intermediary substances, such as cotton, drinking water, or pieces of paper, as *vehicles* for distant healings.

Really I didn't do anything special, just cut an ordinary sheet of paper into small pieces and sign each piece, but even the signing is unnecessary. I learned that everything I take in my hands picks up my energy, even radiates it and becomes surrounded by a sort of magnetic field. The energy is invisible, but its heat can be felt. Every material has this property to a certain degree, but the most responsive are: water, fibrous material, wood, plant, human or animal body and so forth. One day even the "soul," "spirit,"—though not matter—may take this energy, which would be an interesting topic for you as a psychiatrist. With all this energized material, no matter how far from me, I remain in contact for a long time. I believe this is the reason that I can do successful distant healing only on a person treated by me personally before, or on a person who is in possession of material energized previously by me.

The pieces of paper radiate heat as if they were alive. My friends in Hungary use my letters (typewritten too), by putting them under their pillows in order to relieve pain, and they write incredible stories about this. This is not autosuggestion because it was tried on babies and sick people who were not aware that my letter was smuggled under their pillows.

I want to emphasize that it makes a great difference how long I hold it in my hands. Sister Justa in Buffalo, during experiments, handed me for LH treatment a test tube containing an enzyme called trypsin, damaged by ultraviolet radiation which reduced its activity to 68% to 70%. We got the best results when I held the test tubes in my hands for seventy minutes. I do the same now when treating water or cotton balls.

A treated object can pass energy to another nearby object. To prove this, here is another story: a patient of mine, suffering from cystic fibrosis, had a wood-carving, Dürer's *praying hands*, carved by myself. He kept this carving in his hospital bed, hidden in a towel, because it gave him strength when choking; it was his talisman. One day the nurse, by mistake, instead of the hospital towel, put my patient's towel on the chest of some children suffering from the same disease. The children during the treatment uniformly asked: "Why is the towel so nice and warm today? What a good feeling spreads from it." So the woodcarving passed the energy to the towel it was wrapped in.

I use distant healing more and more often recently. I have patients with cancer, gallstones, kidney stones, bladder trouble and so forth, who are exposed to sudden, excruciating pain, so they call me up by telephone, even in the dead of night, asking for help. These patients, relieved from pain, usually fall asleep during my healing.

Even if we don't see each other, or don't think of each other for years, I remain in contact with my distant patients, provided—as mentioned before—they were treated by me at least once personally before, or possess treated objects. If this is the case, the result of the distant healing is usually positive. Regarding the distant healing, as far as I am concerned, with intensive concentration I would imagine the patient in my presence as if he were before my eyes, then I would use the LH methods over the patient's body in thought, believing that I can awake his dormant energy—which is present in everyone—and believing also that I can even strengthen his energy with the still unknown energy I possess. Since the energy, as a result of continued expenditure, is used up to a certain degree, the treatment in most cases has to be repeated. I believe that traces of the energy remain in the human organism for a long time after the last treatment. It cannot be felt, but when required, it can be activated by both the patient and healer: the former by strengthening his dormant energy, or recollection; the latter by trying to make connection for absent healing. This I wanted to achieve by sending small pieces of treated paper to the patient. Thus, the contact between healer and patient is not constant, just a faint memory, which has to be activated.

There are no set rules for healing. People are different according to their physical and mental capacity and spiritual constitution. So every person has to be treated individually.

In answer to the question, "Do you teach healing?" Estebany answers, "No!" Asked, "How do people become healers?" he says:

I could not explain how anyone could develop this energy in question, or pass it on to somebody else by learning. Healing is a gift of God, a talent according to the Bible. True, everybody can relieve some little pain, but this is not considered healing. One cannot develop healing by study, as is done in other physical arts and sciences. Either you have it inside you, or you don't.

He commented on healing energy:

> I don't feel that I get the energy from outside sources. I feel as if I were a magnet myself with a magnetic field around me, which enables me to give energy . . . .The bearer of this energy is the body, not the soul (spirit). In my opinion, when a healer dies, the magnetic energy remains with the corpse.
>
> Beside the body's magnetism, the spirit also works, directs, and differentiates. An artist or sculptor works with the body, but is influenced by spirit. When depressed, he uses different colors than in a happy, balanced state. But soul, spirit cannot be sick. When, for example, a sick person, suffering from schizophrenia, dies, the departing spirit stays whole and healthy. Otherwise, it would remain sick forever, which does not make sense.

Estebany does not feel he is guided by spirits. He is powerless to help himself if he is ill.

Estebany used intermediary materials as vehicles to make connections between himself and his healees during distant healing. It is not clear whether these substances actually store energy or serve as a means for the sick person to draw energy from Estebany or perhaps from the same source from which Estebany obtains his power. Alternatively, Estebany may constantly be sending energy through these sensitized objects.[14]

Research in parapsychology on clairsentience has shown that psychically perceptible imprints can be left in objects by people who hold them. This supports Estebany's observations. Of course, the objects in addition may be placebos—aids to the healer and ill persons to believe more fully in the healing process and to activate self-healing.

There is a rich lore on healing through saints' relics (Gorres) and numerous reports of healings effected through handkerchiefs by Jesus and the Apostles (Appendix A). Many modern-day healers report they can convey healing in this way.

Each healer has his or her own preferred ways of working. Estebany is unusual in preferring to use bits of paper or other materials as vehicles for his healing. Most healers prefer to give healing directly by the laying-on of hands or with a mental focus directly upon the healee in distant healing.

When researchers wish to study healing it is difficult to know which healers to choose. In the early research it was imperative to establish whether healing worked or not. Researchers therefore chose to work with healers who frequently produced strong results, such as Estebany. However, researchers know that if their work is to be accepted it must be validated through repetitions in other laboratories. If other laboratories use different healers who apply healing in ways which are different from the methods of the first healer, the results may differ in each study—not because healing is not effective, but because the research design used with the first healer might not suit the others.

Bernard Grad began research with Estebany giving healing by holding the cages of groups of mice who had skin wounds.[15] Grad demanded this because he was skeptical about the use of vehicles for healing and because he wanted his study to conform to the more common practice of healing by the laying-on of hands so that it could be replicated by others. In order to get measurable effects, Estebany had to hold each cage of mice for 15 minutes twice daily over a two-week period. When 150 mice were being treated, with only a few mice in each cage, this took up a major part of his day. Estebany finally convinced Grad to let him give healing to pieces of cotton which were then placed in the cages of mice in later experiments on the effects of healing mice with iodine-deficient thyroid goiters. While Grad was skeptical at first, he listened to Estebany's stories of successes in sending people bits of paper and finally let Estebany use the cotton. The goiter experiment was successful, and Estebany was pleased that he could still participate in the research while getting on with his treatments of the many people who requested his healing.

Scientists replicating Grad's study are unlikely to have the services of a healer who works like Estebany. Questions will then arise as to whether each experiment was measuring the same healing effect or something different.

It is imperative that researchers describe the normal practices of the healers studied in any experiment. This is rarely done. Many researchers, in fact, demand of healers that they give treatments of a standard length of time, thus attempting to set up a *standard dose* of healing. This requires healers to practice a much shorter time than most usually allow and puts them under a demand stress which can have negative effects on their demonstrations of healing. Some healers may take several minutes to focus their healing, to connect with whatever level of concentration or sources of energies, or to build up a process of readiness for change in the healee. Imposing a five-minute limit therefore handicaps the healers and may produce a weaker effect than otherwise.

Defining a "standard dose" of healing, however desirable scientifically, should not be linked to standard time intervals.

Healing is experienced in broadly similar ways amongst healers and healees around the world. Each culture colors its explanations of healing in the unique language and life experiences of that part of the world. We may learn much about healing both from the overlaps and the differences in descriptions.

Larissa Vilenskaya
Parapsychology in the USSR, 1981

Larissa Vilenskaya studied bioelectronics and healing in Moscow. After moving to the West in the 1970s, she was editor of the journal *Psi Research*. In the following section, she reports on four healers and several aspects of healing research in the former Soviet Union.

Djuna Davitashvili is one of the best known healers in Russia who treated Leonid Breshnev over many years. She reports that she can diagnose which parts of the body are diseased because different illnesses elicit different sensations in her hands as she passes them over the healee. These include "prickling, warmth or other sensations not easy to define." She can *charge* a plant with healing energy, which ordinary people can subsequently sense as a "prickling feeling when passing a hand near the plant."

Vilenskaya refers to an investigation of Davitashvili's diagnostic ability:[16]

> During the course of the six-week period, 43 people who previously underwent examinations in various medical institutions were examined by J. Davitashvili with the intention of diagnosing their conditions. Concurrence of the clinical diagnoses and the diagnoses made by J. Davitashvili yielded 97.3%. It should be noted that in 49.7% of the cases she diagnosed additional concomitant diseases (which were confirmed in 86.9% of the cases during further polyclinic examination).
>
> In another study, a sensitive thermographic (temperature measuring) device was used to demonstrate post traumatic arterial blockage in the right arm of the healee.
>
> Before the session, the right hand was not visible on the photograph because its temperature was equal to the room temperature, due to the circulation disorder. In the middle of his forearm, a place of sharp decrease in temperature was visible—a manifestation of the malfunctions of body thermoproduction because of cicatrix [scar] changes as a result of the wound.
>
> After the recording of this condition, a session for correction of the biofield of the right arm of the patient was conducted. J. Davitashvili carried out characteristic passes by her right hand along the patient's arm, and he felt clearly several specific sensations: heaviness in his hand, later in the whole arm, developing almost to slight pain, then the patient could not ball his hand into a fist because of the sensation of "pushing away" between his fingers, as if they were "the same poles of magnet." In 8-10 minutes all these sensations disappeared and only the increasing warmth remained, which disappeared after the session. After the end of the session the thermograms of the patient's arm were recorded every 15 minutes. The thermograms showed the increasing temperature, widening of the area of higher temperature, with the hand becoming visible. First, blood volume in the smaller vessels increased and then in the larger vessels. In spite of the tissue changes due to the scar in the middle part of the forearm, the area of the "cold" zone decreased. In 45 minutes after the session, the patient's hand was clearly visible at the thermovisor; its temperature increased, comparing with that before the session, at 2.5-3.0 degrees Celsius, although subjective sensation of warmth was lacking.

> It should be noted that the right ("working") hand of the in-
> ductor [healer] became apparently cooler. The thermograms
> showed the difference in temperatures of the right and the left
> hands of the inductor, despite her doing intensive passes by the
> right hand. In a few minutes the equality in temperatures was re-es-
> tablished after the inductor's autogenic suggestion.

Davitashvili's healing was apparently able to open up a blockage to circulation in a person's arm after an injury. Without surgery it would appear
unlikely that circulation could be restored to an injured arm within the few
minutes required for a healing treatment. This would appear to be a clear
demonstration of spiritual healing. However, it has been demonstrated that
people under hypnosis or other forms of suggestion are able to alter circulation. This is very commonly done in biofeedback and Autogenic
Training.[17] Such control may extend even to the point of stopping arterial
bleeding after injury or during surgery.[18]

We are therefore left with questions of whether the changes in the
injured person's arm were due to the effects of suggestion or of healing.

Vilenskaya reports that Vitaly Yokolev frequently treats headaches. Healees
say that the pain seems to move with his hands as he passes them over their
heads. In this way, he "gathers" the pain at the back of the head, and with a
rapid movement of his hands from beside the temples to the chin, "throws
down" the pain. Healees say at that moment the pain disappears.

Again one cannot know whether suggestion or healing brought about
these changes.

> *Heavier-than-air flying machines are impossible.*
> —Lord Kelvin, president, Royal Society, 1895

Vladimir Safonov, engineer and former freelance newspaper correspondent,
developed intuitive diagnostic and healing abilities. He recommends the
following:

> Those aspiring to heal should, in the author's opinion, have the
> following attributes:
>
> - A desire to overcome the inner barrier of disbelief in the possibil-
>   ity of radiating bioenergy from one's body.
> - Good health and no hereditary disease; age ranging from 30 to
>   50 years.

- Lack of blind respect for an "opposing" authority.
- Some knowledge of medicine and human physiology.
- Altruism and humanity.
- The desire to research and share observations and findings.

Distant healing requires the following: . . . the ability of a healer to concentrate on the person for whom the energy is intended; to be able to imagine (without closing the eyes) the basic features of the person (face, tone of voice, clothes), remembering the last visual encounter with him. Of real assistance is a photograph of the person looking directly into the camera. The maximum length of a distant healing session is five to eight minutes. This duration is connected with specific features of one's thought processes and does not allow prolonged concentration on one thought or image.

An interesting phenomenon that sometimes accompanies Safonov's transmission of energy from a distance is the involuntary appearance in his mind of a picture of the surroundings in which the healer is situated.

Distant diagnosis is possible from photographs.
[A]ny photograph, even one taken in childhood, carries information about the state of health of the person on the day when the diagnosis is made. In trying to learn this method of diagnostics, the following points are of great importance:

- Imagine clearly and in detail that the person whose conditions a healer is to determine is sitting on an empty chair near the healer.
- Having imagined as if it were the real person on the empty chair, the healer can begin the diagnostics with his hands. It is advisable at the beginning of training for the actual person to be present in the room.
- An essential condition is to forget for the moment that you are diagnosing an empty space in which you are imagining the object, but rather to think that you are diagnosing the actual person.
- The diagnosing of the imagined "double" gives the same feeling as during ordinary diagnostics of a patient, only in the former case the sensations are weaker and less easily felt; the healer has to concentrate to the maximum degree possible.
- There is also another method of diagnostics. Sometimes a healer can, without analyzing his sensations, simply know that there is a diseased part of the body under his hand. Knowledge outstrips the observation.
- Distant diagnosis is possible via the telephone. Quite by chance the author found that he was able to diagnose a person while

talking to him by phone. Hearing the voice of the person, he could obtain in his mind an impression of the appearance of the person and of his disease.

• Rejuvenation is possible via visualization.

Throughout the ages, mankind has been seeking an explanation for the process of aging of the organism, trying to preserve the body through the most diverse ways and means. However, each of us can direct the "biological clocks" within us, i.e., we can turn the hands of the clock backwards without the aid of any other force or action outside ourselves. In order to do this one has to restore in his memory one day of his life (hour by hour) when he was young, healthy and happy. This means to live again in the past. It may be for an hour or two, or for a day. Having spent one hour in the past, the organism "charges" an enormous supply of bioenergy.

Safonov can also identify the illness that caused the death of a person from a postmortem photograph.

Safonov makes helpful suggestions for applications of healing. However, he does not explain why good health in the healer is required. This contradicts the experience of at least two healers I know who had serious illnesses from which they were cured prior to becoming healers themselves (Lombardi; Shubentsov). Though the suggestion that the healer should lack "blind respect for an opposing authority" is couched in negative terms, it presumably means the healer should be confident of her or his own abilities. This has been noted by other healers to be important. Safonov's recommendation of visualizations[19] for rejuvenation is unique.

Barbara Ivanova (1984), a Moscow parapsychologist, developed a "method for increasing perception of 'intuitive information.'" These are her instructions:

• Imagine some pleasant event or any picture or image which pleases you.
• Try to understand and remember how you have imagined this— what "place" this mental image occupied in your mind.
• "Wipe off" from your "inner screen" everything you imagined and create a "vacuum" in your mind.
• When an experimenter gives a task-program (e.g. to identify the location of a scar on the body of a person situated in another room), wait passively, "filling the vacuum" by a programmed image. In other words, wait for the appearance of "quasi-visual" or "quasi-auditory" images in the same way and in the same "place" of your mind where you had previously a conscious image.

Vilenskaya states

> Using, along with the aforestated procedure, group relaxation and various exercises on visualization of spontaneous and "programmed" images, Barbara Ivanova indicated that many of her students after several training sessions were able to perform remote diagnostics, successfully determining the nature and location of diseases, as well as locations of pains, scars, tumors, etc. The most gifted students sometimes could receive the name of a disease in medical terms, as "quasi-auditory" information, while not possessing knowledge in medicine and in some cases not even understanding what this name meant. More often students gave some features and locations of disorders on the human body, without giving the exact name of a disease.
>
> According to Ivanova, the same method also leads to development in students of the ability to perceive general intuitive (i.e. clairvoyant, including precognitive) information, not connected with medical problems. Possessing these abilities herself, she observed that the results of the training group were much higher when training sessions were conducted by a "psychic" person. Thus, it appears that not only the training method itself is important but rather some kind of "psychic" (wordless) influence of a group leader.

Vilenskaya compares the healing work of Ivanova, who trained herself deliberately for this ability, with that of Brother Macedo, a gifted natural healer in Brazil.

> Both of them are able to perform mass sessions of healing (Barbara Ivanova during her lectures, and Brother Macedo during mutual meditations of participants); neither need to know the exact medical diagnosis to perform healing, believing that their radiations will "find" the diseased organ or system ("weak spots") in the patient's body.
>
> "[T]elergy" applied by the Brazilian healer (as he coined it), and "bioenergy" applied by Soviet healers, are, in my opinion, manifestations of the same process of interactions of human beings which is as yet not understood by science.

Several testimonials to Ivanova's healing ability are presented. A letter from Ivanova describes a series of controlled experiments in which some of Russia's best healers were studied. No measurable changes were noted. Ivanova notes that the officials reporting the results of these experiments omitted many important details.

Ivanova adds:

> [I]f one has the ability to radiate bioenergy, it is not enough to give one the right to heal. First of all, a harmonization of both patient and healer is necessary, and only afterwards one may try to send his energy. There can be no lasting results without a certain ethical and moral level.

Maria Mir visited the Soviet Union and obtained a number of writings by and about Ivanova, which she and Vilenskaya have put together in *The Golden Chalice*. In this work, Ivanova expands upon her experiences in carrying out and teaching psychic diagnosis and healing. She reports that she always uses either direct contact or, for distant healings, a link-up with the ill person via the telephone. She teaches healing very cautiously to a select group of students who must be ethical and moral people. She feels that otherwise healing energies could potentially "boomerang," affecting the healer negatively.

Student healers are led by very gradual steps to longer and longer periods of healing. Ivanova also utilizes a psychic induction procedure to enhance students' healing abilities. Of special interest are her precautions against dissipating one's own energies in healing, instead of transmitting cosmic energy. She notes that the following negative reactions have been observed in the healers (not in people they treat) when proper caution has not been employed:

- Tingling, which can be so strong as to be "exceedingly tormenting," often associated with sensations of heat
- Muscular contractions, which are occasionally quite strong
- Giddiness, which may even proceed to complete loss of consciousness
- Perspiration
- Exhaustion, which can reach proportions of total weakness and depletion, especially when the healer exceeds his capacities and engages in healing beyond the time limits commensurate with his level of skill
- Feeling of fever, which can include shivering, cold, and weakness, again associated with excessive energy depletion
- Loss of weight, "sometimes 800–1,000 grams after thirty minutes of work"
- High concentration of sugar in the blood, even to levels seen in diabetes
- Blood pressure changes, occasionally to dangerous levels
- Stress-like brain waves, similar to those seen under strong emotional excitement

- Heart dysfunctions with pulse rates increasing or decreasing, and electrocardiograms demonstrating arrhythmias
- Loss of coordination, a rare occurrence
- Temporary loss of taste, smell or other senses, with hypersensitivity or even sensory hallucinations
- Disturbance of endocrine system functioning on rare occasions
- Pains, especially in the extremities, but also in other body parts
- Loss or disturbance of sleep—a frequent occurrence
- General depression, "irritability or other signs of exhaustion of the nervous system, as well as many other symptoms of malfunction"
- All of these disorders can be felt for minutes, hours or days, and some of them even for months, if necessary measures are not taken. . . . We can view these disorders as a stress-response. . . .
- We can avoid these negative responses of mind and body by gradually training the psychic and exposing the body to the influence of our psi energies or that of other psychics only to a degree compatible with the psychic's potential.

Ivanova reports on a variety of uncontrolled studies with success in diagnosis and relief of a range of symptoms and illnesses. She states that a negative governmental attitude in the former Soviet Union, with censorship of reports of healing research activities, led to great difficulties for healers.

In personal communication during a visit to Britain, Ivanova mentioned to me an intercontinental healing experiment. A group of Americans visiting in Moscow videotaped her giving group healing. When the videotape was played to an audience in the United States, the audience experienced healing effects.

Ivanova also shared her feeling that reincarnation is one of the most important concepts she teaches.

> It is not that the same person passes from one physical life to another. Rather, it is a part, or facet, of a much more profound entity which expresses itself in physical existence to work out lessons of love and understanding for relationships with itself, with fellow beings and with its place in the cosmos. (In the West you might say "with God," but this is against the beliefs currently acceptable in the Soviet Union.)
>
> I myself have clear memories of previous lives as a German naval officer in the last century; as a courtesan in Spain; as a man in Brazil and more. It is because of these lives that it was easy for me to learn Spanish, Portuguese and Italian. I apparently never had a previous life in an English speaking country or in Czechoslovakia, because these languages have been extremely difficult for me to learn. After only eight months' study, I was doing simultaneous translations in Portuguese. After three years' study I still could barely translate a

Czech newspaper, though Czech is very close to Russian which I have spoken all of my life.

We must also be aware that groups of people, nations and even the planet as a whole have group karma. This can explain some of the trends and events in history. After nations have swung to the dark side, as with Germany in this century, there is a challenge for its citizens to learn karmic lessons and to work out ways to compensate and make amends for their wrongs.

Ivanova possesses clairaudient perceptions for diagnosis and also for information she channels from sources suggesting discarnate entities, the collective unconscious, and higher intelligences.

Ivanova's methods for teaching clairsentience resemble those of Silva Mind Control.[20] Though they seem reasonable, they still require validation studies.

Ivanova's letter on the unsuccessful experiments implies that the negative attitudes of the observers may have influenced the process or the reporting.

The transmission of healing simultaneously to large numbers of patients has been reported by Olga Worrall and others. This might involve the healer making healing energies available, while the healees are the ones who draw the energy to themselves. This is even clearer in the case of Oszkar Estebany, described above.

I am unsure what to conclude from the long list of symptoms Ivanova reports her student healers may experience. She speculates that they may be related to stress. Perhaps the negative atmosphere in the Soviet Union placed healers under pressures expressed through these symptoms. In the West it is common for healers to report temporary sensations ("telesomatic reactions") which appear to correspond with the healee's symptoms, but it is unusual for such symptoms to persist or to be taken as dangerous.[21] In fact, some healers use these sensations to diagnose patients' problems.

There are numerous healer techniques which seem idiosyncratic to particular practitioners. We have no idea as yet which of these may be essential to healing and which are merely superstitious beliefs.

It is encouraging that relations between the West and the East now permit increased sharing of information.

Our next healer, Mieczyslaw ("Mietek") Wirkus, is a strong teacher in Baltimore who has helped many doctors to develop their healing gifts. He was a subject in a study by Elmer Green, a renown biofeedback specialist, who showed that there are altered magnetic fields around healers when they are healing,[22] and produced some encouraging results in a study on the treatment of skin cancers.[23]

Mieczyslaw Wirkus

Personal communication, 1987

Mietek Wirkus was born in Poland and now lives near Washington, D.C. He discovered his healing ability as a child when he was able to relieve his sister's asthma attacks by placing his hands on her shoulders. Healing is called *bioenergo-therapy* (BET) in Poland, where it has been officially approved as a paramedical treatment. Wirkus was officially licensed there to practice biodiagnosis and BET following completion of practical and theoretical courses and examinations under the commission of the Psychotronics Society of Warsaw.

Wirkus can identify the present and future states of health of a person by passing his hands through the biofield, noting

> cold, warm, tingling, pressure and/or pain vibrations.
> . . . Occasionally I also feel stabbing pains. At times it even seems to me as though an invisible force were tearing pieces of flesh from my palm. In order not to feel the patient's illness and deplete my own energy, I prevent his negative currents from entering my body by dint of mental effort. I imagine that I've created a kind of barrier to them in my wrist. Then I "shake them off" or "rub them off" on the wall.
>
> Recently I find it less and less necessary to bring my hands near the patient in order to discover what's wrong with him. I am developing an ability to perceive diseased organs. I "see" them in very different ways. When I close my eyes they appear to me as if on negatives. At times I perceive something like golden flashes. There are also precise pictures, as exact as those in an anatomical atlas. Once, when I approached a patient, I felt a pain in my kidney. The next moment I caught a clear "glimpse" of his diseased suprarenal gland. However the rest of the kidney I was "viewing" was blurred. It turned out later than the patient really did have problems with his suprarenal gland. Another time, in the right lower part of a patient's stomach, I "glimpsed" a sort of needle pointing into her body. Surprised, I asked the patient whether she had pains in that area. She said yes. It turned out that it was ovarian pain radiating into her body.

Sessions usually last 20 to 30 minutes.

> After examining an individual I begin transmitting my energy to him . . . I generally place my palms on his head, on the spot where the brain center regulating the function of the diseased organ is located. In this manner, by means of the nervous system, I balance the energy levels in the diseased organ and in the surrounding area.

> . . . I even sense the organ in my hands as if I were holding it. I transfer my energy to it, eliminate the blockage, and make the "disoriented cells" return to their right proportions and right place.
>
> . . . [I]t seems as if the organ were blocked by a ring that prevents the proper bioenergetic information from entering it. My job is to eliminate this ring and correct the "mistakes" in the patient's biofield by means of my own energy . . . .

Wirkus finds that people often report warmth or heat in the area addressed either during or after sessions. Some report general relaxation and/or sleepiness. Others report no sensation. "In cases of severe pain a temporary increase (12 to 48 hours) in discomfort can occasionally occur but is soon followed by marked decrease in pain." Sometimes one visit suffices. At other times several sessions are needed. BET does not require patients to participate and has been helpful to infants and comatose patients.

Wirkus believes, as do his colleagues in Poland, that BET restores exhausted energies to an organism from the body of the bioenergotherapist. He finds support for his theory in Kirlian photography, which shows that BET therapists have a wider and stronger biofield than the average person. In Kirlian photography an electrical pulse is passed through an object (such as the hand or finger of a healer) onto a photographic plate in a dark room. The electricity creates images of energy fields surrounding the object. These have been correlated with states of health and illness.[24]

In addition to the laying-on of hands, Wirkus feels

> there is one more condition: You must love people, you cannot have any rancor, malice or hatred in you. Concentrating on kindness and love raises the energy level; it is a source of strength . . . .

Sessions with Wirkus have been especially helpful in healing asthma, diseases of the nervous system, gastric ulcers, ovarian cysts, sterility, nervous illness, psychosomatic diseases, childhood deafness, allergies, and pains of all sorts (including migraine, arthritis, and cancer).

He believes that most people possess a modicum of healing ability and, that with a strong desire to help and with practice, most can significantly develop this gift. He runs workshops on his healing methods.

Wirkus objects to the term *psychic,* feeling that these are natural abilities present in most people, whereas *psychic* seems to connote unusual or esoteric abilities.

It is encouraging to learn that in Poland bioenergy diagnosis and healing are being integrated actively and enthusiastically with conventional medical treatment. I hope that medicine in the West may soon follow this example.

The late Bruce MacManaway was an inspiring teacher of healing. He was a very practical man who used a pendulum as a way of bringing his intuitive awarenesses into consciousness—for diagnoses and appropriate treatments.[25]

Bruce MacManaway with Johanna Turcan
Healing: The Energy That Can Restore Health, 1983

Bruce MacManaway, a Scottish healer, shares a treasure trove of experiences from forty years of clinical practice.

- In surrogate healing, MacManaway gave laying-on of hands treatment by proxy, through the healee's friend or relative, who performed the treatments under the healer's direction. This method proved helpful in cases where the sick person was unable to avail himself directly of the treatments because of the severity of illness or distance from MacManaway.
- Group healings, with several healers treating the same patient, seemed to produce superior results. The authors briefly cite experiments of Maxwell Cade which support this contention, demonstrating enhanced effects on electroencephalograms (EEGs) in healees as increasing numbers of healers participated (Cade/Coxhead).
- MacManaway found that focusing his healing on the spine was especially helpful in a wide spectrum of illnesses, even when the sickness did not appear to be related to the spine in Western concepts of physiological and anatomical processes. He noted, for instance, that healing directed to the levels of thoracic vertebrae numbers four and five were helpful in cases of severe psychiatric problems.
- MacManaway saw energy flows corresponding to Eastern theories of chakras and found changes occurred in these areas during healing.
- MacManaway described an instance in which out-of-body healing occurred:

> There was a small girl in Perthshire whom I knew purely on account of my spare-time hobby which was teaching show jumping to members of the Pony Club. She fell ill and as she was not responding to treatment, her mother (whom I did not really know at all) rang up a mutual friend to see if I would be prepared to help. Unfortunately, I was away and could not be contacted. The friend, having talked to me about telepathy in the past, endeavored to send me a telepathic message stressing the severity of the child's illness. The rest of the story came from the child. She was sitting up in bed the next morning, her fever symptoms gone and loudly demanding breakfast. Her mother expressed surprise and delight. "Don't be silly, Mummy," came the response. "You know that man from the Pony Club, Major MacManaway, came to see me last night." Her mother looked blank.

"Yes, he held his hands over my tummy and it was very hot and then he told me I'd be all right in the morning. And I am."

This excellent book shares numerous techniques and a wealth of healing experience.

All of our healers seem to raise as many questions as they answer. Surrogate healers are described by other healers and by kinesiologists. This intervention suggests several possibilities. Perhaps the surrogate person merely is a telepathic link between healer and healee. Perhaps the surrogate is transformed temporarily into a healer. Perhaps the surrogate adds her or his own healing energies to those of the healer.

Many healers use pendulums. These appear to function somewhat like a dial does on a mechanical instrument. That is, the pendulum may swing forwards and backwards to answer "yes" to a question the healer holds in her or his mind, and left and right to answer "no." Pendulums provide a way for healers to let their unconscious minds provide intuitive or psychic information.

The skeptic may suspect that the pendulum provides no more than a chance response or a response generated by the unconscious mind of the healer without any connection whatever to more than that.

The answer to this question, as to many others, must be found in careful research.[25]

Healing is far too often given as a treatment of last resort, late in the course of illness or injuries which are not responding to conventional therapies. Healers uniformly say that healing is much more effective in the acute stages of illness. While most healers see this unfortunate delay in seeking healing as a complaint without remedy, Edgar Chase found ways to treat acute injuries.

Edgar Chase
Personal communication, 1988

The late Edgar Chase, a surprisingly spry and alert octogenarian, was a healer for close to two decades. He worked as an industrial scientist, head of a management consulting group and university lecturer. He discovered his healing abilities while taking his wife to another healer[26] for treatment of her painfully deformed spine. Edgar (as he preferred to be called) studied anatomy and radionics and used a pendulum in his work.

Retired from active participation in sports and from coaching England's hockey team, Edgar was still an avid spectator sportsman. He was understandably proud of his track record in healing, with a national reputation for treating severe sports injuries. Athletes whose doctors predicted they would be sidelined for the rest of the season were back on the field at the end of a week after Edgar treated their injuries. During his late years, he had considerable success treating more difficult diseases, such as cancer, multiple sclerosis and post-traumatic coma. People in coma for weeks and months returned to consciousness after Edgar's treatments.

His methods are noteworthy in several respects:

- In scanning people's bodies diagnostically with his hands, he noted sensations associated with particular dysfunctions: "A fracture feels like a toothache; muscle problems are a dull ache; a trapped sciatic nerve can feel like a serious electric shock in my hands; depression and nervousness like a prickle; cancer like worms moving under the skin; asthma like mites under the skin; and pituitary gland imbalance like an irregular vibrating moped engine."
- With knowledge of anatomy and physiology, Edgar stated he was able to do the following:

    > I can visualize the structure of each part of the body and diagnose problems from imbalanced radiations which emerge from the body, and by treating at this location, the healing energy has a direct route to the centre of the root cause of the problem.

- Edgar found that pebbles which he held for a while (particularly from Iona, known as an earth "power point") seemed to carry curative powers for his patients.
- In distant healings (which he felt were effective when touch healings were not possible) Edgar connected best with the healee if he had a lock of hair and a photograph. He felt he had greatest success if he tuned into the patient's mind by rotating their photograph to a particular orientation indicated by a dowsing pendulum. He felt it was important for the healee to be in a quiet, receptive state when healing is being sent. He also sent distant healing by placing the photograph and hair on a medium-sized stone which he had held in his hands for many hours, saturating it with healing.
- He found he could markedly reduce anxiety if he directed healing through his fingers to particular points on the shoulders and neck which are related to anxiety (according to instructions he received from a Japanese acupuncturist). He also treated hormonal and emotional problems by directing healing to the pituitary, allowing patients to heal themselves.
- When imparting healing to a person or an object, Edgar's thumb, forefinger and the intervening web of muscles would twitch for the duration of treatment. When sufficient healing had been transmitted the twitching ceased automatically.
- Edgar believed healing works by restoring life force to atoms which have been depleted of this energy.

- Edgar was able to treat himself effectively for many problems. Partial loss of vision in his right eye, which had developed four years before, was now fully restored as a result of self-treatment. He had no colds for decades. He subsequently developed arthritis in the hip. He said he was unable to heal himself of this problem mainly because of the physical restrictions in orienting his hands to the correct position.
- Kirlian photographs of his fingers during healing, made at Birmingham University, demonstrated a flare between three and four inches long around his index fingers. The Kirlian aura was only a quarter of an inch long when Edgar was not visualizing healing.

Edgar did not know how his healing succeeded in many cases where even conventional therapies had failed.

> There could be a psychological explanation. Since a treatment session seldom lasts less than one hour, there is a unique opportunity to get to know the patient and his problems in life. The total problem is identified, and it is possible to treat "wholeness." Patients are encouraged to talk about the problems they face and in doing so they defuse their difficulties. Objectives can then be created to optimize the resources available and to identify additional resources that have to be acquired if the objectives are to be achieved. This is "The Cybernetics of Wholeness."
>
> [T]hose patients who recover from "terminal" illness or illnesses classed as incurable by medical technology do so when their own body healing powers are stimulated or regenerated by a gifted healer who can reverse despair and despondency to genuine hope— as a result of experiencing positive responses to the healing energy, which complements and makes effective the treatment given by the orthodox medical consultant . . . .
>
> It is important that patients in hospitals should not be treated by a healer without the knowledge and consent of the doctor. If a change results from the treatment, positive or negative, the doctor might be confused and could draw wrong conclusions as to the effectiveness of his own treatment.

Chase's spectrum of healing practices was broad. His potency may have been enhanced by his understanding of anatomy, as well as bearing witness to his dedication to being a good healer.

I was unable to obtain a satisfactory explanation from him as to why he couldn't heal his own hip by absent healing.

Edgar Chase graduated from many of the practices of radionics into healing without using dowsing devices. This is again typical of some of the better healers. Pendulums and other aids for making intuition conscious are helpful at first, but may not be needed after more experience.

Visual imagery is used by numerous healers in a variety of ways. Dean Kraft focuses on some of these. He has strong psi abilities as well as healing gifts.

Dean Kraft

Portrait of a Psychic Healer, 1981

Dean Kraft, a gifted natural healer, describes a number of loosely controlled experiments in which he participated. In those that were conducted carefully, he was able to achieve the following:

Influencing cancer cells in a laboratory. HeLa cancer cell cultures are standardized cell preparations that grow tenaciously on the walls of the laboratory culture flasks. Few cancer cells are dislodged even if the flasks are vigorously shaken. In five trials (one at the Livermore Laboratories in California and four at the Science Unlimited Research Foundation in San Antonio, Texas), Kraft was able to loosen many more cancer cells than were dislodged in control flasks. Cells were visually counted in a hemacytometer. Four trials lasted 20 minutes each. In the fifth trial, lasting 60 minutes (three 20-minute sessions), the cancer cells appeared not only to be dislodged but also destroyed. Dr. John Kmetz reports these findings are significant, i.e., the possibility they occurred by chance was less than one in a thousand. No data are presented to support these claims.

Influencing an unspecified instrument which measures electrostatic fields. Kraft was able to do this repeatedly, at will, within a Faraday cage to exclude extraneous electromagnetic fields.

Kraft made other interesting discoveries: EEGs recorded during healings demonstrated increased alpha waves. Simultaneous EEGs of the healees showed some activity which was synchronous with that of Kraft.

Kraft was able to influence a magnetometer in an informal test.

He has repeatedly demonstrated strong, focused psychokinetic (PK) ability, moving small objects such as pens solely through intention at will. He has also assisted police with clairsentient clues which helped solve crimes and located missing persons. Kraft finds exercising his clairsentient and PK abilities much more exhausting than healing. He frequently faints with the exertion of PK demonstrations.

He reports he can alleviate headaches, muscle and joint pains, paralysis following trauma, herpes zoster ("shingles") colitis, ocular hemorrhage, congenital deafness, depression, and can cure a variety of cancers, including multiple myeloma.

Kraft describes his methods. He intuitively developed techniques of concentration, shutting out all of his thoughts and tensions, breathing deeply to quiet his mind. After relaxing his body and mind,

> I usually spent five to ten minutes with each sick person, during which it seemed to me that I was giving him or her a "dose" of my energy. I've never been entirely comfortable using the word

energy in connection with what I do, since no one has ever established that there is a transfer of energy involved, but from the first
time I did psychokinesis, it seemed to me that something like energy (in my mind I saw light) was coming out of me and
connecting to the object, and a similar model seemed to apply to
healing. Indeed, almost all the people I worked with claimed to
feel a pulsating energy, like electricity, passing into their bodies,
often accompanied by a sensation of warmth.

Visualizing the person's problem area was very important. If a
person had a cancerous tumor I would visualize the fleshy malignant mass. Then I would place my hands about half an inch
above the skin over the affected area, at the same time imagining
the diseased tumor beginning to disintegrate and dissolve. The
more vividly I could visualize the troubled spot the more satisfied
I was with my interaction with the ill person.

In another example, in curing a woman of shingles he reports that he visualized the stimulation of blood flow to facilitate her healing. He also
visualizes that he is channeling energy from nature during healing.

Kraft once suffered symptoms similar to those of a patient. She had a
small, red rash on her face. On returning home after giving his treatment,
Kraft noticed a similar rash on his face in exactly the same place. The healee
phoned that evening to report that her rash had disappeared.

After I hung up the phone, I studied my reflection in a mirror.
Suddenly I felt a surge of anger, and I yelled aloud to the empty
room, "I won't allow it! I won't be in a position to pick up someone else's symptoms!"

The next morning the mysterious rash was gone, but the incident
made me realize that I had better protect myself. To me that meant
that I must, through concentration, keep my "energy charge" so
high, so positive, during healings that I would be unable to receive
any negativity from the ill person. Since then, no similar incidents
have occurred.

Kraft believes that a whole complex of factors must harmonize in order for
a healing to occur. These may include his own and the patient's mental
state, as well as astrological and electromagnetic factors. He feels that such
factors must be aligned, somewhat like the multiple sights of a gun. When
they are approximately lined up he can achieve a modest result. When they
are precisely aligned, then major changes may occur.

Kraft's descriptions of his observations, experiences, and ideas are
extremely helpful. He is not unusual in demonstrating psi gifts along with
healing. However, the magnetometer and electrostatic field tests are insufficiently described by Kraft to permit comment.

In personal communication, Kraft has shared medical reports and
videotapes of his successful treatment of a woman in advanced stages of

amyotrophic lateral sclerosis (ALS; also called Lou Gherig's disease or Motor Neuron Disease). This is a progressive degeneration of portions of the spinal column and brain, starting with muscle twitches and weakness and eventually producing paralysis and death. There is no known cause or conventional cure for ALS. This is the only report of a cure of ALS which I have ever heard of, by any method.

Thus far we have focused primarily on descriptions of healing methods and the sources of healing energies. Healers also speculate on how healing works. One gets the impression from their varied reports that there may be one or more essential common denominators in their observations, filtered through the personalities and belief systems of each one, so they appear distinct and even contradictory at times.

The following report comes from a seminar I attended with a gifted Russian healer. Unlike Estebany, who felt that healing could not be taught, Yefim Shubentsov firmly believes that most people can learn to develop their healing abilities.

Yefim Shubentsov

Healing seminar, Philadelphia, 1982

Russian healer Yefim Shubentsov emigrated to the United States in 1980. Raised in an orphanage from about the age of two (his parents disappeared, and he does not know what happened to them), he says, "I had to be tough to survive!" He grew up with the mixed careers of boxing instructor, painter, and free-lance illustrator and artist. In 1969 he was hospitalized because of a large tumor on his right leg. A bone graft was necessary after its removal, because the wound healed poorly. A friend introduced him to some people who were exploring healing. He was told he had healing ability and could probably help himself. Though initially skeptical, he successfully healed his own leg wound.

He soon proved to himself he could relieve pain and improve other health conditions. He joined a group of investigators, first as a hobby, but soon became convinced it should be his life's work.

Shubentsov studied aspects of medicine and practiced many techniques of concentration, visualization, and methods of activating diagnostic and therapeutic bioenergetic skills. From 1972 to 1980 he was head of a research group at a bioelectronics laboratory.

Today he lives in Boston, practicing *bioenergetic therapy*. He taught his methods to physicians and others interested in healing. Here are some of his ideas:

There are positive and negative biological fields of two types.

- People sometimes find they have natural aversions to others. This is because of differences in their biofields. It is easy to test this. Two people need only hold up their palms towards each other (as though about to push each other away). At a distance of an inch or two between the palms it is possible to detect a sensation of warmth or cold. If warmth is felt there is a positive interaction between their fields; if cold, the interaction is negative. Positive and negative social/psychological interactions are anticipated in accordance with these sensations. These qualities are permanent characteristics and cannot be changed.
- A person can make his fields positive or negative in another sense. By positive or negative thoughts or with variations in health and disease, a person's field acquires positive or negative characteristics. The positive feels cool to a healer's hands; the negative warm and prickly. These can affect others positively and negatively, producing relaxation, relief of pain and healing, or the opposite. In extreme cases, such as when a person who had a disease makes a present of a piece of jewelry she wore to someone dear to her, she may actually be doing her dear one a grave disservice. The jewelry may transmit negative effects to the next wearer. Such fields can be cleansed from the object by a healer simply through appropriate passes of his hands over the object.
- The healer protects himself and the sick persons from negative effects of such fields with the mental affirmation: "Nothing negative from me to you or from you to me."
- These negative effects are the basis for the "evil eye." In small towns it is easy to identify the person who emanates negative "vibes" when he visits. Everyone knows everyone else. When three neighbors each notice separately that one person's visit is associated with negative vibrations, he is identified as the source of these feelings and accused of the "evil eye."

Shubentsov believes healing can be taught to everyone. This involves no miracles. It is a physiological process, unrelated to belief systems. Basic points about healing include the following:

- Through practice, hands can be sensitized to various emanations from inanimate and animate objects. This provides sensitivity to the biofield for diagnosis. Practice in sensing the biofield leads to a "vocabulary" of sensations associated with various physiological conditions. By repetition the healer can learn which sensations are correlated with which conditions.
- A broken, green twig can provide practice in the sensation of injury.
- Healing energy is emitted by one of a healer's hands more than by the other. With experience one discovers which it is. This is then used as the active hand, which is held over the point of pain or illness and moved with a clockwise motion (facing the patient). The other hand is held immobile on the opposite side of the body to enhance the healing effect.

- The optimal time of day for healing powers can be identified. Very advanced healers who have learned to control their energies can heal equally well at any time of day or night. The beginning healer should take a series of containers with earth and seeds in them and, keeping light and watering constant, give healing to each container at different times of day. The plants growing best will reveal the healer's most potent time of day.

Distant healing is performed with a visualization of the subject. Shubentsov makes his usual passes over the visualized body. This can also be used by the healer for self-healing. In this case, he visualizes himself and gives his visualized-self the healing. The healee can make contact with the healer from a distance, via a picture of the healer. This may be a basis for the efficacy of religious objects such as crosses or pictures of saints.

Healing energy directed with a probe at acupuncture points is many times more effective than insertion of needles at those points. Touch healing is more powerful than auric healing. Healing energy applied to medications can markedly enhance their potency.

One must be careful not to treat a pain that may be caused by an illness of acute nature for which the pain is a danger signal.

Shubentsov prefers to treat specific illnesses, where he has demonstrated success in healing.

These include:

- Allergies of all sorts (These are Shubentsov's specialty. He holds the subject in his therapeutic biofield while having her smell, touch, or taste minute quantities of the allergen for increasingly long periods of time. This desensitization while undergoing healing treatament can produce total cessation of allergic reactions forever with a single treatment of about 15 minutes per allergy. Shubentsov includes Raynaud's and Buerger's diseases with his category of "allergy to cold.")
- Headaches, including migraines; high blood
- Myopia (nearsightedness, which can be markedly reduced with healing in some cases and only slightly in others; the progressive deterioration of vision with myopia can be halted in most cases)
- Nystagmus (tremors of the eye muscles) of various cause; arthritic pains (not deformities); muscle pains of all sorts
- Circulatory insufficiency due to atherosclerotic disease
- Heart disease, including atherosclerotic problems, angina, post-myocardial infarction (heart attack) recuperation; (cardiac arrhythmias may be exacerbated unless proper [unstated] techniques are used)
- Ulcer-pains, not bleeding; constipation; hemorrhoids; impotence; menopausal hot flashes
- Phobias, habits (overeating, smoking), and obsessions respond to a particular healing technique within ten seconds. Shubentsov asks the healee to vividly visualize himself enjoying his habit or experiencing his phobia

or obsession. Shubentsov then visualizes a situation himself, which is extremely negative, while making powerful passes in front of the patient. He claims that single sessions produce cures in the desires or negative thoughts, if the patients do not go back to experience them in the next few weeks.

Shubentsov prefers to treat problems that respond readily and rapidly to healing. A marked subjective or objective response within the first session is a good sign. If no response is obtained after an hour's effort, prospects are generally poor for marked benefit from his healing. This is not to say that his healing cannot help in difficult cases. Moderate improvement is possible with daily treatments of an hour or more for such problems as paralysis following strokes or trauma, or polio-related neuromuscular problems. However, Shubentsov feels such investments in time and effort are inordinate and draining to the healer.

Shubentsov says that aging processes are arrested when people are exposed over long periods to healers' fields. "In the years I worked in my institute in Russia, those who worked within a 16-meter radius of myself did not develop wrinkles!"

Shubentsov feels that healing energy comes either directly from the healer's body or is channeled through the healer from an unidentified outside source. He himself is a tireless person. He literally has never known what it means to be tired and has had to question others in order to gather some concept of what this means. He can work for many hours not only without subjective tiredness but also with equal effectiveness at the end of his work as at the beginning. He sleeps only about five hours nightly.

In the 1970s, Soviet scientists sought to demonstrate the efficacy of this therapy in 100 cases. No controls were required. Healing is an elective subject in some Russian medical schools; Shubentsov taught 400 doctors in his last years there. The government was taking a very serious interest in these phenomena, not only for health reasons but also for potential military applications. For this reason, Shubentsov warns that any information released from old Soviet sources regarding healing is likely to be of minimal value or possibly even deliberately misleading.[27]

Shubentsov suffers from limitations to his practice imposed by the American medical system. He may not diagnose or touch a patient for fear of prosecution. In the Soviet Union, where doctors were all salaried, they were often happy having healers or others help their patients. There was no competition for patients' business that would produce restrictive legislation against healers.

Shubentsov's orientation is extremely pragmatic. He wants to be sure his treatments are effective and therefore chooses illnesses that will rapidly demonstrate observable and preferably measurable response to healing. Having learned healing by arduous and exacting practice of techniques of observation, and sensing/treating with his hands, he is extremely clear on how to teach others these skills.

For this reason, Shubentsov has little appreciation for controlled studies. His observations are likely to include Type I errors. I am skeptical regarding the effectiveness of his treatments for phobias, obsessions, and habits.

Many healers report sensations of heat and cold but do not interpret them as more than indications that healing is occurring.

The caution against removing pains is logical, but I have never heard of a person endangered or harmed through such removal.

Shubentsov's views on teaching healing, diametrically opposite to Estebany's, suggest that healers' opinions may be strongly colored by their life experiences and beliefs. Healers tend to generalize from their personal experiences without checking with other healers to verify whether their views are accurate. Alternatively, perhaps the healing of gifted natural healers differs from that of those who develop their gifts intentionally.

Since the policies of Perestroika have been introduced, healing in Russia has been freed of much governmental constraint. Healers are flourishing in private practice and in collaboration with doctors and other complementary therapists. Some even have popular TV programs, with reports that healing can be received through video transmission.

There are no whole truths; all truths are half-truths. It is trying to treat them as whole truths that plays the devil.

—Alfred North Whitehead

Healing from serious illnesses may be influenced by many factors, such as diet and surgery, as discussed by Joseph Zezulka, a Czechoslovakian healer.

Joseph Zezulka

Biotronic Healing, 1976

Joseph Zezulka had been a healer in Czechoslovakia for about 30 years when he shared this experience and advice. He calls himself a biotronic healer. He identifies *material, psychic,* and *vital* components of a person's being, which contribute to normal growth and health. Vital energies are absorbed through breathing, eating, and sleeping. Vital insufficiency produces disease. Biotronic healers transfer vital energies from the environment to the healee, not drawing from the healers' own vital energies.

Zezulka differentiates between two types of healers:

Magnetizers can passively transfer vital powers, but they do not know exactly what they are or how to regulate them. They use touch healing. "I would presume that the magnetizer's healing is accomplished by strengthening the centers of power in the sick person's body with the translated powers, so that the lines of force regain their balance."

Unconscious coloring of the transmitting power by each magnetizer's own qualities may produce greater success in healing certain kinds of diseases than others.

Sanators can actively and purposely regulate and control the vital powers as they transfer them from the environment to the sick person. Sanators cannot give an overdose of healing energy. Healees will only absorb as much as needed. Sanators correct imbalances of energy at the levels of cells, organs, and total body. Their healing acts through a *morphological center*, which regulates and controls body functions.

Zezulka feels some people can only relieve pain and that this can be harmful because it may mask disease processes which would then go untreated. He makes recommendations for healing cancer. He stresses that diet is a crucial factor, giving the following food recommendations:

Prohibited: smoked and roasted foods (including coffee and chocolate), fried and baked foods, and tinned foods with benzoic acid.

Recommended: Fresh, boiled, or stewed fruits and vegetables, milk and milk products. Cooking should be done with water added.

Dietary recommendations are helpful adjuncts to healing but are not curative.

These suggestions are based on the observation that plants lose their *vital capacity* with time after being harvested. This he apparently deduces from Kirlian photography which shows an aura around plants that gradually diminishes after they have been plucked.

Zezulka then describes his spiritual healing ability.

> Besides the classical "taking off" the plasma [*aura*] spoilt by disease and an overall filling of the patient with vital energy, I influence locally the liver. I try to increase its detoxifying function and to strengthen it generally, especially the part to the right of the sternum.
>
> In the next phase I influence the morphological centre (my view and term) which I presume to exist in the cerebrum. It is a centre which commands the form of the body as a whole, then the individual organs and cells.
>
> I exercise an effort to disturb the pathological neoplasm and to achieve balance in the morphological signals whose chaos may be caused both on the afferent and efferent tracks.
>
> Only in the last phase I exercise local influence on the cancer. I concentrate on its cells and modulate the stream of energy towards tranquillity. I try to pervade the organism of the cells and to disturb their excessive and excitative activity. In this the tranquillity power may be given in greater amounts. This is why I often use water and work with wet hands. In this way the overall vital energy is modified and its tranquilizing part is increased. The same manner is used later to dissolve the tumor. The process of dissolving may not be equally easy in different types of cancer. This is why it is

good to ask the surgeon to remove the tumor after the healing process is over. The afflicted spot is the "locus minoris resistentiae," where new cancerogenous process might start after some time. The surgeon should operate only after the healing process is over because in some cases the operation may not be necessary.

Surgical removal of the remaining tumor decreases the likelihood of metastases. Between 10 and 15 healing treatments are advised prior to surgery, and further healing afterwards. Follow-up healing treatments over five years are advisable, with continued adherence to the diet.

Zezulka's warning of healers who might endanger a sick person by masking a warning pain signal from the body echoes several other healers. This is logical but has never proved a problem in my explorations of healing.

His comments on confirmation of his dietary theory by increased relapse rates if patients stop the diet are questionable. Rather than attribute relapses to dietary indiscretions, why not ask why a person would go off the diet? Not sticking with a very strongly recommended diet seems to me far more likely an indication of psychological self-destructive motives, which could themselves lead to relapse. Of course, no theory can be established without proper controlled experiments.

Alexei Krivorotov and his two sons, all healers reporting from Russia in the 1960s, were well ahead of their time. They describe some of their methods of healing and speculate on ways in which healing may work.

Victor Adamenko

Electrodynamics of Living Systems, 1970

Victor Adamenko, of the former Soviet Union, discusses theoretical issues and the relationship of Kirlian photography[24] to healing. He starts with a description of Alexei Krivorotov:

> A. Krivorotov prepares himself for the treatment session by concentrating in thought on the patient. Thereupon by forcibly rubbing one of the palms against the other he makes his hands dry and in a slow motion over the patient's hair electrifies his hands. If the patient is healthy, he feels at five to ten centimeter distance a "subjective" heat from A. Krivorotov's hands pleasantly spreading throughout his body. The sensation of heat corresponds to a temperature of 45 to 50 degrees Celsius and cannot be measured objectively. Some people experience the feeling of light prickling, easiness, intoxication, or, on the contrary, heaviness.
>
> As A. Krivorotov slowly passes his hands at some distance along the patient's body, there arises in the patient approximately at the

site of the sick organ a strong subjective sense of heat, at times almost unbearable. A. Krivorotov also feels at this place an intensification of heat in his hand. Stopping his hand, he says: "You feel pain here." A. Krivorotov's hand remains at the sick organ until the sensation of heat becomes annoying. It is a signal for the session to be terminated. As a rule, A. Krivorotov has no knowledge of diagnosis in advance. Perception of "heat" in different people is different and is, apparently, related to whether the disease is more or less serious. In the case of a serious disease the treatment session takes less time, whilst as the patient makes progress the treatment increases in length. Sometimes the subjective sensation of "heat" at the site of the sick organ persists in the patient for two days. However, in the process of treatment there gradually sets in an adaptation to A. Krivorotov's field. In some patients the subjective sensation of heat is accompanied by the sensation of vibrations whose frequency differs from person to person. Remote "heat" is not perceived by everybody and, until he met Academician Nikolai Zelinsky, Krivorotov used to place his hands on the patient's body. Zelinsky experienced a very strong sensation of heat and in order to allay the sensation he suggested that A. Krivorotov should keep his hands at some distance. When A. Krivorotov's hands were about five centimeters away, Zelinsky said: "The heat is just as strong as I need it."

A. Krivorotov deals primarily with nervous diseases. Particularly good progress is made in the treatment of nervous exhaustion, but there were cases of the curing of such diseases as lupus. Rather quickly cured is poliomyelitis, but hypertension, bronchial asthma, polyarthritis yield very slowly to treatment, the effect being at times completely absent.

Similarly to A. Krivorotov, the method of bioenergotherapy is possessed by his sons—Vladimir, a physician, and Victor, a mechanical engineer. However, the subjective sensations induced by them in the patients are different. A. Krivorotov produced in the patient, as a rule, the feeling of a strong avalanche as of "heat" whereas his son, Victor, the sensation of slight pricking.

An analysis of A. Krivorotov's work has revealed that participating in the process is a strong electrostatic field. Occasionally slight discharges take place between A. Krivorotov's fingers and the patient's body. Subjective sensations of heat cannot be produced by a low-power source of electrostatic field as is produced by A. Krivorotov and, moreover, it is absolutely inconceivable that this "heat" can persist in the patient's body a few days.

Therefore, it is obviously a question of a reflectory [sic] effect of an electrostatic field from Krivorotov's hands on the patient's skin receptors, whilst a prolonged feeling of heat persists in the patient's memory. Thus, A. Krivorotov's effect on the patient through electrostatic field takes place on the information level.

Semyon Kirlian, after examining A. Krivorotov's integument skin, arrived at the conclusion that during preparation for the treatment process the dielectric properties of A. Krivorotov's hands are improving. This conclusion finds support in high-frequency photos of A. Krivorotov's hands in a high-frequency discharge field. S. Kirlian also cites experimental evidence in support of the electrostatic field being generated by A. Krivorotov. However, as already mentioned, a subjective sensation of heat due to A. Krivorotov's electrostatic field could not be produced with the aid of a technical electrostatic field. The sole conclusion to be drawn from this is that either A. Krivorotov's field is qualitatively different from a technical field, or it merely accompanies the effect of some other agent. In any case there exists a correlation between A. Krivorotov's electrostatic field and the subjective sensation of heat, produced in the patient.

An unusual feature in this report is that as the healee improves, Krivorotov's treatments take longer. The opposite is more often the case with other healers.

It is hard to know what to make of the Kirlian and electrostatic readings. Further studies of the correlations of these with subjective sensations and with results of healing appear warranted.

Heat is the most common sensation reported by healers and healees during healings. It is often used as an indicator of seriousness of illness and as a measure of need for treatment. It is unusual for the sensation to persist for more than a few moments past the termination of the laying-on of hands. Objective measurements of heat during healing do not demonstrate a rise of temperature. This seems to suggest a synesthesia, or crossed-sensory perception. Nerve endings which perceive heat may be stimulated by healing energy of some sort which is different from heat but which overlaps with it in some manner to stimulate the nerves.

The differences reported between the three Krivorotovs in sensations produced in healees is echoed by healers around the world. There appear to be distinctly different sensations with each healer, and there may also be differences with the same healer on different occasions. This implies that there may be differences between healers in healing energies or in other parameters of their treatments as well as differences in healing treatments given under varying conditions.

Victor K., Alexei E., and Vladimir K. Krivorotov

Bioenergotherapy and Healing, 1974

The Krivorotovs assume that healing is biological psychokinesis, using energies originating in the healer. They report their experience and recommendations on a number of parameters of healing:

The healee should relax and focus his attention on the part(s) of the body in need of healing.

> It must be emphasized that the cooperation of the patient is of paramount importance if a cure is to be achieved through bioenergotherapy. If we examine the problem of human illness from the psychological aspect, it is conceivable that any illness, either directly or indirectly, is mentally initiated by the patient. Therefore, the patient himself must be induced to eliminate his own illness. When he begins to resolve the manifold psychological contradictions which can exist in the human mind, bioenergotherapy will have a greater effect.

The healer focuses his whole attention on the patient.

> The healer also imparts biological energy to the treated zone which supplements and reinforces the energy provided by the patient.
> We have all experienced the feeling of cheerfulness which is associated with the application of effort to the achievement of a goal. This is the very inner state which is needed for the healer to engage in bioenergotherapy. Specific sensations in the hands are linked with these feelings. These sensations can be distinguished once a person has developed sufficient experience. Thus a healer can learn how to voluntarily control his internal state to produce the feelings which allow biological energy to emerge.

Duration of treatment is from one to twenty minutes. Duration and depth of healer concentration depend on

- The extent to which the healer is prepared for the activity by virtue of his training.
- The nature of the patient's illness.
- The degree of cooperation elicited from the patient.

Any illness in the healer may be intensified during healing. Certain patients may drain a healer's energy, requiring the healer to rest before treating someone else.

The person being healed may feel the following sensations: tingling, goose-pimples, generalized warmth, and initial focal pain under the healer's hands in touch healings, often fading within one or two minutes. After treatment, some patients feel alert and cheerful while others are tired and may even sleep. Focal warmth may persist for hours after treatment.

The healer identifies areas on the subject's body in need of treatment by a sensation of vibration in the healer's hands.

The Krivorotovs claim the bioheat emitted by healers is distinct from biological energy (heat measured with thermometers). The bioheat can produce sensations of asphyxiation, in which case the healer may have to continue with hands off the body.

Methods of applying biological energy include the following:

- *Static*—hands remaining stationary.
- *Dynamic*—hands moving—for spinal treatments and widespread illness.
- *Linear*—on extremities of spine.
- *Rotary*—in region of heart or solar plexus.
- *Local*—at sites of disease
- *General*—energizes the local site plus the entire nervous system; used in cases of exhaustion and lethargy.
- *Healer's hands held next to each other*—best for general method; hands feel tingly, painful, become warm.
- *One hand*—may have different energy from the other; either hand may be used alone, depending on which is empirically found to be effective.
- *Directional energy application between hands*—hands placed on either side of problem area, with energy directed from one hand to the other; hands feel smooth and quiet, no temperature change, but definite sensation of "current" flow.

Why the Krivorotovs feel heat more than other sensations is not clear.

Many Western healers theorize that if they feel tired after giving healing they may be draining their own body energies. If healers visualize opening themselves to cosmic energies, they often do not tire, and some even find that healing stimulates, strengthens, and refreshes them.

The observation that illness is exacerbated during healings is not reported by others, though pain is commonly aggravated. Such *aggravations* of symptoms are also common at the start of treatment with homeopathic remedies.[28]

The following report on the Krivorotovs expands the possibilities of how healing may work.

Victor K. Krivorotov

Some issues of bioenergy therapy, 1981

Victor Krivorotov explains his understanding of Bioenergy Therapy (BT), based on many years of practice and research. He feels that BT is brought about by activation of energy in the healer's hands. He notes that electro-magnetic phenomena are a part of the process, as demonstrated by photomultipliers (in the ultraviolet range), which picked up an increased emission during BT of 200 percent to 300 percent.

He adds that BT appears to have a "resonant nature"

> because a healer using the method does not become tired. Tired-ness appears in the periods of overcoming the inertia of the ordinary condition of the hand, in the process of maintaining the inertia of its active state, as well as in the process of overcoming passivity of the general condition of the organism. All these attempts require, at times, strong concentration of willed effort. One cannot exclude that a hand is only a means for the energy contact, and the information for the elimination of pathological processes is transmitted by additional channels, which at present are not known to us . . .

He feels BT may act in concert with several other forms of therapy, such as psychotherapy and acupuncture, to bring about a healing, because it works in part via stimulation of acupuncture points.

> The higher stage of BT is not only the treatment of a disease but rather the entire interaction of two systems (two organisms) on all levels. Bioenergy exchange has its necessary place in this inter-action, but not always the first place, because the bioenergy function does not take the highest position in the general hierar-chy of all functions of a human being.

Krivorotov makes the following points:

Healing treatments require concentration by both healer and healee.

Krivorotov recommends treatment be given for 10 to 30 minutes. A shorter time is insufficient for "energy contact." Longer times "decrease the efficiency of therapy; the organism begins an adaptation to this stimulus, and in further sessions it can result in total ineffectiveness of therapy."

Some healers, of less than maximal ability, are effective only at certain times of the day.

Biotherapists of the medium level are able to perform healing only at the time of maximum psychophysiological activity of the organism; usually it occurs from 10:00 a.m. to 1:00 p.m. and from 5:00 to 7:00 p.m. Biotherapist-beginners are active in these intervals not every day, but only during days which are most favorable for their psychophysiological conditions; usually it is connected to climate factors and phases of the moon.

The healer "has to be healthy and an energy active person. A practicing biotherapist has to observe a certain regime of nutrition, sleep and maintain contact with nature."

Krivorotov divides the organismic (in contrast with cellular) functional systems, which he calls the macrobioenergetic systems into the following categories:

- Psychic functions: thinking, emotions, control
- Sexual (psychosomatic) functions
- Somatic functions: digestion, motor function, respiratory function

The interaction of all macrobioenergetic systems has two regimes: an imbalanced regime at the conscious level and a balanced unconscious regime. Mainly the activity of a person occurs in the imbalanced regime: to perform some action one has to highly activate one of the systems, simultaneously suppressing activity of the others. This is a principle of existence of any organism. To solve a complicated mathematical task, one has to almost stop the activity of his muscles, stomach, etc. The degree of the imbalance has its limits; if the organism oversteps them, it often leads to pathology, because a subsequent balanced regime cannot be achieved. This can result in long deformations for some systems of the organism. The balanced regime is manifested considerably in the deep sleep (identified by delta-rhythms) and partly in the paradoxical stage of sleep as well as in the waking state in the periods of decreasing conscious activity (which is of a rhythmic character). The way of life of a contemporary person with a high level of conscious activity can cause an overloading of the organism by these imbalances. This leads to an increasing rate of diseases. Pathogenesis, as a result of imbalance, is a phenomenon characteristic of human beings in the civilized world. Animals cannot overeat or overexploit their sexual function. Human beings received this opportunity from nature but did not acquire enough knowledge to use it. Having lost unconscious ways of regulation, we must learn to use conscious ways.

What is the role of BT in normalizing the balance?

BT includes two essential energy procedures. The first is the attempt to achieve the equilibrium of all macroenergetic systems of a patient. Along with this "tactical" procedure, the strategic approach is necessary: to convince the patient to change his way of life. "Tactical" balance is achieved by the influence of the active hand of a healer, although sometimes it could occur due to the psychotherapeutic factor, i.e., by the patient's effort of will.

In some cases, the first session of BT can occur at the level of achieving the general energy balance until the patient learns how to preserve this state. The second energy procedure is activation of a pathogenic zone (this is the BT itself).

One of the main tasks of BT is to preserve, for a lengthy period of time, the level of activity of a pathogenic zone which was created by the energy-active hand of a healer, without damaging other functions of the organism. This task can be successfully solved if a healer is aware of macrobioenergetic laws . . . a person who has mastered the art of BT, clearly understands that without this inner transformation of a patient his recovery will be only of a temporary nature. . . .

Krivorotov postulates an internal energy system which is correlated with the individual's value system. Behaviors contrary to the value system drain the individual's energy and leave him prey to biological and psychological malfunctions and diseases.

By contemplation, a person may resolve conflicts affecting the macro-bioenergetic and internal energy systems. Krivorotov proposes the following subdivisions:

- *The System of Control:* "The healthy mind creates the healthy body."
- *The System of Thinking:* "Let our thoughts clear the world from vanity and contradictions."
- *The System of Emotions:* "By negative emotions one kills himself and others, by positive emotions one constructs the world, and by microemotions one cognizes it. We came to this world for cognition and creation."
- *The Sexual System:* "It is not reasonable to dig a new well for each sip of water, moreover, if there are springs not far away; i.e., it is not expedient to exploit the system of reproduction for the sake of pleasure."
- *The Digestion System:* "Don't eat for pleasure, but rather eat with pleasure; if you've eaten more than you needed, you've . . . left somebody hungry, because one third of mankind is starving."
- *The Motor System.* "Your muscles are like a hound; when a hunter gives his hound an opportunity to regularly romp, the hunting is successful."

- *The Respiratory System:* "Breathing is like a Genie who awaits his moment; the moment will come when the healthy mind creates the healthy body."

Krivorotov decries the views of modern conventional medical cosmology:

> All methods of intervention ultimately decrease the resistive potential of a person. From the very beginning, these methods were intended to be used in cases of emergency when there was only one choice: death, or further life with decreased potential. In order to save a patient, physicians treated the disease but not the patient. Gradually "the method of intervention" became the main method of medicine, which is applied for all, including non-dangerous illnesses, without vital necessity. This unconscious orientation of contemporary medicine also decreases the potential of a human being as a biological system on the genetic level. In "fighting for life" today, the "medicine of intervention" unconsciously worsens the future of mankind. At present, the majority of people, beginning from infancy, apply one or another kind of medical treatment, and we encounter a sad paradox: in spite of the high development of medicine, the disease rate is increasing each year.
>
> What is the reason for this strange situation? One of the main reasons is the spontaneous development of medicine, without a theoretical and philosophical consideration of global problems. The second reason, which is a consequence of the first one, is that while being spontaneous, it appears to be influenced by patients who demand use of "methods of intervention."
>
> Observations show that the increasing number of patients who demand this method, results from an incorrect way of life and an egocentric being. However, the "medicine of intervention" gradually changed human attitudes, and at present the majority of people cannot accept the idea that diseases result from violation of moral and ethical laws. Therefore, science looks for reasons for disease only on a physiological level, and non-scientists view appearance of disease as an accident caused by fluctuations of external conditions. In this situation all mankind is forced to pay for delusions of mistaken people.

Krivorotov points out possible broad social effects of spiritual healing:

> We see that patients who were subjected to BT increase their level of feedback concerning processes in the organism. They begin to feel a sense of responsibility for their health and actively participate in the process of recovery. Thus, the way to the world of self-regulation will lead people to the way of "self health care" and will free the tremendous social forces which today are spent for health care.

We also mentioned that on the basis of responsibility for their own health, people will become aware of their responsibilities for others. As we excluded religion from our life, we were unable to find a substitute for its function in the regulation of human ethical interrelations.We believe that after BT becomes a widely accepted method of therapy, a physician (who will be at the same time a healer) will take a mission of a spiritual teacher.

Larissa Vilenskaya has translated a gem of wholistic medicine from Eastern Europe.

Viktor Krivorotov's views are strikingly consonant with those of Western wholistic medicine. His observations on the effectiveness of some healers only at certain times of the day echo those of Shubentsov and of acupuncturists. This may explain some of the puzzling variability in results obtained with spiritual healing.

Krivorotov's opinion that cognitive changes must occur in order for benefits of healing to be long-lasting is echoed by many but not all healers. His conceptualizations of the workings of the mind and body closely parallel Western ones but are sufficiently different to be worth studying.[29]

I know of no other healer who claims that too long a healing treatment is deleterious.

The late Olga and Ambrose Worrall are described in three excellent volumes, each providing fascinating views of how great healing gifts are discovered and developed.

Ambrose A. and Olga N. Worrall
The Gift of Healing: A Personal Story of Spiritual Therapy, 1965

This book presents a personal account of the Worralls' lives, recounting how each separately, and later both together, developed healing gifts.

Ambrose A. and Olga N. Worrall with Will Oursler
Explore Your Psychic World, 1970

This series of questions and answers explains the experiences and cosmologies of these gifted healers.

Edwina Cerutti
Mystic with the Healing Hands: The Life Story of Olga Worrall, 1975

Edwina Cerutti reports on discussions with the Worralls, especially Olga, regarding experiences with and understandings of healing; letters and references documenting their work; brief descriptions of several studies in which Olga participated; and Biblical references to psychic phenomena by category: clairvoyance, spirit control, spirit voices, messages from departed spirits, spirit return, levitation, and trances.

Olga laughingly admitted she was no scientist, and did not truly understand how healing works. She was able, however, to share explanations which the spirit world had given her and her husband, Ambrose. She felt that since Ambrose was a scientist, he made more sense out of these explanations.

He said that spiritual healing is a rearrangement of the micro-particles of which all things are composed. The body is not what it seems to be with the naked eye. It is not a solid mass. It is actually a system of little particles or points of energy separated from each other by space and held in place through an electrically balanced field. When these particles are not in their proper place, then disease is manifested in that body. Spiritual healing is one way of bringing the particles back into a harmonious relationship—into good health.

Olga's healing was colored by her psychic abilities. She would receive psychic information about a person's background, sometimes including a diagnosis, which helped her know how to help a person—through healing or in giving information and advice. Thoughts would appear in her consciousness with a clarity which conveyed unequivocally that she had been told something. Occasionally a voice would communicate internally, or she might perceive a spirit form of a man or woman next to the healee, and the messages which were communicated were of great importance and benefit to the healee.

Olga felt that laying-on of hands healing is a vital part of the development of novice healers. In her own healing she found that absent healing was just as effective. This was accomplished through "a universal field of energy which surrounds both her and the patients. . . ." During absent hearings she perceived a "cool kind of power flowing from her solar plexus." In addition, she received instructions and help from discarnate advisors, particularly spirit physicians.

Olga did not feel that prayer was necessary in the form of petitions to powers on high for help. She preferred to make "a request to be used as a healing channel and an expression of deep gratitude for the fulfillment of the request." It is not essential for the healee to pray.

Hiroshi Motoyama, a Japanese biologist, tested Olga Worrall on his meridian-measuring device, which demonstrates findings apparently specific for healers. The device measures electrical potentials at the end-points *(seiketsu points)* of the 28 meridians. In ordinary people, the measured levels are between 0.1 and 0.26. Olga's values were in the range of 1.0, four times those of the average person. Significant changes were also recorded after Olga gave healings. Motoyama interpreted his findings to indicate that Olga projected healing more from her left than from her right hand. The kidney, digestive, and heart meridians reflected the greatest changes during healing. These are correlated with the heart, solar plexus, and throat chakras.[30]

Also helpful are segments from the Worralls' book with Will Oursler. Ambrose Worrall states:

Individualized man expresses his individuality by his ability to select ideas of his own choosing and show them to others in
observable form through the use of his will and the law of creation. This operation of the will of man upon the idea, or that
which is desired, involves faith. The principle of creative law is
without limitations. The demonstration of this principle is limited by the extent of man's belief in it. The passive selection of an
idea, without the act of willing it into motion, will never produce
an active demonstration. Man must believe in the creative law. He
must learn to trust it, to know that it always works.

This combination of belief and trust is the foundation of faith,
the kind of faith that Jesus spoke of when he said: "If ye had faith
as a grain of mustard seed, ye might say unto this sycamine tree,
Be thou plucked up by the root, and be thou planted in the sea;
and it should obey you." That's from the 17th chapter of St.
Luke, sixth verse. Since man cannot escape the results of the operation of creative law, he is selecting new ideas and motivating
them. He can bring about such changes in his condition, environment, and activities that creative law will allow. . . .

Reality is in the imperceptible. Man makes the error of seeing the
effect as reality whereas the Cause is reality. Looking upon effect as
reality brings confusion to man's mind. The enormous complexity
of effect is so great that man's mind cannot encompass it. Yet man
can think of Cause, the single source of all manifestation, God,
without being overwhelmed with the multiplicity of formulas applicable to effect.

On using healing forces negatively, as in killing weeds:

I think it would work that way, too. But we are very, very careful
never to tune in on destructive thinking. The problem with that
would be that if we started to experiment in that direction, thousands of people tuned in to us might be affected. We don't know
enough about the mechanism yet. It may work on plants, and it
may work on a patient who is attuned to us at that time. So we are
afraid to experiment.

On water held by Ambrose Worrall for Dr. Robert Miller:

I [Ambrose] asked him whether he had made any other tests on
the water, and he said he had poured some of the water into a pie
plate, that he had gotten some special photographic film from a
photographer and put it over the pie plate and left it there all
through the weekend. The photographer told him he couldn't
possibly get any reaction on this film from distilled water in a pie
plate. What he actually got was a photograph of the pie plate and

water, which they have been unable to explain. This was special photographic film which was sensitive only in the high ultraviolet range. . . .[31]

On plants:

Ambrose, you say you prayed for the plant. What was your actual ideation? Was it an encouragement of growth, or what?

I think you might say that our attention probably creates a carrier wave and that this other force, whatever it is, modulates that carrier wave in some way and is carried through and does its work at the other end.

Olga Worrall stated that she did not believe healing could be taught (1981). She felt people either have the ability or they do not.

The following quotes from Cerutti clarify the relationship between Olga Worrall's healing, psychic, and spiritual experiences.

You were explaining the "psychic overlay" in your kind of spiritual healing . . . and frankly, it leaves me in a quandary. What I mean is: do I have to have some kind of psychic ability in order to do spiritual healing? Is that a prerequisite

Figure 1-5. Olga and Ambrose Worrall were among America's best-studied early healers.
Photo courtesy of Psychic News, London

for setting up a healing service in a church, or for even attempting spiritual healing? Because I'm about as nonpsychic as you can get!

"Definitely not," Olga reassured him. "The spiritual healing I do is enhanced by my psychic gift, but spiritual healing can be, and usually is, accomplished by people who are neither clairvoyant nor clairaudient, nor mediumistic in any way. The healing current flows through every clear channel available, whatever the healer's psychic abilities or, for that matter, religious beliefs. As a matter of fact, I don't profess to have psychic intervention available in every case. My clairvoyance is entirely spontaneous and can't be turned on and off at will. Many people call me and expect a prompt psychic diagnosis—as if their ten-cent pieces in the telephone should start my motor up like coins in a washing machine. Sometimes it does, and sometimes it doesn't."

Olga Worrall (1982) saw spirits from childhood and was in communication with Ambrose when he passed on before she did. I asked her what she understood of reincarnation. I was surprised at the vehemence of her scathing criticisms of anyone who believed in reincarnation, which she felt was a silly notion.

The Worralls point to a complex interplay between healer and healee, involving, at least, beliefs, visualizations and energy transfers.

Harold Sherman surveyed a number of healers on many aspects of healing, Here, Ambrose Worrall elaborated on his views:

Harold Sherman
Your Power to Heal, 1972

> When I undertake to help a sick person, I sit with the patient and do what I call a "tuning-in" operation. This is done by sitting in a relaxed state and fixing my attention on the patient, but not to any specific part of the body or the condition that may be existing. In this way I avoid being biased in the direction of a particular condition which the patient thinks he has and which may be an effect rather than a cause. After the "tune-in" has been accomplished, the conditions are such that the "force" can flow. It will flow providing the potential in the patient is lower than the potential of the healer. It will always flow from the high to the low potential. This is putting it somewhat in materialistic terms, but I do not know any other way to explain it. The power that flows is entirely impersonal. Although I am instrumental in creating the conditions which permit the force to flow, actually I have no control over it whatsoever. I believe that it will only flow when the conditions are right and that the extent to which it will flow is governed by a condition which can be likened to two batteries, one that is highly charged and one that is not so highly charged. When they reach the same potential, there is no further flowing of power.
>
> During a treatment, I do not feel a power flowing into me from an external source, but I feel that the power builds up within me. However, I do feel the power flowing from me. It seems to flow in the form of heat when I do the laying-on of hands. While using this method of treatment, the power flows from the portion of my hands that are in contact with the patient.

In the case of "absent treatment," I do not feel power flowing from my hands but, instead, feel it flowing like a cool stream from my solar plexus. Usually I have the sensation that something in the form of a cylinder some twelve inches in diameter seems to extrude from my solar plexus to a distance of twelve to fourteen inches. A force then turns my body to focus this cylinder in the direction of the patient. After the cylinder is focused, I feel the power flowing for perhaps ten seconds, and that is the extent of the "absent healing." This force which I feel in "absent healing" is a cool force, quite different from the warm force experienced during the laying-on of hands. I have no explanation for the apparent difference in temperature.

I feel that this discharge of power is probably accompanied by a lowering of my vitality during the treatments. Half an hour after I have finished the treatments, when I once again am in tune with my physical body, I become aware of a tired feeling. However, I think this is purely physical.

After I work all day and then work all evening, it is natural that the vitality of the physical body should reach a low ebb. This has nothing to do with the flow of spiritual power which, I feel, is something entirely independent of the physical body. The physical body is merely a channel through which it flows.

During a healing treatment I do not turn my attention to some far-off place up in the heavens, nor do I look for the source of power anywhere else or ask it to come to me. I just have a feeling that it will be available when the conditions are right and when I permit myself to become the channel for its use.

. . . Unfortunately, some people are not clean. When this situation exists, I do not feel at home and feel a discordant condition. I have a desire to get away from the person. To overcome this feeling requires effort and energy, and under such conditions, one can never attain the attunement which is necessary to get the best results.

Whether or not people believe they can be healed has no effect on me. If a person in active opposition said, "I know you can't help me," it would probably build up a barrier and so prevent his receiving help, although I have no way of proving that this would be so. I have had cases where people have come not believing and received excellent results. I have had other cases where they came believing and received very little help.

When I put my hand on a patient during a healing treatment, I feel as if I am wearing gloves. When my hand touches the skin, something seems to be between the skin and my hand, and the feeling is not the normal sensation one gets in touching a person. There is a difference that is hard to explain. The feeling of some layer between the patient and my hands may be caused by my being out of tune with my physical body. Perhaps there is a dissociation of the spirit from the body to some slight degree which gives me this sense of separateness. I have never been able to explain this phenomenon to myself, although I have many theories.

When the power flows through my hands, I feel heat and sometimes I feel pins and needles. If I am treating a skin disease, I feel the pins and needles very strongly, and I feel it more strongly if I have some part of the body enclosed in my hand.

Ambrose Worrall's scientific background enhanced his observational powers. It may, as well, have shaped the expression of his healing gifts.

The divergence of experiences and opinions of healers is perplexing. While there appears to be a common ground, the differences are often quite striking. It will take much study to tease out the wheat from the chaff.

Most of the healings we have considered thus far have occurred gradually over a period of several days or weeks. The late Harry Edwards was renowned in England for bringing about instantaneous cures. At first the newspapers trumpeted reports of his miraculous healings. Eventually these were no longer news—only another unusual healing by the famous Harry Edwards.

Edwards was a keen observer and shared many of his clinical notes and theories in several books. He believed that spirit guides assisted in healings.

Harry Edwards

The Science of Spirit Healing, 1945

Harry Edwards was one of the greatest healers in modern England. At the peak of his career, he received thousands of letters weekly requesting distant healing.

Edwards distinguished three types of healing:

Magnetic healing ability is possessed by most people, especially if they are in good health. In fact, a healer who is not in good health, is tired, or otherwise not in top condition should not engage in magnetic healing because it can sap her vitality. It is the simplest and easiest type of healing, recommended especially for painful conditions.

. . . The beginner should try lightly resting his hands over the region, and as he does so . . . consciously direct with all the power of his mind that the pain will be smoothed away. The hand need only rest on the part for a short space of time while the mental effort is being made.

A visible sign of healing power experienced by many healers—as with the author—takes the form of subdued light streams of an iridescent pale blue color flowing from the fingertips. These streams are most easily seen in subdued lighting against a dark background.

If the tips of the fingers of both hands are held close together, the stream from one fingertip will join up with that from the opposite finger. On increasing the distance between the fingers the stream or ray becomes attenuated. When the hands are moved alternately upwards and downwards, or in circular movement, the rays still link forefinger to forefinger and so on. When substances like two pieces of wood or card are placed in the centre of the light ray the latter penetrates both and is seen between the two separate pieces . . . .

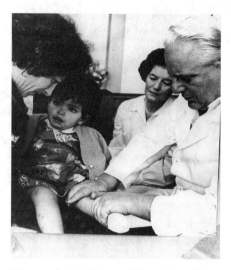

Figure 1-6. Harry Edwards giving healing to Linda Martel, who was born with congenital spina bifida, hydrocephalus, and heart problems, but was herself a powerful healer from age 3 to 5, when she passed on.

Photo courtesy of Psychic News, London

Spiritual healing, in the Edwards terminology, is healing with the aid of spirits of persons who have died but who still wish to help the living.[32] He believed spirits helped in most healings.

There must be a healer to act as the human instrument or medium for the applied spirit-healing forces. Through him are the forces that can transcend and overcome the causes of the illness and restore the physical distortion of harmony. To enable the human instrument to be well used, there must be the willing co-operation of the total organization of the healer: mental, physical, etheric and spirit. Using the human instrument is the spirit-healing Guide or Guides. The two, the healing medium and the healing Guide become co-operators. The human mind interprets the condition of the patient—the spirit-healing minds are concerned with the diagnosis and correction of the disharmony.

Contrary to magnetic healing, the spiritual healer rarely feels tired or distressed after healing, no matter how many patients he treats or how tired he was previously.

[T]he patient also possesses the trinity of bodies. If that were not so, then the patient could not be receptive to the healing forces.

When a patient appears non-receptive, it may be that there is a disharmony between the physical and spirit bodies of the patient, so preventing any "tuning-in" between the healer, his Guides and the patient.

Edwards mentioned that *manipulations* should also be included under spiritual healing. Here the healer allows his physical body to be "used by the Guide through direct control." Edwards reported numerous cases in which severe physical abnormalities such as arthritic, deformed spines were moved into normal alignment with return of physical functioning within seconds by such manipulations. Sometimes several sessions of treatment by manipulation would be necessary, realigning the bones in stages.

In *absent healing* only the intangible medium of thought exists:

[A]bsent healing is directed by the healing medium on behalf of someone at a distance—generally a person whom the medium has never seen . . . distance is immaterial.

Edwards often was called upon by intermediary persons to heal an absent healee. This situation could occur when the healees were too debilitated to apply for help themselves; when they had no familiarity with spiritual healing; when they were mentally unbalanced or minors or even when they and/or their families were opposed to spiritualism. He believed this made no difference to his ability to help.

He believed there was no set formula or procedure for absent (or any other type of) healing. Upon receiving the oral or written request the healer

sends forth . . . a thought force that help may be given to the patient.

This thought emission is generally given at a set time of the day when the healer can sit (either by himself or with friends) in seclusion and silence. He then divorces from his mind all considerations of a worldly nature and "tunes-in" to his spirit Guides.

The healer must have full confidence in the knowledge that through the instrumentality of his mind-directing-consciousness the healing spirit Guides in association with him can receive the thought appeal on behalf of the patient.

Edwards noted that the healee need not be aware of when the healing is sent and that the healing seems to be more effective when the healee does not know that healing is taking place. He speculated that this may be because sick persons are unused to clearing their minds and entering a meditative, receptive state. When they anticipate healing, they may actually tense themselves and therefore make themselves unreceptive to the healing. Furthermore, the healer may not be aware that she is sending healing. In some instances,

Edwards forgot to write down a request for healing or to attend to it consciously, yet patients still reported marked relief from their illnesses.

> The only logical explanation of these spirit healings is that, during the moments when the healer was being told of the patient and the illness, the healer mentally framed the desire to help. The essential thought emission was thus made and received by the healing Guide and acted upon. It may well be that the barest fraction of a second is all that is necessary for this to take place (the conditions for transmission and reception being favorable) to set the healing process into motion.

Edwards noted that he was often aware of the diagnostic condition of the healee during healings. This included perceptions of incidents associated with the cause(s) of the illness, along with the time frame within which the ill health occurred. He also became aware on occasions of the healee's physical surroundings during the distant healing.

> What happens is this. The healer has "tuned-in" to his spirit mentors, his eyes are closed, and his inner self is concerned only with asking for help for, say, "Mr. Griffiths of Bradford, suffering from duodenal ulcers." As the healer's inner self dwells on the situation, so there becomes pictured on his consciousness a vision of the room in which Mr. Griffiths is in. This vision is as vivid and precise as if it were physically visible—as if the healer were actually in the room.
>
> The picture may last only a moment or it may appear to exist for a number of seconds. The vision, however, is so vividly and firmly impressed on the mind that every detail can be remembered with ease: The color scheme of the room, the furniture and its characteristics, whether the patient is in a chair or in bed, the windows, curtains, etc., also the patient himself, whom, it will be remembered, the healer has never seen.
>
> [N]ormally to record such a picture mentally would require an appreciable number of minutes for a mind trained to observation, to absorb, individually, each item and register it in the memory. With spirit traveling, the picture is real and alive and so impressive that the picture lives on in the healer's mind and he can recall every detail without stress.

Edwards found that such perceptions could be verified later as having been entirely accurate in every detail, including the presence of other persons in the room with the healee. His explanation for this phenomenon is that

> man has three main bodies, of which the spirit body with the spirit or inner mind is the principal agent used in spirit healings. This spirit mind is not primarily concerned with recordings arising out

of the automatic reactions of physical associations, such as everyday sounds, touch, etc. It receives these experiences, it is true, but they are inferior experiences. The principal function of the spirit mind is to act as the directive thought agent. This comes into play when the individual consciousness is at issue, i.e. when there is need for mental concentration or for the need of creative thought. It is the repository of human experience, the propelling power for action. It is the reflection of the individual's character, and, most important, applies the motive-power for the spirit body.

When the healer "tunes-in," he surrenders the thought superiority of physical matters to that of spirit healing, which becomes, for the time being, the dominant superior. So that for spirit traveling, the dominant spirit mind, freed from the inferior physical mind, is free to travel to the surroundings to which it is attracted, namely the patient's condition.

Edwards pointed out that, conversely, spirits are able to interact with the physical plane through this same process, using the human medium (channel) as their instrument for communication.

If this is so, then when the spirit mind of the healer travels there should be some human instrument in the visited surroundings which can act as the medium for the recording of the vision. A second hypothesis is that the spirit mind of the healer sees the spirit bodies of the patients, etc., as all are harmoniously "tuned-in" in the same manner as in the case with normal vision, when a visitor calls. The vision of the appointments of the room, etc., being recorded by the spirit mind from their characterized etheric counterparts.

When a patient is ill, he is either very often in a state of slumber or his mind whilst awake is slumberous—in other words, he is not very much concerned with normal physical matters. Thus his spirit self is in the condition to be in harmony with the visiting spirit mind or spirit-healing Guide.

Edwards emphasized that a specific request must be put forth for the healing to occur. It will not take place without this. Spirit guides are available to help but they do not usually interfere of their own volition.

He noted that the trance state in which he performs healings

is the overshadowing of the normal consciousness by that of the Guide. The trance condition may vary from 5 to 99%. Those healers able to work, and at the same time retain sufficient [sic] of their normality to be acutely aware of what is taking place, experience the greatest joy in healing—for there could be no pleasure which would excel the exquisite delight of the inward realization of knowing when the disharmony has been removed.

The ability of the healer to attain to a condition of trance may be described in this way: he divorces from his mind every thought of ordinary things and allows his spirit mind to become superior. This art of surrender is the hardest part of psychic development, but with perseverance becomes a natural change. This change may be described (inadequately) as the healer feeling a sense or condition enshrouding him, as if a blind [curtain] had been drawn over his normal alert mind. In its place he experiences the presence of a new personality—one with an entirely new character—which imbues him with a super-feeling of confidence and power.

An absorbing interest in the patient's condition occupies the entire mind and there is no room for any other thought. Should any outside interference occur, the healer feels it acutely. His whole energy and power is focused upon the patient with zeal and directiveness whilst endeavoring to investigate and remove the cause of the trouble.

The healer is conscious of intelligent movement with a directive purpose behind it. There is no automatic movement. If the hands are being used to dissolve a growth, it seems as if the mind occupies the fingertips. They seem to become mentally sensitive. If the hand is used to remove pain, then the hand possesses the sense of "wiping away" the pain. If the healer, aware that strength must be given to a weak part of the patient's body, rests his hand over the affected part, he feels the flow of vitalizing power pass from himself, through his arm and hand to the patient. There is intelligent effort behind every act the healer performs under the direction of his Guide.

While this takes place, the healer may be only dimly aware of normal movement, speech, etc., taking place around him. If a question is addressed to him about the patient's condition, he will find himself able to respond with extraordinary ease and without mental effort—in other words, the more knowledgeable personality of the Guide provides the answer. Thus does the healer "tune-in"—it is the subjection of his physical sense to the spirit part of himself, the latter becoming for the time being the superior self under the control of the director.

The great joy of healing in this way is experienced when the treatment is nearing completion. The healer becomes aware of a feeling of intense pleasure, as he knows inwardly that the healing has been successful. A feeling of ecstasy pervades his whole being.

No wonder is it that healers feel that the gift of healing is "divine," is beyond price and cannot be commercialized!

Edwards speculated that some *healing rays* or *cosmic forces* may be involved, but felt these are as yet not understood in conventional terms. He felt that spirits affect the body through the heart and/or bloodstream.

Healing is possible, he noted, not only for physical and emotional problems, but also for relational ones. The interactions of people who had not related well to each other often improved with healing.

Edwards was instrumental in forming the first, and now the largest professional group of healers, *The National Federation of Spiritual Healers.*

Edwards was, particularly to me as a psychiatrist, painfully unaware of the unconscious mind and its functions in monitoring the internal and external environment, in storing information and in programming responses according to previous experiences, especially traumatic ones. He may have attributed to spirits much that the unconscious mind could account for. Emotional conflicts and tensions can bring about changes in the physical body. Resolving such conflicts and releasing such tensions can improve a wide range of physical symptoms.[33] Edwards appears to have been ignorant of such mind-body interactions. On the other hand, some of what is currently accepted by conventional psychology as the work of the unconscious mind may in the future be found to be related to higher consciousness or to spirits. Perhaps, indeed, it is just two different ways to characterize the same phenomenon. Though much of his theorizing and speculations on spirit influences may appear unlikely within conventional Western paradigms, anecdotal (M. Long) and scientific evidence is gradually accumulating to support belief in such matters.[34]

I am bemused by the fact that the British Confederation of Healing Organizations discourages healers from mentioning that they sense spirit guidance as a part of their healings. There are potential legal problems here. How would healers be judged in court if they claimed that they were not responsible for a negative effect of healing because it was caused by interventions of spirits?

Edwards was able to alleviate symptoms and cure severe physical illnesses very rapidly. He sought to help healees connect with awareness of their spirituality. I wonder whether he may have alleviated symptoms in such a way that their symbolic purposes to the healee might have been missed. More discussion on this subject will be found in Volume IV.[35]

Edwards deliberately avoided learning medical diagnosis and terminology in order to leave his mind unfettered. Though this may have left him free of conventional biases against unusual healings, it also prevented him from being able to describe in precise medical terminology the problems he was dealing with. This makes evaluation of his reports difficult. For instance, when he reports a "growth on the head," one does not know whether this was a traumatic lesion, a chronic infection, a benign or malignant tumor, or something else entirely.

Edwards' clairvoyance is a psychic ability which is common in healers. Many healers can perceive the condition of the healee from a distance. Edwards was also able to perceive the surroundings of the healee.

The ethics of sending healing to people who are unaware or unwilling to have it are problematic. Most healers will agree to send healing to those who are not capable of deciding for themselves (infants or people in coma, for example) if their relatives agree to it. Many will refuse to send it to people who are of legal age and in a condition to be responsible for themselves and have not requested it.

Edwards was one of the first healers to be studied by a doctor.[36]

Most people appear to have some measure of healing gifts. Even children may be strong healers, as evidenced in the next report.

Charles Graves

The Legend of Linda Martel, 1968

Linda Martel was born on the island of Guernsey with multiple congenital abnormalities. She had spinal bifida (incomplete growth of the lower spine), hydrocephalus (water on the brain), and heart abnormalities. She spent her first two years fighting for her life in a hospital.

At age three, living at home with parents who were not devoutly religious and who did nothing to initiate them, Linda began to demonstrate strong healing abilities. She would lay her hands on a person who had pain or illness, appearing to know intuitively just where on their body her help was needed. Within minutes pains would disappear.

With time, it was found that she could impart her healing to clothing or pieces of cloth. These could be worn or carried in a pocket and would convey the healing.

One would think a child like this might find resonations in church or other religious forms of expression. Linda, however, showed a strong aversion for church and would cry vigorously if taken by her parents to Sunday services, which they attended irregularly. Her upset was so marked that they stopped taking her.

Linda died at age five. By then she was so well-known as a healer that many people, not having heard of her death, were still approaching her parents to have her help. Her parents resourcefully cut Linda's clothing into small pieces which they gave to people in need, knowing that this would still convey healing.

Linda Martel was one of the strongest and best known child healers. I expect there will be more child healers as parents become more comfortable with healing so that such gifts in their children can be encouraged.[37]

Healing through the vehicle of cloth and other materials is common to a number of healers, as we saw with Martel and Estebany.[38] Healing with the use of handkerchiefs and other materials was described in the Bible.[39] I know of a nurse who feels unsafe to give healing openly in her hospital. She gives healing to IV bottles containing cancer chemotherapy medications. Her patients rarely have the usual severe side effects of nausea, vomiting, and headaches.

How healers know intuitively what to do to give healing is a difficult question to answer in concepts of Western science. Here are further clues to this part of the mystery of healing.

Ruth Montgomery

Born to Heal, 1973

Ruth Montgomery describes the life and work of an extremely gifted healer whom Montgomery called "Mr. A." to protect him from undesired publicity. A surgeon named Dena L. Smith worked with him extensively and reports on numerous and very difficult cases in which he was able to provide help or cure. Montgomery describes the cosmology of the healer, a brief excerpt of which follows:

> I . . . asked how he derived his information, and Mr. A. replied, "Why, from tuning in on The Ring." Pressed to explain in terms available to the layman, he said that a protective ring of energy encircles each planet and stores within it all knowledge since time began. All thoughts and inventions, he said, are "taken off The Ring," and all such information is available to anyone who learns to listen. He says that the Ancient Wisdom implanted in his mind as a child is unchanging. The years have merely expanded it and brought to him increasing proof of all he learned as a boy.
>
> "The theory of energy as the life-force and body activity is as old as the ages," he continues, "and there are many well versed in the Ancient Wisdom to whom most of this is known. This world we live in is composed of gases and energy. All substance—plant, animal and human life—results from the unlimited combination of energy frequencies acting on these gases. Every plant, animal and human has its own individual energy frequency to establish and maintain life, growth and development. At birth, the first breath of life is our direct supply, our lifeline with the Universal Power . . . Life itself! At any time that this energy flow is cut off from the magnetic field, the energy which originally sets the field becomes a part of the Power it came from. So long as this energy is established and flows through without obstruction, we are in tune with the Universal supply of energy."

Mr. A. believed that there is a *master brain* in the abdomen, a magnetic field which controls the nerves throughout the body. The lungs are strengthened by this magnetic field and enabled to draw in energies from the cosmos. When the magnetic field is depleted by fears, angers, hatreds, or trauma, a person may be nervous, restless, and confused, suffer shortness of breath, be irritable and have other physical symptoms.

He said that children inherit strong or weak nervous systems, dependent on their parents' energies. If the mother's and father's energies are
strong and well matched at conception, the child inherits a healthy and
strong nervous system. If there is a mismatch in the parents' energies or if
they are nervous or unhealthy, the infant may have a weak nervous system.
This weakness could be reflected in a difficult birth. Treatment by a healer
around the time of birth can strengthen the child's energies and capacity to
absorb and utilize energies from the universe.

Mr. A. believed that people with healthy abilities to connect with natural energies could become healers.

Montgomery's book is written in easy style but is uncritically enthusiastic. Nevertheless, it provides a wealth of data on the views and experiences
of a very gifted healer.

Mr. A. seems to attribute the source of healing energies to a universal
energy pool, channeled through the body of the healer. Mr. A's identification of the lower abdomen as the source of a magnetic field is of interest.
This may correspond with reports of chakras (Kaptchuk; Motoyama) or the
hara, energy centers described by Eastern medicine and those who see auras
(e.g. Brennan 1987; 1993). His views on genetic interactions with parental
fields are unique.

The source of intuitive knowledge which Mr. A. identified as the
"ring" is reported by other highly gifted healers such as Tony Agpaoa
(Stelter) and Edgar Cayce (Sugrue; Stearn). Could this represent an intuitive description of a collective consciousness?[40] Why a ring?

Mr. A. is revealed in a later Montgomery book to have been the late
William Gray.

---

*There is no source of deception in the investigation of nature
which can compare with a fixed belief that certain kinds of
phenomena are impossible.*

—William James

We have surveyed a spectrum of views on how healing works. Let us now
consider just a few of the enormous variety of ways and settings in which
healers apply their gifts.

The first two reports come from healers who work closely with doctors.

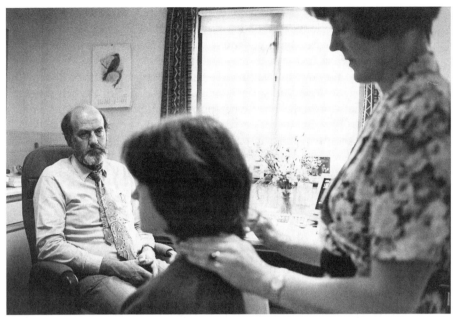

Figure 1-7. Hillary Morgan giving healing in the office of Dr. Rindy Bakker

Photo by Tony Sleep

Hillary Morgan

Working as a healer in a National Health Service doctor's practice, Personal Communication 1996

For nearly ten years Hillary Morgan has been working closely with Rindy Bakker, a general practitioner near London. Dr. Bakker[41] is open to helping people through acupuncture, which he practices himself, and through a range of other complementary therapies. He makes many of these available in his office. He obtained the agreement of the local health authorities to pay for these treatments—a pioneering achievement in the integration of complementary therapies in the National Health Service. He is also one of the founding members of the Doctor-Healer Network.

Morgan reports:

> A spiritual healer in a doctor's practice brings in fresh dimensions to working with patients. Healers can bring fundamental spiritual healing elements into a busy surgery (British term for a doctor's office). A surgery can be less than an optimal healing environment—under the pressures of large numbers of patients and limited time available. (Doctors in England usually have only seven to ten minutes to give each patient.) One healing contribution is a change of pace or en-

ergy, a stilling of the all-too-common franticness and fear and frustration of patients and doctors. Just visualizing harmony in the waiting room can have a beneficial effect, not only on patients but also on the receptionists.

I can offer another approach—a stepping back from the problem, pain or ache and an acceptance of the person, wherever they are at that moment. From that point, healing starts to happen as a person will begin to feel better for just being heard and from relaxing into the problem, the pain, fear, distress or disease.

We can share some healing energy work with relaxation. Often these healing approaches invite people to identify what is really going on inside them.

Spiritual healing is a gentle approach that fits well with a medical system. It introduces dimensions of gentleness, creating a harbor of rest from all the storms of dealing with life. It only takes a moment to sit quietly, take a few deep breaths and link into a peaceful energy. This complements the medical work nicely. If people need surgery, they make a good recovery and heal quickly. The medicines they take may be more effective. They may require lower doses, and eventually may no longer need to take medications at all.

An important focus of the work is in addressing the fears of letting go of the pain or illness, as it has been a familiar companion for so long.

People have reported back that they find they feel better able to cope with life and whatever that brings to them. A sense of taking responsibility for their illness begins to grow within them. A good example of this was a woman who had experienced a hearing loss after an airplane trip when she had a head cold. There was nothing medically that could be found, yet her hearing continued to deteriorate. She adapted to her disability and learned to concentrate on one person at a time. She admitted that regaining her hearing would be traumatic in that she would have to learn all over again to cope with all the noise of listening to several people at once and this would be hard for her. She also agreed her hearing problems had not all been negative. She had gained a lot of empathy for people who have hearing problems.

I have also worked with some patients in the surgery who are at the end of their life and who have asked to die at home. Along with the doctor, district nurse, and sometimes a hospice I have been able to go and give healing wherever the patient is. This has helped them let go without fear and to die a peaceful death. Such spiritual healing has also helped other family members. Death is a part of life. It is not a failure. I find this spiritual healing experience to be very beautiful. Because doctors are taught to cure or at least relieve symptoms and because the attitude in our society has been to fight death at all costs, death can sometimes be viewed as a failure. Having a healer working in the practice can offer another dimension to this end.

I work with women experiencing difficulties getting pregnant, with some satisfying successes. For nausea in pregnancy I get them to relax and talk to their baby—before as well as after it is born. This is another way of relieving physical and emotional stresses.

A healer can act as a reminder of bringing in a sense that we are more than just our physical bodies. It is not about pushing beliefs onto anybody but rather about accepting people and feeding in a loving vibration.

Working as a healer in a doctor's National Health Service surgery is different from working in my private practice. The people referred to me by the doctors trust what their doctors say. If he or she recommends seeing a healer they are prepared to give it a try, although they might not have considered such an approach on their own initiative. Indeed, they may not even be aware of spiritual healing. So as they cross the threshold to see me they are often anxious, wary, or even frightened, with all sorts of misgivings as to what might happen to them in a healing session.

One woman told me that she did not want to see her dead grandmother (probably confusing *spiritual* healing with *spiritualist* healing). I assured her that I did not want to see her either.

Some people come because the doctor told them to, or at least that is what they seemed to hear. They come with some hostility, an attitude of "So what do you think you can do to fix me?" I have found that healing can cut right through this aggressive negativity and transform the fear. Once that is released, their own inner healer can get to work.

Others come along determined that they are not going to be helped. One woman used to screw up her eyes and almost hold her breath in her attempts to block the healing. She could then return to the doctor and report that healing had not helped her—adding to the list of other treatments she felt had been a waster of time. She didn't want to give up on her illness. Despite her negative attitude, I was able to hold this woman in a loving vibration and at some level I intuited that she felt it—though I would never expect her to admit it openly.

Children referred by the doctors normally are open and respond well to healing. The real challenge is with the parents, and I do my best to bring them into the healing. Sometimes tears are shed and there is a release of fears that the child may be carrying for their mother or father.

Many are interested to hear that there is a healer in the practice and ask to see me. Sometimes this is out of curiosity. At other times it is with an awareness of finding a missing part of themselves that the more conventional medical treatments have not addressed.

Some come in search of a miracle, hoping that by passing my hands over their body they will have an instant cure and be able to carry on with their lives as before. These people often receive a miracle—but not in the ways they are expecting. For example, a man came to me with depression and pain, wanting to have the whole lot taken away. He discovered that rather than me, as a healer, being able to take it all away, he could do that for himself by getting in touch with his intuition and letting his own inner healer help him.

Working with a doctor gives me a stamp of approval. It says that this doctor thinks healing is effective and is willing for a healer to work in the surgery. This gives people the confidence to come and experience healing in the knowledge that this is a legitimate and worthwhile form of treatment.

People who come for healing in my private practice are often desperate. They feel let down by conventional doctors and come with the attitude, "I have tried everything else so I thought I would give healing a go." This does not happen in my work in the surgery, as most people there feel they have received a lot of support from the doctors. Spiritual healing is seen as part of that support.

Others come who have been referred by someone who benefited from healing. On the positive side, many of these people come with reasonable expectations. Others sometimes come to please the enthusiastic person who has referred them rather than for their own benefit. Nevertheless, changes occur as long as they are willing to keep an open mind.

Healing in my private practice is more relaxing, without the noise and pressure of the surgery—where phones are constantly ringing and there is an underlying pressure to deal with people, some of whom are angry and frightened. However, there is not the back-up in my private practice that I have with the doctors. For instance, when a woman who saw me for healing at the surgery relaxed so much that she afterwards collapsed in the toilet, it was very reassuring for both of us to have a doctor on hand to check her vital signs while I gave healing to reduce her fear and ease her tensions.

In my private practice I treat animals. Even in the enlightened doctors' surgery in which I work this might cause a bit of a stir. Animals can reflect their owners' dis-ease. As I think of this, I wonder whether a group animal healing in the doctors' waiting room might do a lot towards sorting out their owners as well!

Hillary Morgan has a warm personality and the lovely combination of strong intuition in a person whose feet are planted firmly on the ground. She also has an open, questioning mind. This is the sort of healer that most doctors would enjoy working with.

Julie Motz developed her healing gifts after healing herself for back pain. She worked for a period of time with Dr. Mehmet Oz, a cardiothoracic surgeon at Columbia-Presbyterian Medical Center in New York City.

Julie Motz
Energy work for patients with cardiothoracic surgery and breast cancer, unpublished report 1996

Motz assesses the patient's biological energies at the chakras.[30] When she senses blocks of energy flows she may guide and aid patients in seeking awareness of the causes of the blocks and ways to remove them. Powerful emotions and traumatic memories may be released.

Motz also works on what she calls *cellular consciousness*.[42] This assumes that every cell in the body has its own awareness which can be addressed by healees and healers. The focus may be upon blood, muscle, or bone. With cardiac patients, Motz may sense a sadness prior to surgery. "When I ask these patients to allow their blood to thank their old heart for all it has done for them, and to lovingly say good-bye to it, the sadness gradually eases."

At the request of the patients, Motz began working in the operating room during surgery. She directs energy into the kidney and liver acupuncture meridians to enhance their functions under surgery. As soon as patients are under anesthesia she gives healing to bring their biological energy fields down to their feet, because these fields tend to rise around the head with anesthesia.

During surgery she gives healing through her hands to the patient's head. She speaks to the brain, helping it anticipate the shock of receiving blood with chemicals from the heart-lung bypass machine.

The body may store memories of old traumas, which can be released during surgery. Motz helps patients with healing to release these. She also gives healing to the replacement heart when it is brought into the operating room. This heart may be helped to release feelings it retains about the death of its donor. She tells of one heart which seemed to harbor resentment towards the brain of the person who abandoned it when he committed suicide. Motz may suggest to the patient ways in which to address the new heart and to help it adjust to the trauma it has experienced.

When patients regain consciousness, Motz works with them to harmonize their energies with the energy of their new hearts. Motz notes that people she has worked with have had lower pulse rates, fewer rejections of transplants, and less depression than people who have not had healing.

Motz has also worked with Dr Allison Estabrook and Dr. Freya Schnabel to help patients who are undergoing surgery for breast cancers. Motz found again that patients stored old traumas in their bodies, and helped them to release these during anesthesia.

> During the surgery, when the breast was just about to come off the body, I experienced the sense of a tremendous burden being removed. An image came to me of the patient's mother, and of the burden she felt the patient had been to her as a child. I told the patient, under anesthesia, that I knew that she had been a delightful child, and that this sense of burdening her mother would leave her body with the breast.
>
> When I shared this with the patient in the recovery room, immediately after the surgery, she breathed a sigh of relief, and told me that she hoped she had, indeed, released the energy of that memory from her body. I worked with her once more before she left the hospital, and she called me a week later to tell me that she was recovering faster than had been expected, and felt that the work we had done together was largely responsible for this.

Multiple benefits for both patients and caregivers result from the integration of spiritual healers into conventional medical practice.[43] It may be even more helpful when the doctor and healer are the same person, as with the next two reports.

Ursula Thunberg

Crossing the Rim into Healing Consciousness, *Bridges* 1997

Ursula Thunberg is a medical doctor trained in psychosomatic medicine, specializing in adult and child psychiatry, and has worked in the last few years in New York City with hundreds of people who have AIDS. She developed her own healing gifts under the tutelage of Mietek and Margaret Wirkus.[44] She gives healing with her hands near to but not touching the body.

> Besides initially learning to move and control more consciously the energies which make up my own body, I learned over many months of daily exercises how to draw healing energies through my system to be able to change in a healing manner exhausted or damaged energy fields of clients in need. This process is experienced by me as

if I am aligning myself as a conscious transformer with existing energy fields of a healing quality. . . .

We are trained to work with the field of energy that deals with human vitality and seems to be responsible for much of the physical healing and repair, and to work with the emotional and mental fields, and other energy aspects of the composite living organism that we call a human being.

Thunberg gives healing by holding her hands on opposite sides of the healees' bodies without touching them, or by absent healing.

She reports on a sampling of problems that responded to her healing treatments:[45]

- Pains of all sorts respond dramatically, including injuries, bursitis, and arthritis. Improvements may be immediate or may come within 24 hours.
- A 68-year-old cousin of Thunberg had a hard fall, landing on her hands, knees and shins. Both hands and both knees started swelling rapidly, and her palms and shins were discolored with hematomas. Because of commitments to patients who were waiting for her, Thunberg could only give healing for a few minutes to the injured hands. Returning home several hours later, Thunberg noted that her cousin's hands were no longer swollen, the hematomas on her hands and shins had disappeared, the swelling in her knees had disappeared, and she was happily free of pain.
- Fractures heal noticeably more quickly than expected when healing is given.
- Shock following severe injuries responds within minutes.
- Diarrhea, a common problem with AIDS, responds well but may require several treatments for a lasting improvement.

Thunberg points out that there is much to be learned from sharing such clinical experiences about the benefits of healing

Dr. Thunberg has a commanding presence, which may help healees to feel confident in her healing. She also has an open mind and is keen to explore questions about how healing can best be applied.

Stefania Szantyr-Powolny is a sprightly, cheerful, retired general practitioner. She completed her medical studies after serving eleven years of slave labor in Siberia. Losing all her family there, she had promised to study medicine if she survived. She is the first Polish physician to integrate bioenergy healing in her work.

She shared the following observations at the Healing Energy Medicine Conference sponsored by the Doctor-Healer Network in London in 1992. She was very pleased to be able to discuss with medical colleagues her clinical experiences of healing, which was impossible for her to do in Poland.

Stefania Szanter Powolny

Notes from a doctor-healer in Warsaw, *Doctor-Healer Network Newsletter,* 1993

The truth about a man is enclosed between a myth and scientific knowledge.
—Professor Wlodzimierz Sedlak

I am a medical doctor and have been a bioenergy practitioner for twelve years. I have followed the improvements in my patients and collected documentation on bioenergy therapy treatments. Though the results are impressive, we are still searching for ways to explain them.

Let me share a few examples from my work. There is a clinic of the Society for Deaf Children in Warsaw where I have seen over 500 patients as a bioenergy therapist. The children suffer from the full range of causes of deafness. Work at this clinic illustrates a good example of cooperation between medical staff and bioenergy therapists. The specialist examines patients and tests their hearing with an audiometer. He then refers the patients for bioenergy therapy. After several sessions the audiometer test is repeated.

A few examples will illustrate the effects of the bioenergy therapy treatment.

Patient Z.L., 25 years old, had been deaf in both ears for 22 years because of streptomycin toxicity at age two. On his fourth visit I was really moved when he entered the room and announced: "Doctor! I can hear! I can hear water in the bathroom. I can hear my mother saying something in the room next to mine. I can hear a dog barking." The audiograms below show the changes with his treatment.

Is there anything more wonderful and satisfying than such a response?

I must admit that such miraculous achievements as the one I shared are not very frequent. Sometimes patients need several treatments and improve only gradually to a partial recovery of hearing.

What is important is that the improvements with bioenergy therapy occur in the range of high tones. These are due to alterations in the nerves of the ear, where conventional medicine cannot offer treatment. The audiograms repeatedly have shown these changes.

Together with the specialist we have come to the conclusion that bioenergy overcomes blockages in growth of the central nervous system. Improvements in hearing are often connected with improvements in speaking abilities and abilities to communicate, so

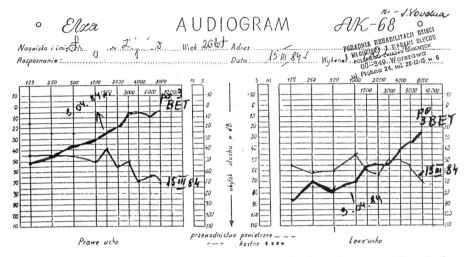

These observations were shared on the Healing in Medical Practice panel at the Healing Energy Medicine Conference Dr. Stefania Szantyr-Powolny is a General Practitioner and Bioenergy Therapist. ul Bonifacego 87 m.50, 02-945 Warsaw, Poland.

Figure 1-8. Audiograms of Patient Z.L. of Dr. Powolny. The higher lines in the right graph show hearing levels after healing, with a lower threshold for response to standard tones.

vital to the psychological, social and educational development of children.

Patient P.Z., age nine, suffered since infancy from bed-wetting. He was examined by many specialists because this was very troublesome to him. It was interfering with his socializing with other children, and he was starting to develop different complexes. After five treatments the boy kissed me spontaneously, telling me his problems had disappeared.

Specialists are not able to explain what functions and in what systems bioenergy therapy produces changes. With bed-wetting I find about 98% have positive results.

Patient C.K., age 35, had suffered for many years because of failure of the bones to knit after a fracture of his right leg. He had undergone many different surgical operations, including one with the Elizarow method, without positive results.

He came to see me, walking with crutches, supported by a metal brace on his leg. His attitude to unconventional medicine was rather negative. After the third treatment he had a new X-ray, and it was evident that the bone had started to knit. The surgeon following the patient acknowledged this. We met six more times. Half a year later I found him walking easily, without crutches or brace. He was very grateful for what I had done.

Alternative methods of medicine cannot replace conventional medicine and I would never suggest we even consider this. These methods can be used to save human lives and reduce suffering. They should be known and available to all people in the world. Fortunately, the world of conventional medicine is increasingly in agreement with this.

Science is not eager to accept some old laws of Nature. We know that apples have been falling from trees for ages, but only Newton gave a scientific explanation for this phenomenon. Research work on bioenergy therapists can open a new era in alternative medicine. At present we should enjoy every single possibility given to us by Nature, using all approaches to help others and ourselves. No one knows what potentials are hidden in human beings.

Healing gifts, present in many people without their awareness, should be developed as much as possible.

We are pleased to find that in Poland today there are many different centers of unconventional medicine as well as individual practitioners using different methods. The State licenses bioenergy therapists when they can prove their abilities through very rigorous tests in diagnosis and treatment under the Bioenergy Section of the Psychotronic Society. Medical schools are introducing courses in bioenergy therapy, acupuncture, homeopathy, iridology, and more.

I want to stress one thing. Each session with a person has physical-psychic-spiritual aspects. The hands of a healer discover energetic disturbances over ill places and transform healing energy, needed to restore balance and normal functioning. The most important thing in all bioenergy therapists is their approach to people. They must love their fellow men, should be warm and kind-hearted to everyone, and should want to help others.

Very often conventional health careers and patients must be taught how to treat health in a wholistic way. One ought to remember about a unity between body, mind, and spirit. Harmony between living things, including humans, and the environment is a necessary condition to one's well being.

In this crazy, hectic life which seeks to conquer the world, we should know how to say, "No!" No to selfish thinking. No to negative feelings. Start to be positive!

As a medical doctor and a bioenergy therapist I would like to suggest a simple prescription:

> Three times daily, for ten minutes:
> Calm down and meditate.
> Hold kindness in your heart for others.
> Smile, smile more often.

Reports from physicians who are doctors have a particular richness and depth of appreciation of illness and of the healing process. I look forward to receiving further reports as more doctors develop their own healing gifts and share their experiences.[46]

Healers are well accepted in China. Doctors learn traditional medicine or Western medicine. More recently they are training in both.

David Eisenberg is a Boston physician who was one of the first Westerners to study natural medicine techniques in China. He now teaches complementary medicine methods at Harvard Medical School.[47]

David Eisenberg with Thomas Lee Wright
Encounters with Qi: Exploring Chinese Medicine, 1985

In this book, Eisenberg explores theories and practices of *qigong* (literal translation is *breathing skill*), part of which is the Chinese equivalent of spiritual healing.

Qi[48] is the Chinese name for energies believed to imbue the body with its life force. The Chinese feel that this energy flows through lines in the body which correspond to the acupuncture meridians.

Qigong is the study of harnessing and focusing these energies. People may do this for themselves through meditation and physical exercises, with special attention to breathing techniques and to visualizations of the energy being concentrated in the center of the body, and then flowing where needed to other body parts. This, termed *internal qigong,* is contrasted with *external qigong* in which healers project energies outside their bodies.

Eisenberg describes qigong masters who display extraordinary physical prowess, including great strength; resistance to harm when crushed by great weights or pierced by sharp objects; reduction of body weight, even to the point of levitation; psychokinesis; ability to light fluorescent bulbs with their hands (as long as they are not in a building higher than the fifth floor); and healing.

Eisenburg provides numerous anecdotal reports of healings. He echoes Chinese claims, based on unpublished studies, that qigong can help with arthritis, asthma, bowel problems, cancers, coronary artery disease, diabetes, hypertension, chronic kidney disease, "neurasthenia," peripheral vascular disease, and peptic ulcers. He briefly quotes a study of myopia[49] and another in which bacterial culture growth was enhanced and decreased at will by a qigong master. He also mentions that qigong energies directed to acupuncture points can be used sometimes for anesthesia.

He cites Chinese claims that the emission of qigong energies can be measured as heat and infrared radiations on various instruments. In addition, "nuclear magnetic resonance scanners, CAT scanners, and other so-phisticated electromagnetic devices have been employed to document and quantify *external* qigong activity. Our hosts made available no details of this research."

Eisenberg describes sensations he and other Westerners experienced when qi was directed to their bodies by various masters. These included "pins and needles," "electrical impulses," pressure, numbness, and dulling of consciousness or confusion. The latter was noted during an experiment in which the master apparently caused a subject to move in various directions by merely directing qi energy at him from several feet away.

After extensive studies, including many visits and a year's fellowship at various Chinese medical facilities, Eisenberg notes that a comparison of Chinese and Western methods of treatment is very difficult. He gives the instance of a patient with pneumonia. In the West, this infection is presumed to be caused by specific bacteria or viruses. The treatments are aimed at the elimination of the infecting organisms.

> You have a high fever, chills and cough. When you arrive at the office of a Western doctor, a detailed medical history is taken and a physical examination and laboratory tests are performed. Evidence from your physical examination and abnormalities in your chest X-ray lead the doctor to decide that you have pneumonia. A sample of your sputum, stained for bacteria, confirms the diagnosis. You are treated with appropriate antibiotics and sent home to rest in bed.
>
> Now imagine going to the office of a traditional Chinese doctor with the same symptoms. The physician listens to your story and then asks a number of questions about the "type" of chills you've had and the manner of your sweating. He takes your pulse and examines your tongue. The doctor is aware that your lungs are troubling you, but his diagnosis, according to traditional medicine, refers to the underlying imbalances in your body. The pneumonia with its associated fever, cough, and sputum production is the *manifestation* of the underlying imbalance. It is the "uppermost branch," not the "root," of the illness. By studying your tongue and pulse and by listening to your story, the physician identifies the precise excess or deficiency affecting your body. This may involve an imbalance of an organ distant from the lung. The doctor treats your imbalance rather than a condition known as pneumonia.[50]

This is a valuable book on traditional Chinese medicine. It illustrates the caution with which Western scientists must examine therapeutic systems from other cultures in order to learn what might be meaningfully applied to their own. The authors take no cognizance of Western studies of healing, and their reports and assessments in this book appear cautious. Type II errors (rejecting a useful treatment) are likely.

Therapeutic Touch (TT) is one of the most widely used methods of healing in the United States. It was developed by Dolores Krieger, R.N., Ph.D., at the New York University School of Nursing, with Dora Kunz, a gifted natural healer and psychic. TT is being increasingly accepted in professional and academic circles as a result of the fine work of Krieger and others who have researched TT and demonstrate its efficacy in their clinical work. Krieger has personally taught many thousands of nurses these simple methods of diagnosis and healing. An estimated 40,000 nurses use TT, and more than 90 nursing schools offer courses in this healing method. A growing number of hospitals have nurses utilizing these techniques, though TT may often be given quietly and unobtrusively. These methods clearly provide an exciting adjunct to conventional therapies.

Carefully controlled studies have validated the efficacy of TT[51] and more are planned and in progress. The full range of efficacy of these techniques is just beginning to be uncovered.

Dolores Krieger

The Therapeutic Touch: How to Use Your Hands to Help or to Heal, 1979

Krieger explains the steps in giving TT:

1. *Centering*—The healer clears his mind and relaxes his body, finding within "an inner reference of stability."
2. *Scanning*—The healer passes her hands around the body of the healee, sensing for any asymmetries or irregularities in the energy field that might indicate a portion of the body in need of healing. Often a second healer will simultaneously scan the opposite side of the body, after which the two switch places and scan the opposite sides of the body, comparing impressions at the end. The consensual validation obtained through working in pairs is helpful in learning to trust one's diagnostic and healing abilities.
3. *Unblocking the healee's field*—The healer may sense areas that do not have a normal energy flow. She will direct her healing energy to these areas to smooth them out.
4. *Transferring energies to the healee*—The healer consciously sends energies, often with visualizations of light of particular colors for healing.

Healing is given with a light touch or with the hands held near to, but not touching, the body. Krieger feels that to become healers people must have clear intentionality, motivation to help, and an ability to understand their own motivation for wanting to heal. She observes that people practicing TT also improve their intuitive and psi abilities.

She recommends TT for relaxation, alleviation or elimination of pain (e.g. arthritic, traumatic), acceleration of natural healing processes, nausea, shortness of breath, rapid pulse, pallor from peripheral vascular contraction, poor circulation in the extremities, physiological development of premature infants, assistance in pacifying irritable babies, and more. She does not know of any illness in which she feels TT is totally or always ineffective. She has found (per Estebany) that cotton can both store and facilitate healing.

Krieger finds that belief does not affect the success of healing. She feels skeptics can be helped. "However, two personality variables—denial of illness and hostility—do have a negative effect on TT, perhaps because they both may translate themselves graphically to the healer and inhibit the healer's efforts."

Krieger teaches healing to relatives of healees so that they may give treatments at home.

Her approach has been one of the most effective of all the methods in opening professionals and lay persons to healing, as well as in generating research.

Krieger's book is an extremely helpful introduction to anyone interested in learning about TT. It also contains excellent "how-to" exercises. Krieger gives poetic descriptions of the inner changes accompanying the learning and development of healing skills—some of the best descriptions I've seen of how healers learn to heal.[52] This book is more clinically than research oriented, however, and potentially open to Type I errors.

Many TT healers say the definition of TT as an exchange of biological energies between healer and healee should be expanded to include the vision that healers may be channels or transducers for love, God, universal, cosmic, or other transcendental energies. Others insist that TT as originally formulated should not be adulterated with other belief systems, lest current and future research may not be comparable with earlier research.

A modification on TT called *Healing Touch* is growing in popularity, again pioneered mostly by nurses. Healing Touch adds the use of pendulums to help healers bring their intuitive impressions into conscious awareness, beliefs in cosmic rather than personal energies, directing healing to the chakras, and more emphasis on psychological interventions as an essential part of the healing process. The formal TT steps of centering and sensing of the aura prior to healing are maintained within Healing Touch.[53]

Healing takes different forms in the hands of different people. The following are healers whose healees appear to self-correct some of their problems through various movements of their bodies during treatment.

Jane Tinworth

Dynamic healing, Personal communication, 1992

Jane Tinworth's healees often move about in unpredictable ways during the course of treatments. They may arch their backs, enter complex yoga positions, postures or motions, and both she and the healees are often surprised at the complex contortions. Healees experience these as strong

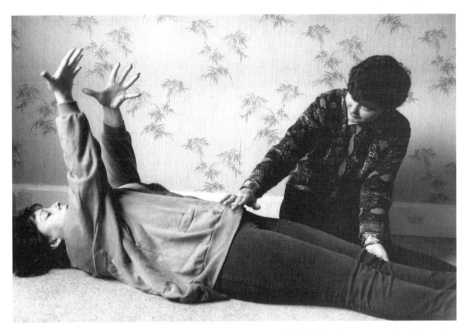

Figure 1-9. In dynamic healing, patients may arch their backs, wave their hands, and make many other corrective movements.

Photo courtesy of John Stubbs.

urges which they simply comply with because they the movements will be beneficial. They may resist with an effort of conscious willpower, if they wish, or may shake portions of their body vigorously. Tinworth does not suggest these.

Tinworth writes:

> However skilled a description of dynamic healing may be, it has to be experienced to be accepted. Even witnessing the phenomena is only part of the picture. A familiar remark from clients at the end of a session is "I wouldn't have believed it if I hadn't experienced it myself."
>
> The term *dynamic healing* is given to a particular manifestation of spiritual healing in which clients respond to the healer's energy by performing spontaneous movements with no conscious direction or control. For example, a person with a structural or arthritic problem may "observe" their trunk, limbs or head moving around in certain patterns or vibrating, rippling or stretching. Movements may be slow and gentle or rapid and strong. The body may be in a prone position or it may execute a variety of seemingly impossible movements over a lengthy period. It is not unusual for even elderly clients to have an hour of really vigorous movement and yet feel

relaxed both during and after the session. The experience is of the movements "doing themselves" and of a sense of "rightness."

Dynamic healing is a density of the healing force and I have no doubt that it demonstrates our innate ability to heal ourselves. Results are always positive, even when the movements seem to bear little or no relation to the presenting problem. Injury through making movements which were previously difficult is unknown. Pain is only occasionally experienced in the process but seldom to the point of the client wishing to stop.

Dynamic healing does not always involve physical movement as this obviously is not appropriate for all conditions. During healing many clients access underlying causes of problems—physical, mental, emotional and spiritual—together with their own intuitive guidance for resolving them. Others may enter altered states of consciousness akin to deep meditation.

It is important to be aware that these responses during healing are quite spontaneous and not the result of therapy or suggestion.

Clients are often startled by their own unusual movements, which are often very funny to observe. Their resulting laughter and light-heartedness can also be a part of the healing process.

Once they have experienced dynamic healing, clients can be shown how to put themselves into the healing "mode" and continue the process alone by attuning directly to the energy source.

The only side effect is improved well being.

I had been healing for about 15 years without such visible effect before the dynamic aspect began to occasionally and gently manifest. The first strong session came in 1987 when a man, severely disabled and in pain for fourteen years through a spinal injury, arrived for healing, hardly able to get himself onto the treatment couch. I was taken by surprise as his body contorted violently from head to foot and I actually thought he was having an epileptic fit. However, when I asked him if he was all right, he answered very calmly, "I am in your hands. I am content." An hour later he walked upright and pain free from the room. After that the self-healing manipulations grew to become everyday occurrences.

Spontaneous self-correction has been known to happen for some time, but until a few years ago researchers in England were aware of only three healers consistently producing dynamic effects. Now I am delighted to report that a significant number of colleagues and other healers who have passed through our development courses are having similar effects on their clients. This reinforces my belief that by dealing with our own problems and constantly seeking to raise our levels of love and awareness, many of us have this potential.

Margaret[54]

Personal communication, 1990

Margaret found at the age of 17 that she could calm a woman diagnosed as "mental breakdown, homicidal" by rubbing the bottom of her spine and talking with her. She did not immediately pursue her healing career after that.

> I was put off by a family friend who offered to train me to develop my skills. The little purple light and the nasty smell (probably joss sticks) were totally alien to my experience. They thoroughly put me off healing at that time.

At age 24, skiing in an international event, Margaret severely injured her leg, sustaining a compound fracture of the right tibia and multiple fractures of the fibula.

> I was left on the dump heap, told I'd never ski again. After five months in casts and another 18 months of physiotherapy, I was back on the slopes and racing again. The fibula had a cartilaginous union which left the leg unstable. Healing from a doctor who was also a healer helped that. He showed me how to put my hands over a trouble spot and thus to develop my own healing abilities.
>
> Initially I worked on animals. My first patient was my Labrador retriever, who was cured of an infected claw and later of scabies. I worked on a cat with viral pneumonia with good results. Hearing this, a woman with viral pneumonia requested my help, and she was cured too.

Margaret studied physiotherapy for 18 months and radionics in order to understand and focus her efforts in a more professional manner. Later she abandoned the radionics, relying on her intuition to guide her work.

Soon after taking up healing she found that her healees moved their bodies in unusual manners during healings.

> The first person who did that was a 21-year-old woman with severe cervical disc problems and headaches as well as bad asthma. She had been warned not to turn her head when it was inclined forward. The first thing she did when I started my laying-on of hands was to go down on all fours and turn her head rapidly and vigorously from side to side! Then she went into complex yoga postures which I had never seen before, though I'd done a little yoga myself. Then she did ballet steps and belly dancing. This is all the more remarkable because she was totally unathletic.

A remarkable series of healings followed over the course of several decades. Margaret will typically have a healee lie on her couch and will place a hand on or near his head. Within a few seconds to a few minutes, he develops an altered state of consciousness. His eyes will often be glazed and unfocused, and he will blink only a very few times per minute. He may lie still for many minutes or for a whole treatment. She may move her hands to the spine, chest, abdomen, to points of pain or dysfunction, or to other portions of the healee's body as instinct directs her. At times he will move his body in a wide variety of ways. Limbs may be stretched or exercised vigorously; his back may be twisted or arched backward; he may rise from his recumbent position to enter yoga asanas, to perform classical dance exercises, to stand on his head or to do other exercises and contortions. Movements may be in twitches, rhythmic motions, or coordinated sequences. Often the motions the healee goes through are new and unfamiliar to him and beyond his capabilities when he is in his ordinary state of consciousness. Margaret reports she cannot predict and is often surprised by the particular motions displayed. "I have several times had to go to books to find out what they were up to!" She finds that they may repeat particular patterns within sessions and from one session to another, but she in no way directs or leads them.

> It all seems to come from within them. They do what they need to do to release their old patterns and to correct their problems. Though their contortions may seem strange to an observer, the healees themselves often sense which particular muscles or joints are being exercised for self-correction. They are not directing this consciously, however. It is purely an instinctual process.

These varied exercises appear to be self-corrective for neural and musculoskeletal disorders. A person with a bad back might produce loud "cracks" in her back during such exercises, much as are heard under chiropractic or osteopathic manipulations. Animals, including a horse, treated by Margaret also went through such self-corrective contortions. This is further support for the claims that these movements are not consciously directed by Margaret or her healees.

During healings healees may be totally unconscious, conscious of their inner and outer surroundings but unresponsive to the environment, or totally conscious and interactive with the environment. If conscious, they will report they move as they do in response to a very strong inner urge or compulsion to do so. It is not a voice or "spirit guidance" directing them. People may experience further inner urges to resume their unusual exercises after leaving Margaret's presence. One healee reported, "I need only to lie down to reinvoke this process. It is usually more a matter of resisting a frequent urge than of setting up a mental state to commence these exercises." In relaxed social situations, some have succumbed to such urges in public, much to the amusement of their friends. Healees feel their self-healings are more intense when Margaret is providing healing than when they are on their own.

Margaret seeks to work as closely as possible with physicians, osteopaths, physiotherapists, and other health professionals. Although she addresses her work in a very serious and responsible fashion, the atmosphere in her treatment room is light and often jocular. Margaret is able to engage in healing without the need to be in a special meditative state. She is able to converse freely while ministering to as many as four healees at a time—limited only by the number of limbs she has to extend a touch or healing presence to each person. The light atmosphere, particularly the laughter, is reported by some healees to intensify the effects of her healing.

Margaret's healings generally last from one to two hours but may go even longer. Though they may continue their self-corrective exercises without her touching them constantly, she feels she needs to be available to each person for healing touches, emotional and physical support, and protection from danger of banging and injuring themselves while moving about her living room (though no one ever has been hurt).

How and why healees perform their self-corrective "dances" during and after dynamic healings is unclear. A few other healers, including the late John Cain (see following review), produce similar movements in healees. Hans Engel, a physician-healer in California, reported uncoordinated gross muscle contractions in two people with *tic doloreux* and one with osteoarthritis of the hip.

I have reviewed videotapes of the healings of Tinworth and Margaret, as well as those of another dynamic healer, Ron Staley. Dramatic improvements have occurred with many musculoskeletal and neurological problems, including severe osteoarthritis, chronic fatigue syndrome, and multiple sclerosis.

These healings seem to hold bold clues to what healing may be about. I must admit the answers elude me, though I have many theories about these movements during healing.

Several sensitives who see auras report that the healings of Margaret affect people through very refined levels of their being.

The spontaneous appearance of *yoga asanas* may indicate innate human physiological patterns in the origins of yoga. F. Smith explains some yogic healings through involuntary movements (*kriyas*) which occur as body energy blocks are apparently released.

Ron Staley gives healing in the name of Christ. He does a laying-on of hands, turning the proceedings over to the care of Jesus. In addition to seeing his healees engage in movements, he finds that a small percent lie very still, experiencing an intensely blissful state. He calls this "resting in the spirit."

All three dynamic healers find intense emotions may be released during healings. These appear to be the stresses, perhaps long buried in the unconsciousness, which precipitated their illnesses.

I expected all healers would be highly evolved spiritually. My disappointment was second only to that when I entered medical school expecting I would be joining a sort of elite club of gentlemen. Neither doctors nor healers are any different from other folk, with all the same human limitations, foibles, and failings.

I was not yet aware of this when I met John Cain, our next healer.

Pat Sykes

You Don't Know John Cain? 1979

Valerie Wooding

John Cain Healing Guide, 1980

Peter Green

Heal My Son, 1985

Pat Sykes interviewed a number of healees treated by the late John Cain. Cain could induce altered states of consciousness in individuals or groups. He sometimes worked in a hall with up to 70 healees to whom he simultaneously "beamed" his energy. They usually went into a trance-like state, partially aware or totally unaware of their surroundings. It was a calming and restful state for most, during which anxiety and depression were markedly diminished. Many physical symptoms also abated, either instantaneously or gradually, with repeated healings over a period of several weeks or months.

In about five percent of cases, unusual processes developed. Healees experienced sensations of warmth or tingling rising through their backs from the base of the spine. There was initially a sexual arousal, then an intense feeling of love with a desire to share the love. Shortness of breath and intense feelings of peacefulness were common. These states lasted about one to two hours. Such sensations have been reported by meditators, usually occurring only after many years' practice. The feelings are known as the raising of kundalini energy in the spine.[55]

Healees might involuntarily assume various yoga asanas, dance intricate patterns, move their bodies rhythmically and vigorously, tumble about, and even grab Cain in various judo holds. Such motions were usually totally unknown to the subjects in their waking states, and often were clearly beyond their normal capabilities. The actions seemed to facilitate recovery from various musculoskeletal problems, but may also have been related to internal organ systems according to yogic traditions.

Valerie Wooding suffers from multiple sclerosis, which improved greatly under Cain's treatments. She reports that while not receiving healing, she could not stand up straight, sit up from a prone position, or bend her spine. Her muscles did not atrophy because of the exercises she performed while in an altered state of consciousness during Cain's healing treatments. She felt that her awareness of the exertions her body could tolerate during healing also increased her optimism.

> I frequently exercised in ways which *I never* considered within my capabilities—yoga, ballet, judo, even headstands. . . . I am fully conscious of what my body is doing almost as if I am observing it—but I am also aware of the reasons for it.
>
>   When I cannonball (backward forward rolls at great speed) across the hall at Bromborough my head can be heard cracking loudly against the parquet floor. I am aware of this, I, too, could hear it— and feel the contact. But *it does not hurt,* nor have I ever pulled a muscle or received a bruise. I have exercised in the most athletic manner in the midst of a crowded hall without ever hurting myself or anyone else present, occasionally negotiating a patient's out-stretched arm or coming to a sudden stop inches away from a chair. There is an inbuilt safety device—and it seems to include radar!

Many people asked Wooding how she was able to do these things. She had no answer other than that she could not do them in her normal state of consciousness.

> [I]t is an amazing sight to watch Cain's patients whilst healing is taking place. Some lie unnaturally still, not moving a muscle throughout the session. Others move un-self-consciously as the needs of their body dictate. Stomachs dilate, spines bend, arthritic joints crack as they move with full mobility. Yoga exercises, Eastern dancing, physiotherapeutic exercises could all be seen side by side with patients banging the floor or practicing judo on Cain.

Wooding cites a patient-helper who was of the opinion that Cain's healees had access to some source of universal knowledge. This helped them to know what to do for their own benefit.

  Cain had no idea how or why these phenomena occurred. He never saw anyone hurt himself, even in the most violent of physical manipulations. He was familiar with judo, yoga, and dance, though not particularly adept in these activities.

  Cain also differed from most healers in his distant healing. He asked healees to gaze at a photograph of himself in order to make contact.[56] Treatment could be successful with or without his awareness that a healing was being sought. On occasion he asked healees to focus the healing on a particular part of the body by placing the photograph there. Another method he used was a link-up between himself and the healee via a surrogate person who did a laying-on of hands under his instructions (usually over the telephone). This was even more effective if the surrogate had been conditioned by a healing treatment from Cain.

Cain reported he had several spirit guides who directed his treatments. He occasionally produced dramatic, instantaneous cures of physical disabilities with a direct request to a spirit entity to intervene, without resorting himself to a laying-on of hands.

In healing circles Cain was a somewhat controversial figure because he was extremely blunt in his manners and outspoken in his opinions. He smoked almost constantly, even during healings. He openly derided healers who produced more modest results. He sometimes gave telepathic commands to healees to perform certain actions which appeared to be more for exhibition of his own powers than for the good of the healees.

He was able to help especially in cases of arthritis, emotional problems, multiple sclerosis, and circulatory and neuromuscular difficulties. Dramatic improvements were also noted on some occasions in cancers and hormonal difficulties. He estimated that 95 percent of his healees showed some improvement.

Cain was undoubtedly a powerful and unusual healer. Other healers have demonstrated some of the same effects, including the kundalini phenomenon.

In 1987 I observed Cain treating a group of seven select healees who experienced kundalini effects. They reported energies running up their spines and experienced a blissful state.

My reaction as an observer was very mixed. Though obviously seeking his healees' improvement, Cain also appeared to be seeking his own aggrandizement. This was especially evident when he gave telepathic commands for various actions even when one of the women healees seemed to be clearly opposed to these. Subsequent discussion with these healees, however, revealed nothing but positive regard for Cain and his treatments.

The kundalini phenomena in Cain's healees seemed to be limited to blissful sensations, not extending to transcendent experiences.

Perhaps Cain produced some of his effects of apparent healing by hypnotic suggestion, possibly unconsciously. However, reports in the books, cases related by Cain himself, and discussion with the seven healees I met all suggest that some of his results represent genuine healings.

As in any situation of power, there are temptations to misuse and abuse it. Doctors are not the only ones who sometimes seem to believe they are God.

Most reputable healers I know do their best to avoid taking too great a credit for healings, even when they occur dramatically and frequently. The danger is not only to the healee when power goes to a healer's head. The healer may shift towards pushing healees to improve for the benefit of the healer's reputation rather than for the healees' benefit. In healing tradition it is said that when this happens, healers often lose their powers.

One could hardly ask for a sharper contrast with Cain than Ethel Lombardi, to whom I owe a great personal debt for introducing me to the dramatic effects of spiritual healing.

Ethel Lombardi
Personal communications, 1982

Ethel Lombardi, a peppery, Scottish-Irish, middle-aged woman with red hair and sparkling green eyes, is trained as a *Reiki* master. Reiki is the Japanese word for the life force or energy, a variant of qi.

The Reiki system of healing originated in Japan toward the end of the nineteenth century.[57] Healers learn the Reiki method through practice under a master's tutelage, enhanced via an induction procedure in which the master attunes the student's vibrations to healings. Power symbols which enhance healing are taught by the Master.

The basic Reiki methods involve a standardized set of laying-on of hands treatments given to the entire body. The healer allows universal energies to flow through him or her to the healee and does not visualize anything other than the healee receiving as much energy as needed to heal whatever problems are present. The healer does not presume to know what the true problems are, inasmuch as symptoms apparent to the healee and the healer may only be manifestations of more severe or causal factors at a deeper level than can be seen from physical examination. These could also be on psychological or spiritual levels, which can be reached only through the deep, unconscious mind of the healee.

There is a strong psychological component to Reiki healing. Feelings may often be activated, with the healer encouraging their release. This release may clear up physical symptoms.[58] The Reiki tradition suggests healing is effective through energy fields that permeate the body, involving chakras and other energy centers.

Lombardi learned Reiki from the late Hawayo Takata, who brought this method to America from Japan. Lombardi came to appreciate Reiki healing through being healed herself of severe arthritis and other illnesses. When giving her a healing, Gordon Turner correctly predicted she would one day be a great healer.

Lombardi was long frustrated by the fact that far more people applied for healings than she had time to help. She appealed to the cosmic intelligences who guide her (she hesitates to call them spirits, inasmuch as she feels they are not the spirits of departed humans) to instruct her in faster methods.[59] In answer to her request she was given a new and extremely potent method of healing which she calls *MariEl,* a name coined by herself from the combination of *Mary,* Mother of Christ, and the Biblical *El* meaning God. This method requires only about a minute to achieve results, while a Reiki healing would take 20 minutes or longer.

Lombardi is a very powerful and innovative healer and teacher, constantly honing and refining her methods to achieve ever better results. At times she will project energy from her eyes, use gemstones, or gather a whole group of student healers around the healee to enhance the potency and effectiveness of a healing. She feels that a very important part of her work is the healing of the earth itself and of all living things as part of a preparation for a new age of consciousness, which many psychics and healers report we are on the threshold of entering.

Ethel has participated in various research studies, including Elmer Green's—showing that electromagnetic field changes can be registered in copper walls surrounding a healer in the act of healing.[60]

My own interest in healing was awakened through observing Ethel Lombardi producing in half an hour a physical change which was medically, impossible. A lump under the nipple of a young man shrank, softened and was no longer tender—making the surgery scheduled to remove the lump unnecessary.

At that moment, my skepticism about spiritual healing was healed as well.

The original Reiki Masters have empowered many new Masters, and these, in turn, have empowered others. Not all Masters have the same standards for selection of new Masters, so a student or healee is best advised to do careful comparative shopping before selecting a teacher.

The publisher of *Healing Research*, William Rand, is himself a Reiki Master, trained by several of the Masters empowered directly by Takata. He has taken the unusual initiative of studying with a number of different Reiki Masters, receiving the induction of a Master several times. He discovered that power symbols taught for facilitating healing differed from Master to Master. It appears Takata gave different teachings to the various people she empowered.

Crystals are recommended by some healers to augment their healings and to facilitate self-healing, as with our next healer.

Ronald S. Miller

The healing magic of crystals: an interview with Marcel Vogel, *Science of Mind*, **1984**

The late Marcel Vogel, a scientist who worked for IBM for many years, studied crystallography. He then developed and taught methods of healing. He believed that when a crystal is properly cut, a person's mind can induce it to emit vibrations which are, in effect, amplifications of the user's mind. He felt that because a crystal has a very regular molecular organization in its structure, the healing energy emitted by crystals is similar to that emitted by lasers, i.e. coherent and concentrated.

Vogel believed that emotional distress weakens the energy field around the body, which may then permit disease to enter the physical body. A healer can use a crystal to release the negative patterns of the energy body, which then permits the physical body to become whole again.

At the start of a healing, Vogel said a brief prayer and took a deep breath. He projected his consciousness lovingly into the crystal, seeking a resonation with it. After holding his breath briefly, he exhaled quickly and forcefully. This produces the sensation of a vibration in the crystal. Vogel scanned the subtle body of the healee with the charged crystal, seeking areas that appeared out of balance and in need of healing.

He believed the focal point for healing should be in the chest at a point he calls the *witness bone,* located at the sternum over the thymus gland. He felt this is where thought forms and inner feelings are manifested.

> During treatment the patient draws in a deep breath and mentally scans this area, to discover the root cause of his disturbance. The patient, not the healer, makes this appraisal. Then, by amplifying the field through the use of the crystal, I help the patient visualize and bring to awareness the root cause of the physical disturbance in his system. Then I suddenly say the word "Release!" As I snap the crystal like a whip cracking, the sudden movement of subtle energy—directed to the root cause of his disturbance through visualization—evokes a complete relaxation in the patient's system. Stress leaves the body, and he quickly is restored to wholeness.

Miller noted that releases appear to be caused by a healee's "willingness to face the truth of his own being," in addition to the energies supplied by the crystal. People may not have the energy to face their problems on their own.

Vogel responded:

> Exactly right. I call this process *transformational medicine,* because it gives the soul the opportunity to reconnect with the body, and the resulting wholeness is equivalent to good health. One of the main tenets of transformational medicine is that all forms of disease are the result of inhibited soul life. So, the art of the healer involves assisting each person to align himself with the soul and to release those patterns which inhibit the soul's activity.

Vogel briefly mentioned cases of blindness, herpes simplex, an ovarian cyst and an abscessed tooth which responded to his methods. He taught his techniques widely and had an active following throughout the United States. He felt the students' main work is to relinquish their rational thinking, utilizing their intuitive sides. He believed that healing may occur without love, but that such healings will be only superficial and temporary. He theorized that interactions of mind and crystal are possible because both of them process information holographically.

Crystals may provide an important tool for understanding how the human mind functions and interacts with energies and matter. Much work must be done before Vogel's speculations can be accepted at face value. It might seem that a crystal may be no more than a placebo, suggesting to healer and healee that healing can occur. It is essential to have more detailed reports of treated cases. Blindness, for instance, may be caused by hysteria and its cure due to suggestion rather than to healing.[61]

I was delighted to find the double-blind, controlled study of C. Norman Shealy et al. (1993), which shows crystals help significantly in the treatment of depression.[62] Other reports (Baer/Baer; Silbey) describe the use of crystals as adjuncts to healing, but these are not based in research. Sensitives who see auras report they see healing effects with crystals.

I have attended workshops with healers who use crystals, and have interviewed many sensitives who see aura changes suggesting improved health through healing with crystals. My impression is that crystals do facilitate healings and may create energy fields and/or provide ancillary healing powers.

The authors of the next book posed a standard set of questions to five gifted healers about their beliefs and practices.

Nancy Gardner and Esmond Gardner
Five Great Healers Speak Here, 1982

The following excerpts are noteworthy:

Guruder Shree Chitrabhana, a Jain healer in India, states:

> [A] true religious leader . . . is the small boat which takes the spiritual pilgrim from the shore to the deep-water vessel of spirituality out in the harbor.
>
> The limitations [to healing] are karma. Karma is an all-important factor in a healing or a blessing. If the karma is heavy, the efforts of the healer cannot succeed. Karma is the sum to date of your past actions in this life and in your previous lifetimes. It is the reaction and boomerang return of your deeds and thoughts and is constantly being modified by your present actions and thoughts. It is an absolute law, as forceful as an invisible wind that bends us with its power like so many trees, uprooting some and, when we die, blowing our souls into new situations like so many seeds.

During your lifetime, your karma can be recorded in four ways.

- It is written on the water and is gone before you can read it.
- It is written with pencil and can be erased.
- It is written with ink. A special substance is needed to erase it.
- It is carved in stone and written in blood. It can only be expiated with deeply carved suffering and understanding.

The first two types of recording are generally acts of light-hearted carelessness, some little wound, an unkind joke, a thoughtless bit of character assassination. You feel sorry and—it is gone. The third is done with intention and is erased with difficulty. A special soul substance is needed such as deep, true compassion.

The fourth karma is cold sin, done without compunction. It is carved so deep in stone that no master, healer or saint can help to remove this in one lifetime. The patient should understand that if his karma is caused by something that is written in blood, only a counterbalance through good karma accumulated in the passage of time can cure it. An enlightened healer can only point the way to awareness and the building of a clean future.

No healer can take complete responsibility on his head and say, "I am going to heal you." That disturbs the law of the universe, which is not governed by one healer or one person. If he claims that he is able to heal any kind of disease, that is ignorance of the law, or he is on an ego trip, setting himself above the laws of the universe.

However, instead of saying to sick people as so many do who accept the law of reincarnation, "It is your fate, you have earned it, endure it," the healer should point the way out of this condition. With the present disorder of the body, he should point out that it is important to keep a strong spiritual level. When we are negative, we are below our level and then illness comes. We have gone out of nature, out of balance, and we have not lived a life in tune with the natural laws of love, compassion and humanity. We must know constantly that our thoughts are living things with vibrations that can bless or harm us. (Send out only thoughts that will come back to you with high vibrations bearing interest. Interest is the extra compassion we give.)

The authors asked Brother Mandus of England, "What is the most cooperative and ideal behavior on the part of the patient?" He answered:

[L]ove . . . is the central flame of life. . . .
[S]o many miracles of healing take place when we turn our attention away from ourselves and seek an objective for living joyously so that others may be prospered and blessed because we pass their way.

> We must realize that . . . in this whole area of spiritual experience must lie the prevention of so much human disease and disaster, and that, in the end prevention was even better than miraculous cure.

Mama Mona Ndzekelli, president of the African Spiritual Church of South Africa, blends African tribal traditions with Christianity in her healings. Mama Mona feels she need not diagnose problems in order to cure them, though demonstrating her diagnostic skills to a skeptic may provide confidence in her ability to help. She reports that shaking hands casually in social settings is a drain on her healing powers. A lot of her healing has been done by a special handshake.

> [H]ealers . . . project a light, the quality of which depends upon the giver. . . . Mama Mona has seen and described balls of fire falling upon the heads of the persons being helped, even upon her own head.

Oh Shinnah, an American Indian, has been instructed in the Native American ways of healing and holds a master's degree in experimental psychology. She uses crystals in healing.

> The crystals that are used for healing have their own power and energy, and do their work by just being in the proximity of the one in need of healing. When held in the hands, they can be programmed to specific ills. They will magnify the intentions of the healer, and through their purity, combine the forces of nature and spirit to channel healing vibration, promote clarity, help one to be less emotionally reactive, refract disharmonious energies, release negative ions, collect positive ions and work with one's dreams, without any help from the two-legged. They have memory and attract the spirits of light.

When asked, ". . . can the healer use any method at will?" she answered:

> We too often become more attached to method than to the actual healing. Many years ago, I asked Dr. Karl Menninger if he had one lesson to give me to guide the rest of my life, what would it be. He very quickly answered, "If it works, do it, and do it Now."

On other topics she observes:

> Healing is innate within most of our natures. It is society that closes us off to inborn abilities.
> Anyone who wishes to help "make better" must develop a deep sense of love and compassion, which is a reflection of one's spiritual self in union with the nature and Source. One must be willing to explore his own illnesses and loneliness and welcome change.

Through the looking within, we may become truly empty, leaving space to be filled by That which is Above. We attach to and personalize our illnesses, claiming them as our own—my migraine, my cancer, my broken life. It seems the two-legged has a propensity for suffering. We cling to our psychosis and disease. If we give over our pain, what then will take its place?

We must practice surrender in our every moment, in our everyday lives. If we develop the quality of balance and emptiness, we will be working in harmony with the forces of nature and spirit all the time, therefore having a stronger effect for good in the world.

The views of Harry Edwards, the last healer interviewed by the Gardners, are summarized later in this chapter.

In a modest way, the Gardners approach a few of the questions addressed in this book. They identify some of the common denominators of healing through the views of these healers.

The skeptic will point out that it is hard to prove whether the theory of karmic influences provides a valid explanation or is merely a *hedge* used by healers against disappointment or losing face when treatments are unsuccessful.

Love, acceptance, and compassion are repeatedly mentioned by healers and healees as vital components of healing. Love is felt as an active force, not merely experienced as a positive bedside manner.

The Gardners' book is highly recommended for its rich descriptions in the words of the healers.

Traditional healers can be found in every country. These are people who either spontaneously exhibit innate healing abilities or have studied with other healers to develop their gifts. They often assume complex roles within their cultures, serving as counselors, social mediators, peace-keepers, and priests. Their ritual practices have been well described in literature on *shamanism*, but their potent spiritual healing abilities have been given insufficient attention. Some of the best clues to the mystery of healing may come from shamans.[63]

Max Freedom Long lived for many years in Hawaii and delved into the secrets of the local medicine men, the *kahunas*.

Max Freedom Long
Recovering the Ancient Magic, 1936

Long presents observations of his own and of others on a broad gamut of native practices involving the full range of psi phenomena.[64] Long explains kahuna healers' understanding of psychology and mind-body connections, tracing these back to India, the presumed origin of the people of the Pacific Islands.

> [I]n India there has been an ancient teaching that there exists a
> *Body* (subconscious), *Mind* (conscious), *and Soul* (superconscious).
> The kahuna names for these are *unihipili*, *uhane* and *aumakua*. To
> be certain that we are right we have but to go to the ancient scrip-
> tures which Sri Ramakrishna studied and accepted in part, to find
> there the division of the human consciousness into the Lower Self,
> the Self and the Higher Self.[65]

The *unihipili* (subconscious) is believed to consist primarily of memory and
morals without reason, stored in computer-like fashion. It also maintains
vital life functions. The memory includes behavioral complexes associated
with belief systems. For instance, if the person is taught "Thou shalt not
steal!" the command is ingrained in the unihipili. Should the person steal,
his unihipili suffers from guilt and expects expiation or punishment.

The *uhane* (consciousness) has reasoning but no memory. It may
partially separate from the body in sleep or other states of awareness. The
kahuna may use his uhane to influence the unihipili of a healee in order to
heal. Long notes that for these interventions to be effective the kahuna
generally had to touch the person being healed.

> As one of my friends was involved in this case—a Chinese-Hawaiian
> gentleman—I was able to observe from the side lines, from the in-
> ception of the trouble to the cure, and to see that the trouble never
> returned once in the six years that followed.
>
> "Henry" was a healthy young man who worked in a salt factory
> several miles from Honolulu. One morning, while driving along
> the open road to his work, he fainted. His car was wrecked and he
> was badly bruised. For over a period of two months these fainting
> spells recurred. In one of them he fell into an open fire. In another
> he fell on his bed and his cigarette set the bedding on fire, result-
> ing in a narrow escape.
>
> After three doctors had been consulted and had failed to discover
> the cause of the trouble, the young man's Hawaiian mother in-
> sisted that he should go to a kahuna for help. Henry did not
> believe in kahunas, being a modern young man and well-educated,
> but in desperation he did as his mother advised.
>
> The kahuna listened to the story with half-closed eyes, and when
> it ended closed his eyes entirely. He sat there quietly for several
> minutes, then addressed Henry sharply:
>
> "I think you hurt some Hawaiian girl, no? You hurt bad and she
> grumble to spirit friends. They find you got shame feeling eating
> you inside, so they find easy for punish you. Come! Confess up!"
>
> Henry was amazed, but he confessed. He had intended to marry
> the girl some day, but his Chinese father had another young lady in
> mind for his son. In the end Henry had allowed his father to have

his way and had stopped calling on the Hawaiian girl. He did not know how she had taken his action.

"It is bad kind of hurt," said the kahuna. "Your shamed feeling is eating you inside, and when something is eating inside, then spirits can do bad things to you. Now, you got to go to the girl and make present and aloha until she forgive you. You do that and then come to me some more."

Henry did as he was directed and found the girl not unreasonable when she heard of the father's part in the matter. In due time she forgave him and accepted his present.

Upon his return to the kahuna, the old man again closed his eyes and made an examination of the case. He reported that the attacking spirits of "grandma and old auntie" had gone away content.

"But," said the old man. "Funny kind thing is inside of everyone. That spirit live inside you got no sense. It's not very smart. Long time it take to throw away your shame feeling. Even when other spirit in you know you make all right with girl, that spirit what make body grow thinks you still got to be punished. Even when grandmama and auntie spirit go home, it going keep on make for same kind push uhane outside body so you fall down and hurt you. You not understand this kind. All you got to do is like I tell to you to do. You think you can believe I know what everything about?"

Henry nodded. He had been convinced that the old kahuna knew his business.

"Good! That fine! All you need is be good in faith in me. Now I tell you something. In me is power from gods to forgive you for hurt girl and for everything bad you ever do. I going forgive you in kahuna way what lots more better than church way. Kahuna way forgive both spirit in you. Now I take this raw egg. I hold it over cup. When I do that, both of us hold breath. I put cleaning *mana* into egg. I break in cup. I give to you, you swallow quick and all at once. Then we breathe again. You understand?"

Henry understood. He obeyed orders. The egg was poised over the cup. Henry held his breath. He was nearly bursting when the egg was finally broken and handed to him. The moment he had gulped it down, the kahuna seized him and rubbed his stomach violently, at the same time panting out compelling words:

"Egg and mana is inside! It clean away all your sin! You clean like baby now! You not need shame for anything! You all clean now! No one can punish! You no can punish yourself! You never go black and fall down some more! You all new and clean and happy and well!"

The kahuna smilingly declared the cure complete and permanent. He collected his modest fee, and Henry went back to his work. Never did the fainting spells return.

The kahuna treated illnesses of infectious origins as well as apparent psychosomatic illnesses like Henry's. They were successful with Western people as well as with natives:

> A young white woman, once an ardent Christian, and married, developed a deep sore on the ankle. The doctors found it to be caused by a tubercular bone. They proposed an operation which would stiffen the joint for life.
>
> The kahuna examined the case and was none too anxious to take it. The girl was almost hopelessly complexed by the dogmas of "sin" absorbed in early life.
>
> The kahuna set to work to *kala* the guilt complexes after preparing the patient by having her fast and do penance that she might be consciously convinced that she no longer deserved punishment at the hands of God. He left the *unihipili* to overcome the infection and heal the sore. This it did in a few weeks.
>
> In the meantime, to keep the complex from being reformed, the kahuna had used a method which is a last resort, but which will have to be used on this generation, perhaps in the West. The method is this: Where complexes are so deep-seated and spring into action at once because the convictions of the *uhane* cannot be changed, the commission of "sins" under the complex must be avoided. In this case the patient had considered many harmless things either sins of commission or omission. Cards, drink and normal sex life were sins to her way of thinking. The kahuna could not convert her to his saner "test of hurt" philosophy, so he ordered her to give up all things she considered sins.
>
> She obeyed orders. He *kala-ed* her in the name of Jesus Christ, a wise thing to do considering the source of her faith—and so freed her guilt in *uhane* and *unihipili*. At once the *unihipili* responded and healed the sore, as I have said. But soon after the sore was completely healed, she disobeyed the injunction to cease to do things she considered sinful. Thinking her cure permanent, she again went back to her gay parties and to the few healthy activities which were sins against her dogma-complex which the kahuna could not remove because he could not change the beliefs of her *uhane* or mind by his most reasonable arguments.
>
> Suddenly the sore broke out again as if the unihipili had resumed the old punishment for sins or had ceased its protective work. The kahuna refused to renew his treatment. The operation was performed successfully by the doctors, but the ankle left stiff.

The kahuna may also enslave the *unihipili* of a deceased person by a process akin to hypnosis. The kahuna can then direct that entity to be an agent for influencing people at a distance. Kahunas may even hex a person to death using such methods if they feel a social or moral wrong has been committed. If the target of the hex is innocent, they will not be harmed. The accuser of the hexed person who acts maliciously may be hit by the rebounding hex. The goal of the kahunas was not vengeance but redressing wrongs and maintenance of social order. The victim who sought out the hexing parties could be given ways in which to make restitution for transgressions, and then the hex would be lifted.

These methods were learned by non-native Hawaiians through processes of discussion and deduction. The kahunas always remained secretive and would not deliberately teach their magic techniques.

The *aumakua* (superconscious) is presumed by long to be the agency for more far-reaching changes in healing, including instantaneous, miraculous cures. Long arrives at this conclusion by inference and analogy, as no kahuna would reveal his secrets.

Long writes of an old Hawaiian woman, known to be a most powerful kahuna and generally considered more or less a saint, who lived in a house built on a sand beach.

> One afternoon a car drove up and visitors began to get down. The car stood high on solid ground beside a hollow filled with soft sand. One of the visitors, a kindly Hawaiian man, missed his footing and fell, breaking a bone in his leg just above the ankle. He was slightly intoxicated at the time—a thing not too unusual on a holiday.
>
> The kahuna was standing by to receive her guests. The man fell and the sound of the breaking bone was plainly heard. Immediately she knelt beside him and took his leg in her strong old hands. The skin was pushed out over the ragged end of the protruding bone and the swelling had commenced. Forcing the bone back into place, she commanded the man to remain quiet. She closed her eyes for a moment, then opened them and spoke the words of power, "Be healed," in Hawaiian.
>
> The healing was instant. The man rose to his feet and walked with the other guests to the house. No one was more amazed and intrigued than was my friend. He had seen and heard everything and had been convinced that the bone had been broken.

Kahuna healers make clairsentient or telepathic diagnoses. They direct healees to mend the emotional and relational wrongs underlying their problems, and then help the healees to relinquish their guilt complexes from their subconscious minds. When the guilt complexes are released, physical symptoms improve. The treatment seems to involve psychotherapeutic techniques that are little different from Western ones. The kahuna utilizes the full range of suggestion, from exhortation to hypnosis. This parallels the methods of hypnotherapy, Neurolinguistic Programming,

Western psychoanalytic theory[66]and the conceptualizations of Victor Krivorotov.[67]

Long shares many of his own experiences in searching his mind via dream and meditative states for processes that might explain the kahuna healings. He hypothesizes that *realization*, a *being-one-with* the healee, nature, and the powers of the universe are involved in the miraculous cures.

His methods of linguistic analysis for teasing out kahuna healing secrets (Long 1976) are also worth reading.

"Let both sides seek to invoke the wonders of science instead of its terrors. Together let us explore the stars, conquer the deserts, eradicate disease. . .."

—John F. Kennedy, Inaugural Address

Hexing has been associated in many cultures with shamans. Shamans use such energies either to heal or to harm. Some observers point out that these negative effects are utilized to maintain social order within the community, as described by Long, above. The next discussion expands upon these issues.

Daniel A. Slomoff

Traditional african medicine: voodoo[68] healing, in Ruth-Inge Heinze, *Proceedings of the Second International Conference on the Study of Shamanism*, 1986

Daniel Slomoff studied healers in Togo. In taking their professional vows, healers in this society agree to harm as well as to heal people in order to maintain the social order. For instance, a theft puts the entire community out of balance. The healer's task is to restore order as rapidly as possible.

> The victim believes he knows who stole the property. He approaches the healer and requests that a spell be cast on the perpetrator. . . . The healer then casts the spell and the accused thief becomes ill. The person suffering now approaches the same healer or another healer. . . . The diagnosis is quickly made that a spell has been cast and a substantial sum must be paid for a healing ceremony . . . and the community gathers for the ceremony. It may last six hours or six days, depending on the nature of the illness. During the ceremony, members of the community go into trance and . . . the voice of the spirit comes through one of them and reveals that harm has been done, the truth shall be known and the guilty punished. Everyone suspiciously looks around the group,

knowing that the gods have spoken. Anxiety builds because this is a close society and people know each other's business. It is difficult to hide and often someone in trance will blurt out the name of the culprit . . . it may be the person who is ill if he is guilty or another. In either case, the illness will lift when the guilty party has paid his debt and the harmony in the society is restored. . . .

The guilty man gives the victim twelve goats and this man must slaughter two goats and make an elaborate feast in honor of the person who has done him harm and who has paid just retribution. In this way, the community returns to a state of comradeship and balance very quickly and efficiently.

Without the healer's agreement to utilize his healing powers to harm, social justice cannot be carried out unless police, courts, and jails are established. Hexing traditions provide for confessions of crimes without leaving animosities. When the gods resolve the problem, no grudges are held.

In Western society the use of healing for negative purposes is strictly avoided and denounced by most healers. I have talked with hundreds of healers and scores of teachers of healing. All, without exception, are totally committed to using healing solely for positive purposes. The use of hexing as a social regulator would seem limited to more homogeneous and less mobile cultures than those of Western society.

The potential to harm via these processes remains, however. Fear of misuse of healing may be one of the reasons that Western society has consciously or unconsciously avoided involvement with it. It is not surprising to find distrust and anxiety regarding potential misuse of healing in a world where the media highlight ever more exciting episodes of fictional and real violence, where weapons of war are still stockpiled, and where the killing of certain segments of the population is contemplated or implemented as a deliberate strategy.[69]

Clues to the mystery of healing come from many quarters. Here, David St. Clair described the use of healing in dentistry and psychiatry.

David St. Clair

Psychic Healers, 1979

David St. Clair describes a number of healers,[70] including the following:

Brother Willard Fuller and his wife, Sister Amelia Fuller, are Pentecostalist healers specializing in dentistry. Brother Willard is reportedly able to materialize gold and silver-colored metal fillings by praying to God. The material is said to be "a metal unlike anything known to science today."

Sometimes cavities simply disappear under his ministrations and the teeth are restored without fillings.[71]

Bob Hoffman is a psychic-psychiatrist, a healer of the mind. He has a spirit guide named Dr. Siegfried Fischer, who was a psychiatrist friend of Hoffman prior to his death. He is able to zero-in on core psychiatric conflicts with Dr. Fischer's aid and cure them. His treatments last three hours, and a month of weekly visits often suffices to produce a cure.

St. Clair excerpts a number of letter testimonials to Hoffman's methods.

The reports in this book provide a spectrum of healer phenomena in a descriptive, noncritical manner.

At a lecture/demonstration by Fuller I attended in Philadelphia, no visible results were obtained. I spoke before and after this session with several people who said they had witnessed fillings appearing at other sessions.

While most healers rely upon subtle energies to bring about changes, some healers intuitively diagnose problems and prescribe unusual remedies. The most famous of these healers was Edgar Cayce.

Mary Ellen Carter and William A. McGarey
Edgar Cayce on Healing, 1972

Edgar Cayce was a gifted intuitive who was able to make accurate diagnoses at a distance, given only the name and location of a healee. Under hypnotic trance, Cayce gave many details of ailments and then recommended treatments, some for conventional medications and a large number for unconventional approaches, including chiropractic and osteopathic manipulations, special diets, colonic irrigation, electrical stimulation, and unusual chemotherapies. For instance, Cayce would recommend application of castor-oil packs to the chest for pneumonia, with resultant dramatic relief of the illness (in the days prior to antibiotics). He reported he got his information from *Akashic* (universal) records in another dimension. The treatments were reported to be successful even in most difficult cases.

Cayce's methods of diagnosis seem very strange in Western medical terms. This is healing of a different kind from that of most described in this volume.[72]

Sadly, no scientific assessments of Cayce's abilities were made during his life. Retrospective review of 150 randomly chosen case reports (Cayce/Cayce) showed 43 percent with documented, confirmed diagnosis and positive results from treatments; no effects in 7 percent; and no information on the rest.

The Association for Research and Enlightenment (A.R.E.) in Virginia Beach, Virginia, was founded in 1932 for exploration of modern applications of these cures. Records of thousands of cases are preserved at the A.R.E. Drs. William and Gladys McGarey, American physicians, have been studying these remedies on their patients for many years (W. McGarey), finding some of them to be effective.

Clairsentient diagnosis is yet another area where healing may make a major contribution to modern medicine.[73]

Items from several other reviews of healing deserve special mention. Materials from these books are also cited in other volumes of *Healing Research.*

Alfred Stelter

Psi Healing, 1976

Psi Healing is an excellent review of healing literature. It focuses on material published in German, but also includes studies in English. The author, a chemistry professor, has broad experience with healers from the Philippines and a displays a scientific approach to the subject. Here are several highlights:

German engineer Fritz Grunewald describes a biomagnetic effect when he studies Johannsen, a medium, around 1920.

> Johannsen could do simple feats of psychokinesis such as depressing one side of an evenly balanced scale. Grunewald found that each time, just before the scale descended, the magnetic field strength in the medium's hands—which he held out toward the object to be moved—grew markedly weaker, only to increase after the psychokinetic act. It looked as if something which had produced the strong magnetism in Johannsen's body . . . displaced itself outward and released psychokinetic effects.
>
> A few times Grunewald, by means of iron filings strewn on glass plates, was able to obtain pictures of the magnetic field within Johannsen's hands. In this way, he found several magnetic centers in the hand's magnetic field which Grunewald believed were evoked by electrical eddies in the medium's hands . . . . But strangely, the magnetic centers seemed at times to lie outside the medium's hand. We must recall the hypothesis that the biofield can move outside the body.

Electromagnetic measurements have been made on and around the hands of healers by other researchers, with mixed findings. It is possible that the magnetic effects of Johannsen were produced by psychokinetic mind effects upon the measuring instruments rather than by electromagnetic effects.[74]

Preservation of food using healing has been reported occasionally, usually with desiccation ("mummification"). Citing a report by Alan Vaughan (1972), Stelter notes that if healers "treat" unrefrigerated food, it keeps much better than control samples. Stelter speculates this is due to the killing of bacteria by the healing energies. He then postulates that this effect could explain how healers can help cure infected wounds presumably by killing infecting microorganisms.

Stelter briefly reviews the life and work of Tony Agpaoa, a Filipino healer renowned for doing psychic surgery—operating to treat diseased tissues with his bare hands. [75] When Agpaoa was asked how he learned, he replied:

> From earliest childhood, Phil A., another healer, received a steady stream of instructions and explanations from "higher powers" about life and the production of human energies. He could not describe this more fully to others, but it seemed so natural that he assumed everyone must be receiving similar knowledge. He believed these instructions and information were available to everyone who understood how to "listen." . . . Agpaoa said more or less the same thing when he explained that all human knowledge is somehow stored up perhaps in some sort of cosmic memory and that meditation could draw out all kinds of instruction from it.

Agpaoa seemed able to project intense energy from his eyes. He reportedly used his gaze to start fires, prepare blossoms for herbal medicines and heal skin disorders. He claimed he lost this ability at the age of fourteen because he was not mature enough in his use of it.

Stelter quotes Edward Naumov, a Russian scientist who studied the gifted healer Nina Kulagina (no reference cited):

> It is difficult to explain to some scientists that emotions have a profound influence on the medium's achievements. These scientists believe people can be turned on and off like machines. They do not seem to understand that their own force fields can also affect the medium. Some of them, who have no understanding of psychology and bioinformation, radiate hostility and mistrust, emanations caught by the medium.
>
> Generally, we can give demonstrations of psychokinesis at any time, but if the observers include people with a negative attitude, the medium often requires up to four, even seven hours before phenomena take place. On the other hand, if the medium is surrounded by people with a friendly attitude, it only takes five minutes.

The phenomena at Lourdes are generally attributed to some *healing powers of the location.*[76] Stelter suggests otherwise:

Decades ago the French physician and parapsychologist Dr. E. Osty, reported on a well-to-do lady of his acquaintance who spent much time in Lourdes as a voluntary helper at the spring in the grotto of Massabielle. Her chief activity consisted in helping the patients into the pool and immersing them briefly. In the course of her long activity, more than once she witnessed extraordinary spontaneous cures of severely disabled persons bathing in the spring. During the patients' submersion in the cold spring water, at the moment in which the cures presumably set in, she always felt as if all her strength were withdrawn from her. She required several days to recuperate from these attacks of weakness.

In a discursive, easily readable style, Stelter presents evidence and expounds his theories in a critical though not comprehensive manner. It is sometimes difficult to distinguish where presentation of evidence ends and discussion and speculation begin.

The projection of healing through the eyes has not been well studied, but has also been mentioned by other healers, including Lombardi.

In psychic surgery the healers open the body with their bare hands or with an ordinary knife, operating swiftly without producing pain, bleeding, or infection. As fantastic as this sounds, reliable witnesses have made consistent observations of such operations. Some psychic surgeons have been caught faking operations. This does not invalidate the work of *all* psychic surgeons.

With 326 references, *Psi Healing* is one of the better surveys on theories of healing and is rich in detail. It is especially useful on psychic surgery.

In one of the best overall discussions on spiritual healing I have found, George Meek briefly describes healers from Brazil, the United Kingdom, the United States, the former Soviet Union, and the Philippines and analyzes many aspects of healing.

George W. Meek (Editor and Contributor)
Healers and the Healing Process, 1977

Especially noteworthy are the discussions on:

- The acceptance healing has attained in the British hospital system. Healers are permitted to assist either at the request of the patient or of the physician.
- Theories of healing.[77]
- Paranormal healing in the Philippines.
- Information concerning healing from trance mediums who claim to act as channels of communication for discarnate spirits.

Though the authors provide stimulating material, they exhibit uneven style, depth and breadth of expertise, and writing clarity. The editor, an American engineer, shares a wealth of knowledge from his broad experience with healers and healing.

Spirit communications need careful and cautious scrutiny. Experts in the field have repeatedly observed that information from spirits does not necessarily represent the last word from on-high. Furthermore, the information can be subject to severe distortions in transmissions and translations through the medium.

> *To be uncertain is to be uncomfortable, but to be certain is to be ridiculous.*
> —Chinese proverb (Dossey 1998a, p. 109)[78]

Stanley Krippner, a parapsychologist with vast field and laboratory research experience, and Alberto Villoldo, a psychologist with considerable field experience with healers in various cultures, review the practices of many fascinating healers[79] and discuss various theories of healing.

Stanley Krippner and Alberto Villoldo
The Realms of Healing, 1976 (rev. ed. 1986)

The following points are of particular interest:

• There are difficulties in assessing the validity of psychic surgery, as practiced in the Philippines,[75] with the yardsticks and cultural assumptions of Western science.
• South American spiritual healers have an uninterrupted tradition of healing over many centuries, from which much can be learned.
• Evidence from Kirlian photography[24] suggests that healing may involve a transfer of energy from healer to healee.

This book is a must for anyone seeking to comprehend the intricacies of healing phenomena.

Anthea Courtenay
Healing Now, 1991

This is the best survey of British healers, written by a journalist who was a grateful recipient of healing. It provides an excellent survey of a spectrum of healers and sensible discussions on aspects of healing, though it is a little naive in its description of the British healing organizations.

Richard Gerber

Vibrational Medicine, 1988; Revised edition 2000

Richard Gerber presents an excellent discussion on healing as energy medicine. His style is easy to read, and his diagrams and illustrations greatly facilitate understanding. His discussion covers extensive theories for healing, self-healing, and ways of integrating subtle-energy models with conventional scientific models.

Lawrence LeShan

The Medium, the Mystic and the Physicist, 1974

Lawrence LeShan is a psychologist well known for his work with people who have cancer. He started out a skeptic, approaching spiritual healers with the intent of exposing them as frauds who were harming his clients by giving them false hope and encouraging them to delay or avoid effective medical treatments. He came away from his study of healers a firm believer.

This book shares LeShan's explorations of healing, how he came to be a healer himself, and how he developed a program to teach others to develop their healing gifts.

LeShan also describes inner levels of awareness, worlds in which the laws of action and reaction are different from those of our everyday world, and through which we may understand what appear to be extraordinary healing effects in the external world.[80]

Rounding out this series of cameos of healing, Ruth Benor suggests another area where healing can help. Ruth worked for many years as a nurse, midwife, health visitor, genetics counselor, and lecturer in palliative care. She pioneered the introduction of complementary therapies into nursing courses and clinical care, and is the founder of the Holistic Nurses Association in Britain. In the following testimonial, she shares from her wealth of experience in assisting people to make the most important journey of their lives.

Ruth Benor[81]

Healing Unto Death, 1999

> *Healing unto death begins with the awareness that we are not merely a physical body. The person extends beyond the discernible mass as we know it.*
>
> —R.B.

Perceiving the Spirit or Soul of a person leaving the body was not discussed within my family, although other family members also had similar perceptions.

Spiritual matters were not taught in nursing school. I was distressed in my introduction to care of the dying patients and their families—focused principally on how to relieve physical suffering, how to lay out the body and how to break bad news to relatives. Discussion of spiritual issues was limited to religion, such as requirements to call in the appropriate clergy, not touching a Muslim body and ignoring those who had no religious affiliation.

I knew there was much more than I was being taught. I experience most of life through my intuitive senses first. These come as sudden flashes and sometimes as deeply felt phenomena which refuse to be ignored. I know "healing unto death" through my senses, through observing people as they make their final life transition into death. This has been a normal part of my everyday experience.

The transitions during the process of dying, death, and bereavement encompass physical, psychological, subtle energetic, and existential realms. I do not consider myself to be an authority or special person but share my experiences, having come to realize in recent years that other sensitives— many of them health care professionals—also have such awarenesses.

My family was very fearful of death, seeing it as a robber, a thief in the night. They were unable to talk about it for fear of evoking it. I realize now that my mother and my grandmother were gifted psychics but through fear and negative conditioning were haunted by their abilities rather than feeling helped and nurtured through them. My mother saw spirits, particularly garden devas, and only in her later years would share how she perceived and talked with them. It was good to see her sitting in a garden in Cornwall, renewed by the beauty of this garden and uplifted by witnessing the work and frolics of the various nature devas and fairies. But just as she could relate to the positive aspects of this intuition/insight, she could also feel afraid of the less childlike images. This is what caused her to deny her intuition when I was a child, and what denied me, in turn, the opportunity to share and validate my similar experiences—until much later in life.

As a child I would wake up in the morning and thank God for the return of my spirit to my body, realizing that my spirit may not have been present while I was asleep.

When I heard of a person's death I would pray for the safety of their spirit, knowing somehow that their spirit might not go easily into its proper place after leaving the body. This had never been discussed in my family. It was a strong intuitive knowing that the genuine prayers of a person on behalf of a soul which had just crossed over from life would be a help to the soul on its journey.

Coming from a family who were death-denying and fearful of death, I was a fish out of water. I just couldn't understand what their fears were about.

I first saw energy and spirit in the transition process of dying when my grandfather was near his death. I was eleven. On my way to school I stopped to pick up my cousin, who lived with our grandparents. My grandfather was sitting in his chair. He was naturally pale of skin, but that morning he looked different. He seemed somehow translucent. I could see through him. He was asking to have an egg for breakfast. Though he seemed somehow "vague," there was no indication that he was ill. It was just another morning, my cousin and I rushing not to be late to school. However, I remember thinking as we opened the front door that this was the last time I would see him alive. I hesitated as I called goodbye and felt a fullness in my chest that made me want to cry and try to hold him back, but I was hurried along and could not share any of what I sensed. That day he died, peacefully.

Drawing on these senses and experiences to present a tangible and coherent story is no easy task. To describe this in professional, clinical terms is relatively easy. It is far more difficult to put into words how I reach into the spiritual, into the essence of Being.

I cannot speak of death without also speaking of bereavement—which is not only the reaction to the death of others but an anticipation and preparation for our own deaths. During these formative years I observed many people dying. We lived in a large Victorian house on the edge of a park. Britain was recovering from the Nazi bombings and struggling with the scarcities of food and resources following the War. In this generation, which had known many war deaths, death was not covered up or hidden. It often happened at home, with family members nursing and caring for the dying, helped by local community members. Certain people would help lay out the body. Funeral directors played only a minor role—in contrast to present practices where the impact of death is diminished and it is more usual for death to occur in a hospital or hospice. In many instances these modern ways interfere with the healing process of grief. Death is isolated and sanitized and therefore not fully experienced, resulting in unresolved feelings and more difficult adjustments. The physical dimensions may be addressed but the psychological hurts of bereavement are too often avoided, leaving unresolved grief which scars those who run away from these pains—in effect burying the hurts inside their unconscious minds, where they remain to haunt them.

I remember many ways the community honored the dead and their families. Various rituals were carried out as a mark of respect for both the deceased and the bereaved, aiding the grief process with rites of passage. Our community honored the lifeless body, displaying it in its coffin in the family home until burial. There was no fear of the body. It was considered an honor to view and say goodbye to the dead spouse, child or friend. Curtains at the windows would be drawn and all mirrors covered with a dark cloth. This sharpened the focus on the loss by blocking any reflection which might distract from the grief of the family. Neighbors and friends would visit, finding ways to support and help. Members of the family wore a black arm band on the sleeve of their jacket. These mourning rituals demystified death, giving the family the time and ceremony through which to grieve and to be socially recognized for their loss. These emblems marked a transition for the mourners, integrating the grief and loss of the family with that of their community. The outcome was usually a healing. This was a great contrast with my nursing experience.

As I grew into my practice of nursing, my visions, my intuitive aware-ness and my healing gifts developed further. There were healings of many sorts but I was particularly drawn towards healings into death. I cared for many people who came to the hospital to die. Not infrequently, families of the terminally ill patient had not witnessed a death or seen a dead body and hesitated to speak of the impending end of life. Healing took the form of gentle support for them to enter this final separation. This sort of healing is more a state of being than an act of doing. Often I find people speaking to me of their deep, personal spiritual experiences spontaneously, or with the barest of prompting on my part.

It is only recently that a shift in our society back to the old ways is gradually occurring, with better education about death and with improved medical science and technology to ease the physical discomforts which may precede death. There is also the home-like atmosphere of hospices which involve the family of the dying person to the extent they are ready for this. Hospice care can also be arranged in a person's own home. A sense of community is thus re-established.

When people are unfamiliar with death it can feel like an enemy. My healing may simply be to calm them. I recall a woman who was out of control with fear about dying. The room was full of hysterical vibrations. My healing on the physical level came through my calming touch and voice. I prayed silently for peace to come to her, grounding the energies in the room, inviting the angelic presences to help. She calmed down within a few minutes. It was not uncommon for patients to ask for 'the nurse with the voice' to tend to them when they were upset like that.

Losing confidence, feeling overwhelmed and vulnerable, are common experiences when one receives news of life threatening illness or approach-ing death. It has been said that there is no dress rehearsal for dying, but we frequently experience losses throughout life. It can be helpful to recall times in your life when serious things happen in order to reconnect them to how you coped. In raising your awareness, fear and anxiety can be reduced and a sense of confidence and ability to cope can be developed.

As I cared for patients I increasingly saw with my inner eyes and noticed more and more the subtle energies around the body. These looked like vapor, sometimes like a core of color. I started to understand the changes in patients as they journeyed through the course of their terminal illnesses towards death. The energy shifts also involved those who were significant to them.

I am aware of people who are preparing, either consciously or unconsciously, to die. There is a special feel to them which draws my attention. As they make their transition I may see the spirit move from the body in any of several ways. The body may be an empty shell, still alive, but with its spirit partly detached—something like a skin being shed. The spirit may look like a vapor, or may appear more solid. At other times it is invisible but I know with my inner awareness it is there. At death it often moves out through the crown chakra or through the solar plexus. Sometimes there is a complete separation and it looks to me like there are twins in the bed. The spirit then walks away and may turn to look at what is going on before departing.

Some people who are dying deliberately hold onto their spirit, waiting for relatives to arrive for their final farewells. I was called to my mother's deathbed in the hospital, after many years of her deterioration into an Alzheimer oblivion. When I arrived, her soul was floating close to the body and still attached to it. Over 15 minutes a gradual separation occurred. When her physical body died, her spirit was still in the room. It was escorted out of the room by another spirit.

Even knowing about these issues, my emotions sometimes dominate my reason. My stepfather had severe neurological impairment for two years, following two cardiac arrests. His spirit was still strongly attached. A part of him wanted to go but he held back, not wanting to abandon his family. I also held onto him, praying for him not to die, hoping that somehow he would recover. When he started having epileptic fits and had further deterioration, drifting in and out of semi-consciousness, I spoke with him through my inner voice about leaving. I told him how much he would be missed but that he need not prolong his suffering for our sake, and that we could all take care of ourselves. Three days later he passed on. I was not present when his spirit departed but I sensed from 200 miles away he had gone.

Sometimes when people are dying a number of spirit entities will gather around the bed. Though others might see an empty room, to me it appears crowded. After death they may remain to honor the transition and to interact with the bereaved relatives and hospital or hospice staff.

What is the spirit? It is that essence or spark which works with ego to express the will of the eternal soul through the garments of flesh in the play of life. Spirit wants to be lived. It is impossible to box it into descriptions with words.

The soul, on a higher level, is beyond human feelings of anxiety, pain and suffering. The soul is the wind, which cannot be seen. The spirit and body are manifestations of the soul, and can be seen—like the effects of the wind.

In healing into death I make friends with the very essence of the dying person—engaging in spiritual healing on all levels.

On the level of flesh I help to relieve unnecessary suffering, physical and psychological. While conversing with a person on the physical level I often communicate as well with the spirit. I might acknowledge the movement of the spirit towards letting go, returning to the source. The person in the flesh might be afraid, but the spirit would be free of fear and preparing to depart. My healing is to help people make their peace with being at the end of their life. They must deal with all the stages of their own grief about leaving—from denial, through sadness, anger, guilt, and finally into resolution to leave. We may never mention death, but inside I know they know, and know also that I know and that we are communicating on some other level about this.

It is somewhat like being a midwife to the spirit. A midwife attends the coming into the physical world of a new being, seeing that there is a safe delivery. Healing into death is being there to help the spirit into another world.

It is hard for me to put these awarenesses into words without feeling what I am saying must sound inflated. Many intuitive healers simply refuse to speak of this. It is beyond reasoning. It is an inner knowing which is as certain as any knowing from the physical world, actually much more real when one is used to awareness in these other dimensions.

Sometimes the healing is through talking with the relatives, explaining that the situation is terminal, but always being patient and respectful of their state of readiness to let go or insistence to hold on. If they are resistant and fearful, I can only talk with them, never pushing, till they are ready to accept the inevitable. At some point there is a conference between our spirits at a transcendent level, and there may be a resolution of conflicts and agreement that the dying person should depart. In other instances the relatives won't let go. I often feel then I must side quietly with the ones who are dying, giving them the emotional and spiritual strength to make their own decision if their family members are closed to the possibility of releasing them.

I tended a woman who was terminally ill, lying comatose in her home, physically exhausted and ready to die, but unable to depart because her frightened daughter refused to let go. I stayed with them through most of the night. It was like when a guest overstays her welcome, not knowing it is time to go. I sensed on a spiritual level that the mother was prepared to go, and told her with my inner voice I was there not just for her but also for her daughter. Feeling the mother had heard me, I accepted her daughter's offer to drive me home. Her mother died before we arrived at my home. When I was called back to the hospital by the daughter, I saw her mother's spirit hovering anxiously near her. Shortly after I comforted the daughter, the spirit moved on. Though the daughter was angry at having missed the last moments of her mother's life, we were able to talk this through to a healthy resolution.

I have worked as a genetic and bereavement counselor with babies who died stillborn or shortly after birth. I often feel the mothers know on some level what has happened. In some cases there seemed to have been decisions made at a spirit level about the baby dying.

I have seen abortions under anesthesia at the request of mothers where the spirit of the mother was awake and the spirit of the baby was shocked by this trauma. I have seen the spirit of the fetus lingering around the body for the period that the fetus was still breathing. I tended intuitively to the spirits of the babies without words and they soon departed.

Many obstetricians and midwives avoided speaking with the mothers. They didn't know how to accept the seemingly unfair death of a baby before life had properly begun or how to deal with their own sense of in-adequacy, failure and anger. They had had no preparation in their training to deal with infant deaths or parental bereavement. The parents' grief was compounded in being abandoned by the medical staff. I would be called in to relieve them of the responsibility of resolving their relationships with the parents.

I may connect without words with other nurses or doctors, as though my spirit expands to dock next to theirs in a mutual caring interaction, helping them deal with the parents' grief and their own. This is a healing for the staff.

Today there are many schools where doctors and nurses are taught to deal better with death and bereavement.

Though I have participated in many deaths over many years, each is unique. I have witnessed peaceful deaths and stressful ones, predictable and surprising ones. It is important to begin to sort our what contributes to each. We must learn from our experiences and find ways to share them. How else will we grow in our abilities to avoid unnecessary suffering and how else will we find ways to teach what we learn? This is particularly so in a society which is so death denying.

A good death is one where the individual has had opportunities to be involved in the decisions surrounding physical care, where distressing symptoms and pain were controlled, where family or friends were involved, where clear communications were shared, based on honesty and respect of feelings and needs and where spiritual needs were honored.

Healing means to *make whole*. What I have come to advocate is a wholistic approach, which addresses physical, intellectual, emotional, social and spiritual dimensions and needs of all participants: of the person who is ill, of their family and friends, and of the caregivers. Healing through a wholistic framework in terminal illness, even more clearly than in other illnesses, is not about cure. This healing is a gentle, pervasive reaching into all the dimensions of the individual to help her or him arrive at a state of acceptance—not through passivity but through a gradual awakening aware-ness, touching those parts of themselves which are damaged, hurting, blocked or unexpressed, to develop a quality of wholeness within them-selves, thereby initiating a process of self healing. Through wholistic healing we shift from just putting days into life to putting life (quality) into the remaining days.

Healers have much to contribute to health care and to people who are approaching the end of their lives. I was taught in medical school that if a person under my care in the hospital had the affront to die, it was probably my fault—either in failing to make the right diagnosis or in failing to prescribe the correct treatment. I was not taught about helping people to die. Death was (and still is, in too many minds) considered a medical failure.

It is difficult to omit many fascinating and, no doubt, relevant descrip-tions of healing experiences, but publishing limitations dictate I must do so. This chapter may be daunting in the range of practices and beliefs it presents, but this is the challenge to anyone wishing to understand healing to a depth greater than the teachings of any one individual.

Adding to the confusion is the fact that healers evolve in their own practice and understanding. F. W. Knowles (1954, 1956), for example, was initially taught healing rituals but later discarded these as unneces-sary. Most of the more successful healers find that their healing develops different characteristics over time.

We have much to sort out to unravel these mysteries.[82]

A BRIEF SUMMARY OF HEALING APPROACHES [83, 84]

It is common sense to take a method and try it. If it fails, admit it frankly and try another.

—Franklin Delano Roosevelt

There are obviously many systems of healing, each with its strengths and weaknesses. Any may be appropriate as an entry into learning to develop one's own healing gifts. Lack of inclusion in this list is not an indication that I disapprove of any method. There are many more approaches to healing than I can summarize here. Indeed, there are many more methods than I am familiar with. Many are small schools led by a particular person or group. I have included here the ones I have personally encountered, whose practitioners I have found to be generally reliable. This does not mean that I endorse any of these methods uncritically. The individual practitioners as the vehicles for the healing are the most important aspect of whether healings are likely to be helpful—far more important than the methods they use.

Spiritual healing in religious settings

Many churches include healing services. Often the clergy are the healers, using prayer and the laying-on of hands to convey healings and encouraging congregants to pray for their own healing. Congregants with strong gifts of healing may be invited to participate in conveying healing to others. Rituals—such as communion, anointment with blessed water or oil, visits to shrines, and touching or observing holy or blessed relics—may facilitate healing.[85] Speaking in tongues and exorcisms may also be practiced.

Some churches teach that faith is required in order to receive healing. This may mean faith in God, Christ, the Holy Spirit, the Pope or the clergy. Faith in the doctrines and teachings of the church and loyalty to these may be emphasized. Others teach that one must have faith in one's own ability to be healed.[86]

Strengths:
- Long traditions of healing which may have accrued wisdom of experience.
- Mantles of authority which may enhance healees' belief that they can be healed.
- Regular healing prayers either during services or in healing circles sometimes including gifted nonclergy.

- Pastoral counseling for emotional and relational healing.
- Support of a community—emotional, social, and spiritual.
- Encouragement, facilitation, and teaching of love, acceptance, forgiveness, and healing.
- Acknowledgment of spirit survival and the availability of loved ones and saints in other dimensions who can comfort, advise, and heal.
- Awareness of evil spirits and possession, with rituals and prayers to deal with them.
- Practices of *deliverance* which provide relief from negative self-image, old hurts and guilt.
- Hundreds of studies showing correlations between religious affiliation/ practice and health (J. Levin).

Limitations:
- Limited scope of healing approaches, as in traditions that may not offer the laying-on of hands, discourage or proscribe practices that conflict with church teachings, doctrines, and dogma, or warn that healing outside the true faith may be evil or involve the devil.
- Instilling guilt and fear rather than love and hope through teaching that lack of response to healing indicates lack of faith.
- Emphasizing the power of healing of the clergy, thereby discouraging congregants from developing their own gifts of self-healing and of healing others.
- Teaching sectarian exclusivity and self-righteousness, denigrating other religious teachings and healing traditions, such as acupuncture, yoga, and other complementary therapies, which may be pejoratively labeled *new age practices.*[87]
- Encouraging *spiritual bypassing* of emotional and social responsibility and healing—assuming religious practices can assuage or cure all ills; overlooking psychological problems which may often include personal projections of negativity upon others; and condoning communal projections of negativity upon others.
- Inappropriate labeling of symptoms as manifestations of *possession*[88] and inappropriate use of exorcisms in treating people with emotional disturbances.[89]
- Variability in supervision and certification.

Qigong healing

Qigong evolved out of ancient Chinese traditions of healing (K. Cohen). Internal qigong teaches profoundly effective methods of relaxation, meditation, gentle movement exercises, and self-healing. External qigong, or *weiqi,* is healing done by qigong masters, often involving physical movements to shape and project the healing energies.

Strengths:
- Emphasis on self-healing, even when external qigong is used.
- Extensive research base in China.

Limitations:
- Most qigong healers, particularly in China, tend to view emotional problems exclusively in terms of physical and energy disharmonies.
- Lacks formalized structure for clinical teaching, supervision, and regulation.

Medical dowsing

Dowsers have been well known for using intuition to locate water and other materials underground. Some dowsers develop intuitive diagnostic and healing gifts as well. I am impressed that the feedback of field and map dowsing are excellent ways for many people to develop their intuitive gifts. Many healers in various traditions such as Healing Touch use pendulums to connect with intuitive knowledge for diagnosis and healing.

In Britain there are practitioners of radiesthesia and radionics—dowsers who use instruments with dials, affectionately called *black boxes*, for dowsing and distant healing. These have been outlawed in America by the Food and Drug Administration, which has been very vigilant and at time merciless in prosecuting people who promote the use of these instruments.[90]

Strengths:
- Pragmatic orientation, training dowsers to look for feedback to enhance learning.
- Focus on diagnosis, which can be very specific.
- Ability to recommend specific treatments based on the same methods.
- Identification of *geopathic stress*, a type of illness apparently due to negative earth energies.[91]

Limitations:
- Danger of assuming that the dowser has "the" picture rather than "a" picture of the problem.[92]
- Responses of dowsing instruments that are very concrete and literal, limited to the precise wording of the questions asked, and possibly misleading.[93]
- No research support for this methodology in healing, although there is good research in identifying geopathic stress and other earth-energy related matters.
- No formalized structure for clinical teaching, supervision, and certification.

Reiki healing

Developed in Japan by Dr. Mikao Usui in the early 20th century, this method is growing in popularity around the world.

Sixteen Reiki masters were empowered by Usui. It appears that each master was empowered with individualized gifts, which may differ from those of other masters in subtle or substantial ways.

Reiki is taught at several levels of competence. Reiki I teaches beginners a pattern of laying-on of hands on the head and torso. Reiki healers initially adhere to this pattern in each healing treatment, being taught that this ensures they will not overlook aspects of people's problems or introduce energy imbalances through addressing only the symptomatic sites. A pain in the head, for instance, might be due to local muscle spasms from tiredness, but it might also be due to poor posture, emotional imbalances such as anger or depression, or to systemic dysfunctions such as hypertension. A part of level one teaching involves an *induction* of healing abilities in the healer by the Master.

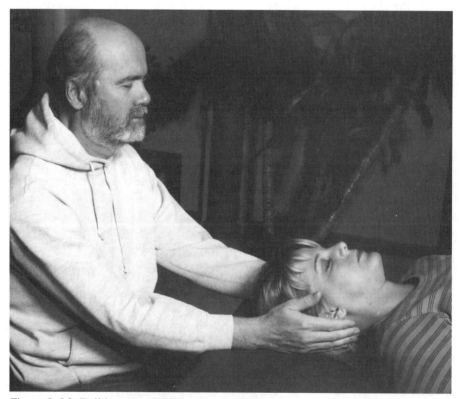

Figure 1-10. Reiki master, William Lee Rand administers a Reiki treatment.

Reiki I teaches laying-on of hands healing; Reiki II teaches distant healing. Reiki-III is an induction to Master level. Originally masters were carefully selected by teachers. Now it seems that there is less and less selectivity.

Modest fees are charged for Reiki I and II courses, fees of several hundred to several thousand dollars are charged for Reiki III.

Strengths:
- Learning is facilitated by an induction from the master, which is said to be able to open anyone to connect with a healing ability.
- Whole-person orientation encourages wholistic healing.
- Emotional releases are encouraged, and approaches such as *pull-outs* facilitate this.[94]
- Healees are given the respectful space to draw the energies they require from the healer, rather than the healer manipulating the energies or pushing for change.
- Power symbols facilitate healing.
- Some Masters encourage their students to work on themselves to clear their own channel for healing
- Several research studies support the efficacy of Reiki healing.[95]

Limitations:
- Some in the later generation of Masters may not have been selected with careful discrimination for advanced experience or abilities.
- No generally accepted formal structure exists for supervision or certification of healers.
- High fees may sometimes be charged for Master level training.

LeShan healing

This method was developed in the late 1960s by Lawrence LeShan, a clinical and research psychologist who specializes in psychotherapy for people with cancer. LeShan was initially a skeptic, as noted earlier, believing that healing was at best some combination of wishful thinking, suggestion, and avoidance of facing up to one's problems. He set out to observe healers in order to expose their charlatanism, but was surprised to find some with actual abilities to bring about unusual arrests or remissions in various diseases, occasionally with such rapidity as to be instantaneous or "miraculous."

He carefully observed some of the better healers, noting common denominators in their practices: they were able to focus or *center* their minds; they found ways to unite with the healees in a profound way; and they felt themselves and the healees to be "one with the All." LeShan practiced meditation and then practiced healing as he had observed it, with very positive results. He then taught others to develop their healing gifts. For three decades Joyce Goodrich has focalized the teaching of the LeShan method, while LeShan has continued to focus on self-healing for people with cancer and other serious illnesses through psychotherapy.

LeShan focuses primarily on distant/absent or what he calls "Type 1" healing. Healers are encouraged to work in pairs.

Goodrich has been working for years to develop collaborative research on LeShan healing, with modest success.

Strengths:
- Is whole-person oriented.
- Allows/facilitates healees' finding their own way to their highest potential
- Strongly emphasizes healers' personal clarity and centering.
- Standardizes mental procedures for engaging in healing, which provides some measure of a known healing process for research.
- Has a modest body of research that supports the efficacy of this approach.[95]

Limitations:
- Acknowledges "Type 2" (touch/near) healing but does not teach this.
- Provides a standardized mental process which may limit healers from the broader spectrum of available healing approaches.
- Though healers are encouraged to practice in pairs, has no structure for formal supervision or certification.

Therapeutic Touch (TT)

Therapeutic Touch was developed by Dolores Krieger, Ph.D., RN, professor of nursing at New York University and Dora van Gelder Kunz, a gifted clairsentient and healer. Taught to a conservatively estimated 40,000 nurses and others in America and around the world, it is now taught in more than 90 nursing schools in America.

TT teaches people to *center* themselves and to develop their awareness of biological energy fields around the body. Students learn to scan the body, passing their hands a few inches away from the body from head to toe, front and back. They note any asymmetries or abnormal energy sensations and address these energetically, holding their hands over these parts, and may image that they are conveying energy to the healee if energy depletions are noted, or drawing energy from the healee if excesses of energy are found. Healers may project images of particular colors to correct or counteract energy imbalances. The aura may be *combed* or *smoothed* if negative energies are to be removed.

Dora Kunz warns that only the most advanced healers should give treatments to the head, as they may inadvertently cause severe energy imbalances. The source for the healing energy may be imaged as coming from the healer or from a universal source of energy.

Strengths:
- Many TT healers have a grounding in conventional medical practices.
- Has the strongest base in research of any healing system, with about 40 doctoral and masters dissertations as controlled studies or grounded theory studies, plus other studies exploring its efficacy in treating anxiety, pain, hypertension, and more.[96]
- Teaches healers to *center* themselves;
- Is problem/symptom-oriented, with a focus on correcting energy imbalances.
- Provides multiple diagnostic and therapeutic inputs through practicing in pairs and lessens the likelihood of missed diagnoses or skewed treatments.
- Focuses on diagnosis and is problem-oriented and grounded in research; it can be taught to health caregivers without stretching their belief systems.
- May empower healees to work wholistically on themselves, addressing body, emotions, mind, and spirit.
- Healers may teach family members to give TT healing to each other.
- Well-delineated guidelines for certification.

Limitations:
- As practiced by some, TT may be mechanistically focused on correction of energy imbalances and may limit healers and healees from awareness of emotional and spiritual aspects of healing.
- Some practitioners exhibit an elitist attitude, with claims that TT is research-based and that other approaches of healing are not, as though TT were not "healing."
- As practiced by some, the focus may be on healer-identified problems rather than on allowing healees to find their highest potential.
- Although practicing in pairs is encouraged and beginners are to practice with more experienced healers for several months, there is no formal structure for supervision.

Craniosacral therapy

Craniosacral therapy relies for diagnosis upon sensations of energy pulsations around the head and spine and by more sensitive practitioners, anywhere around the body, and relies for treatment upon movements of the bones of the skull and of visualizations of alterations of these energies. Though few craniosacral practitioners consider themselves healers, I see sufficient overlap to consider this a form of healing. I am impressed that the combination of visualizations with subtle energy interventions is most potent.[97]

Strengths:
- Is excellent for (but not limited to) neurological and other problems, including many that find little help from allopathic medicine (post-traumatic stroke, musculoskeletal problems, cerebral palsy, coma, and hormonal dysfunctions).
- Teaches practitioners to rely on subtle energy sensations and grounds these with visualizations of cranial bones.
- Combines energy interventions with physical manipulations of the musculoskeletal system.
- In America, osteopaths (primary practioners of this therapy) have full medical training in addition to their osteopathic training.
- In America, regulation is similar to that of medical practitioners, but with no certification of healing aspects of craniosacral therapy.

Limitations:
- For the most part, it ignores or denies the subtle energy nature of practices, and therefore does not encourage consideration of other spiritual healing methods.[98]
- Few practitioners are trained to deal with psychological aspects of problems.
- There is limited research support.[99]
- It lacks formalized structure for clinical teaching, supervision, and certification of healing aspects of craniosacral therapy.

The Bowen Technique

The Bowen Technique was developed in the 1950s by Tom Bowen, a gifted Australian intuitive. The methods he developed are claimed to be effective 85 to 90 percent of the time, in one to three treatments. The method involves a very gentle rolling of particular muscles under the hands of the therapist. A standard set of manipulations is used to treat most problems. Particularly responsive are musculoskeletal problems, even when they have been present for many years and are unresponsive to conventional medical treatments. Particularly helpful for frozen shoulders, asthma, emphysema, irritable bowel syndrome, hiatal hernia, skin conditions, hyperactivity, and depression. This method helps on organic, emotional, and psychological levels simultaneously.

Strengths:
- Is rapidly and potently effective for many problems.
- Can help emotional problems, even though these are not addressed through talking interventions, with the belief that the treatment itself takes care of whatever needs attention.
- Given permissively, allows healees to improve as much as they are ready to.

Limitations:
- Is somewhat mechanistic.
- Avoidance of talking may leave healees with unresolved underlying psychological or stress problems and unchanged attitudes, and therefore open to recurrence of problems.
- Lacks research to demonstrate efficacy.
- Lacks structure for supervision and certification.

Barbara Brennan healing

Barbara Brennan was an astrophysicist who left her job with NASA in the mid-1970s to work on strengthening her clairsentient and healing gifts, which were present from childhood. She founded a prestigious school of healing, attended by many doctors and other health caregivers, where there is a strong emphasis on psychological and energy approaches, including intuitive diagnosis of energy field abnormalities based upon the theory and practice of bioenergetics.[100] The training is very costly, with modular sessions over a four-year course of studies in New Jersey.

Strengths:
- Four-year, thorough training.
- Emphasizes diagnosis.
- Includes healing for psychological dis-ease.
- Includes healing for relationships with other people.
- Includes past life healing.
- Includes healing for relationships with Gaia.
- Strongly emphasizes healers clearing their own problems.

Limitation:
- Cost of training.
- Is somewhat prescriptive—more "my will" than "Thy will" be done.
- Has no research evidence to support its efficacy.
- Has no mechanisms for formal supervision or certification after graduation.

Polarity Therapy

Polarity Therapy was developed by Randolph Stone, an osteopath, naturopath, and chiropractor. This form of healing balances energies between various points on the body. It relates to positive (top/head, right) and negative (bottom/feet, left) polarities of energies in the body. Massage, light touch, and near-the body healing are used.

Strengths:
- Focuses on specific symptoms, prescribing specific points for dealing energetically with problems.
- Includes awareness of the cosmic cycles of rebirth.

Limitations:
- Symptom focus may lead to ignoring the person as a whole.
- Lacks formalized structure for clinical teaching, supervision, and certification.
- Lacks research to confirm efficacy.

SHEN healing

SHEN therapy was developed by Richard Pavek, an American scientist. It addresses emotional tensions which manifest in physical symptoms, using light touch at particular points on the body. It has been helpful with a number of conditions, including anorexia, bulimia, migraine, pains of all sorts, panic attacks, post-traumatic stress disorder, premenstrual symptoms, and irritable bowel syndrome.

Strengths:
- Is rapidly and potently effective.
- Healers are strongly encouraged to clear their own emotional tensions.

Limitations:
- Is somewhat mechanistic.
- Avoidance of talking may leave healees with unresolved underlying stress and unchanged attitudes, and therefore open to recurrence of problems.
- Lacks research.
- Lacks formalized structure for clinical teaching, supervision, and certification.

Healing Touch (HT)

Developed out of Therapeutic Touch, Healing Touch extends the focus of healers to include chakra diagnosis and treatment, the use of pendulums to augment intuitive awareness, and spiritual awareness. Healing energy is perceived as being channeled through the healer from a universal source.

Strengths:.
- All the strengths of TT
- Broader cosmology than TT, including spiritual awareness.
- Greater emphasis on the healer's self-awareness and self-development.
- Well-delineated guidelines for certification.

Limitations:
- Tends to be symptom-focused.
- Has slight tendency toward elitism.
- Lacks formalized structure for clinical teaching, and supervision.

It is clear from the diverse views and clinical descriptions of healers that we are challenged to define precisely what spiritual healing is and how it works. The clues, as in any mystery, are probably all there. It is a challenge to the sleuths of the science and the art of healing to sort them into the patterns which will explain them.

The next chapter extends the descriptions of healers, examining studies on their abilities to influence inanimate materials.

CHAPTER TWO

MEASUREMENTS OF HEALERS' EFFECTS ON THE PHYSICAL WORLD

Unfortunately, Nature imposes her own conditions for the manifestation of her phenomena and is tactless enough to ignore man's criteria or convenience.
— Edward W. Russell

If you have built castles in the air, your work need not be lost; that is where they should be. Now put the foundations under them.
— Henry David Thoreau

This chapter reviews technical studies showing that healers can influence and bring about physical changes in various nonliving materials. These are relevant in several ways to spiritual healing:

- They show that spiritual healing occupies a place on the spectrum of mind-matter interactions.
- They point to biochemical effects and mechanisms through which spiritual healing may act within the body.
- They demonstrate that more than a placebo effect is taking place.
- Healing may be administered via *vehicles* such as water, gauze pads, medications, or other materials.
- Physical effects may be developed as tests of healing abilities.
- Clues to the mystery of healing may emerge from studies of healers' interactions with various forms of matter.

"Zena,"[1] a hospital nurse who is also a strong healer, cannot wear watches because they malfunction. Electrical equipment in her home and in her husband's business office often malfunctions when she is nearby. Her laptop computer was returned to the store four times with major malfunctions. Oddly, electrical equipment she uses in the hospital has not malfunctioned.

Zena's interactions with material objects are not all negative. She finds that she can give healing to gauze pads and people who use these on cuts and abrasions have little pain and seem to heal very quickly. She can *charge* crystals so that people who wear them as jewelry find they have healing effects.

Healing Effects on Water

Robert N. Miller (1977), an industrial research scientist, instructed a gifted healer, the late Olga Worrall, to treat several containers of copper salt solutions as though she were healing someone. When the copper salts were crystallized out of solution, they were noticeably different in color and coarser than those of control samples which had been handled identically by a non-healer.

Miller hypothesized that the healing had altered the water in the copper solution. Samples of treated distilled water were then examined for viscosity, electrical conductivity, capacitance, refractive index, infrared (IR) absorption, and surface tension. Consistent reductions in surface tension were noted, which was measurably reduced in the Worrall samples. Miller gives specific details of the procedures he follows to measure the healers' production of what he termed *paraelectricity*. He used wires held at one end by the healer while the other ends were immersed in water. IR spectrophotometry of the water indicated changes consistent with an alteration in hydrogen bonding. Changes in the other measures were not consistent.

Miller also found Worrall could create a pattern in a cloud chamber by holding her hands around the unit. Cloud chambers are instruments which identify subatomic particles which pass through them. In a later experiment, Worrall produced similar patterns in the cloud chamber from a distance of many miles.

Miller then investigated the effects of magnetic fields. He found that a very strong field[2] applied for 15 minutes to water produced changes in the crystallization of copper salts that were similar to changes in the Worrall experiment. Surface tension was also reduced when six magnets were inserted in half a liter of water for more than four-and-a-half hours. The surface tension of the water treated with magnets gradually returned to normal over a period of 30 hours. If the water was swirled in a stainless-steel beaker the surface tension returned to normal within minutes.

Further tests revealed that when rye seeds were sprinkled with water held by a healer or with water treated by magnets, sprouting increased 28 percent and 60 percent, respectively, over that of control seeds (for which untreated water was used). Further clarification of these comparisons is required because Worrall had held the water 30 days prior to the running of the experiment.

Miller proposes that the reduction in surface tension be used as a measure of a healer's ability to produce healing energy. He would call the energy *paraelectricity* according to the designation of the late Ambrose

Worrall, Olga's husband. Ambrose, also a healer, said "It is recommended that the unit of quantity for paraelectricity be named a 'Worrall' and be defined as the energy required to reduce the surface tension of 100 ml of distilled water from its normal state (72.75 dynes/cm at 20°C) by 10 dynes/cm."

Douglas Dean and Edward G. Brame (1975) also studied healer-held water with IR spectrophotometry. They demonstrated changes in the water which persisted for three years after the treatment. Calorimetric (temperature) measurements were consistent with altered hydrogen bonding.

Dean (1982; 1986) reported further on measurements of healer-treated water. Dilution of this water produces measurable heat. When a healer treated a fluorinated polymer film, the same IR effects were observed in the film. Ultraviolet (UV) spectrophotometry demonstrated a peak peculiar to the treated water.[3] Both IR and UV measurements must be made on special equipment.[4]

Dean found that healers who produced strong effects in the UV range might generate weak results in the IR range and vice versa. More intense effects were noted when the healers treated water in partly filled bottles than when they treated water in full containers. Distillation of treated water sometimes did and sometimes did not eliminate the effect. Treatment of steam in a distillation apparatus produced the same alterations in the distillate. The *half-life*[5] for the spectrophotometric effects in water varies with different healers. About three days is most common, but it may be up to two-and-one-half years in a partly empty bottle. Another discovery that Dean reported was that just prior to re-melting, a new crystal structure could be observed in the water (1982).[6]

Glen Rein (1992) reports that non-Hertzian electromagnetic fields may impart a patterning in water which conveys healing properties. These are waves hypothesized to exist in the vicinity of *caduceus coils*—coils of wire which are wound in opposite directions to each other.[7]

Stephan Schwartz et al. published a detailed study of IR effects produced by healing on water.[8] Some of the people he studied were actively engaged in spiritual healing outside the experimental situation and some were volunteers with no healing experience. Schwartz et al. placed water in vials which were held against the palms of subjects' hands during healings. New vials were placed in this way for consecutive periods of five minutes after the start of healing, covering the first 15 minutes of treatment. Samples were taken as controls for calibration of the spectrophotometer and for the treatment situation. The treatment room control samples were taken to the room where the healers were studied but were not placed in the healers' hands. Measurements performed by two independent researchers under double-blind conditions were consistent with each other. When all treated samples were compared with all controls, a significant difference was noted ($p < .02$). When treated samples were compared only with calibration controls (which had not been taken to the treatment room), the difference was even more pronounced (p < .002). The difference between the treated versus the session-control samples was not significant. The intensity of effects did not vary at the various time segments which were sampled. The results suggest that water in the vicinity of healers can be affected even when healing is not focused directly or even intentionally on the water.[9]

The Institute of HeartMath in California teaches techniques for developing self-healing and spiritual healing abilities.[10] In the meditative state that is taught, people develop coherent heart frequencies which provide a measure of their meditative focus. Glen Rein and Rollin McCraty (1994) individually studied five people trained in these methods. They were given distilled water in sealed test tubes and told to focus on them for five minutes with the intent of altering their molecular structure. Control samples from the same source were kept in another room. Water samples were analyzed with a computerized UV spectrophotometer, programmed for sequential automated measurements at 10 second intervals in the 200-204nm region of the spectrum. The average absorbence over a 15-minute period was calculated. The overall mean absorbence value for the control samples was -0.00160 to -0.0009 and for the treated ones +0.0039 to +0.0044. These differences were significant (p < .01),[11] with treated water having higher absorbence values at 200nm while controls had higher values at 204nm.

A second test measured spectra before and after treated water was added to human placental DNA samples, 20 mg/ml. Three control and three treated samples were measured. Control water produced a mean decrease in absorbence of 0.46 percent (0.36) while treated water produced a 1.35 percent (0.61) decrease, a difference which is significant (p < .05).[12]

V. Patrovsky, a Czechoslovakian scientist, studied the effects of electromagnetic (EM) fields and of healing on water.[13] He reports that two distinct types of effects can be produced in water.

Polarised water is produced by electrostatic or static magnetic fields. Traces of hydrogen peroxide and free radicals are formed via a magnetohydrodynamic effect, but the physical properties of the water are unchanged. Polarised water is effective for stimulating plant growth but will not prevent calcified sediment in mineral solutions.[14]

Resonant water is produced when EM or magnetic fields break hydrogen bonds in water molecule clusters. A peak for this effect is found around 16 Hz. According to Patrovsky (1978),

> In this water, $(H_2O)_5$ and $(H_2O)_6$ clusters predominate as detected from the IR spectrum (3.9 microns) and from reduced surface tension. This type has little effect upon plant growth, but can prevent sedimentation of calcified deposits . . .
>
> There appears no difference in the actions of suitable magnetic, electrostatic or biologic (healer's) fields, showing that: The biological field is the only physical field generated by living matter.

Table 2-1. Comparison of resonant and polarised water

	RESONANT	POLARISED
Origin	Alternating magnetic or electric fields of optimal frequency 5-25 hz & HF (Ghz)	Static magnetic/electric fields; ultraviolet light and ultrasound
Physical changes	Infrared absorption increased at 3.9 polarization	None, or small change in ion microns; surface tension reduced
Chemical	Little or not observable	Traces of hydrogen peroxide and free radicals
Technological and biological action	Sedimentation and crystallization retarded; little effect on plants	No influence on dissolved salts; stimulation of plant growth and seed germination
Detection	Infrared spectrum and surface tension change	Detection of hydrogen peroxide with luminol: seed germination
Probable	Resonant molecular absorption: reduced H-bonds; paramagnetic nuclear	Magnetohydrodynamic effect; increased negative charges on ions resonance UHF
Stability*	20–25 hours stoppered; 3–5 hours exposed to air; decomposes with healing	14–30 days; Decomposes with healing

* Inserted from Patrovsky 1983 b

Patrovsky says that the biological field consists of at least two components: a direct current (DC) aspect (e.g. electrostatic charges) which may emanate from eyes or fingers; and an alternating current (AC) aspect which may emanate from the brain and muscles. In healer-activated water, therefore, one may detect free radicals and a diminution of surface tension. Patrovsky demonstrated this with 10 samples treated by a Czech healer, J. Zezulka, in which surface tension was measured by capillary elevation. Zezulka's samples averaged 8.7 centimeters; 30 control samples measured between 9.3 and 9.6 centimeters. This is a 9.4 percent decrease, close to the 10.3 percent decline produced by Olga Worrall (Miller, 1977).

Patrovsky speculates that natural water may become activated by passing through magnetic gradients in the earth or through action of solar flares.

Jerzy Rejmer (1985) of Warsaw mentions in a very brief translated note that when deuterium plus normal water "with a solution strength under one percent plus DSS indicator" was subjected to bioenergetic influence for five minutes the entire spectrum was displaced 0.3 parts per million under Nuclear Magnetic Resonance (NMR) spectrometry.

Patrovsky's last observation is extended by yet another study, which is unfortunately also sketchily reported.[15] J. Schonenberg Setzer placed water in three church sanctuaries (Catholic, Episcopal, and Methodist) before Sunday services and collected them an hour after the services. Plants treated with the church water grew faster than the control samples *but only during the second and fourth lunar quarters*.

In 1974 Brame repeated the experiment, examining the church water with IR spectrophotometry. His results confirmed an effect on Sundays close to full and new moons.[16] He reports that "neither the number of worshipers in the sanctuary nor the religious importance of the date had any significance on the results."[17] No measurements or statistics are given for either study.

Alok Saklani demonstrated effects of an Indian healer's treatment of water for enhancing plant growth. He found no spectrophotometric effects in healer-treated methanol.[18]

Peter Fenwick and Roy Hopkins (1986) found no effect of healing on water but reported that their equipment was not as sensitive as Dean's.

Two researchers report that healer-treated water tastes distinctly different from untreated water (Dingwall 1968, VII, p. 60; Leichtman 1986). Leichtman observes that wine treated by healers tastes smoother and less acidic. Dingwall adds that he found one patient who was sensitive to whether the water was *magnetized* by her own magnetizer or by another; that she could say how many *passes* he had made over it; and that if she drank water magnetized by another she experienced cramp. In several casual trials, I have not found that healed water has a different taste from other water. The study seems worth repeating.

Confirming Miller's findings, Jan A. Szymanski (1986a), a Polish scientist, reports on an experiment in which five bioenergy therapists held their hands one to three centimeters from a laboratory plate containing copper chloride solution and concentrated intensely. After 24 hours, visible differences were noted in samples on which three of the healers were focusing. "The samples had smaller but more densely distributed crystal grains and because of this the optical density of the pictures was greater." Their color was darker than the control samples. Five people who were not healers were unable to produce crystal changes in such a procedure.

Further study of chemical systems is warranted.

Photon Emission

S. Grabiec et al. report that photon emission can be used as an indicator of "degree of activation by the biofield." They state:

> A freshly prepared 0.1% pyrogallol solution in a 0.15 M phosphate buffer medium with pH 7.2 + 0.1% hydrogen peroxide was exposed for about 30 seconds to a "biofield" at a distance of 2 - 3 cm from the "biofield" source. The same freshly prepared solution

without exposure to a "biofield" served as the control sample. Temperature and pressure were kept constant during the tests and efforts were made to eliminate any other possible effects of the infrared radiation. Photon emission of the control samples fluctuated from 370 to 425 pulse/minute and those of the experimental samples from 464 to 950 pulse/minute.

It is unfortunate that more details are not provided.[19]

Photographic and Electromagnetic (EM) Effects

Several researchers have reported on photographic effects produced by healing. Graham Watkins and colleagues performed a series of experiments on accelerated awakening of anesthetized mice through the intent of psychics.[20] He reports that when photographic film was placed in light-proof envelopes under target animals the film was exposed. The degree of exposure decreased with distance from the animal. Watkins notes that several plates underwent exposures resembling pictures obtained with electrical discharges. He also observes that one of the PK (psychokinesis) subjects demonstrated a high static charge which tended to recur rapidly after grounding and that another successful PK subject was found to have similarly high electrostatic charge. He hypothesizes that healing may, therefore, involve electrostatic or EM fields. An alternative, he points out, is that the electrostatic phenomena may merely be concomitants of the PK process that are not essential to its occurrence. If this is so, they could still be theoretically useful indicators of healing. In Watkins's experience, however, they did not prove to be reliable indicators. A third possibility, Watkins suggests, is that healing involves a form of energy, the properties of which overlap with electrical energy.

Gordon Turner (1969) reports that when photographic film is interposed between the hands of a healer and parts of a living organism in need of healing, images can be produced. He points out that these effects do not occur when the film is placed between the healer's hand and a part of an organism that does not require healing.[21] Similar effects are reported by the *Chinese Academy of Science* and by Zhao Yong-Jie et al. Researchers found that nuclear emulsion film and thermoluminescent film shielded from light were exposed in the vicinity of the target during studies of clairvoyance.

Benson Herbert[22] (1973) observed unusually high skin resistance in Suzanne Padfield, a healer and PK adept.

A unique Austrian healer, Leonard Hochenegg, produces sensations of electric shocks during healings, can light a fluorescent bulb with his hands and has been found to discharge up to 30,000 volts from his hands (Hochenegg; Playfair 1988).

Support for healer EM effects is suggested by Michael Shallis (1988). In a survey of people who experienced "unusual electrical phenomena," he found many who produced unusually strong electrical discharges from their bodies. About 70 percent of these people were gifted with psi abilities, including healing.[23]

The most impressive study to date of EM effects of *healers* was set up by Elmer Green et al. (1991) at the Menninger Clinic. Green had read of a Tibetan meditative practice for student monks *(chelas)*, reported by A. P. Sinnett in an English newspaper in India (Barker, 1882):

> The methods used for developing lucidity in our chelas may be easily used by you. Every temple has a dark room, the north wall of which is entirely covered with a sheet of mixed metal, chiefly copper, very highly polished, with a surface capable of reflecting in it things, as well as a mirror. The chela sits on an insulated stool, a three-legged bench placed in a flat-bottomed vessel of thick glass. . . . A magnet with the North Pole up is suspended over the crown of the chela's head without touching it. The chela is left alone gazing on the wall. . . .

This started Green to thinking whether this arrangement might isolate the student from electrical ground, allowing an electrical charge to build up in his body. He speculated that if this is the case, it might be possible to measure such buildups of electrical body-potentials.

Four studies were conducted over a period of eight years. In the first researchers used a single copper wall, attached to an electrometer. In the other studies a room with four copper walls was used, each wall wired to an electrometer. Another electrometer was wired to the subject's body. The walls measured electrical effects at the front, back, top, and bottom of the subjects' bodies. When normal subjects were studied, the maximal voltage variation noted was two volts, associated with small body movements.

The third study is of most relevance to *Spiritual Healing*, as it explored electrical effects during nine healers' and five other sensitives' meditative states while they were engaged in noncontact or distant healing. Healees were either in the copper-walled room or several rooms away from the healers. Anomalous surges of more than four volts were noted in many of the sensitives *during periods when no discernible movement was evident.* One might speculate that tensed muscles could cause such surges, and indeed surges of up to 50 mV could be observed with emotional activation. The surges in the sensitives were 4-221 volts (median 8.3 V)—over 1,000 times greater than those of ordinary people. Such surges were noted in six of the subjects, five of whom were healers. Body potential surges occurred for the most part simultaneously with surges in the walls. The meaning of these findings is as yet unclear.

Cyril Smith and Simon Best review further evidence for overlaps of EM fields with biological processes. They tell of experiments in which EM fields reproduced allergic symptoms in sensitive patients and where appropriately tuned fields could also neutralize such symptoms. Water could be *patterned* by EM fields and used as a vehicle for these therapeutic effects. Details of these controlled trials are not provided, nor are statistical analyses of results.

Glen Rein (1992) studied the magnetic field emissions from the hands of a healer, Dr. Leonard Laskow. Laskow calls his healing "holoenergetic" healing.

> The magnetic fields were measured using a flux-gate magnetometer sensitive from D.C. to 500 Hz. Laskow cupped his hand over the probe but did not touch it . . . . Non-healers were unable to influence magnetometer readings. Touching or moving the probe gave characteristic, sharp patterns which were readily distinguishable from energetic patterns.
>
> An initial and critical part of the holoenergetic healing process is opening the crown chakra. The magnetic field pattern generated when Laskow opened his crown chakra was recorded. It appeared distinctly different from other patterns obtained in that it had a very sharp onset, an equally sharp dissipation and only lasted eight seconds. This result implies that the event was short-lived and caused a shift in the magnetic field pattern only during its duration. The return to normal baseline was characteristic of patterns produced by other states of consciousness when Laskow consciously chose to shift into another state or end the particular experiment . . . in some tracings the energetic pattern shifts down, implying a decrease in the magnetic field strength in the environment around Laskow's hand . . . .
>
> Since we had observed that only certain contents of consciousness resulted in magnetic field patterns which were different from an ordinary state of mind, it was of interest to compare the patterns from two states which gave different biological responses measured as an inhibition of tumor cell growth. We therefore compared the magnetic pattern obtained when Laskow was in an *unconditional loving state* and in the *return to natural order state*. The results indicate that indeed these magnetic patterns were different from each other. Compared to the robust effect with the natural order state, the unconditional loving state produced a weak, non-specific pattern . . . .
>
> In general these patterns were obtained most consistently when Laskow was allowed to generate the different states and contents of consciousness spontaneously, rather than being told a given sequence. One of the most interesting spontaneous magnetic field patterns was obtained when Laskow inwardly asked that Spirit flow through him. He asked Spirit to demonstrate its presence to science with a characteristic signature pattern. The tracing obtained gave a uniquely different pattern from the other patterns obtained and was characterized by sharp, frequent peaks in the negative direction.

Rein speculates that the effects of healing may be mediated by non-Hertzian waves. Non-Hertzian waves cannot as yet be measured directly on scientific instruments. Rein placed a caduceus coil (a device which is believed to generate non-Hertzian waves) in Laskow's energy field in the course of one of his studies.

> The tracing obtained indicates that prior to addition of the device, the magnetic pattern was repetitive, containing numerous sharp, small positive peaks. Upon addition of the device, the magnetic field pattern was substantially altered. The new pattern was qualitatively similar in shape but gradually increased in overall magnitude. These results suggest that non-Hertzian quantum fields enhanced the magnetic field emitted from Laskow's hands during holoenergetic healing.[24]

R. Macdonald et al. (1977) studied three well-known healers: Rev. John Scudder, Dean Kraft, and Olga Worrall. The researchers attempted to replicate the experiments with cloud-chambers, magnetic-fields, high voltage and passive photographic film exposures, object-weight measurements, spectroscopic analyses of water, and animal blood pressure and EEG measurements. The authors report, "Most of the attempted replication did not confirm the reports of the previous experimenters." They did note that small changes in electrical-field strength near the subjects were detected by means of a 10-ohm input high-impedance voltmeter (HIVM).

In a brief, controlled experiment, the healers were asked to hold saline which was then used to water rye grass seeds. Kraft's water produced significantly less growth in the experimental versus the control plants (various measurements gave a confidence range of $p < 0.05$ - 0.001). Worrall's water produced growth which was significantly greater ($p < 0.05$) on all measures.[25]

Discussion

Experiments by Miller, Dean, and Brame, and Schwartz et al. showed changes suggesting a decrease in hydrogen bonding in healer-treated water. It is unclear what effect a decrease in hydrogen bonding and reduced surface tension of the water might have on chemical reactions in animals and plants. Because water constitutes about 65 percent of the human body, the changes in water alone might account for some of the effects of healing, either directly or through enhancements of biochemical reactions secondary to the presence of altered water. Many of the consequences of healing are manifested as an acceleration of natural recuperative processes. Changes in body water might, for example, account for more rapid wound healing after treatment with spiritual healing by altering enzyme activity.

Dean (1985) observes that the water effects may represent something other than altered hydrogen bonding because the effects are sometimes carried over to a distillate (after the water is boiled to a steam and condensed), which would not be expected if they were due to hydrogen bonding alone.

Since the effects of the hydrogen-bonding and treated-water experiments (together with the crystallization results that Miller noted) are similar to those produced by a strong EM field, this may mean that some healings are produced by an energy similar to magnetism.[26] The impact of healing on the crystallization of copper salts may result from interactions with the salts or may be due to alterations in the water in which they are dissolved.

Watkins's and Turner's studies on photographic effects of healing provide another indication of some sort of transfer of energy between healer and healee, or of EM/photographic effects secondary to a healing influence. A word of caution in assuming that healing produced the observed effects comes from studies of *thoughtography* which show that some psychics can create images upon photographic film without known physical means of influencing the film.[27]

These observations find parallels in Kirlian photography, in which a high-voltage/low-amperage pulsed charge creates images on film of objects which are placed against the film. The Kirlian aura of the healer may decrease in size and intensity after healings. Conversely, the aura of the healee may increase in both respects, a phenomenon that also suggests a transfer of energy from the healer to the healee.[28]

Rein's work on quantum energy fields may be a breakthrough in linking quantum physics with healing. One must be cautious, however, in jumping to conclusions before these results are replicated by Rein and others. For instance, it is possible that the enhancing study with Laskow was due to suggestions which created expectations in Laskow and led to his producing different effects for psychological rather than energetic reasons.

Some of the physical effects reviewed here may be used to screen or test for psychic effects which correlate with healing ability. Particularly promising are spectrophotometry and surface tension of water; crystallization of copper salts; and exposure of photographic film. Further research is required, however, to establish whether any or all of these results are produced by all healers, only by some of them, or only under certain circumstances.[29]

Where, oh where is the modern day Madame Curie who will clarify what energies are involved in healer effects on water and on photographic film?

—D.B.

We must likewise clarify whether any of these physical effects correlate regularly with the degree of healing ability in healers or to the particular ranges of conditions which respond to treatments by different healers. For instance, Miller's suggestion that surface-tension results be used as a measure of healing energy seems premature. If the expression of healing ability follows the patterns of distribution of PK gifts, this may mean that while each healer may be gifted in healing, not all will be able to produce water, photographic, or other effects.

Olga Worrall's ability to create a pattern in a cloud chamber may give us further clues about healing. The experiment obviously needs replication and clarification before any serious conclusions can be reached.

Some healing effects reported in Chapter I were produced as readily over great distances as they were locally. This contradicts conventional theories of energies known to classical physics. Ordinary energies act more powerfully upon objects which are closer to their source than at greater distances. A radio receiver picks up the signal from the transmitting station more weakly the farther it is from the station. The diminution of effect with distance is readily measurable and mathematically predictable. Healing and other psi effects seem to act at great distances with no apparent diminution of their power—even over thousands of miles. Simple studies could clarify whether healers are able to alter water or crystallization of copper salts from a distance.

Many of the above reports overlap with psi research. Chapter 3 examines psi effects in greater detail.

CHAPTER THREE

PSI PHENOMENA

On trying to formulate a theory of psi phenomena, one has first to proceed like the hero of a medieval mystery play: he must slay, or come to grips with, the dragons guarding the entrance to the sanctuary of science. The first dragon is the challenge of scientific fact-finding. The data of parapsychology have to be assembled and validated by the consensus of qualified workers in the field, while doubtful or spurious evidence must be discarded. On the other hand, all the evidence that has stood the test of scientific scrutiny has to be included— regardless of the consequences. The second dragon is the paradox that although we feel duty-bound to apply the principles of the scientific method to our findings, they run counter to some of the basic propositions of science itself. The third, fourth, and fifth dragons stand for the classical Kantian categories of Time, Space, and Causality which are clearly incompatible with direct action and thought at a distance implied by telepathy, clairvoyance, and psychokinesis, while precognition seems to arrest time's arrow in its flight and to reverse the purportedly irreversible chain of causal events. The sixth dragon guards our conventional doctrine of cerebral localization, confining consciousness and other specific functions to more or less circumscribed areas of the brain cortex, or perhaps to lower echelons of the central nervous system. The seventh dragon is the picture of personality structure, suspended in splendid isolation in classical Euclidian space, functioning in Newtonian, pre-relativistic time, and subject to strictly foreordained laws of cause and effect.

—Jan Ehrenwald

My 11-year-old daughter, Becky, came to me with a question one morning, shortly after we returned from living for six years in Israel. "Daddy," she asked, "Is there such a name as Kevin?"

"Yes," I answered. "Why do you ask?"

"I dreamed last night that I was teaching a little boy named Kevin. I never heard that name before."

I thought nothing more of this until I returned from work that day and Becky was waiting eagerly to tell me her story. "Daddy! You won't believe this! Our teacher took us today to tutor children in the first grade. The little boy I tutored was named Kevin."

I sat with Becky to explain that dreams sometimes are windows into the future. She seemed pleased with herself for having had this experience.

The next day, however, she came to me and said, in a very thoughtful tone, "Daddy, I don't want to have those kinds of dreams."

"Why not?" I asked.

"Because I'm going to worry now, when I have bad dreams, that they might come true too!"

The psi (from the Greek letter, Ψ) phenomena include telepathy, clairsentience, psychokinesis (PK), precognition, and retrocognition. Though such phenomena are well accepted in most cultures around the world, in Western society many people have difficulty with them.

Everyone has a measure of psi abilities. Think whether you ever do the following: know who is phoning before you pick up the ringing telephone; feel an intuitive urge to phone a friend and find that he or she is in need of your support; have dreams which come true; wish mentally for something and find it arrives without conscious effort on your part; or know when someone dear to you is in trouble or passes on.

First, let us define our terms: (See also Table 3-1.)

Extrasensory Perception (ESP)

Telepathy: Extensive experiments carried out by Joseph B. Rhine at Duke University in America, by Leonid L. Vasiliev in Russia, and by many other researchers around the world have demonstrated that some people are able to obtain information directly from the minds of others. People can also transmit information via mind-to-mind communication. Distance does not appear to weaken telepathic effects even when thousands of miles separate sender and receiver.

Clairsentience: Experiments have shown that some people obtain information about a person or object through extrasensory perception (ESP) not involving telepathy. This knowledge seems to come to the mind of the perceiver directly from the object. For instance, J. B. Rhine showed that there are people who can identify the order in which cards lie in a deck after the experimenter shuffled them face-down but before she turned them over.[1] It has been demonstrated that people can know clairsentiently what is happening at a distant location without sensory cues or other contact (e.g. telephone) with that place.[2] Some clairsentient people have identified the location of dead bodies (Pollack).

Table 3-1. Definitions of psi phenomena

Telepathy: The transfer of thoughts, images or commands from one living being to another, without use of sensory cues.

Clairsentience: Knowledge about an animate or inanimate object, without the use of sensory cues (sometimes called psychometry). This may appear in the mind of the perceiver as visual imagery (clairvoyance), auditory messages (clairandience), or other internal sensory awareness.

Precognition: Knowledge of a future event prior to its occurrence.

Retrocognition: Knowledge of a past event, without use of sensory cues.

Extrasensory perception (ESP): The above four modes of acquiring knowledge without cues from any of the external senses: sight, sound, smell, taste, touch, or kinesthesia (position-of-body sense from muscles or tendons).

Psychokinesis (PK): The ability to move or transform an object without use of physical means; commonly referred to as "mind over matter."

Psi (from the Greek letter Ψ): ESP and PK.

Sheep/goat effect: Believers ("sheep") score significantly better than chance, while disbelivers ("goats") score significantly poorer than chance expectancy on psi tasks.

In such cases telepathy could not have been involved. Clairsentient impressions may be perceived as sensory information (visual images, voices, smells, etc.) or as broader pictures and feelings, such as positive vibrations in a church, or negative vibrations in an empty room after an argument occurred there. They may be experienced as inner impressions or as images perceived outside the perceiver.

Precognition and retrocognition: Gifted subjects are able to read the future for themselves or others. To initiate the perception they may hold an object belonging to a person, be in his presence, or be given her name. Such individuals can often give information about a person's or object's past. Laboratory subjects have been able to guess correctly series of cards before they were shuffled (Rhine 1961) and to describe places visited by experimenters before these places were selected (Jahn/Dunne).

Extrasensory perception (ESP): a term referring to the above abilities.

Psychokinesis (also called *PK* or *telekinesis):* Rhine (1970), Helmut Schmidt (1974), and others have shown in repeated, highly significant experiments that matter can be manipulated by the mind. Rhine used dice, asking his subjects to roll the desired faces (chosen by a random number table). Helmut Schmidt developed sophisticated electronic devices which subjects were able to influence at will.

Much has been published on the PK effects produced by Uri Geller and many others who are able to bend metal without the use of any normal physical force. The successful bending of metal objects sealed in transparent containers and observations of objects disappearing from sealed containers is even more impressive (Hasted).

In Eastern Europe, studies and films have been made of gifted subjects who move small objects by PK. Western observers have confirmed these effects.

Psi refers to ESP and/or PK abilities.

Psychokinesis resembles spiritual healing since both entail the mind influencing matter. In fact, healing may simply be biological PK. Similarly, clairsentience appears to be the basis for psychic medical diagnosis and is probably the means by which healers know how to help healees. Telepathy and clairsentience, which can both span vast distances, may prove to be an aspect of distant intuitive impressions and healing. For these reasons I present this summary of psi phenomena prior to presenting research specifically related to healing.

Sheep/goat effect: When groups of subjects are tested for psi powers the data taken as a whole are often totally random. It appears as though subjects are merely guessing answers and obtaining purely chance results. Gertrude Schmeidler suggested that such data be divided according to whether the subjects believed or disbelieved in the existence of ESP. The results of this exercise showed that believers tended to score as a group significantly better than chance on ESP tests and disbelievers scored significantly poorer than chance on the same tests. Schmeidler applied the term *sheep* to the believers and *goats* to the disbelievers.[3] Analyses have been made of data from experiments both before and after Schmeidler made her proposal. The preponderance of evidence supports the sheep-goat hypothesis (Palmer 1971).

Psi phenomena have been investigated with sufficient rigor to convince the *American Academy for the Advancement of Science* that Parapsychology is worthy of inclusion as an academic field.

GIFTED PSYCHICS

Sai Baba

A holy man in India, Sai Baba claims to be in his second of three reincarnations devoted to the progress of mankind. He teaches that there are many paths of spiritual advancement and may punctuate his teachings with amazing displays of psi powers. To impress people, he has materialized objects such as jewelry with intricate designs deeply meaningful to them. He also materializes *vibhuti,* a so-called holy ash with alleged medicinal powers. He is gifted to the point of appearing almost omniscient. He is able to provide his millions of devotees with the most intimate details of their lives—past, present, and future. He has reportedly healed many illnesses, including fractures, arthritis, blindness and cancers. Western observers have scrutinized him carefully during materializations for sleight-of-hand tricks and have even searched his garments for pockets which might conceal objects, but no one has been able to find any hint of trickery.[4]

Sai Baba uses his gifts to enthrall his devotees, convincing them of his deep understanding of themselves, of the meaning of their lives and, above all, of the wisdom he teaches. It is difficult to imagine him submitting to scientific scrutiny for purposes of analyses of his talents; indeed, he has declined all invitations to submit to laboratory investigations.

Gustavo Adolfo Roll

Paola Giovetti, an Italian reporter long interested in psi, is one of a privileged few who have been well received by Gustavo Adolfo Roll, an Italian with a wide range of psi talents (W. Roll et al. 1982). Roll is able to materialize and psychometrize objects, to read minds and to perform other unusual feats. He refuses to submit to formal laboratory testing, maintaining an independent attitude towards his gifts. For the select few to whom he demonstrates his abilities, he has produced drawings and oil paintings through PK without touching the paints, even designing these to the specifications of a group of observers, each of whom suggests an element which Roll then includes in the piece of art. He destroys most of his work, not wanting to create commercial products. Giovetti, however, has preserved some of Roll's productions in photographic slides.

Roll is extremely intelligent. His complex demonstrations of his talents are original. For example, he had an investigator pick cards from a deck to determine the volume, page and line in an encyclopedia where a certain quotation he cites could be found. Asked why he refuses to be studied formally by parapsychologists, he answers, "I am but as a rain gutter for the rain. You should analyze the rain, not the gutter!"

Thomas G. M. Coutinho

Thomas G. M. Coutinho, or "Thomas," as he is known in Brazil, has PK and healing gifts. He has been seen to materialize coins; transform coins of his country into those of another; bend metallic objects; reunite pieces of torn paper; produce flashing lights around vehicles in which he and others are driving; dematerialize his body and disappear; and perform unusual feats of near and distant healing, involving apparent removal of diseased portions from the subject's body. Western scientists have studied Thomas, including William Roll, an American parapsychologist (no relation to the above-mentioned Roll) Elson Motagno, a South American physician, and Lee Pulos, a Canadian psychologist.

Pulos describes Thomas as being totally in the present, in the *now*. He shows little concern for past or future. He derives great amusement from the spontaneous, unplanned appearances of his PK abilities, such as when a metal chair on which he was sitting in a restaurant collapsed because the legs bent. He is warmhearted and emotionally responsive. When exercising his gifts, he often consumes large quantities of alcohol and may also ingest copious amounts of table salt and lime juice with no ill effects. He charges very high fees for healings and spends money lavishly. Pulos makes the interesting observation that Thomas (as well as another 19 out of 23 children Pulos studied, who were gifted with metal-bending abilities) received severe electric shocks at some time in his life prior to being able to demonstrate PK abilities.[5]

I find even more convincing the reports of children who are found to have telepathic, clairsentient, precognitive, psychokinetic, and other psi abilities (Easton; Peterson). The children are often confused both by their psi interactions with the world and by the fact that most adults do not understand, much less possess them.

A Spectrum of Psi Effects

The above observations of subjects highly gifted with psi powers were made by people familiar with such phenomena. Their comments contribute to our appreciation of psi, yet leave us with questions and doubts. Could the subjects have been clever magicians, deceiving their investigators? Could accomplices have participated in the demonstrations without the knowledge of the observers?

For this reason parapsychologists have worked diligently in the laboratory to isolate and describe the nature of psi effects more precisely. For example, Montague Ullman (1974), a noted parapsychologist, describes two very gifted Soviet psychics. The late Nina Kulagina, a 47-year-old housewife, could move objects such as matches lying on a flat surface without touching them, under conditions that preclude physical means of interacting with the objects. She could also levitate objects and deviate magnetic needles. Kulagina experienced severe physiological stress when performing many of her PK feats, with racing pulse, pain in her spine and weight loss of up to two kilograms in an hour. Kulagina also demonstrated strong healing abilities.

Alla Vinogradova, a child psychologist in her late 30s, can also move objects by PK and perform healings. She demonstrates far fewer and less severe physiological effects from her psi activities. During some of her PK demonstrations, electrostatic charges appear on and/or around target objects.

Soviet researchers have concentrated more on the telepathic sender than their Western counterparts. Leonid Vasiliev describes experiments in which telepathic inductions of hypnotic trances were achieved from a distance in controlled, statistically significant studies. Though similar experiments were successfully performed in the West in the nineteenth century, they were abandoned for no apparent reason (Eisenbud 1983).

Vasiliev also reports on hypnotized subjects who could be made to contract specific muscles merely by the approach of an experimenter's finger near (but not touching) the involved muscles or near the nerves innervating those muscles. Vasiliev reviews further research on insect muscles that contracted when the experimenter approached the recently killed but still responsive insect bodies. The insect muscle contractions sometimes were synchronous with the rate of breathing of the experimenter. It is unclear whether these represent PK or interactions of biological fields of the participants.

Julius Krmessky reports on tests in which delicately balanced objects were moved by PK. The power appeared to be projected from the eyes of subjects.

Graham Watkins and Anita Watkins (1974) studied a gifted psychic, Felicia Parise. She was able to use PK to deflect the needle of a compass so that it would not respond to an iron knife or small magnet so long as the compass remained where it was when she had focused on it. When the compass was moved a few feet away it reacted normally. Returned to its original position, the deviation and unresponsiveness to iron objects were again present. This effect lasted about 25 minutes. Photographic film lying under the compass was exposed, the intensity of exposure decreasing with distance from the compass in all directions. There is no conventional scientific explanation for such phenomena.

Harold Puthoff and Russell Targ comment on the ability of Uri Geller and Ingo Swann to produce apparent magnetic effects which registered on sensitive instruments. Geller also affected a laboratory balance by PK, raising and lowering the balance pan with a force of up to 1.5 grams.

Walter Uphoff and Mary Jo Uphoff (1980) provide many scientific and personal details about two Japanese PK subjects. Particularly noteworthy was the detection of ultrasound waves in the vicinity of 30 mega-Hz which emanated from the left frontal regions of their brains during PK activity. Another report (Larissa Vilenskaya) notes that Nina Kulagina was able to produce a burning sensation on the skin of a subject through quartz glass.

The Metal Benders

John Hasted, Professor of Experimental Physics at Birkbek College, University of London, published a series of observations on mental metal bending, outstanding both in scientific rigor and in appreciation of motivational factors in the subjects.[6]

Clear parallels exist between these gifts and those of healing. The metal benders are able to demonstrate their abilities only some of the time; they are able to transfer these powers to others; they sometimes report associated aura effects; and they may conduct experiments that involve instantaneous transportation of metal from inside sealed containers to places outside. No dangerous side-effects with such abilities have been noted, though laboratory instruments and other metal objects are occasionally damaged unintentionally.

Mark Shafer pointed out that the relaxed social atmosphere of a small group can facilitate metal bending. This was the start of a new research technique which accommodates to the nature of the psi phenomena. An extension of Shafer's theory is the metal bending party,[7] at which several experienced metal benders are interspersed among a group of people. The group is encouraged to bend metal and many with no prior experience are often able to do so.

I participated in a metal-bending party during meetings of the *Combined Society for Psychical Research/Parapsychological Association* at Cambridge, England, in 1982. The organizers selected about 50 participants for their openness to experiencing psi phenomena and for their social compatibility. They explained that metal bending is a common latent psi ability which can be brought out in such a group setting. Three experienced benders who circulated among the participants facilitated the group process. In the preparation phase, silverware, metal bars, and other items, which had been bent in other groups, were displayed.

The leaders then laid out a collection of normal silverware, urging participants to choose a piece that appealed to them intuitively or with the aid of a pendulum. Within minutes the experienced benders were demonstrating their successes in twisted, rolled, and curled forms. The inexperienced participants were soon exclaiming excitedly as they found their silverware suddenly *gave* and became malleable to slight pressure. Most impressive among the more exotic bends and twists were the pigtail curls, and tight spirals (in spaces of 1/4 to 1/2 inch) in stems of heavy cutlery—twists that would have been difficult even with the use of heavy tools. By the end of the evening 75 percent of the participants had succeeded in bending metal.

My own experience? I worked on a spoon of fairly rigid construction. Applying moderate force, as permitted, I found the threshold of muscular effort required to bend the spoon with normal pressure. I suddenly found the spoon gave and bent easily until the bowl lay folded back against the stem. I wondered, however, if in the charged, excited atmosphere I had exerted more pressure than I consciously realized.[8]

This questioning is termed *retrocognitive dissonance* in psychological lingo (Inglis 1986). It is what we commonly experience when we witness psi events that so clearly and grossly contradict everyday expectations of the way things ought to be. The mind simply balks at digesting such a bolus of strange experience and seeks every possible maneuver to expel, reject, and explain it away.

*It is much easier to rationalize experience than to re-examine
and alter the commonly held axioms of our existence.*

—D.B.

Such internal mental quarrels between unusual observations and conventional expectations occur also with spiritual healings.[9]

Thoughtography—Mental Photographic Effects

Another form of PK involves the intentional production of images on photographic film. The Western pioneer in exploring this area is Jule Eisenbud, a Denver psychiatrist. He studied Ted Serios, an eccentric man who could project mental images onto film. In a typical instance, Serios would stare at a Polaroid camera held in his hands or in the hands of someone else, the picture would be taken, and the film immediately developed. Instead of the face of Serios, a picture of a building or other scene would appear on the film. Skeptics were certain that trickery must be involved because Serios liked to hold a hollow plastic tube over the lens of the camera. Numerous observers examined this tube and found it to be no more than a psychological prop for Serios, as it was hollow and contained nothing which could account for the enormous variety of images which appeared on the film.

In other instances, investigators would hold the camera themselves with no tube in front of the lens. They would point the camera at any part of the room and take a picture. They were very surprised to find that the pictures which came out had perspectives of the room which were not within the range of the camera when the shutter was opened, and which included distortions which they found impossible to explain or to reproduce.

Many times the picture taken would be entirely black. Although this could be produced by overexposure of the film, there was no way they could have done this with the light that was available. Similarly, pictures that were entirely white might appear. These are impossible to explain, as the lens was opened with no obstruction between it and objects in the room.

Pictures of specific remote buildings and other scenes which appeared on the film were clearly identifiable by unique features, sometimes including names printed on the buildings. Yet these pictures also contained distortions. As with other psi phenomena, the pictures could not be produced regularly.

Eisenbud speculated that the distortions were due to mental blurring in Serios' memory or psi perceptions of these buildings.[10]

The reactions of observers to the process of producing thoughtographic pictures were just as fascinating as the pictures themselves. People who just heard about it simply would not believe it was possible. People who observed it found it disorienting, particularly when a camera pointed in one direction produced a picture of the same room from a different angle. Everyone, including Eisenbud, kept looking for ways in which they could explain away these thoughtographic photos, despite numerous and varied successful repetitions.

Eisenbud (1983; 1989) gave careful thought to these reactions.

> I was aware that similar reactions were not uncommon among experienced investigators of psychical phenomena and had led some of them, in fact, to leave the field because of their inability to resolve them. The irrationality of this kind of morbid doubt was beautifully expressed by a brilliant British investigator, Everard Feilding, in his delightfully written notes on a series of sittings (carried out in 1908 with two other experienced investigators) with the noted physical medium Eusapia Palladino. This illiterate but quite remarkable Italian peasant woman, who on occasion had been caught in flagrant fraud, nevertheless on other occasions could be observed under conditions of more stringent control to cause objects to move . . . without physical contact of any discoverable sort, and to cause other strange things to happen that I won't even mention here for fear that the reader with all his buttons will lay this book down and turn to something like good science fiction or a James Bond bit of nonsense. "If Eusapia's psychology is a puzzle to us," Feilding wrote, "we find that our own is scarcely less so." He observed that so marked was his and the other investigators' need to resolve the painful ambivalence occasioned in them by the contradictoriness of what they saw when stacked up against ordinary experience and their habitual ways of regarding things that they hailed with relief some minor break in control technique that theoretically made it possible for their already mentally indicted culprit to outflank some precaution, and kept looking hopefully for the definite indications of fraud that would once and for all put their minds at rest. Again and again their eagerness to resolve an almost unbearable emotional confusion tricked them into believing that such signs had been found, only to discover, upon reference to the notes carefully dictated to a shorthand stenographer present at the sittings, that what they had hoped would prove to be a lapse in some condition of control was in fact not such at all (Eisenbud 1989, p.43).

Such reactions of incredulity help to explain some of the difficulties experienced in Western society in dealing with psi phenomena and healing.

Table Tilting and Rapping

Another form of PK, *table tilting* and *rapping*, has been familiar in the seance room for at least a century. Typically, a group of people gathers around a table in a darkened room. They may pray and sing hymns or other songs to help invoke the intervention of spirits with whom they wish to communicate. After a time, the table may start to emit raps, rumbles, or other sounds and tilt or even levitate. A code is often suggested by the participants in which one rap or tilting to one side may signal *yes* and two raps or tilting to the opposite side, *no*. Questions are asked aloud and the table proceeds to answer them in code. Often there is one member of the group who is felt to be the medium facilitating such phenomena.

In the past few decades table tilting and rapping have been researched by several investigators. Kenneth Batcheldor was the first to conclude that such occurrences were manifestations of the participants' PK abilities rather than interventions of spirits from outside the group. He studied such seance phenomena extensively but published very sparingly. The New Spiritual Science Foundation in England is now pursuing this line of research, with a focus on communication with discarnate spirits (Spiritual Scientist).

Research into seance phenomena resembles in many respects the metal bending parties. An atmosphere of levity facilitates the occurrence of the phenomena.

One of the most impressive bits of evidence for a paranormal effect comes from oscilloscope analyses of the raps produced in these settings, which gives a visual picture of sound waves. A normal physical rap shows a gradual decrescendo pattern, as the energy of the initial impact dissipates. PK raps show a distinctive crescendo and/or very rapid falloff pattern (Owen).

Random Spontaneous Psychokinesis (RSPK)

Outbreaks occur in which household objects move around without apparent cause (Bayless 1967). Such events are often violent, with objects falling off shelves or flying across a room. These occurrences were once thought to be caused by mischievous or malicious ghosts or spirits and were labeled *poltergeist* phenomena.

Many such cases have been investigated to rule out fraud, and they appear to be genuinely attributable to PK.[11] A force/distance relationship to the presumed subjects was noted in one report (Roll 1972). The further from the subject, the weaker was the effect. This has not been confirmed by any other investigator.

In recent years parapsychologists have often linked such occurrences to the presence of a particular individual in each series of RSPK events. One hypothesis is that unexpressed, unconscious emotions may be the motivating forces behind these PK events. An angry person might release anger by using PK to smash a mirror or another object. Further evidence is adduced from the observation that psychotherapy with presumed PK agents and their families may bring about cessation of poltergeist activity. This suggests that when emotional conflicts are resolved the anger is no longer projected by PK.

Spirit entities are reported to produce poltergeist effects as well. A classic example is the stopping of clocks in the homes of relatives and friends of the deceased when a person dies. (There is even a popular American song, *The Grandfather Clock*, with this theme.) Some will argue that such effects are due to the living, who use psi unconsciously, both to identify that a relative has died and to bring about the physical effects.[12]

I am personally familiar with a related instance:

Over a period of several months I met regularly with "Nadya," a psychic reader. I asked her many questions, being at the time especially interested in the range of psi abilities she possessed. The one area in which she was definitely lacking was green-thumb ability. She said, "I have a black thumb! Any plant I touch quickly withers." When I moved to another town I gave her as a parting gift a glass vase with a plastic flower. Although pretty, the vase was obviously inexpensively made. (A seam showed where two halves of molded glass had been bonded together.)

Several years later I visited Nadya. She related to me that her elderly mother, who had lived in a distant city, used to visit her home several times a year. For some reason she liked the vase and requested that it be placed close to her bed whenever she stayed with Nadya. A few months prior to my visit Nadya awakened during the night to the sound of a loud bang. She found the vase split in half along its seam. She immediately felt that her mother, who was at her own home, had died. Indeed, a few hours later a telegram arrived confirming her mother's death.

To the uninitiated, such claims for PK must sound far-fetched. Even veteran investigators in this field admit to being uncomfortable with these effects. They question their own eyes and ears, searching for a misperception or alternative ways to explain phenomena which so grossly contradict everyday experience that major shifts in views and understandings of reality are demanded.

It is impossible to prove definitively whether such events represent PK activated by the deceased person just prior to death, PK by the spirit of the departed, or PK by a member in the household where the activity occurred.

Statistical Studies of Psi Powers

The above examples come from highly gifted psi subjects or from settings in which psi is encouraged—consciously or unconsciously—to occur. Though many people possess psi abilities, they are expressed so subtly or infrequently that they often go unnoticed or are dismissed as chance occurrences. However, if ordinary people are tested many times for such abilities it is often possible to demonstrate statistically that they do possess them. These tests can be rather tedious and boring. It is often easier to gather the necessary numbers of trials for statistical analysis by using groups of subjects. Such studies clearly show that most of us have some psi powers but that we are unable to express them on demand. Oddly, we may experience them either in times of need or on apparently random occasions, with no apparent motivation or reason.

Helmut Schmidt devised boxes on which a series of lights were lit at irregular intervals through a link with a random number generator (RNG).

It did not matter whether the RNG functioned on electronic scramblers or even on the random emissions of radioactive particles. Subjects were able to influence these devices in the direction the experimenter demanded, producing highly significant results over long series of trials. PK effects were also demonstrated by Robert Jahn, emeritus professor at the Princeton School of Engineering, and Brenda Dunne, his assistant, with computer RNGs and with a mechanical cascade of styrofoam balls. Unexplainably, "goats" as well as "sheep" sometimes produced results in directions opposite to those which were requested.

> *Now, if consciousness, via its own expressed desire, can bring some degree of order into a simple random string of ones and zeros emerging from a rudimentary machine, is it so unreasonable to suspect that it can invoke similar, or subtler, processes to influence the far more elaborate, relevant, and precious information processing systems that underlie our own health?*
>
> —Robert Jahn (1995, p. 310)

Remote Viewing and Enhanced Psi

In one variation of this phenomenon, a psi viewer sits in a laboratory with an experimenter. Another experimenter goes to a remote place which is randomly chosen from a pool of such locations and revealed to the outward bound experimenter after she leaves the laboratory. The subject then uses her psi abilities to describe as many aspects of this location as she can. This experimental format has repeatedly produced significantly positive results in a number of different laboratories (Jahn/Dunne; Puthoff/Targ). The successful research on remote viewing supports the possibility that healers can diagnose illnesses from a distant location.

Charles Honorton and others have developed the *ganzfeld technique* for enhancing psi expression. They have the subject in a quiet room, viewing diffuse white light through plastic eyepieces and hearing a nondescript hiss (*white noise*) through earphones. Under these conditions, psi occurs more often. Statistical meta-analyses of series of ganzfeld studies show astronomically significant results (Utts). This confirms both the existence of psi phenomena and the facilitation of psi through the ganzfeld technique.

Psi Displacement in Time and Space

Jahn and Dunne showed that subjects could describe the remote places accurately prior to the arrival of the outward-bound experimenter at the target location.

Helmut Schmidt (1976) explored backwards-in-time PK effects. He pre-recorded a series of outputs from an RNG. At a later time he played these back through the RNG output display for subjects who were asked to alter the output of an RNG. The subjects did not know that the RNG output was prerecorded. Subjects produced highly significant deviations of the RNG from random output. No such deviations occurred in the RNG when subjects were not focused on altering the later output display of the recordings which had been made earlier.[13]

This may compare with healing effects that appear to be displaced in time.

General Observations on Psi

Stephen Braude (1979a) summarizes:

> [T]here is a growing (if not always coercive) body of evidence that success in PK experiments does not depend, or depends very little, on subjects' knowing (at least by normal means) such apparently relevant facts as the nature, mechanics, or existence of the PK target system, or even whether they are being tested for PK.
>
> There is evidence, also . . . that subjects tend to perform best when they do not actively try to affect the experimental outcome . . . we begin to get a rather surprising picture of PK. In fact, to some, it begins to look as though success in PK tasks might be accomplished without any form of computation or information-processing by subjects.

Rex Stanford developed the *conformance theory of psi events*.[14] This predicts that psi will function best when an organizing force or intention is influencing a random system. Several studies seem to confirm this theory, including a few on animal systems.[15]

The *conformance theory* may be directly relevant to healing. The factor of healee need may be a potent organizing force which activates psi powers latent in most people.

Many of the body's biochemical and neurological processes include a random aspect in their functioning. For instance, chemical reactions occur randomly between molecules. Theoretically, this places healing in a strong position to succeed under experimental conditions, assuming the validity of the conformance theory. Meta-analyses of numerous psi experiments lend support to these speculations. When overall results of research with living targets are compared with those of other psi experiments, there is a much higher success rate with the healing studies (Braud 1989).

The idea that psi powers operate in our lives is disconcerting and disorienting. Such abilities appear to contradict our everyday experience. They show that our usual perception of the world is a limited-range experience. Acceptance of psi may require a paradigm shift in our thinking.

This is similar to what happened when classical (Newtonian) physics was found to be a limited-range explanatory system relative to modern, *quantum* physics. The observations and rules of classical physics describe properties and relationships of objects which we experience through our senses. These rules *make sense* to us.

The observations and rules of quantum physics relate to particles and waves which are deduced to exist through various experiments designed around complex instruments. For instance, we are told that an electron may be either a particle or a wave, depending on how we examine it. We are told that objects such as billiard balls, which appear solid to our senses, actually consist more of space between atomic particles than of matter. Though these observations are counter to our intuitive grasp of nature, we have come to accept them.[16]

Observations from psi research are confusing when we apply everyday linear reasoning to them. Most experiments can be explained by more than one psi power. Receptive telepathy may be a special case of clairsentience. That is, a person might read information from the brain of a sender rather than from his mind or thoughts. Broadcasting telepathy may be an instance of PK, or direct effects of a sender's mind on the brain or mind of a receiver. Clairsentience may in some cases involve reading the mind of the experimenter who placed a given object in the experimental room. Ostensible clairsentience or telepathy may actually be precognition. The subject may see the results of the experiment or obtain her information from the future rather than from the telepathic sender or object she is supposed to be viewing clairsentiently.

Everyone seems to have some measure of psi ability. In most of us it only occasionally becomes conscious. It is unclear whether this is because it occurs only rarely or because it is a function of the unconscious mind and occurs frequently but goes unnoticed most of the time. Much evidence supports the hypothesis that psi acts via the unconscious mind. In addition to the sheep/goat effect, we find psi speaking to us more often in dreams they in waking states (L. Rhine 1961; 1967). If this is the case, in most instances psi ability would be as inaccessible as most of the other unconscious materials we hide from conscious awareness for various defensive psychological reasons.

People sometimes worry that all their private, intimate secrets will be revealed to sensitives. Psi doesn't work that way. People cannot be read psychically like books from beginning to end. Sensitives perceive whatever information is relevant to the highest good of the person in the context of their consultation. Very often the perceptions received are symbolic and only partial answers to the question posed by the psychic, and need to be checked out with the person whose thoughts are being perceived in order to make sense of them.

For example, in giving healing during psychotherapy to a woman with a chronic backache I got the image of a car rushing towards me. When I shared this with her, she suddenly recalled having had a head-on collision fifteen years earlier. Though not physically injured, she had been emotionally shaken and angered. Upon releasing the anger, her pain was relieved.

Why are psychic perceptions cloaked in obscure symptons and images? This probably serves to protect people from revelations—to themselves as well as to others—with which they would not be comfortable if they were to enter conscious or social awareness. Ask several people what they would think of a situation in which everyone had telepathic powers. You will find that most people are very uneasy about such a proposition. Ask psychics how people responded to their psi abilities when, as children, they revealed telepathic or clairsentient glimpses uninhibitedly. Most will say that the reaction was discouraging, sometimes including fright and occasionally (Peterson) even anger.

Olga Worrall, the gifted healer, told of her difficulties with psychic perceptions when she was a child. Friends of her parents visited her home and complimented her mother on her choice of some new curtains in the living room. Olga was utterly confused when her mother responded with embarrassment and anger to her question, in front of the guests, "Why are they lying about liking the curtains?"

Western society generally inhibits the expression of psi abilities so that gifted subjects tend to withhold them. With sufficient discouragements psi powers may then be repressed by the unconscious mind. This spares the person the discomfort of confrontation with an unaccepting environment. For instance, about 20 percent of children report that they see colors, probably the biological energy field (*aura*) around the bodies of people— before they enter school. After they are in school a while, very few report they see these colors (Peterson).

Schmeidler's *sheep/goat* dichotomy seems to indicate that everybody has psi ability but that it is used in directions consistent with their beliefs. We may speculate that believers use psi to obtain positive results. Conversely, disbelievers filter the psi perceptions through their belief system and produce negative results in order to avoid the cognitive discomfort a positive outcome might produce. This comforts them that no such thing could happen—ironically using the very psi powers they find uncomfortable to produce results which appear to prove their disbeliefs.

Psi effects occur irregularly and infrequently. Many people therefore question whether psi phenomena are more than random fluctuations in observations.

There is a marked tendency for *hits* (successful attempts) to occur at the beginning and end of a series of trials. This effect is like that observed in the testing of retentive memory for nonsense syllables and similar psychological tasks. Items at the beginning and end of the list are retained more frequently. It may be related at least partially to attention, which is greater at the beginning and end of a series of trials.

The problem of unrepeatability of experiments is much more vexing and serious. Subjects may do well in one series of trials and poorly in another for no apparent reason. Attempts to increase successful performance by rewards, feedback, and other methods have been largely ineffective. Many skeptics cite this as reason to question the existence of psi. They claim that people should be able to demonstrate psi powers repeatedly and reliably if they possess them. There is no a priori reason, however, that psi phenomena should conform with expectations of repeatability and reliability, just as procrustean measures taken from any given scientific field need not apply to any fields outside their own.[17]

> *We often give more attention to the weeds in our gardens than to the flowers.*
>
> —D.B.

Summary

An enormous body of research presents convincing evidence that psi phenomena exist.

Psi phenomena exhibit a lawfulness of their own:
1. They occur more often in early and late trials in a series of tests.
2. They are frequently demonstrated in the first of a series of experiments but not in attempted replications of the same experiment. Jule Eisenbud (1989, p.1-2) observed, "I concluded . . . that the repeatable experiment in parapsychology would take its place, alongside the alchemist's stone and the cabalist's tetragrammaton, with those dreams of mankind that would remain forever dreams."
3. Psi perceptions are often cloaked in images and metaphors in a similar manner to dreams and other unconscious material.
4. Even gifted psychics have only a partial success rate over large series of trials.

Hasted and Shafer, referred to earlier in this chapter, and Iris Owen and Margaret Sparrow, among others, have noted that *willing* PK effects to occur is counterproductive. Being in a frame of mind that *allows* them to happen without conscious direction works much better. Rex Stanford (1974) has found support for this approach in the psi lab. He gives the example of a young woman who was very successful in a psi experiment. Upon questioning, it became apparent that she had not even understood the instructions properly. Her technique was simply to hope that everything would turn out well.

Perhaps this unfocused state of mind is also produced by the ganzfeld method.

Though single studies of psi may demonstrate significant effects, skeptics claim there is still the possibility that the rare occurrence of one chance in twenty, in a hundred, or even in a thousand has occurred merely by luck. That is, the results may represent a random, rare, but nevertheless possible chance combination of results rather than any psi effect. A way to address this argument is to do a *meta-analysis* of a series of studies. This assesses what the statistical probability is that the *entire series* could have occurred by chance.

Meta-analyses of psi research are beginning to refute the criticisms based on poor replicability, demonstrating very robust statistical probabilities across series of studies. Meta-analyses are confirming that highly significant results are obtained in studies of general psi research,[18] PK on random number generators (Radin/Nelson); PK on tossed dice (Radin/ Ferrari); studies of PK on biological systems by Braud and Schlitz (Braud/ Schlitz 1991); and psi phenomena under ganzfeld conditions (Honorton et al.; Utts), under hypnotic induction (Schechter), and in forced-choice precognition (Honorton/Ferrari).

The unrepeatability of many psi experiments is cited as a basis for discounting the existence of psi. This is a problem that also concerns psi believers. It is not exclusive to this field. H. M. Collins points out that similar repeatability problems exist in the harder sciences, such as in studies of laser design and gravitational fields. It may be that too many unnoticed and uncontrolled variables enter into psi effects and produce unrepeatable experiments.

Jule Eisenbud (1989, p.167-8 footnote 10) observes,

> [P]hysics itself has had to "give up physics"—or at least physical-type radiation hypotheses—as a basic means of clarification in certain problem areas. One of these is the domain of all events, large and small, where attractive, or gravitational, "forces" are held to apply, and the other is the mystery of how light gets across empty space. The former "action at a distance" problem remained a basis of lively and at times acrimonious controversy from the time of Newton, who throughout the eighteenth century was indicted in many quarters as being "occult," until Einstein simply outflanked it by replacing "force" assumptions with geometrical ones dealing with masses in a curved time-space manifold. In the other problem area, physicists have had to content themselves with the position expressed by Einstein when he wrote (with Infield in *The Evolution of Physics*), "Our only way out seems to be to take for granted the fact that space has the physical property of transmitting electromagnetic waves, and not to bother too much about the meaning of this statement."

We could conclude from the unrepeatability of psi effects that psi has natural laws different from those of other phenomena. However, the sheep-goat effect has been helpful in clarifying one source of discrepancies, suggesting that there may be others which are explainable in linear terms. There is evidence that geomagnetic activity may contribute to variability of telepathic transmission.[19] Psi perceptions are more successful on days when planetary geomagnetic field activity is quieter. Anecdotal evidence has also been produced for variability of healing with thunderstorms (Turner 1969) and with lunar phases (Setzer). Psi effects may be more sensitive to these influences than are other phenomena. This may ultimately provide clues to the nature of psi energies and processes. Moreover, the experimenters themselves may be a part of tests to a far greater degree than has been appreciated, which could account for variability that precludes repeatability.[20]

The lack of definitive clarity in this discussion is partly due to our limited explanations for psi. However, sufficient experiments have been performed to demonstrate beyond reasonable doubt that psi exists. We know enough to realize that psi effects occur with less intentional control than other types of interactions with the environment. Perhaps we shall never produce these effects entirely at will. My own belief is that the lessons from psi research require restructuring of our conventional scientific paradigms. Our discomforts with psi have more to do with inadequacies in our Western scientific models than with psi phenomena.

For those interested in skeptics' views on psi, I recommend the comments of reviewers along with the original works.[21] Skeptics' views are often laced with selective presentations of poorer evidence for psi, while ignoring the better evidence; application of procrustean standards and measurements using yardsticks which are not properly applicable to psi; demands for stringent scientific methodology which far exceed those applied in other fields of research; and even misrepresentations of materials.[22]

Psi and Healing

Skeptics claim that although there have been studies of healing for various problems, these have not been replicated. This is simply untrue. A robust body of research, reviewed in the next chapter,[23] confirms many healing effects.

There has not been a meta-analysis of healing studies as a whole. Braud and Schlitz (1991; 1997) showed highly significant effects of healing in a series of studies on electrodermal responses.[24] Other meta-analyses of clusters of healing studies have found highly significant effects (Astin et al; Braud/Schlitz 1989; Winstead-Fry/Kijek) and one, which included dissertation abstracts and pilot studies, did not find significant results (Abbot).

The studies reviewed in this chapter point to a variety of interesting possibilities in unraveling the mystery of healing.

Healers' reports of healing-conducive states-of-mind parallel laboratory studies of psi-conducive states. As Lawrence LeShan and Joyce Goodrich summarized, the healing state of mind is not one in which the healer actively pursues changes in the person being healed. The healer seeks a oneness with the healee and allows whatever healing can take place to occur. This suggests that investigators of psi and healing ought to alter their laboratory techniques to accommodate the practices of those who do not usually produce psi phenomena and healings on demand. Pressuring them to do so may be counterproductive.

How are we to understand this need for a nondirected state of mind if psi and healing are to occur? LeShan suggests that the healer enters alternate realities in order to heal. In these mental states, matter and mind and time may have different relationships from those in our everyday, sensory reality. Healers may be able to bring about unusual changes in the physical world because of different laws of nature in those alternative realities. The nondirected, meditative state may be a way to gain access to the other realities. A second possibility is that the psi and healing functions reside in the right hemisphere of the brain.[25] Meditative states may help either to activate the right brain hemisphere, to deactivate the left one, or to synchronize both (Cade/Coxhead). Another hypothesis is that by quieting the mind one relinquishes counter-productive beliefs and habits of bodily tensions and other malfunctions, allowing healthy, normal functions to reassert themselves.

The irregular occurrence of psi and healing in a laboratory environment may relate in part to their being *need-determined*. A strongly felt need in someone associated with the situation may facilitate expression of psi abilities. In natural settings one would expect the greatest need to reside in the healee, followed by the healer with altruistic and/or ego-involved needs (such as reputation or financial gain).

In the laboratory, the needs of the healee are often subordinated to those of the experimenter. With respect to healers, the laboratory situation where the experimenters' needs are clearly paramount is often little better. Most people tested for psi or healing say that the laboratory is not only boring but also irrelevant to their work. Healers often dedicate much or all of their lives to helping large numbers of people in serious need of healing or counseling. Working on bacteria or mice is not something on which they want to waste valuable time. Some even say that such frivolous use of their healing gifts might lead to a diminution of their powers.

The intrusion of others into the healer-healee relationship has to be distracting at the least. The monitoring of physiological parameters by means of various instruments with their wires can cause the relationship to lose much of its healing quality. Neither healer nor healee is likely to feel the experimenters' needs are as strong as their own, and they will probably not experience their own needs as being as important as when they are outside the experimenters' frame of reference. The challenge is for experimenters to take their studies to the field or to create an encouraging atmosphere in the laboratory. It is almost surprising that despite such obstacles healing and psi experiments have produced convincing evidence.

Healing involves clairsentience and/or telepathy. Many healers are able to detect and identify specific bodily dysfunctions without being told by the healee or by anyone else what the health problems are. In some cases the healers may be obtaining information from the minds of the healees, those who accompany them or those who know their diagnosis (such as their physicians). In other instances the healer clearly transcends the information available via such telepathic sources. Healers have been known to make detailed diagnoses which were previously unknown to anyone but were later verified on medical examination. Very talented clairsentient diagnosticians have been able to name the patient's illnesses, using medical terms that they never learned and do not comprehend. Precognition may also explain some of these diagnoses.

PK seems to be involved in some healings, according to the definition that the mind of one person acts on an object outside itself. This seems more likely in instantaneous, miraculous healings and psychic surgery,[26] where the interventions of the healer are quite dramatic. Tissues may be dematerialized and materialized. We cannot be certain, however, that this is healer PK. Healers may be activating processes within healees rather than acting upon the healees. In this case it seems as though telepathy may be invoked because healers can work at a distance and without the knowledge of the healees, while still obtaining significant effects.

Montague Ullman's descriptions of the different styles of psi and healing of Kulagina and Vinogradova suggest that several very different channels or modes may exist whereby psi and healing are expressed. This is supported by the observations of effects of healers on water which may show up either on IR or UV studies. Alternatively, healer methods may be identical but may be colored and distorted by personalities and belief systems of the healers and healees, and by multitudes of extrameous factors.

Leonid Vasiliev's observations on apparent PK-induced muscle contractions seem open to several interpretations. Simple PK may be involved. This appears more likely in the case of the insect muscles, because here the experimenter knew the desired result. Supporting the PK proposition is harder in the case of the hypnotized subjects, because the experimenters were naive with respect to the anatomical structures involved. They could, of course, have obtained the required information telepathically from experimenters or others who did have the knowledge.

This would be what is commonly called *super ESP,* which has been demonstrated in other instances (Stanford et al. 1975; Solfvin 1982).[27] In Super-ESP psi powers are used to scan for information and to influence the environment.

Another possible explanation of the muscle contractions is some sort of a biological-field interaction between experimenter and subject, per the synchronization observed of insect muscle contractions with the experimenter's breathing. In any case, these experimental situations suggest overlap with aspects of healing.[28]

The metal-bending and the less rigorous observations of Sai Baba and Thomas suggest that a subject may be able to cause matter to alter or even disappear instantaneously from one place and appear in another. This suggests that either the healer or healee may be able to materialize or dematerialize body tissues to bring about a healing. Reports of mediumistic materializations may also be relevant here.[29]

Psychic subjects have been able to induce PK and healing abilities similar to thcir own in other subjects who did not previously display such abilities. Uri Geller is especially noted for transferring his ability to soften and bend metal and possibly also to restart broken timepieces. Filippino healers reportedly bring out healing and psychic surgery abilities in others (Stelter).

The induced healers often report that their healing was effective only when they were in contact with their mentors. The precise distance relationship is impossible to ascertain from the limited information given in the reports. In one case Stelter stated that a student healer was able to reproduce psychic surgery while in the Philippines but not when he returned to Germany. Confounding factors may also include confidence/skepticism in the healer and/or belief/doubt/negative effects of other participants and observers.

Some healers report they regularly induce healing abilities in relatives of healees, initiating absent healing over great distances.

Any study of PK or healing force/distance effects should, therefore, exclude investigators from the vicinity of the target objects. The experimenter close to the object could be a secondary, induced agent for PK, thereby complicating the study.

Another parallel between metal bending and healing is the report of observers that they may sense a tingling when they place their hand between that of the bender and the target object.

Hasted and Shafer both comment on the need for a proper atmosphere for the metal bending to occur. Again this parallels reports in healing. Hasted (1982) mentions that a significant percent of metal benders in time develop healing abilities. They complain the metal bending gets boring after a while.

The Uphoffs' report on ultrasonic waves with PK is a novel observation which is worthy of further investigation. I do not know of any studies on healers involving these frequencies, but qigong healers have been found to emit infrasonic waves (Peng/Liu).[30]

Larissa Vilenskaya's report on Kulagina's ability to produce a burning sensation through quartz glass suggests ultraviolet radiation maybe related to this effect, as UV light passes through quartz glass.

Stanford's theory that PK may occur most readily when an organizing need acts upon a random system seems a reasonable description of many of the physiological processes that may respond to healing. The body's immune system, for example, requires that antibodies and white blood cells, which circulate randomly throughout the body, attack invading organisms. The healer may aid the targeting of these elements. This may also be the case on a chemical level. Many body processes entail complex biochemical reactions of molecules distributed randomly throughout the body. They often require specific enzymes to facilitate reactions with each other. The healer's psi might facilitate the completion of these random chemical processes. Research confirms that healers can alter enzyme activity.[31]

Helmut Schmidt's random number generator study, demonstrating backwards-in-time causation, closely parallels healings that are reportedly displaced in time.

As with all psi phenomena, differentiating who is producing the effects in a given case is impossible. For example, the experimenter could conceivably be the true agent for Schmidt's effects, using clairsentience and PK. The subjects could also be precognizing the future experimental situation and affecting the RNG prior to reaching the laboratory. The same is true of healing. We can never know whether healer or healee produce given results.

> *The wise man says, "I am looking for the truth," and the fool,*
> *"I have found the truth."*
> —Russian proverb (Dossey 1998a, p. 109)

Several aspects of RSPK investigations have bearings on our understanding of healing. All of the propelling force in moving the object in RSPK can be reasonably presumed to originate in the human agent. This may then impose force/distance limitations on the abilities of the subject to affect the object. In the case of RSPK it is usually inanimate objects that are affected. If inanimate objects are influenced by RSPK it is only to move them in gross, bodily fashion from one place to another. In healing, there are energies, awareness, and intelligence which are available in the healees to help in effecting changes. This adds a possible dimension of participation of the healee, which would generally not occur in instances of RSPK. The range for healer effects may be far greater, therefore, than for RSPK effects.

The mechanisms for healing may or may not be different for distant (versus present) touch healings. Healers are of the opinion that there is little difference in effectiveness between distant and present healings. Careful investigation is required to substantiate these clinical impressions.

Broader Psi Perspectives

If psi communications occur between individuals, then psi consciousness may occur as a group phenomenon. A collective consciousness may exist within humanity, within other species, within the entire planet (as Gaia), or even beyond, to the entire cosmos.

Experiments performed by Dean Radin (1997) appear to confirm this possibility. RNGs—which function randomly most of the time—were found to deviate significantly during periods of time when large numbers of people were focused upon an exciting event such as the final football game of a season, the media coverage of the O.J. Simpson trial verdict, and the like. There was clearly no intention on the part of participators/observers in these instances to produce deviations in random number generators, but some sort of space-time influence was generated. The effects were small but repeatably measurable.

This suggests that massed healing prayer may be a potent intervention. It also begins to confirm what many healers and mystics say: Each of us is as a brain cell in the mind of the cosmos. A healing of any individual contributes to the healing of the All.

In summary, major components of psi phenomena are relevant to healing:
- Telepathy, clairsentience, and PK may be components of the healing process. They have been demonstrated conclusively in the laboratory.
- Telepathy and clairsentience have been shown to occur at vast distances, which may be a basis for, or parallel with, distant diagnosis and healing.
- The undirected state of mind which is psi-conducive may be identical with or similar to states of mind that are healing-conducive.
- Psi awareness and influences on the world appear to have no limits. There may be no limits to healing effects other than our disbeliefs.

CHAPTER 4

CONTROLLED STUDIES

> *There is really no scientific or other method by which man can steer safely between the opposite dangers of believing too little or believing too much. To face such dangers is apparently our duty and to hit the right channel between them is the measure of our wisdom.*
> —William James

> *If you make people think they're thinking, they'll love you; but if you really make them think they'll hate you.*
> —Don Marquis

Does healing work? If so, how does it work? By carefully examining the published research, this chapter begins to answer these two questions in a more precise fashion. The studies in this chapter explore in a methodical way the effects of healing on people, animals, plants, and other living matter such as bacteria, yeasts, and enzymes.

There are more scientific studies on spiritual healing than on most of the other complementary therapies. Hundreds have been performed over the past 30 years.[1] If we could use the number of studies as a measure of success, healing would automatically be an impressive therapy. However, quality of research must be considered as well as quantity. In the pages that follow, we'll be looking at these studies with an eye toward their strengths and weaknesses.

No single study can answer definitively whether or not healing works. But we can begin to show a pattern wherein a number of studies provide solid evidence of the efficacy of healing. What's more, by demonstrating the clinical efficiency of healing in specific situations, individual studies also provide a sense of where healing is effective and how it works. They show healing alleviating specific symptoms and treating objectively identifiable diseases as well as the more subjective dis-eases. Studies in humans and animals explore whether or not healing can be of benefit for wound healing, hypertension, diabetes, pain, anxiety, and much more.

The studies also suggest some of the mechanisms for the action of healing—how it works. These look at healing on both human and nonhuman subjects, examining the biology behind healing reactions. Animals, plants, bacteria, and other organisms lend themselves to more structured studies because they are less complex than humans, and their environments can be more carefully controlled. Studies on human subjects are always open to such extraneous influences as psychological, social, dietary, and environmental factors. These may alter the subjects' responses to healing. The experimenter's challenge is to limit these factors as much as possible.

Only rarely, if at all, can science produce answers of absolute certainty. A modicum of doubt as to the validity of research results must therefore remain, even in the best of all scientific studies.

Studies and summaries

A note before we proceed further.

This book, Volume I of *Healing Research*, has been published in two parts: a main text and a supplement. In the chapter that follows, the descriptions of research studies that you will encounter are concise and direct. Intended primarily for the layperson, they provide a basic, clear summary of what was done in each study and what the results were. In their total, these summaries provide a good, solid introduction to the research that is currently available.

Those who seek more detailed information should consult the supplement, where most of the studies in this chapter and the next are discussed at greater length, often with more attention to research methods and complex statistical data.

The end of the study summary is marked by the study title and journal or dissertation reference.

Discussions following each study may include a spectrum of comments, some ranging even to polar analyses of the results. Not infrequently, these differing interpretations demonstrate that research does not prove or disprove the existence or efficacy of healing. Research presents data that we must interpret, and our interpretations can vary widely—depending on our basic assumptions about life processes, levels of acceptance of psychic and healing phenomena, and the validity of research designs.

My analyses are shaped in two major ways by my professional training and clinical experience. First, I am a psychiatric psychotherapist and a practicing healer. While I am eager to see how healing can be studied within the frameworks of rigorous, randomized controlled studies, I believe that healing is as much a gift and its administration an art as it is a potent therapeutic intervention per se. Boxing the delicate, unconditionally loving interactions of healing into a research protocol may make it difficult to allow healing a full opportunity to demonstrate its efficacy. To some degree this is like wanting to study how people make love—in a laboratory, with a certain length of time allotted to the interaction in order to standardize the research protocol, with physiological measurements and psychological tests before and after the interaction, and in some studies restricting the participants from speaking with or touching each other. From this perspective, my analyses favor the likelihood that healing effects are confirmed by the research evidence when statistical significance of the results suggests that they are beyond chance levels. Even if there are flaws in aspects of the research design, it is possible that the effects were produced by the healing.

Second, I am a medically trained psychiatric researcher. I am very keenly aware that if there are any flaws whatsoever in the research design or in the reporting of the study, we cannot know with any degree of certainty whether the results were due to effects of healing or whether they might have been produced by any of the confounding variables discussed above. To the extent that it is possible, we must methodically identify and control every variable of the spiritual healing interaction and assure ourselves that the research design is adequate to eliminate every variable other than spiritual healing that might have produced the differences between the experimental and control groups. Unless we do this, we cannot know if spiritual healing is more than a placebo. Ethically, we are bound to research spiritual healing with randomized controlled studies—even though the studies impose limitations upon the delicate processes of spiritual healing that may make it more difficult for the healing to express itself and be confirmed by the research.

The review and assessment of studies is a complex matter. At the end of the discussions following each study I have placed my ratings of the studies according to the following ranking system.

I.   **Excellent study**, including all the items required for a blinded, randomized controlled study, with adequate reporting of data to confirm the results.

II. **Study lacking in some details**, but reason suggests this is not significant.[2]

III. **Reporting of details is seriously deficient** (as when I only have a dissertation abstract summary) or details such as essential data to support reported findings are missing. Post hoc findings are also in this category.

IV. **Critical elements are missing**, such as blinds, any form of randomization,[3] or a clear confound was identified by the researchers or by myself.

V.   **Poorly designed study**, where it is unlikely that significant effects could be found. The otherwise excellent study of Schlitz/Braud (1985) is in this category because healers were required to produce a healing effect within a timeframe of 30 seconds, alternating with 30 second periods of nonhealing.

I have been stringent in ranking the studies. I feel that we must be as careful as possible in assessing these studies, to rule out any shred of possibility that confounding factors other than healing might have produced the observed results.

This is not to say that studies ranked III or IV are necessarily poor studies. Some are simply limited by a serious flaw in an otherwise excellent design and execution—such as neglecting to check whether medications taken (types and timing) by subjects in the experiment and control groups were similar. Other apparently good studies are limited by inadequate reporting of their methodology, data, or analyses.

Clinical researchers of healing would be wise to consult someone experienced in healing research during the design phase and again prior to writing up their results for publication.[4]

Finally, each of the summaries in this chapter ends with my own analyses, weighing the strengths and weaknesses of each study. Research provides observational data. Observations are reduced to numbers for statistical analyses, such as numbers of healees with backache who improved compared to numbers who remained unchanged; millimeters of growth in plant size; or rates of enzyme activity. While we would like to have definitive answers from research studies, this is rarely the case. What you make of the results may depend on your interpretation of the numbers. Widely differing interpretations may be suggested by believers and by skeptics who discuss the same figures.

The test of a first-rate intelligence is the ability to hold two opposed ideas in the mind at the same time and still retain the ability to function.

—F. Scott Fitzgerald (1936)

I am reminded of a Woody Allen film in which he is lying on the analyst's couch, complaining that his wife is always making excuses and avoiding him and that he hardly ever has any sex. The analyst asks, "How often do you have sex?" Woody answers, "Only twice a week." In the next scene, his wife is lying on the couch, complaining that her husband is all over her, all of the time, insisting they have sex all of the time, and that she's completely fed up with so much sex. Her analyst asks, "How often do you have sex?" She replies, "It's twice a week." Taking into account the subjectivity of any interpretation of results, at the end of each study, I suggest how a believer and how a skeptic might view and interpret the findings.

Beyond that, look for the discussions at the end of studies and preceding them. These place the adjacent studies in a larger context of other research, medical science, and the history of healing. You can get an overview of the research by skimming these sections.

What to look out for: ideas and terms that matter

Here are some of the basic concepts that you will want to keep in mind as you read the studies.

Quality—In general, we look at the rigor and thoroughness of the researchers, their work, and their reporting of their work. We look for adequate description of the research procedures so that the study might be repeated by another experimenter. We want to see a solid description of the healers, their methods, and their beliefs. Finally, we want to see a comprehensive presentation of the study's results. This chapter and the next are highly focused on these questions of quality.

Selection of subjects—Here, by way of limiting potential variables, it is important to consider the selection processes and criteria for selecting the healers and their subjects. Factors in the selection may have an unintended effect on the outcome of a study. These might include the duration of illness, whether or not subjects are taking any medication, and whether healees are volunteers or are chosen by the researchers. There may be a selection bias on the part of a researcher, or a volunteer's motives may introduce an effect.

Controls—It is important that scientific studies be performed in a controlled manner, with variable factors limited as much as possible. In healing research, this means that when an experimental group is given a specific healing treatment, a control group is not given that treatment. The control group must resemble the treated group as much as possible, both in its demographic background as well as the way it is handled by the experimenters. To the extent possible, the only difference between the groups remains the actual treatment.

Some studies may be performed with an experimental (treated) group, a nontreated control group as a baseline, and a second control group that receives a simulated (mock) treatment to see if the belief that one is undergoing treatment actually produces healing effects. Other studies include control groups receiving treatments of known benefit.

Randomization—To further avoid uncontrolled variables, the subjects need to be randomized between the experimental and control groups as evenly as possible so that both groups resemble each other as nearly as possible. The best way to do this is to randomly divide the whole subject pool, but this can be harder than it sounds. For example, a researcher who divides the subject pool may be unconsciously concentrating the stronger or the younger subjects into the experimental group, unintentionally skewing the results. To avoid such biasing effects, participants are assigned according to random numbers generated independently of the researcher.[5]

Blinds—The outcome of a study may be unintentionally affected by the attitudes or the expectations of an experimenter or a subject. Results may be produced through suggestion or placebo effects.[6] Blinds are techniques for keeping both subjects and experimenters unaware of which person is receiving which treatment. Blinds prevent experimenters and subjects from responding according to expectations attached to experimental and control conditions. For example, without blinds, a researcher who believed in healing might be inclined to notice more improvements in the treated group than in the control group. Blinds can be complex and so thorough that in some cases, subjects may have no idea at all of the nature of the experiment. As well, blinds may extend to those who handle the animals in animal research or to judges who are called in from outside to analyze data.

Significance and statistical analysis—Statistical analysis of differences between the experimental and the control groups assures us that the observed differences are unlikely to have occurred by chance. We may be told that in the experimental group, 25 out of the 38 people who were treated with healing improved, while in the control group, only 19 out of 41 improved. However, we would not know if these are meaningful differences. It is possible that such differences could occur by chance. Statistical analysis can tell us how likely it is that differences occurred by chance. We would love to have result where the likelihood that chance plays a part is one in a million. Such an outcome is rare, though, and most scientific studies look at a likelihood of one time in 20 as the minimum criterion for acceptance of results as being unlikely to have occurred by chance.

In statistics, that likelihood is reported as probability. In a standard formula, that one in 20 minimum is given as a probability of less than five times in a hundred (.05) or p < .05.

Naturally, it is more convincing to find results that are even less likely to have occurred by chance, perhaps less than one in a hundred (p < .01) or less than a thousand (p < .001).

When probability reaches .05, it is said to have reached significance. For the purposes of this book, I am designating that a probability of .02 to 05 is of modest significance, .01 is significant, and .001 or higher is highly significant.[7]

Post hoc analysis—In some cases, researchers will report *post hoc* (after the fact) analysis, which is made subsequent to the conduct of the study, as a reconsideration. While such analysis may be valid, it is often suspect because it goes outside the structure of the original study design.

Type I and Type II errors—As noted previously, these are assessment errors that can stem from the researcher's attitudes toward the results of the study. In a Type I error, the researcher accepts as true something that is actually false. In a Type II error, the reverse applies: one accepts as false something that is actually true.[8]

Replication—Perhaps one of the most important of research endeavors, replication builds on earlier work. In replication, researchers attempt to repeat a previous study. Two or three good studies with similar results are much more convincing than a lone study, no matter how well done.

It is one of the paradoxes of science that the more precise the question one studies, the more limited the information one obtains, because of the narrow, exact focus of the research. Only a serious commitment to extensive research in spiritual healing can overcome this paradox, providing us with such a sufficient volume of this narrow, limited information that we can have a clearer sense of the nature of healing.

Personally, I am impressed with the overall quality of evidence in favor of healing. Considering that we are in the early days of healing research and that most of the studies were done without financial support, the body of evidence is all the more impressive.

The mechanisms of spiritual healing are still a mystery. Healing appears to transcend the ordinary, accepted laws of science.[9] Clues that point to a resolution of the mystery must certainly be found in the pages of this chapter and the next.

HEALING FOR HUMAN
PHYSICAL PROBLEMS

*In research the horizon recedes as we advance . . . and
research is always incomplete.*

—Mark Pattison (1875)

A growing collection of controlled studies on human subjects has been
published since the mid 1980s. These are generally of greatest interest to
those of us who are seeking healing for our own problems or those of
people close to us.

Distant healing offers an excellent way to set up a double blind study.

Coronary Care Patients and Intercessory Prayer
Randolph C. Byrd

Byrd, a physician, assessed the progress of patients on an illness severity
scale that he devised, as no other scale existed for such evaluations:

> To evaluate the effects of. . . intercessory prayer (IP) to the Judeo-
> Christian God. . . in a coronary care unit (CCU) population, a
> prospective randomized double-blind protocol was followed. Over
> ten months, 393 patients admitted to the CCU were randomized,
> after signing informed consent, to an intercessory prayer group
> (192 patients) or to a control group (201 patients). While hospi-
> talized, the first group received IP by participating Christians
> praying outside the hospital; the control group did not. . . . After
> entry, all patients had follow-up for the remainder of the admis-
> sion. The IP group subsequently had a significantly lower severity
> score based on the hospital course after entry ($p < .01$). . . .

There were no differences between groups on admission in degree of severity of myocardial infarction or in numerous other pertinent variables.

"Intercessors" were "born again" Christians who prayed daily and were
active with their local church. Intercessors were given patients' first names,
their diagnoses and updates on their condition and ". . . each intercessor
was asked to pray daily for a rapid recovery and for prevention of complications and death, in addition to other areas of prayer they believed to be
beneficial to the patient." Significantly fewer patients in the prayer group
required intubation/ventilation ($p < .002$) or antibiotics ($p < .005$), had
cardiopulmonary arrests ($p < .02$), developed pneumonia ($p < .03$) or
required diuretics ($p < .05$).

Despite the differences between groups, the mean times in CCU and duration's of hospitalization between groups were nearly identical.

Positive therapeutic effects of intercessory prayer in a coronary care unit population (*Southern Medical Journal*, 1988)

The study shows significant effects of distant healing on cardiopulmonary patients. It is curious, however, that as Byrd reports, the duration of hospitalization was not affected. This is an excellent study. It would be of help to have more details as to how blinds were maintained. Rating: I

The Byrd study is one of the most cited studies in the healing literature. It was well designed, included large numbers of subjects, had excellent blinds, and produced positive results with distant healing in patients with severe cardiac problems. It is puzzling that despite the improvements in physical conditions, duration of hospitalization was not shortened.

The following is a deliberate replication of the study of Byrd.

Coronary Care Patients and Intercessory prayer: replication

William S. Harris and colleagues

Effects of intercessory prayer were studied in a randomized, controlled, double-blind study of 990 consecutively admitted patients[10] on a coronary care unit (CCU) at the Mid America Heart Institute (MAHI). Kansas City, MO. There were 466 in the E group and 524 in the C group. No significant differences were noted in other health conditions, age, or sex between the groups. Neither patients nor staff knew the study was being done, and therefore informed consent was not obtained.

Teams of Christian intercessors were recruited from the local community. A secretary (blind to the subjects' diagnoses and severity of illness) phoned the prayer group team leader, providing only the subject's first name. Prayer was offered individually. The secretary kept the records of E and C assignments and no one else had access to them till the end of the study. The secretary had no contact with the subjects, data collectors, or statistician. Intercessors were requested to pray daily over the following 28 days.[11]

As no standard scales exist for the assessment of CCU cardiac status or progress, the researchers developed their own scales, and also used the scale from the study by Byrd.

Results: On the AHMI-CCU scales, the E group scored 10 to 11 percent improvements ($p < .04$). No significant differences were noted between E and C groups on the Byrd hospital course scores, although there was a trend in favor of the E group.

Interestingly, median hospital stay was 4 days and no significant differences were noted between the two groups.

Authors' Comments: It is puzzling why no significant effects were noted in this study on the Byrd scores. One possibility is that in Byrd's study the informed consent resulted in 12.7 percent of the patients refusing to participate, making the Byrd subjects a self-selected group. In the Byrd study the intercessors were given the diagnoses, severity of illness, and progress notes on subjects throughout the hospital stay and prayers were sent only until the time of discharge. In this study, no information was provided to the intercessors other than subjects' names. Prayers were sent for 28 days in every case, regardless of length of hospitalization.

A randomized, controlled trial of the effects of remote, intercessory prayer on outcomes in patients admitted to the coronary care unit (Archives of Internal Medicine 1999)

A modest but significant effect of distant healing is demonstrated in this study. However, it is difficult to know how to evaluate very limited effect with an assessment scale that has not been validated. Rating I.

Significant effects of distant healing are again demonstrated in patients on a cardiac intensive care unit.

There were differences between this study and the study of Byrd, in the information given to patients (and consequently in the selection of patients), in the information provided to healers, in the number of days during which healing was sent, and in the assessment scales that demonstrated significant differences. The scale used by Byrd did not show significant effects in this study.

Another significant aspect of the studies of Byrd and of Harris et al is that they are published in respected, conventional American medical journals. Until recently, mast medical journals would routinely reject articles on spiritual healing.

These significant effects of distant healing introduce Newtonian medicine to the action of mind from a distance, "non-local consciousness" (Dossey 1993). One would hope that the benefits of such an inexpensive intervention would appeal to those who are claiming concern over the high costs of medical care.

Many people feel that there is a distinction between prayer healing and healing done outside of religious settings or frameworks. As yet there is no research which would validate this view.

The specter of a global increase in AIDS is very worrisome. While palliative therapies are available, many of these have negative side effects and as of this writing no curative treatments have been found.
    It is helpful to have two exploratory studies of healing for AIDS.

Advanced AIDS and Distant Healing

Fred Sicher, Elisabeth Targ, Dan Moore, and Helene S. Smith

To examine the effects of distant healing on people who have advanced AIDS,[12] this randomized, double-blind study was done through the California Medical Center's Complementary Medicine Research Institute. The 40 volunteers (37 men, three women) all received regular medical care at several medical centers and were randomly divided into two groups to receive either distant healing or no healing. Healing was sent by 40 healers who lived in various parts of the United States and came from several religious backgrounds, including Christianity, Buddhism, and a number of shamanic traditions. All of the healers had at least five years' healing experience and were accustomed to distant healing. The healing lasted 10 weeks, and healers were randomly rotated throughout. Subjects and doctors were blind as to who was receiving healing and when.

At the outset, there were no significant differences between the experimental and control groups. After six months, the experimental group had significantly fewer AIDS-related illnesses (modest significance: $p < .04$) and lower severity of illness (modest significance: $p < .02$). Visits to doctors and hospitalizations were less frequent and days in hospital were also lower, all to a significant level. Improvements in mood were also noted ($p < .04$).[13]

A randomized, double-blind study of the effects of distant healing in a population with advanced AIDS (*Western Journal of Medicine*, 1998)

This excellent study demonstrates significant effects of healing on AIDS.

No comparisons were made regarding medical treatment for different patients at various participating medical centers, although treatments were given with a standard combination of medications. It is theoretically possible that the experimental group might have received some medical treatment that gave them an advantage over the control group. However, there is no known conventional medical treatment that can produce the results seen here. Rating: II

It is particularly encouraging to have a study showing significant benefits of distant healing for AIDS. I hope this study will encourage replicating research. It would be particularly helpful to have research with a tighter design, having both experimental and control groups treated at the same center under the same treatment regimen.

AIDS and Therapeutic Touch

Clare Thomasson Garrard

Clare Garrard explored the effects of Therapeutic Touch (TT) and mock (simulated) Therapeutic Touch (MTT) treatments on 20 men between the ages of 22 and 34 who were HIV positive.[14] A TT healer with six years' experience administered treatments for 20 minutes to the men in the TT group. The healer used five minutes for assessing the energy field and the rest of the time for treatment. Subjects all wore headphones and sleep masks so that they would not be aware of the presence of the healer. In the MTT group, the healer entered the room silently and stayed there for 20 minutes without giving healing. Subjects were matched and randomized to either TT or MTT.

To measure the healing effects, CD4 cell (a type of white blood cell deficient in people with AIDS) counts were made before the treatments, and then at three, six, and nine weeks after. As well, a test that measures the ability to cope with stress was given before treatment and after nine weeks. Stress has been shown to contribute to the deterioration of health in HIV-positive people.

By week nine, the two groups showed significant differences in CD4 counts, ($p < .05$) as well as in resources for coping with stress ($p < .001$).

***The Effect of Therapeutic Touch on Stress Reduction and Immune Function in Persons with AIDS* (Immune Deficiency) (doctoral dissertation, Birmingham: University of Alabama, 1996)**

This study demonstrates that Therapeutic Touch has significant effects on white blood cell counts and on stress reduction. MTT subjects may have had greater stress then TT subjects. Though it does not confirm that Therapeutic Touch is effective in the long-term treatment of AIDS, it does appear promising. Rating: IV

Garrard's study is of great importance because thus far there have been no effective treatments for AIDS. It is of particular note because stress contributes to the deterioration of health in HIV positive people, and HIV illness is very stressful. A treatment which can improve both aspects of this disease with no known side effects is most welcome.

Anxiety and stress bring about changes in the immune system. Changes in circulating immune proteins such as immune globulins (Ig) and lymphocytes may thus provide measures of physiological stress responses, as in the following study.

Stress, the Immune System, and Therapeutic Touch

Melodie Olson, Nancee Sneed, Mariano LaVia, Gabriel Virella, and Ramita Bonadonna

The researchers anticipated that students about to take their professional board examinations would be highly stressed and would show changes to their immune systems. This study tested whether or not Therapeutic Touch (TT) could influence the students' immune systems, compared with students who did not receive the treatment. A group of 22 medical and nursing students were randomly divided into experimental and control groups, while stress and immune function were measured with standard tests at three points during the experiment. Three TT treatments were given by an experienced practitioner. The control group had no intervention.

Experimental and control groups showed comparable levels of stress at the beginning of the study. After treatment, on the day before exams, there were modestly significant differences ($p < .05$) for the three immune system values measured.

The experimenters note that dietary intake might have had an influence on the outcome, along with the presence of a caring person (the practitioner) for the experimental group, a presence missing from the control group.

Stress-Induced Immunosuppression and Therapeutic Touch
(*Alternative Therapies,* 1997)

This was a well-designed and well-reported study, with a significant effect on the immune system, all the more impressive for the small numbers in the study. As the authors note, the relaxing factor of the caring person cannot be eliminated as a cause of the changes. Rating: IV

The results of this study are a good start at confirming a healing effect on the immune system. Further suggestive evidence can be found in the animal studies on qigong healing reviewed later in this chapter and in the study of Quinn and Strelkauskas in Chapter 5.

In England healing is finding increasing use by general practitioners. Some refer patients to healers, and others, like Michael Dixon, have invited healers to work in their offices. This study suggests ways in which healing can be helpful in clinical practice.[15]

Healing and Chronic Symptoms
Michael Dixon

Following a successful pilot study,[16] Dixon studied 57 people with chronic problems in a clinic where he works with seven other primary care physicians. The patients had an assortment of physical and psychological conditions that had been present at least six months. The nurse assigned alternating patients to either the experimental group or the control group. The experimental group received 10 weeks of healing from healer Gill White for 40 minutes each week. After discussing the healee's health with each, White passed her hands over that person's body while visualizing white light passing through her to the person. The control group received standard medical care and then received healing 12 or 24 weeks later, after the study was completed. Standardized tests were used to assess physical and mental function; immune functions were measured through assays of natural killer cells (CD 16 and CD 56.)

After three months, the experimental group scored significantly better on symptom scores (modest significance: $p < .05$). At six months, no significant differences were found in the immune cells. On the several self-assessment tests, the experimental group showed consistently higher scores. **Does 'healing' benefit patients with chronic symptoms? A quasi-randomized trial in general practice** *(Journal of the Royal Society of Medicine, 1998)*

Significant effects of healing are demonstrated for patients in general practice. However, the lack of randomization and the failure to impose blinds leaves the results of this study open to questions. Rating: IV

Most patient visits are to a general practitioner. Dixon's study is very encouraging, showing that a wide variety of chronic problems can respond to healing. The study also confirms the impression of healers and other wholistic practitioners that quality of life is enhanced with healing, despite the fact that symptomatic improvements may not be effected or maintained over a long period of time.

The fact that the immune cells did not respond to healing is an important finding. Healers speculate that healing probably enhances immune system functioning. This study suggests that if that is so, it is not generically so. It is more likely, in view of the studies showing significant effects of healing on immune cells in AIDS, that healing enhances immune functions when there is a specific need for this enhancement.

The next four TT studies explore healing effects on hemoglobin, a protein found in red blood cells, carrying oxygen to every cell in the body. These were done by Dolores Krieger, one of the originators of this method of healing, and are some of the most frequently cited in the spiritual healing literature.

Human Hemoglobin Levels and Therapeutic Touch
Dolores Krieger

Dolores Krieger was intrigued by Bernard Grad's 1965 research[17] suggesting an increase in chlorophyll in plants that were watered with healer- treated water. She hypothesized that hemoglobin levels in humans could also be increased through spiritual healing, since hemoglobin is chemically similar to chlorophyll.

In the first three of four experiments, Krieger employed Oscar Estebany, the Hungarian healer studied in Grad's experiments. In a fourth experiment, she used as healers 32 nurses who were taught to do Therapeutic Touch.[18] In all four, Krieger reports significant increases in her experimental groups (from $p < .01$ to $p < .001$), as opposed to her control groups.

Therapeutic Touch: the imprimatur of nursing *(American Journal of Nursing,* 1975); **Healing by the "laying-on" of hands as a facilitator of bioenergetic change: the response of in-vivo human hemoglobin** (*Psychoenergetic Systems,* 1976)

Krieger's pioneering studies show that spiritual healing in humans is effective. However, the studies suffer from a lack of details regarding the Therapeutic Touch treatments and data on the results. Moreover, she does not say how long the effects lasted, nor do we know whether or not the results were clinically significant.[19] Rating: III

Scientists are always skeptical about research reports, particularly when they involve a therapy that is new or unfamiliar to them. Even though a given study may suggest that healing is effective, there might have been unusual, unnoticed conditions which produced the observed results of TT healing on hemoglobin in Krieger's studies. The laboratory may have made errors in measurements, the researcher may have made errors in calculations, and so on. It is therefore extremely important for studies to be replicated by independent scientists. The next study is a replication of the first one, using a different form of healing.

Human Hemoglobin Levels and Reiki
Wendy S. Wetzel

Wendy Wetzel replicated Krieger's work, using Reiki,[20] a different form of healing. Wetzel's subjects were a self-selected sample of 48 adults who were taking Reiki training in California. A blood sample was drawn for each of the 48, then they were given first-degree Reiki training. A second blood sample was drawn 24 hours after the first. Two blood samples were similarly taken 24 hours apart from a control group of ten healthy medical professionals who were also involved with Reiki.

Wetzel notes that her study is limited by a lack of randomization, a small control group, and a lack of blinds for the experimenter who performed the fingersticks and read the hemoglobin and hematocrit values. She reports a significant change in both hemoglobin and hematocrit values for the experimental group at the level of p < .01, while the control group demonstrated no significant change.

Reiki healing: a physiologic perspective (*Journal of Holistic Nursing*, 1989)

Again, an effect of healing on hemoglobin is demonstrated, but it is difficult to assess the importance of Wetzel's observation, as there is no differentiation here between Reiki training and Reiki healing treatments. The implication is that in learning to activate their own healing gifts, the healers also activated their own self-healing mechanisms. The healers may also have received healing from their teacher through the process of inducting them into the Reiki healer state. The lack of randomization may have introduced unknown biasing factors. Rating: IV

These studies suggest further positive answers to the question, "Does healing work?" Significant effects of healing on hemoglobin are demonstrated in Krieger's and Wetzel's studies.

However, it isn't clear how meaningful these changes are. There can be statistical significance of a study while there is not a whole lot of clinical significance. In other words, there might be small changes which we can definitely identify but which wouldn't make a whole lot of difference in terms of a person's health. Regarding hemoglobin levels, further studies must be done on people with too little and too much hemoglobin to see whether their clinical conditions are improved as a result of the changes.

If valid, these studies suggest one possible mechanism whereby healing may improve health. With anemia the lack of oxygen-carrying capacity of the blood can weaken an organism. If the anemia is corrected, then the blood can carry increased oxygen to the tissues and organs of the body, helping one maintain health and fight off all sorts of illnesses.

The decreases of hemoglobin in Wetzel's study are unusual and unexpected. My personal experience and observations contributed by others indicate that Reiki seeks to return us to whatever physical state is most beneficial and in the greatest harmony. Snel and Hol found decreases in hemoglobin in a study of healing for amyloidosis in mice.[21] Interestingly, a study of healing on red blood cell cultures produced effects in both directions.[22]

W. H. Sullivan observed, "It is much easier to make measurements than to know exactly what you are measuring."

Healers believe that spiritual healing harmonizes the body's functions, facilitating and enhancing ordinary body processes so that the best possible physiological state of health is achieved. It is difficult to comprehend the functional benefits of a decrease in hemoglobin and hematocrit to the well-being of normal individuals. This suggests that conventional medicine might yet find benefits in a re-examination of the ancient treatment of bleeding, which was discredited as an effective treatment in a study of an influenza epidemic in the middle of the nineteenth century. It may be that there are problems other than influenza for which bleeding is helpful. It is of course helpful in polycythemia, a condition in which excessive numbers of red blood cells are produced. It may be helpful in other conditions as well, or there may be more people suffering from polycythemia than we appreciate.

Surgery is stressful. Healers claim healing can help people come through surgery with less debilitation from physical and emotional stress and pain. The next two studies explore this possibility. Relaxation touch, a relatively new method, was the focus of the first study.

Abdominal Hysterectomy and Relaxation Touch

Concepcion Silva

Relaxation touch is an "energy-based technique . . . consisting of modulation and stimulation of the patient's energy," with the investigator in a meditative state. This study examined 60 patients who had undergone abdominal hysterectomy,[23] ages ranging from 35 to 65. They were randomly assigned to one of three groups, receiving either relaxation touch for 20 minutes, a 20-minute back rub by the investigator, or no treatment. Recovery was measured with the Recovery Index developed by Silva.

Relaxation touch produced earlier recovery (particularly in the pulmonary and gastrointestinal systems) than either of other conditions in the study, with highly significant results after one ($p < .00005$), two ($p < .0001$) and three ($p < .00005$) treatments.

The effects of relaxation touch on the recovery level of postanesthesia abdominal hysterectomy patients (Summary: *Alternative Therapies in Health and Medicine*, 1996)

A benefit of relaxation touch is demonstrated. However, blinds are not mentioned for those assessing the status of the subjects, nor are raw data presented, and it is difficult to assess the study's validity without these. Further, the massage group had, on the whole, longer times in surgery, and this could account for their poorer responses. Rating: IV

Here we find evidence that healing may be effective in relaxing surgical patients, but too few details were presented to allow for full assessment of validity.

The following pilot study was done by Zvi Bentwich, an Israeli doctor I met when he was working in America.[24] Bentwich started out a complete skeptic but felt the research that had been done on animals deserved to be extended to humans. He was kind enough to credit me for designing the study protocol, the results of which he presented to my pleasant surprise at a wholistic medicine conference in Israel at which I was invited to present my work.

Surgical Recovery and Distant Healing

Zvi Bentwich, S. Kreitler, R. Pfeffermann, and Daniel J. Benor

This Israeli study examined 53 men recovering from inguinal hernia surgery. The men were divided into three groups to receive distant healing (from 30 miles away), suggestion (administered through taped messages), and no additional treatment. The study was double blind, except for the suggestion group.

The healing group did significantly better than the other groups, according to nine major variables used in the study (modest significance: $p < .05$).

Effect of distant healing on recovery from surgery (*Presentation at 2nd International Dead Sea Conference on the Anatomy of Well-Being, Tiberias, Israel, 1993*)

The study demonstrates a healing effect in enhancing recuperation from surgery. However, Bentwich provides too few details to allow confidence in this report. He prefers not to publicize his results until he is certain that they are replicable. Rating: III

The next series of experiments deals with the effects of healing on autonomic functions of the human body, such as blood pressure.

Hypertension and Remote Healing

Robert N. Miller

To examine the effectiveness of remote healing on hypertension, researcher Miller brought together eight healers and 96 patients in a study that was double-blind and randomized, except for an attempt to maintain male/female balance in the control and experimental groups. Measurements focused on diastolic and systolic blood pressure, pulse, and body weight.

Four healers used Science of Mind methods, including relaxation, visualization, and attunement with a higher power. For these four, there was highly significant ($p < .014$) improvement in systolic blood pressure for the experimental group over the control group. There were no significant differences in the other measured factors. Not enough of the patients treated by the four other healers returned for post-treatment blood pressure measurements to permit statistical analysis.

Study of absent psychic healing on hypertension (*Medical Hypotheses*, 1982)

This study supports the idea that healing is helpful for treating hypertension. Even a modest reduction in blood pressure can be clinically helpful, both directly and in reducing needed medication. One serious flaw in the study is that prescribed medications given to the patients are not mentioned. These could have produced the differences between the groups. Further, it is a questionable practice to select only the best results for analysis without reporting the rest. Rating: V

Anxiety and Therapeutic Touch

Janet F. Quinn

Quinn studied the effects of Therapeutic Touch on anxiety.[25] In a *post hoc* review of her results, diastolic blood pressure was reduced (highly significant: p < .007). In the study, no prediction had been made about diastolic pressure, since it usually remains constant while systolic pressure usually varies with stress.

Therapeutic Touch as energy exchange (*Nursing Science Quarterly*, 1989)

Since diastolic pressure is not greatly influenced by anxiety, this finding may indicate that healing reduces hypertension by means other than relieving anxiety. Strict research methodology proscribes acceptance of *post hoc* findings. Further, insufficient data is presented to know if the finding is clinically significant. Results could also reflect different medications given to the experimental and control groups, as well as the timing of medication use in different subjects. Rating: IV

Ethel Lombardi (1982), a Reiki Master, reports that iliac pulses transiently disappear periodically during her healings. I have witnessed this phenomenon. When testing for blood pressure changes during and immediately after healing, measurements ought to be continuous or frequent.

Hypertension and Paranormal Healing

Jaap J. Beutler, Johannes T. M. Attevelt, et al.

Chosen according to specific research criteria from a group of 587 volunteers, 120 patients with hypertension were placed into three groups based on their levels of systolic blood pressure. Each group was in turn divided into three subgroups: those receiving no healing; those receiving distant healing from behind one-way mirrors (so that neither patients nor experimenters knew who was receiving healing); and those receiving laying-on of hands. Twelve healers, all members of Dutch healer societies, participated.

Results were mixed, with no single treatment consistently better than the other. After 15 weeks of treatment, 83 percent of the patients in the first group felt improved well-being, compared with 43 percent in the second group, and 41 percent in the third group.

Paranormal healing and hypertension (*British Medical Journal*, 1988)

Healing may have produced the greater well-being in the laying-on of hands group. Subjective improvement may have been due to psychosocial or suggestion factors related to the presence of the healer. The study appears to have been carefully performed, but shows no results for healing on hypertension. Rating: I

A study by Catherine Leb on healing for depression[26] also found mild effects of healing on systolic blood pressure in subjects without hypertension.

These studies of healing on blood pressure leave us with inconclusive results. Anecdotal reports from numerous healers indicate that blood pressure appears to respond to healing. Many healees are able to reduce the amounts of antihypertensive medications they take, and some are even able to discontinue medication. Perhaps the results of these three studies indicate that in hypertension it is suggestion and self-healing which are effective, more than spiritual healing. The exclusion of patients with complications of hypertension may have removed those who would have responded best to healing. Healing often appears to be most effective where serious needs for healing exist.[27]

Healing frequently relaxes healees. Relaxation may lower blood pressure. Spiritual healing might thus help indirectly by reducing the stress response, which then lowers the blood pressure.

This speculation may find support in the studies of Byrd and Harris, et al, where highly significant effects of healing were noted on patients hospitalized for heart problems.

Asthma and bronchitis have been reported by many healers to respond to healing. The next study investigates this application of healing.

Asthma and Healing

Johannes T. M. Attevelt

In a design similar to that of the Beutler, Attevelt, et al. study, this study looked at the effect of healing on 90 patients with asthma and/or asthmatic bronchitis. Severity of asthma was measured by examining breath volume and flow rate. Patients also reported on other aspects of their asthma, including the frequency of attacks, the color of sputum, and further details.

The most important outcome of this study was a lack of significant differences among the control group, the laying-on of hands group, and the distant healing group.

***Research into Paranormal Healing* (doctoral dissertation, University of Utrecht, The Netherlands, 1988)**

The lack of results of the study may reflect possible experimenter bias, since the authors appear skeptical about distant healing. As well, the fixed duration of healing treatments, 15 minutes, does not follow the general practice of healing, in which the length of treatment varies according to the types of healing done. The study is meticulously designed and described, except that effects in the distant healing group are not delineated. It is flawed by the lack of blinds for the experimenters. No evidence is found for healing, beyond that produced by suggestion or expectation. Rating: IV

It is difficult to know why some studies show no effects of healing. Believers will say there must have been negative confounds. Skeptics will say that this reflects the true worth of healing.

It may seem unfair to criticize studies for limiting the duration of healing treatments when some experiments show significant effects with only 5 to 15 minutes of treatment. I believe the criticism is valid because some healers may be able to produce effects within a brief period and others may need a longer time.

Mothers of premature infants often have difficulties with milk letdown. They express milk manually from their breasts with a suction pump because their babies are often in incubators and in any case cannot suck as vigorously as babies born at term.

Breast Feeding and Therapeutic Touch

Cynthia A. Mersman

Mersman looked at the effect of Therapeutic Touch (TT) on mothers of premature infants. She wanted to see if mothers who received the treatment would give milk with greater letdown, quantity, and fat content than would women who received no treatment or a fake (mock) TT. The study looked at 18 mothers of diverse racial and ethnic background. Mothers kept diaries of their breast feeding, and at the end of the study answered questionnaires and graded their perceptions of their babies on a standard scale.

Statistical analysis showed no significant difference among the three groups in amount of expressed milk or its fat content. Supplementary analysis showed that significantly more milk was expressed by the TT group than the other groups (modest significance: $p < .05$).

***Therapeutic Touch and Milk Let Down in Mothers of Non-nursing Preterm Infants* (doctoral dissertation, New York University, 1993)**[28]

The study finds a significant effect of Therapeutic Touch, though Mersman does not specify what "supplementary analyses" are. One must be skeptical of analyses made on a *post hoc* basis rather than through the procedures set out in the original study design. Rating III.

Chemotherapy can severely reduce the quality of life of people who may have only a short while to live. It can directly cause nausea, stomach cramps, vomiting, diarrhea, headaches, dizziness, dysmenorrhea, edema, weakness, and hair loss, and can indirectly cause anxiety and depression. The symptoms are so severe and unpleasant that treatments are usually interrupted for several weeks of rest, so that body and spirit can recover before treatments are continued. Once they experience these symptoms, even the anticipation of receiving chemotherapy can evoke the same symptoms.

Anecdotal reports indicate that healing can reduce or eliminate many of these negative effects. It is good to have a study that begins to confirm this benefit of healing.

The Anticipatory Effects of Chemotherapy with Therapeutic Touch and Relaxation

Kathleen Anne Sodergren

Sodergren looked at the possibility of using Therapeutic Touch (TT), nonevaluative information, and progressive relaxation to help overcome the vomiting and nausea that patients often undergo before receiving chemotherapy, symptoms that they anticipate will occur during chemotherapy. The subjects were 80 people who had undergone anticipatory nausea and vomiting in their courses of chemotherapy. They were randomly assigned to one of four groups in the study. The three kinds of treatment were made over three cycles of chemotherapy, and the subjects assessed themselves regarding a number of criteria.

Nonevaluative information and TT increased positive affect and decreased the severity of symptoms after chemotherapy. TT and relaxation lessened symptom distress before and after chemotherapy.

The Effect of Absorption and Social Closeness on Responses to Educational and Relaxation Therapies in Patients with Anticipatory Nausea and Vomiting During Cancer Chemotherapy (doctoral dissertation, University of Minnesota, 1993)[28]

Possibly significant effects of healing are demonstrated. It is impossible to assume that true effects are demonstrated with the brief report available, particularly without statistical data. Rating: III

It is not surprising, in view of the studies showing healing effects on anxiety and depression, that these effects of healing would be of help to people receiving chemotherapy.

It is a sad commentary on conventional medical care that healing is not used more widely with toxic chemotherapies. Even when hospital staff know how to give healing, they may not feel safe to do so because of the skepticism and criticisms of their peers, which could even jeopardize their jobs and careers.

One nurse who worked in a setting that is hostile to healing found a way around this. She quietly gave healing to the chemotherapy IV bottles prior to hooking them up to patients' veins. Her patients had far fewer side effects than those of other nurses. This was noticed by her supervisor, who even checked to see that she was correctly following the procedures for administering chemotherapy. Her supervisor simply could not understand what was going on!

Even when we have further, confirmatory studies of these benefits of healing, it will probably take a while for conventional medicine to offer healing instead of giving other medications to handle the side effects of the chemotherapy.

The following study is of clinical interest but has serious faults in its design and the limited details provided in the report. It may be a victim of limited publication options and poor reporting of the results included here. In any event, this pilot study of leukemia is of interest because of its subject.

Leukemia and Prayer

P.J. Collipp

Ten families in a church prayer group were asked to pray daily for ten leukemic children. The ten children were randomly chosen from a group of 18 and were given otherwise routine medical treatment. Neither treating physicians, patients, nor the praying families knew they were participating in this study. Evaluations were made by doctors and parents on unstated criteria and at unstated intervals. Results were not significant.

The efficacy of prayer: a triple-blind study (*Medical Times*, 1969)

The study of cancer in humans is critically important. Unfortunately this study is so flawed as to be useless. The results of the study are not statistically significant. Weaknesses of the study include: unstated criteria and measurement intervals, a small number of patients, and different chemotherapy for different patients, possibly affecting the outcomes. In addition, leukemia includes many varieties of blood cancers. Some of these respond very well to chemotherapy. Some have been reported in rare instances to remit under self-healing approaches. Healers have also reported favorable responses. Considering all of the variables that were not controlled in this study, we await a well-designed study of healing for leukemia. Rating: V

Overall, the evidence from controlled studies for healing of physical problems is strongest though still modest, for cardiovascular problems in an intensive care unit and for AIDS; and modest for surgical problems and for a spectrum of problems in general practice. Because of problems in research design and reporting, it is only suggestive for hypertension, and changes in hemoglobin levels.

Qigong healing, taught by masters in Chinese healing, is for the most part self-healing through mental focus and physical exercise (K. Cohen 1997; Kuang et al.). A biological energy called qi (pronounced chi) has been recognized over many centuries as the active component of acupuncture. Qi is a life force which flows through the body. Qigong masters may also give healing by transmission of external qi (waiqi), again using combinations of mental focus with physical movements.

Kenneth Sancier, a senior scientist in the Materials Research Laboratory of SRI International, and Vice President of the Qigong Institute at the East West Academy of Healing Arts, has an extensive database of research on qigong. These studies were reported at international conferences on qigong, and are mostly from China. With Sancier's kind permission, I include here several studies of external qi treatments.

Sancier's qigong summaries are inserted at the ends of appropriate sections with a minimum of comments because so many questions are raised by the limited information provided in the original reports.[29] Some of these studies might be of a level equal to studies included earlier in this chapter, if attention was given to randomization, if blinds for the animal handlers and laboratory staff counting cells were included, if data and methods of data analysis were included in the reports, and if methodologies were adequately described.

Although the studies may not be up to Western standards, they point to ways in which healing may act upon people, animals, microorganisms, and cells. There are more studies from China than can reasonably be included in this chapter. The breadth of scope of these studies is witness to the enigmatic, wakening giant China.[30]

There are various ways of studying blood flow. One of them, a laser Doppler flow meter, showed positive effects of healing in this next study.

Human Physiology and Qigong

Ruijuan Xiu, Xiaoyou Ying, Jun Cheng, Chouggao Duan; Tao Tang
Institute of Microcirculation, CAMS, Beijing

During a test of qigong, a computerized measurement system was used to examine a number of body parameters, including heart rate, respiration, blood pressure, and skin microcirculatory blood flow (SMBF). Of all the parameters measured, the most significant effect of qigong was on the SBMF of both the qigong master and recipients of qigong (modest significance: p < .05).

Studies of qigong effect on the human body [via] macro and micro-circulatory parameters measurement (*1st World Conference for Academic Exchange of Medical Qigong, Beijing,* 1988—from qigong database of Sancier.)

The dilation of blood vessels in the skin with qigong healing tends to confirm healers' reports that healees feel relaxed and flush when receiving healing. It may also explain reports of heat sensations during healing.

Acupuncture treatment is given at points along meridians (energy lines) which run the length of the body. All of the points have reference numbers and many have names such as the *Laogong* point on the palm of the hand. Qigong healers focus on emitting qi energy from particular acupuncture points on their hands (and sometime on other parts of their bodies), directing the energies to acupuncture points on the healee's body.

Changes in Skin Temperature and the Practice of Qigong

Tokuo Ogawa, Shigemi Hayashi, Norihiko Shinoda; Norkazu Ohnishi-Aichi Medical University, Japan/Chinese-Japanese Institute of Qigong, Japan/Shakti Acupuncture Clinic, Japan/Aichi Medical University, Japan

This study used an infrared color thermograph to measure skin temperatures of two qigong masters and several volunteers of both sexes who received the emitted qi. The skin temperatures of the palm and fingers elevated after the start of qigong, with temperatures rising as much as 4° C in three to four minutes.

Changes of skin temperature during emission of qi (*1st World Conference for Academic Exchange of Medical Qigong, Beijing,* 1988, from qigong database of Sancier)

Is it dilation of capillaries that produces sensations of heat or is it a subtle energy? Western studies have not shown increased skin temperatures with healing.

Nearsightedness and Qigong

Guo and Ni

Eighty myopic (nearsighted) children aged 12 to 15 were selected randomly from an ophthalmology clinic. They were divided into four groups: the first received no treatment, the second placebo eye drops, the third instruction in the practice of qigong meditation, and the fourth received treatment by a qigong master. The first two groups showed no improvement; in the third, two improved; in the fourth, 16 improved.

Study of Qigong in treatment of myopia (near-sightedness) Cited in: (David Eisenberg with Thomas Lee Wright, *Encounters with Qi*, 1985)

The study appears to show a significant healing effect on myopia. Unfortunately however, too few details are reported, and the research is unconvincing.

A similar study by Wengguo Huang showed that qigong treatments for hypermetropia (long-sightedness) were effective, and that improvements continued for weeks following treatments.

Healing of myopia is also reported in America. Jacob Liberman, an ophthalmologist, and a few other pioneering researchers have shown that visual perception may be altered through various self-healing exercises, some of them taken from Chinese traditions. Liberman finds that vision is not limited by the physical apparatus of the eye but is often limited by the psychological mind-set of the people he treats. When they release the fears of looking at various aspects of their lives, past and present, and relax into a state of allowing the eyes to see rather than forcing them to focus, their vision may improve dramatically.

Liberman himself has improved his vision from 20/200 to better than 20/20.

This appears to be a psychological self-healing rather than an energy healing, although the mechanisms for this might involve the energy body.

In Eastern Europe healing was frowned upon by the communist authorities when they were in power, especially if it was used with any connotations of spirituality. Healers and researchers had to use terminology which was culturally neutral, so they coined the term bioenergotherapy, referring to the biological energy field that is apparent around the bodies of humans and other organisms. They drew support from Kirlian photography, which was developed and widely used in Eastern Europe. This electrophotographic technique shows an apparent energy field around living things. The auras of color in Kirlian photography and related photographic techniques have been interpreted as reflecting the states of health and illness of plants and animals.[31]

The next study comes to us from Eastern Europe. It explores healing effects on epilepsy and on the electroencephalogram (EEG), which measures the electrical brainwave activity.

Epilepsy and Bioenergytherapy

Ewa Purska-Rowinska and Jerzy Rejmer

Bioenergotherapy was used with 42 epileptic patients. There was a definite reduction in the severity of epileptic attacks, with no change in frequency. No distinct alterations in the EEGs were noted. Some improvement was seen in mood, with increased talkativeness in adult patients.

The effect of bioenergotherapy upon EEG tracings and on the clinical picture of epileptics (*Psychotronika*, 1985)

Though this translated report is too brief for proper assessment, it is encouraging to learn that healing may be a helpful adjunct for treatment of epileptics.

Extensive anecdotal observations of synchronizations of EEGs between healers and healees have been reported by Maxwell Cade and Geoffrey Blundell. Sometimes the EEG patterns of healers and healees will lock into an identical pattern during the time of healing. These observations are fascinating, but it is impossible as yet to know what they indicate. The obvious suggestion is that a resonation or harmonization of biological energies occurs which may enable healers to suggest or induce changes in their healees. Much further research will be required to clarify how this works and whether the synchronization is a primary, causal interaction or a secondary effect of other processes.

A growing body of research shows that the brainwaves of healers and of healees may become synchronized during healings.

Emitted Qi and Spectrum Analysis of the Brain

Desong Li, Qinfei Yang, Xiaoming Li, and Jiming Shi, Institute Qigong Science, Beijing College of Traditional Chinese Medicine, Beijing

"It is still disputable as to whether or not a qigong master can emit qi to influence others without any psychological suggestion. The spectrum analysis is a technique for the study of brain function." In these experiments, the EEGs of a qigong master and twelve normal subjects who took part in the experiments were synchronously recorded. The study was so designed that psychological suggestion was prevented. A second group received a form of mock qi.

The qigong master and the recipients of qi both showed statistically significant elevation in the beta frequency section, while the mock qi group showed no obvious change.

Spectrum analysis effect of emitted qi on EEG on normal subjects (*2nd World Conference for Academic Exchange of Medical Qigong, Beijing 1993*—from qigong database of Sancier)

Synchronization of EEGs of healers and healees during healing suggest some sort of resonation occurring between them. Healers and healees often sense heat, tingling, vibrations, and other sensations during the laying-on of hands. This is often interpreted as an energy exchange. Numerous Western scientists have measured a broad spectrum of electromagnetic radiations without consistent findings of emissions from healers that might be correlated with healings.

Researchers in China are reporting that infrasonic sound[32] is emitted from acupuncture points on the healer's body, and that this may be, at least in part, what produces healing effects.

Lu Yan Fang, Ph.D., of the National Electro Acoustics Laboratory in China, recorded infrasonic sound emitted from the hands of qigong masters during external qi healings. She was able to produce healing effects with synthetic infrasonic sound at similar frequencies, reporting benefits for pain, circulatory disturbances, and depression. Infrasonic qigong, based on these explorations, is now being studied in the United States.

Electroencephalograms record the electrical activity of the surface of the brain, relying on electrical contacts which are placed on the scalp. This provides a very crude measure of what is happening in the enormous complexity of the brain. In order to sharpen the focus of this method, it is possible to see what responses are evoked within the extreme complexity of the EEG by a standard, repeated stimulus to the body of the subject (somatosensory evoked potential), as in the following study. The many repetitions of the standard stimulus to the body become identifiable as corresponding electrical responses in the brain. Changes in the evoked response can then be used to check whether qigong influences the nervous system.

The Effects of Emitted Qi and Infrasonic Sound

Xueyen Peng and Guolong Liu; Beijing College of Traditional Chinese Medicine, Beijing

Healthy subjects were exposed to either emitted qi or infrasonic sound. The intensity of the qi was measured at more than 70 dB; the infrasonic sound instrument could generate sound in the range of 60 dB to 90 dB. The subjects' somatosensory evoked potential (SEP) and slow vertex response were measured before, during, and after exposure. An equal number of subjects were examined as a control group.

In changes similar to those produced by medication, the amplitude of most SEP waves changed significantly (p < .01), but the latency of the waves did not change significantly.

**Effect of emitted qi and infrasonic sound on somatosensory evoked potential (SEP) and slow vertex response (SVR) (*1st World Conference* *for Academic Exchange of Medical Qigong, Beijing 1988*—from qigong database of Sancier)

This study suggests that infrasonic sound produced from the healer may be an active force in bringing about changes in nervous system activity. However, there is no evidence in this study that infrasonic sound in itself is able to bring about changes similar to healing. It would also be of great interest to clarify how the healer emits the infrasonic sound.[33]

The studies of the effects of Qigong on EEGs suggest that the nervous system may be the site of primary spiritual healing influence. As the nervous system is one of the main controlling systems in the body, many other effects of healing might be mediated through the brain, spinal cord, the peripheral nerves, and via the neurohormonal and neuroimmunological systems.[34]

Many healers believe that the nervous system is a secondary site of influence for spiritual healing. They sense that there are biological energy fields around the bodies of healers and healees and that these are the primary transformers for healing, bringing the subtle energies of healing from more refined vibrations into more dense vibrations, which can influence the nervous system and then, secondarily, the rest of the body.[35]

It is entirely possible that both theories may be valid, and that healing works through several pathways simultaneously.

It has been suggested that there may be some sort of resonations between healers and healees that puts them in tune with each other and allows healing changes to happen. This might be like a crystal which resonates with a given radio frequency.

EEGs provide a way of checking whether resonations might be occurring in the brains of healers and healees, as explored again in this next report.

Effects of Qigong on Healers and Healees
Masaki Kashiwasake

This Japanese study looked at the EEGs of qigong masters and their normal, healthy male healees during healing. Blood flow, activity in the meridians, biochemical blood tests, and psychological tests were studied under double-blind conditions, as were psychological factors.

> Results showed synchronization between the transmitters and receivers in their EEGs, a remarkable increase in electromagnetic emission from the receiver, and an increase in the number of white blood corpuscles in the transmitter.

Double-blind test of qi transmission from qigong masters to untrained volunteers (*Journal of Mind-Body Science*, 1993)

The report suggests that there may indeed be a resonation between healers and healees, but this brief English translation of a Japanese language report provides too few details to permit assessment of the validity of the findings.

Measuring the Infrasonic Waves from Emitted Qi

Xin Niu, Guolong Liu, and Zhiming Yu; Beijing College of Traditional Chinese Medicine, Beijing

In a search for the physical mechanism behind qi, these Beijing researchers looked at the infrasonic waves that emanated from qigong masters when they were emitting qi. Tests were made in a sound-proof room, with the microphone suspended over the acupuncture point at the center of the hand known as Laogong. The study examined 27 qigong masters, three of whom were female. Individuals who were not qigong masters were examined in a control group.

The study found statistically significant differences between the groups, including exceptionally high-intensity infrasonic emissions from the more seasoned masters. The study showed that the bodies of healers also emit infrasonic sounds at particular acupuncture points

Measurement and analysis of the infrasonic waves from emitted qi (*1st World Conference for Academic Exchange of Medical Qigong, Beijing, 1988*—from the qigong database of Sancier)

It appears that infrasonic sound may be a factor in healing. This study does not show that healing effects are produced by sound, nor does it clarify whether or not qi is emitted from other acupuncture points.[36, 37]

Infrasonic healing

Zhifu Yuan, Family Acupuncture Center, San Clemente, California,

Doctors across the United States are using a device that emits infrasonic sound as a form of simulated qi. Its use has produced results that are not as dramatic as those of leading Chinese qigong masters, but it has apparently been of value. More than 100 doctors who use the simulator regularly in their practice were surveyed about its use. Doctors report patients feel relaxed after using the machine and patients have greater energy and clarity of thinking. The respondents also saw relief from pain and chronic fatigue, and other effects.

Survey of 100 doctors using simulated qigong in the USA (*2nd World Conference for Academic Exchange of Medical Qigong. Beijing, 1993*—from the qigong database of Sancier).

It is still too early to know whether infrasonic sound conveys the total effects of spiritual healing. Anecdotal reports I have heard indicate that only partial healing is brought about by devices that produce infrasonic sound. My expectation is that the human instrument is far more subtle and potent than any other instrument.

I would also question whether the infrasonic devices act purely in and of themselves, or whether they might be variations of radionics devices (instruments which project healing without any known radiation), which are known to be linked to the operators of the devices. That is, the devices seem to amplify the healing of the operators, projecting them to any location around the globe, though many attribute healing powers to the devices themselves.[38] *Clearly, infrasonic waves could not bring about healing effects at a distance of more than a few hundred feet, so they cannot account for the entire range of known and scientifically demonstrated healing effects.*

Western healers generally do not specify parts of their bodies other than their hands as conveyers of healing energies. Chinese healers identify specific acupuncture points on the hands and face for emission of healing energies. One must wonder about qualitative or quantitative differences in energies emitted from the various healers' foreheads and hands, and whether qigong healing differs from Western healing methods in substantial ways.

HEALING FOR SUBJECTIVE EXPERIENCES

Presently, science is not yet able to capture the spirit of life in order to quantify it, but it continues to try to reduce the infinite source of existence into a finite research study.

—Catherine Leb, p. 45

Having reviewed studies on human problems for which there are objective observations and measures, let us consider now a range of problems that are subjective in nature, such as pain and stress. Science tends to be even more cautious of reports of successful healings in these areas. Skeptics are suspicious that these reports merely represent effects of such techniques as relaxation, suggestion, placebo, and hypnosis.[39] Carefully controlled studies are therefore particularly important.

The first series of studies explores the benefits of healing for headaches, back and neck pain, arthritis, surgical pain, and chronic pains of multiple causes.

There is no direct measurement for pain. People may respond very differently to what is apparently a similar injury or other cause of pain, with some reporting excruciating distress and others saying that their pain is modest and tolerable.

Attempts have been made to use objective measures that appear to correlate with pain. For instance, skin resistance (used as the basis for the lie detector test) reflects states of tension and relaxation in the body. Pain generally makes a person tense, so measures of tension should theoretically correlate with intensity of pain. However, there can be great variability in people's skin resistance, in comparing one person to another or even in the same person over a period of time. This makes skin resistance an unreliable indicator of pain. The same is true of measures of muscle tension which bear a rough correlation with subjective pain experiences.

Research shows that people's serial assessments of their own pain over a period of time appear to be reliable indicators of their subjective experiences. A simple way of quantifying pain is to have people put a mark on a 10-centimeter line which is labeled "no pain" at one end and "worst possible pain" at the other end. This sort of Visual Analogue Scale (VAS) is widely used in pain research (McCormack et al.). Several pain questionnaires are also used, relying on a standard series of self-assessment questions.

Pain and Johnston Healing

Robin Redner, Barbara Briner, and Lynn Snellman

B. Johnston (1975) developed a method of healing that begins with the treater's assessment of the bioenergy field around the patient's physical body. Through the hands, "the treater senses only imbalances, (which may evidence as heat, a dense quality, or a sense of blockage), and treats the imbalance by visualizing the energy becoming balanced and free flowing. This visualization continues until the treater senses a change towards balance or the free flow of energy in that area."

With a superficial review of research on Therapeutic Touch (TT), and citing Clark and Clark's (1984) criticisms of the early TT studies, the authors dismiss TT as of unproven value. They feel their study introduces a major improvement by including an attention placebo control group, which is intended to control for expectancy effects and for the relaxation effects that occur when one receives attention from a caring person.

The 47 participants, recruited with ads in local papers, suffered from arthritis, headaches, and low back pain separately or in combination of all three. They must have had the arthritis for six months, or the headaches or backaches for six weeks, and must not have been taking narcotic medications or have been receiving massage, physical therapy, acupuncture or acupressure during the study. They were randomly assigned to experimental or control groups, with equal numbers of each diagnosis in both groups. They were told that there were two possibilities but remaining blind regarding assignment. They were randomly assigned to a treater pair for the duration of the study.

Treaters followed a prescribed treatment regimen for placement of their hands near to but not touching the body, with visualizations of providing more energy or removing excess energy as intuitively perceived to be appropriate.

For the placebo group, treaters made random motions of their hands around subjects' bodies for the same length of time. Treaters engaged in various mental exercises intended to block potential healing energy flows, such as rehearsing multiplication silently.

Participants were assessed before and after healing. Pre- and post-healing physical exams were done by six osteopathic doctors and one advanced medical student, looking at a variety of factors. Assessors were randomly assigned and blind to the experimental or control group assignments. The same assessor was assigned each pre- and post intervention pair of examinations.

Treaters made a "Bioenergy Evaluation," rating such items as energy flow, vitality, and health status of physical organs and systems. They also rated each session, estimating how effective they had been in healing and in mimicking healing. Participants filled out standard self-evaluation tests, and "Manipulation Check" was made by an independent bioenergy treater who had four years' experience, assessing the quality of energies at six major energy centers of several participants selected randomly from High-Intensity and Low-Intensity groups.

Several of the evaluation scales showed modestly significant (p < .05) differences in ratings of pain reduction.

An increase in anxiety in the High-Intensity group is unexplained.

Effects of a bioenergy healing technique on chronic pain,
(Subtle Energies, **1991)**

A well-designed study, well reported. A significant decrease in pain and anxiety, lasting a week, is demonstrated in the healing group.

It is of note that these effects were obtained with healers including some who were only partially trained in the Johnston methods. The authors offer no breakdown of results by level of healer training.

I am not impressed with the authors' assessment of TT as being inferior to the Johnston method. A controlled study would be required to support such claims. Rating: I

Postoperative pain is reasonably well handled by analgesic and narcotic medications. However, these have side effects including drowsiness, unsteadiness, constipation, allergic reactions, and more. Healing may offer a treatment which relieves pain without side effects.

Postoperative Pain and Therapeutic Touch

Therese Connell Meehan

This study compared the effectiveness of five minutes of Therapeutic Touch (TT) healing with routine treatment by pain medication in alleviating pain after "major elective abdominal or pelvic surgery at a major North American urban medical center."

The study was conducted on 74 women and 34 men under the approval of the institutional review boards of both a university and a medical center. Consent was sought from participants, who received an explanation of TT procedures the evening prior to surgery. Subjects were informed that "many nurses who use it believe that it can decrease pain but that this had not been scientifically tested." They were told that they would still have the option to request an injection for pain if the nursing intervention did not provide adequate pain relief.

The 108 who agreed to participate (out of 193 who were approached) were randomly divided into three groups of 36, to receive TT, mock TT (MTT), or standard intervention (SI) alone. Healing was administered by three TT healers, who were nurses with at least two years' experience. MTT was given by seven female registered nurse research assistants who had no previous experience with TT. They were instructed by Meehan in how to move their hands around the body to mimic TT treatment, while counting backwards mentally by sevens. A Visual Analogue Scale (VAS) was used to assess pain immediately prior to and one hour following interventions, timed to coincide with the anticipated period of maximal medication effect, and was administered blindly.

A substantial reduction in pain occurred in the SI group, with a slight reduction in the TT group and no reduction in the MTT group.

Statistical analysis showed SI to be superior to TT and MTT for pain relief. TT just missed showing a significant advantage over MTT (.05 < p < .06). None of the patients in the TT group reported increased pain in the hour after initial assessment, whereas 27 in the MTT and three in the SI groups did. The TT group showed a modestly significant longer duration of pain relief than the MTT group (p < .05).

Therapeutic Touch and Postoperative Pain: a [M. Rogers] Rogerian Research Study (doctoral dissertation, New York University, 1985; *Nursing Science Quarterly,* 1993)

This study was reasonably well designed, considering the constraints of doing healing research in an American hospital at a time when healing still appeared strange to most medical authorities. It suggests that TT healing might offer mild reductions in postoperative pain and extend the time between injections of analgesics. In view of the near significance of the effects of TT on pain, it would seem likely that a replication of this study with larger numbers is warranted.

The negative results may have occurred due to negative suggestions from the research staff regarding the possibilities that the "nursing intervention" might not be effective. As it stands, it appears that healing had less effect on pain than pain medication. Further replications are required before any firm conclusions can be drawn. Rating: I

Meehan replicated her earlier study

Postoperative Pain and Therapeutic Touch

T. C. Meehan, C. A. Mermann, M. E. Wiseman, B. B. Wolff, and R. G. Malgady

This study investigated the effect of Therapeutic Touch on postoperative pain in 159 patients who underwent major elective abdominal or pelvic surgery.

Patients were assigned through a randomized blocking procedure to one of three treatment groups: an experimental group receiving TT, a single blind control group receiving mock Therapeutic Touch (MTT), or a standard control group receiving standard care (no study treatment). "Subjects received the assigned treatment the evening before surgery and seven times during the postoperative period. The number of doses and amount of analgesic medication received over the postoperative period was calculated." Using a Visual Analog Scale, pain "was measured before and at four intervals following one treatment administered in conjunction with a narcotic analgesic on the first postoperative day, . . . and the time lapse calculated until the next analgesic medication was administered."

Subjects who received TT in conjunction with the analgesic waited a significantly longer time before requesting further analgesic medication (p < .01). "No significant difference was found in pain intensity scores during the initial three-hour post-treatment period. Subjects who received Therapeutic Touch requested fewer doses of analgesic and over the entire postoperative period and received less analgesic medication than the control groups, but this decrease was not significant. . . ."

The effect of Therapeutic Touch on postoperative pain (*Pain*, 1990)

It is good to have a replication of research showing that TT healing is significantly effective in prolonging the postoperative efficacy of pain medication.

It would be helpful to have more details, such as the length of time TT was administered and the levels of experience of the healers. The available summary is too brief to permit proper evaluation of its procedures, results, and conclusions. Rating: III

The reduction in total pain medicine used when healing was given together with pain medicine is worthy of further research.[40]

It is curious that in the Meehan et al. study women responded better to the TT compared to the previous study. Perhaps this has to do with the specific types of surgical procedures[41] *that were used on the men and women.*

The next study examined effects of distant healing for pituitary (brain) surgery, which can be very anxiety-provoking in addition to being painful.

Anxiety and Intercessory Prayer

William Michael Green

William Green explored the effects of having 10 people pray from a distance for reduced anxiety and enhanced recovery in 57 people who had pituitary tumor surgery. People praying received the name and date of surgery for each subject but had no contact with subjects. Green simultaneously studied the effects of heightened expectation for recovery in the same subjects.

Subjects were randomly assigned to one of four groups: those receiving distant prayer and enhanced expectations; those with enhanced expectations only; those receiving prayer and normal expectations; and those with normal expectations only.

Green established enhanced expectations through the following statement to subjects selected for the first two groups:

> Since I don't know myself at this point, I cannot tell you if you will be in the experimental prayer group or not. But whether or not you are in that group, it is important for your part in the study to really expect and hope for an enhancement of your recovery process beyond what has been normally predicted based on the fact that you may be included in the experimental prayer group.

To establish normal expectations in the other groups, Green said:

> Since I don't know myself at this point, I cannot tell you if you will be in the experimental prayer group or not. You may be in it and you may not. But whether or not you are in that group, it is important for your part in the study to expect a normal recovery from your surgery as would ordinarily be predicted.

Assignments to distant healing were made by Green after the establishment of normal or enhanced expectations. Green physically left the hospital before making the healing assignments. Strict double-blind procedures were maintained.

Before surgery, no significant differences in levels of anxiety or in beliefs in prayer were found between the groups. For the group that received prayer and enhanced expectations, mean daily pain ratings decreased (highly significant: $p < .001$). For the group with no prayer and normal expectations, ratings also decreased (highly significant: $p < .001$).

Significant decreases in state anxiety were found only in the group that had normal expectations and prayer (highly significant: $p < .0002$).

Decreases in trait anxiety were found in both groups with enhanced expectations, while trait anxiety actually increased in the groups with normal expectations. In the group with prayer and enhanced expectations, the decreases in trait anxiety were of modest significance $p < .023$). The differences between the enhanced and normal expectation groups was also significant ($p < .041$).

The Therapeutic Effects of Distant Intercessory Prayer and Patients' Enhanced Positive Expectations on Recovery Rates and Anxiety Levels of Hospitalized Neurosurgical Pituitary Patients: A Double Blind Study (*doctoral dissertation, California Institute of Integral Studies, San Francisco, 1993*)

A significant effect of distant prayer healing on anxiety is demonstrated in this well-designed and well-reported study. It is unusual to find a change in trait anxiety over a brief time period, as this is meant to be a measure of inherent personality characteristics that relate to anxiety responses.

The small numbers may have limited the significance of the findings. As with Byrd and Harris, there is no way to know whether nonresearch prayers may have been sent to subjects in the control group.

Green also may have missed some instances of objective physical findings by relying on discharge notes rather than on specific questionnaires, which would require notations of presence or absence of the problems. Rating: I

Distant healing appears to be helpful for surgical patients. While some are of the opinion that prayer healing is different from Reiki, LeShan, or other, nonreligious methods, I know of no evidence to support such an assertion. It would be most interesting to explore this question, and not at all difficult to design a study to do so.

*In the next study, people with chronic postoperative pain were given Healing Touch by experienced and inexperienced practitioners, with an interview serving as a control treatment. Each person received all three interventions, but the sequence of interventions was randomized (a **Latin square** research design) so that there would be no systematic bias of the study due to a particular treatment being given first, second, or third.*

Postoperative Pain and Healing Touch

Victoria E. Slater

This study looks at the effects of Healing Touch (HT) on chronic non-malignant pain and examines the experiences of giving and receiving HT. Twenty-three men and women had three sessions: Healing Touch (HT) given by a trained provider, HT given by a naive provider, and a placebo control interview. Subjects acted as their own controls. Thus, treatment order was randomized, rather than the subjects themselves. All had non-malignant post-operative pain lasting more than six weeks after abdominal surgery.

Two standard HT techniques, magnetic unruffling and wound-sealing/ filling, were taught to all trained and naive HT providers via videotape and written instructions. All were female RNs.

The responses to the HT treatments differed from the placebo interview qualitatively at a statistically highly significant level ($p < .0001$), indicating that HT is not a simple placebo. Quantitative and qualitative results comparing the two HT treatments contradicted each other. Quantitatively, subjects had fewer pain sensations after naive HT than after trained HT. Qualitative descriptions of recipients' responses indicated that they experienced relaxation, some pain relief, and various physical sensations during both naive and trained treatments, but more so during treatments by trained HT providers. In addition, recipients reported more unpleasant non-pain sensations such as nausea and headache after receiving trained HT than after naive HT. Three recipients reported total pain relief after trained HT; two of those three were treated by the same nurse. More than half of the trained and naive provider/ recipient pairs reported similar sensations during the treatments. Naive providers reported more uncomfortable sensations while giving treatments than did trained providers.

Both trained and untrained HT providers gave treatments that recipients report as relaxing and pain relieving. The most experienced providers' treatments were followed by the most dramatic and long lasting pain relief. ***The safety, elements, and effects of Healing Touch on Chronic Non-malignant Abdominal Post-operative pain* (doctoral dissertation, University of Tennessee College of Nursing, 1996)**[42]

Significant effects of healing on pain are demonstrated, and Healing Touch appears to be effective even when given by very inexperienced healers.

Skeptics would say that it is difficult to maintain that anything more than suggestion produced the pain relief, when naive "healers" produced as much improvement as trained healers. Rating: I

Headache Pain and Therapeutic Touch

Elizabeth Keller and Virginia M. Bzdek

Elizabeth Keller tested the following hypotheses (1986): Therapeutic Touch (TT) will reduce tension headache pain and the initial reduction will last four hours; TT will be more effective than a placebo simulation of TT, both at the time of intervention and four hours later.

To qualify, the 60 volunteers had to have tension headaches, "defined as dull, persistent head pain, usually bilateral, with feelings of heaviness, pressure, or tightness, which did not involve a prodrome, neurologic deficit, infectious process, or recent head trauma" and had to be free of headache medication during the four hours preceding the study. Patients were randomly assigned to TT or placebo touch groups and were blind regarding their treatments. Subjective experience of headache pain was evaluated on three scales of the McGill-Melzack Pain Questionnaire (MMPQ), which was completed just prior to and five minutes after the treatments.

The researcher gave both the TT and the placebo (mock TT). In the latter she focused her mind on subtraction of sevens from 100, while holding no intent to help in her consciousness. Subjects in both groups sat quietly and were asked to breathe slowly during the five minute procedures.

The effectiveness of TT was supported by the 28 (90 percent) of patients who had reduced headache pain on post-test compared to pre-test scores on all three MMPQ tests, both five minutes and four hours after TT treatments (highly significant: $p < .0001$). The immediate superiority of TT over the placebo simulation was also supported on all three MMPQ tests, but superiority after four hours was not supported in the initial data analysis. Removing from the analysis data of all who used other treatments, highly significant differences between the E and C groups became apparent (p < .005-.01), depending on the MMPQ test).

Effects of Therapeutic Touch on tension headache pain (*Nursing Research, 1986;* E. Keller, master's thesis, University of Missouri, 1983)

This well-designed study shows that healing is effective for headache pain. However, several factors were not reported which might have influenced the study, including the overall duration of the tension headaches and possible use by subjects of medication that was effective for longer than four hours. Either of these factors could have biased the results if present to a greater extent in one group than in the other.[43] Rating: IV

Millions of work days are lost annually due to backaches. While most clear up in a few days or weeks, a significant number persist for months or even years. Many treatments are available, including medications for pain, muscle spasm, and stress; massage to relieve muscle spasms and help to relax tensions; spinal manipulation; and even surgery. Many of these treatments have side effects, such as habituation or addiction to pain medicines. Some carry serious risks of worsening the problems, as with surgery.

For pains of this sort many healers and grateful healees report that healing has much to offer. It is good to see a growing body of research evidence confirming that healing helps to bring about pain relief and relaxation and produces no known dangerous side effects.

Chronic Back Pain and Light-Touch Manipulative Technique

David Dressler

David Dressler developed a technique for spinal manipulation that he claims relieves "muscular hypertonicity and vertebral joint motion dysfunction due to muscular and fascial restriction." Light-Touch Manipulative Technique (LTMT) claims to move displaced vertebrae back into position, and its terminology and conceptualizations seem to derive from chiropractic or osteopathy. In practice it is clearly a form of healing, as the author notes that treatment may be given with the practitioner holding his finger near the body (up to several feet away). Dressler speculates that this may be explained by interactions of the energy fields of the participants.

Dressler solicited subjects for a clinical study of his technique through a newspaper ad for "neck pain/back pain wanted." He offered free professional assessment in return for participation in the study. All 27 subjects had chronic neck and back pain which had been either untreated or had been unresponsive to (unspecified) treatments.

A physiotherapist and chiropractor assessed "each cervical restriction of flexion or extension found between C2 and C7 in every subject before and after the author examined the subject." The assessors did not know which subjects were treated by Dressler and which were in the control group. Assessments for the study were based on motion testing and palpation of the cervical spine. Criteria for improvement are not mentioned. Treatment was given during Dressler's palpation, without subjects' knowledge.

Of the 16 treated subjects, 14 improved. Of the 11 controls, only 4 showed improvement (significant: $p < .01$).

Light Touch Manipulative Technique *(International Journal of Alternative and Complementary Medicine, England,* 1990)

It is fascinating to find a study of healing under a different name and discipline that helps relieve back and neck pain significantly. Dressler's clinical observations parallel those of John Upledger, a craniosacral osteopath.[44]

While patients with both back and neck pain were included, the numbers of each allocated to treatment and control groups are not mentioned, nor is there mention of checks to see that both groups were comparable in severity of initial symptoms. Criteria for assessment of symptoms and of improvement are not described. It is therefore unclear precisely what benefits were produced by LTMT and how valid the study might be. Rating: III

It is fascinating to have numerous anecdotal reports similar to Dressler's from complementary therapists who report heat, tingling, and other sensations during their hands-on treatments.[45] These sensations are identical to those reported by healers.[46] Few of these other therapists are aware of this similarity, and fewer yet will acknowledge it lest they be branded as healers rather than recognized as offering a manipulative therapy. Healing has been considered by many to be a fringe therapy, despite the fact that there are more controlled studies on healing than on all of the other hands-on complementary therapies.[47]

The next study examines the effects of healing on people with chronic pains from several causes. I was particularly pleased to find this study because it is relevant to my personal practice of psychotherapy combined with healing. I find these to be a particularly effective combination of interventions.

Chronic Back Pain, Laying-on of Hands, and Psychotherapy

Jerri Castronova and Terri Oleson

This study explored whether healing by the laying-on of hands would produce significant reductions in pain, somatization, anxiety, and depression compared to supportive psychotherapy or control conditions.

An advertisement in a local newspaper produced 37 volunteers, aged 20 to 60, "whose back pain was not due to spinal abnormalities or congenital spinal defects, and who were not currently in psychotherapy, healing, or seeing a chiropractor." They were randomized into healing (12 subjects), psychotherapy (13), and control (12) groups. All participants underwent standard tests to evaluate psychological distress and pain.

Healing included scanning with the healers' hands through the healees' energy fields to identify where there might be physical or emotional distresses, energy blocks, or pains. Supportive psychotherapy included discussions of pains which were present and behavioral methods for reducing pain.

Healing and psychotherapy groups both showed nonsignificant decreases in somatization, anxiety, and depression relative to the control group. Various tests showed somewhat greater differences in therapy and healing groups, but none were significant. Healing group subjects reported after weeks one, three, and six that their pain was either all gone or nearly gone and "that they were now coming to terms with the causes of the pain and its symbolization in the body."

A comparison of supportive psychotherapy and laying-on-of-hands healing for chronic back pain patients (*Alternative Medicine*, 1991)

Though the basic design idea of this study is good, details are missing in the report and significant effects of healing are not demonstrated. Rating: III

Arthritis is a crippling illness for which Western medicine has only limited treatments. Some of the conventional treatments carry serious side effects. Many healers have reported they are able to relieve pain and increase mobility in arthritis. The following studies examine this scientifically.

Arthritis Pain and Therapeutic Touch

Susan D. Peck (Eckes)

Susan Peck compared the effects of routine medical treatments plus six sessions of either Therapeutic Touch (TT) or progressive muscle relaxation (PMR) on symptoms of degenerative arthritis in 108 people aged 55 or older. Subjects were assigned randomly to either treatment after a four-week baseline period without TT or PMR. No significant differences in demographic variables were identified between the two groups. Treatments were given once weekly, with 84 people completing all six sessions and also completing pain assessment questionnaires.

Significant differences were demonstrated by both TT and PMR when comparing pain and arthritis assessments before and after treatments. TT decreased pain and distress (both highly significant: p <.001).

***The Effectiveness of Therapeutic Touch for Decreasing Pain and Improving Functional Ability in Elders with Arthritis* (doctoral dissertation, University of Minnesota, 1996)**

This excellent study shows significant effects of healing for both the physical and functional aspects of arthritis. Regretfully, it is impossible to evaluate solely from the brief dissertation abstract available. Rating: III

Peck's study of healing confirms clinical reports of healers that healing can be effective in treating functional disabilities of arthritis as well as in treating pain.

Osteoarthritis of the Knee and Therapeutic Touch

Andrea Gordon, Joel H. Merenstein, Frank D'Amico, and David Hudgens

Andrea Gordon and colleagues explored the effects of six weekly Therapeutic Touch (TT) healings on pain and physical disability in people aged 40-80 who had osteoarthritis of one or both knees. "Those who had knee replacement(s) in their affected knee(s) were excluded from the study. Of 31 people recruited, 27 completed the study."

Subjects were divided into three levels of severity of disease and were randomly assigned within each level. Severity was assessed through symptom questionnaires and radiographic readings, assuring equal severity of illness across the groups, including eight TT, 11 mock TT (MTT), and eight nontreatment control subjects.

TT was given by a healer, MTT by a woman of similar age and appearance who had experience in health care. TT and MTT treatments were videotaped to assure that naive observers could not distinguish between the two. Pain was measured with several standardized tests and assessment scales, as well as depth interviews.

The TT group demonstrated significant improvements ($p < .04$ - $.0003$) on 10 out of 13 of the Multidimensional Pain Inventory scales, and on activity levels ($p < .01$ - $.0005$).

The effects of Therapeutic Touch on patients with osteoarthritis of the knee (*Journal of Family Practice,* 1998)

Significant effects of TT on arthritis pain and movement limitations are demonstrated in this study. However, as no blinds were used for experimenters, it is impossible to rule out the possibility of suggestion as a cause for the observed changes. Rating: IV

The next study of healing for arthritis is very limited.

Rheumatoid Arthritis Pain Treated with Reiki

Randi Anderson Bucholtz

Randi Bucholtz studied the effects of Reiki touch healing compared to casual touch for relief of pain in patients with rheumatoid arthritis. This was a single-blind, randomized, crossover study in which subjects served as their own controls. Six subjects 18 years or older were studied. The healer, a nurse with two years of experience in Reiki, level 2, administered both the healing and casual touch treatments.

Though consistent decreases in pain were noted in comparisons of the measurements before and after healing, as well as over the series of treatments, the results did not reach significance.

The use of Reiki therapy in the treatment of pain in rheumatoid arthritis (master's thesis, University of Wisconsin, 1996)[28]

This study suggests a positive effect of healing on arthritis, but it is sad to see efforts wasted in a study that is unlikely to bear results. Though the design is in principle a reasonable one, the small number of subjects makes it highly unlikely that significant results would be found. This is a problem not only in terms of the absolute numbers, but also because arthritis is a disease in which patients frequently experience spontaneous waxing and waning of symptoms. Further study appears warranted. The available abstract is too brief for proper evaluation. Rating: III

It is helpful to have several studies by different researchers confirming that healing can be helpful for pain and functional disabilities of arthritis.

These studies show that chronic pains of headaches, backaches, and arthritis respond to healing.

The following study comes from Finland, where the medical profession is so skeptical of healing and other complementary therapies that they tend to discount reports of scientists in other countries, accepting only studies done by scientists they know personally. The healer, Marja-Leena Aho, is widely acclaimed in Finland for helping people who have serious illnesses. Some of her healees spontaneously move their bodies into postures that appear to contribute to self-healing.[48]

This study examines how healing can be effective for chronic pain. Chronic pain is one of the most common symptoms treated by healers, with anecdotal reports indicating great successes in relief of pain from almost any cause.

Chronic, Idiopathic Pain and Spiritual Healing

D. Markus Sundblom, Sari Haikonen et al.

Idiopathic pain syndrome (IPS) describes people who suffer from chronic pain with no known somatic problem or whose pain is not adequately explained by a lesion (when no major psychological disturbance is also present). Some believe that IPS is an expression of an underlying depression. Patients included in this study "were preoccupied with severe pain of at least six months' duration" and "lacked any organic pathology or pathophysiological mechanism that would account for the pain."

The 24 patients were randomly divided into treatment and control groups. The healing group was given three to eight 40-minute healing treatments by Marja-Leena Aho. Healees lay on a bed while the healer held her hands about 20 cm above them. Healer and healees recorded their impressions of the healings. Multiple standard tests and pain scales were used to assess pain and psychological condition.

Data from medical and psychological interviews and questionnaires indicated that two patients believed healing had been successful, four reported some relief, and six had no benefit. Ten patients reported sensations during healing, most commonly warmth and relaxation. All patients found healing to be a pleasant experience.

Visual Analog Scale pain scores before treatment and two weeks after showed no significant differences between treatment and control groups. Moderate decreases in pain were noted more in the treated than in the controls both at two weeks and one year. Use of analgesics was somewhat higher in the controls at two weeks but not at one year. Improvements in responders were noted in increased recreational and sexual activities at two weeks, but sexual activity returned to previous levels at one year.

There were significant decreases in scores for hopelessness and increases in acceptance of psychological factors influencing the pain problem (modest significance: $p < .05$). All changes, except for recreational activity, returned to baseline levels by one year, although there remained a tendency for decreased social isolation and increased denial of symptoms.

The authors note that this study is weak in having small numbers of patients and not including blinds for those who assessed the patients.

The effect of spiritual healing on chronic idiopathic pain-A medical and biological study (*Clinical Journal of Pain,* 1994)

This is a most thorough investigation of medical and psychological variables that might be related to healing effects. Despite the low numbers of patients, significant findings were found of increased hope and acceptance of underlying psychological factors associated with pain, although no direct effects on pain were found.

It is sad to see so much effort invested in a study of such few subjects, when it is unlikely that statistically significant effects could be anticipated. The very large numbers of tests applied actually weaken any credence one can give to the results, as one would expect five positive results in one hundred trials by chance alone. The lack of blinds and placebo controls leaves one to question whether factors of expectation and suggestion could have been causal rather than any healing effects. Rating: IV

The findings in this study are consistent with the observations of others and with my own clinical observations that spiritual healing significantly enhances progress in psychotherapy.69

It seems a lot to expect that a brief healing intervention alone would bring about significant changes in so complex a problem as that of severe chronic pain. Problems of self-image and secondary gains are deep-rooted and unlikely to change with brief interventions. This makes these findings all the more remarkable.

A better design would have had the healer continue treatments with larger numbers of patients over the course of the year, adding psychotherapy with some of the patients.

These studies show that healing can help significantly in reducing acute and chronic pains. In clinical practice, most healing treatments last for 20 to 60 minutes, with the duration determined by the intuitive assessment of the healer. Much of the early research on healing for anxiety and pain has studied the effects of a standard five-minute healing intervention. Though significant effects have been noted with these brief interventions, it is reasonable to anticipate even better results with longer treatments, as in Redner's study.

Pain, Anxiety and Depression in Chronically Ill Patients and Reiki healing

Linda J. Dressen and Sangeeta Singg

Dressen and Singg randomly assigned 120 cronically ill patients who experienced pains of various sorts to one of four groups: Reiki, Progressive Muscle Relaxation, Control (no treatment), and false-Reiki.

Patients had pains that had been present for at least one year. Pains included: headaches, coronary heart disease, cancer, arthritis, peptic ulcer, asthma, hypertension, and HIV infection. Groups were matched to have equal numbers of men (12) and women (18). Following baseline measurements, each of the three treatment groups received ten 30-minute treatments, administered twice weekly over five weeks.

Measurements: Patients were assessed before and after the series of treatments, using a series of pain and anxiety scales. Reiki patients had another assessment three months after completion of treatment.

Results: There were no significant differences between groups in medical condition, age, or on any of the measures prior to treatments.

Comparing pre- vs post-treatment scores, Reiki proved significantly superior ($p < .0001-.04$) to the other treatments on 10 out of 12 variables.

At the three-month follow-up, these changes remained consistent and there were further, highly significant reductions in Total Pain Rating Index ($p < .006$) and in Sensory ($p < .003$) and Affective ($p < .02$) Qualities of Pain.

Depression decreased significantly more in the men than in the women in the Reiki Group, while there were significantly greater increases in faith in God in women in the Reiki group than in women in all the other groups.

The authors note that there were variables that were not assessed which might have influenced the results: "seriousness of the illness, multiple experimenters, multiple sites, religiosity, and social support available to the patients."

Effects of Reiki on pain and selected affective and personality variables of chronically ill patients (*Subtle Energies* 1998)

Significant effects of Reiki healing on anxiety, pain, and depression are demonstrated in this study. However, it is difficult to rely on these results because medications and several other important variables (mentioned by the authors) were not controlled. Rating IV

Menstrual and premenstrual symptoms, particularly pain, cause much suffering to uncounted numbers of women. Medications for pain and other symptoms often provide only partial relief and add problems through their side effects.

Menstruation and Therapeutic Touch

Margaret M. Misra

Misra studied the effects of Therapeutic Touch (TT) on women's experiences of menstruation during the first days of their cycle. The 31 women (age 18-41) were either given TT or rest. Pain prior to and following interventions was measured with the short form McGill Pain Questionnaire (MPQ). Significant effects of TT were noted.

The Effects of Therapeutic Touch on Menstruation **(master's thesis, California State University, Long Beach, 1994)**[28]

Significant effects of healing on menstrual pains are demonstrated, but the available abstract is too brief to lend serious credence to the reported results. Rating: III

Lawrence LeShan was impressed that healers have such widely differing practices that it could be very confusing to investigators attempting to find out whether healing works and if so, how. He developed a method of healing that he hopes will provide a pool of healers who will presumably be reasonably equivalent in how they work.

The next two studies focus on LeShan healers.

Joyce Goodrich has devoted her career to teaching the LeShan methods of healing and to healing research. Her doctoral dissertation examines sensations experienced by healees during LeShan distant healing.

Distant Healing Sensations and LeShan Healing

Joyce Goodrich

This study examines what patients feel upon receiving distant healing treatments and questions whether or not independent judges are able to identify from healees' subjective reports when a distant healing treatment has occurred.[50][51] In Type 1 healing,

> the healer establishes an altered state of consciousness in which reality is experienced as a unitive state and anything or anyone held within the healer's focus of attention, within his or her consciousness becomes a part of that experience of oneness with all. There is no attempt to "do anything" to the healee (in Harry Edwards' words, "All sense of 'performance' should be abandoned"), but simply to include him or her in the experience of oneness with depth, purity, and intense caring. . . .

Type 2 healing involves the laying-on of hands. "It does not require the unitive, clairvoyant reality state of consciousness," although it can be done while in that state.

Goodrich carried out an experiment involving 12 people with physical problems who were unsophisticated in theories about healing. Change in their physical condition was not a focus of the study. "The only indications of change in their conditions came from subjective evaluations." Six healers trained by LeShan were used.

A series of Type 1 healings was scheduled for each of the 12 subjects. The first and the fifth healing for each person were "present" (healer and healee in the same room) and the remaining eight were distant (healer and healee separated by unspecified distances, all presumably in their own homes). A few healings were conducted over greater distances. Healers and healees were told that healings would be done at specific times of day scheduled by Goodrich. Unknown to them, half of the distant healings for each healee were scheduled at least an hour after the participants expected them (nonsynchronously).

Healees reported such sensations as relaxation, drowsiness, heaviness, decreased anxiety, increased energy, and peacefulness. Sensations reported by healers included a more intense awareness of self and feelings of peacefulness.

Three judges who were blindly given healers' and healees' self-rating forms on their subjective experiences successfully identified whether the healings were synchronous or nonsynchronous (modest significance: $p < .005$). Goodrich, disclaiming recall for coding of data, also rated the forms and found significant results.

Table 4-1 Judges' assessments in Goodrich Healing experiment

HEALINGS IN CHRONOLOGICAL SEQUENCE	THREE JUDGES' EVALUATIONS IN PERCENTAGES	
	RIGHT	WRONG
1. present - synchronous	98 %	2%
2. distant - synchronous	45	55
3. distant - synchronous	55	45
4. distant - nonsynchronous	70	30
5. distant - nonsynchronous	87	13
6. present - synchronous	96	4
7. distant - nonsynchronous	29	71
8. distant - nonsynchronous	59	41
9. distant - synchronous	78	22
10. distant - synchronous	75	25

An interesting finding was that accuracy in judging whether distant healings were synchronous or nonsynchronous methodically and consistently increased with the length of time between distant healings and the very first healings for each healee in which both healer and healee were present.

***Psychic Healing: a Pilot Study* (doctoral dissertation, Union Graduate School, Yellow Springs, Ohio, 1974)**

This is an excellent study. It shows that healees can identify subjective sensations during distant healings with a high degree of accuracy.[52]

One must keep in mind that physical changes were not the subject of this study. Though healees experienced subjective sensations during distant healings, this is not meant to be proof that healing is effective.

Goodrich provides abundant raw data to permit readers to make their own evaluations of her study and conclusions, as well as to appreciate qualitative aspects of the healer-healee interactions.

The inclusion of Goodrich's judging data in the grouped statistical analysis seems questionable. She had some awareness of the assignments of codes to data and was therefore not completely blind in making evaluations. Significant results were obtained independent of her input, however. Rating: I

Beginning students of healing and healees both often question whether they are feeling something related to healing if they sense heat between the hands of a healer and the body of the healee, or whether they merely feel the natural heat of a warm hand. This doubting of one's own experience is even more marked with absent healings. It is most helpful to have the confirmation of Goodrich's thesis that such sensations are frequent enough and distinct enough to be reliably identified by healees and by independent judges who reviewed reports of the healees' perceptions.

Goodrich's research suggests that, contrary to common expectations, the less close (socially) the healer and healee were, the greater was the likelihood of sensations being experienced during healing.

Shirley Winston followed up on the observations of Goodrich in the next study.

Personal Relationships and Psychic Healing
Shirley Winston

This study asks: Is psychic healing based on a personal relationship between healer and healee or a relationship of a nonpersonal or transpersonal nature?

Four LeShan healers treated 16 healees. Healers and healees were cycled through through a series of one-week healing schedules. By the end of the study, each healee had undergone four conditions:

- "Healer and healee meet, converse, get to know each other, then healing is done in the presence of healee, with feedback afterwards." The next two healings are at a distance.
- "Healer and healee meet, healing is done in presence of healee, but there is no conversation. . . ." The next two healings are at a distance.
- "Healer receives a letter in healee's handwriting and a photo of healee." Three healings are done at a distance.
- "Healer receives a lock of healee's hair." Three healings are done at a distance.

The results show "a trend toward more effective psychic healing when interpersonal information and communication are lower, but miss statistical certainty."

Research in Psychic Healing: a Multivariate Experiment **(unpublished doctoral dissertation, Union Graduate School, Yellow Springs, Ohio, 1975)**

It is impossible to say whether the null results are due to lack of actual differences between the study conditions or to other factors, such as lack of need for healing in the healees. As no statistically significant results were obtained we cannot draw any conclusions from this study. Rating: I

Winston's inconclusive results leave unanswered questions about the importance of interpersonal closeness in healing effects. The trend towards significance is suggestive but would require further study for confirmation.

The largest series of studies of healing for human clinical problems focuses on anxiety, as treated by Therapeutic Touch.[53] Patricia Heidt is a pioneer in healing research, among the first to study the effects of healing in humans.

Anxiety in Hospital Patients and Therapeutic Touch

Patricia Heidt

The effects of Therapeutic Touch (TT) were explored with 90 people hospitalized on a cardiovascular ward in New York City. State anxiety was measured prior to and following the interventions given to each of three matched subgroups: (1) five minute healings, which were given with the hands touching the body; (2) five minutes of mock healings ("casual touch"); or (3) no intervention.

> Subjects who received intervention by therapeutic touch experi-enced a highly significant (p < .001) reduction in state anxiety, according to a comparison of pre-test to post-test means on A-state anxiety . . . Subjects who received intervention by therapeutic touch had a significantly (p < .01) greater reduction in post-test anxiety scores than subjects who received intervention by casual touch or no touch.

Effect of Therapeutic Touch on anxiety level of hospitalized patients (*Nursing Research* 1981; doctoral dissertation, New York University, 1979)

We have here clear evidence for a significant reduction of anxiety with healing. It is hard to judge whether results were attributable entirely to TT or whether suggestion may have played some part in this study, since no blinds were employed in the evaluation phase. The person administering the anxiety tests was fully aware of who had TT and who did not. How-ever, we should also consider that the test instrument is self-administered by the subject and tester influence may presumably be minimal.

Subjects matched for pre-test scores were assigned to each of the three groups, but no randomization procedures are mentioned. Random assignment of subjects to experimental and control groups would hope-fully even out extraneous differences between the groups.

More serious is the possible confounding of medications that patients were given, which may well have included tranquilizers and beta-blockers. If these were given closer to the time of the TT intervention in the control group than in the experimental group, the observed results may have little to do with TT. Rating: IV

Janet Quinn's study closely replicates Heidt's, with the difference that the healer's hands were held *near the patients' bodies but not touching them.*

Anxiety in Hospital Patients and Therapeutic Touch
Janet Quinn

Quinn designed her research to test the theorem that Therapeutic Touch (TT) without physical contact would have the same effect as TT with physical contact. This theorem was derived from the broader conceptual system developed by Rogers (1970), which suggests that the effects of TT are outcomes of an energy exchange between two human energy fields. Since the effects of TT with physical contact on state anxiety are known, state anxiety was used as a measure of the efficacy of TT without physical contact.

Sixty male and female subjects between the ages of 36 and 81, hospitalized on a cardiovascular unit of a metropolitan medical center, were randomly assigned to the experimental group, which received noncontact Therapeutic Touch (NCTT), or the control group, which received mock TT. Each subject completed the A-State Self Evaluation Questionnaire before and after the assigned intervention. It was hypothesized that subjects receiving NCTT would have a greater decrease in post-test state anxiety scores than subjects receiving the control intervention. This hypothesis was supported at a high (p >.0005) level of significance.

In treating subjects with NCTT, the nurse performed a complex intervention of five minutes duration. The control group was treated identically in all outward appearances. However, in the control treatments the nurse did mental arithmetic while going through the outward motions of a TT treatment. Nurses who administered the control treatment had no experience in TT. Checks were made with observers naive to TT and they could not distinguish which treatments were being given.

An investigation of the effect of Therapeutic Touch without physical contact on state anxiety of hospitalized cardiovascular patients (*Advances in Nursing Science,* 1984; doctoral dissertation, New York University, 1982)

This study, paired with the previous one, demonstrates the close similarity in results from contact and noncontact laying-on-of-hands treatments for state anxiety. As Quinn notes, this may be a benefit to patients who need quick relief from anxiety and are unable to take drugs. However, one must be cautious in interpreting the results of this study. Here, as in Heidt's, a possible confounding variable is the medications that were given to patients. Rating: IV

Replications of studies are important, both to confirm that the original studies were not due to chance and to explore healing in different settings for different healees. It is of interest to see whether or not repeated studies of the same healer can yield consistent findings, and whether or not different healers can achieve equivalent results. The following studies do just that.

Hospital Patients' Anxiety and Therapeutic Touch: Replication
Janet F. Quinn

Quinn again tested the effects of Therapeutic Touch (TT) in reducing postoperative anxiety after open heart surgery, with the elimination of eye and facial contact to see whether these are necessary to the reduction of anxiety. She gave real and mock TT (MTT) treatments for five minutes from beside patients so that no eye contact was made. Independent observers, naive to TT, could not distinguish between the two treatments. A third group was included which received no treatment (NT). Subjects were randomly assigned to groups, and no significant demographic differences were found between the groups.

Anxiety was assessed by self-evaluation, pulse rate, and systolic blood pressure in 153 patients. No significant differences were found between the groups, though the greatest differences were noted in the TT group and the next greatest differences in the MTT group.

A *post hoc* finding was that diastolic blood pressure was significantly lower in the TT group than in the NT group. Another *post hoc* finding was that 114 patients (76 percent) were receiving cardiovascular medication, with 108 (72 percent) receiving calcium channel blockers or beta-adrenergic blocking agents, or both. These were given to stabilize pulse and blood pressure and would have limited the response ranges of both. Beta-blockers may also decrease anxiety.

Quinn notes that it was difficult for her to ensure that she would not be healing during the MTT treatments, as the healing rituals are so habitually associated with giving healing that this might automatically have occurred to some degree despite her intentions and efforts to preclude it.

Therapeutic Touch as energy exchange: replication and extension (*Nursing Science Quarterly*, 1989)

Though no significant effects of healing were found, there was a positive trend in favor of the healing group. Larger numbers of subjects might have produced significant effects. Again, Quinn presents a well-done and meticulously reported study.

It is unfortunate that in setting up the study with blinds to avoid Type I errors, Quinn was also blinded to the fact of the patients being on medications, which may have seriously influenced the responses on the study measures. Similarly, the provision of MTT by the healer seems a poor procedure. However, the question remains as to why positive results were found by Quinn with a similar design in her previous study. The finding of lower diastolic blood pressure is of interest and bears replication, as discussed earlier. Rating: IV

Anxiety and Therapeutic Touch

Elizabeth Habig Hale

Hale studied the effects of Therapeutic Touch (TT) on adults hospitalized on three private medical-surgical acute care units. The 48 patients were randomly assigned to either eight minutes of TT (excluding centering), eight minutes of placebo/mock TT (MTT), or control/untreated groups. Diagnoses included 16 musculoskeletal (33.4 percent) and 12 gastrointestinal problems, and the rest with peripheral vascular, respiratory, genitourinary, or neurological disorders.

Hale gave the TT, and MTT was given by nurses who had no TT training but were instructed in making the appropriate hand movements. Systolic and diastolic blood pressure (BP) and pulse (P) rate were recorded along with the State-Trait Anxiety Inventory (STAI) as indicators of stress. All variables were measured twice before and after the interventions, and the placebo group had measurements at corresponding times.

Results showed no significant differences between the groups in their starting state on any variable. The control group had lower postintervention measures of STAI (modest significance: $p < .05$), and the second systolic BP measurement was higher than the third (modest significance: $p = .03$).

Hale points out that the STAI in this study was administered two hours after interventions, compared to five minutes in most other studies. This may indicate that TT has an immediate effect which is not sustained. This is the only study of TT for anxiety showing a greater effect for the control group.

A Study of the Relationship Between Therapeutic Touch and the Anxiety Levels of Hospitalized Adults (doctoral dissertation, College of Nursing, Texas Woman's University, 1986)

It would appear that the TT and placebo interventions may have prevented the patients from relaxing, if one is to take the control group's greater reduction in anxiety as an indication of the normal course of events for this population. This would imply that the TT healer might not have been very effective. I could find no reference to Hale's expertise in TT in the dissertation. Rating: I

The negative effects of TT and mock TT on anxiety are difficult to explain.

Many health caregivers are learning to develop their healing gifts through TT and other methods. Anecdotal reports indicate that with practice one may enhance healing ability.[54] The next study examines the effects of healers with various levels of experience in TT.

Measuring Experience in Therapeutic Touch
Cecilia Kinsel Ferguson

Cecilia Ferguson assessed the internal consistency, reliability, and validity of content, construct, and prediction of the Subjective Experience of TT Survey (SETTS). This questionnaire is used to differentiate between experienced and inexperienced practitioners of TT. It was developed by Dolores Krieger with the help of Judith Wilcox, a meditation expert. It contains 68 items tabulating the frequency with which a healer feels specific physical and emotional changes.

Ferguson administered the SETTS and the Adjective Check List (ACL), which evaluates people's self-descriptions, to 100 nurses who practice TT (50 experienced and 50 inexperienced) and to 100 nurses who were unfamiliar with TT. With the latter, she arranged for 50 to "read a brief description of the actions the practitioner of therapeutic touch performed. They were then asked to complete the SETTS and the ACL while imagining that they were practitioners of therapeutic touch." Nurses in the last group of 50 answered questions modified from the SETTS to relate to their experiences in their ordinary treatment of patients. The two TT level nurses did not differ in demographic variables, but the non-TT nurses were younger, less experienced, and less educated to a significant degree (all at a high level of significance: $p < .0001$) than the TT nurses.

TT nurses were asked to administer (to any patient of their choosing) the Self-Evaluation Questionnaire for state anxiety before and after a healing and an Effectiveness of Therapeutic Touch Scale (ETTS) after a healing. The ETTS asks healees to choose a number between 0 (representing not at all helpful) and 100 (extremely helpful), to characterize their response to the TT treatment.

Ferguson found that the SETTS significantly differentiated the experienced practitioners from the other three groups combined and the inexperienced from nonpractitioners of TT (both at $p < .01$). Experienced TT nurses scored higher than the other three groups combined on the nurturance and creative personality subscales of the ACL. Healees showed highly significant decreases in anxiety scores (experienced nurses $p < .0001$; inexperienced nurses $p < .001$). The differences between the scores of the two groups were also highly significant for the anxiety and the ETTS measures (each $p < .001$).

***Subjective Experience of Therapeutic Touch Survey (SETTS): Psychometric Examination Of An Instrument* (doctoral dissertation, University of Texas, 1986.)**

The decrease in anxiety with TT is again impressive. The study is well designed and well run, demonstrating a healing effect on anxiety.

The significant difference in reduction of anxiety between those treated by experienced and inexperienced nurses supports the contention that healing treatment can be learned. The positive self-evaluations of the patients suggest that the degree of experience with TT makes a difference in the response to the treatment. It is unfortunate that no mention is made of types of problems treated or qualitative patient criteria for improvement, making this study difficult to evaluate.

Because there were highly significant demographic differences between the practitioners and nonpractitioners of TT, it is impossible to draw conclusions with any certainty regarding the SETTS or ACL test results. Rating: I

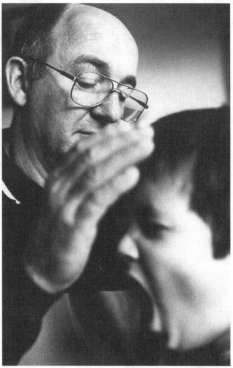

Figure 1-11. Healees regularly sigh, breathe deeply and relax as healing is being given. Children respond very readily (not knowing so many reasons not to). *Photo by Tony Sleep.*

The following report explores healing for anxiety in cancer patients, but regretfully is too brief.

Anxiety Levels in Oncology Patients and Therapeutic Touch

M. S. Guerrero

The briefest of summaries[55] states that state anxiety was reduced in oncology patients receiving chemotherapy (modest significance: $p < .05$). **The Effects of Therapeutic Touch on State-Trait Anxiety Level of Oncology Patients, (Masters Abstracts International, 1985)**
This report is far too brief to allow any assessment of its value. Rating: III

While cancer is one of the illnesses for which people frequently seek healing, there are so few studies in this area that I include here a study barely worth mentioning.

Cancer Patients' Anxiety Level and Therapeutic Touch
Louise Marie Kemp

Louise Kemp randomly assigned eight people with terminal cancers who were receiving palliative care to have five or seven minutes of either TT or mock TT (MTT). She measured their anxiety on the State-Trait Anxiety Inventory (STAI), finding that all five TT subjects had reductions in their anxiety. The sample was too small to provide meaningful statistical analyses. *The Effects of Therapeutic Touch on the Anxiety Level of Patients with Cancer Receiving Palliative Care* (master's thesis, Dalhousie University, 1994)[28]

There is a growing awareness of post-traumatic stress disorders (PTSD) in people of all ages following physical and emotional traumas. Clinical reports that healing can help with PTSD[56] are now supported by the evidence from the following study.

Stress after Hurricane Hugo and Therapeutic Touch
Melodie Olson, Nancee Sneed, et al.

In the post-traumatic period 6 to 12 months following natural disasters, people are more prone to exhibit stress-related problems (Madakasira/ O'Brien). The health care community was challenged to deal with such stress during Hurricane Hugo. As with most post-traumatic stress, memories and unresolved feelings about earlier losses and stresses were re-activated.

This study explored the benefits that Therapeutic Touch (TT) had to offer in the treatment of post-traumatic stress following the hurricane. Correlations were studied between subjective reports and physiological measures of stress, though the literature generally has shown poor correlations (Fagin). Correlations were also studied in healees' and healers' physical sensations as the TT treatments were given over various parts of the body.

TT was given with the hands near to but not touching the body, following the usual procedures of centering the mind and focusing upon the intent to help. Healers redirected "areas of accumulated tension in the subject's body by movement of the toucher's hands," while "concentrating attention on the specific direction of excess energies using hands as focal points." Healers were allowed to continue treatment until they felt maximum benefits had been achieved.

Volunteers came from the university, including faculty, staff, and students. They had either "worked during the hurricane itself or had suffered loss in the form of injury, property damage, or power outages for extended periods . . . . The subjects' perception of increased personal stress was confirmed by a short questionnaire that addressed the effects of the hurricane on their lives."

Following treatment, mean anxiety scores were significantly reduced relative to pretreatment scores (modest significance: p < .05), as they were when the scores after treatment were compared with the control sessions (modest significance: p < .05). Anxiety scores in the treatment group were reduced by about half, while those in the control group were unchanged or slightly higher.

Physiological changes in the treatment group compared with the control group were lower for heart rate (in all but one subject), blood pressure, and respirations and were higher in skin temperature, but not to a statistically significant degree.

Therapeutic Touch and post-Hurricane Hugo stress (*Journal of Holistic Nursing*, 1992)

It is good to see TT taken into a natural environment where its effects on stress can be observed. The authors are to be commended for having done a study that demonstrates, despite conditions that were obviously less than optimal, that TT is effective in reducing stress and that length of treatment appears to contribute to positive response. Their use of self controls would appear to have provided a measure of safeguard against the influence of extraneous factors upon the results.

It is unclear whether the control subjects were taken as a group to compare with the treatment group or whether only those eight in the control group were studied for comparison of TT versus self-controls. It would appear fairly certain from the wording of the study that the former is the case. If this is so, then the study is weakened, as no demographic data are given to compare those in the control group with those in the total group, leaving the possibility that extraneous differences might have contributed to the differences in test results. Rating: III

It is good to have the study of healing taken from the hospital into the outside world. If healing can help with severe stresses such as hurricanes, it is likely it can help with lesser stresses of everyday life.

Once it becomes apparent that healing is effective for anxiety, we want to have some assessment of how healing might compare with other complementary therapies in treating this problem. The next study makes a good start in this direction.

Anxiety Reduction with Therapeutic Touch and Relaxation Therapy
Deborah Gagne and Richard C. Toye

Psychiatric inpatients at a Veterans' Administration hospital were randomly assigned to either Therapeutic Touch (TT), Relaxation Therapy (RT), or mock TT (MTT) on two consecutive days. Out of 44 patients referred, 31 completed the study.

TT was administered for 15 minutes by a nurse or a nursing assistant; MTT for the same length of time by a different nurse; and RT by a chaplain who normally provided RT for patients at the hospital. TT was a novel intervention for the participants.

Anxiety was measured on the State-Trait Anxiety Inventory (STAI) for State Anxiety, and with a behavioral assessment. Despite randomization, the MTT group had lower anxiety than the other two groups at the start of the study. No blinds are mentioned for staff performing the behavioral assessments. Participants' confidence or belief in the treatments they received was assessed with a 10-item questionnaire. Results were analyzed by a psychology intern who had no contact with the patients.

Results showed that TT appears to have an anxiety-reducing effect equivalent to that of RT when subjective anxiety is the measure. Behavioral measurement favors RT as an agent for reducing anxiety (highly significant: p < .001), perhaps because the RT is directed at relaxing muscles.

The effects of Therapeutic Touch and relaxation therapy in reducing anxiety (*Archives of Psychiatric Nursing,* 1994)

It is of interest to note that TT healing appears to provide a subjective reduction in anxiety in psychiatric patients that is equivalent to relaxation therapy. It is good to have a start at demonstrating that TT healing may produce more than transient reductions in anxiety. Certainly further study is warranted.

However, it is difficult to assess the results of this study because the MTT group started out with lower anxiety. No assessment is given as to whether or not this was significantly different from anxiety in the treatment groups. Further, there is no indication that those assessing the behavioral measurements were blind to the treatments. If not, this could result in bias. Finally, raw data are not given for individual days.

This comparison of TT and RT may relate more to the clinical efficacy (or perhaps the bedside manner) of the two therapists than to the therapies. Replications of this study are in order to clarify these questions. Rating: IV

The next study explores the benefits of Reiki healing for test anxiety, a very common experience among students of all ages.

Test Anxiety and Reiki

Lucia Marie Thornton

Lucia Thornton studied the effects of Reiki healing on the stress of undergoing examinations in 22 women nursing students, while 20 students received mock Reiki treatments from a research assistant. Prior to and following the interventions, each student was tested for anxiety State-Trait Anxiety Inventory (STAI) and personal power (Barren Power as Knowing Participation in Change Tool), and each answered questions about her well-being.

The STAI showed significantly lower anxiety for both the experimental and control groups, with no significant differences between them. No other significant changes were noted.

Effects of Energetic Healing on Female Nursing Students (*master's thesis, California State University, Fresno,* 1991)

The available abstract is too brief to assess properly. No effects of Reiki healing on anxiety are demonstrated. Rating: III

Healers claim that distant healing works as well as contact healing. The next study examines distant prayer healing for anxiety, depression, and self esteem.

Self-Esteem, Anxiety, Depression and Distant Intercessory Prayer

Sean O'Laoire

Fr. Sean O'Laoire is a Catholic priest and clinical transpersonal psychologist in the San Francisco Bay area. He advertised for local volunteers to pray for the health of others or to be prayed for. He trained 90 volunteers as agents in directed and nondirected prayer. Directed prayer specifies a desired outcome, such as for improvement which will be demonstrated on their assessments at the end of the study. Nondirected prayer seeks "alignment with divine will."

The 406 volunteers who were prayed for were divided randomly into three groups, one for directed prayer, one for no prayer, and one for nondirected prayer. Agents had no particular gifts or experience in healing and subjects had no particular problems or pathology. Prayers were offered over 12 weeks, 15 minutes per day. Multiple standardized tests were used to assess the mental states of both the agents and the subjects.

All of the 406 subjects showed highly significant improvement ($p < .0001 - .01$) in every objective and subjective score. There were no differences between the directed and nondirected prayer groups, nor between the prayer and control groups. All of the 90 agents showed significant improvements on 10 measures (p < .0001 - .05). Neither method of prayer produced significantly better results. Agents who prayed more showed significantly greater improvement (p < .0001- .0004) on five objective measures, but subjects showed no differences related to amount of prayer sent.

An experimental study of the effects of distant, intercessory prayer on self-esteem, anxiety, and depression (*Alternative Therapies*, 1997)

An excellent study, well designed and well reported. Significant post hoc correlations are demonstrated between the amount of prayer and improvements in agents, and between belief in the power of prayer and improvements in subjects. The findings are impressive in view of the fact that neither agents nor subjects identified any focused needs for prayers.

The primary focus of the study, directed vs. nondirected prayer, did not demonstrate significant differences. A likely explanation for improvement in all subjects are suggestion/placebo effects. Rating: I

The design of the O'Laoire study may have mitigated against demonstration of differences in efficacy of directed versus nondirected prayer healing. A specific need for healing, plus clearer instructions and more training of agents in nondirected prayer, might contribute to more positive findings. Including any mention of outcome in the nondirected prayer would seem to shift it towards being directed prayer.

The fact that agents who prayed more improved more may be due to self-reinforcement. That is, as agents noted improvements in themselves, they were encouraged unconsciously to pray more. Conversely, agents who noted little improvements in themselves might have been discouraged from praying. Although improvements in agents were not a stated focus of the study, the fact that agents were given symptom assessments at the start of the study would have suggested this expectation to them.

Healers debate whether focused, directed prayer, in which healers specify the desired outcome, is more or less effective than nondirected prayer, in which healers just wish for the best to happen to the healees. This is not just a philosophical question but a very practical one, if one wants to maximize the effects of healing. This is a question still waiting to be resolved.

Most of the studies of healing for anxiety focus on adults, though healers and parents give ample anecdotal reports of children's sensitivity and more rapid responses to healing. The following studies explore this promising area of therapeutic intervention.

Stress in Premature Infants and Therapeutic Touch

Rosalie Berner Fedoruk

Fedoruk studied the effects of noncontact Therapeutic Touch (TT) on seventeen premature infants in intermediate and intensive care. Such babies are easily agitated by routine handling because of the immaturity of their nervous systems. The effects of TT in alleviating the stress of having their vital signs (such as blood pressure or temperature) taken during routine nursing care were studied. Stress was measured behaviorally using the Assessment of Premature Infant Behavior (APIB) scale and physiologically by recording transcutaneous oxygen pressure ($tcPO_2$), the amount of oxygen in the infant's blood, which is thought to reflect stress.

Two types of controls were used: mock TT (MTT), in which a nurse untrained in TT mimicked the motions of TT while calculating simple arithmetic backwards out loud, and no TT (NTT). Blinds were used in $tcPO_2$ measurements, but not in APIB measurements. Fedoruk did the observations, and reports "I can tell even when a TT practitioner is working and when she isn't, and everyone in the NICU knew who did TT and who didn't."

Results indicated a significant decrease in stress on the APIB compared with baseline (modest significance: $p < .05$). A suggestive increase in stress on the APIB was noted for the MTT condition, possibly related to the stimulus of the nurse counting out loud and to her distress in doing this exercise. No significant differences were noted on any of the $tcPO_2$ measures.

***Transfer of the Relaxation Response: Therapeutic Touch as a Method for Reduction of Stress in Premature Neonates* (doctoral dissertation, University of Maryland, 1984)**

Healing effects for anxiety are demonstrated in premature infants, for whom tranquilizing medication would not be prescribed. The work appears to have been carefully done, with the exception that blinds were not used for APIB measurements. This leaves the possibility that the person making these clinical assessments might have biased the results in the anticipated direction. Rating: IV

It is gratifying to see evidence that healing may help premature babies to relax. These infants often find themselves in the harsh world of a hospital environment, with glaring lights, all sorts of hustle and bustle and noise, plus various intrusive and often painful medical and nursing interventions. While all of these are clearly necessary to save their lives, they are still emotionally disruptive and potentially traumatic. A healing intervention, carrying no risk of side effects and promising some measure of relief, would be most welcome to these vulnerable motes of life.[57]

Hospitalized children have many painful experiences, including physical pains from their illnesses and injuries, restraints, needles and surgery, as well as psychological pains due to stressful separations from family and many other factors.

Stress in Hospitalized Children Treated with Therapeutic Touch and Casual Touch

Nancy Ann Kramer

This study examined the effects of six minutes of Therapeutic Touch (TT) healing on children aged two weeks to two years who were hospitalized for surgery, injuries, or acute illnesses. Thirty children were selected from routine admissions to a pediatric unit over a five-month period, without regard to cognitive or psychosocial development. Children were excluded if they had cancer or other chronic illnesses or had received medications to lower fevers within the previous four hours or sedatives within eight hours. To provide a comparison with TT, casual touch was given to children while they remained lying in their cribs.

Physiological measures were gathered between six a.m. and two p.m., the period of the greatest number of stresses from investigative procedures, and when parents are least often present. Baseline measures were taken at times when the children were noted to be under stress, and measures were repeated three and six minutes following initiation of touch intervention.

TT brought about greater stress reduction than casual touch at both the three minute and six minute intervals (modest significance: $p < .05$ for each).

Comparison of Therapeutic Touch and casual touch in stress reduction of hospitalized children (*Pediatric Nursing*, 1990)

It appears that TT healing can reduce stress reactions in hospitalized children. This is impressive despite the limited healing time allotted. Unfortunately, this study is seriously flawed. No randomization is mentioned in assigning children to TT or casual touch intervention, nor is any mention made of checks to see whether children assigned to each of the intervention groups were comparable in severity of presenting problems or in severity of stresses which challenged them. As the experimenter was presumably biased towards finding an effect of TT, she might have behaved toward the children in the casual touch group in subtle manners that were not as soothing.[58] Rating: IV

At first glance it might seem a waste of time to publish and review studies on anxiety, such as the next few in this series, which show no significant benefits of healing. For several reasons it is actually important that we do not ignore them.

Skeptics are suspicious that the positive studies might represent a few chance successes out of hundreds of failures.[59] *However, as funds for studies of healing are extremely limited, this is not the case. Of the few studies in the literature, many have been done for professional degrees and are available as academic references to any who wish to see them.*

One can learn much from studies with no significant results. Thomas Edison was once asked, after he had spent many weeks without success in examining various materials as potential light bulb filaments, "Aren't you discouraged with so many failures?" "No," he replied. "Now I know 100 things which don't work!"

Relaxation and Noncontact Therapeutic Touch

J. W. Collins

Collins explored how Therapeutic Touch (TT) affects the physiology of normal adults, measuring skin temperature, pulse, respiration, galvanic skin response (GSR), and electromyograms (EMG), and using a relaxation assessment scale developed for this study. Each of the 24 subjects had both TT and mock TT (MTT) in a randomized, double-blind design.

The TT group demonstrated mild relaxation on EMG, temperature, pulse, and GSR but not reaching statistical significance. The MTT group also demonstrated mild relaxation and the differences between the groups was not significant on any of the measured variables.[60]

The Effect of Non-contact Therapeutic Touch on the Relaxation Response **(master's thesis, Vanderbilt University, Nashville, Tennessee, 1983)**[28]

I have not seen the original of this thesis. It seems that TT in normal, healthy people cannot be expected to produce a greater effect than placebo. It may be that in cases of mild anxiety any attention can be calming. TT did not reduce anxiety in this study. Rating: III

Test-Taking Anxiety and Therapeutic Touch

Melodie Olson and Nancee Sneed

Normal, healthy professional students in nursing or health-related graduate programs were studied prior to and following the stress of an exam, a paper, or a presentation that represented at least 30 percent of their course grade. Subjects were not on any anti-anxiety medication. With a standardized stress test, they were divided into 20 high-anxiety and 20 low-anxiety students. The high-and low-anxiety groups were then randomly divided into experimental and control subgroups.

Both groups then followed a routine of treatment and test, using three tests, including the Spielberger State-Trait Anxiety Inventory (SSTAI). The control group sat quietly for 15 minutes in lieu of treatment

No significant differences were noted between the experimental and control groups with either high anxiety or low anxiety. "Power analysis (Cohen) using the variability of SSTAI in the high-anxiety group showed that a sample of 76 individuals in each of the two high-anxiety groups . . . would be needed to document statistical significance."

Anxiety and Therapeutic Touch (*Issues in Mental Health Nursing,* 1995)

The study provides a bit of useful information: Groups of 76 subjects in each of the experimental and control groups may be necessary in some situations in order to demonstrate significant effects of healing on anxiety. It is difficult to know how to evaluate this study when the authors indicate, without further data, that the type of stressor may have been a confounding variable. Any differences between groups may have been due to the type of stressor rather than to the healing treatments. Rating: IV

Stress in Female College Students and Therapeutic Touch

Gretchen Lay Randolph

In this randomized, double blind study, Randolph examined physiological responses of women students in college to stressful stimuli as they were treated with Therapeutic Touch (TT). She used a film, *Subincision*, validated as a stressful stimulus. Sixty students were divided into two groups of 30 for experimental and control conditions. Both groups saw the film while their skin conductance, skin temperature, and muscle tension were monitored. The experimental group received TT with the healer's hands on their backs and lower abdomens for 13 minutes. The Casual Touch (the control) group was given the same outward touch without the intent to heal from a nurse who imitated TT but had no knowledge or training in TT.

No significant differences were noted between the two groups on any of the measurements.

The Differences in Physiological Response of Female College Students Exposed to Stressful Stimulus, when Simultaneously Treated by Either Therapeutic Touch Or Casual Touch (*Nursing Research,* 1984; doctoral dissertation, New York University, 1974)

The summary speaks for itself. Most healers believe that healing works primarily on those who are truly in need. I think this is the most important limiting factor in the study. Another possibility is that the healer might not have been as potent as healers in studies that demonstrated significant findings.

In mild anxiety, it may be that healing is no more effective than suggestion. Rating: I

Anxiety in the Hospitalized Elderly and Therapeutic Touch

Brenda Sue Parkes

Parkes studied the effects of Therapeutic Touch (TT) on the anxiety of 60 hospitalized patients aged 65-93. Parkes assumed that elderly patients would be anxious since they were hospitalized. Patients were randomly assigned to three groups. There were no differences between groups in mean age, sex, religion, numbers of previous admissions, medical/surgical diagnosis, and practice of meditation. Patients with 43 different diagnoses were included. Group 1 received five minutes of TT; Group 2 had mock TT; and Group 3 had a nurse hold her closed hands over the shoulder of the subject "with no intent to transfer energy."

There were no differences between groups in the pre- to post-treatment State-Trait Anxiety Interest scores. In fact, all three groups evidenced a slight increase in anxiety.

Parkes notes, "The mean pre-test scores were very close to the mean scores of what Spielberger termed the normal means for this question-naire." She speculates that elderly patients may actually experience reduction of anxiety because they are hospitalized.

***Therapeutic Touch as an Intervention to Reduce Anxiety in Elderly Hospitalized Patients* (doctoral dissertation, University of Texas at Austin, 1985)**[28]

This study would seem to be an embarrassment. It appears useless to study the effects of healing on anxiety when no significant anxiety is present. Rating: V

The next study proves the point of learning from studies which fail to show significant effects. Following up on Parke's study, above, Simington and Laing designed a study with sharper focus in a similar elderly population.

Anxiety in the Hospitalized Elderly and Therapeutic Touch

Jane A. Simington and Gail P. Laing

Anecdotal reports suggest that Therapeutic Touch (TT), given along with back rubs to promote sleep can alleviate state anxiety (Blazer) and other symptoms of psychological distress found in the institutionalized elderly, reducing agitated behaviors in the following day.

Simington and Laing hypothesized that TT given as a back rub would be more effective in reducing state anxiety than a back rub given by a nurse unfamiliar with TT (Control Group 2); that TT would be more effective than mock TT in reducing state anxiety (Control Group 1); and that significant differences in state anxiety between Control Groups 1 and 2 would not be found following the interventions.

Subjects were drawn from two large urban and two small rural long-term care facilities. Clearance was obtained from the ethics committees of the involved facilities. Subjects were included if they were cognitively capable of participating according to a team of senior nursing personnel at each institution. A sample of 105 was used, after seven refused and three left the study for various reasons.

Research Assistant 1 (RA1) helped the subjects complete the Spielberger State-Trait Anxiety (STAI) test after their treatment, remaining blind to the assignment to treatments. RA2 was a registered nurse who randomly assigned subjects by drawing numbers 1, 2, or 3 from a hat. She also gave treatments to Control Group 2. The Primary Investigator (PI), a registered nurse experienced in TT, gave the TT treatments. The PI also gave the intervention for Control Group 1, mimicking TT treatment while counting backwards in her head from 100 by threes to help her refrain from entering a healing mode of awareness. Subjects were blind to the treatment modality they received, which in each case lasted three minutes.

The TT group had significantly lower STAI scores than Control Group 2 (modest significance: $p < .05$). No significant differences were noted between the STAI scores of the TT group and Control Group 1 or between Control Group 1 and Control Group 2.

Simington and Laing conclude that TT significantly enhances relaxation, produced by a back rub. They hypothesize that the efforts of the PI at blocking TT in Control Group 1 were only partially successful.

Effects of Therapeutic Touch on anxiety in the institutionalized elderly (*Clinical Nursing Research*, 1993)

A well-designed and adequately reported study. A significant effect of healing for anxiety is demonstrated with TT given as a back rub, compared to back rub treatments without TT. However, no checks were made on medications taken by patients that might have influenced anxiety.

Randomization by drawing numbers from a hat is a poor procedure. It leaves open the possibility that either subtle sensory cues or psi cues (clairsentience or precognition) could have guided the person randomizing the subjects, so that subjects with less severe symptoms or greater chances of improvement would be selected into the various groups. This is called *intuitive data sorting* in parapsychology. Rating: IV

It is good to see research evidence show that healing is more potent than another therapeutic modality: in the case of the previous study, a back rub. While it is important for research to establish the efficacy of individual therapeutic components, in the real world therapists apply many combinations of treatments to help people get better. I have spoken with numbers of hands-on therapists who note that their hands get warm and tingly when they are treating clients, with no awareness on their part that spiritual healing might be involved.

The period of palliative care is a very sensitive time at the end of the lives of people with cancer and other serious illnesses. Anecdotal reports indicate that healing can bring marked relief to people suffering from pain, stress, and other problems in palliative care. The next study explores this possibility in a focused manner.

Cancer and Therapeutic Touch

Marie Giasson and Louise Bouchard

Giasson and Bouchard studied the ways in which noncontact Therapeutic Touch (NCTT) could alleviate the suffering of people with cancer (primarily lung cancer) who were hospitalized on a palliative care unit. The 20 selected subjects did not have confusion and were able to fill out a visual analogue scale (VAS) assessment of nine specific items, plus an overall assessment of "general well-being."

The subjects were randomized into two groups: the experimental group had NCTT for 15 to 20 minutes and the control group had a rest period of the same duration, always scheduled one hour following a regularly prescribed analgesic. Giasson was the healer and the investigator for the study, with 150 hours of supervised learning in TT and 3 years of using it. Relaxation was used rather than mock TT (MTT) because NCTT was given for 15 to 20 minutes and it was felt by the investigators to be unethical to give MTT for longer than 5 minutes.

There was a significantly greater improvement in scores in the experimental versus control groups (highly significant: $p < .0015$). The former demonstrated highly significant increases in Well-Being scores ($p < .001$), while the latter did not show any significant increases.

Effect of Therapeutic Touch on the well-being of persons with terminal cancer (*Journal of Holistic Nursing,* 1998)

The study shows a significant effect of healing on the well-being of people who are in terminal care. Significant effects were found in the treatment group from before to after treatment, as well as when comparing experimental and control group results. Sadly, because no blinds were used and the healer was also the investigator, there is a clear possibility of suggestive effects, and no firm conclusions can be drawn from this study. Rating: IV

This study shows that healing can enhance well-being in patients in palliative care, where there is much suffering from pain, anxiety, depression, loss of appetite, nausea, and other symptoms.

Enhancing the quality of life for people in terminal care is an important contribution of healing. Not only is there suffering from the cancers and other illnesses, but also from the side effects of many of the medical treatments that are given. Healers have reported anecdotally that they can

enhance quality of life in palliative care, at a time when people's remaining days are very precious to them. It is helpful to have this exploratory study which begins to confirm these reports.

The next study comes as a brief note from Poland, where healing is increasingly being accepted as a useful therapy.

Anxiety and Bioenergytherapy

Jan Gulak

Jan Gulak, a bioenergotherapist, studied the anxiety levels of his patients before and after his 15-minute treatments. His measure was a standard anxiety questionnaire administered 14 days prior to and 21 days after his treatment of 76 people. Various statistical analyses showed the results to be significant (p < .01 and p < .001). Accompanying the decrease in anxiety were cessation of migraines and sleeplessness, improvement of circulatory insufficiency, and relief of digestive and reproductive organ pains.

Lowering the anxiety levels in persons undergoing bioenergotherapy (*Psychotronika*, 1985)

The results of this translated study appear impressive. Again, as neither blinds nor randomization are mentioned, the results of this study may represent experimenter or placebo effects.[61]

Major depressive disorders are found in 3 to 5 percent of the American population (Cancro). Of those started on antidepressant medication, 10 to 15 percent stop their medications, and 30 to 40 percent of the remainder fail to respond (American Psychiatric Association, 1993). Antidepressants often produce unpleasant side effects, diminishing quality of life.

There is clearly a place for exploring the benefits of healing for depression, the subject of the next studies.

The first of these studies explores the effects of six sessions of Healing Touch (HT) on depression. HT is an extension of TT, including longer sessions and a focus on the chakras.[62]

This study breaks new ground by including several types of energy field assessments as measures of the efficacy of healing treatments.[63] A subjective grading was made of the severity of disturbance in the energy fields palpated by a healer's hands around the bodies of the subjects. In addition, a healer used a pendulum to assess the degree of openness, which is taken to be a measure of health of the seven major chakras. The pendulum appears to act like the dial on a meter. It amplifies minute, unconscious movements of the healer's hand, thereby externalizing the healer's intuitive impressions, making them clearer.[64]

Depression and Healing Touch
Catherine S. Leb

Catherine Leb explored whether Healing Touch (HT) could be of help to volunteers with depression that ranged from two months to 36 years. The volunteers were referred to the study from psychotherapy practices. The mean length of time in therapy prior to the study was 6 to 9 months for the experimental group and 9 to 12 months for the control group. Of the 30 participants, 27 had used therapies other than psychotherapy and antidepressants; 18 were using some form of medication.

The treatments involved two 30- to 45-minute HT sessions per week over a three weeks period. A depression inventory was given to all subjects before and after treatment, and to the experimental group again one month after treatment. Higher scores on that test indicate greater depression. There were significant score differences between the two groups prior to treatment (p < .03).

The energy fields of subjects were assessed with two types of hand scans by the healer who gave the HT treatments. A pendulum assessment was made of each of the seven major chakras, with higher scores representing greater health.

The change scores for the two groups reflected a highly significant decrease in depression for the treatment group (p < .001), which were sustained at one month after treatment. The mean hand scan measures showed highly significant changes (p < .001). Scores for change in the seven chakras were significantly higher for the experimental than for the control subjects (p < .001). The chakras in the control group were initially closed and remained closed during the study. Systolic blood pressures in the experimental group were significantly lower after HT in sessions 2, 3, and 6. Both pulse and respiration were significantly lower in sessions 2 to 6.

***The effects of Healing Touch on depression* (master's thesis, University of North Carolina, 1996)**[28]

The study shows a significant effect of healing in depression, both via the depression inventory and by energy field assessments. However, no firm conclusions can be drawn from this study because the experimental group started out with higher depression scores, leaving greater room for improvement. Further, one cannot rely upon subjective assessments of energy fields by the same person who is giving the treatment because of expectancy effects. To rely upon the swings of a pendulum of the same person in no way makes these observations more objective or reliable. Rating: IV

This is an important study because it introduces measurements that rely upon the intuitive perceptions of a healer. The human instrument is currently the most sensitive one available for assessment of the biological energy field. If a person (other than the healer) who was blind to the assignments of subjects to the two groups, made these assessments they would be more objective and therefore of far greater value.

The next study of healing for depression is of special interest because of the method of healing used.

Crystals and gemstones of various sorts have been reported by many healers to enhance the efficacy of their healing.[65] Many have viewed this practice as a magical belief, reminiscent of the nostrums and amulets of superstitious gypsy rituals or even of witchcraft. It is easy to see that if an authority figure such as a healer attributes healing powers to an object, the suggestion alone may bring a person to expect to feel better when holding or wearing the object. This is another example of a placebo effect.

It is good to have a scientific study, the first of its kind, examining whether crystals might enhance healing. C. Norman Shealy is a pioneering neurosurgeon who has been exploring and using a wide range of complementary therapies for pain and other physical and emotional problems over several decades.

Depression and Healing with Crystals

C. Norman Shealy et al.

This study explored Cranial Electrical Stimulation (CES),[66] autogenic training,[67] photostimulation, brain wave synchronization (BWS),[68] and music[69] in the treatment of 141 patients with chronic depression who had not responded to antidepressant drug therapy. Education and treatment with the above therapies was provided in groups of 8 to 12 patients in 44 hours over two weeks.

In addition, patients were blindly assigned to carry with them either glass or quartz crystals that were "mentally programmed to assist a positive mental attitude." Assignment to crystal or glass was arranged by having a person who was not involved with the study draw slips of paper from a box, without informing the research staff of the assignments. Patients could not distinguish the glass from the quartz, and 85 percent believed they received quartz.

> [P]atients were guided to pass their "crystal" through a candle flame while willing the "crystal" to be cleared of all stored energy. They then were asked to breathe out onto the "crystal" three times while thinking their agreed upon positive healing phrase. Each patient chose a phrase meaningful to them, similar to "I am happy and joyous."
>
> They then placed their "crystal" in a white satin pouch to be worn on a cord around the neck, with the pouch over the anterior mid-sternum every day. They were instructed to avoid allowing anyone else to touch their "crystal" and to reprogram it positively every morning for one week and once a week thereafter.

Clinical assessments and Zung tests for depression were administered prior to the start of the study. Blood was drawn from the first 103 patients for norepinephrine, serotonin, cholinesterase, betaendorphin, and melatonin.

After the two-week instruction/therapy period, patients were given a musical tape with 20 minutes of their preferred classical and relaxation music and a guided imagery tape. They were instructed to play one of their tapes twice daily over three months during relaxation practice. Their crystal pouch was to be worn during all waking hours (with the exception of bathing).

After the three-month period, patients returned for a repeat of the Zung test and repeat blood tests (for the same 103 patients).

> Prior to treatment, 90 percent of the patients had one to seven [blood test] abnormalities (levels above or below the laboratory normal ranges), with a total of 337 abnormalities (out of 927 possible) in 103 patients.
>
> Three months after the treatment program, 29 of the patients had one to four abnormalities, with a total of 46 recorded abnormalities (out of 927 possible) in 103 patients. Of even greater interest, only four of those who had residual abnormalities after therapy were classified as being out of depression. In other words, 25 of the 29 were still depressed.
>
> At the end of two weeks 119 of the 141 patients had Zung scores 10 points or more lower than their initial scores or below 50, which is the minimal level for diagnosis of clinical depression. Seventy-five of the 88 who received quartz were improved. Forty-three of the 53 who received glass were improved initially. Thus 84 percent of all patients improved initially.

Statistical analysis of the Zung scores from before to after three months of therapy showed a significant improvement for the entire group. The differences—61 of the 88 patients (70 percent) who received quartz versus 17 of the 53 (31.5 percent) who received glass—were significantly in favor of the quartz crystals ($p < .001$). Zung scores between patients with glass versus quartz prior to therapy revealed no significant differences.

Shealy et al. observe that no drug has been known to produce 84 percent improvement in depression over two weeks. The quartz crystal group improved almost twice what could have been anticipated with most antidepressants, and there were no side effects. The cost effectiveness of this program is about 35 percent of usual rehabilitation programs for depression.

Non-pharmaceutical treatment of depression using a multimodal approach (*Subtle Energies*, 1993)

This is an excellent study, well designed and well described. Significant effects of crystal healing on depression are demonstrated. No flaws are apparent in the research design. Randomization procedures could be automated to minimize possible intuitive sorting of subjects. Replications would be good to have. Rating: I

There is a vast anecdotal lore on healing with crystals and gemstones. It is a help to have research suggesting that crystals can augment healing, particularly for a problem like depression, which is widespread and often incompletely helped by conventional therapies. Hopefully this study of Shealy and colleagues, confirming that crystals can reduce depression, will encourage explorations of the benefits of such treatments.

The use of distant healing for depression is explored in the next study. Bruce Greyson is a psychiatrist who has been studying Near Death Experiences. He was recruited by Joyce Goodrich for this study of LeShan healers.

Depression and Distant Healing

Bruce Greyson

This double-blind study evaluated LeShan distant healing as a complement to conventional depression treatment with antidepressant medication and psychotherapy. Forty randomly chosen patients in a psychiatric hospital in Connecticut were assigned at random to either a distant healing group or a control group. There were no differences in severity of symptoms between the two groups.

Healing was sent by two to four healers who never met the healees or knew their names but were given brief narrative descriptions of their problems. Multiple healers were assigned by Joyce Goodrich to ensure that healing would be sent daily over six weeks.

Greyson made periodic clinical assessments, remaining blind to the assignments of the patients for healing throughout the 14-month course of the study. A structured interview provided information for the completion of four tests measuring mental status. In addition, healers scored their degree of satisfaction with each healing, ranging from exceptionally strong through moderate to least strong.

In the final results, there were no significant differences in length of hospitalizations or in readmissions between the two groups. Scores on three of the four tests were lower for the experimental group, but not significantly so. Ultimately, the more healing sessions received and the higher the healers rated the quality of the healing, the lower were the ratings on depression, general psychopathology, and general distress, often to significant levels.

Distance healing of patients with major depression (*Journal of Scientific Exploration,* 1996)

Although depression scores did not show straightforward significant decreases, a healing effect was suggested by the correlation with lower scores of both the numbers of healing sessions and the healers' assessments of the quality of the healing treatment. Goodrich is to be commended for her explorations of healers' qualitative awareness of the efficacy of their healing sessions. Considering the possible confounds she discusses, a study with larger numbers of subjects appears warranted.

The study would have to be repeated to be convincing as to any healing effects on depression. Rating: I

Many people think that because antidepressant medications are readily available we can deal effectively with depressive disorders. This is far from the truth. Numbers of people cannot find an effective antidepressant. Others suffer from unpleasant, sometimes severe side effects. They are faced with the horrible choice of living with a markedly diminished quality of life because of such problems as dizziness, drowsiness, blurred vision, diminished sexual drive, and constipation—or discontinuing medication and suffering from the depression. Healers have reported anecdotally that they can help deal with depressions. It is good to have studies such as the last ones which make a start at confirming this possibility.

Death is a problem that every one of us will face. Approximately 16-20 milion new mourners face bereavement every year. Healing could help mourners, as it is effective in treating depression and anxiety. Grief may be a problem not only in and of itself. People who are bereaved are at greater risk for getting serious illnesses.[70]

Grief and Therapeutic Touch

Loretta Sue Robinson

Robinson studied a convenience group of 22 adults who had recently been bereaved. She assigned them randomly to receive either three Therapeutic Touch (TT) or three mock TT (MTT) treatments.

Demographic data and assessments with the Grief Experience Inventory (GEI) were gathered from each subject prior to their first treatment and after their third treatment. GEI responses were obtained again at one and nine weeks after the last treatment. At the last assessment, subjects were invited to report any effects of the treatment on their grief.

Statistical analyses confirmed that TT was beneficial in helping people deal with grief.

The Effects of Therapeutic Touch on the Grief Experience, **(doctoral dissertation, University of Alabama, Birmingham, 1996)**[28]

While this study is reported too briefly to permit proper analysis, it would appear that a positive effect of healing on grief may be demonstrated. Rating: III

Alzheimer's disease affects over 3 million people in the United States today, and it is estimated that this figure will rise to 10–15 million in the next two decades. Alzheimer's and other dementias can include a range of disturbed behaviors. Caregivers are left with the difficult choice between having to give these people tranquilizing and sedating medicines, which diminish their mental alertness and can increase their confusion, or allowing them to suffer with the disruptive behaviors. Healing offers a treatment intervention that does not cloud consciousness.

Alzheimer-type Dementia and Therapeutic Touch
D. L. Woods, R. Craven, and J. Whitney

This double-blind study explored the responses to Therapeutic Touch (TT) of people with Alzheimer's disease who exhibited disruptive behaviors. Fifty-seven patients were randomly assigned to TT, mock TT, and control groups in each of three special care units in Canada. TT was given once in the morning and again in the afternoon for five to seven minutes over three days.

The experimental group showed a marked decrease in vocalizations compared to the control group (modest significance: p < .04). The mock TT group showed a decrease approaching significance (p < .074) compared to the control group.

The effect of Therapeutic Touch on disruptive behaviors of individuals with dementia of the Alzheimer type (*Alternative Therapies*, 1996)

An apparent benefit of TT in disruptive behaviors of Alzheimer's disease is demonstrated. Again, the study is reported too briefly to allow for proper assessment of the results. Randomization procedures, blinds, raw data, and statistical procedures are not described. Rating: III

The use of healing for agitation in people with disruptive behaviors of dementia appears promising, particularly where healing—with no side effects—might improve quality of life.

My personal impression from my practice of psychotherapy combined with healing is that the two modalities together are more potent than either alone. It is good to see research that helps to validate this, as in the following study.

Self-Esteem, Group Counseling, and Intercessory Prayer

Barbara Schutze

Schutze addressed the question: "Does group counseling with the addition of intercessory prayer for psychological (inner) healing change self-esteem more than counseling without the intercessory prayer condition?"

The subjects were 37 young adults in a suburban youth organization. They were given a Self-Esteem Inventory pre-test followed by five consecutive weeks of counseling in small groups. Each group had two facilitators. The Self-Esteem Inventory was also used as the post-treatment measure of change.

Ten subjects were randomly selected for the experimental group out of participants in small-group counseling sessions. They were assigned randomly, one each to a facilitator, to receive intercessory prayer for inner, psychological healing. The experimental condition was not revealed to the subjects until the study was completed. Experimental (E) and control subjects (numbers not specified) received identical treatment. The experimenter was the only person who knew who was in the E group until after the final assessment tests were given. Facilitators were instructed to tell no one who was assigned to them for healing. None of those subjects who participated in the E group participated in the group counseling session which would be facilitated by the person who was assigned to pray for them.

Statistical analysis demonstrated modesty significantly greater improvement in the subjects who had intercessory prayer (modest significance: $p < .05$).

Group counseling, with and without the addition of intercessory prayer, as a factor in self-esteem (*Proceedings of the 4th Internat ional Conference on Psychotronic Research, Sao Paulo, Brazil,* 1979)

Intercessory prayer (presumably a form of distant healing) was apparently helpful in enhancing self esteem. The available report is too brief to permit proper assessment of procedures such as methods of randomization and firmness of blinds. Data are not presented to support the reported results. Rating: III

Use of alcohol and other addicting drugs is often associated with stress, anxiety, depression, and low self-esteem. Considering the positive effects of healing demonstrated with these problems in earlier studies, it would appear likely that healing should be of help with addictions, as explored in the next study.

Alcoholism and Intercessory Prayer
Scott Walker et al.

This was a prospective, double-blind, randomized study of intercessory prayer for people who entered a standard treatment program for alcohol problems. Over six months, the 42 recruits were told that "they may or may not have prayers offered for their problems with alcohol by outside volunteers."

Periodic assessments included several psychlogical tests, urine screens, and such factors as involvement with Alcoholics Anonymous

Volunteers with experience in intercessory prayer were recruited from the local community to pray daily for six months. They agreed to refrain from prayers for religious conversion of their subjects, as well as to maintain confidentiality. Formats for prayer were not specified. Volunteers who completed the six-month period of research had Protestant, Catholic, and Jewish affiliations. Subjects were assigned to volunteers of diverse affiliations, with three subjects assigned to each volunteer, identified only by their first name and a research number. Subjects had three to six volunteers praying for them.

No significant differences in alcohol consumption was found between groups. Of all the variables studied, none differentiated between the two. However, the control group subjects demonstrated a greater loss to follow-up by a factor of five (modest significance: p < .05), despite efforts to track them through whatever contacts were provided. Regardless of group assignments, those who said that there were people already praying for them prior to the start of the study were drinking significantly more at the six month assessment than those who had no outside intercession (modest significance: p < .04).

Walker observes that the common expectation that prayer by people who are involved with a person will be beneficial may bear re-examination.

Intercessory prayer: a pilot investigation funded by the Office of Alternative Medicine (*Alternative Therapies,* 1997)

While a suggestive benefit of healing is found in the increased attendance in the treatment program of those receiving healing, no firm conclusions regarding healing can be drawn from this study without further replication. Rating: I

Though no effect of healing on drinking behavior was demonstrated, healing prayer by intercessors who were not personally involved with the subjects appeared to significantly increase attendance in the treatment program. As addiction is a long-term problem, this effect of healing is likely to contribute to beneficial responses over a period of time.

Those who reported that people were already praying for them at the start of the study had poorer results. I would hypothesize an even stronger negative effect of intercessory prayer by family members of people who are addicted than does Walker. Addictions tend to appear as a part of codependent relationships. Prayer from family members of addicts are likely to be colored by their codependency wishes, which could lead the addicts to avoid a treatment which threatens the codependent relationship.

Here are two more studies, although neither adequately describes the problems healing was intended to affect.

Deteriorating Disease and Prayer

C.R.B. Joyce and R.M.C. Welldon

This study examined matched pairs of patients suffering from "chronic stationary or progressively deteriorating disease," either psychiatric or joint disease such as rheumatoid arthritis. Subjects who were being seen by a psychiatrist or a specialist in physical medicine were divided into an intercessory prayer treatment group and a control group. Neither the patient, the physician, nor the participating prayer groups knew to which group each patient belonged, and the patients were unaware that a trial was in progress. The first six valid and definite results available all showed better results in the treated group. Five of the next six showed better results in the control group.

The objective efficacy of prayer: a double-blind clinical trial (*Journal of Chronic Diseases,* 1965)

Clinical criteria used in evaluations are not specified. Although the patients were allegedly matched, criteria for matching are not given. Neither specific psychiatric diseases, specific joint diseases, nor even numbers of patients in each of the two gross categories included in the study are mentioned.

Combining patients with very different chronic illnesses in the same controlled study seems questionable, even when the experimenter matches them in some way. With a small sample and insufficient data regarding the prayers and evaluation methods, this is a poor study, despite a basically good underlying strategy of matching patients. Rating: V

Psychic Healing
Julio C. di Liscia

Journal abstract:

An experimental test of psychic healing at a distance is reported. Jaime Press, a well-known healer in Argentina, was the subject. . . . A physician selected two patients with similar medical conditions and gave the experimenters a sheet of paper on which were written the names and ages of the patients only. One of the patients was selected later by the experimenters, without the doctor's knowledge, as the experimental target. The healer was informed of the name of the person to be healed. Meanwhile, the physician continued medical treatment of the patients with no knowledge of the previous selection. The names of the selected patients were mailed to a third person and were unopened until the research was finished. It was planned to include 100 patients in the study, but the healer could not continue the work due to legal problems concerning his healing activity. A total of 58 patients was available for statistical analyses. Chi-square analyses of control and experimental groups were made in relation to improvement, worsening, and no change categories, but there were no significant differences.

Psychic healing: an attempted investigation (*Psi Comunicacion*, 1977; *Parapsychology Abstracts International*, 1984)
Though my high school Spanish is somewhat rusty, my reading of the original report suggests the author is biased against healers, in that he labels their overstatements about their prowess as "megalomania." Unfortunately, the original article does not describe the conditions treated or criteria for inclusion in the "improved," "unchanged" or "worse" categories. Evaluation of this report is therefore impossible. Rating: III

This concludes the review of available studies on subjective experiences. Even if we take a conservative view that one cannot rely upon single studies for evidence of efficacy, there are replicated studies showing that healing is effective for pain in adults and for anxiety in adults and children. There are multiple reports suggesting healing can help with depression.

Pain and anxiety are the symptoms most frequently reported anecdotally by healers and healees to respond to healing. It appears warranted to recommend healing for these problems as a treatment of choice in nonsurgical pain, considering that healing has no known deleterious side effects. In surgical pain, healing may be recommended as a complementary intervention to ordinary postsurgical care.

An observation from anecdotal reports (which I have not found in the research literature) is worth repeating here. There may be temporary increases in chronic pain with the first few healing treatments, usually followed in further healing treatments by decreases in pain. The initial pain is actually a positive sign, interpreted by many healers to mean the healing is producing some sort of beneficial shift in biological energies.

INTUITIVE (CLAIRSENTIENT) ASSESSMENT

It is through science that we prove, but through intuition that we discover.

—H. Poincaré

Clairsentient[71] assessment is reported frequently by healers[72] and promises to become an important adjunct in medical evaluations. Unfortunately, relatively little has been done as yet to evaluate this aspect of healing because too few physicians are willing to risk criticism by their colleagues for collaborating with psychics and healers.

Assessment of the energy field by healers is one basis for treatment. This is a particular focus in Therapeutic Touch healing, where healers may give healing according to the intensity and other characteristics of the field. For example, they may project energy mentally to boost areas they sense are deficient, or draw off excesses of energy when they feel an area is overactive.

While many studies have focused on the clinical efficacy of healing in influencing various organisms with various problems, the next is a first attempt at validating the abilities of healers to sense the energy field.

Testing the Validity of an Energy Field Assessment Form

Susan Marie Wright

Susan Wright developed an energy field assessment (EFA) form to identify particular qualities during assessments of the human energy field. This study was set up to develop the validity and reliability of the EFA in assessing the location and intensity of pains, as well as in identifying generalized fatigue and depression.

Wright and an assistant each scanned the energy fields (a process of two to four minutes) of 52 people experiencing chronic pain of various sources. The two examiners noted with each scan sensations of heat, tingling, and cold, as well as any right-left differences in the energy field.

The subjects filled out a demographic questionnaire, the Brief Pain Inventory (BPI) and the Profile of Mood States (POMS). The pair of healers sensing the fields were blind to any information about the people whose fields they sensed and recorded. Of primary interest in the BPI is a drawing of a person, front and back, upon which subjects indicated the locations of their pains by shading in the relevant body parts.

Highly significant correlations were found between the sensed field abnormality and pains in the neck, upper back, and lower back (p < .0008-.00001).

There were not enough subjects with pains at other locations to reach the experimental criterion of p < .01 level of significance through the statistical analysis used. Of note is the additional finding that left shoulder pain assessment was modestly significant at the level of p < .03. Wright notes that the numbers of subjects with pain in right and left shoulders were barely over the minimum frequencies required to calculate statistical significance. Also, highly significant positive correlations were found between the background field strength recorded and the presence of fatigue (p < .002).

Development and Construct Validity of the Energy Field Assessment Form *(Western Journal of Nursing Research,* **1991; doctoral dissertation, Rush University College of Nursing, 1988)**

It is very helpful to have a study confirming with high significance the validity and inter-rater reliability of the sensing of biological energy fields. One would hope to see replications of such a study before drawing any serious conclusions from it.

Though the results appear highly significant, a serious breach of the blinds in this study is possible. The fact that subjects filled out their assessment forms before and after the sensing of the energy fields by the healers, combined with the healers' asking subjects to close their eyes during the sensing, leaves open the possibility that healers might have looked at the subjects' assessment forms. Rating: IV

This study is most encouraging and should stimulate further research of aura sensing. It would be helpful to examine whether the sensing of symptoms other than pain and fatigue could be validated, and whether changes could be reliably identified in the energy field that correlate with changes in the conditions of subjects due to conventional and energy field treatments.

Another factor to study is the presence of strong heat, cold, or electrical sensations, which Gordon Turner found to correlate with subjective reports of cures.[73]

The next study explores in a different manner the abilities of people to identify the presence of someone else's hand near their own hand.

Perceiving the Presence of a Nearby Hand

Gary E. Schwartz, Linda G. Russek, and Justin Beltran

Schwartz and colleagues noted that various measurable energies of two people may interact when they are close together. For instance, electrical cardiac energy interactions occur and may vary with the degree of openness of the participants to interpersonal information (Russek/Schwartz). The electrocardiogram (ECG) patterns of each of two people sitting near each other appear in each other's electroencephalogram (EEG) patterns.

The researchers also noted that the hands carry direct current (DC) skin potentials, as part of a complex, dynamic energy pattern around the hands and other parts of the body.

Two experiments were performed to establish whether ordinary people who were blindfolded could identify the presence of the hand of an experimenter which was held several inches above one of their hands. (Subjects had no claims to any healing abilities.)

In the first experiment, the subjects' mean guesses were above chance (58.5 percent; modest significance: $p < .02$), while estimates of their own performance were 12 percent lower (not significant). Subjects' mean confidence ratings were higher for correct guesses than for incorrect ones (high significance: $p < .004$). This suggests that they were partially aware of when their guesses were correct.

In the second experiment, guesses were 69.8 percent correct, highly significantly above chance ($p < .00001$). Again, estimated performance was 12 percent lower than actual performance.

In the combined experiments, results were highly significant ($p < .00005$). There were no differences between men and women in percent of successful guessing. Both groups also had higher confidence ratings regarding correct guesses compared to incorrect ones ($p < .007$).

The Authors note that they did not control for possible sensory cues such as faint sounds, body heat, or electostatic effects.

Interpersonal hand-energy registration: evidence for implicit performance and perception (*Subtle Energies*, 1995)

This study clearly demonstrates significant evidence that ordinary people can sense when another person's hand is near their own. This supports the claims of healers to be able to sense an energy field around the body.[74]

In a contrary view, as noted by the authors, the results of this study could have been produced by heat, electrostatic effects, or electromagnetic effects. No firm conclusions can be drawn as to anything relevant to healing, other than that healers might experience sensations in their hands and healees might experience sensations in their bodies because of effects of known physical energies. Blindfolds are nototiuosly poor at blocking vision. Rating: IV

These studies of Schwartz and colleagues suggest that unselected subjects can identify when another person's hand is held near their own. Schwartz et al. suggest that electrostatic and/or electromagnetic effects may contribute to these sensations.

The fact that temperature sensations were correlated with subjects' overall estimates of correctness of their guesses need not point to physical temperature as the energetic component causing the sensations, and likewise for electrostatic and electromagnetic effects. Despite the frequent reports of sensations of heat in healers' hands or at the site of healing in healees during healings, measurements with sensitive thermometers usually do not demonstrate changes in skin temperature (Engel).[75] Healing sensations may be synesthesias, or crossed-sensory perceptions. Another such example is that people are able to identify colors through their hands (Duplessis).[76] It seems that we have far broader abilities to interact with our environment through the nerve endings in our skins and/or through the biological energy fields around our bodies than conventional science accepts. This is further supported by the study of Gordon Turner (1969a),[73] showing that during absent healings people also report sensations of heat, tingling, cold, electrical sensations, and the like. Such effects at a distance cannot be caused by electromagnetic, electrostatic, or temperature effects.

The mystery of healing is truly starting to be addressed through such pioneering work as that of Wright and of Schwartz and colleagues. It is only through methodical confirmations and eliminations of various hypotheses that we will come to understand the true nature of healing.

In contrast with the last two studies, the next one is of interest primarily for its publication in a prestigious American medical journal, and for its demonstration of the readiness of conventional medical journals to present what they perceive to be negative results of healing studies.[77]

Hand Sensing and Therapeutic Touch

Linda Rosa, Emily Rosa, Larry Sarner, and Stephen Barrett

For a fourth grade science fair project, Linda Rosa's nine-year-old daughter, Emily, did a study of Therapeutic Touch (TT) healers' abilities to sense biological energy fields. A casual search for local TT practitioners gathered 21 out of the 25 contacted who agreed to participate in this study. Experience with TT was between one year and 27 years. Fifteen TT healers were tested over several months in 1996 at their offices or homes. The study was published in 1998 in the *Journal of the American Medical Association* under the title "A Close Look at Therapeutic Touch."

In the study, healers laid their hands on a table, palms up, 25 to 30 cm apart. The experimenter sat opposite them, screened from sight by a tall barrier. Healers inserted their arms through holes at its base, with the further precaution of a towel placed over their arms so that they could not see the experimenter through the arm holes. Each healer was tested 10 times, being allowed to prepare themselves mentally for as long as they wanted before each set of trials. The experimenter held her right hand 8 to 10 cm above one of the healer's hands (chosen by coin toss) and alerted the healer, who then identified over which of her or his hands the experimenter's hand was located. Healers were given as much time as they wanted to make their selection (ranging between 7 to19 minutes per set).

An earlier pilot study with seven other subjects who were not TT healers demonstrated that tactile cues such as heat or air currents did not give away the presence of the experimenter's hand.

To reach a significance level of p < .04, healers had to identify the targeted hand correctly 8 out of 10 times. In the first series only one healer scored 8, but on a retest scored only 6.

The healers gave a number of explanations for their failures, including the following:

1. In each series of trials, a tactile afterimage made it difficult for healers to distinguish the actual hand from the "memory" perception. However, the initial trials in each series did not score greater than chance.
2. Healers' left hands are usually more sensitive receivers of biological energies than their right hands, which are usually more potent projectors of such energies. Out of 72 trials with healers' right hands, 45 (62 percent) demonstrated incorrect responses. Out of 80 incorrect responses, 35 (44 percent) were with the left hand. These differences are not statistically significant.
3. Healers would do better if they were given feedback (in a practice trial prior to the experimental test series) as to which hand was being tested. Rosa et al. feel that this should not be necessary, but concede that such a procedure would eliminate this objection.
4. Healers felt that the experimenter should be more active, holding the intentionality of projecting her energy field. Rosa et al. feel that this should not be necessary, as such a demand is not placed upon patients whose energy fields are being sensed by TT healers.
5. Some healers reported that their hands felt so hot after several trials that they either had difficulty or were unable to sense the experimenter's field. Rosa et al. observe that this contradicts the statements of TT healers that they can deliberately manipulate patients' energy fields during the course of 20-30 minutes of a typical TT session. This objection is also not supported by the fact that only seven out of 15 first trials had correct responses.

A second series was completed in a single day in 1997 and recorded on videotape by a TV broadcasting crew. Healers were permitted to sense the experimenter field and each also selected which of her hands she would use for their test (seven chose her left hand; six chose her right). Healers identified which of their hands was being tested in 53 out of 131 trials (41 percent). The range of correct responses was 1 to 7.

Healers made the following additional objections at the end of the second study:

1. The towel over a healer's hands was distracting (1 healer).
2. A healer's hands were too dry (1 healer).
3. The televising of the proceedings interfered with concentration and increased stresses (voiced by "several" healers). Rosa, et al. believe that the presence of a TV crew should not distract or stress healers more than the usual hospital settings in which many TT healers practice.

The 123 correct responses out of 280 trials (44 percent) in the two series obviously did not support claims of healers to be able to sense the energy field. Rosa et al. note that if healers had responded correctly in 2/3 of the trials their results would have been significant at $p < .05$; if in 3/4 of the trials, at $p < .0003$. "However, if TT theory is correct, practitioners should always be able to sense the energy field of their patients." Accuracy would also be expected to correlate with the length of practice of healers. No significant correlation was found in this study between healers' performance and their levels of experience.

Rosa et al. conclude that TT healers have no ability to sense the biological energy field because the 21 TT healers they studied did not succeed in identifying which of their hands was being tested. "To our knowledge, no other objective, quantitative study involving more than a few TT practitioners has been published, and no well-designed study demonstrates any health benefit from TT."

They also point out that "In 1966 the James Randi Educational Foundation offered $742,000 to anyone who could demonstrate an ability to detect an HEF[78] under conditions similar to those of our study. Although more than 40,000 American practitioners claim to have such an ability, only 1 person attempted the demonstration. She failed, and the offer, now more than $1.1 million, has had no further volunteers despite extensive recruiting efforts."

George D. Lundlberg, M.D., then editor of the *Journal of the American Medical Association*, adds the following comment on this study in the issue in which it appears:

> The American public is fascinated by alternative (complementary, unconventional, integrative, traditional, Eastern) medicine. Some of these practices have a valid scientific basis; some of them are proven hogwash; many of them have never been adequately tested scientifically. "Therapeutic Touch" falls into the latter classification, but nonetheless is the basis for a booming international business as treatment for many medical conditions. This simple, statistically valid study tests the theoretical basis for "Therapeutic Touch": the "human energy field." This study found that such a field does not exist. I believe that practitioners should disclose these results to patients, third-party payers should question whether they should pay for this procedure, and patients should save their money and refuse to pay for this procedure until or unless additional honest experimentation demonstrates an actual effect.

A close look at Therapeutic Touch (*Journal of the American Medical Association,* 1998)

I wrote to Lundberg, informing him that a doctoral dissertation examining the sensing of auras by healers showed positive effects. Phil B. Fontanarosa, M.D., the senior editor of JAMA, replied that my letter "did not receive a high enough priority rating for publication in JAMA" and no interest was indicated in this dissertation.

On the face of it, the study by Rosa et al. seriously challenges the ability of healers to sense energy fields. However, the study itself presents its own challenges. It is surprising, for example, that a study done by a 9- to 10-year-old girl would be published in a prestigious medical journal such as this. The standards for accepting research reports in such journals usually require that they must have been performed by a medical practitioner.

The first, third, and fourth authors of this article are self-identified skeptics, the last two being members of an organization called Committee for the Study of the Paranormal. This organization is known to be dedicated to discounting any evidence for the existence of parapsychological phenomena. The methods it uses are not always of the highest scientific standards, and to many observers appear to be deliberately misleading. Several examples of such methods are evident in the study of Rosa et al.

For instance, regarding healers' objection number two, that the right hand is not as good a sensor as the left: Rosa et al. state in their summation of results with healers' right hands, "only 27 (38 percent) had correct responses" instead of noting that *45 (62 percent) demonstrated incorrect responses*. This makes it more difficult to see that the findings of the study are in a direction which supports healers' claims. With larger numbers it may be possible to show that this is a significant finding.

Another example of misdirection is in the statements by Rosa et al. about published TT research that "Of the 74 quantitative studies, 23 were clearly unsupportive."[79] The authors make no mention of the remaining 51 studies which one would guess from their analysis must be supportive. I know of several, and Rosa et al. cite some of these in footnotes (nos. 76-86 inclusive) to their article. No discussion of the positive findings is presented, and I find no reference in the text to footnotes 76-86.[80]

With these omissions, the article looks, at first reading, quite convincing in its damnation of published TT research. It would appear, however, that these omissions contain material that opposes the authors' and editor's beliefs, and one must wonder whether the omissions were deliberate.

The authors make clever use of language in stating, "To our knowledge, no other objective, quantitative study *involving more than a few TT practitioners* [italics mine] has been published. . . ," language that is again misleading. Most studies of healing are done by only one or a few healers. This is in no way a criticism of the research, which in fact has in many cases produced significant results. The last part of their sentence, "and no well-designed study demonstrates any health benefit from TT" is clearly untrue.

Rosa et al. and the Journal editor assume that there is no validity to claims of healers to sense an energy field or to be able to influence it. They therefore dismiss any suggestions of healers regarding factors in the test situation which might influence such a field.

Healers' objections that performing in front of TV cameras could be a negative influence appears to me a valid criticism of the second part of

274 Ch. 4 - Controlled Studies

this study. While the ambiance of a hospital ward might be stressful (particularly to outsiders), it is composed of elements familiar to nurses and therefore not as distracting as the unfamiliar presence of a TV crew and the research situation. Furthermore, in the hospital the intent is to provide a caring intervention, not to prove one's abilities to sense an energy field.

There is evidence that one can influence one's energy field and the process of healing through one's mental state and intent. Several nurses were able to produce significant results with TT given with the intent to heal versus going through the motions of TT while doing arithmetic in their heads to avoid activating TT healing (Keller 1983; Quinn 1989).

Skin resistance in the hands can be altered by changes in mental state.[81] This would produce a concomitant change in the electromagnetic field around the hand. Kirlian photography has demonstrated that when people have positive feelings for each other, their energy fields merge, and conversely, when they feel negatively towards each other, their energy fields retract from each other.[82]

I can add to the above some anecdotal evidence from workshops I give on developing one's healing gifts. It is possible for one person to project energy from a hand or foot and for another person to identify when the first one discontinues this projection of energy. I would personally support healers' suggestions that it is possible for experimenters to withdraw or to not project their energy fields, thus making it difficult for a healer to identify the energy field.

A further objection is that part of the experience of sensing energy fields is a dynamic one. When I sense someone's field, I move my hand towards and away from their body, as well as across their body. This provides far stronger sensations than simply holding my hand still near the body.

I would also suggest that the presence of a skeptical person in a parapsychological or healing study could dampen or inhibit the effects under study. While this must appear to skeptics to be an unfair proposal, this is the nature of parapsychological effects, which are very much influenced by the mental states of participants and observers. Skeptics are likely to obtain negative effects, believers positive ones. This has been amply supported by the studies of sheep and goats in psi research.[83]

The picture is not all that clear, however. In the testing of energy fields, two studies of sensitives' abilities to see auras produced negative results (Ellison; Gissurarson/Gissurarson). Ellison, despite his claims of being an impartial scientist, comes across in discussions as a sharp skeptic. I have no personal knowledge of the Gissurarsons.[84]

The offer of Randi is couched in terms that leave him as the arbitrator of what is acceptable evidence. There is very little liklihood he would ever pay out his reward.

The sweeping dismissal of TT as a valid therapeutic method by Rosa et al and by the editor of the journal, based upon the evidence of this limited research by a 9- to 10-year-old girl, is patently ridiculous. This study simply explored the ability of healers to sense the energy field of one experimenter under specific test conditions. In no way did it test healing abilities.[85 86]

Though the next study (along with two later ones) is not a controlled study, and this one is translated, these are included here by way of introducing how intuitive assessments can contribute to integrative care.

Biodiagnosticsian and Doctor's Diagnoses

Karel Mison

Karel Mison of Prague presents a brief note on 2,005 diagnoses each made by a physician and by a "biodiagnostician." Six physicians and eight biodiagnosticians participated. The Supplement presents Mison's findings in table form. Here, it must suffice to say that the eight biodiagnosticians achieved diagnostic congruences with the physicians that ranged from 49 percent to 85 percent.

Statistical processing of diagnostics done by subject and by physician (*Proceedings of the 6th International Conference on Psychotronics Research*, 1968)

This study is a good beginning, indicating that in some instances clairsentient diagnosticians can achieve as high as 85 percent congruence with medical diagnosticians. However, the report does not tell us whether the various diagnoses were validated by objective laboratory data. No controls or statistical analyses are presented.

This translated study suggests that in some cases a clairsentient diagnostician might work well with a physician. As this is a quick, safe, and inexpensive method for diagnosis, it seems well worth further study. It would be interesting to know whether any particular characteristics differentiated the physicians and biodiagnosticians as individuals or as pairs whose diagnoses were more often congruent or incongruent.

Medical diagnosis is far from a perfect science. This percentage of congruence in a study of healers and doctors is as good as several different medical diagnosticians might achieve.

Many workshops and courses in psychic development are advertised. The following studies examined whether one such course produced any positive results.

Silva Mind Control

Robert Brier, Barry Savits, and Gertrude Schmeidler

The researchers note that "The Silva Mind Control organization advertises that it enables its graduates to develop E.S.P." In an experiment, a surgeon selected 25 cases and divided them into five groups. Five enthusiastic mind-control graduates each received one group of data and made their clairsentient diagnoses. No significant results were found.

Researchers noted a slight tendency for more positive results in more recent graduates of the Mind Control Program and ran a second experiment with subjects tested on the day after graduation from training. Although the overall results were not significant, this was misleading. "Two of the subjects were children, aged 10 and 12, and their readings were meager and uninformative." One subject's results taken alone were modestly significant ($p < .05$) and "If the scores of the three older subjects had been examined separately, they would have been significant." Another graduate of the same course volunteered to be tested and also achieved significant results ($p < .05$).

Experimental tests of Silva Mind Control graduates (*Research in Parapsychology 1973*, 1974)

The second experiment suggests that some positive results are obtained with this training, assuming that the subjects did not have clairsentient abilities prior to taking the course. It would appear reasonable to request more careful research be done on more subjects before reaching any firm conclusions.

Gertrude Schmeidler, in personal communication, added that her impression was that the Silva graduates attended very closely to verbal and nonverbal cues which led them towards diagnoses that were known to the experimenters and that little if any psi was likely to have been involved. Rating: I

Silva Mind Control

Alan Vaughan

Vaughan notes:

> [A] nurse . . . who had completed the Mind Control course and had received her diploma . . . asked me to arrange for an objective test of her and her fellow graduates' distant clairvoyant diagnosing ability. Accordingly, with cooperation from a physician, I sent her

the first names, last initials, sex, age, and city of residence of five patients whose conditions were unknown to me. The nurse and 20 other Mind Control graduates attempted to make clairvoyant diagnoses for these and returned them to me.

To evaluate the readings quantitatively, I selected two patients of the same sex and comparable ages, put their 21 readings each (total of 42) on coded cards, randomized them by flipping a coin, and sent them to the physician for judging, asking him to guess which of the two patients was being described by the diagnosis. Chance would give 21 "hits." The physician's judgings gave 16 "hits." In addition, he indicated on the cards any apparently correct diagnostic statements that guided him in his choice. Only one card bore a correct diagnostic statement. . . . I then sent the physician the remaining 63 readings (for three patients by 21 students) and asked him to report to me any additionally correct statements. He found no other striking correspondence to his patients' conditions. These findings would seem to put in doubt the claims of Silva Mind Control.

Investigation of Silva Mind Control claims (*Research in Parapsychology 1973*, 1974)

Before dismissing totally the claims of the Silva methods, one would want more substantial studies. However, the author's conclusions seem warranted. Rating: III

My personal impression is that the claims of Silva Mind Control are greatly inflated, based on my attendance at a course, personal contact with a number of graduates, and experience with many healers. Few of the better healers and fewer of the average ones are good at distant diagnosis, so I would hardly expect the inexperienced, with just a few hours' lessons, to have more than very modest success.

There are people with highly refined gifts of clairsentience who are clearly in a different category from the average person who takes a course in psychic development. These people are usually untrained in medicine or in scientific research, so few studies have been made of their diagnostic abilities. When intuitives team up with physicians we begin to get a clearer picture of their abilities. In the next studies we again we have an important contribution from Norman Shealy, who has been brave enough to publish the results of his work with Carolyn Myss, a gifted clairsentient diagnostician, and with other sensitives at a time when these subjects are not well accepted by his medical colleagues.

Psychics and Medical Diagnosis

C. Norman Shealy

Shealy performed several studies of intuitive diagnosis.

In a pilot study, Shealy selected 17 patients for eight psychics, including Henry Rucker, to diagnose. "We found this group to be 98 percent accurate in making personality diagnoses and 80 percent accurate in diagnosing physical conditions. For instance, they clearly distinguished between three totally separate cases of paraplegia—paralysis from the waist down—one traumatic, one infectious, and one degenerative in nature."

In a more formal study, Shealy diagnosed a series of patients by his own physical examination and administration of the Minnesota Multiphasic Personality Inventory. Six clairvoyants were given photographs, names, and birth dates of the patients; a numerologist was given just names and birth dates; a graphologist was given a handwriting sample; and a chirologist was given palm prints. Each diagnostician was asked, "Where is the difficulty or pain?" and "What is the major and primary cause of the patient's illness?" Two of the clairvoyants were 75 percent accurate and a third was 70 percent accurate in locating the site of pain. (Numerology was 60 percent accurate, astrology 35 percent, and palmistry and graphology 24 percent—the same as chance.) In determining the cause of the pain, the clairvoyants ranged from 65 percent accuracy down to 30 percent. Here there was only a 10 percent probability of obtaining the correct diagnosis by chance.

A psychologist who was given the photographs did not exceed chance levels with his guesses.

In informal testing, Shealy gave Caroline Myss, a gifted clairsentient diagnostician, only the names and birth dates of 50 patients. He found her to be 93 percent congruent with his own diagnoses.

The role of psychics in medical diagnosis (*Frontiers of Science and Medicine, 1975*); C. Norman Shealy—Clairvoyant diagnosis (*In: Energy Medicine Around the World,* 1988).[87]

A significant intuitive diagnostic ability is demonstrated in this study.

Regretfully, Shealy does not give sufficient details to permit independent evaluation of his results, nor is statistical significance analyzed.

Shealy's results suggest that clairsentient diagnosis may be a most useful adjunct to conventional diagnostic techniques, especially with the consensus of multiple psychic diagnosticians. Rating: IV

Further study might clarify whether the successful intuitive diagnoses are achieved via clairsentience or via telepathy with the medical diagnostician. Doctors often achieve no better than 70 to 80 percent consensus in diagnosis with each other. The high rates of success of one diagnostician with Shealy suggest that she might have been reading his mind in some of the cases.

Another gifted clairsentient diagnostician, Dora Kunz, worked closely with Shafica Karagulla, a physician. Kunz sat for two years with Karagulla, exploring the correlations of her aura perceptions with medical findings. Their descriptions of their collaborative explorations make fascinating reading. (Karagulla; Karagulla/Kunz). Though rich in detail, they are not systematically summarized or tabulated.

Let us return to another more formal study of clairsentient diagnosis.

Medical Diagnosis and Extra-Sensory Perception
Nils Jacobson and Nils Wiklund

The Swedish Mind Dynamic method claims that its practitioners learn to diagnose illness at a distance from patients' names and addresses. The researchers investigated the diagnostic abilities of a teacher of this method, Mr. B.A. They did two experiments, one with 10 male patients, the other with 10 female patients. With experimenter blinds in place, Mr. B.A. was asked to first diagnose the names on a list, then match those names with a list of given diagnoses. In the second experiment, the names and diagnoses were made up, a fact unknown to both Mr. B.A. and the experimenter conducting the trial. Mr. B.A. showed distress in making the second set of diagnoses.

In neither experiment was there a correct diagnosis, which could occur purely by chance.

Investigation of claims of diagnosing by means of ESP (*Research in Parapsychology 1975*, 1976)

No evidence is found for intuitive diagnosis in this study. The imposition of restrictive and misleading laboratory conditions on a clairsentient diagnostician is poor practice, muddying the experimental waters. It may be that he is able to make correct diagnoses under the conditions with which he is familiar and comfortable. The distress of the subject in the second experiment suggests he was unconsciously aware of irregularities in the procedures.

The first experimental design is simple, but the number of trials is too small for assessment with any confidence. Rating: V

There is only a modest body of research on intuitive diagnosis and the scientific evidence for its validity is limited. My personal impression is that this is a valid and vastly underrated, understudied, and underutilized aspect of spiritual healing.

MISCELLANEOUS THESES AND DISSERTATIONS

A variety of other doctoral dissertations and master's theses mention healing briefly. Though of peripheral interest, they support the view that there is a broad, growing interest in spiritual healing. These are summarized from the CD-ROM *Dissertation Abstracts International* without comment.

Registered Nurses' Knowledge and Practice of Therapeutic Touch (master's thesis, Gonzaga University, 1997)

M. Joanne Green

A mail survey of 176 nurses queried their knowledge about TT and whether they practiced TT. One tenth reported they use TT and two thirds were interested to learn about it. Common uses for TT included relaxation, anxiety, pain, and nausea.

Meanings of Intuition in Nurses' Work (master's thesis, University of Victoria, Canada, 1994)

Wendy Ellen Copeland Cooper

This study explored three nurse educators' use of intuition in making decisions. Authentic, trusting relationships facilitated the use of intuition. Storytelling was the language they found most helpful for this modality of communication.

The Effects of Therapeutic Touch on State Anxiety and Physiological Measurements in Preoperative Clients (master's thesis, San Jose State University, San Jose, California, 1997)

Mary Margarita Bacon

A stratified random sample survey of 160 nurses using herbal and other alternative therapies showed the highest familiarity with TT and lowest for Reiki. Acupuncture was seen as having the greatest helpfulness, Reiki the least. There was little familiarity with herbal medicine.

Therapeutic Touch and Complementary Therapies: A Public Policy Paper (master's thesis, New York Medical College, 1997)

Donna Elizabeth Schuller

Cost and care changes with TT and complementary therapies.

Attitudes of Women with Breast Cancer Toward Therapeutic Touch (master's thesis, Michigan State University, 1996)

Donna Blanche Zambetis

Over three quarters of 73 women with breast cancer who answered a questionnaire describing TT said they would be willing to receive TT.

Attitudes Toward Therapeutic Touch: A Pilot Study of Women with Breast Cancer (master's thesis, Michigan State University, 1991)

Julie Gwen Thomas-Beckett

Women with breast cancer responded to a written description of TT. Three open-ended questions and a 30-item Leikert scale showed that people who were familiar with TT developed a more positive attitude to it, with 39 percent indicating readiness to receive TT.

Effect of Therapeutic Touch Concepts on the Anxiety Levels of Nursing Students in a Psychiatric Setting (master's thesis, Bellarmine College, 1995)

Suselma D. Roth

Nursing students on their psychiatry rotation received a course on TT theory and practice. There was no significant decrease in anxiety (normally present during psychiatric rotations) as a result of the course.

HEALING ACTION ON ELECTRODERMAL ACTIVITY AND MUSCLE STRENGTH

I'm not the one for putting off the proof. Let it be over-whelming.

—Robert Frost 1928

The following set of studies examines the more limited influence of one person upon another via mechanisms that do not involve physical, psychological, or social interactions, although healing to improve a problem condition is not the intent. The studies may also shed light on relaxation responses from healing, because electrodermal response parallels relaxation.

Before we proceed, several fundamental comments:

First, feedback devices have been developed to provide information that people can use to alter their internal physiological states. These devices give users data on parts and functions of their bodies of which they normally have no awareness because such functions are controlled automatically by the autonomic (unconscious) nervous system. For example, there are feedback devices that monitor electrodermal activity (electrical resistance in the skin), which correlates with states of tension in the body. These devices transform the electrical resistance measurements into auditory tones or movements of the needle on a dial.

Second, Rex Stanford's conformance theory to explain psi (1974; 1978) postulates that the will of a subject can act upon random elements in a system to introduce greater order. This theory has been supported by research on the influence of people's minds upon random number generators (RNGs) that are activated by electronic microswitches or by radioactive emissions, as well as upon RNGs that rely on mechanical devices.[88]

In an extensive series of experiments, William Braud introduced an innovation into the feedback model. Braud provides an observer (O) with information on the electrodermal activity of a subject (S), who is in another room. O is then told to influence S by psychokinesis, in order to reduce or increase S's electrodermal activity. Braud also extends Stanford's conformance theory, suggesting that "under certain conditions, a system possessing a greater degree of disorder (randomness, lability, noise, entropy) changes its organization so as to more closely match that of another system possessing less disorder, less entropy, greater structure." Over a period lasting from 1978 to 1995, Braud and several colleagues explored these ideas in several projects that comprised more than 23 experiments.

Electrodermal Activity and Healing

William Braud

Braud conducted experiments to determine the effects of the efforts of Matthew Manning, a gifted healer, on electrodermal activity (EDA).

Blindly scored polygraph records show highly significant results (p = .002).

Conformance behavior involving living systems
(Research in Parapsychology 1978, **1979)**
Significant healing effects on EDA are demonstrated. Though the studies appear to be well designed and well executed, the descriptive data is too meager for proper assessment.[89] Rating: II

Electrodermal Activity and Psychokinetic Influence

William Braud and Marilyn Schlitz

Braud and Schlitz "conducted a 'bio-PK' experiment to determine whether target persons with a relatively strong need to be influenced (calmed) would evidence a greater psi effect than would persons without such a need." They achieved significance levels for calming effects of p < .035 for the 16 active (needy) versus 16 inactive subjects; p < .014 for the active subjects versus chance expectations; probability was nonsignificant for inactive subjects.

Psychokinetic influence on electrodermal activity
(***Journal of Parapsychology*** 1983)
In this well-performed and well-reported study, response of EDA to healing is again demonstrated, significant where active subjects were used. This would seem to indicate that healing acts where needed, where a calming effect might be beneficial. Activation of self-healing in the healee by the healer appears to be another possible mechanism for healing. The experimenters were not blind to the activity type of the subjects, and thus an experimenter rather than a subject need effect may have been demonstrated. The authors consider this possibility but dismiss its significance with the observation that this would still demonstrate a need—of the experimenters. Rating: I

Psychokinesis: Further Studies

William Braud, Marilyn Schlitz, John Collins, and Helen Klitch

Three experiments were run that utilized the same experimental arrangements for allobiofeedback as in the previous study (Braud and Schlitz 1983). The experimenters looked at the ability of influencers to increase or decrease the EDA of volunteer subjects, and to affect levels of other physiological variables. They also looked at the ability of volunteers to block the attempted psi influence. Several of their results reached modest levels of significance.

Further studies of the bio-PK effect: feedback, blocking, specificity and generality (*Research in Parapsychology 1984*, 1985)

The experimenters were rigorous in their application of statistical procedures, taking as significant only those findings that were predicted from the start of the experiment. The first experiment was similar to distant healing, with positive results. The third experiment suggests healing may have selective physiological effects. Significant healing effects are demonstrated. One would need confirmation of the blocking and specificity effects before one could place much confidence in them. Rating: I

Blocking of healing by healees was not confirmed in this study. Many healers believe that such blocking occurs. They propose that people may need their illnesses to manipulate their relationships (for instance, to get more attention, or to avoid various obligations) or to have the lessons which suffering can bring. It would be of great interest to pursue this issue further, in light of the suggestive blocking noted in this study.

Reiki and Electrodermal Activity

Marilyn J. Schlitz and William G. Braud

Schlitz and Braud studied Reverend David Jarrell, who uses and teaches a modification of the Reiki healing system.[20] He includes spirit guides, etheric bodies, chakras, and past lives in his healing. The object of the study was to determine whether distant healing of this sort could alter the skin resistance response (SRR) of a subject in 30 second periods, while feedback, consisting of a measurement of SRR, was given to the healer. The study employed three healers. No significant distant healing effect was noted for the healers as a group. "However, consistent calming effects (46.32 percent and 45.48 percent, respectively) were obtained for two of the Reiki practitioners, and consistent *reversed* (activation) effects were obtained for the third practitioner."

Reiki plus natural healing: an ethnographic/experimental study (*Psi Research*, 1985; *Research in Parapsychology 1985*, 1986)

While methodologically well carried out and well reported, this study is seriously flawed, in that the healers were required to function in a fashion inconsistent with their ordinary healing practices, limiting their healing to only 30 seconds. No effects of healing are demonstrated in this study. Rating: V

Electrodermal Activity: Intuitive Data Sorting and Psychokinesis

William Braud and Marilyn Schlitz

This study explores the possibility that the observed effects of allobio-feedback may be

> contributed totally or partially by an intuitive data sorting (IDS) process in which the influencer or experimenter psychically, yet unconsciously, scans the future electrodermal activity stream of the subject and begins an experimental session at a time that maximizes the degree of fit between the ongoing electrodermal activity and the prescribed schedule of influence and control periods. . . . According to this "informational" model, psi functioning is still in evidence but is of an informational rather than a causal (psychokinetic) sort.

The study did not produce significant effects.

Possible role of intuitive data sorting in electrodermal biological psychokinesis (*Research in Parapsychology 1987*, 1988)
     The EDA effects that are observed in these experiments appear to be exerted intentionally by the influencer rather than selected by IDS to match the expectations. The IDS hypothesis is not ruled out by this experiment. There is no way to rule out the possibility that IDS was occurring at the instigation of the experimenters by the influence of super-psi. In line with their investment in producing this long series of experiments, one would anticipate that the experimenters could unconsciously orchestrate the results to agree with a preferred hypothesis. Rating: I

Electrodermal Activity: Allobiofeedback Studies Summarized

William Braud and Marilyn Schlitz

This article summarizes the entire series of allobiofeedback studies, providing descriptions and data not previously published. There were 323 sessions with 4 experimenters, 62 influencers and 271 subjects. Of the 15 assessments, 6 (40 percent) produced significant results. Of the 323 sessions, 57 percent were successful (high significance: $p < .000023$). Qualitative information is also provided. Subjects frequently reported subjective responses correlating closely with influencers' images.
     Braud and Schlitz mention very briefly two additional experiments of 30 and 16 sessions. In a footnote they add that the first of the additional

studies focused on "whether increments or decrements in SRR activity might be easier to produce via distant mental influence." The second studied "whether the magnitude of a distant mental influence effect could be self-modulated by the influencer." They promise to expand upon this in a later publication. No significant results were obtained in these experiments.

A methodology for the objective study of transpersonal imagery (*Journal of Scientific Exploration,* 1989)

The overall significance of the series is most impressive.[90] It is disappointing to have so little detail on an experiment which produced no significant results. Rating: III

It is important to have replications of studies by several laboratories in order to determine the credibility of a new observation. Dean Radin and colleagues at the Department of Parapsychology at the University of Edinburgh invited William Braud to their laboratory to help them set up a replication of his allobiofeedback model. Braud's participation assures us that the replication followed his model closely.

Electrodermal Activity: Replication

D. I. Radin, Robin K. Taylor, and William G. Braud

Radin and colleagues tested the hypothesis that "mental intention can influence a remote person's autonomic nervous system, as measured by changes in electrodermal activity." In 16 sessions, influencers attempted to either "calm or activate a remote person's electrodermal activity in randomly assigned 30-second epochs over a 32-minute session. . . . "A paired activate/calm analysis "showed a significant tendency for electrodermal activity to be higher during activate periods and lower during calm periods. . . ." (modest significance: $p < .03$). A *post hoc* test found evidence that "remote attention alone, independent of the assigned direction to calm or activate, tended to raise autonomic activity over baseline levels" (high significance: $p < .001$).

Remote mental influence of human electrodermal activity, (*European Journal of Parapsychology,* 1995)

This is an excellent study, well designed and well reported. Modest effects of mental intent of one person to calm or activate the skin resistance of another person from a distance of 25 meters are demonstrated. The more highly significant *post hoc* findings cannot be accepted without further replications. Rating: I

Correlations of findings in the study by Radin et al. with geomagnetic activity furthers our appreciation of the nature of subtle energies and their interaction with other natural fields and forces.[91]

With this very impressive series of successful replications of the allobiofeedback model, we can be more confident that this is a real effect of mental intent of one person upon another, and a confirmation of yet another healing effect.[92]

The implication is that healing can relax people, because skin resistance is correlated with states of tension and relaxation. This is why skin resistance is used as a basis for lie detector tests. People who are not habitual liars become tense when they tell a lie. It is unclear whether the observed healing effects are due to direct action on skin resistance or whether the skin resistance changes are secondary to changes in tension in the subjects.

Of related interest are the similar effects of mental intent on electrical potentials in plants.[95] *The significance of these changes is unclear. Could this mean that plants have various levels of tension that correlate with their electrical potentials, as do humans? Or conversely, are these changes less related to emotions and more a manifestation of some as yet undefined physiological mechanisms?*

An interesting research observation is that there appears to be a decline in significant findings through the series of studies of Braud and colleagues. Similar declines are found in the series of two studies of anxiety by Quinn, and the studies of motility of algae by Pleass and Dey. Declines are noted in many series of individual trials in parapsychological studies. It is speculated that boredom with routines of research (such as guessing which cards are being focused upon telepathically by someone in another room) might be the cause of the decline effect, but it seems premature to speculate further on the reasons for the declines.

Distant healing is so alien to our materialistic culture that very firm evidence is required to confirm that such nonlocal effects actually occur. Objective measures of distant healing effects on physiological measures could provide such evidence. In the following study, several experimenters explored whether they could influence each other's heart rate, electrodermal activity, and the dilation of blood vessels in their fingers.

Human Physiology and a Ritual Healing Technique

Janine M. Rebman, Rens Wezelman, Dean I. Radin, Paul Stevens, Russell A. Hapke, and Kelly Z. Gaughan

In two experiments, Janine Rebman and colleagues monitored the electrodermal activity (EDA), heart rate (HR), and finger blood volume (BVP) of study subjects while an experimenter sought to calm them from a distance, with no ordinary means of communications between influencers and subjects. Reasoning that lessons might be learned from traditional cultures about distant mental influence on living subjects (DMILS), the authors included in this study the use of ritual objects. Traditional cultures claim that the focus of a magician on a person is enhanced when such ritual objects are used.

In the first experiment, study authors alternated between being healer, patient, and experimenter. Personal belongings, bits of hair, and soft clay models that each subject made of himself or herself served as ritual objects. Healing was done according to a specific protocol in an acoustically and electromagnetically shielded room, in series of three 12-minute sessions. The experiment resulted in significant increase in BVP and significant decrease in HR, both as predicted. The EDA showed a slight arousal rather than relaxation, but did not reach statistically significant levels

Based on the first experiment, increases in HR and EDA and a decrease in BVP were predicted in a second experiment. Highly significant results were found as predicted, with EDA and BVP increased (respectively, $p < .0004$; $p < .002$), and HR decreased ($p < .001$).

Remote influence of human physiology by a ritual healing technique (*Subtle Energies*, 1995)

This well-designed and well-reported study demonstrates significant effects of distant mental influence on electrodermal activity, heart rate, and peripheral blood volume. The interpretation of the unexpected EDA results awaits further replications and evaluations. Rating: I

This study confirms yet again that healers can significantly influence a healee from a distance. It is good to have a study with the multiple measures of electrodermal activity, heart rate, and peripheral blood volume. While logic would seem to predict that EDA should decrease (consistent with measurements of EDA in a relaxed state), the EDA increased in this study. The authors suggest that the imagery and rituals of healers massaging a doll representing the healee may have caused this elevation in EDA. EDA in horses has been found to increase when they are stroked.

When objective instruments demonstrate effects of an experimenter upon a subject from a distance, it becomes clearer from the one side that there is evidence to support what healers have been claiming, and more difficult from the other side to reject the possibility of nonlocal influences.

The next three studies explore healing effects on muscle tension, which provides another measure of anxiety and stress. Such tension can be measured with electrodes on the skin above the muscles.

The first study of physiological effects of distant mental intent more closely approximates a healing situation.

Relaxation and Therapeutic Touch

Daniel P. Wirth and Jeffery R. Cram

Wirth and Cram studied the effects of noncontact Therapeutic Touch (NCTT) on a number of human physiological responses, including measures of neuromuscular activity. These responses in turn all reflect general levels of autonomic nervous system (ANS) arousal and therefore provide measures of relaxation effects of healing.

The 12 volunteers were all associated with a Northern California yoga retreat center, 11 being daily mantra meditators. Of these, five were also trained in advanced Kriya yoga meditation and one was self taught in another meditation technique. Subjects were led to believe that the study was about meditation and were not told that it focused on healing, nor were they informed of the design of the study.

In a randomized, double-blind study, baseline recording periods were alternated with experimental and control (mock TT) conditions. NCTT and mock treatment were given from behind each subject by one of two TT practitioners, without the subject's knowledge (eight by an independent TT practitioner and four by the first author).

All of the measures showed general gradual reductions in arousal levels over the course of the study. Significant decreases in readings were shown in all measurements for both NCTT and mock TT, compared to the baseline. A comparison of the mock TT value and the TT value (both minus the baseline values) showed significant differences on the measure of neuromuscular activity during and following the NCTT treatments.

Multi-site electromyographic analysis of non-contact Therapeutic Touch (*International Journal of Psychosomatics,* 1993)

A well designed and well reported study. It is helpful to have an independent measure confirming the relaxation effect of healing almost universally reported by healers and healees. As the authors note, it is difficult to know how much to attribute the relaxation to meditation practiced during the study and how much to NCTT. However, it is unfortunate that subjects were regular practitioners of yoga and meditation. No mention is made by the authors of a check to see whether the experimental and control group differed in their experiences or practices of these techniques. The results may therefore represent differences between the groups in self-healing rather than in spiritual healing. Rating: IV

Muscle Relaxation and Nontraditional Prayer

Daniel P. Wirth and Jeffrey R. Cram

Here Wirth and Cram measured the electromagnetic energy flow of the body at energy points known to ancient Eastern tradition as chakra centers. The study used a randomized, double-blind, within-subject, crossover design to examine the effect of nontraditional distant prayer on the electromyogram (EMG), which measures electrical activity in muscles.

The 21 subjects were not taking medication, suffering from heart conditions, pregnant, or subject to other significant medical problems. Each subject was randomly assigned to two sessions, one with treatment and the other with control conditions. Treatment was by simultaneous Reiki and LeShan distant healing, with no contacts or communications between healers and subjects. Although healers used these approaches to access healing, they shifted into prayers at deeper healing states. Sessions were 30 minutes long, including 21 minutes of physiological monitoring.

The results showed highly significant reductions in EMG activity for two of the four muscle regions studied: the lumbar area ($p < .001$) and the T6 paraspinal ($p < .0002$). Reductions in EMG activity were noted primarily during treatments, and especially shortly following the start of the healing sessions. During control periods, there was usually an increase in overall muscle activity, presumably due to back muscle fatigue. The T6 paraspinal region corresponds to the area of the heart chakra, an energy center identified in Eastern traditions with healing.

The psychophysiology of nontraditional prayer (*International Journal of Psychosomatics,* 1994)

This well-designed and well-reported study confirms that EMG measures can validate subjective reports of relaxation with healing treatments. It is noteworthy that healers identified prayer states that they felt accessed deeper states of healing than LeShan or Reiki healing did. Significant healing effects were demonstrated.[94] Rating: I

Another study measured electromyography during Therapeutic Touch treatments.

Muscle Tone and Therapeutic Touch

Nancy Whelan Post

Post studied effects of Therapeutic Touch (TT) on muscle tone in 38 students and faculty at her university. Volunteers were randomly and blindly assigned to TT or placebo groups. Forehead muscle activity was monitored by an electromyographic device and automated recording equipment. All subjects demonstrated significant decreases in muscle tone and no significant differences were found between the groups before and after interventions.

The Effects of Therapeutic Touch on Muscle Tone (master's thesis, San Jose State University, 1990)[28]

Therapeutic Touch healing demonstrated no significant effects on muscle tension. The *Masters Abstracts International* summary from which this report is taken was too brief for proper analysis of the study. Rating: III

The effects of healing in reducing muscle tension, as measured by electromyography, appear significant. They suggest that the tension of muscle fatigue can be reduced by healing. It is unclear whether the healing acts on the muscles or on the general state of emotional and/or physical tension of the subjects, as healing appears to act in a general way to reduce several physiological measures of tension states.

It seems that where there is no apparent need for relaxation, as in the Post study, no relaxation is produced.

With relaxation, the autonomic nervous system brings about dilation of blood vessels in the skin, which raises the temperature of the skin. Skin temperature can thus be used as a rough indicator of shifts in tension and relaxation.

The next two studies explored effects of Therapeutic Touch healing on skin temperature.

The Relaxation Response and Therapeutic Touch

Mary Miller Sies

Mary Sies studied relaxation in eight experienced Therapeutic Touch (TT) healers who scored higher than 97 on the SETTS test[95] and who had at least one year's experience. Skin temperature was monitored during TT healings, presuming that elevations in temperature indicate relaxation.

Half of the healers showed a highly significant relaxation response ($p < .0007$). Durations of healing greater than 15 minutes were required to achieve relaxation responses.

An Exploratory Study of Relaxation Response in Nurses Who Utilize Therapeutic Touch (master's thesis, University of Arizona, 1987)[28]

While this brief report requires caution in interpreting the study, highly significant elevations in skin temperature of healers were demonstrated with TT healing. This appears to confirm that TT produces a relaxation response in healers during healing. Of note is the need for 15 minutes of TT to achieve an effect. However, with such a brief report and without controls, it is impossible to accept the conclusion of Sies that TT promotes relaxation. One would want information on factors that might have influenced the results, such as the temperature of the room, the emotional states of the healers, stress, or relaxation factors which might have been present. Rating: III

The next study employed controls in studying TT healing effects on skin temperature.

The Parasympathetic Nervous System and Non-contact Therapeutic Touch

Christine Ann Louise Tharnstrom

Christine Tharnstrom explored changes in subjective reports of stress and superficial skin temperatures over a period of 15 minutes. A rating scale from 1-10 was used to assess subjective stress in 39 subjects divided into three groups: TT, mock-TT (MTT), and control. Significant reductions in skin temperature and stress levels were found in all groups, with no significant differences between the groups.

The effects of Non-contact Therapeutic Touch on Parasympathetic Nervous System as Evidenced by Superficial Skin Temperature and Perceived Stress (master's thesis, San Jose State University, 1993)[28]

No healing effects are demonstrated in this study, which is too briefly reported for reasonable analysis. It would appear that changes in skin temperature can be produced by suggestion. An alternative explanation might be that the person giving MTT treatments had innate healing abilities. Rating: III

These master's theses, which focused on limited numbers of subjects, must be taken as pilot studies. The use of skin temperature to assess stress appears promising but requires further study.

Another form of muscle testing widely used in wholistic practice is the testing of muscle strength as an indicator of physical and mental health and illness. It assumes that the body functions as an energetic unity. When the awareness of people is focused upon their dis-ease or disease, their muscular strength is weakened. One may thus present a question to people about their psychological or physical states of being and while they focus upon that question one may test their muscle strength. If the answer to the question is positive, their strength is unchanged from their baseline strength or even stronger. If the answer is negative, their muscle strength is weaker. This is a very basic "truth detector."

This sort of test originates in the tradition of Applied Kinesiology (AK), a derivative of acupuncture theory and practice. AK uses this test to explore the integrity of the acupuncture meridians and organ systems.

One may use this method as well to explore allergies. One may put the suspected allergen in a person's left hand, while testing the strength of their right arm. If they are allergic to it, their ability to resist one's pushing down on their outstretched right arm will be noticeably decreased. Some therapists do this by simply having the person think about the suspected allergen.

One may also use this method to explore the unconscious mind. I will sometimes ask psychotherapy clients to focus on whether a relationship is good for them, or on whether there were problems in the past with a particular member of their family which may have left emotional scars. I once had a paranoid client who would not believe the evidence of his own bodymind, when his arm was markedly weaker upon focusing on the question of whether he had any resentments or hurts from his relationship with his father. He insisted that I must have pushed harder on his arm after asking that question. I had to have him hold a weight in his outstretched hand and support the weight with my hand, removing my support as the question was asked. In that way he could see that the identical weight produced a markedly different response as he focused on the sensitive question.[96]

This method of muscle testing was used in the next study by researchers who studied the effects of healing on normal, healthy people.

Muscle Strength and Qigong
Kenneth M. Sancier and Effie P. Y. Chow

Sancier and Chow used an arm muscle test to show changes in a subject's muscle strength affected by "changes in external qi emitted by a qigong master or by internal qi that resulted from negative or positive thoughts of a subject." The latter were produced by allowing only the subject see a flash card that was marked "well" or "sick." Measurements of pressure applied to the arm and its duration. A computer was used to record and analyze the reponses. Of the two measurements, the duration until the arm gave way to downward pressure proved to be more sensitive.

For 12 subjects in the study of changes in internal qi, "there was a significant difference in the value of the [time duration]" (p in the range of .0001 to .049) and for three subjects "there was no significant difference." The most highly significant correlation (p < .0001) "was attained by a subject who reported using strong visualization of what it meant to him to be sick or well."

The qigong master emitted external qi with the intent to "either weaken or strengthen each of the eight subjects." For the resistance duration, the mean values "were approximately two seconds for the weakened state and approximately four seconds for the strong state" (highly significant: p < .0001).

Sancier maintains that the "results affirm the often stated belief that visualization and positive thinking are an essential part of the healing process."

Healing with Qigong and quantitative effects of Qigong *(Journal of the American College of Traditional Chinese Medicine,* **1989)**

A simple and rapid test of the influence of a healer appears to be demonstrated with muscle testing. However, though blinds were included with the external qi tests, the fact that a standard sequence was repeated by the healer in all subjects could have inflated the results. The experimenter doing the muscle testing would presumably note the effects and their order. He or she might then apply more or less pressure on the arms of the subjects, in line with expectations. No data are provided on the amount of pressure applied. One must therefore be cautious in accepting the validity of these results.[97] [98] Rating: IV

One would think that the benefits of healing in treatment of infectious diseases could be studied rather easily. Oddly, I have found few reports on this topic. A Chinese study by Chu Chou, listed in the bibliography, showed that candida yeast infections in women could be improved with qigong healing.

Other problems await study: burns, heavy menstrual bleeding, intrauterine fetal growth retardation, improper fetal position during labor, infant colic, eczema, cancers, and psychotic decompensations.

Let us now turn to research on more narrowly focused effects of healing. These and subsequent studies on other organisms may provide further clues to some of the underlying mechanisms of healing.

HEALING ACTION ON ANIMALS

It has recently been discovered that reasearch causes cancer in rats.

—Anonymous

Studies show healers can influence the health of animals, supporting the claims that healers can be helpful to humans with similar problems. Such studies are also important because they eliminate the placebo effect as a cause of results.

Among early studies of healing on animals, the work of Bernard Grad is classic. He was the first to study healing in a laboratory setting.

It was Oscar Estebany[99] who interested Grad in this work. He volunteered to have Grad study his abilities so that more people, including those in health regulating bodies, might come to accept healing as a legitimate aid in health care.

"I think you have the wrong address," said Grad. "I'm a Ph.D. doctor. I don't study people. I study mice."

"That's okay," said Estebany. "I can work with mice, too."

Grad had studied biological energies with Wilhelm Reich, and was thus open to such propositions. He designed and ran a number of studies of healing on his own time, with only occasional, minimal funding, and at great risk to his professional standing and continued employment at McGill University.

Wound Healing in Mice and Spiritual Healing

Bernard Grad

In a pilot study Grad anesthetized 48 mice and created similar sized wounds on their backs by the removal of a piece of skin approximately one-half inch by one-inch. He describes his procedures in great detail. The mice were divided into three groups of 16: the first group received healing for 15 minutes twice daily, the second was an untreated control, and the third was an untreated control whose cages were heated as much as the cages of the mice held by Estebany (to control for the possibility that heat from Estebany's hands might induce faster wound healing.) The lab workers were unaware of which groups they were handling.

At 14 days, the wounds of the experimental group had healed more rapidly than those of either of the control groups (highly significant: $p < .001$), and the rate of wound healing of the two control groups did not differ from each other.

Grad repeated this experiment with similar results. As no blinds were employed, no further details were provided.

Some biological effects of the "laying-on of hands": a review of experiments with animals and plants (*Journal of the American Society for Psychical Research*, 1965a[100])

Science requires methodical replications to be certain that observed results were actually due to healing.

Wound Healing in Mice and Spiritual Healing: Replication
B. Grad, R.J. Cadoret, and G.I. Paul

This study replicated Grad's pilot experiments, this time using 300 mice, careful controls, random assignments of mice to experimental and control groups, and blinds. The mice were divided into an experimental group treated by Estebany; a control group held by nonhealers in a manner similar to the way Estebany held the treated cages of mice; and a "heated cage" control group. Half of the cages held by Estebany were placed in closed paper bags and the other half in open paper bags during the healing treatments in order to preclude (with the sealed bags) or minimize (with the open bags, into which Estebany could insert his hands) any physical interventions by the healer which might influence the mice to heal more quickly. C groups were also placed in bags, half of them sealed and half open, in identical manner to the E group. Mean areas of wounds in the three groups were not significantly different at the start.

Results were significant on days 15 and 16 of the study, with E group in the open bag healing more rapidly than the two C groups (p <.01). On subsequent days, the differences in wound size were not significant because nearly all had healed completely. The trend of more rapid healing in the mice in the closed bags in the E group was similar to that of those in the open bags but did not reach significance.

The influence of an unorthodox method of treatment on wound healing in mice (*International Journal of Parapsychology*, 1961)

These first controlled experiments on mammals suggest that spiritual healing helps heal wounds. In personal communication, Grad reported that Estebany had to hold each cage twice daily for 15 minutes in order to obtain the noted effects. This was more intensive treatment than Estebany usually requires to obtain results. These are nicely designed, performed, and reported studies. Significant healing effects are demonstrated. Rating: I

The most useful part of these experiments is that mice do not respond to suggestion. It is impossible to claim this is a placebo effect.

These studies are in the best tradition of scientific inquiry. Anecdotal reports from a healer that healing could help people with wounds led to pilot studies, which were followed up by increasingly precise controlled studies.[101]

Grad was pleased with the wound healing studies. He proposed to Estebany that they could study the influence of healing on hormones, potentially a more profound demonstration of a healing effect. Though Estebany had agreed, he found that the many hours demanded of him in the laboratory were limiting his ability to give healing to the numerous people who needed his help.

When Grad indicated he wanted to run the following study, Estebany proposed, "Why don't I just give healing to some cotton? You can put this into the cages and this will be every bit as good as if I hold the cages for all those hours." Grad was at first skeptical, but gave in when Estebany told him of the many people he had helped by mailing them bits of paper to which he had given healing. Estebany received testimonials from successful healings with babies and with people in coma who had had this type of healing, where suggestion could not have been an adequate explanation.[102]

Goiters in Mice and Spiritual Healing Using Cotton

Bernard Grad

Goiters were produced in mice by withholding iodine from their diets and by giving them Thiouracil, which produces goiters. The rate of thyroid growth was measured by weighing the thyroids as the mice were serially sacrificed over 40 days. Seventy mice were divided into three groups: a no-treatment control group; a group treated regularly by Estebany and then another healer, and a group undergoing heat control, to simulate the elevated heat attained by the treatment group.

In a second experiment, 37 mice were divided into two groups: the first were placed in cages with healer-treated cotton cuttings; the second placed with untreated cuttings.

In the first experiment, the thyroids of the healer-treated group of mice grew more slowly than those of both controls (high significance: $p < .001$). The thyroids of the third group (simulated heat) did not grow significantly more slowly than those of the no-treatment group. In the second experiment, mice in contact with the healer-held vehicle for healing developed goiters significantly more slowly than the controls (high significance: $p < .001$).

Upon return to normal diet, the thyroids of goitrous mice receiving direct or indirect healing returned to normal more quickly than those of the control group. (No numbers or statistics are cited for this last portion of the study.)

The biological effects of the "laying-on of hands" on animals and plants (In: G. Schmeidler, Ed., *Parapsychology: Its Relation to Physics, Biology and Psychiatry*, 1976)

These are excellent studies, with details adequately reported. These studies once more demonstrate a significant healing effect in mammals. As with healer-treated water for plants,[103] we have in healer-treated cotton a vehicle which appears to convey healing. We should also note that the healing is this study may be preventive rather than curative healing. Rating: I

It is ironic and sad that mice and other animals are sacrificed in studies to demonstrate effects of healing. Grad, in personal communication, explained that neither he nor Estebany could find any doctor willing to study Estebany's abilities with human patients. Their choice was either to study animals or nothing. As it took 24 years to repeat Grad's skin wound experiment in humans, and as the study on goiters has not yet been repeated in mice or other animals, Grad's point is well taken.

Healers are very well accepted in the Netherlands, where Frans Snel, a parapsychologist, published a number of studies (with various colleagues) on animal healing, including the following one and several others, below.

Amyloidosis and Healing in Hamsters
Frans Snel and P. R. Hol

Amyloidosis is a disease in which amyloid (abnormal protein) deposits are formed around cells in various organs, eventually compromising their function. Amyloidosis usually occurs in late life with no known cause. It is also one of the possible causes of Alzheimer's disease, though dementia is not part of the usual course of illness when there are amyloid deposits in other parts of the body. Several animal species may also develop amyloidosis, providing a basis for this study of hamsters.

In two experiments, groups of hamsters (42 and 50, respectively) were randomly divided into treatment and control groups. All hamsters were injected with casein. Using randomly distributed photographs of the hamster cages, healers worked to prevent the onset of amyloidosis. At specific intervals, the animals were sacrificed and their blood analyzed for three parameters: hemoglobin, lactose dehydrogenase (LDH), and gamma-GT. Differentiation of white blood cells was studied in the first experiment, but not in the second because the researchers considered the results too dependent on the varying daily interpretations of the analyst.

With Experiment 1, significant effects in predicted directions were noted for differentiation of band forms, which indicate infection (modestly significant: $p < .017$), and other parameters. For Experiment 2, on day 4 the level of he moglobin was lower in the treated animals (modest significance: $p < .05$).

Snel and Hol note that some of the healers disapproved of the animal experimentation and that in the second experiment the randomization ("designating which were to be the experimental and control animals after the experiment was finished") and daily injections may have limited the opportunity to get "through" to the animals.

Psychokinesis experiments in case in induced amyloidosis of the hamster (*European Journal of Parapsychology,* 1983)

The significant positive effects in the first experiment support claims of healers that they can ameliorate the progression of chronic illnesses. The lower number of bandforms in the experimental group suggests that their disease was not as severe as that of the control group. The significant reduction in hemoglobin on day 4 of Experiment 2 is worrisome but is not sustained and may have been due to chance factors.

One would want to have further tests to see whether lowering of hemoglobin occurs in mice, as it does in some humans with healing (Wetzel). Rating: I

Though amyloidosis is not a common illness, it is somewhat similar to other such diseases as rheumatoid arthritis, lupus, and other collagen diseases. If healing can produce positive effects on amyloidosis in mice, there is reason to believe it may be helpful in these other diseases, as healers commonly report.

The next study is most intriguing—an ignored classic in scientific research. In addition to showing how healing may influence infectious disease in animals, it reveals how psychic experimenter effects may creep into research.

Experimenter effects are fairly well documented in research with humans. Gross or subtle verbal and nonverbal cues may lead subjects to behave in manners expected by the experimenters. For instance, when teachers are led to believe that particular students in their classes are especially bright, the students perform better and their IQs even increase. If people are told they are being given a stimulant, they may report feeling that they are stimulated—even when they are actually given a sedative. Experimenter effects are also possible in animal studies. It is believed that animal handlers may unconsciously handle animals differently in experimental and control groups, biasing the results according to their expectations. The following study explores such possibilities, with the addition of possible psi and healing effects.[104]

Malaria in Mice: Expectancy Effects and Psychic Healing

Gerald F. Solfvin

Gerald Solfvin set up a highly unusual, complex study of several experimental variables. He hypothesized that animal handlers' expectancies could produce different rates of illness in mice in their care. In addition, he studied the effects of healing expectations in the animal handlers without actual use of healers and without knowledge on the part of anyone during the experiment as to which mice were designated to be healed. The manipulations in the experiment were of the expectations of the student assistants.

> The mice all were inoculated with the rodent version of the malarial blood parasite. Each student was assigned 12 mice housed in a single cage and was told that half of them would be inoculated with babesia while the other half would receive a sterile injection. The students themselves randomized and marked their mice with either yellow (babesia) or black (nonbabesia) markings to indicate which were which, thus this condition remained nonblind to them. In addition, the students were led to believe that half of each of these two groups would be receiving distant healing from a psychic healer, when in fact there was no such healer in the study. . . . The students were not aware of which mice were supposed to be healed and which not, these being randomly assigned to the healing and control conditions by the author.

The study followed complex and extensive randomization and blinding procedures.

In Experiment 1 Solfvin had three handlers. Two were clearly *sheep* and one was clearly a *goat*.[105] The sheep produced random results. The goat produced modestly significant results ($p < .021$) on the dimension of illness expectancy and a suggestive trend ($p < .092$) for healing expectancy, *both in the direction opposite to that predicted by experimental hypotheses.* That is, the results were strongly in the direction a goat would predict.

In Experiment 2 Solfvin had five handlers. "The babesia and nonbabesia designations (used for inducing expectancies in handlers) were changed to high or low babesia." The results were uniform across the five groups, showing a modestly "significant main effect for the healing expectancy factor" ($p < .05$) and "a marginal trend for the illness . expectancy factor (p between .05 and .10). Both of these are in the direction of the induced expectancies."

Psi expectancy effects in psychic healing studies with malarial mice
(*European Journal of Parapsychology*, 1982a)

This is a key study for understanding possible errors of interpretation that may arise even in controlled studies. Mice in this study were all inoculated with the same dose of malarial parasites, yet some became sicker than others. On the surface this seems to indicate a healer effect. Though no known healer participated in the study, one must postulate that one (or more) of the experimenters was responsible for the significant healing effects. Solfvin points out that this need not be so. Differentials in the handling of mice in the various groups in line with handler expectations (perhaps augmented by clairsentient or precognitive perceptions of mouse group assignments) could have produced portions of the results.

The experiment was well-designed and adequately reported. The levels of significance are too modest for any far-reaching conclusions without further replications. Rating: I

The implications of this study are truly revolutionary. If reproduced, they would indicate that psi healing influences can be produced selectively in an experimental group of mice despite apparent totally controlled, double-blind conditions. If substantiated by repetitions under a variety of circumstances, this will force science to re-evaluate one of its most valuable tools in research, the double-blind experiment. The expectations of experimenters should be clearly stated in future studies, as this may be one of the variables affecting the results.

Rupert Sheldrake (1994) has developed a theory of morphogenetic fields—similar to a collective consciousness which is specific for each species. He speculates that experimenter effects such as those in Solfvin's study may be present in the hard sciences as well as in the biological sciences.

The man who cannot occasionally imagine events and conditions of existence that are contrary to the causal principle as he knows it will never enrich his science by the addition of a new idea.

—Max Planck

In many parts of the world, collars, bracelets, anklets, and earrings are recommended for protection against illness. Their potency is usually attributed to the materials they are made from, such as gold, silver, copper, iron or plant materials. To most educated Westerners, this must seem to be a fairy tale.

Would you believe there may be demonstrable effects of various collars on the progress of malaria in birds? See the following study for precisely such evidence.

Malaria in Birds and Protective Collars
P. Baranger and M.K. Filer

At the age of six days, chicks were injected intravenously with malaria. Groups of six to eight birds were used in repeated trials, until more than 350 birds were included in the studies. Birds in control groups were given nothing or had 12 doses of either 1 mg of chloroquine or quinine, medicines that control malaria.

Treated birds were given metal collars 1 mm. in diameter, of either open, closed, or spiral design, measuring about 20mm across. Metals used included: aluminum, brass, copper, gold, iron, lead, magnesium, manganese, molybdenum, nickel, nickel alloy (nickel, iron, chromium and manganese), silver, German silver (copper, nickel and zinc), tin, and zinc. Plant fiber collars, also about 20mm across, were made from twisted threads of cotton, linen, nylon, rayon, silk, sisal, and wool. Chicks were acclimated to the collars for two days prior to the injection of parasites.

Gold, iron, and copper appeared most effective. The average survival of the birds wearing these collars was 20 to 30 days compared with only 11.6 days for the controls. The appearance of the parasites in the blood of birds with collars of these metals was delayed dramatically relative to the controls. In the second experiment the results were comparable to or exceeded the results obtained with quinine or chloroquine. Tin and silver increased survival to 20 days, while other metals only slightly increased the average length of survival or had no effect. In several instances, birds lost their collars. Their infections increased markedly by the next day.

The protective action of collars in avian malaria (*Mind and Matter,* 1987)

The effects of metal collars on prolonging survival with malarial infection seem clear. How to explain the findings is a problem, however. I have deliberately placed this study following Solfvin's study, as the experimenter effect seems a likely possibility. One might also postulate that the presence of the metal or fiber collar alters an energy field around or within the body so that the defense mechanisms of the organism function more efficiently. This seems a possible explanation since particular metals appear to have greater influence. Again, the apparent healing responses could be an experimenter effect, particularly as blinds are not mentioned in the study. Further, randomization is not described and no statistical analyses are presented. Blinds could be easily arranged with coated materials. Ultimately, one cannot put any reliance in these results.[106] Rating: IV

The positive effects of wearing bracelets of various materials on malarial infections (and other conditions) does appear to warrant further study. If this is not an experimenter effect, it would certainly provide one of the least expensive ways of improving health.

The following unusual study explores healing for malaria in rats. Its novel aspect is that it explored whether healing might be able to act backwards in *time. That is, at the end of the study a healing effect is projected to the rats, several weeks after they have been injected with the malarial parasites.*

This might sound like a very far-out, most improbable way of studying healing (or any other) effects. Several facts suggested that this might work. Healers sometimes receive thanks from healees for healings before *the healers have sent absent healing. It would thus appear that healing might occur backwards in time. Another line of evidence comes from experiments in parapsychology demonstrating apparent backwards-in-time effects by psychics who can influence random number generators prior to the time the psychics focus upon them (Schmidt 1976).*[107]

Rodent Malaria and Backward-in-Time Healing
F. W. J. J. Snel, and P. C. van der Sijde

It has been shown in a few studies of psychokinesis (PK) that it is possible for a person to produce PK effects retroactively. That is, conditions are set up so that a person's influence upon a physical measuring device is recorded prior to the time when the person consciously makes the effort to exert an influence upon that machine.

In this study, a professional healer (with one year's experience) sent healing to rats who had been injected with malarial parasites. The healer's intent was to prevent the spread and multiplication of the parasites in the red blood cells of the rats (Nu/Nu variety) who were specially bred with no thymus gland and thus with no T-cells. The healer lived 20 miles from the laboratory and was given only photographs of the rats that were to receive healing. Healing was sent after the completion of the study.

The rats were injected with the malarial organisms 12 days prior to the start of the experiment. They were randomly assigned, using a random number table, to healing and control groups *after day 42 of the experiment*. Neither healer nor experimenters knew which animal would be assigned to the healing group prior to that time.

Segregated by sex, the rats were randomly distributed in cages that included both experimental and control animals. "Every rat was individually marked and recognizable. A photograph was taken of all four cages and sent to the healer by mail. The healer was asked to prevent the spread and multiplication of blood parasites (malaria) in the red blood cells of the target rats." The healer sent healing for 10 to 15 minutes every evening over the six weeks of the experiment.

"[T]he infected red blood cells in the experimental groups are generally lower than those in the control groups, except on day 42. The differences on days 14 and 28 are modestly significant ($p < .02$ and $p < .015$, respectively), suggesting a healing effect."

The lower percent of infected red blood cells in the control group compared to the treated group on day 42 might be explained by a loss of interest on the part of the healer over a period of six weeks.

Particular white cell types showed differences between experimental and control groups during the experiment.

The effect of retroactive distance healing on babesia rodhani (rodent malaria) in rats, (*European Journal of Parapsychology,* 1990)

A significant healing effect is demonstrated, with less severe evidence of malarial infection in red blood cells in rats that were assigned at the end of the study to be given healing.

The authors call this a *probable retroactive healing effect* because the rats that were to be given healing were not assigned to this treatment until after the study was completed. Another possible explanation is that the healer precognitively recognized which rats would be selected at a later time for healing and sent absent healing during the study.

The fact that all but one of the mice survived much longer than expected suggests that all the mice may have benefited from the healing. This might be due to control and experimental mice being held in the same cages, with the healer receiving a photo of all the mice. Even though they were clearly marked, the healer may not have been able to send healing only to experimental mice.

As apparently it is not known what the normal course of illness is for Nu/Nu rats infected with malaria, it is difficult to assess the results of this study. There appear to be sex differences and there may be other contributing factors causing the differences attributed to healing. No blinds are mentioned for the person reading the microscope blood slides, which leaves open the possibility of experimenter bias.[108] Rating: IV

Effects of healing that transcend the usual limits of time stretch our credulity and our understanding of nature. Effects that appear to be caused by future events are not unknown in quantum physics, however. It appears that spiritual healing and quantum physics may demonstrate ways of interacting that are outside of our ordinary, Newtonian ways of conceptualizing the world. Rather than reject the evidence that contradicts our ordinary laws of science, we need to re-examine our understanding of these laws. Strange and difficult as this may be, it may lead to important progress in health care.

Though no rigorous studies of healing for cancers are available in humans, several have been done on animals.

Tumor Growth and Paranormal Healing

Frans W. J. J. Snel and Peter C. van der Sijde

Frans Snel and Peter van der Sijde explored the effects of a variety of healing methods on cancers in rats. Prior to randomizing animals into groups, they were matched in sex, age, and weight. An animal handler who was not a participant in the study cleaned the cages and fed the animals, handling them briefly in the process. Room temperatures in the laboratory and the healers' homes were recorded during the study and did not differ or vary significantly. Healing was given in the healers' homes at times of day which were convenient to the healers. All healers were interested in working with animals.

The four experiments explored the effects of healing on rats that had been injected with rat liver tumor cells in one case and acsites tumor cells in the other three. Experiment 1 studied direct healing effects on tumor growth (measured by weight) versus tumor growth in the control group, predicting no differences between these groups. The experiment used one professional male healer. Experiment 2 studied direct healing together with gentling (stroking, cuddling) on female rats, using one professional female healer.

Experiment 3 studied the effect of distant healing on survival time, predicting rats in this experiment would survive longer than those in Experiment 2, and using four professional male healers who live 25 to 70 kilometers away from the laboratory. Experiment 4 studied the effects of direct healing combined with gentling and distant healing on tumor growth in a control group, and used the same healer as in Experiment 1.

No spread of tumor was found in any animal beyond the local sites of injection. In the four experiments, the first two did not achieve significant results. For Experiment 3, out of 118 rats, 76 died during the experiment. No significant differences amongst the survivors in survival time were noted in experimental (distant healing) vs. control groups, or in survival according to sex. Half of the rats treated by healer 1 survived the entire period, while only 17 percent of the animals of healers 2 and 4 combined survived, a significant difference ($p < .01$). Of note was the survival of the female rats of healer 1 longer than any other female rats, while his male rats survived the shortest time.

For Experiment 4, the differences between experimental (distant healing) and control groups was modestly significant ($p < .05$), as was the difference in mean survival time between the combined treated groups and the control group ($p < .05$). No other significant differences were noted between conditions.

The effect of paranormal healing on tumor growth (*Journal of Scientific Exploration,* 1995)

Significant effects of healing on tumor growth in rats are demonstrated. This is the more impressive in experiment 4, which had small numbers of animals. The fact that the animals were left in the healers' homes leaves open a question of what else might have been done to produce these effects. Rating: IV

This modest, exploratory study produced several helpful findings. It confirms that healing can be helpful in slowing the growth of cancers, and in one instance appeared to prevent the growth of cancer completely. It also confirms commonly held clinical impressions that some healers are more successful with particular problems than other healers.

Franz Snel and Peter van der Sijde are to be commended for doing a study of healing in healers' own homes, which would allow for the most comfortable application of healing as far as healers are concerned. While skeptics might question whether this model opens questions as to the treatment of the animals because they were not under the constant observation of the experimenters, the benefits appear to me to outweigh the risks.

This study by Frans Snel and Peter van der Sijde confirms that healing can produce significant effects on cancers in rats. There is every reason to believe, both from the logical extension of this study and from numerous anecdotal reports from healers and grateful healees, that healing can produce significant effects on cancers in humans.

While people suffering from cancer naturally are hoping for a cure when they come for healing, it is rare in my informal surveys of healers to hear of such complete healings. Far more common, but not less appreciated, are the dramatic alleviations of pain and physiological dysfunctions caused by cancers. Relief of many of the side effects of chemotherapy, radiotherapy, and surgery are also commonly reported. Healing is not usually recommended as an alternative but rather as a complement to conventional therapy.

At present it is very difficult to find doctors willing to participate in healing research, and studies on cancers in humans await such opportunities.[109] *While studies on animals are deplorable, they have provided information which gives hope to people who suffer from cancers and from the diminished quality of life which accompanies many treatments for cancer.*

Screening Healers

Gary Null

Gary Null sought to understand healing when his brother had a stroke at the age of 35. In this, the fourth of a series of articles, Null details his explorations of healers, the healing process, and subjective aspects of the healing experience.

In a test of healing abilities, 50 healers were screened for demonstrable ability to prolong the lives of mice injected with cancer cells. Healers were assigned one mouse for touch healing and one for distant healing, with another two as controls. Each mouse was inoculated with a highly lethal strain of cancer. Healers were allowed to employ whatever methods they felt would prolong the lives of their mice.

Only one of the 50 healers was consistently successful. Rabbi Abraham Weisman produced total tumor regression in one of his mice and the other survived longer than average. Rabbi Weisman then participated in further double-blind experiments. In the second, "Weisman was able to extend the average life of the treated mice to 12.8 days, compared to 8.9 days for the control group" (a 43.8 percent increase); in the third, to 14.9 days, compared to 12.9 days for the controls (a 15.5 percent increase).

Healers or hustlers (*Self-Help Update*, 1966)

Significant effects of healing are demonstrated in slowing the growth of cancers. The use of only two mice each seems likely to lead to Type II errors in all but the very best healers. Randomization is not mentioned, raw data are not provided, and no statistical analyses are reported. It is therefore difficult to accept these results as more than suggestive evidence for healing effects. Rating: IV

This is the first published broad screening of healers to determine healing ability. While the intent seems good, the method may have problems. Some healers may be squeamish about mice, unprepared for working with animals

in general, or uncomfortable in a laboratory. The problem of healer assessment, other than by demonstrated clinical effects in humans, remains a challenge.

This series of studies shows that healing can be of benefit in treatment of cancer. Several lessons may be drawn from the studies. Various healers may differ in the efficacy of their treatments. A person with cancer who is seeking treatment would be wise to find a healer who has had success with cancer. Furthermore, if there is no benefit from the treatments of one healer, there is reason to believe that another healer may still be helpful.

The following studies examined the growth of mice who were given healing. The possibility that healing can enhance normal animal growth seems feasible, in the light of studies (reviewed later in this chapter) which show healing increasing the growth of plants, bacteria, and yeasts. These are translated studies.

Growth Rates in Mice and Emitted Qi

Lida Feng, Shuying Chen, Lina Zhu, Xiuzhen Zhao, and Siqi Cui; Chinese Immunology Research Center, Beijing

Experimenters looked at the effect of the emitted qi on the growth of over 60 mice, and achieved statistically significant results ($p < .05$). They also explored the effect of emitted qi on the amount of growth hormone in mice's serum, achieving more significant results ($p < .01$).

Effect of emitted qi on the growth of mice (*2nd World Conference for Academic Exchange of Medical Qigong, Beijing, 1993*—from qigong database of Sancier)

If healing can truly increase the rate of growth of animals, it might prove helpful to babies who are small in utero (fetal growth retardation) and to premature infants. This would be a great boon to these children, who often suffer neurological damage if they survive.[110]

Mice Appetite and Distant Healing

Sergei V. Speransky

A Russian electronic engineer, Leonid M. Porvin, "developed a 'technology' for achieving altered states of consciousness conducive to 'distant influence.'" Porvin focused on one out of a pair of successive groups of mice from a distance of 1,700 miles, with the intent of either increasing or decreasing their weight gain. Groups were chosen randomly, in a double-blind design, and their weights recorded as the criterion of change. In 70 trials, the results were highly significant (p < .0000000002).

May and Vilenskaya, summarizing this work, present confusing figures. They state that there were five groups of 13 mice each in target and control groups, with a total of 260 mice. Not only do these figures not add up correctly, but it is unclear how the numbers divided into 70 trials.

"Distant influence" on the eating behavior of white mice (May and Vilenskaya, *Subtle Energies,* 1992)

An effect of healing on weight gain in mice appears to be demonstrated. However, without more details, such as the actual figures for weight change, it is difficult to assess the significance of this report. It is also difficult to know what to make of a report which includes obvious errors in numbers.

Next, we have several studies in which animals were injured or injected with tumors and then given healing. Again we decry the use of animals for healing studies, but must appreciate that the intention is to help people with cancer and other illnesses, when human research has not been possible.

Rabbit Bone Fracture and Emitted Qi

Lin Jia and Jinding Jia; National Research Institute of Sports Science, Beijing

Here, experimenters investigated the biological effect of the emitted qi on healing fractures, using sixteen healthy male rabbits divided into a control group and an emitted qi group. The research found that the "amount and density of callus formation were better in the emitted qi group than in the control group," with a significant difference in the second week (p < .01) and a difference of modest significance in the third week (p < .05).

Overstrain caused pathological changes ("including muscle fibers edema, shortening or lengthening of sarcolemmas, disorganization, breaking and disappearance of myofibrils as well as Z lines, accompanied by edema and damage of mitochondria") were seen less frequently in the emitted qi group than in the control group. "The difference of density between the two groups was significant" (p < .01).

Effects of the emitted qi on healing of experimental fracture (*1st World Conference for Academic Exchange of Medical Qigong, Beijing, 1988*— from qigong database of Sancier)

It is helpful to have this confirmation of healers' anecdotal reports that healing can accelerate the healing of bone fractures.

The next studies explore the effects of spiritual healing on a variety of animal cancers. Even though they include many technical details, I feel they are important because they provide a wealth of evidence to reassure those who might need the help of a healer to deal with cancer.

It is extremely difficult to find medical settings in which to do research on spiritual healing effects (or of any other treatment) for cancers in humans. Most people choose to have chemotherapy and/or radiotherapy. It is rare to have access to groups of people with similar cancers who are receiving a standard treatment. This makes it very difficult to set up equivalent experimental and control groups for a proper study of healing.[111]

Too often, healing is sought as a treatment of last resort for cancer. This again makes it difficult for spiritual healing to demonstrate its full potential. The studies of spiritual healing for cancers in animals are therefore extremely valuable in helping us to have confidence that healing can help with this difficult disease. Again I am saddened that animals are sacrificed for the sake of humans, but I see this as the lesser evil.

Mouse Tumor Growth and Psychokinesis

Brenio Onetto and Gita H. Elguin

Onetto and Elguin looked at the potential of psychokinesis to inhibit tumoral growth in living organisms. In a preliminary study, the area, weight, and volume of such growth in a group of 30 tumorogenic mice treated with "negative PK" showed significantly less growth ($p < .01$) than that of 30 untreated control mice. "A second group of 30 mice were treated for an equal period of time with 'positive PK' in an attempt to increase the tumoral growth, but these mice did not differ from the untreated control animals. Anthony Campbell (1968) adds that at 16 days and 22 days, the average tumor area was significantly smaller (high significance: $p < .001$ in both instances), "and when the animals were killed (at 23 days) this difference was confirmed by direct measurement and weighing of the tumors ($p < .01$). The animals...lost significantly less body weight than did the controls" (modest significance: $p < .05$).

Psychokinesis in experimental tumorogenesis *(Journal of Parapsychology,* **1966; thesis for a professional degree in psychology, University of Chile, 1964)**[112]

This appears to be a sound and significant study. However, insufficient raw data are provided in the brief translated abstract for evaluation of procedures or independent confirmation of statistical analyses.

It is interesting that attempts to increase the rate of tumor growth failed in the study of Onetto and Elguin. Many healers claim that a "native intelligence" in the healing process guides healing to act only in directions that are beneficial to the healee, in line with the intentions of the healer.

In the treatment of cancer we have a complex situation. The healer may be slowing the growth of the cancer cells or decreasing the activity of their enzymes (as shown to be possible in experiments reviewed below). In addition, the healer may be influencing the host animal's own defense mechanisms to act on the cancer cells. Host antibodies against cancer might be increased; blood supply to tumors might be shut down; or other, unidentified processes may be involved.

Clinical reports indicate that healing not only helps with the primary illness, but also reduces side effects of chemotherapy and radiotherapy, and improves emotional states. While it may be difficult to mount studies of healing for cancer in humans, hopefully research can be initiated soon. See Steven Fahrion's preliminary study showing success with basal cell carcinomas in the next chapter.

The study of Onetto and Elguin and the Chinese qigong studies strongly suggest that healing can slow the progress of many types of cancer.

There is an enormous body of research on healing from China.[113] As the translated reports available are fragmentary and leave many questions about this research, only a few samples have been included in this volume.

In China many people practice internal qigong as a way of maintaining and promoting health. These self-healing practices are credited with curing many illnesses, including cancers. It is unclear whether internal and external qigong involve the same or different processes. Internal qigong is now following yoga into health promotion practices in the west.

The Chinese usually recommend meditation and qigong exercises either before or along with the Master's healing. One study (T. Liu et al. 1988) confirms that self-healing by internal qigong may enhance healer-healing (external qigong). In the West, exercises in relaxation, meditation, and imagery (collectively labeled psychoneuroimmunology or PNI)[114] have been shown to slow and sometimes halt or reverse the progress of cancers. I know of no studies focusing on the possible additive effects of PNI and spiritual healing, but this could well be a potent combination.

While we are eager to learn whether healing can help people with cancer, scientists hope also to discover how healing brings about these positive effects. Several qigong studies, reviewed in later sections, begin to explore this question. For instance, studies have demonstrated that healing can influence the growth of cancer cells in animals and in laboratory cultures.

Western studies have not yet included microscopic analyses of cancer cells treated by healers. Chinese qigong reports suggest that healing may disrupt the chromosomes of cancer cells and cause other nuclear damage which could destroy them. The nucleus is the brain of the cell, directing its metabolic and reproductive functions. Disrupting or destroying the chromosomes in the nucleus would make it impossible for the cells to multiply.[115]

Healers report healing can reduce the side effects of radiotherapy given for cancer. The following translated study makes a start at exploring whether this might be so.

Mouse Cancer and Healing

Dmitri G. Mizra and V. I. Kartsev

In three experiments mice were exposed to lethal doses of ionizing radiation from cesium.[116] Experimental (E) and control (C) groups of 10 mice each were irradiated together with 30 rads/minute. Survival time of the mice was recorded as the measure of healing effect. In the first experiment, healing was given at 15 minutes following irradiation. In the second, healing was given 15 to 20 minutes prior to irradiation to four experimental and four control groups. All of the mice in the C groups died by the 19th day after irradiation. In the E groups, the mortality was 90 percent, 50 percent, 40 percent, and 22 percent respectively. Eighteen months later, 15 mice from the E groups were still alive. Most of the healers gave healing from a distance of meters away from the mice. The most successful healer was 800 miles away.

In the third, healing was given both before and after irradiation. "[N]ine out of 10 animals in one test subgroup and all 10 in another subgroup survived, as compared to three mice in the control group."

Mental influence on grey mice exposed to lethal doses of ionizing radiation (May and Vilenskaya, *Subtle Energies,* 1992)

This translated study demonstrates an impressive effect of healing in counteracting the lethal effects of radiation. It is unclear why there were such wide variations in survival of animals, though mention of varying doses of radiation suggests this could have been the cause.

If this study can be replicated and healing can be confirmed to reduce mortality after exposure to radiation, then healing may also reduce the illness which occurs as a side effect of radiation therapy.

This concludes the review of foreign studies of healing on animals.

The following is an exemplary series of American studies in which the objective of the healing is to hasten the recovery of mice from anesthesia. Many healers report that they can appreciably reduce the morbidity of surgery by adding healing to the routine medical care of the surgical patient. Healing is often given prior to, during, and after hospitalization.

Reducing the amount of time patients spend under anesthesia could reduce all sorts of complications which accrue the longer the anesthesia is applied. These may include irritation of the airways in the lungs and pneumonia—which can lead to death even though the operation is a "success."[117]

This series also demonstrates how experimenters sharpen their methods to focus with increasing clarity on possible mechanisms of healing.

Arousing Anesthetized Mice through Psychokinesis

Graham K. Watkins and Anita M. Watkins

"Twelve subjects (nine of them professed psychics or known to be exceptional performers on PK or ESP tests) were tested for their ability to cause mice to arouse more quickly from ether anesthesia than normally would be expected." Three experiments were conducted, with different experimental conditions and varying numbers of runs. For all experiments, 24 pairs of mice were serially anesthetized in each *run* (group of single trials). Care was taken to randomize mice that were more easily anesthetized between the experimental and the control conditions.

In the first experiment, "the mean sleep time for the control group was 32.63 seconds," while that of the experimental group was 28.72 seconds (modest significance: $p < .036$). In the second experiment, for all subjects the overall "mean control time was 27.90 seconds, as compared with the mean experimental time of 21.54 seconds" (highly significant: $< .001$). In the third experiment overall, "the mean time to arousal for the control group was 30.14 seconds;" for the experimental group the time was 24.91 seconds (highly significant: $p < .001$).

Possible PK influence on the resuscitation of anesthetized mice (*Journal of Parapsychology*, 1971)

Significant accelerations of recovery from anesthesia are demonstrated. This is an excellent study, meticulously reported, with significant results. Rating: I

There were a few instances in which the control mice woke more quickly than the experimental mice, although these effects were not statistically significant. Such negative results bear clarification. Healers report that they never obtain negative effects from healings. This study suggests that healers' reports might be in error, and that careful scrutiny might yet turn up some negative effects.[118]

Arousing Anesthetized Mice through Psychokinesis: Replication

Roger Wells and Judith Klein

Journal abstract:

An attempt was made to replicate the findings of a previously reported experiment by G.K. and A.M. Watkins. In the present experiment, four subjects previously determined to be *gifted* were tested for their ability to cause mice to arouse more quickly from ether anesthesia than normally would be expected. One mouse of each pair tested was an experimental mouse; the other, a control. The subject's task was to try to awaken the experimental mouse more quickly than the other. Eight experiments, each consisting of

24 trials, were conducted. Seven of the eight were in the expected direction, one being independently significant at the level of p = .01. There was an average difference of 5.52 seconds between the time the experimental mouse awoke and the time the control mouse awoke (p < .05). Of the total 192 trials, 110 were hits (p < .05).

A replication of a psychic healing paradigm (*Journal of Parapsychology, 1972*)

These are significant results in nonsuggestible subjects. A true healing effect seems to be demonstrated. Questions remain, however, as randomization was done by casual distribution of mice between groups. Rating: IV

Although significant healing effects are found in this study, as in the previous example, the experimenters could have caused the observed effects because mice were not randomized thoroughly. Perhaps the experimenters clairsentiently or precognitively selected mice with short waking times to be targets, relative to slow wakers, who were selected for the control group. Perhaps the person timing the waking biased the results.

Resuscitating Anesthetized Mice: Further Studies
G. K. Watkins, A. M. Watkins, and R. A. Wells

The previous experiment was replicated seven times with more careful controls and with attempts to rule out possible factors, other than psychokinesis, that might influence results. Mice were assigned randomly to experimental and control groups. Subjects sat behind a one-way mirror. Experimenters monitored the waking of anesthetized mice in blind fashion. In the first half of each run (16 or 24 trials), mice on one side of the table were targeted; in the second half, mice on the other side were targeted. The seven experiments saw various modifications in procedure and testing.

Experiment 1, with simple replication using two new talented subjects, reached modest significance (p < .026). Experiment 2 used mice pairs preselected for similar wakening times, anesthetized in the same container (high significance: p < .002). With Experiment 3, the belief in ESP of nontalented subjects (p = nonsignificant in previous tests) was positively related to scoring (modest significance: p < .05). "Those who did not think they would do well in fact did better than those who had a more confident attitude" (p < .01).

In Experiments 4 and 5, subjects were monitored for EEG, EKG, respiration, finger plethysmograph, and galvanic skin response (GSR). "Both series yielded highly significant PK scoring" (p < .004 and p < .00003).

In Experiments 6 and 7, two series were done to find out why there had been chance results in previous work when the target side was randomly changed from trial to trial, rather than remaining the same for each half of the run. The subjects had complained that they could not shift their focus of concentration fast enough, which led the researchers to hypothesize that a lag effect might exist in which the PK exerted on the previous trial would continue to have an influence on the mouse's performance in the current trial. To test for such an effect, the subjects did half of a normal run, concentrating exclusively on one side or the other. The subjects then left the room and occupied themselves with other activities while the experimenters, who were unaware of which side had been the target, continued the procedure to the end of the run. In the first of these series, the same experimenters performed both halves of the run; in the second, as an added precaution against experimenter effects, two different experimenters conducted the second half.

> Linear regression analyses showed the two halves of the run to be similar in overall scoring. This was true in both series (p = .02 in each). In addition, both halves of the run showed independently significant high scoring levels in each series. In the first series, the first half was highly significant at p = .003 and the second half at p = .002. In the second series the significance levels were p = .04 for the first half and   p = .05 for the second half.

Further studies on the resuscitation of anesthetized mice (*Research in Parapsychology 1972*, 1973)

Significant effects of healing are demonstrated. Though this study is reported very briefly, the meticulous report of Watkins and Watkins (reviewed above) suggests it is highly likely this study was equally meticulously designed and run. This is an excellent study, but too briefly reported to allow serious consideration. Rating: III

This series of studies on waking mice from anesthesia is a demonstration of work carefully done to tease out alternative explanations. Experiment 2 rules out the possibility that the results were due to biased selection of mice because experimental and control group mice were selected for similar lengths of waking times and anesthetized in the same container.

Studies 6 and 7 explore an apparent lag or linger effect of a healing, in which a healing effects linger at the site where healing was given. Healers felt uncomfortable when the experimenters wanted them to shift their healing randomly from the mouse on one side to the mouse on the other. The healers intuitively felt that the effects of their healing lingered for about 20 minutes at the spot where they directed the healing. The researchers' observations suggested that this claim of the healers might be correct. Healing directed to a given side of the table seemed to linger after a given trial so that subsequent mice on that side benefited from the healing sent to the previous mice at that spot. Further possibilities remain, however, which might explain the apparent linger effect.[119]

It is still possible that the experimenters caused the observed effects. One would have to clarify: Did the experimenters who monitored the wakening of mice know that mice on one side of the table would always be experimental (or control) for a number of consecutive trials? How many subjects participated? What were raw scores and physiological measures?

If healers knew the purpose of the experiment, they could continue to send healing energy from a distance.

If animal handlers knew the nature of the study they might sense via psi which side of the table had been the target side and might then cause the observed waking effects themselves. This would, in itself, be a healing effect, but it would not be evidence of the supposed healers' abilities.

Healing Anesthetized Mice and Linger Effects
Roger Wells and Graham K. Watkins

Wells and Watkins proposed that in their previous studies, results may have been influenced by a "linger effect," in which a subject's healing might not immediately dissipate when the subject stopped concentrating, but could linger on to affect other trials.

In the first of two experiments, in eight runs of 24 trials each, the target side for each run was randomly chosen. The subject healers left the building (from behind the one-way mirror) after the first half of each run. The second half of the run was begun immediately, as though the subjects were still present. "The first halves showed significantly faster awakening for the mice on the target side" (high significance: $p < .001$), and in the second halves, "the mice on that side continued to awaken first" ($p < .001$).

In the second experiment, "both halves of this series were significant in the expected direction . . . ($p = .024$ for first halves; $p = .015$ for second halves), but only the second halves were significant . . . [$p = .05$ with another statistical method]."

The researchers concluded that "the second series of experiments seemed to indicate that the linger effect is not only a reality but may be a more reliable finding than the main effect."[120]

Linger effects in several PK experiments (*Research in Parapsychology 1974*, 1975)

We continue to see significant healing effects. Again, scanty reporting mars otherwise apparently excellent studies. Rating: III

The fact that the experimenters handling the mice appear to have known the purpose and design of the experiments introduces a possibility that experimenter effects might be demonstrated rather than a linger effect. It is also unclear whether subjects knew the experiment was being continued after their departure. Distant healing might also explain the so-called linger effect.

Further experiments could be conducted to ensure that experimenters and subjects are blind concerning the existence of the second part of the experiment. Assuming the linger effect to be possible, experiments could be done to measure the area within which it appears to function.

Arousal of Anesthetized Mice: Further Studies
Marilyn Schlitz

A random-number generator determined the experimental/control assignment for pairs of mice. For each of 60 trials, subjects viewed the experimental mouse on a computerized television monitoring system from 30 feet away. Debra Weiner reports that the three subjects

> were instructed to use any strategy they wished in trying to make the experimental mouse awaken faster than the control. Arousal time was determined by the mouse moving sufficiently to expose two photocells. . . . Subjects received feedback for hits or misses . . . at the end of each trial.
>
> Hits and misses and time differences between arousal of experimental and control animals were examined statistically. Each subject was treated as a separate series. There were a total of 168 usable trials. . . .

Subject 1 obtained nonsignificant results on hits and misses, but significant differences in arousal times ($p < .05$). The results of subject 2 approached but did not quite reach significance in the opposite direction to that intended ($p < .08$). Subject 3 obtained nonsignificant results.

PK on living systems: further studies with anesthetized mice (Weiner, Debra H., *Journal of Parapsychology*, 1982; Schlitz, *Parapsychology Review*, 1982)

Modestly significant positive healing results are evident. It is reassuring to see persistent research in pursuit of ever refined methods and paradigms. Although these marginally significant results are encouraging, it would be useful to have further replications with this design.

A full report with raw data is still needed for independent analysis of the results. Rating: III

Methodological problems appear to have been solved by this last study, which yet again showed significant effects of healing in waking anesthetized mice.

This is one of the most impressive series of studies in the healing research literature. The meticulous attention to detail narrowed the possible explanations for the results.

The studies of healing on animals demonstrate a spectrum of healing effects that could be helpful to humans.

Grad and Cadoret showed that skin wounds in mice healed more quickly when the mice were given healing.

Grad's study of healing to slow down goiter growth suggests that healing may have beneficial effects upon hormonal processes. It also confirms that cotton may serve as a vehicle for healing.[121]

Solfvin's study of healing effects in malarial mice is among the most interesting of all the healing studies. Because no one in the study had direct knowledge of which mice were designated for healing while healing effects were demonstrated, it would appear that super-psi may bring about confirmations of experimenters' expectancies.

The study of Baranger and Filer of materials that appear to retard the progression of malaria in chicks suggests that various materials may have inherent healing properties that apparently act through being near the animal in need of healing. It appears possible that an energy field around the given material may interact with the energy field of the animal. The alternative of an experimenter effect cannot be ruled out, particularly because no blinds were included in this study.

The studies of healing for tumors in mice strongly suggest that healing may have a place in the treatment of cancers in humans.[122]

The series on healing for waking mice from anesthesia is one of the clearest in demonstrating significant healing effects. Consistent with these results are anecdotal reports of healers treating people prior to and during surgery, which indicate that less anesthesia (and other medications) may be needed.

Hopefully it will be possible to do more studies to confirm in humans the benefits demonstrated in the studies on animals.[123]

HEALING ACTION ON PLANTS

There are very few human beings who receive the truth, complete and staggering, by instant illumination. Most of them acquire it fragment by fragment, on a small scale, by successive developments, cellularly, like a laborious mosaic.

—Anaïs Nin (1969)

The effects of healing upon the growth of plants may be somewhat similar to the effects of healing upon humans, because plants are complex, multicellular organisms. Plants are convenient, inexpensive, and easy to study because one can be reasonably certain of controlling the conditions to assure that spiritual healing is the only influencing variable. The rapid growth rates of plants also make it possible to conduct studies over brief periods of time.

Many excellent studies of healing on plants have been published. Some, which were not studied or reported with the same rigor as those in this chapter, are reviewed in Chapter 5.

Biological Effects of the Laying-on of Hands: a Review
Bernard Grad

Barley seeds damaged by watering with one percent saline solution were divided into experimental and control groups. Saline was used to damage the plants so there would be a greater chance a healing effect would be evident. The healer could significantly mitigate the subsequent retardant effect of the saline on plant growth by holding the beaker of saline with which the plants were initially watered (highly significant: $p < .001$). The experiment was repeated three times, with results of modest significance in the same direction: ($p < .05$) and ($p < .02$). The experimental group of plants were a darker green, suggesting higher chlorophyll content.

Some biological effects of the "laying on of hands": a review of experiments with animals[124] and plants[125] (*Journal of the American Society for Psychical Research*, 1965)

Significant effects of healing on plants are demonstrated. How the saline mediated the effects is a challenge for further research. Grad's studies are carefully done and well controlled, with procedures and data reported in satisfactory detail. Rating: I

In addressing the second question posed at the start of this chapter, "How does healing work?" we seem to gain important clues from studies which show that vehicles such as water can convey healing. How to interpret the clues is a challenge.

These significant experiments suggest that the healer transmitted healing by one of the following:

- *influencing the saline solution in a manner that mitigated its damaging effect on seeds;*
- *affecting the saline in such a way that it had a positive effect that may have been transferred as healing energy in the water; or*
- *making a link between the healer and the seeds via the water and then acting by distant healing on the plants.*

It is unclear whether this is an example of a healing effect or a prevention of injury.[126]

Grad's speculation that healing increased the chlorophyll in plants led Dolores Krieger to hypothesize that healing might increase hemoglobin in humans. Her pioneering study of TT effects on hemoglobin was the first of a series on spiritual healing for humans.

Some healers are recognized for their unusually strong healing abilities. Early studies often focused on these healers because researchers had no other way to know who was a healer worthy of investigation and who might be a weak healer or even a charlatan.

The next report examines the healing abilities of three well-known, strong healers, Rev. John Scudder, Dean Kraft, and Olga Worrall.

Three Healers Examined
R.G. MacDonald, H.S. Dakin, and J.L. Hickman

Under double-blind conditions, sterile saline in sealed bottles was treated by the healers and was then used to water 16 identical sterile peat pots, each containing five rye grass seeds. An identical number of pots and seeds was watered with untreated saline. All pots were randomly distributed close together to ensure equivalent conditions of ambient air and sunlight. Following the initial watering with treated or untreated saline, each pot was daily watered with 15 ml. untreated distilled water.

The trials of Dean Kraft achieved significantly negative results (p < .001-.05), while Worral achieved significantly positive results (p < .05), with the "total and mean heights of the treated group . . . on the average 27% and 18% greater than the heights of the control group, respectively." No significant differences were seen with Scudder's plants.

Preliminary physical measurements of psychophysical effects associated with three alleged psychic healers (*Research in Parapsychology 1976, 1977*)

The language and content of the report suggest the authors are skeptical regarding healing. Despite this, significant effects were found. Kraft's negative results with plants warrant the questioning of Kraft as to his attitudes towards plants.

The data are too scanty to permit independent judgment of these results, so any conclusions must be tentative. Rating: III

An occasional healer may develop rare and unusual abilities. Geoff Boltwood, an English healer, found that plant seeds would sprout in his hand if he gave them healing for just a couple of minutes.

The following study examines Geoff Boltwood's ability to enhance the sprouting and growth of plants over a period of days.

Rapid Sprouting of Cress Seeds

Tony Scofield and David Hodges

Tony Scofield and David Hodges, lecturers in animal physiology at Wye College, London University, studied the effects of healings by Geoff Boltwood on cress seeds. Seeds were stressed by soaking overnight in half saturated saline solution, which ordinarily lengthens the time required for germination. In other cases, seeds were left unstressed. Six carefully randomized experiments were performed, each with careful blinds. In each, a number of seeds were placed in Boltwood's right hand after he washed and dried his hands. He held them either with or without the intent to heal, covering them with his other hand, for two minutes. Seeds were washed before and after his intervention. The seeds held by Boltwood were studied as the experimental group. Control group seeds, identical in all other ways, were not held by Boltwood. The healing was supervised by Scofield, who took care to observe Boltwood constantly to prevent substitution of seeds. In a seventh experiment, water that was used to soak the seeds was held for two minutes, rather than treating the seeds directly. In the final experiment, the entire procedure was filmed.

The rate of germination of treated seeds was often nearly double that of the control seeds. In Experiment 1 this reached modest statistical significance at p < .05; in experiments 2-6, p < .0001 or less (high significance).

The normal appearance of a fully-hydrated seed, after soaking in either saline or distilled water . . . appears to be plump and smooth-surfaced and is surrounded by a well-developed mucilaginous coat. Details of the root, shoot and cotyledons are clearly visible through the seed coat. . . . After healing many of the seeds were dried up, closely resembling dry seeds from a freshly-opened packet; others retained a developed mucilaginous coat, whilst the remainder seemed to be partly, patchily dried . . .

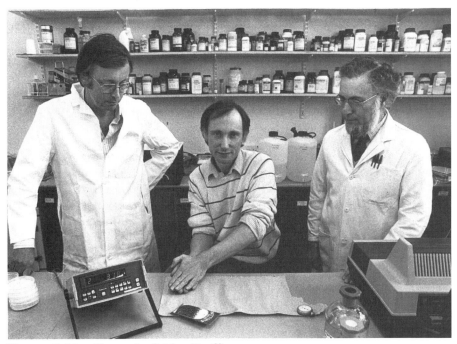

Figure 1-12. Tony Scofield, Geoff Boltwood and David Hodges study the sprouting of cress seed, which may commence within minutes of a healing treatment.

Photographs by Barry Marsden

Unstressed seeds grew more rapidly and more robustly than stressed, healed seeds. Unstressed seeds that were given treatment germinated significantly more rapidly on the first day than unstressed, untreated seeds. Thereafter the differences were not significant. No significant results were noted in the filmed session.

Demonstration of a healing effect in the laboratory using a simple plant model (*Journal of the Society for Psychical Research*, 1991)

This study was rigorously run and the results were significant. The finding that significant results were not obtained during videotaping has been reported in other psi studies and could be due to self-consciousness in the healer. The study reports the drying out of some of the seeds, and this may be similar to the dessicating effects of some healers on fruit, fish, and meat reported by Cassoli and by Grad.[127] Though the study was well performed on the whole, seeds were not marked to preclude substitution by Boltwood with sleight-of-hand techniques. While significant results were found, the fact that no significant results were obtained when videotaping was introduced suggests caution in accepting the results. Rating: I

I have myself observed Boltwood sprouting cress seeds in his hand. I took care to watch that his hand was always in view from the time he opened it, empty, to grasp the seeds, until he opened his hand again to show the sprouted seeds. I am convinced this is a genuine phenomenon.

In countries with unbroken traditions of healing, where industrialization and Western scientific views have not discouraged people from believing in spiritual healing, healers are accepted by the general populace as an important part of the health care system. It is helpful to have controlled studies of such healers in India to confirm that they can produce demonstrable healing effects, as in the following two reports.

Shamanic Healing and Wheat Seeds

Alok Saklani

In two experiments, Alok Saklani asked an Indian shaman to treat randomly selected wheat seeds by holding them in her hands for 45 seconds. Experimental and control groups were established, with blinds in place. Growth was determined by measuring plant height to the longest leaf. In the first experiment, using fresh water, "the mean length of the treated group as compared to the control group was significantly greater ($p < .01$) on days 15 to 18, and of borderline significance ($p < .05$) on days 14 and 19." In the second, the seeds were injured with saline solution. "The total number of seeds germinated per pot was . . . significantly greater in the treated group as compared to the control group ($p < .01$). Also, the number of plants per pot was significantly greater on day 12 ($p < .01$) and of borderline significance on days 7, nine and 11 ($p < .05$). . . ."

Psi-ability in shamans of Garhwal Himalaya: preliminary tests (*Journal of the Society for Psychical Research*, 1988)

The results of these well-run and well-reported experiments suggest that, through influence either directly upon the seeds and/or on the water, the healer was able to enhance plant growth. Rating: I

Shamanic Healing and Wheat Seeds: Further Studies

Alok Saklani

In this series of four experiments, Saklani continued to study wheat seeds that were undamaged by saline. He explored whether random variations in growth of two groups of plants might produce significant differences that could account for differences observed when healers treat plants. Saklani selected the seeds, divided them into packs of 50 each, coded them, and handed them to an assistant, who assigned them (by drawing lots) to pots filled with earth from the same source. All were given identical water and ambient light and temperature conditions in the laboratory. Only plants germinating on the same initial day were considered. Plant height above earth was the only measure of growth. The only significant results were with the third experiment: day 10 ($p < .001$); day 18 ($p < .05$)

In a fifth experiment, two shamans treated packs of seeds to influence them to grow better. These packs, along with three packs of untreated seeds (totaling 900 seeds), were coded as A and B and given to an experimenter. These were randomly assigned to 30 pots and treated as above.

On day 7 both A and B had more growth than the controls (high significance: $p < .001$). On day 13 A showed more significant growth ($p < .001$) than B (modest significance: $p < .05$), when each was compared with the controls. When the three controls were compared with each other, sample 1 showed significantly more growth than sample 3 ($p < .05$) on day 7. All other comparisons of controls versus controls showed no significant differences.

Psychokinetic effects on plant growth: further studies (*Research in Parapsychology 1989*, 1990)

Experiment 3 produced significant results, and under the conditions of Experiment 5, the effects of the healers were more highly significant than the those found between two of the controls. Some of the results obtained might be due to chance variations in the results rather than to the healer's influence. Although in one control-only experiment a highly significant difference ($p < .001$) was obtained, in Experiment 5 the control versus control difference was not as significant. One cannot compare with any confidence results obtained from separate experiments because there is a possibility that different conditions extraneous to healing produced the results.

As Saklani selected the seeds and sorted them by hand, it is possible that he produced the results by intuitive sorting of seeds into groups with better or worse growth potentials.

Studies by other researchers have included further measures, such as the numbers of plants germinating in each pot, days until initial germination, and root length. Inclusion of these data might have shed further light on what occurred in this experiment.[128] Rating: I

Mental Healing and Growth in Corn
Gerald F. Solfvin

Gerald Solfvin performed six experiments of healing on the growth of corn seedlings using a healer and also including botany students who did not claim healing abilities. As with his study of malaria in mice (Solfvin 1982a), he included false expectations in the design. In this plant experiment, he led the laboratory workers to believe that some of the seeds were damaged by immersion in saline and that some were normal, although in actuality all were damaged. He selected seeds randomly and maintained conditions for each seed that were as equal as possible, planting experimental and control seeds in a checkerboard pattern.

No consistent significant effects were found, although occasional suggestive effects were noted. Solfvin concludes that this model is so riddled with problems he does not recommend it for further studies.

Studies of the effects of mental healing and expectations on the growth of corn seedlings, (*European Journal of Parapsychology,* 1982b)

No effects of healing are demonstrated. There may be a problem in Solvin's checkerboard fashion of distribution of E and C groups of seeds. This might make it difficult for a healer to focus attention on seeds to be healed as opposed to those to be ignored. Rating: I

Though not producing significant effects, this report is a model for the careful observations and reports required in plant experiments. Such reporting allows a reader to appreciate the details attended to by the experimenter and identify possible extraneous factors that might have influenced the results.

Solfvin himself noted that despite his best efforts to provide the same environment for each seed, some cups were drier than others, possibly because of variation in the tightness of the packing of the sand around the seeds.

Solfvin's randomization procedures may also have been faulty. His methods could permit the experimenter to select seeds in nonrandom fashion via subtle sensory cues, clairsentience, or precognition. Such intuitive selection of seeds, rather than healer or expectancy effects, might account for some of the suggestive results he obtained. Solfvin noted that the weights of a particular group of seeds were heavier than those of the comparison group, supporting a possibility that some such selection bias could have occurred.

I disagree with Solfvin about the usefulness of the seed model for future study. I would recommend that:

- Randomization be instituted with procedures less open to experimenter bias.
- Larger numbers of seeds be used.
- Seeds be planted in separate rows, at least, and perhaps better in separate trays, with proper alternation of their placement in the lab to ensure the randomization of extraneous factors.
- Watering be done from above, with measured amounts of water for each tray.

Corn Germination and Psychokinesis

Joseph Michael Wallack

Wallack studied "a possible psychokinetic effect on plants from the 'laying-on' of hands of a self-claimed 'psychic healer'. . . ." Randomly drawn corn seeds were pre-soaked for 12 hours in a 2 percent saline solution and were then "randomly assigned to three prepared petrie dishes: healing, control, and a control for the temperature of the healer's hands." In three experiments, "statistical analyses yielded nonsignificant effects."
Testing for a psychokinetic effect on plants: effect of a "laying-on" of hands on germinating corn seeds (*Psychological Reports*, 1984)
The author probably correctly speculates that further testing (especially observation) might provide different results and notes that root growth may not be the best measure for healing effects. Also, the soaking time and concentration of salt may be variables contributing to negative results.

Wallack soaked his seeds in 2 percent saline, while Grad used 1 percent saline. The 2 percent saline may be a damaging threshold value beyond which no healing effects are obtainable. Though the experiment appears well designed, run, and reported, it is unduly brief to provide much evidence against healing. Further descriptions of the healer would be welcome. Rating: III

Corn Germination and Therapeutic Touch

Anita M. Bush and Charles R. Geist

Anita Bush and Charles Geist explored whether an electromagnetic field (EMF) pulsating around the hands of a healer could account for healing influences on the growth of plants. Considering the healing model used by Grad and by Wallack, in which seeds were damaged by soaking in saline solutions and then incubated on pads watered with distilled water, Bush and Geist suggest that a flow of ions would be created across seed membranes. This would, in effect, establish a living "battery." Replicating Wallack's experimental design in a pilot study, Bush and Geist found that corn seeds injured with saline developed a current bias with a positive measurement at their rounded ends and a negative one at their pointed tips.

They cite research that showed that plant growth occurs "in the direction of decreasing magnetic field intensity" of externally applied fields (Andus 1960). They call this "magnetropism" and suggest that in a laying-on of hands an inhomogenous magnetic field might be the stimulus for plant growth.

Bush and Geist hypothesized that corn seeds injured by saline would not recover and grow better than control samples when treated by a healer.

Commercial seeds were prepared following Wallack's methods. Seed dishes were randomly subjected to either: heat pulse, electric pulse, magnetic pulse, Therapeutic Touch, "naive touch" (a mock TT treatment), and no treatment. All conditions were applied simultaneously, and seeds were incubated replicating Wallack's methods. No significant differences were noted at 42 hours. At 66 hours the heat-pulsed seeds (92 percent) showed significantly more sprouting than the TT group (76 percent; $p < .05$). The TT group showed no increase in sprouting between 42 and 66 hours. The naive touch group was the only one to show significant increase in sprouting between 42 and 66 hours ($p < .05$).

Geophysical variables and behavior: LXX. Testing electromagnetic explanations for a possible psychokinetic effect of Therapeutic Touch on germinating corn seed (*Psychological Reports*, 1992)

The authors note that Wallack used a 2 percent saline solution to damage the seeds and obtained no healing effects, while Grad used a 1 percent solution and obtained significant effects. It is not clear why the authors chose Wallack's methods if they were hoping to demonstrate a healing effect. It is also possible that the healer in this study was not particularly gifted or effective in healing.[129]

While no effects of healing are demonstrated under the conditions of this experiment, the negative effects in this study cannot be taken as a general evidence of a lack of healing efficacy. Rating: I

The electromagnetic hypothesis to explain effects of healing appears worthy of further study.

Plant Growth and Loving Attention

Chris Nicholas

This study focused on influencing plants through thought. The experimenter sent loving, caring vibrations to one of two groups of 19 radish plants. Otherwise, both groups received similar physical treatment. Healing intent was applied for 15 to 20 minutes daily over 30 days. At the end of the study the weight and height of each plant were measured. The love group was heavier than the ignored group (modest significance: $p < .02$) but there was no significant difference in height between the groups.

The effects of loving attention on plant growth (*New England Journal of Parapsychology,* 1977)

Despite the small numbers of plants, an effect of healing seems evident.

This appears at first glance to be a carefully run experiment. Procedures are adequately described regarding weight measurements, though whether height was measured to include the roots or only the sprouts is not specified. However, no blinds are mentioned nor is randomization described either for selection of plants or in distribution between experimental and control groups. This leaves open a possibility of unconscious experimenter bias in distributing or measuring the plants. Rating: IV

Bean Growth and Healing

Mary Rose Barrington

Matthew Manning, the noted British healer, was challenged to treat half of a group of mung beans to make them grow faster. "[F]our beans were placed in each compartment of ice cube containers, the compartment having been lined with two layers of white blotting paper." Manning was to have treated beans in randomly selected compartments, but he objected to this design. He was therefore given three entire trays to treat and three were kept as controls. Because of further problems only 48 beans were ultimately treated, with another 48 as controls. Appearance versus non-appearance of radicles and plumials within seven days was taken as the measure of success or failure.

More radicles and plumials were found in the promoted than in the control trays, (modest significance: $p < .02$).

In another experiment, Manning was given a sample of beans in a sealed container and asked to retard their growth. "The retarded beans did slightly worse than the promoted, but better than the controls, in neither case to any significant degree."

Bean growth promotion pilot experiment (*Proceedings of the Society for Psychical Research,* 1982)

This experiment demonstrates a healing effect on plants. It would be interesting to know whether Manning has reservations about using healing to retard plant growth.

Procedures are too meagerly described to be certain these experiments were properly run. For instance, experimental and control samples were given to a third party for nurture and observation, presumably to ensure blinds, but Barrington does not specifically mention whether or not he was blind as to which tray was experimental and which was the control. Rating: III

The above studies of healing on plants relied on healers treating the plants directly or on using vehicles for healing such as water or saline solutions.

The next study explores whether the psychological state of a person might influence plant growth.

Effects of Depression on Plants

Bernard Grad

Grad examined the possibility that depression might produce a negative healing effect on the growth of plants. He postulated that if depressed people hold water that is then used to water plants, the plants might grow more slowly.

The study looked at three subjects, two of whom were patients in a psychiatric hospital. Each person held a sealed bottle of normal saline between their hands for 30 minutes.

The solution was then poured on barley seeds embedded in soil, which was then dried in an oven for 48 hours. Following this, the pots containing the seeds were removed from the oven and watered at suitable intervals with tap water not treated by anyone. When the seedlings appeared above the soil their number was counted and their height measured. . . . The watering with saline, the subsequent drying, and the restricted watering with tap water were used as forms of experimental stress to the plants. This experiment was carried out under multi-blind conditions, the information necessary to identify the treatment of each potted plant being divided among five individuals.

The seeds watered by the saline held by one man (who was in a confident mood at the time of hand-treatment on the saline) grew significantly [p < .02-.05] faster than those in the remaining three groups. Thus, this part of the hypothesis was supported by the experimental data. However, the plants treated by a woman who had a neurotic depression had a slightly higher growth rate than that of the controls, and this was contrary to expectations.

Her attitude towards the experiment was extremely positive.

The laying-on of hands: implications for psychotherapy, gentling and the placebo effect (*Journal of the American Society for Psychical Research*, 1967)

This study suggests that emotions may influence healings. Data and statistics are not presented adequately. However, in view of *green thumb* and *brown thumb*[130] people who seem able to influence plants positively and negatively—identified and demonstrated by Loehr (see Chapter 5)—Grad's research on single cases of depression are only hints, at best, of a possible connection between emotions and healing on plants. Grad may have had one green-thumb and one brown-thumb subject. Further clarification is needed. In either case, a healing effect is demonstrated. Rating: III

The next two studies focus on radionics. Radionics deals with the diagnosis and cure of illness with the help of various devices with dials and calibrations (affectionately called black boxes) designed to help the user tune into vibrational frequencies of the target. It is similar to dowsing in that the operator of the device is a part of the diagnostic/treating system. The device is probably a feedback mechanism that aids users in applying their psi diagnostic and healing abilities, though many radionics specialists insist the devices themselves have psi powers.

Radionics is a recognized and accepted relative of dowsing[131] and healing in Britain. In America, the Food and Drug Administration takes strong exception to the use of these devices and has actively prosecuted radionics practitioners.

A Look at Radionics
Edward W. Russell

Russell presents a concise history of the development of radionics, along with descriptions of numerous experiments that demonstrate its efficacy. The book summarizes many experiments (which are sketchily described). One involves enhancement of plant growth with radionic treatments. Significantly increased yields were noted for potatoes.

Another looks at pest control in fields with various crops. Here the radionics device is tuned first to a particular field, usually by a photographic negative of that field. It is then tuned to vibrations noxious to pests infesting crops in that field. Counts were made of damaged plants in sample rows in the experimental field and in adjacent control plots.

In 1950 four out of six trials were significantly positive over one year. The targets were Japanese beetles and European corn borers. In 1952 78,360 corn stalks were inspected on 81 farms, covering 1,420 acres. Significant results were obtained in 92 percent of the cases for Japanese beetles and 58 percent for European corn borers. In 1953, 13 out of 14 tests against European corn borers produced significant results.
Report on Radionics: Science of the Future, the Science Which Can Cure Where Orthodox Medicine Fails, 1973

Significant effects of radionics healing appear to be demonstrated. No blinds or randomization are mentioned in these experiments. However, the fields were planted by various farmers, so randomization may have occurred. This still leaves the possibility of experimenter bias in counting infested stalks. Statistical analyses are also lacking. Rating: IV

Healing to protect crops from insect pests could be a major contribution, not only to enhancing food production, but also to lessening the need for pesticides. If these experiments could be repeated and verified, radionics might provide methods that would not contaminate the environment for enhancing crop growth and for controlling pests. Both applications would be far less expensive than existing methods.

If healers can protect seeds from chemical damage, enhance their growth, and control plant pests, they may be able to help humans in similar fashion.

Energized Water and Rye Grass Growth
Robert Miller

Robert Miller reports:

> Tests were conducted to determine the effect of energized water on the growth rate of rye grass. Exactly 25 rye grass seeds were placed in each of six plastic cups filled with potting soil. Holes were punched in the bottom of the cups and each cup was placed on a saucer. The seeds were watered by placing the water in the saucers. This permitted the water to reach the seeds at a uniform rate by capillary action.
>
> Two of the cups were watered every day with measured amounts (50 ml.) of Atlanta tap water, two with tap water which had been energized by an individual who could produce large changes in surface tension by the standard test, and two cups . . . with tap water . . . exposed for 16 hours to a horseshoe magnet having a field strength of 1500 gauss. At the end of four days eight percent of the seeds in the control cups had sprouted, 36 percent of the seeds in the cups watered with the subject-energized water had sprouted, and 68 percent sprouting occurred in the cups watered with the magnet-energized water.
>
> After eight days the length of each blade of grass was carefully measured. The average height of the control blades was 2.8 inches, the blades watered with the subject-energized water averaged 2.9

inches, and the grass blades watered with the magnet-energized water had an average length of 3.6 inches—28.6 percent more than the control blades.

The relationship between the energy state of water and its physical properties *(Research paper, undated, Ernest Holmes Research Center)*
An effect of healing on plants is demonstrated. It seems that magnets impart to water the equivalent of a healing influence in some instances stronger than the effects of a healer. This study adds to those of Smith and Edge with enzymes and magnets.[132]

No blinds were used, statistical analyses were not done, and data are not presented to permit independent assessment of the results. Rating: IV

Chinese healers have studied effects of emitted qi on plants, as have healers in the West. A few of these translated reports are summarized here.

Rice Germination and Emitted Qi

Fan Yiji, Hu Gang (Laboratory of Photocatalysis, Shanghai Teacher's University, Shanghai), Qiu Yuzhen, Chai Jianyu (Shanghai Qigong Institute, Shanghai—from Sancier, 1991)

To determine the effects of qi on the germination rates of rice seeds (*Japanese indica*), two qigong masters separately emitted qi from their Laogong point for 30 minutes to different batches of dry rice seeds held in the palm of their hands. "Each procedure was repeated for three different batches of seeds over five periods during the day. The treated seeds were germinated on a wet paper surface in the dark. After 36, 40, and 44 hours, germination rates were determined by counting the number of sprouts. For controls, germination rates were determined for (1) batches of seeds that were treated with a mimic qigong by individuals without qigong experience and (2) seeds that did not receive qi."

The "germination rates for three batches of seeds treated by a given qigong master in a given 30-minute period of time were averaged." For one qigong master, "the percentages of seeds that germinated after 40 hours for the above five time periods were 56, 43, 43, 41, and 52, . . . compared with the control value of 30." The other qigong master obtained similar results. The percentages of seeds that germinated "were generally greater for the Qi-treated seeds than for those of the controls," reaching significance during two specific periods during the day.
A study of emitted Qi on the germination rate of rice seeds (from Sancier, 1991; *American Journal of Acupuncture,* 1991, reprinted with permission)

Rice Germination and Qigong

Gang Hu, I. Ji Fan, Yuzhen Qiu, Jianyu Chia; Laboratory of Catalysis, Shanghai Teacher's University, Shanghai, China; Qigong Institute, Shanghai, China

> The influences of qigong waiqi on germinating capacity of rice . . . are different when the rice is exposed to qigong waiqi in different times from 8:00 to 16:00 o'clock. The germinating capacity tested is increased greatly at 8:00 and 16:00 o'clock but unchanged in the midday. We think that effects of qigong waiqi are controlled by [a] biochronometer.

Biological effect of emitted qi with the biochronometer (*3rd National Academy Conference on Qigong Science. Guangzhou, China, 1990;* from qigong database of Sancier.)

The greater effects of healing at particular times of day, as in this study, is a fairly well-accepted phenomenon in several healing traditions, including those of China[133] and Russia.[134] Applied kinesiology and acupuncture are felt by some practitioners to be more effective in the treatment of disorders associated with particular meridians at particular times of day (Thie). One must wonder whether spiritual healings of humans and other organisms would also be more potent at particular times of day and whether this is due to factors in the healers or in the treated organisms.

Most Western research on healing has focused on effects upon the whole organism or upon cells within the organism. In China there has been considerable exploration of effects of healing on elements within cells.

The next study examines positive and negative healing effects on chromosomes in pollen.

Pollen Chromosomes and Emitted Qi

Sun Silu and Chun Tao; Weifang Medical College, Shandong Province, China

This study sought to determine whether the "qi emitted with the intention of protecting flowers" decreases the rate of appearance of micronuclei in the dividing chromosomes of the pollen mother cells; and "qi emitted with the intention of injuring the flowers increases the rate of appearance of micronuclei. . . ."

Results show a significant difference between the experimental group and the control group, indicating that the "qi emitted under control of the mind has a bi-directional effect on the chromosomes of hereditary material. It may protect and also destroy."

Biological effect of emitted qi with tradescantic paludosa micronuclear technique *(1st World Conference for Academic Exchange of Medical Qigong, Beijing, 1988;* from qigong database of Sancier)

If plant chromosomes can be influenced by healing, it is possible that animal and human chromosomes can also respond. This could be a mechanism for healing of cancers, where the chromosomes develop in abnormal ways.

Though the foreign studies may lack rigor in design or details in reporting, they suggest a wide range of experiments that could further our understanding of how healing works.

A number of reports indicate that plants may have greater sentience than normally assumed in Western society.[135] *Fascinating as they are, no firm conclusions can be drawn from these preliminary studies.*

HEALING ACTION ON SINGLE-CELLED ORGANISMS

Whoever thinks a faultess piece to see,
Thinks what ne'er was, nor is, nor e'er shall be.

—Alexander Pope (1711)

The next series of reports studies movements of living, single-celled organisms. Since they seem to represent telepathic instructions to the organisms to move in a particular direction, some may argue they don't belong here. However, they might represent psychokinetic influence over the organisms, actually moving them through the agency of mental powers.[136] *Theoretically, they could be of assistance in immobilizing infesting parasites so that the body could more easily attack and eliminate them.*

Paramecia and Psychokinesis

Nigel Richmond

In experiments designed to study whether or not an ability of PK exists that could influence the behavior of protozoa, "[p]aramecia were chosen as suitable subjects for these tests because they are very common, are easily recognized, and usually swim about in random fashion. . ." The direction in which a paramecium would swim was to be influenced by thought alone.

Each attempt was made under a low-power microscope (magnification x75), with the field of view of the microscope divided into four by cross wires in the eyepiece of the instrument. "The attempt was timed by a stopwatch for a given period, and the quadrant containing the paramecium at the end of this time was noted." Each destination quadrant was selected by "turning up cards from an ordinary pack of playing cards, each suit indicating one of the 4 divisions."

"A series of 794 experimental trials was run," with a control series of 799 trials in which "no conscious effort was made to influence the paramecia and the card was not turned up until the end of the 15-second period."

A second series of 701 experimental and control trials was then run, with minor improvement in technique. There were 444 successes in experimental trials (253 in the desired direction; 191 opposite). Richmond states that his results are highly significant.

Two series of PK tests on paramecia (*Journal of the Society for Psychical Research*, 1952)

In the second experiment, where successful chosen-direction trials are tabulated, there was a significantly positive result of healing for that category alone. The inclusion of "opposite direction" movement with "chosen direction" movement seems questionable, since "opposite" can be defined in any way convenient. Richmond does not provide comprehensive data to permit full evaluation of his results. No firm conclusions about healing can be drawn from this study. Rating: V

While significant effects of intentionalality are demonstrated on paramecia, the fact that they moved in diretions other than those intended by the researcher leaves many questions.

Protoza and Psychokinesis

J. L. Randall

Randall repeated Richmond's experiment, using *Stylonychia mytilus*, a protozoan similar to the paramecium that tend to make "sudden darting movements about the slide. . . . [I]t was thought that they might be amenable to psi influences." The targets were chosen randomly, of the 560 trials, half were controls.

There was no "evidence for psi, either of the direct or reverse variety."
Randall reports:

> The writer did not embark on these experiments in an attitude of disbelief; on the contrary, he fully expected to obtain positive confirmation of the Richmond effect, and was somewhat disappointed when he failed to do so. The fact that no such effect was detected does not necessarily prove that Richmond's results were faulty, since we know that psi effects are extraordinarily elusive. However, the work of any experimenter cannot be regarded as more than suggestive until it has been confirmed by others.

An attempt to detect psi effects with protozoa (*Journal of the Society for Psychical Research,* 1970)

The details of this study are adequately reported, and no healing effects are demonstrated. It is a pleasure to find a researcher who mentions his attitudes and intentions, variables that may influence the results in a variety of ways. Rating: I

Numerous questions remain: Does Stylonychia Mytilus respond differently from paramecia? Was Richmond more gifted with psi than Randall? Did other factors account for the disparity in results between the two studies? Knowles also reports an attempted replication of Richmond's experiment with no positive results, though he does not provide details (1954).

Algae and Psychokinesis

Charles M. Pleass and N. Dean Dey

Using a light scattering spectrometer, Pleass and Dey developed a highly sophisticated, mechanized, and computerized model for observing the motility of marine algae *Dunaliella tertiolecta* in laboratory test-tube culture. They were able to calculate the speed of movement of algae with approximately 99 percent accuracy, taking up to 75 measurements per second.

Participants were told "to be with the algae" during experimental periods compared with control periods. Calmness and relaxation of the participants, without ego involvement in the outcome, seemed to be very important in their success. Great care was taken to insure that ambient physical factors were equal in both measurement periods.

In 251 trials with 18 subjects, the results were highly significant (p < .000000005).

A second series was run with further physical controls. Under these conditions, 118 trials with 14 participants approached but did not reach significant levels (p < .059).

Pleass and Dey also ran experiments with the marine algae *Tetraselmis suecica*, where they measured the response of algae to the killing of a portion of the culture that had been removed from the main batch. Pilot trials produced significant results, while results of formal trials did not differ from chance.

Using the Doppler effect to study behavioral responses of motile algae to psi stimulus (*Parapsychological Association Papers*, 1985)

Conditions that appear to favor extrasensory interaction between Homo sapiens and microbes (*Journal of Scientific Exploration*, 1990)

The very highly significant results in the first series suggests that microorganisms may be influenced to move in particular directions through intent. The nonsignificant effects in the second series might be explained by the decline effect, which has been noted in numerous psi studies. There could, in addition, be differences in susceptibility to psychic influence between various types of algae. Different environmental factors might also have played a part, as the experiments were run several months apart.

One must be cautious in accepting evidence that cannot be replicated. There is always the possibility that unrecognized, chance factors might have produced the positive results, though this seems improbable with such a high level of significance.[137] Rating: I

The highly significant effects of intention on the motility of algae appear worthy of further study.

The next study examines the ability of a healer to influence the movement of moth larva. Strictly speaking, it does not belong in this section on single-celled organisms. I placed it here because it could conceivably be relevant to healing used to treat parasitic infestations.

Psychokinesis and Lepidoptera Larvae
Louis Metta

Journal abstract:

The subjects in this exploratory experiment tried by PK to influence Lepidoptera larvae to crawl into specified sectors of an experimental box. The box was a petri dish provided with a hole in the cover through which the larva was dropped. The dish was placed on a background marked into 12 sectors. Half of the sectors were designated "good" and half, "wrong." The subject tried to influence the larva to go to the "good" sectors. There were two experimental subjects. Subject 1 obtained a significant negative deviation in his overall scoring (p = .012). The negative effect was weakened by inconsistency in the individual run scores; of the four runs, run 2 was comparable in size but opposite in direction from the other three runs. An analysis which considers only size of deviation yielded p = .0006. It appeared that this subject demonstrated a strong psi influence but could not control its direction. Subject 2 gave insignificant results.

Psychokinesis on Lepidoptera larvae (*Journal of Parapsychology,* 1972)
    The importance of this significant study is that a subject could influence the larvae to move in a given direction.
    Technically, the study is sound and produced significant results. Lack of raw data precludes proper assessment of the results. The fact that the movement was in a direction opposite to that intended is a problem if this mechanism is suggested as a manner in which healing could be effective with parasitic infestations. Rating: III

These studies suggest that healers may be able to influence single-celled organisms (and possibly also moth larvae) to move in selected directions. A healer might inhibit the mobility of infection-bearing organisms, thereby assisting people's natural defenses against them.

Similar studies have been run on telepathic control of animal movement (with cats and rats).[138] I do not see such experiments as being directly relevant to healing except in demonstrating telepathy or PK with animals, which lends some credence to healers' reports that they are effective in diagnosing and healing animals.[139]

HEALING ACTION ON BACTERIA

This affair must all be unraveled from within.
—Agatha Christie (1920)

Bacteria grow happily and harmlessly on the skin, the mucous membranes, and in the gut. The body seems able to get along with, ignore, or contain these potentially damaging parasites, except when 1. particularly virulent bacteria gain entry to the body through wounds, breathing, or eating; 2. the body is weakened by malnutrition, toxins (for example smoking, pollutants, or drinking), or other diseases (for example influenza or AIDS); or 3. when chemotherapy or radiotherapy weaken the immune system. It has also been shown in recent years that the presence of a wide variety of bacteria, including some with potentials for producing illness, may be normal and even necessary for health.

A growing series of studies shows that growth of bacteria in the laboratory can be accelerated and slowed by healing.

Psychokinesis and Bacterial Growth

Carroll B. Nash

Journal abstract:

The experiment was conducted to determine whether the growth of the bacterium *Escherichia coli* can be psychokinetically accelerated and decelerated during a 24-hour period with subjects not known to be psychically gifted. Each of 60 subjects was tested in a single run consisting of a set of three tubes of bacterial culture to be growth-promoted, a set of three to be growth-inhibited, and a set of three to serve as controls. The growth was greater in the promoted tubes than in either the controls or the inhibited tubes . . . $p < .05$. Post hoc correlations between the three treatments for the 60 subjects yielded the following results . . . between promoted and inhibited tubes . . . $p < .001$ . . . between inhibited and control tubes . . . $p < .02$. Post hoc analyses showed that the intersubject variance in growth was 1. greater between the three treatments than within them . . . $p < .05$, and 2. greater in both the promoted and the inhibited tubes than in the controls, with $p < .01$ in each case. The results are interpreted to indicate that bacterial growth was psychokinetically accelerated in some of the tubes intended for growth promotion and psychokinetically retarded in some of the tubes intended for growth inhibition.

Psychokinetic control of bacterial growth (*Journal of the Society for Psychical Research*, 1982)

An excellent study, rigorously performed and adequately reported, confirming significant healing effects on bacterial growth. This study shows that healers can decrease and increase the growth of bacteria in the laboratory. Rating: I

This study suggests yet another answer to the question, "How does healing work?" Infectious diseases may be cured if healers can inhibit the growth of infectious agents. The mechanism itself is still a mystery. Perhaps it works via inhibition of bacterial enzyme activity, a hypothesis supported in the studies of healing on enzymes, later in this chapter. Other possibilities include alteration of cell membrane permeability and interference with cell nutrients.

It seems likely that if healers can decrease *bacterial growth in the lab, they can also do it within living organisms. Likewise, if healers can* increase *bacterial growth in the lab, it appears likely they could increase the growth of helpful or harmless bacteria in the body. Whether they could do both simultaneously is explored in a later study by Carroll Nash.*

It is particularly interesting that the nonhealer *college student subjects in Nash's study produced highly significant healing results. My experience in teaching people to develop intuition and spiritual healing ability leads me to believe these potentials exist in most caring people. This echoes the experience of uncounted numbers of teachers and students of healing.*

The next study evaluates the healing abilities of high school students.

Psychic Influence on *E. Coli* Bacteria

William C. Leikam

William Leikam trained 23 high school students "to enter light trance through a standard relaxation response." Using double-blind procedures, he studied their abilities to psychically influence the growth of *E. coli* bacteria.

Three sets of twelve test tubes containing bacteria were set up. One set served as a control, the second as a visual treatment set, and the third as a remote treatment set. Subjects were directed to look at the visual set. They did not know where the remote set was located, other than that it was somewhere in the science lab, about 50 meters away.

Leikam reports: "Taking into account the standard deviation of each set the calculations showed that in the remote set there was an increased growth over the control set of 3.2 percent, and in the visual set an increased growth of 7.5 percent over the control." He claims that the results were statistically significant, though he does not provide data to back this claim.

A pilot study on the psychic influence of E. Coli bacteria (*unpublished report*), 1981

The results appear to indicate healing can be taught. It is unfortunate the report is so brief, precluding a clear assessment of results. It is also perplexing to read there were five students in the visual group but 12 tubes and that each tube was influenced by one student. No conclusions can be drawn from this study. Rating: III

The next study focuses again on the powerful healing abilities of the late Olga Worrall.[140] *She was asked to help bacterial cultures to survive when they were poisoned with two types of antibiotics or with phenol.*

Healing and Bacterial Cultures

Elizabeth B. Rauscher and Beverly B. Rubik

Rauscher and Rubik, both scientists, studied the effects of the laying-on of hands by the well-known healer Olga Worrall on the growth and motility of *Salmonella typhimurium* bacteria. Worrall held her hands near the bacteria for two minutes but did not touch them. The bacteria had been treated with chemicals to retard either their growth or their motility. Motility was measured under a microscope and growth of cultures with a spectrophotometer.

Motility was totally inhibited by phenol in the control sample after one to two minutes, while seven percent of the healer-treated samples remained motile after 12 minutes.

Healing treatments of bacteria growing in normal (untreated) cultures showed enhanced growth if the treatment was given in the bacterial life phase of active growth (mid-logarithmic growth phase). There was no difference between treated and control samples if healing was carried out in an earlier growth phase (lag phase).

In bacteria inhibited with antibiotics, the aim of the healer was to protect the bacteria from the antibiotics. A consistent dose-response effect was found. Healing produced a greater differential in the growth rate between experimental and control samples when the dose of antibiotics was lower.

Human volitional effects on model bacterial system (*Psi Research*, 1983)

These experiments begin to tease out possible mechanisms for aspects of the healing process. Unfortunately, the published report lacks details of data, procedures, and statistical analyses to allow readers to evaluate the results independently. Neither blinds nor randomization are mentioned. Drawing more than very tentative conclusions from these experiments prior to their replication is premature. The variability of healer effects or other factors may have contributed significantly to the results in addition to (or rather than) the proposed differences in bacteria or antibiotics.[141] Rating: IV

Phenol and the two types of antibiotics used to poison the bacteria in the Rauscher/Rubik study act upon different aspects of bacterial metabolism. This may explain some of the different healing effects on the bacterial cultures that were poisoned with each of these chemicals. By expanding upon this sort of research, it may be possible to tease out some of the biochemical processes that are sensitive to healing. This, in turn, might provide clues as to the nature of the biological energies that appear to be involved in healing.[142]

Worrall related in personal communication that she had been asked to kill bacteria as part of the previous experiment. She refused to do so, feeling that a negative use of healing on her part could have unknown consequences, possibly extending to negative effects on healees receiving distant healing from her.

The next study explores alteration of genetic processes as another possible mechanism for healing. Carroll Nash explored the possibility that healing might shift the rates of bacterial mutation. This is a logical possibility according to Stanford's conformance theory, which postulates that psychokinesis may work better on systems with elements in a state of random flux.[143] *When cells are replicating, the genes in their chromosomes rearrange themselves in random fashion between the chromosome pairs.*

Psychokinesis and Bacterial Mutation
Carroll B. Nash

"Three experimenters each tested 20 subjects not known to be psychically gifted." Each subject was asked to mentally promote mutation of lac-negative strains of *Escherichia coli* (bacteria) to lac-positive strains in three test tubes and mentally inhibit mutation in three tubes. Three tubes served as controls. Careful blinds were instituted to preclude awareness of lab workers as to which tubes were selected for which conditions. "Because of procedural errors, results were obtained for only 52 subjects."

"The mutant ratio of lac-positive to total bacteria was greater in the promoted tubes than in the inhibited tubes," at $p < .005$ (highly significant); "less in the inhibited tubes than in the controls," at $p < .02$ (significant); and "greater in the promoted tubes than in the controls, although not significantly so."

Test of psychokinetic control of bacterial mutation (*Journal of the American Society for Psychical Research*, 1984)

This is a carefully designed, executed, and reported experiment. A significant effect of healing is demonstrated on bacterial mutation or on selective growth and inhibition of bacteria in a mixed laboratory culture.[144]
Rating: I

This study suggests how healing may help the body to fight off infections of pathogenic organisms and simultaneously promote growth of benign organisms that normally grow in the body. Healing can selectively promote or inhibit bacterial mutation or growth.

If the effect of healing upon bacterial mutation is a real one, we begin to have evidence for a more reliable healing mechanism. Healing might be able to alter the processes involved in DNA synthesis. This possibility is in fact supported by studies reviewed in the section on enzymes and DNA later in this chapter.

Just as healing may have varying effects on different mammals, a Chinese qigong study shows it that may have varying effects on different bacteria (Z. Liu et al. 1993a).

HEALING ACTION ON YEASTS

Yeasts, like bacteria, grow normally and harmlessly on the skin as well as in the gut and on mucous membranes. Yeasts may also infect the body and cause illness. When the natural balance of microorganisms in the body is altered by antibiotics that kill off normal bacteria in the gut or mucous membranes, a field is left open for the pathological growth of yeasts. Once yeast infections occur, special diets and antifungal medications may be required to eliminate them.

Reports of effects of healing as "psychokinesis" upon yeasts closely parallel effects of healing on bacteria.

Psychokinesis and Fungus Culture

Jean Barry

Journal abstract:

The objective of this research was to discover the effect of thought on the growth of a fungus. The fungus was cultured in petri dishes in a laboratory incubator, each subject being assigned five experimental and five control dishes. At each session, the dishes were placed 1.5 meters from the subject, who tried for 15 minutes to inhibit the growth in the experimental dishes while disregarding the controls. The results were measured by outlining the boundaries of the colonies on thin paper, cutting them out, and weighing them. If the total of the experimental dishes was less than that of the controls, the trial was a hit.

There were 10 subjects. Three to six subjects worked during a session, and there were nine sessions. Out of 39 trials, 33 were successes ([highly significant:] $p < .001$). This success was consistent to an extra-chance degree: out of 11 subjects or combinations of subjects, 10 scored above chance ([significant:] $p < .01$); and out of 194 experimental dishes, 151 were hits ([highly significant:] $p < .001$).

General and comparative study of the psychokinetic effect on a fungus culture (*Journal of Parapsychology,* 1968)

This study appears sound. A highly significant effect of healing on yeast growth from a distance of 15 meters is demonstrated. Barry gives us no clues as to the nature of healing employed. Rating: I

In our pursuit of answers to the question, "Does healing work?" we must confirm beyond reasonable doubt the assertions of healers that they can heal at great distances. The next study adds evidence to support these claims.

Fungal Cultures and Psychokinesis from a Distance
William H. Tedder and Melissa L. Monty

Tedder and Monty studied effects of distant PK on the inhibition of growth of fungal cultures. One author handled the cultures and had no knowledge regarding the subjects or choice of experimental and control targets. The other organized the PK subjects. Two groups of subjects participated. The first consisted of people familiar to Tedder; the second were volunteers who at best infrequently interacted with him. All were shown pictures of the target location and were told to concentrate on the cultures in any way they wanted for at least 15 minutes daily, from a distance of up to 15 miles.

The first group "had 16 hits and no misses, producing a highly significant p = .00003. . . . Collectively, the seven subjects produced a mean growth differential of -9.81 mm per trial, or almost -2 mm per dish over a total of 80 dishes" (highly significant: p < .00006). The second group had "four hits, eleven misses, and three ties over the two series" (nonsignificant: p < .08). The "mean growth was also non-significant."

Exploration of long distance PK: a conceptual replication of the influence on a biological system (*Research in Parapsychology 1980,* 1981)

This study demonstrates that distant healing can produce significant effects on yeast growth. The study design is excellent, but again too scantily reported to permit independent analysis of the results.

Aspects of this study of *distant healing* require clarification. First, no mention is made of preclusion of approach by experimental subjects or by the second experimenter to the target area during the three days of fungal culture incubation. As the authors themselves note, unconscious PK may have been working during intervals between periods of conscious concentration.

Second, the authors assume that the first experimenter (in charge of culture handling) would have had to perform a difficult psi task, probably of impossible complexity, in order to act as agent for the observed effects. Solfvin (1982) demonstrated that PK of the complexity required for the second experimenter to be the PK agent is possible.[145] Alternatively, the agents may have used the first experimenter as an auxiliary (*proxy*) agent to themselves. That is, the distant agents may have telepathically directed the energies of the first experimenter to act locally on the cultures near her. Healers occasionally report they will do this, using friends, family, or chance observers as "proxies" or "surrogates" to relay or augment their own healing powers.[146] Rating: III

Yeast Growth and Psychokinesis

Erlendur Haraldsson and Thorstein Thorsteinsson

Seven subjects tried to "increase the growth of yeast in a group of ten test tubes, without touching them. . . . An experimenter who was 'blind' regarding the experimental and control tubes measured yeast growth in a colorimeter. In 12 sessions, 240 test tubes were run, half E and half C. . . . Each experimental tube was paired for analysis with a control tube used in the same session, and the yeast growth in the two tubes was compared."

Results were significantly in favor of the experimental tubes (modest significance: p < .02). Of the seven subjects, "three were engaged in healing, two as mental healers and one as a physician." They did the bulk of the positive scoring (high significance: p < .00014), while the nonhealers gave chance results.

Psychokinetic effects on yeast: an exploration experiment (*Research in Parapsychology 1965*, 1966)

A significant effect of healing is demonstrated on yeast growth. However, this report is too brief to permit proper evaluation. It poses many questions: Were precautions taken to ensure similar temperature for control and experimental tubes? Were tubes paired randomly? What accuracy of measurement was achieved? What range of error in measurements existed? Rating: III

The finding that believers in psi effects (sheep) achieve better results than nonbelievers (goats) is common.[147] It is not unexpected that such effects should be found with healing, since other studies of psi show similar results. For instance, believers in telepathy, clairvoyance, or precognition will produce significantly better results than chance, while disbelievers will produce significantly poorer results than chance.

This is why reports on the attitudes of the experimenters towards healing are important in interpreting the results, and why I have highlighted every reference to skepticism in these reports. If experimenters have positive or skeptical beliefs they could influence the results in line with their expectations.

In the next study, Grad explored the possibility that healers might be able to influence physiological processes in yeasts just as they are able to do in other organisms.

Yeast Fermentation and Psychokinesis

Bernard Grad

Grad reports that "Eighteen bottles with sterile, vacuum-sealed five percent dextrose and normal saline solutions were arranged in six sets of three bottles per set." In five sets, one bottle was treated by a man, another by a woman, and the third was untreated. "The sixth set, the control, consisted of three untreated bottles. Treatment involved holding the bottles between the hands for 30 minutes." Scoring was done under a multiple-blind system. "In each experiment, 20 milliliters (ml) from each bottle were placed in each of 16 randomly selected fermentation tubes to which five ml of 20 percent yeast in solutions of five percent dextrose and 20 ml saline were added and the rate of carbon dioxide production was measured eight times over the next five and a half to six hours."

"Statistically significant differences were observed in four out of five sets," three at the highly significant level of $p < .0005$.

PK effects on fermentation of yeast (*Proceedings of the Parapsychological Association Meeting,* 1965)

A highly significant effect was obtained, perhaps from a healing energy. The direction of the healing effect was not noted, but in personal communication, Grad clarified that it was an increase in carbon dioxide.

Insufficient data are presented in this brief report. Specific numbers and statistical methods are not provided for the summarized measurements. Rating: III

Results of healing on human illness are difficult to study because of factors that are difficult or impossible to control, such as dietary, psychological, relational, and environmental influences. Researchers have sought to develop simpler models of illness on which to base healing research. In the following study yeast cultures were poisoned and the healer was challenged to help the yeasts resist the toxic effects.

Standardizing the Study of Healing

Harold B. Cahn and Noel Muscle

The researchers describe a technique in which a culture of baker's yeast, *Saccharomyces cervesiae,* is poisoned with cyanide. This inhibits oxygen consumption and thus provides a system that a healer can influence. Measuring the volume of oxygen uptake with a manometer can provide feedback on healing effects within seconds.

Cahn and Muscle prescribe precise procedures for setting up this apparatus. In a pilot study with a female "psychic healer":

The overall effect is clear: both the slope and cumulative ten-minute readings for the "hands on" interval is greater than for either the pre-run or post-run controls. Statistically, only the difference in cumulative uptake between the pre-run and "hands on" run is significant . . . (p < .02).

Examination of the graph [showing rates of oxygen consumption] will reveal an interesting anomaly. The first four minutes of the post-run series is nearly identical with those of the "hands-on" series. Could this be due to a residual effect of "laying-on" of hands? . . .

Toward standardization of "laying-on" of hands investigation (*Psychoenergetic Systems,* 1976)

This report presents a method wherein immediate feedback of in-vivo effects of healing can be demonstrated. This could prove valuable in showing the effectiveness of healing; exploring further some of the biochemical mechanisms involved in healing; providing feedback to student healers; and testing whether someone has healing abilities.

A well-done study, but raw data again are not provided in sufficient detail.[148] Rating: III

The next study examines whether psychotic people might have a negative effect on yeast growth via vehicles of water they have held.

Yeast Fermentation and Effects of Psychotics
Carrol B. Nash and Catherine S. Nash

Each of 19 psychotics held a separate sealed glass bottle containing an aqueous solution of dextrose and sodium chloride for 30 minutes. Six ml. of the solution in the bottle held by the psychotic was placed in each of 12 fermentation tubes and six ml. of a similar solution in a control bottle (held by no one) was placed in each of 12 other fermentation tubes. To each of the 24 tubes, four ml. of a yeast suspension was added. The total amount of carbon dioxide produced in the 12 experimental tubes during an interval of approximately two hours was compared with the amount produced in the 12 control tubes.

The bottles were divided into groups on the basis of how long after they were held by the psychotics they were tested, i.e., withing two weeks and from two to six weeks. While the results are only marginally significant and have not been corrected for selection, they suggest the inhibition of yeast fermentation by a solution when held by psychotics, the deterrent effect of the solution lasting for approximately two weeks after being held.

Effect of paranormally conditioned solution on yeast fermentation (*Journal of Parapsychology*, 1967)

This brief report hints at many interesting points. Assuming some legitimacy to the trend noted, one must look for answers as to whether or not emotional states of humans can affect life system processes in organisms outside themselves. Are there agents other than the participants' emotional state that could account for the results?[149]

The study presents insufficient detail. One would want to know exact numbers or units of measurements observed; specific statistics used and what the authors consider marginally significant; diagnoses of the psychotic people (schizophrenics vary widely in their symptomatology, and paranoids are quite different from schizoaffectives); information on the degree and nature of understanding and co-operation of the participants in the study; and attitudes and expectations of subjects and experimenters. Rating: III

If the growth of yeasts in vitro can be slowed by healing, it is reasonable to believe that this could be true of the growth of yeasts causing infections in the body.

The fact that yeast growth may be increased in the laboratory may seem a cause for concern, lest the giving of healing might worsen a yeast infection. Two observations mitigate against this concern. First, the growth of yeasts in vitro was promoted by the healers' intent that they grow better. Second, healing given to humans with positive intent has not produced deleterious effects. Furthermore, healing might selectively promote the growth of benign yeasts which normally populate the body. These yeasts appear to prevent invasion by pathological yeasts. It appears that healing can selectively influence the human target towards greater health while influencing the infecting organisms towards being eliminated.

HEALING ACTION ON CELLS IN THE LABORATORY (*in vitro*)

We do not understand much of anything, from . . . the "big bang," all the way down to the particles in the atoms of a bacterial cell. We have a wilderness of mystery to make our way through in the centuries ahead.

—Lewis Thomas

Cells can be studied as living units removed from the body. They also can be grown in laboratory cultures, either suspended in liquid or on flat dishes of chemical nutrients.

Several studies show that healing can influence cells in the laboratory. By exploring how healing influences cells *in vitro*, it is possible to learn some of the ways in which healing may influence cells in the body.

Many healers are gifted with additional psychic abilities. Matthew Manning is a well-known English healer who had wildly uncontrollable psychic abilities during his teenage years. For instance, fires would break out spontaneously around him without his conscious intent (Manning 1974).

The fifth experiment with Manning in the series of Braud, Davis, and Wood is reviewed here in detail because of its focus on healing effects with cells.[150]

Red blood cells (*erythrocytes*) can be stored for long periods of time if kept in fluids of similar concentration to normal body fluids. If placed in more dilute (*hypotonic*) solutions, water seeps into the cells in an attempt to balance the pressures inside and outside. The cells then tend to swell and rupture (*hemolyze*), spilling hemoglobin into the surrounding solution. The hemoglobin then colors the solution and its concentration outside the cells can be measured with a spectrophotometer. Matthew Manning was asked to protect the cells from bursting.

Psychokinesis and Red Blood Cells

William Braud, Gary Davis, and Robert Wood

Manning attempted to decrease the rate of hemolysis of human red blood cells that were being stressed by being placed in dilute saline. He "imagined the erythrocytes as intact and resistant to the hypotonic saline and sometimes he mentally projected a 'white light' around the cells."

The results were highly significant ($p < .00096$). "The test run with the most significant results was one in which Manning sat apart from the experimenter."

The authors also briefly report on a study on Manning (which they observed first-hand) by Dr. John Kmetz of the Science Unlimited Research Foundation in San Antonio, Texas. Here Manning "was able to exert dramatic influences upon cancer cell cultures, ranging in magnitude from 200 to 1,200 percent changes, compared with the controls." In one experiment with 38.02 percent deviation from chance, statistical significance reached p < .00002.

Experiments with Matthew Manning (*Journal of the Society for Psychical Research,* 1979)

The studies by Braud et al. were well run, adequately described, and highly significant. A healing effect is demonstrated. The hemoglobin study suggests that cell membranes of the red blood cell may be strengthened through healing. Rating: I

Manning's ability to kill cancer cells with near and distant healing is also impressive. The study by Kmetz is tantalizingly interesting, but lacks sufficient detail for proper consideration.[151]

Matthew Manning was able to slow the rate of hemolysis (bursting) of the red blood cells. Eventually, he abandoned his collaboration with researchers. He became bored and frustrated when the positive results he produced in various laboratories did not seem to convince the scientists that healing actually is a potent intervention. "They kept asking me to produce the same effects over and over again. We didn't seem to be getting anywhere."

It is important to establish whether healing is an ability possessed by only a gifted few or whether many—including people who make no claims to possess healing abilities—are able to produce the same effects. The next study, a replication of the previous one, adds evidence that the latter is likely.

Red Blood Cells and Distant Healing

William Braud

Braud wanted to determine whether or not "a relatively large number of unselected subjects would be able to exert a distant mental influence upon the rate of hemolysis of human red blood cells. For each of 32 subjects, red blood cells in 20 tubes were submitted to osmotic stress (hypotonic saline)." With 10 of these tubes, the subjects attempted to "protect the cell" using "visualization and intention strategies;" the remaining 10 tubes served as noninfluence controls. Both subjects and experimenter were blind to critical aspects of the procedure, and "subjects and tubes were located in separate rooms."

Braud found that "a significantly greater number of subjects than would be expected on the basis of chance alone showed independently significant differences between their 'protect' and 'control' tubes" (highly significant: p < .000019).

Distant [healing] mental influence on rate of haemolysis of human red blood cells (*Research in Parapsychology 1988,* 1989)

This was a most carefully performed and meticulously described study. Again we have very highly significant confirmation of the healing abilities of subjects claiming no healing gifts to influence a biological system. Rating: I

Braud suggests that we must be cautious in interpreting such results. Control of hemolysis in the lab may differ from influence over hemolysis within the body, as body chemistry is far more complex.

The studies of red blood cells show that the membranes that make up the walls (the "skins") of cells can be strengthened to withstand the physio-chemical stress of being placed in water that is more dilute than body fluids. Just how the cell membranes were able to do this was not clarified.

Cell membranes are extremely complex gateways and pumps for fluids and chemicals which enter and leave the cells. They carefully regulate the internal environments of cells, and actively promote or block the passage of molecules moving in and out so that a healthy environment is maintained inside the cell. If healing can enhance the activities of cell membranes, this would be an important way in which healing could facilitate states of health and illness within the body.

Red blood cells can be grown in laboratory cultures. Though the following study summary is rather brief and somewhat technical, it appears tantalizingly interesting.

Blood Cell Formation and Therapeutic Touch

Jo A. Eckstein Straneva

This study evaluated the effects of Therapeutic Touch (TT) on *erythropoiesis* (the formation of blood cells) in the laboratory. It was anticipated that with TT treatments there would be more rapid differentiation of cells as they grew, shown by enhanced formation of hemoglobin, more rapid maturation, and greater numbers of red blood cell colonies growing in the laboratory cultures. Three TT healers and one mock healer gave treatments to the samples twice each day. Controls included simulated or mock TT (MTT) and no treatment.

Out of eight cultures treated with TT, three showed reduced hemoglobin, an effect opposite to that which was anticipated. In eight studies, five revealed significant differences between the TT and the MTT and control groups, but "only half occurred in the direction hypothesized."
Therapeutic Touch and In Vitro Erythropoiesis (doctoral dissertation, Indiana University School of Nursing, 1993)[28]

The study demonstrates significant effects of TT on red blood cell growth. The variability in direction of effects parallels the variability in hemoglobin levels noted by Wetzel when people received Reiki healing. Despite that, it is difficult to accept these findings as significant or valid when they occur in some instances in one direction and in other instances in the opposite direction. This brief summary is inadequate for full evaluation. Rating: III

It is puzzling to find healing sometimes enhancing blood cell growth and at other times decreasing growth. While skeptics will say that this invalidates the research, I believe the truth is just the opposite. Here are effects of healing which beg for further study and clarification.

One possibility is that there are factors such as sunspot activity which might have influenced this study if samples were run on different days. Sunspots have been found to influence protein reactions in the laboratory. Many other factors may influence healings. By studying these and other unexplained effects we will learn more about the nature and processes of spiritual healing effects.

Cancer cells lend themselves to scientific study because their aggressive ability to grow in the body also allows them to grow readily in the laboratory. The following study explores a gifted healer's abilities to slow the growth of cancer cells in the laboratory.

Malignant Cells Growth and Psychokinesis

Frans Snel

In this study, "a psychic healer attempted to inhibit the growth of mouse leukemia cells in tissue culture, as compared to controls. One gifted subject was available and the experiment was designed around him. Three experiments were conducted using closely similar procedures."

First, the subject was asked to inhibit the growth of cancer cells which were being incubated in an oven. The healer was given photographs of the bottles containing the cell cultures. He performed the healings (method and duration unspecified) from a distance of 15 kilometers. In the second experiment, the healer did not come to the laboratory again. Instead he only received a photograph. In the third, all the available people in the laboratory "(analysts, researchers, students)" were used as subjects. "Generally they did not think it possible to influence the mitosis [cell division] in this way, but they cooperated."

A fourth experiment was a replica of the third, with the healer trying to repeat the results of experiment 2.

All the bottles in the first experiment contained only dead cells, the targets as well as the controls. There was therefore nothing to count. The results in the remaining experiments showed statistically significant differences between cultures remotely treated by a healer and the control samples. However, in two of the three viable experiments (2 and 3), results were contrary to the intended direction.

An analysis of variability in the results relating to the placement of the samples in the incubator leaves room to question whether the observed differences were due to healer effects or to unknown factors associated with the stove that was used.

PK influence on malignant cell growth (*Research Letter No. 10, Parapsychology Laboratory, University of Utrecht*, 1980)

The fact that much larger differences were obtained in experiments in which healing was involved suggests that some of the observed differences were a result of healing. More subjective information on the healer might help us understand why he did not retard cancer cell growth in the second and third experiments and why he was successful in the fourth.

This is a meticulously performed and reported study with significant results. Despite these positive results, Snel indicated in personal communication (1992) he is now skeptical about the reality of healing because of repeatability problems. Rating: IV

If healing can inhibit the growth of cancer cells in the laboratory, there is reason to believe it could also do so within the body, adding a further possible answer to our original question, "How does healing work?" [152]

The next study explores healing effects on isolated nerve cells. Pacemaker cells in the giant marine snail, **Aplysia californica,** *are similar to human nerve cells. At regular intervals they emit electrical action potentials at a steady rate.*

Detecting Psychokenesis in Healing

S. Baumann; J. Lagle, and W. Roll

"Subjects were asked to perturb the firing rate of pacemaker neurons so there would be a statistically significant difference between interval lengths during target and control periods. . . ." While experiments were performed with seven subjects, "preliminary analysis of the results was completed on work done with only four subjects." Of these, for the first subject (a parapsychologist), one out of three series with the pacemaker detector was highly significant (p < .002), with an increase in firing rate of the neuron despite the subject's aim to decrease it.

For the second, a trance medium who claimed she could "channel energy through her hands," one of two experiments with pacemaker cells was significant (p < .01). The third, a woman also claiming to channel energy through her hands, had one experiment that was significant (p < .01). For subject four ("a teenage girl who had been the focus of ostensible RSPK activity for several months"[153]), four out of four experiments were significant, and most at high levels.

Preliminary results from the use of two novel detectors for psychokinesis (*Research in Parapsychology 1985*, 1986)

Highly significant effects of healing on isolated nerve cells are demonstrated. This study was well done and well reported. Rating: I

This simple research model is most productive. If healers can significantly influence the conduction rate of single cells in the laboratory, they may be able to influence nerve cells in intact organisms. This would provide access to a human subject's nervous system whereby far-reaching alterations in mind and body processes could be produced. For instance, altering the rate of activity of parts of the brain could be a way to calm down a stressed person. The nervous system regulates many of the activities and functions of the body, including the muscles and all of the internal organs. Some of the nervous system influence is indirect, through its control of hormones. Hormones, in turn, regulate many aspects of body functions. Inmune functions may also be influenced by neurohormonal processes.

It would be most interesting to extend this study to see whether the same effects could be obtained with distant healing. If not, then the influence on nerves might be through local energy field effects.[154]

Many Western healers will not deliberately focus healing energies to "negative" purposes. If they are treating a person, they are mentally focused on improving that person's health, not on killing the cancer within the person.

It appears that Chinese qigong healers do not hesitate to use what they term negative qi energies. We have much to learn from healers in other cultures. Here are a few brief samples from Chinese qigong healing studies on cells.

A study of effects of healing on protein synthesis (C. Chinhsiang et al. 1991) reports:

> The results show that Peaceful Mind Qi increased the growth and respiration of cultured cells, whereas the protein synthesis rate was affected minimally. By contrast, Destroying Mind Qi decreased all of these biochemical reactions. The researchers suggest that Peaceful Mind Qi is accepted by the cells as a signal to stimulate the above cell functions. Destroying Mind Qi decreases the cell function rates by generating a large energy that results in changes of the cytoplasm fluidity, the nuclear matrix or the cell membrane.

We believe that this *in vitro* study provides strong support for the reality of emitted qi and its potential for changing the metabolism of living cells. The dependence of the outcome on the intent of the qigong master has profound implications for medical qigong in clinical applications. . . . (Sancier, *American Journal of Acupuncture*, 1991, reprinted by permission)

In another study healers reported anecdotally that their treatments seem to enhance the effects of radiotherapy. One qigong study on cells appears to offer early support for such claims (Q. Cao et al. 1993).

Several studies examine the microscopic effects of healing on cellular components within cancer cells (L. Feng et al. 1988; C. Yuantegn 1991). I know of no Western studies that explore this dimension of healing effects.

Nerve cells conduct electricity by transferring ions (atoms with positive and negative charges) across their cell membranes. One qigong study showed healing effects on sodium transport in nerve cells (A. Liu et al. 1993).

In summary, healing produces significant effects on cells in the laboratory. This shows that healing is effective and suggests that within the body healing may influence cells individually and collectively to improve health.

HEALING EFFECTS ON THE IMMUNE SYSTEM

The most exciting phrase to hear in science, the one that heralds the most discoveries, is not 'Eureka!' (I found it!) but "That's funny."

—Isaac Asimov

Healers have hypothesized that a logical way in which healing ought to work is to strengthen the immune system. Several studies in humans explore this possibility.[155] The next series explores this hypothesis through laboratory studies of immune system cell cultures. These studies are highly technical and suffer as well from being translated research. All but the medically trained readers will probably prefer to skim between this point and the conclusion.

The immune system includes several components. A variety of *lymphocytes* (white blood cells/WBCs) produce antibodies that chemically disable foreign materials in the body. WBCs engulf and dismantle foreign matter such as debris from normal physiological functions or injuries, or viral or bacterial invaders. Among these cellular defenders, the *natural killer (NK) cells* are particularly potent in attacking invading cells. *T-cells* are WBCs from the thymus gland (under the breastbone) that direct other WBCs in their defensive activities.

Antibodies are chemicals designed to neutralize specific invading organisms, toxins, or allergens. Numerous antibodies are produced by the immune system, including interleukin. These components of the immune system are examined in the next studies.

Immune System Cells and Emitted Qi

Ye Ming, Shen Jiaqi, Zhang Min, Wang Yao, Ahang Ruihua, and Wu Kiaohong; Shanghai Academy of Traditional Chinese Medicine and Materia Medica, Shanghai Qigong Institute, China

Blood samples from human subjects were divided into three groups: one "[s]timulated by external qi from a qigong master," one given "placebo treatment by non-Qigong exercisers who imitated the observable actions of the Qigong master," and one considered as a control to which qi was not emitted. Up to six qigong masters participated in different aspects of the experiments. Four cell functions were measured.

Blood analyses showed that emitted qi caused significant increases in NK cell function and in Interleukin2 production, among other factors.
An in vitro study of the influences of emitted Qi on human peripheral blood lymphocytes (PBLs) and natural killer cells (NK cells) (from Sancier 1991, *American Journal of Acupuncture*, 1991; reprinted with permission)

This study shows that healing may enhance the activities of various types of white blood cells and antibodies.

Natural Killer Cells and Emitted Qi

Lida Feng, Juqing Qian, and Shugine Chen, General Navy Hospital, Beijing

> NK cells, playing an immunosurveillance role in production, transplantation and virus infection of cancer, is not only important effective cell, but opsonic immunity cell as well, so that NK cell attracts us more attention.
>
> We have recently reported that qigong waiqi effects on killing cancer cells. To further reinforce the effect of qigong waiqi killing cancer cells, we isolated NK cell from the health's blood and immediately combined with qigong waiqi to kill adenocarcinoma cells of stomach cultivated out of the body using the density gradiental method.
>
> The result shows: that the killing rate of qigong waiqi effect on adenocarcinoma cells of stomach is 36.60%, the killing rate of NK cell's effect is 39.78%, the killing rate of combining effect of both qigong waiqi and NK cell is 81.61%. The difference is statistically remarkably significant (p < .01) between test group and control group.

Research on reinforcing NK-cells to kill stomach carcinoma cells with waiqi (emitted qi) (*3rd National Academy Conference on Qigong Science, Guangzhou, China, 1990;* from qigong database of Sancier)
This study shows that healing may enhance the ability of natural killer white blood cells to kill cancer cells.

These studies provide early support for the hypothesis that healing can enhance immune system activity.[156]

HEALING ACTION ON ENZYMES AND CHEMICALS

It is the theory which decides what we can believe.
—Albert Einstein (1971, p.63)

Enzymes are substances in the body that facilitate various metabolic processes. They are chemical ushers and matchmakers which help other chemicals to find each other, to interact and combine much more rapidly and smoothly than they would on their own.

Several studies show that psi healing can improve the rates at which enzymes work.

Enzyme Activity and Healing

Justa M. Smith

Researchers studied the effects of the laying-on of hands by a healer, Oscar Estebany,[99] on the enzymatic activity of trypsin under carefully controlled conditions.

> Solutions of trypsin[157] were divided into four aliquots; one was retained in the native state and will be referred to as the control; the second was treated by Mr. Estebany in the same fashion as he treats patients, this is, by the laying-on-of-hands (simply putting his hands around the stoppered glass flask containing the enzyme solution for a maximum of 75 minutes from which 3 ml portions were pipetted out after 15, 30, 45, and 60 minutes); the third was exposed to ultraviolet light at 2537 A, the most damaging wavelength for protein, for sufficient time to reduce the activity to 68 to 80%, and then treated by Mr. Estebany as above; the fourth was exposed to a high magnetic field (3,000-13,000 gauss) for hourly increments to three hours. Three to five activity measurements were made on each of the above samples for each time interval.

Enzyme activity was increased 10 percent over 75 minutes when Estebany carried out his laying-on of hands treatment. His effect on the native enzyme and on the enzyme exposed to ultraviolet is practically the same.

Smith repeated the experiment with three people who did not claim to have any healing power, and three who did. None had a positive effect on enzymes.

Mr. Estebany returned in the late fall of 1967 for a two-week period at Rosary Hill College campus in order to repeat the experiments. It should be noted that during his summer visit there was little college activity and a very tranquil atmosphere, with Mr. Estebany completely composed. However, in the fall it was not possible for him to live in a residential hall, and because of circumstances personal in nature, he was not at ease. As a result, in the same type of tests, he had no influence upon the enzymes. Therefore, it may be deduced that the ability of a healer depends upon his personal state of mind.

Paranormal effects on enzyme activity, *Human Dimensions,* 1972

Smith demonstrated a healing effect on enzymes in the laboratory. These studies were well run, however, Smith does not present statistical analyses. The trends as graphed in the report appear to be significant in the directions indicated, but a clearer statement of outcome significance is needed. Lacking this, it is impossible to assess the significance of these results.

Though this report does not mention temperature controls, Smith reassured me in personal correspondence that these were strictly maintained.

In her report, Smith assumes that Estebany's state of mind in the second study negatively influenced the results. This is clearly an educated guess rather than a demonstrated fact.

A number of replications would be necessary before one could begin to accept the validity of her report and conclusions. Her results may represent effects due to very different causes such as chance variations, differences between healers, expectations of healers concerning the "proper" direction for results, similar expectations on the part of the experimenter, and other causes. Rating: III

Enzymes are catalysts for enormous numbers of chemical reactions in the body. Without enzymes the chemical reactions required for life processes would proceed so slowly that life as we know it would be impossible. If healers can influence the action of enzymes in the lab, there is reason to believe they may enhance enzyme activity in the body of a living organism. This could bring about healing by either hastening enzyme activity (as in wound healing, blood clotting, fighting invading infective agents), or slowing detrimental processes (as in growth of cancers, hormonal imbalances).

To accept Smith's speculations on reasons for the different results with various enzymes would be premature. However, healers feel that a natural intelligence is inherent in the spiritual healing process, so that the healer does not have to know such disciplines as biochemistry or anatomy in order to bring about physiological changes. Smith's results are in line with this assumption.

Repeating experiments may seem a tedious and uninspiring task. It actually helps us gain confidence in healing effects, as in the next study on an enzyme.

Enzyme Activity and Healing: a Replication
Hoyt Edge

Hoyt Edge replicated Smith's study with the help of Anne Graham, a well-known Florida medium and healer. In five experiments using undamaged trypsin, only one showed an effect (modest significance: $p < .05$). If data from the series are combined, significance reaches $p < .01$. In experiments with trypsin damaged by ultraviolet light, no significant results were found.

Trypsin held in magnetic fields of 1,300 gauss for 75 minutes was likewise not affected to a significant level.

The effect of laying-on of hands on an enzyme: an attempted replication (*Research in Parapsychology 1979*, 1980)

This study begins to confirm that healing may influence enzymes.

Edge mentions that conditions seemed unfavorable for the healer although details are not provided. Smith obtained positive results when more powerful magnetic fields were applied for twice the length of time used in this study.

Although this study supports Smith's findings of a healing effect on trypsin, it is too scantily reported, omitting details which would allow the reader to make an independent evaluation of the results. Rating: III

The similarity between effects of a healer and of very strong magnetic fields suggests that there may be overlaps in the mechanisms involved in these effects. However, most electromagnetic measurements of healers during healing have not revealed electromagnetic field alterations except with the most sensitive magnetometers.

Nerve cells communicate with each other by exchanging complex chemical messages in addition to their electrochemical messages. Glenn Rein studied spiritual healing effects on some of these neurotransmitters.

Neurotransmitters and Noncontact Healing
Glenn Rein

Rein studied the effects of noncontact (hands near mice) healing on the neurotransmitters dopamine (DA) and noradrenaline (NA) in the peripheral nervous systems of mice. Two healers "were asked to alter the impulse flow of the peripheral nerve which innervates the adrenal gland." Ten pairs of inbred mice were studied under double-blind conditions.

In half of the animals, NA increased up to 130 percent (modest significance: p < .05).

> In the remaining animals, NA levels either remained the same or were slightly decreased (approximately 10 percent) relative to the controls . . . DA levels also increased in the same five animals showing increased NA, reaching a similar maximum of 130 percent relative to controls. In the remaining animals the decreased DA levels observed (approximately 25 percent) paralleled the smaller decrease in NA (p < .04).

Rein suggests that individual animal variability in response to healing (of unspecified type) may account for the differences noted between responders and nonresponders. Such individual variability in response to many types of treatments is common in animals and even in yeasts. Healer performance variability may also be a factor. For instance, one of the healers was menstruating during a particular study in which three-quarters of the animals demonstrated decreased neurotransmitter levels, an observation that has also been reported in some other psi studies (Schmitt/Stanford; Keane/Wells).

An exosomatic effect on neurotransmitter metabolism in mice: a pilot study (*Presentation at 2nd International Conference of the Society for Psychical Research, Cambridge, England 1978*)

Here we see that healing can influence enzymes in a living organism. This is a well-controlled study with clearly significant results of healing. It is surprising that others have not studied hormone responsiveness to healing. This would appear to be a fertile area for further work. Rating: I

Neurotransmitters and Psychokinesis

Glen Rein

Matthew Manning (a well-known British healer) "treated blood platelets isolated from healthy human volunteers. . . . These blood cells contain monoamine oxidase (MAO)," an enzyme involved with metabolising critical neurotransmitters in the brain. "Enzyme activity was measured before and after PK exposure in intact cells and in those which had been disrupted. For both preparations, activity of the enzyme either increased [9 trials], decreased [7 trials], or did not change [2 trials] relative to untreated blood cells" (highly significant: p < .001). "Only five minutes' treatment was required." Enzyme measurements were done on a blinded basis.

A psychokinetic effect of neurotransmitter metabolism: alterations in the degradative enzyme monoamine oxidase (*Research in Parapsychology 1985*, 1986)

This is an important pioneering study, well performed. MAO is an enzyme associated with neural transmission. Its function in the brain is to aid the degrading of certain chemicals which are active in the junctions between nerve cells. Activity of this enzyme has also been roughly correlated with depressive mood states.

Why PK should sometimes increase and at other times decrease MAO activity in the laboratory is unclear. Further research is needed to clarify whether this is a consistent finding. The possibility of laboratory error (highly unlikely to be of this magnitude) or extraneous factors influencing the system would have to be ruled out in replications of this study. Rating: I

Rein's studies suggest yet other mechanisms whereby a healing might occur in humans. If spiritual healing can influence the chemicals that nerve cells use to communicate with each other and with organs in the body, then healing may enhance the activity of the entire nervous system. Healing might also override the routine activities of the nervous system. This would allow healers to introduce new patterns of awareness and behavior, moving healees towards wellness.

Some antidepressant medications act by altering MAO activity in the brain. An alteration in MAO activity through spiritual healing could produce changes in nerve function or mood that are conducive to recovery from depression. Healing might act by improving mood alone. This may explain why some healees report they feel better even when no objective improvements are noted by medical examiners.

The next study explores biochemical reactions with proteins found in muscles. It also explores whether healing influences can penetrate metal barriers. While it is highly technical, it gives the reader a sense of the complexities involved in research with enzymes.

Qigong and Enzyme Reaction in Muscle Cells

David J. Muehsam, M. S. Markov, Patricia A. Muehsam, Arthur A. Pilla, Ronger Shen, and Yi Wu

This study explored the effects of healing on the phosphorylation of myosin light chains (chemical reactions in muscle cells), involved in regulating contraction of smooth muscles (found in the digestive tract, arteries, and elsewhere). Myosin light chain kinase (MLCK) is an enzyme that catalyzes the phosphorylation. The binding of calcium to the protein calmodulin is required for the chemical reaction to proceed. The rate of this process may be influenced by weak environmental range electromagnetic fields (EMF), as clarified prior to the healing study.

> In order to assess the effect of ambient (geomagnetic and environmental) magnetic fields, a specially designed shielding box (mu-metal), allowed shielding of the exposure system and samples

from any natural and extraneous time-varying and static magnetic fields. . . . Very small alterations in ambient DC magnetic fields can affect myosin phosphorylation.

In the study of healing effects on this enzyme system, the procedures were exactly the same as those for testing EMF effects. The healing samples were studied at precisely the same place in the laboratory as the EMF exposure samples. Ambient baseline fields were monitored, and no significant changes were observed during any group of healing treatments. Controls were measured immediately prior to or following qigong treatments, and healers were absent from the lab during control studies. For each treatment at least five repetitions of measurements were recorded in the scintillation counter, and reports include mean deviations from controls.

The healers were two Soaring Crane qigong masters, Ronger Shen and Yi Wu. They were asked to treat enzyme samples just as they would treat patients. No illness was specified as reference for their treatment and healers were free to direct healing as they felt appropriate. The reactions were started at a signal from the healers after they had prepared themselves for healing. They stood two to five feet from the samples during healings. The reaction was stopped after six minutes of healing.

All qigong treatments produced reductions in myosin phosphorylation (modest significance: $p < .05$). Healer Shen contributed three treatments, each producing myosin phosphorylation reductions (modest significance: $p < .05$). Healer Wu contributed six independent treatments, each with reductions (modest significance: $p < .05$).

Effects of qigong on cell-free myosin phosphorylation: preliminary experiments (*Subtle Energies*, 1994)

An excellent study, well designed and well reported, with modest significance in healing effects on an enzyme. If any of the controls were run immediately after the healing trials, there is a likelihood that some of the healing effects lingered at the location of the measurements, thereby lowering the control trials as well—in line with the observations of Wells and Watkins (1974), reviewed in the section on healing effects on animals. These linger effects of healing and PK reportedly last about half an hour. If trials were done consecutively, with little time between trials, then the control measurements before the healing trials may also have been influenced by previous healing trials. The observed differences, measured as control figure minus healing figure, may thus have been smaller than actually produced by the healers.

The possibility of an electromagnetic component to healing might be clarified with mu-metal shielding and distant healing, where healers are not informed of this variable. Rating: I

The enhancement of enzyme activity in muscles may explain one of the ways in which healing can help. Healers report that spiritual healing can relieve tired, painful, and injured muscles.[158]

If healing can penetrate to influence enzymes shielded by mu-metal, then it is unlikely that healing is conveyed by electromagnetic radiations. This would appear to support the contentions of healers that a subtle biological energy is involved in healing that differs from electromagnetic energy. Although no mechanical instrument has been found to record these apparent energies which can penetrate mu-metal, their effects are clearly evident upon biological systems. Healers and healees report they can sense these energies during clinical healings.[159]

We await replications of this excellent study.

Evidence reviewed here suggests healing may enhance the activity of a variety of enzymes. Whether only these enzymes are responsive or whether all enzymes can be influenced by healers remains to be seen.

HEALING ACTION ON DNA

The contemplation of things as they are, without error
or confusion, without substitution or imposture, is in
itself a nobler thing than a whole harvest of invention.
　　　　　　　　　　　　　　　　　—Francis Bacon

Deoxyribonucleic acid (DNA) is a protein found in the chromosomes of cell nucleii. DNA transmits hereditary information in all living organisms, for the individual's development, for maintaining organismic stability, and for genetic continuity from one generation to another.[160]

The structure of this protein includes a pair of chains of nucleic acids (nucleotides) which are wound around each other in a double helix. The chains are held together by hydrogen bonds.

By studying DNA with ultraviolet (UV) spectroscopy, scientists can identify its molecular composition. It is thus possible to observe changes in DNA when it is treated with healing.

The Institute of HeartMath has developed a method of mental focus that brings about electrical coherence in heartbeats. The subjective awareness of people in this state is a deep feeling of love. People who achieve this loving awareness claim that they are able to project healing energies. The following study demonstrated alterations of conformance (winding) of DNA in the laboratory through their mental focus.[161]

Psychokinesis, Healed Water, and DNA
Glen Rein and Rollin McCraty

In a total of 10 trials, five subjects each held a beaker containing a sample of distilled water in a sealed test tube. The "subjects were asked to focus on the samples and intentionally alter their molecular structure for five minutes." Control samples measured from the original stock solution into identical test tubes were in an adjacent room.

Water samples were analyzed using "a computerized UV spectrophotometer" to measure structural change in the water. The spectrophotometer was programmed to measure the difference in absorbence values.

To study the ability of the treated water to influence conformational changes in human DNA, treated and control samples "were added to a 1.0ml aqueous solution of human placental DNA (20 mg/ml). . . . The results are expressed as a percent change in absorbence values. . . ."

Results from the first analysis show significantly higher absorbence values for treated water ($p < .01$). "Preliminary results from the DNA experiments indicated that treated water caused a significantly greater decrease in absorbence (modest significance p < .05). The results suggest that the water structured in the these experiments facilitates the spontaneous tendency of DNA to rewind (decrease absorbence). . . ."

Structural changes in water and DNA associated with the new physiologically measurable states (*Journal of Scientific Exploration*, 1995)

The effects of healing on water and of the healed water in affecting DNA are significant findings. It appears that healing can influence the winding and unwinding of DNA chains. However, the lack of clarity regarding the numbers of subjects in the trials and the lack of raw data leave the reader without the means to validate the report.[162] Rating: III

Healing, Subtle Energy, and DNA

Glen Rein and Rollin McCraty

In a blind study to examine the hypothesis that subtle energy information (SEI) could be read by DNA, Rein and McCraty measured "the ability of healers and individuals capable of generating coherent heart frequencies to influence DNA samples in sealed test tubes at a distance of either one mile or one foot. . . . Subjects were asked to focus on winding or unwinding the two DNA strands which make up its double helix conformation." In control experiments, no intentionality was directed to the DNA samples.

Both the local and long-distance effects were significant at the p < .01 level. In some experiments there was a

> 250 percent change in DNA indicating a very robust effect 25 times greater than controls. . . . In general, there was a correlation between the intended winding/unwinding direction and the increase or decrease in absorption values. Decreased absorption is known to reflect increased winding. . . . Experiments with multiple samples indicated that individual DNA samples responded differently and intentionality could be directed to specific samples. This effect was independent of distance.

In another study, the experiment was repeated, "except that the treatment consisted of adding control and charged water (10 percent by volume) to the DNA. Water charged with SEI produced an 8 percent increase in the absorption of DNA, whereas control water produced changes from zero to 3 percent."

> In the second series of experiments with inanimate objects, a test tube containing DNA was placed over a color photograph of a Russian healer and an individual highly skilled in generating coherent heart frequencies. DNA samples were continuously exposed to

the SEI from the photographs for up to three hours and measurements were taken at 30-minute intervals. In these experiments, the percent change in absorption of DNA was measured as a function of time. Both photographs caused a decrease in absorption that gradually increased with time, indicating that the DNA was gradually winding up. The different photographs, however, showed a different time course. The photograph of Doc Lew Childre produced larger increases (10 percent) in DNA absorption compared to the photograph of the healer which produced a maximal 3.8 percent change in DNA absorption. Control DNA absorption values varied between 0.5 to 1 percent.

DNA as a detector of subtle energies (*Proceedings of the 4th Annual Conference of the International Society for the Study of Subtle Energy and Energy Medicine, Boulder, Colorado,* **1994**)

The first experiments show a significant influence of healers on DNA in near and distant healing. The second series demonstrates that photographs of healers may convey healing. This is consistent with other studies in which vehicles such as water and cotton wool were used to convey healing. Absorption ratios of about five to nine times larger than control samples are impressive.

Without raw data to allow independent assessment of the effects of healing on DNA, it is difficult to accept these findings. Although means of results of several studies are provided, numbers of subjects and numbers of trials are not mentioned, nor is there a specification of the statistical tests which were applied. The studies of vehicles to convey healing also lack raw data and statistics to assess the significance of the findings.[163]

The mention of the electromagnetic field influence on DNA is of interest, suggesting that electromagnetic fields in the laboratory where these studies were conducted might have produced the observed effects rather than the healers or vehicles.[164] Rating: III

Chinese qigong studies also explored whether distant healing could produce effects on DNA (M. Sun et al. 1988; F. Zhang et al. 1993), demonstrating significant effects of healing on DNA.

The implications of the studies on DNA are far-reaching and the potential for healing oneself and others by influencing DNA synthesis appears to be immense. In normal maintenance of the body, atoms and molecules are _replaced periodically. It is estimated that the entire substance of the body is completely replaced every seven years. When bodies grow, whenever repairs are made to injured tissues, and when white cells and antibodies are produced for defense against infections, DNA in our chromosomes programs the cell divisions and protein syntheses. Healing could readily enhance our defense mechanisms by influencing DNA.

How healers influence the DNA is an obvious question. Some speculate that electromagnetic (EM) radiation might mediate such influences, but EM radiations have not been detected consistently in investigations of healing.

This concludes the review of the available studies of healing as of January 2000.[165]

FUTURE RESEARCH

Research is to see what everybody else has seen and to think what nobody else has thought.
— Albert Szent Gyoergy

Clearly, there are many areas where healing may prove effective which have just begun to be explored or have not been studied as yet. Here are some problems which I feel might be respond well to healing and also lend themselves well to research.

Surgical procedures: Abdominal hysterectomy, prostatectomy, cardiac bypass, heart valve replacements, joint replacements. Factors which may show measurable healing effects: anxiety, blood loss, post-surgical pain, rate of wound healing, attitudes towards physical and emotional challenges.

Anesthesia: The series of studies on waking mice from anesthesia produced the most consistent significant results. Waking people more quickly after surgical anesthesia would decrease the grogginess which lasts for days and keeps people in the hospital longer. This may not be needed as much— following the development of newer anesthetic agents which allow much more rapid post-op recuperation.

Infections: These are likely to respond to healing, since healers can slow the growth of bacteria and yeasts in the laboratory.

Burns: Factors that may show measurable healing effects, as in surgery, plus body fluid loss, fluid and blood replacements, infections, responses to antibiotics, need for and success of skin grafts, and scarring. Healing may be given through vehicles of medications and dressings applied to the burn wounds, as well as through touch/near/distant healing.

Cancers: Factors that may show measurable healing effects: best when healing is given immediately upon diagnosis—degree of tumor abnormalities at surgery, presence of metastases in nodes, rates of growth of tumors that cannot be removed, fears of illness and death, all of the factors above under surgery, and long term survival and quality of life.

Transplants: Any organs may show measurable healing effects, as in surgery plus immune rejection rate, intercurrent infections, complications of surgery.

Intrauterine fetal growth retardation (IUGR): Some babies who are identified on routine sonograms as much smaller than normal. IUGR has about 20 known contributing factors (e.g maternal smoking, small stature of parents) none of which can be counteracted when the IUGR is identified. These babies are often born premature and very small and often end up with serious, permanent neurological impairments. Factors that may show measurable healing effects if healing is given during pregnancy include: duration of pregnancy, duration and ease of labor and delivery, APGAR scores (of neonatal health immediately following birth), birth weight, length of stay in neonatal ICU, time before discharge from hospital, weight gain after birth, and presence/severity of neurological impairments.

Labor and delivery: The miracle of birth can be a blessed event, but it can also be a time of anxiety, fears, and pain, as well as an experience of physical and emotional trauma. Spiritual healing can help mothers deal with anxiety and pain, and can ease the process of bringing life into the world. Healing can also help with babies who have not turned head-down in readiness for delivery. This works especially well when the mother is encouraged to talk mentally with her baby, explaining what it needs to do. A study that examines the effects of suggestion alone, as well as the effects of suggestion *plus* healing, would be most interesting.

Insulin Dependent Diabetes Mellitus: In severe, unstable diabetics (not stable diabetics) with severe illness: instability of blood sugars, doses of insulin required, attitudes and moods, and stress tolerance.

Long-term effects of healing: Almost all of the studies of healing have been for short-term benefits. It would be most helpful to have long-term assessments of people receiving healing for a variety of problems.

I am available to consult on the design, planning, and reporting of healing research projects. Many serious errors in design and reporting could be easily avoided with prior consultation.[4]

SUMMARY

You have to study a great deal to know a little .
—Charles de Secondat, Baron de Montesquieu (1899)

Let us return to our first question, "Does spiritual healing work? Does research confirm that healing is an effective therapy?"

An impressive number of studies with excellent design and execution answer this question with a "Yes."

If we take a broad view, out of 191 controlled experiments of healing, 83 (43.4 percent) demonstrate effects at statistically significant levels that could occur by chance only one time in a hundred or less ($p < .01$); and another 41 (21.5 percent) at levels that could occur between two and five times out of a hundred ($p < .02$ - $.05$). In other words, close to two thirds (64.9 percent) of all the experiments demonstrate significant effects.

At the start of this chapter I proposed the following rating system:

I   *Excellent study*
II   *Study lacking in some details*
III   *Reporting of details is seriously deficient*
IV   *Critical elements are missing*
V   *Poorly designed study*

If we scrutinize the reports for standards of experimental design and reporting, using this rating system, the following totals emerge for each rating:

I – 50 reports; II – 2 reports; III – 41 reports; IV – 39 reports; V – 6 reports.

Of the 50 reports in combined categories I and II, 38 (76%) demonstrate significant effects. Of these, 29 (58%) have a significance level of $p < .01$ or greater, and 9 (18%) have a significance level of $p < .02$-$.05$.

See Table 4-26 for a summary of all the categories. Interestingly, the distribution of modestly significant, highly significant, and questionable and/or nonsignificant reports is fairly constant across the three main categories (I, III, and IV). The discrepancy between the total of 138 reports in the table and the 191 of total experiments is due to my tabulation of the ranking summary by research reports rather than by individual experiments. That is, some of the reports covered more than one experiment, which is reflected in the grand total of 191 experiments.

Table 4-1. Numbers of rated healing reports*

Rank	p < .01 –.00	p < .02 – .05	Unclear	Non-significant	Total
I	25 (50%)	12 (24%)	1 (2%)	12 (24%)	50 (100%)
II	1	1			2 (100%)
III	11 (27%)	11 (27%)	9 (22%)	10 (24%)	41 (100%)
IV	16 (41%)	10 (26%)	7 (18%)	6 (15%)	39 (100%)
V	1 (17%)		1 (17%)	4 (67%)	6 (100%)
Totals	54	34	18	32	138

*Some reports include several experiments

Ranks I and II: Research to establish that healing works must be repeatable on a range of subjects, in different settings, under the investigation of different scientists to assure its validity. The following are studies that in my opinion are of high quality, with adequate design, execution and reporting and demonstrate statistically significant effects to support an assertion that healing is a potent intervention (ranks I and II): Barry 1968; Brier et al. 1974; Bauman et al. 1986; Braud 1979; 1989; 1990b; Braud/Schlitz 1983; Braud et al. 1979; 1985; Byrd 1988; Ferguson 1986; Garrard 1996; Goodrich 1974; Grad 1963; 1964a; 1964b; 1965/1976; Grad et al. 1961; W. M. Green 1993; Hale 1986; Muehsam et al. 1994; Nash 1982; 1984; O'Laoire 1997; Pleass/Dey 1990; Radin et al. 1995; Rebman et al. 1996; Redner, et al. 1991; Rein 1978; 1986; Saklani 1988; 1990; Scofield/Hodges 1991; Sicher et al. 1998; Slater 1996; Snel/Hol 1983; Solfvin 1982; Watkins/Watkins 1971; Watkins/Watkins/Wells 1973; Wells/Watkins 1975; Wirth/Cram 1994.

This is ample replication of healing research as a generic treatment.

Even if studies with major question marks regarding details of methodology and reporting are excluded, an impressive array of decent evidence remains in 38 studies—covering a broad spectrum of human and nonhuman subjects.

Rank IV: The following studies are reasonably suggestive but include serious questions which leave their results uncertain: Attevelt 1988; Baranger/Filer 1953; Dixon 1998; Fedoruk 1984; Gagne/Toye 1994; Giasson/Bochard 1998; Gordon et al. 1998; Heidt 1981; Keller/Bzdek 1986; Kramer 1990; Krieger 1974/1976; Leb 1996; Miller 1972; 1982; Null 1981; Olson, Sneed 1995, Olson, Sneed et al. 1997; Peck 1996; Quinn

1982/1984; 1989; G. Rauscher/Rubik 1980; Sancier/Chow 1989; Schwartz et al. 1995; Shealy 1975/1988; 1993; Silva 1996; Snel 1980; Snel/van der Sijde 1990; Snel/van der Sijde 1990; Tedder/Monty 1981; Wells/Klein 1972; Wetzel 1993; Wright 1988.

Rank III: These studies that reported significant findings were either available to me only as abstracts of masters theses and doctoral dissertations or were poorly reported: Barrington 1982; Bentwich et al. 1993; Bucholtz 1996; Cahn/Muscle 1976; Dressler 1990; Edge 1980; Grad 1965b; 1967/1976; Guerrero 1985; Haraldsson/Thorsteinsson 1973; Keller 1986; Leikam 1981; MacDonald et al. 1977; Meehan 1990; Mersman 1993; Metta 1972; Misra 1994; Nash/ Nash 1967; Olson/Sneed 1992; Onetto/Elguin 1964; Peck 1996; Post 1990; Rein/McCraty 1994; 1995; Robinson 1996; Schlitz 1982; Schutze 1979; Sies 1987; Smith 1972; Sodergren 1993; Straneva 1993; Tedder/Monty 1981; Tharnstrom 1993; Wirth/Cram 1993; Woods 1996.[166]

Replications: While we cannot be certain of the results of any single study in the last two groups, hopefully replications will some day clarify which are valid. Though we must hold our judgments until such validations are in, the fact that some of these produced highly significant results is very probably indicative (in the light of the significant studies ranked I and II) that healing was a causative factor in at least some of these instances.

The following are studies of healing *for specific targets* that have been replicated. They are designated with "**" indicating high quality studies; "*" for possibly high quality studies with a good research design,[167] and no stars for studies with more serious deficiencies in design or reporting.[168]

Influencing human subjects' electrodermal activity—**Braud 1979; **Braud/Schlitz 1983; **Braud et al. 1985; **Radin, et al. 1995; Post 1990; **Rebman et al. 1995; *Schlitz 1982; Schlitz /Braud 1982.

Lowering human hypertension—*Quinn 1989; Miller 1982.

Reducing muscle strain—Wirth/Cram **1994; 1993.

Enhancing human immune functions—**Garrard 1996; Olson/Sneed et al. 1997.

Altering human hemoglobin levels—Krieger 1976; Wetzel 1989 (See also Straneva 1993).

Reducing anxiety—Dixon 1997; *Fedoruk 1984; **Ferguson 1986; *Gagne/Toye; Guerrero; *Heidt 1981; Kemp 1994; **Kramer; *Quinn 1982; *Olson, Sneed, et al. 1992; **Simington/Laing.

Reducing pain—Bucholtz 1996; Dixon 1997; Dressler 1990; Gordon et al. 1998; *Keller/Bzdek 1986; **Meehan 1985/1993; Meehan et al. 1990; *Peck 1996; **Redner et al.; Slater 1996; Sundblom et al. 1994.

Improving depression—*Leb 1996; Robinson 1996; **Shealy et al.

Enhancing wound healing in mice—**Grad 1965; **Grad et al. 1961.

Slowing progress of malaria in animals—Baranger/Filer; *Snel/van der Sijde 1990; **Solfvin 1982.

Slowing cancer growth in animals—Null 1966; Onetto/Elguin 1966; **Snel/Van der Sijde 1995.

Waking mice selectively from anesthesia—Schlitz 1982; **Watkins/ Watkins 1971; Watkins et al. 1973; **Wells/Klein 1972; Wells/Watkins 1975.

Enhancing plant growth—**Grad 1965; MacDonald et al. 1977; Nicholas 1977; **Saklani 1988; **1990; **Scofield/Hodges 1993.

Influencing bacterial growth—Leikam 1981; **Nash 1982; **1984; Nash/Nash 1957; Rauscher/Rubik 1983.

Influencing yeast growth—Barrington 1982; **Barry 1968; Cahn/ Muscle 1976; Haraldsson/Thorsteinsson 1973; *Tedder/Monty 1981.

Altering enzyme action—Edge 1980; Smith 1972; **Muehsam et al. 1994; *Rein 1978; *1986 replicate healing effects on enzymes as a category of target for healing.

Influencing motility of single-celled organisms—**Pleass/Dey 1985; Richmond 1952 replicates in this category.

Strengthening red blood cells against hemolysis—**Braud et al. 1979; **Braud 1989.

Influencing DNA—Rein/McCraty 1994; 1995.

This is ample replication of research in healing for specific problems, showing there are repeatable effects across varieties of subjects in different laboratories. While there will always be room for improvement in design, and greater assurance regarding conclusions about research evidence when more and improved studies are published, the evidence as it stands is impressive.

Distant healing effects have been demonstrated in Bentwich et al.; **Braud 1988; **Braud/Schlitz 1983; **Braud et al. 1985; **Byrd 1988; **Goodrich 1973; **W. M. Green 1993; **Nash 1982; **Nash 1984; O'Laoire; **Radin, et al. 1995; **Snel/Hol 1983; *Snel/van der Sijde 1990; **Solfvin 1982; **Wirth/Cram 1993; *Braud 1979; *Tedder/Monty 1981; Walker 1997; Miller 1982; Schutze 1979; Snel/ van der Sijde 1995.

A meta-analysis of distant healing studies appeared just prior to the publication of *Healing Research*, Volume I. The June 6, 2000 issue of the *Annals of Internal Medicine* assesses the significance of the effects of distant healing in a series of studies (Astin et al). Three types of studies were analyzed in their review: prayer, Non-Contact Therapeutic Touch, and other types of distant healing. Literature reviews of available databases through 1999 brought to light 100 studies of distant healing. Of the 23 studies that met their inclusion criteria (including 2774 participants), 13 (57 percent) demonstrated positive treatment effects, 9 (39 percent) showed no effect, and 1 (4 percent) had a negative effect.

Inclusion criteria required random assignment of study participants; placebo, sham, or otherwise "patient-blindable" or adequate control interventions; publication in peer-reviewed journals; clinical rather than experimental studies; and that the study be of humans subjects with any medical condition. The authors conclude that on the basis of the evidence, further studies are warranted.

This meta-analysis is of great significance for several reasons. The reviewers were very careful in their selection of studies and in their application of methods of mets-analysis. One of the authors, Edzard Ernst, is known to be very conservative in assessing studies of CAM reports. The conclusions that further studies of healing are warranted is a vote of confidence in the distant healing research they reviewed. Though this may sound less than a full endorsement that the evidence suggests that healing is beneficial, this is as far as skeptical scientists are willing to go at this time in their assessments of CAM therapies. The publication of the analysis in *Annals of Internal Medicine*, a mainstream US medical journal, is further acknowledgement of the evidence accumulating to support a belief in the efficacy of healing.

The authors make excellent suggestions for factors that should be included in healing research design and reports. There were 6 other published studies that in my opinion could have been included in this meta-analysis, and several doctoral dissertations. It is not clear whether the authors were unaware of these or rejected them for lack of elements in their inclusion criteria for their review, as they do not include a list of rejected studies in their bibliography. Assuming my assessment of the excluded studies to be accurate, I believe these would have significantly enhanced the positive findings of the meta-analysis. This meta-analysis also lends credence to the reports of a large number of people availing themselves of healing treatments and praying for healing. It suggests that they are engaging in a beneficial therapy, not just wishful thinking, religious ritual (as rote) practice, or placebo therapy.

This is ample confirmation of healers' claims that healing works from a distance. It is particularly impressive that most of these studies are ranked I and II, that is, they are of higher quality.[169]

Distant healing, probably more than any other aspect of spiritual healing, challenges our credulity within Western scientific paradigms. Volumes III and IV of *Healing Research* present further evidence and discussion on this and related questions.

If healing were a drug I believe it would be accepted as effective on the basis of the existing evidence. Healing is certainly more than a placebo, unless DNA, enzymes, yeasts, bacteria, plants, mice, and rats are subject to suggestion, and unless the dozens of researchers of human subjects in the better quality studies were unable to maintain proper research blinds. This is highly unlikely.

Unlike most drugs, which are specific for very limited problems, healing appears to act as a general tonic, improving the health of the entire organism. Healers claim that there seems to be no limit to the ability of healing to help any and every problem, though not everyone with any given problem will respond to the same degree. The extent to which this is true remains to be validated by further research.

Spiritual healing appears to be a therapy with vast potential for enhancing health care. In Britain and the Netherlands healing is being integrated into conventional medical settings. Elsewhere, progress is slower, with individual practitioners introducing it in their clinical work and people with dis-ease and disease seeking it on their own.

Skepticism on the basis of lack of high quality studies or lack of repeatability is contradicted by the existing evidence.

Skepticism on the basis that we have no theories within conventional science to explain this mass of evidence is not logical or reasonable. Conventional medicine has used many treatments, particularly medications, without explanations for their mechanisms of action. We still do not understand precisely how aspirin, tranquilizers, or antidepressants work, but we do not hesitate to prescribe and use them in vast quantities.

This evidence appears sufficient to respond with a firm "Yes" in answer to the first question, "Does healing work?"

How healing works is far more difficult to answer. Further evidence is presented in Chapter 5, as well as in the next three volumes of *Healing Research* to address this challenging question.

CHAPTER 5

FURTHER CLUES TO THE MYSTERY OF HEALING

The reticence of medical orthodoxy to accept every healing claim which surfaces or which attracts the public eye has been and should continue to be a public protection. On the other hand, the role of public protector all too easily can be an armor for the protection of limited self interest and a professional insulation inimical to the public good. Although the contributions of medical science well may be considered—with gratitude—one of the blessings of mankind, there also may be useful contributions outside the medical mainstream.

At what point should the individual be permitted freedom of choice in the regulation of his/her own health and healing practices? At what point does the medical profession's "right" to arbitrate these matters cease? These are weighty questions calling to be answered.

It seems clear that these matters cannot usefully be reconciled without recourse to an informed public and a healing profession educated beyond the confines of its own orthodoxy.

—Jeanne Pontius Rindge

This chapter is a varied feast of clues to continue to answer our second question, "How does healing work?" It also adds evidence to the first question, "Does healing work?"

As in the previous chapter, the items that you will encounter are summarized briefly here. Those who seek more detailed information should consult the Professional Supplement to Volume I, where most of the studies are discussed at greater length.

We start with several historical items that give a bit of the flavor of how research in healing evolved. We then consider clinical surveys of the effects of specific healers, demonstrating that healing is not a standard medical procedure but is more an art shaped by each individual practitioner. Next we look at studies that attempt to tease out possible mechanisms for how healing works, and other studies which seek common denominators in the beliefs and practices of healers. Finally, we conclude with a few words about cultures in which healing has an unbroken tradition over many centuries. Although Western society is just waking to the serious potentials of spiritual healing, there are deep wells of wisdom in other cultures. From these cultures we are just beginning to draw a few droplets—as they are just beginning to trust us enough to share.

It is difficult to know in some cases which findings may be legitimate effects of healing and which are chance occurrences, placebo effects, or spontaneous waxings and wanings of chronic illness. The reader will have to judge which cases might lean towards a Type I research error and which a Type II.[1]

I selected the contents of this chapter because they are rich in descriptive clues enhancing our understanding of healing. Selection was made on the basis of unique observations, particular healee populations, special methods of healing, and originality of opinions. Articles based on clinical observations, especially those with more objective perspectives, were given preference over articles advocating more narrow belief systems.[2]

HISTORICAL NOTES ON HEALING RESEARCH

The outcome of any research can only be to make two questions grow where one question grew before.
—Thorsten Veblen (1908)

Mesmerism

Franz Anton Mesmer

Mesmer (1734-1815) was one of the earliest scientists to study healing, although he did not recognize or label it as such. He developed a method he called animal magnetism, in which he made passes (hand movements) around the bodies of his patients, inducing hypnotic trances and relieving a wide spectrum of symptoms.[3] In deep trance, mesmerized patients were able to diagnose their own problems with apparent accuracy (Dingwall). Mesmerists were also able to hypnotize subjects telepathically from a distance (Eisenbud).[4]

Far ahead of his contemporaries, he explored realms which they found too dissonant with their materialistic theories. At the time he lived, there were neither sufficient understanding of psychological mechanisms nor theories which could coherently account for these phenomena. It is not surprising his methods were questioned, criticized, and even condemned in some quarters.

Mesmer believed that his approaches would eventually explain these difficult questions (G. J. Bloch):

- How is a sleeping man able to consider and foresee his own illnesses, as well as the illnesses of others?
- Without any instruction whatsoever, how is he able to prescribe the most accurate means of cure?
- How can he see the most distant objects and have presentiments of events?
- How is a man able to receive an impression from a will other than his own?
- Why is a man not always endowed with these faculties?

With today's understanding of the unconscious mind, we can appreciate Mesmer's keen powers of observation and appreciate his willingness to explore the frontiers of therapeutic science of his time. Were he alive today, he would be among the foremost researchers in healing. Though many of his cures were probably due to relief of conversion (hysterical) symptoms,[5] his work appears to have included a spectrum of healing phenomena as well. He did not know to differentiate between hypnotic and psi phenomena. This is not to say that making clinical and scientific distinctions on the basis of modern knowledge is necessarily the correct approach. We can only observe that there are definite similarities between Mesmer's approaches and modern studies of healing.

Modern hypnosis uses brief inductions, usually without passes of the hypnotist's hands around the body. In Mesmer's day, passes would be made for many hours, achieving profoundly deep (plenary) states (Dingwall) in which psi effects were demonstrated. The extensive hand passes around the body practiced by the Mesmerists strongly resemble laying-on of hands healings, and the telepathic influences of hypnotists over their subjects appear to overlap with distant healing. The latter may indicate that healers (and probably other health caregivers) can introduce suggestions telepathically to their healees.

Early Research and Healing through Prayer

F. Galton

Galton reasoned that if prayer were efficacious, then clergymen who pray frequently or monarchs for whom people pray frequently should live longer. "There is a memoir[6] by Dr. Guy . . . in which he compares the mean age of sovereigns with that of other classes of persons." Dr. Guy's results are presented in Table 5.1.

Statistical Studies into the Efficacy of Prayer (*Fortnightly Review*, 1872)

As Galton himself notes, no clear conclusions can be drawn from this line of approach. Although the entire group of clergymen lived one to two years longer than lawyers or members of the medical profession, when eminent members of these other professions are compared, the results are reversed. Other factors, such as residence of the majority of clergy in rural settings versus most other professionals in urban settings, might introduce variables that render such comparisons questionable. One would also think the longevity of royalty must be influenced by more critical variables than prayer.

Galton's discussion highlights the limitations of this report. Nevertheless, as the first recorded effort to establish the effects of healing scientifically, it is a historical gem.

Table 5-1. Mean age of various classes of males living beyond 30, 1758-1843 (Deaths by accident or violence are excluded)

	Number	Average age	Eminent men
Members of royal houses	97	64.040	
Clergy	945	69.409	66.42
Lawyers	294	68.104	66.51
Medical profession	244	67.301	67.07
English aristocracy	1179	67.310	
Gentry	1632	70.220	
Trade and commerce	513	68.740	
Officers in the Royal Navy	366	68.400	
English leterature and science	395	67.505	65.22
Officers of the Army	569	67.070	64.74
Fine Arts	239	65.960	

Rapid healing responses occur rarely, but often enough to attract the attention of the media. It is unfortunate that the trumpeting of healing miracles leads people to have unrealistic expectations. They are often disappointed when they do not experience immediate, dramatic results for their own problems and abandon healing after only a few treatments, when they might have benefited from the more common, gradual response which most people experience with healing, with repeated treatments over several weeks or months.

It is often difficult to know what to make of Biblical and other reports of unusual healings through the ages. Rex Gardner presents evidence to suggest there may be more to such reports than is commonly thought.

Historic and Modern Reports of Unusual Healings
Rex Gardner

Gardner, a British physician, describes healings recorded by Saint Bede the Venerable, a respected historian of the seventh to eighth centuries. Gardner points out that there is a tendency in modern times to dismiss first-hand observations and records of healings from earlier centuries as exaggerations or distortions. Gardner makes a strong argument for giving them greater attention. He describes a number of remarkable modern healings for which he tracked down first-hand observations from reliable reporters.

In one case, an 11-month-old boy was admitted to Royal Victory Infirmary, Newcastle-upon-Tyne in August 1977, who "had difficulty breathing without exertion, with pronounced retraction of his chest wall, indicating severe airway obstruction." He had had measles at age eight months and never fully recovered. Chest X-rays revealed chronic infection and air escaping from the lung into the chest cavity. The doctors told his mother the prognosis was hopeless, and he was discharged.

The child's doctor suggested the family might take him to a Pentecostal healing service. Five days following the healing treatment, he appeared to be happier and more ready to play. Two weeks later he was clearly stronger, even able to stand up by himself for the first time in four months. He continued to improve steadily. By the age of five years and two months, he had fully recovered.

In another case, in 1975, a general practitioner trainee contracted meningococcal septicemia (blood infection) with meningitis and was admitted in moribund condition to hospital with an illness diagnosed as Waterhouse-Friderichsen syndrome. No such case had ever survived in that hospital. Four healing groups simultaneously but separately prayed for her and

> believed that their request that she might be healed with no residual disability had been granted. At the same time, 8:30 p.m., there was a sudden improvement in her condition, though it was four days before she regained consciousness. Physicians were unable to explain how her chest x-ray film, which had showed extensive left sided pneumonia with collapse of the middle lobe, could, 48 hours later, show a normal clear chest.[7]

Gardner also presents paired cases of similar medical problems from the Bede records and from his own experience. For example:

> Bede . . . records a story. . . . A woman, because of possession by an evil spirit, had contracted hideous (ulcers [of the skin]). As long as she remained silent nothing could be done for her; but when she had told all that had happened she was cured by prayers and by application of holy salt, together with the doctor's medical aid. Only one stubborn ulcer remained, against which no remedies prevailed. At last, by her own suggestion, based on previous experience, oil blessed for the sick was applied, whereupon the remaining ulcer immediately responded to treatment by priest and doctor.

From Gardner's own experience:

> About 1970 the captain of the Girls' Brigade. . .had a deterioration in a large (varicose ulcer of the leg) which had been troubling

her for many years. Each morning her bandage was soaked with pus. Her doctor told her to give up her activities. She asked for prayer at the monthly charismatic prayer meeting. A general practitioner present examined the leg and judged that even were the ulcer to heal, it would require skin grafting. The pastor requested one of the women present to join him in praying for the patient. By next morning almost the whole ulcer had dried up with healthy skin covering; but one spot continued to exude pus. One week later one of the Girls' Brigade lieutenants called on the pastor and with embarrassment stated that she felt she should have joined in the prayer for the patient. They immediately visited the patient and the lieutenant laid hands on the area and prayed. Healing became immediately complete.

This story is so bizarre that it would not have been included were I not one of the doctors who examined the patient's leg at the next monthly prayer meeting, and were not all the people who had been present available for interrogation. Against the background of such cases one can no longer shrug off the miracles of the sixth and seventh centuries.

Miracles of healing in Anglo-Celtic Northumbria as recorded by the Venerable Bede and his contemporaries: a reappraisal in the light of twentieth-century experience (*British Medical Journal,* 1983)

Healing appears to promise to help diseases for which medical treatment in the West is still inadequate. The cases observed by Gardner seem to me most convincing; those for which he vouches somewhat less so; those of Bede far less so. Gardner's point is well made. First-hand testimony of a physician can clearly be given greater credence. However, reports of unknown persons—even though they be educated, competent in their own fields of work, and of good reputation—are still somewhat suspect. Reports filtered through second-hand observers, especially from many years past, are easily subject to exaggeration or inaccurate diagnoses. Yet as Gardner points out, with careful clarification one may confirm that a reported healing of dubious certainty may actually prove as impressive as it is claimed to be.

What Gardner does not point out is that the converse is also true. Seemingly clear-cut cases may prove to be hysterical reactions, misperceptions, misdiagnoses, or exaggerations.[8]

HEALINGS AT SHRINES

Take nothing on its looks; take everything on evidence.
—Charles Dickens

Sometimes *the place* appears to be the healer and this attracts pilgrims from all over the world, hoping for cures. Out of the millions who visit such shrines, only a few are cured. One of the most famous is Lourdes in France.

In 1858 a peasant girl named Bernadette Soubirous was gathering wood by the River Gave, at the base of a cliff known as Massabieille. A vision of the Virgin Mary appeared to her, standing at a split in the rock. Miraculous cures were alleged to have occurred at this spot within a few weeks of the first appearance of the Virgin. This became a healing grotto where millions of people with all varieties of illnesses have come to ask the Virgin for a cure. Thousands bathe daily in the waters of the grotto.

Because a few have experienced miraculously rapid cures of intractable, serious illnesses, much interest has been stirred in religious and medical circles. A local medical board has reviewed cases of cures since 1885, staffed by volunteers and supported by donations from private, nonclerical sources. An independent body, the International Medical Commission (IMC) sits in Paris so they cannot be biased by the emotional atmosphere of Lourdes. There are 25 members of the IMC, all practicing Catholics, 13 from France and the rest from other European countries. Their specialties include surgery, orthopedics, general medicine, psychiatry, and radiology, among others.

Here is how the Lourdes cases are evaluated. When an unusual recovery is noted, the patient is examined by members of the local medical bureau. Medical documents accompanying the patient are reviewed, along with the testimonies of the patient, of those accompanying the patient, and of those witnessing the cure. One of the physicians of the medical bureau is designated as the case reporter to gather information for presentation to the full bureau. Visiting physicians are also invited to participate. If there is agreement that the case is sufficiently unusual, a physician near the patient's home is enlisted to seek further testimony and to follow the case during the next year. At the end of that time, the patient is again examined by the Board. The physicians deliberate on whether the cure still appears inexplicable. If this is their decision they forward the dossier to the IMC, which likewise assigns a coordinator to review the case and to report to the entire Commission.

The IMC scrutinizes the medical records of patients from before and after their cures to decide whether each exceeds the normal expectation for recuperation from that particular illness. Critical analyses are applied under 18 headings, including diagnosis (by physical examination, supported by laboratory and X-ray findings), determination that the problem was organic rather than psychological, that the improvements could not have occurred through a natural waning of symptoms, that treatments given could not account for the cure, that both objective and subjective signs of the illness disappeared and laboratory results were negative, and that sufficient time elapsed to assure results were permanent. A majority vote of the IMC determines whether the case is declared "a phenomenon that is contrary to the observations and expectations of medical knowledge and scientifically inexplicable."

If the Commission considers the case inexplicable by ordinary laws of nature, the dossier is submitted to the Archbishop of the diocese of the healed person. He designates a Canonical Commission to review the case afresh. They take separate testimony from the witnesses and express their opinions on whether the case can be considered miraculous by the Church's standards. It is only on the favorable recommendation of the Canonical Commission that the Archbishop may pronounce the cure attributable to the miraculous intervention of the Virgin Mary.

John Dowling notes that in recent years, over four million pilgrims have come to Lourdes annually. Around 65,000 are registered with documentations of their illnesses. The specially built local hospitals can accommodate more than 1500, and many more stay at local hotels. The Medical Bureau reports that over two million sick people visited Lourdes from 1858 to 1984. Of these, around 6,000 claims of cures were examined by doctors. Only 64 were accepted as miraculous cures by the Catholic Church.

Since the inception of the IMC in 1954, 38 files were forwarded through its hands to the Medical Bureau, which felt that full study was justified in 28 cases. Of these, 3 lapsed without formal decisions being rendered, 6 were rejected, and 19 were felt to be cures which were inexplicable. Of these, 13 were accepted by the Church as miraculous. In 1983, 11 were still alive and well. One of the two nonsurvivors was killed in an accident and the other died of "late complications of her original illness nine years after the IMC had passed her as a cure." Retrospective review of the last case produced the opinion that the IMC had been "insufficiently aware of the natural history of Budd-Chiari syndrome and the possibility of natural remission" (Dowling).

The Miracles of Lourdes Reviewed

D. J. West

D. J. West, an English physician, critically reviews a number of cases that had been declared "miracles" by the church after extensive medical and ecclesiastical reviews. He presents a thorough analysis of 11 cases (nine of these prior to the founding of the IMC) and a sketchy overview of another 87. He is clearly a disbeliever of miracles. He states:

The present study is concerned solely with the evidence relating to remarkable or unexplained cures, the aim being to keep as far as possible to factual matters and to limit discussion to consideration of the plausibility or otherwise of various natural interpretations. The fact that these particular cures are believed to have religious significance is irrelevant to the purpose of the study. A critical survey of the factual evidence would be equally valid whether the cures were brought about by a new drug or by the intervention of the Virgin Mary.

West points out that in most of the 11 cases there were possible diagnoses which were not seriously entertained by the Board or the Commission (including malingering) and in some cases diagnoses such as tuberculosis were not supported beyond reasonable doubt by the available laboratory data. The declarations of miraculous cures relied heavily on clinical impressions and a variety of testimonies that could conceivably have been erroneous.

He concludes:

The rarity of the cures, and the incompleteness of the medical information on most of the cases put forward as miracles, makes any kind of appraisal exceedingly difficult. As far as it goes, and taking the dossiers at their face value, the evidence for anything "miraculous" in the popular sense of the expression is extremely meager. Self-evidently impossible cures, involving something like the regeneration of a lost eye or limb, are not in question because they are never claimed. The great majority of the cures concern potentially recoverable conditions and are remarkable only in the speed and manner in which they are said to have taken place. In no case is a sudden structural change confirmed by the objective evidence of X-rays taken just before and just after the event.

In his survey of other cases, West grudgingly notes that there are chronic suppurating wounds that had not responded to conventional treatments, and that closed rapidly and completely at Lourdes.
***Eleven Lourdes Miracles*, 1957**

West is the most stringent of the reviewers of Lourdes healings. His cautious tone underscores a careful scrutiny of the reported cures. This is an excellent review, with details of methods of inquiry and criteria for inclusion or exclusion of cases as miraculous cures. The review is weak in that it is a retrospective survey of work performed by other physicians and other evaluators. It is also clearly biased against the possibility of the truly miraculous that might occur among these cures.

It is impressive that positive findings remain after the many siftings of the evidence. Although X-ray evidence of instantaneous physical cures is not observed among the Lourdes cases considered in review, there are witnessed reports from apparently reliable sources testifying to instantaneous total healings of chronic fleshy suppurating wounds. These are impossible to account for in any conventional way. They appear to constitute recoveries from infections of chronic nature and enormous acceleration of the rate of wound healing, particularly impressive when these had previously resisted all conventional treatments. We are left yet again to postulate new ways of understanding what is possible in the healing of the human body.

A Further Review of Lourdes

St. John Dowling

St. John Dowling discusses the history of Lourdes and provides a detailed description of the process of assessments. He then reviews a recent cure that was agreed by the IMC to be medically inexplicable. The case involves Delizia Cirolli who

> was 12 years old in 1976 when she complained of a painful, swollen right knee. She was examined by Professor Millica at the Orthopedic Clinic of the University of Catania in Sicily. X-rays and a biopsy produced the diagnosis of a metastatic neuroblastoma. The family refused the amputation that the surgeon advised. Though they agreed initially to radiotherapy, the family took her home before she had any treatment because she was very unhappy in the hospital. She had another consultation at the University of Turin but again had no treatment. In August 1976 she spent four days at Lourdes with her mother, participating in ceremonies, prayers in the Grotto, and baths in the water.

Within several months, she was cured. Annual examinations at the Medical Bureau at Lourdes from 1977 to 1980 found no signs of the typical calcifications of neuroblastoma on X-rays of her chest or abdomen.

Though she was cured beyond doubt, the precise diagnosis was questioned. Professor Cordaro of Catania was of the opinion that the histological evidence suggested a metastasis from a neuroblastoma. The Medical Bureau submitted the same slides to eminent French bone specialists. Professor Payan of Marseilles, Dr. Mazabraud and colleagues at the Curie Institute, and Professor Nezel of Paris concurred that this was a Ewing's tumor, although they allowed that a metastasis from a neuroblastoma was also a possibility. Spontaneous remissions of neuroblastomas occur in rare instances but never after the age of five years, while spontaneous remissions of Ewing's tumors have never been reported.

The IMC reviewed the case three times between 1980 and 1982, finally deciding that it was a Ewing's tumor and that its cure was inexplicable. It was not considered relevant that the moment of cure was not at Lourdes. It was left to the church to decide whether this was to be declared miraculous.

Dowling briefly notes how difficult it is for many people to accept that miraculous cures can occur. They tend to doubt the diagnoses of the Medical Board, or to seek other explanations for these unusual improvements in conditions which are normally intractable.[9]

Lourdes cures and their medical assessment (*Journal of the Royal Society of Medicine,* 1984)

Though opinions vary as to the validity of findings in some cases of Lourdes healings, a core of convincing evidence remains.

Detectives working on a mystery examine samples of evidence in the laboratory. Using research methodology reviewed in Chapter 2 of this volume, Douglas Dean (1989) reports that analysis of water from Lourdes and from several other holy springs and places regarded as geological power points demonstrates altered infrared spectrometry readings that are characteristic of water treated by healers. This was true of some but not all samples from Lourdes. Dean clarified that this was dependent on whether the samples were taken from the grotto spring itself or from other locations.[10]

Healings of physical illnesses at shrines appear to be rarer occurrences than the media might have us believe. Nevertheless, those which are accepted by the medical and church authorities are among the best documented complete healings available. How similar these are to spiritual healings brought about with the direct help of healers remains to be clarified.

The Virgin Mary is believed to be a healer by those who visit Lourdes. Cures at Lourdes may be considered cases of distant healing, transcending space and time.[11]

The spiritual uplift experienced by pilgrims appears to be much more frequent than cures.[12] This, in fact, is the aspect of healing that many spiritual healers value the most.

CLINICAL AND LABORATORY OBSERVATIONS ON HEALING

It is the glorious privilege of academics to know that they are on the track of knowing everything. It is the humble gloom of the practitioner to know that nearly everything remains uncertain and paradoxical.
—Edward Whitmont

Healing is a gift most varied in its expressions. One healer may be able to help with a particular spectrum of problems, while others may have no success at all with the same problems. Not uncommonly I hear a healer say "Healing has little to offer in diabetes, or in depression, or in neurological problems." Different healers will tell me "Oh, yes, healing can reduce the amount of insulin needed by diabetics, can bring people out of depression more quickly than medication or talking therapies alone, can bring people out of coma or can halt or reverse the course of multiple sclerosis."

Similarly, healees report they may experience no change in their condition with one healer and receive great results with another. Even with the same healer over a period of time, they may find that their responses differ with successive healing treatments.

It is a challenge to identify patterns from these reports, which clarify the nature and mechanisms of healing as it is expressed by healers and by healees. Without control groups, it is often difficult to assess the validity of these reports. However, they do provide many suggestions for further explorations.

Our first study comes from Germany. This is a highly unusual report, as German medical authorities have not only been uninterested in integrating spiritual healing with medical care, but have prosecuted healers for practicing medicine without a license.

An Early Study of Healing

Inge Strauch

Strauch[13] studied patients in a rural setting treated by Kurt Trampler, a "mental healer." They were examined before and after his treatments. Characteristics of the patients are described in some detail. Categories of illnesses treated are mentioned, but not specific diagnoses or numbers of patients in each category. "Within the major disease groups, most of the objective improvements (15 %) occurred in diseases of the digestive tract."

The statements of the patients themselves in regard to their subjective feelings show great deviation from the results of the objective checks. All those who were objectively improved also stated that they felt better. But the group of those who showed no objective change by no means regarded their condition as unchanged: 61% of these patients thought that it had improved during the time of the investigation. And of those whose condition had objectively worsened, 50% nevertheless declared that they were considerably better, at least temporarily.

Medical aspects of mental healing (*International Journal of Parapsychology*, 1963)[14]

This is the earliest published clinical study with assessments before and after healing by the same group of researchers on a large number of patients. Descriptions of methods and general criteria for evaluations are reasonably presented. More detailed reports on the types of problems treated and those improved would have helped readers appreciate more precisely the nature of the problems addressed.

Because no control groups of untreated patients were used for comparison with those receiving healing, readers are left, at best, with a choice of accepting the opinions of researchers they do not know and cannot evaluate or with the alternatives of suspending judgment or of expressing severe doubts, at the worst.

Of help are the observations on types of patients likely to benefit from healing. The larger number of objective improvements reported where a functional (psychosomatic) component was present implies that suggestion may still be a major component in the response to healing, or that the same illnesses which respond to suggestion may respond to healing. This is further supported by a report of a better response in less intellectual and analytical personality types, whom one might expect to be more receptive to suggestion. Caryl Hirshberg and Marc Barasch (p.115) make a similar observation from their study of people who had remarkable recoveries from illnesses, many of them through apparent self-healings. "[T]hose most likely to experience supposedly miraculous healings do not interpose much critical thought between themselves and a higher power."

The functional illnesses may also be more susceptible to healing because they involve neuronal or hormonal influences; may be related to smooth muscle tension (in gut, bronchioles, blood vessels); or may involve the immune system—and are all therefore subject to mental control. Biofeedback and psychoneuroimmunology[15] confirm that such control is possible in these body systems. Self-healings may be enhanced via telepathic suggestion.

Strauch's report that people who are less tense respond better is hard to reconcile with the above alternatives. Many healers say a relaxed state in healees contributes to a positive response. If anything, it seems to me one would expect *more* response from suggestion in patients who were more anxious. These would have more pressing needs for relief and more room for improvement on a parameter that is notoriously responsive to suggestion. This discrepancy hints at the possibility that something other than suggestion may be occurring.

Many healees reported subjective relief of symptoms even when no objective changes were measurable. Even if this is only due to suggestion, it appears to be a very worthwhile addition to the management of the dis-ease associated with disease. Surveys of healees, considered near the end of this chapter, strongly confirm this finding.

Healing and other complementary therapies are in wide use in Eastern Europe because limited medical resources over many years have forced people to seek every available form of care. Though most doctors in these countries have little awareness of the efficacy of healing, a few are beginning to appreciate its worth and work with healers.[16]

Biotherapy in Poland
Zofia Mialkowska

Mialkowska, a psychologist, reviews the "biotherapy" work of Dr. Jerzy Rejmer in a Polish clinic between 1982 and 1985. Rejmer saw 2,820 people (1,913 women and 907 men). Many had more than one problem, with 3,837 (2,699 women; 1,138 men) clinical complaints registered. Results of Dr. Rejmer's treatments are mentioned for only 1,684 of the 3,837 problems (44 percent) since many healees had only one treatment and no follow-up data are available. Many of the cases had been unresponsive to conventional therapies. In 293 instances (7.64 percent), hospital testimony to this effect was obtained.

Dr. Rejmer treated each person by giving healing to the local body region requiring help (3,090, or 85 percent of problems). Alternatively, "when the organism was remarkably weakened with a generalized character of complaint, he used a generally strengthening technique. . . ." Biotherapy was clearly used in a complementary (rather than alternative) manner, with attending physicians and specialists consulted in 917 cases (27 percent). In 83 percent of cases, patients reported improved well-being. In 53 percent, "the effects of Dr. Rejmer's procedures were confirmed by the appropriate analytical and medical examinations." The greatest objective changes were in the urinary and nervous systems (especially epilepsy); the lowest in the digestive system.

Statistical Assessment of Dr. Jerzy Rejmer's Biotherapeutical Activity at an IZIS Clinic in Warsaw (*Proceedings of the Sixth International Conference on Psychotronic Research,* 1986)

Again, we have a tantalizing report indicating that healing can be helpful in some ways with some illnesses. But again we lack details of diagnosis, criteria for improvement, and control groups against which to judge the results.

Mialkowska reports an occasional occurrence of pain early in the course of healings that has been echoed by numbers of healers and may be a clue to how healing works. No one has proposed a mechanism to explain this, however. Anecdotal reports suggest that it generally bodes well when this happens.

The spectrum of illnesses responding to Rejmer's treatments is at variance with those responding to Trampler's treatments. It is very common to find that particular healers have better responses to a specific assortment of symptoms and illnesses and that these assortments differ for different healers.

In England, I founded a Doctor-Healer Network which is a forum for doctors, nurses, and other conventional therapists to meet with healers and other complementary therapists and clergy engaged in spiritual healing and energy medicine. A member of this network, Dr. Michael Dixon, is among a growing number of physicians in British clinic and hospital practices who are inviting healers to work with them.

A Healer and Doctors Working Together

Michael Dixon

Dixon reports on a clinic in which seven doctors work in general practice in rural England. Despite his colleagues' initial skepticism, Dixon employed a healer, Mrs. Gill White. White had been "coming into Dixon's office every Thursday morning since 1992, seeing an average of five patients for 45 minutes each." In a review of this practice 25 patients

> were asked to score their main symptoms both before and after healing on a nine-point scale and also to assess any changes that they had perceived. As far as self-rated symptom scores were concerned, 72% showed some improvement, including 32% who reported *substantial* improvement in their symptom score. As far as perceived change was concerned, 16 percent felt slightly better, 20% felt much better, and 32% felt very much better. Doctors' perceptions of change largely agreed with perceptions of their patients. All eight patients with stress, joint pains, and abdominal pains reported some improvement, while the improvement was less predictable in the patients with back pain (3 out of 5), depression (2 out of 3), and chronic fatigue syndrome (1 out of 2). Patients with agoraphobia and headache were not helped.

In assessing the healing, "all but one of the patients felt that healing had been a positive, pleasurable, and useful experience in some way."

Dixon discusses at length further examinations into the results of Gill's healing, looking at possible cost savings involved. "We also examined changes in prescriptions," he writes. "Out of the 25 patients, eight either reduced or stopped their medication. The annual saving in prescription costs amounted to a little over £1000 a year, which more than paid for the annual cost of the clinic. The reduction in costs from fewer consultations has not been calculated but is clearly significant."

A healer in GP practice (*Doctor-Healer Network Newsletter,* 1994)

Dixon's pilot study demonstrates that healing is an effective complement to conventional outpatient care. This study is the first to demonstrate that healing can be cost effective, with reduced medication use and fewer patient visits. Dixon almost regretted using those two words because for several months after he published his study he was besieged by the media who were eager to publicize his results. Never mind that his patients improved—it was the fact that the government could be saved a bunch of money which was news.

The healer, Gillian White, heals within a firm personal Christian belief system (which she does not impose upon healees). White is sensitive to counseling issues and does a fair bit of talking with healees in addition to the healing.

The cost-effectiveness of healing appears self-evident to those involved in spiritual healing. It is good to have medical confirmation of this clinical impression.

Craig Brown is another general practitioner member of the Doctor-Healer Network who has two healers working in his offices. He is president of the National Federation of Spiritual Healers.

Another Doctor Working with Healers
Craig K. Brown

Brown works in a practice serving 12,000 patients in South England. He and his five partners referred patients for healing when they had chronic problems of at least six months' duration and had not responded to conventional treatments, including drugs, specialist referrals, and counseling. Healing was given as a complement to ongoing treatments.

The healers (Del Ralph and Brenda Watters) saw patients for 20 minutes weekly over eight weeks, including a minimum of 15 minutes of healing, with the healers' hands held near the body at each visit. The rest of the time was given to discussing the patients' conditions. Patients could choose which of the healers they preferred, and saw the same healer each time.

Patients were interviewed prior to the start of healing to record their main complaint and its duration. The Medical Outcome Study (MOS) questionnaire was administered prior to the first healing, after eight weeks, and after six months. Significant improvements were noted, per scores in Table 5-2.

Table 5-2. The mean scores of the SF-36 questionnaire study group at zero and eight weeks

Scale	Mean score			
	No.	0 weeks	8 weeks	Significance
Physical function	32	70.2	73.4	NS
Role limitation - physical	31	21.8	47.8	p < .01
Role limitation - emotional	32	32.3	54.2	p < .05
Social function	33	52.1	66.4	p < .01
Bodily pain	32	44.6	56.8	p < .01
Mental pain	32	49.6	63.5	p < .001
Vitality	32	32.5	52.7	p < .001
General health	30	48.7	55.4	p < .05

Spiritual healing in a general practice: using a quality-of-life questionnaire to measure outcome (*Complementary Therapies in Medicine,* 1995)

Dixon and Brown are to be commended for taking the trouble to study the efficacy of healing in the midst of very busy and demanding medical practices. Their reports confirm healers' impressions that healing can be of benefit to patients with many problems. It behooves researchers to look for a spectrum of symptomatic improvements with healing, rather than to focus on single presenting symptoms.

The efficacy of healing for anxiety has been confirmed in several studies, as well as in the everyday experience of most healers. The next study begins to examine factors that may contribute to reductions of anxiety when treated with Therapeutic Touch.

Patient Expectations and Therapeutic Touch

Ellen Schuzman[17]

Schuzman made a clinical observation that Therapeutic Touch (TT) reduced anxiety in preoperative patients. She set up a study to explore whether patients' expectations or their trait anxiety (natural, characterological tendency to be anxious) might be associated with this effect.

TT was given by three experienced nurses. Their expertise was confirmed by their scores on the Subjective Experience of Therapeutic

Touch Scale (SETTS).[18] The State-Trait Anxiety Inventory (STAI) and a Credibility Scale for expectations of TT were assessed with 81 women who were scheduled for either gynecological surgery or breast biopsy in an outpatient surgical unit. The STAI was repeated after a five-minute TT healing.

Significant reductions in state anxiety were found in comparing presurgical with postsurgical, post-TT anxiety scores. Further analyses showed that the higher the *trait* anxiety, the lower the *state* anxiety.

The expectations of subjects did not correlate significantly with the reduced state anxiety, nor was trait anxiety correlated with expectations of TT.

The Effect of Trait Anxiety and Patient Expectation of Therapeutic Touch on the Reduction in State Anxiety in Preoperative Patients Who Receive Therapeutic Touch (doctoral dissertation, New York University, 1993)

It appears from this study that TT healing can reduce presurgical state anxiety. It is unusual to find a study that includes explorations of trait anxiety. Most researchers assume that characterological anxiety will not change as a result of treatment, and so they ignore it. These observations suggest further studies.

Healing Touch expands upon Therapeutic Touch to include longer treatments (up to an hour), Native American methods, healing directed to the chakras, and other innovations. The following study explores Healing Touch for chronic pain.

Chronic Pain and Healing Touch

Madelyn M. Darbonne, Tamera L. Fontenot, and Wanda Thompson

The authors studied the effects of Healing Touch (HT) for chronic pain in rural outpatients, as measured on a visual analogue scale (VAS) and Chronic Pain Experience Instrument, before and after four HT treatments.

The authors report that "[n]o attempt was made to control for confounding variables such as: (a) additional treatments in concurrent progress, (b) natural healing processes unrelated to the treatment, (c) the placebo effect, (d) the experimenter effect, or (e) changes in life style and reduction of stress factors. . . ."

Treatment was given by six expert HT practitioners, who also gathered the data. The 19 subjects in the study were over 18 years old, had pain for at least six months, including "chronic neck and/or spinal pain, chronic arthritic-type pain, or those with fibromyalgia syndrome (FMS)."

Reductions in pain were registered on both the VAS (highly significant: $p < .005$) and CPEI (significant: $p < .01$). Subjects also reported greater relaxation and felt a "better overall perspective toward everyday life."

The Effects of Healing Touch Modalities with Chronic Pain *(Journal article in preparation)*

This is an excellent exploratory study of Healing Touch for chronic pain. Giving healing for up to an hour is much more common in clinical healing practice than the usual "standard doses" of five minutes of healing that have been used in much of the initial research on healing treatments for pain.

Pain and Therapeutic Touch
Carolyn Estelle Dollar

Dollar studied the pain of tension headaches in seven adults who were treated with Therapeutic Touch (TT). Intensity of pain was assessed with a Visual Analog Scale (VAS), audiotaped interview, pulse, blood pressure, and respiratory rate. Assessments were conducted prior to, immediately after, and one hour after healing was given.

Significant reductions in pain (highly significant: $p < .0006$) and respiratory rate (significant: $p < .017$) were noted from the pre-test measures to both of the post-test measures. There were no significant differences between the two post-TT measures. Interview data added the factor of greater relaxation with TT.

Effects of Therapeutic Touch on Perception of Pain and Physiological Measurements from Tension Headache in Adults: A Pilot Study (master's thesis, University of Mississippi Medical Center, 1993)[17]

The abstract is too brief to permit detailed comment.

Irritable Bowel Syndrome and Therapeutic Touch
Ronda Evelyn Cooper

Rhonda Cooper studied the responses to Therapeutic Touch (TT) of 29 women with irritable bowel syndrome (IBS). Each woman recorded her symptoms daily in a diary for two weeks before TT was given and during the two weeks when TT was given.

Seven IBS symptoms were reduced by TT, with the reductions in pain being modestly significant ($p < .05$). Flatulence was *increased* by TT.

The Effect of Therapeutic Touch on Irritable Bowel Syndrome (master's thesis, Clarkson College, 1997)[17]

The abstract is too brief to permit detailed comment. Healees often have rumblings in their stomachs within a few minutes of commencement of healing treatments. This is probably the second most observed response with healing, after relaxation.

Healers around the world are gathering clinical reports to demonstrate the efficacy of healing. The following notes come from China. Qigong is practiced primarily as self-healing exercises but may include *external qi* healings given by qigong masters.

While cancer and neurological problems are some of the illnesses for which people frequently seek healing, there are so few clinical notes in these areas that I include here two reports barely worth mentioning in terms of their technical merits.

Cancer and Qigong

Chen Guoguang

Guogang summarizes his treatment of 15 women and nine men, ages 18 to 75, all of whom had cancer diagnosed by physicians. Duration of treatment ranged from eight months to 12 years. He states,

> In an ancient Chinese medical book we read, "where there is a pain, there must be some part in the body blocked up. . . . The pain removes when such a part becomes dredged." Applying this theory, a qigong doctor makes use of his "waiqi" (outside breathing) to put in order the patient's blocked breathing, blood, sputum and undigested food. The doctor concentrates his effort to stimulating the circulating of the blood through the "jing" (channel) the patient falls ill with. Stimulation may at the same time be applied to other channels.

Cancers were present in 14 different parts of the body (cell types of cancer not mentioned). "Cures" occurred in seven healees (29 percent), with decreased pain, lessened swelling, improved appetite and sleep, and reductions in frequency of stools and blood in stools. Notable effects were seen in 13 healees, with greatly decreased pain and relief of other symptoms. **The curative effect observation of 24 cases under my outward qigong treatment (*Proceedings of the 2nd International Conference on Qigong, Xian, China, September 1989*—from Qigong Database of Sancier)**

The conference summary is very brief. It is difficult to know whether the flows of energy that Chen describes in the energy channels along the spine are a particular product of qigong healing or are present in healees receiving other types of healing. If the latter, these may not be sensed by healers who are not educated in the acupuncture energy channel systems. It would appear that Guoguang's definition of cure may be considerably short of Western definitions of cure.

What is of particular note is a warning that Chen makes against stimulating (again, it is difficult to know what type of stimulation is indicated) a particular point lest the growth of malignancies be accelerated. I know of no other healer who gives such a warning.

Healing with Qi

Meiguang Huang

Emitted qi, combined with self-practice of qigong, was used to treat 43 cases of paralysis, 19 cases of hemiplegia, and 24 of paraplegia. "Qigong masters emitted their qi from the *ogong* (P 8) and *shixuan* points," and used emitted qi to "massage points of the patient once every other day. . . . The patient did a qigong exercise one to two times a day. . . ."

The experiment saw symptom relief. In most cases, the ability to perform active movement improved. Some of the cases recovered completely.

> [B]efore treatment, 37 of the 43 paralytic patients had needed support in walking. After treatment, 23 could walk without any help. Only 20 were still dependent on crutches. Some patients who previously used wheelchairs now could walk with crutches, and those who originally walked with a pair of crutches now use only one crutch.
> . . .Before treatment 36 of the 43 cases could not manage their own daily life. After treatment 34 were capable of taking care of themselves.

Comparison of the indices before and after treatment shows a significant difference.

General Hospital of P, Beijing—Effect of the emitted qi combined with self practice of qigong in treating paralysis (*Proceedings of the 1st World Conference for Academic Exchange of Medical Qigong, Beijing, 1988*— from qigong database of Sancier)

It is helpful to have confirmation from China of anecdotal reports from the West of the efficacy of healing for paralysis. Without control groups, however, it is impossible to know whether these patients might have improved without the healing.

South American healers are renowned for helping people with difficult problems.[19] Until recently, only anecdotal reports were available. The following is the first systematic study by doctors and psychologists with assessments before and after healing.

Healing in Brazil

M. Margarida de Carvalho

Carmen Ballestero is a Brazilian trance medium and healer. She is leader of a Spiritualist Center where she and a group of about 200 healers donate their time without payment. Clients come for help with physical, psychological, and spiritual problems. Carmen used to be an English teacher, but now works full time at her center. She claims to channel Saint-Germain, an 18th-century aristocratic French mystic.[20] The other healers have other spirit helpers.

Treatments at the Center include spiritual healing, group discussions, and rituals for patients, together with family and friends. Treatments are given every evening by 20 to 30 healers standing in a circle around the patients. With prayers, meditations, and music, they give healing by moving their hands near the patients but not touching them. The healers feel they are channeling divine energy.

This study was conducted over a period of 10 months. Receiving no other medical treatments, the participants had to have physical (not psychological or spiritual) problems and had to have been diagnosed by an independent medical doctor, with appropriate medical tests. At the end of the study, they were evaluated with repeated medical tests by medical doctors. Out of more than 100 patients, 25 were included in this study, and 20 finished all the evaluations. These patients had serious illnesses, and the research doctors anticipated that all would deteriorate during the course of the study. Carvalho, together with another psychologist and two medical doctors, interviewed and examined the patients and reviewed medical reports from patients' doctors.

Most of the patients attended other healing centers simultaneously.

The research doctors felt that the treatment at the healing center was beneficial. They observed that patients who were emotionally unstable tended to become physically unstable. Improvements appeared to correlate with patients' faith in the Center's healing treatments and with positive attitudes and optimism. Conversely, less improvement was seen in those who expressed little faith in the treatments, many of whom attended primarily because relatives or friends had pressured them to come.

The researchers felt that their own participation may have contributed to improvements, in the form of extra attention to these patients.

An eclectic approach to group healing in Sao Paulo, Brazil: A pilot study (*Journal of the Society for Psychical Research*, 1996).

Healers who come from unbroken cultural traditions of healing may have much to teach us about spiritual healing. It is so helpful to have confirmation from Western health professionals that observable improvement occurs with healings in these contexts. Without such observations, we would be left wondering about the validity of claims of people who are not aware of the distinctions between physical and psychosomatic illnesses.

While clinical studies help to answer the question "Does healing work?" and establish the range and limits of its efficacy, further studies are needed to clarify *how* healing works.

It is quickly apparent that many variations on the theme of healing are practiced. Some feel that a single thought may be enough to bring about healing. Others believe that special states of meditation or prayer are needed. Others feel that the *qualities* of one's awareness influence the healing.

The following two studies examine the effects of spiritual healing on protein synthesis in cancer cells. Of particular interest are the states of mind identified by the healer and the apparent differences in effects with each state.

Healing and DNA Synthesis in Tumor Cells
Glen Rein

Rein explored the effects of a healer upon DNA synthesis of tumor cells in culture. The healer was Dr. Leonard Laskow, an American gynecologist who is now giving and teaching healing.

> Leonard Laskow shifted into a specific state of consciousness and mentally and energetically focused on three petri dishes held in the palm of his hand. Another aliquot of cells from the same stock bottle was being held simultaneously by a non-healer in an adjacent room. The non-healer was reading a book to minimize the interaction of his consciousness with the cells. Both sets of petri dishes (n = 6) were brought back to the tissue culture hood where they were labeled (blindly) and scrambled. The author then labeled the cells with radioactive thymidine and processed them after 24 hrs growth to measure cell proliferation. The same exact protocol was also followed in another parallel set of experiments done with distilled water contained in a plastic lid-sealed test tube, instead of cells in a petri dish. This water, as well as control water, was then used to make standard tissue culture medium which was then added to the cells at the beginning of the 24 hr. growth period.

In the first of three experiments, Laskow explored "five different mental intentions," all built around varying structures of love and harmony, and in one case, "dematerialization."

Laskow reports,

> I had two forms of dematerialization, one was dematerialized into the light and the other one was dematerialized into the void. I wanted to see whether there was a "reluctance" on the part of the cells to go into the unknown. Or is it better to give them a direction into the light. Obviously, this has import for people who are doing healing work in terms of giving direction to tumor cells and energy forms that you want to release. . . .

In the second experiment, Rein and Laskow looked at the extent to which "intention, as a focused mental thought, might contribute to the healing response." Laskow intended and instructed the cells to "return to their normal order and rate of growth," while holding no visual image. Thus there was intent with no imagery.

Rein then proceeded to study the efficacy of water as a vehicle for healing. In the third experiment, he wanted to determine whether there were differences in the energetic patterns associated with different states and contents of consciousness and whether these patterns could be transferred to water used to make tissue culture medium.

For the first experiment, three of the five intentions showed a "significant effect on inhibiting the growth of the tumor cells," with a "return to the natural order and harmony of the normal cell line" was the most effective (39 per cent inhibition). "Allowing God's will to manifest" was half as effective (21 per cent inhibition). "Under the same experimental conditions, unconditional love neither stimulated or inhibited cell growth."

In the second experiment, "focused intent for the cells to return to the natural order of their normal growth rate produced the same inhibitory biological response (20% inhibition) as did imagery alone." That effect was doubled when imagery and intent were combined.

In the third experiment,

> water treated with the intention to return the cells to their natural order and harmony resulted in a 28% inhibition of cell growth, quite similar to that obtained when the cells were treated directly. Even more surprising, however, was the fact that two other focuses which were ineffective when the cells were treated directly, were effective when the water was treated. Thus unconditional love caused a 21% inhibition of growth and dematerialization caused a 27% inhibition. . . . The practical application of this observation is that healers can give their clients water to drink which has been previously charged with their healing energy. This may also be the basis for blessing food and wine.

Quantum Biology: Healing with Subtle Energy, 1992

In other studies Rein demonstrated that non-Hertzian electromagnetic fields can have marked effects directly on biological systems (1988; 1989: 1991), on water (1990) and on biological systems via the water as a vehicle for the effect (1991).[21] He also demonstrated that Laskow could generate a specific magnetic field pattern from his hands when he was in a particular state of consciousness.[22] [23] Rein speculates that non-Hertzian energies may be a mechanism explaining some or all healing effects.

Rein did not include the data from the third experiment in his monograph. The results appear highly significant. Without the data to permit independent assessment of the significance of the results, however, one must suspend judgment upon this experiment.

It is fascinating to have a healer who can demonstrate different effects on biological systems with different states of consciousness and intent. The studies of Spindrift[24] also appear to support this observation, which is often stressed by healers (for example: LeShan 1974a).

Mental Focus and Cancer Cell Growth

Glen Rein and Leonard Laskow

Rein and Laskow further studied the effects of various states of intent and mental focus during healing, specifically on the growth rates of human mastocytoma cancer cells in tissue culture. The uptake of radioactive thymidine was used to measure the rate of cell growth.

Laskow, the healer, held in his hand three petri dishes at a time containing cell cultures while focusing on one of several states of mind, as he was giving healing to the cultures. Three control petri dishes with cells from the same culture were held by a nonhealer in an adjacent room.

A third person labeled all the petri dishes and returned them to Rein, who was blind as to which had been given healing. Rein added radioactive thymidine and at the end of 24 hours measured the rates of cell growth. The same procedures were followed with Laskow treating sealed tubes of distilled water, which was then used in preparing tissue culture medium for the growth of cells.

Varying mental states produced a range of effects, including the following: allowing the cells to "return to their natural order and harmony" produced 39 percent inhibition, while "circulating the microcosmic orbit" produced 41 percent inhibition. "Allowing God's will to manifest" produced 21 percent inhibition. No effects were found from unconditional love.

"[W]hile in the microcosmic orbit state of consciousness, with no specific thoughts, the mental image of visualizing many more cells in the petri dish at the end of the experimental period" produced a 15 percent increase in growth. Visualizing fewer cells produced 18 percent inhibition.

Regarding the healing effects of water, varying intent produced the following effects: "natural order and harmony intention" produced 28 percent inhibition; unconditional love produced 21 percent inhibition; and dematerialization produced 28 percent inhibition, suggesting that water can store qualitative information about the healing.[25]

***Role of consciousness in holoenergetic healing: a new experimental approach,* 1992(b)**

In personal communication, Rein mentioned that in order to control for environmental factors that may influence the performance of a healer, the studies of various types of mental focus and intent were performed on a regular day of the week, over a number of weeks, according to the availability of the experimenters.

This report raises many interesting questions. Though it would appear that the different intents and mental imagery produced the varying rates of inhibition or enhancement of growth, numbers of repetitions of the experiment would be required to rule out other factors. No blinds are mentioned for Rein as regards the mental focus and intent of Laskow, nor are the experimenters' beliefs and expectations detailed. There remains the possibility that the results reflect these or other factors. The fact that different conditions were studied on different days, at least one week or more week apart, leaves open the possibility that extraneous factors might have brought about the observed differences. These could include the phase of moon, sunspots, and geomagnetic activity[26]—which have been shown to influence psi and healing effects[27]—or other, unidentified extraneous factors. While this may seem confusing, such is the nature of early stages of research.

The spectrum of effects for healed water appears different from those of direct healing to cells, but again we would have to have repetitions of this study before we could rule out other confounding factors. While this may seem confusing, such is the nature of early stages of research.

Louis Rose was a doctor in England who took great interest in spiritual healers. He was a skeptic but was willing to see whether healers could prove to his satisfaction that they were able to help people.

A Survey of Healing
Louis Rose

Rose reviews healing anecdotally through ancient and modern history. He describes in detail his efforts to investigate various healers, with all the attendant problems of obtaining reliable examinations by physicians before and after the healings in cases where there was no conventional treatment to obscure the effects of healing. His major focus was Harry Edwards, the renowned English healer.

Rose analyzed 95 instances of purported faith cures. Of these, 80 either could not be documented or were at great variance with the medical

record. The rest show differing levels of healing effect, ranging from no
benefit to actual "amelioration of an organic condition."

Faith Healing, 1971[28]

Rose presents an excellent clinical survey of carefully screened healing reports. Unfortunately, the screening was done retrospectively with multiple,
independent evaluators, so we don't know what criteria were used. This
book should be read in conjunction with any of the enthusiastic writings
of Harry Edwards himself.[29]

Rose raises many interesting questions. How can one obtain reliable
medical evaluations when doctors are reluctant to be involved with healing
and healers? Do people go to healers without checking with their
physicians? If so, for which types of illnesses? A number of doctoral
dissertations in sociology and public health wait to be written in this field.

The variance that Rose found between the claims and the medical
records points out how claims made by people unfamiliar with suggestion,
placebo response, or ordinary changes in disease processes can diverge
widely from an assessment by a physician, who will have a very different
perspective.

The findings reveal 14 cases in which some healing effect was verified
by medical reports. This is a lower percentage than Strauch, Dixon, or
Brown report. Several British healers have indicated to me in personal
communication that they considered Rose extremely skeptical about
healing, so he may have applied excessively stringent criteria in his survey.
It is therefore even more impressive that he still finds healings which
cannot be explained away by conventional medical models.

Again it is good to have this critical review which confirms commonly
heard claims that there are no detrimental effects from healing. Healing
either helps or is ineffective. It does not harm.

It is to Rose's credit that he acknowledged Harry Edward's frustrations
in being investigated by Rose. Edwards felt that there was simply no way he
could provide proof that Rose would not dismiss in one way or another.

Doctors' in-depth case reports on individual spiritual healings are
unfortunately very rare. I am dismayed that patients may improve
dramatically with spiritual healing—after years of chronic pains, physical
disabilities, and various illnesses which did not respond to conventional
medical care—and their doctors do not take the time to investigate what
made the difference.[30] Doctors tend to dismiss these as *spontaneous
remissions* without questioning what caused the remission.[31]

Here is an individual case report from a doctor in America—the best
one that I have been able to find.

Lupus Erythematosus and Healing in the Philippines

Richard A. Kirkpatrick

Kirkpatrick is a physician in the state of Washington. He contributes a case study of a 28-year-old Philippine-American woman who had systemic lupus erythematosus (SLE) in 1977.

This is a disease of unknown cause, suspected to involve malfunction of the immune system. It can manifest as any combination of anemia, arthritis, vasculitis (inflammation of the blood vessels), enlargement of lymph nodes, nephritis (kidney inflammation), hepatitis (liver inflammation), rashes, and other symptoms. It may improve with aspirin, other anti-inflammatory agents, anti-cancer drugs, steroids, and other medications —most of which have toxic side effects.

The diagnosis of this woman was confirmed by laboratory tests indicating kidney damage, among other factors. Substantial doses of prednisone (60 mg/day) reduced her liver enlargement and the albumin in her urine; her enlarged lymph nodes returned to normal; and she felt well. The steroid medication was lowered. A month later hypothyroidism was diagnosed and thyroid hormone replacement was started.

Her disease smoldered on, however, necessitating repeated increases in prednisone. She started to have edema (water retention) and steroid-related (cushingoid) obesity, with periodic irrationality. Because this was presumably due to the prednisone, a toxic anticancer medication was prescribed so that the steroid dose could be reduced. Her serum creatinine levels then rose, indicating kidney damage, confirmed on kidney biopsy. This showed changes typical of SLE. High doses of prednisone and another toxic drug were recommended.

The patient refused, choosing instead to return to her remote Philippine village.

> Much to the surprise of distraught family members and skeptical physicians, the patient came back three weeks later. She was neither cushingoid nor weak. In fact, she was "normal." She declined medications and refused further testing of blood or urine, as directed by the village witch doctor, who had removed the curse placed on her by a previous suitor. Twenty-three months later she gave birth to a healthy girl. During the pregnancy she had intermittent minimal albuminuria [proteins in the urine, a sign of kidney malfunction] and mild anemia. Even now she insists that her lupus was cured by removal of the "evil spirit" that had caused her original symptoms. No signs or symptoms of adrenal insufficiency or myxedema [hypothyroidism] have developed.

Kirkpatrick points out that it is unlikely the patient's SLE burned out. When she discontinued medication, her SLE was quite active, according to numerous laboratory tests. Kirkpatrick asks:

> [B]y what mechanisms did the machinations of an Asian medicine man cure active lupus nephritis, change myxedema into euthyroidism, and allow precipitous withdrawal from corticosteroid treatment without symptoms of adrenal insufficiency?

Witchcraft and Lupus Erythematosus. (*Journal of the American Medical Association*, 1981)

Although the symptomatology of SLE is known to fluctuate, a person requiring the high doses of the medications this patient received is extremely unlikely to improve so abruptly, dramatically, and completely—and to maintain that level of recovery over several years. Furthermore, abruptly discontinuing steroids is stressful (sometimes even fatal) and usually leads to a return of SLE symptoms. The same is true of discontinuation of thyroid replacement therapy and hypothyroidism, though to a lesser degree.

This case of dramatic improvement in a chronic, severe disease is well documented. I have spoken with numerous physicians who mention cases of healings but who have not taken the trouble to gather the findings or have hesitated to publish them. The sharing of such reports can make important contributions to our understanding of the range of effectiveness of healing.

Skeptics commonly suggest that spontaneous remissions of illnesses may be mistakenly perceived as spiritual healings. I believe that the reverse is more likely. Brendan O'Regan and Caryle Hirshberg of the Institute of Noetic Sciences collected 3,000 cases of spontaneous remissions from serious illnesses. Some of these may be found to involve spiritual healing if the doctors will only ask whether patients received healing.[32]

Some healers hold healing meetings for large numbers of people. These are usually healers with particular religious beliefs who include prayer as a major portion of the healing service. Much of this seems designed to heighten the emotional pitch of the audience, which may even reach what appear to be emotional frenzies. This vastly enhances the suggestibility of participants and may well help them be more open to changes initiated by healers' suggestions and healing powers.

I review the work of Kathryn Kuhlman, of this healing tradition, having found several detailed reports on her work. In fact, the first is the best medical documentation of a series of individual healings I have ever seen.

The Healings of Kathryn Kuhlman (I)

H. Richard Casdorph

Casdorph, a physician, describes in detail ten patients who were cured with healing, most of them by the late Kathryn Kuhlman. These are detailed case presentations, including confirmation of organic disease by examining physicians, with laboratory and X-ray reports (reproduced in the book) prior to and following healing treatments, and personal reports by the healed and their families.

Casdorph describes cured cases that include bone cancer, malignant brain tumor, disabling arthritis, and multiple sclerosis. He holds that a belief in Jesus and the Holy Spirit played an important part in these healings. In his opinion, the full healing syndrome generally includes the following:

- Often, but not invariably, someone among the family or friends of the healee feels a burden for their healing.
- Physical deformities due to the illness are corrected.
- There are changes in the healee's personality and spirit.
- After miraculous healings the healees begin to speak and teach about Jesus.
- Spontaneous healings occur in members of audiences who hear the testimonials of those who were miraculously healed, "and souls are saved for the Lord Jesus Christ."

Casdorph discusses the possibility that healing abilities reside in every person, and provides examples of untrained people who appeared to act as agents for healing.
The Miracles, **1976**

Casdorph's investigation of Kuhlman provides an interesting contrast with those of W. A. Nolen and Allen Spraggett, reported below.

Although Casdorph's cases were collected retrospectively, they are carefully supported with reports from physicians who examined the healees before and after healings, and include convincing x-rays and other laboratory data. The medical documentation of individual cures presented here is the most precise and convincing collection of all the healing literature reviewed in this book.[33]

One would think that these impressive medical case reports of cures of chronic and fatal diseases would have excited the medical profession to study the phenomena of healing. It is a testimonial to the capacity of humans to ignore the unusual and unexplainable that these observations have been relegated to the obscurity of library shelves and almost totally ignored.

Allen Spraggett, a journalist, also describes the spiritual healing services of Kathryn Kuhlman.

The Healings of Kathryn Kuhlman (II)
Allen Spraggett

Spraggett discusses many healings, presenting medical evaluations to support the claims of unusual physiological changes. The healings include curing of a collarbone fracture, corneal laceration, a heart condition, clubfoot, and deafness. He outlines in a sketchy way a few possible explanations for these occurrences. A detailed section of the book includes criteria for judging the validity of healings.

How do these miracles occur? Kuhlman believed it was the power of God acting through her that produced the healings.

***Kathryn Kuhlman: The Woman Who Believes in Miracles,* 1970**

Although pleasant and easy to read, this book is technically much weaker than Casdorph's, lacking medical details that would support the diagnoses and changes brought about by healing. It is obvious that the author is not trained in medicine or research and did not have adequate medical consultation in writing his review.

Skeptics who doubt that healing is more than suggestion or charlatanism abound. Few of them take the trouble to consider the research evidence, and fewer yet are qualified medically to judge the evidence. We have the next report on Kuhlman from a skeptical medical doctor.

The Healings of Kathryn Kuhlman (III)
William A. Nolen

Nolen, an American surgeon, presents discursive and extremely detailed descriptions of his investigation into the work of Katherine Kuhlman, Norbu Chen, and many of the better known Philippine psychic surgeons.[34] Through direct observation and follow-up of treated cases, Nolen reaches the conclusion that no physical effects of spiritual healing could be demonstrated in any of the cases and that all of the positive results could be explained by mechanisms of suggestion or normal fluctuations in disease processes.

Nolen makes a good case for the gullibility of a wide variety of average people. He suggests a number of reasons for seeking psychic healers and points out dangers in denying conventional treatment. He speculates that healers may stimulate patients' self-healing and discusses possible forms that suggestion may take within a person, which could have unusual effects. He also considers the unpredictability of cancer and its treatment.

Healing: A Doctor in Search of a Miracle, 1974

Nolen's discussion contrasts markedly with reports by Spraggett, Casdorph, Krippner and Villoldo, Meek, Stelter and others who studied some of the same healers and reached very different, often opposite conclusions to Nolen's.

Stelter directly contradicts Nolen on specific information concerning Philippine healers. He suggests that Nolen is selecting and distorting evidence to support his contention that psychic surgery is fakery.

I am impressed that the balance of evidence seems to support the genuineness of Kuhlman's healing cures.

Proceeding now from general surveys and case reports to studies on specific effects of healing, we have one study exploring healing for slow-growing skin cancers, a second for healing effects on the immune system, and a third for cigarette addiction.

Skin Cancer and Healing

Steven Fahrion

Basal cell carcinoma (BCC) is a skin cancer that rarely metastasizes. It is fairly common, with 480,000 estimated new cases in America annually. Standard treatment is surgical removal. BCC does not remit spontaneously.

Fahrion explored the benefits of healing on BCC, following anecdotal reports that healing could shrink BCC or even eliminate it. Patients were referred by local dermatologists, supplemented by recruitment through newspaper ads when referral rates were low. Though 20 patients were wanted, only 10 were found for the study.

Mietek Wirkus and Ethel Lombardi, well-known healers who had participated previously in research, gave healing for 30 minutes every other day for five days. Healing was given with the hands one to two inches away from the body. A week was allowed for assessments, followed by a second five-day period of treatment.

Assessments of the tumors were made in the laboratory and by the patients' own physicians. Tumor size was recorded photographically through a clear grid with millimeter ruling. Patients were also assessed for psychological responses to healing.

Four patients showed tumor reduction or elimination during the three-week treatment period, confirmed by photographs. One patient had had hundreds of these tumors removed. Healing stopped his recurrences. Patients' doctors made assessments at variable times after the study. In some cases early improvements did not hold.

Healing appeared to be cost-effective. The healers would normally charge $40 per session, which would total $240 for six treatments. For the 10 patients this would have come to $2,400. Dividing this by 15, the numbers of tumors treated, gives a cost of $160 per tumor. This is comparable to conventional surgical excision of the tumor, which would cost about $195 per tumor. Advantages of healing included absence of pain, other side effects and scarring, and improvements in co-existing conditions.

Fahrion recommends that photographic measurements be made in color to provide a more sensitive indication of improvement, and that the distance of the camera from the tumor should be standardized.

Application of Energetic Therapy to Basal Cell Carcinoma (*pilot study, Topeka, Kansas, supported by the Office of Alternative Medicine,* 1995)

This pilot study of healing for skin cancers is most encouraging. Considering that cancer is usually a chronic condition, the benefits that were obtained in six treatments over a treatment period of only three weeks are impressive.

It is encouraging to have preliminary research confirming that healing can help in treatment of cancers.

It is a common finding that healing does not always bring about improvements in problems that are targeted for treatment, but may produce beneficial effects in other physical, emotional, or spiritual aspects of the treated healees. While only four out of ten people with skin cancers showed physical improvements, for one the improvement was dramatic.

The Immune System and Therapeutic Touch

Janet F. Quinn and Anthony J. Strelkauskas

David McClelland has shown that compassionate feelings and unconditional love may enhance the potency of experiencers' immune systems (Borysenko 1985). Therapeutic Touch (TT) appears to enhance health, and it seems reasonable to assume that one of its mechanisms might be the strengthening the immune system. Quinn and Strelkauskas studied this hypothesis in four recently bereaved people, because it has been shown that bereaved people often experience temporary suppression of their immune systems.[35] This pilot study explored whether or not there were changes in immunological and psychological profiles after TT treatments and whether or not there were similarities between these patterns in the two TT practitioners and the recipients of their treatments.

The TT healers initially followed the standard TT procedures but were then free to give treatment as they felt appropriate. This approach was favored over a standard time (often set arbitrarily at five minutes) because it allows practitioners to follow their normal treatment procedures.

The State-Trait Anxiety Inventory (STAI) of recipients showed a mean decrease of 29 percent in state anxiety in recipients over the four days of the treatment. Other testing showed a marked increase in nearly all the separate measures of positive affect (joy, vigor, contentment, and affection) and a marked decrease in negative affect (anxiety, guilt, hostility, and depression)

Sophisticated immunological profiles were studied. Only one lympho-cyte immune cell assay showed consistent changes in response to TT healing.

Psychoimmunologic effects of Therapeutic Touch on practitioners and recently bereaved recipients: a pilot study (*Advances in Nursing Science,* 1993)

It has been postulated by healers that healing must enhance immune sys-tem functions because they see healees improving from infections of many sorts. It is good to have this pioneering contribution towards confirming the hypothesis that healing improves immune system activity. It would be helpful to know what the intervals for treatments and measurements were, in order to have a clearer picture on how the immunological changes progress, as well as to give other researchers the opportunity to replicate the study.

Healing has demonstrated its efficacy in treating anxiety and depression. These are major components of addictions. It is good to see the next investigation of how healing might help with cigarette addiction.

The title of this study suggests skepticism on the part of the researchers or the publisher about healing.

Cigarette Addiction and Laying-on of Hands

M. Gmur and A. Tschopp

Gmur and Tschopp studied 532 heavy smokers at the University Psychiat-ric Clinic in Zurich. The healer, called Hermano, treated by placing his hands on the healee's head with a vibrating movement. He claimed to "put out of action. . .[the] cerebral nicotine addiction center, from which the smoker's repeated reaching for a cigarette was triggered."

Of the total, 40 percent stopped for four months; 32.5 percent for one year; 20 percent for five years; and 15.9 percent for 12 years. At the final check, 37.5 percent were not smoking.

The investigators compared 75 discontinued smokers with 23 who re-sumed smoking within four months. Of 21 variables, only the item, "smoked in bed" significantly differentiated the two groups. Other items tending to point toward poor results were concomitant drinking, rare church attendance, and the attitude that the treatment will help "if you believe it."

Factors determining the success of nicotine withdrawal: 12-year follow-up of 532 smokers after suggestion therapy by a faith healer (*International Journal of the Addictions,* 1987)

Sadly, without a control group it is impossible to guess whether the healer helped by healing, suggestion, or indeed if he helped at all beyond strengthening the will of the smokers to cease.

Next, let us consider more studies that explore subjective responses and suggest yet further clues as to how healing may work.

Healers report that pain is one of the symptoms which responds most readily to their treatments.

Frederick Knowles examined healing effects on several types of pain. Knowles (1954) learned methods of healing used in India and then studied medicine to better understand what he was doing. Though initially instructed in secret rituals for healing, he found with experience that these were not essential for beneficial results. He also demonstrated that suggestion alone was insufficient and that a period of concentration on his part was necessary in addition to suggestions in order to effect healings. Neither alone was nearly as effective as both together.

Pain and Healing: Three Studies

Frederick W. Knowles and Kenneth Richmond

Knowles sees a healer's mental concentration as vital to the healing process, no matter what actions and rituals the healer performs. He describes his own procedures for visualizing improved health and reports that his own healings were made more effective by concentration. Knowles speculates that the need for such concentration cancels out the possibility that suggestion is happening instead of healing. He also sees a need for the healer to establish in the healer's own mind "a vivid expectation of benefit to the patient."

Richmond chronicled Knowles's treatment of 43 cases of painful conditions such as chronic osteoarthritis, rheumatism, and sciatica, selected for chronicity and absence of concomitant medical treatments. Knowles was observed concentrating for about two minutes per patient visit, with between three and five visits per patient. He checked patients' responses between periods of concentration, asking questions regarding decreases in pain and increases in the range of motion of joints. He allowed up to three weekly visits in cases of no response before withdrawing from a case. When he was partially successful he would continue for up to 12 weekly sessions. He preferred skeptical patients. The best results were in conditions such as osteoarthritis, in which definite physical lesions were observable.

Knowles (1956) and Richmond report on experiments performed by Knowles to try to tease out mechanisms of healing action. Experimental pain was inflicted on volunteers by prolonged blockage of circulation with a pressure cuff applied to the arm. Healing was not effective in such cases. Knowles did have some success in instances where only the brachial artery (in the arm) was experimentally blocked. The authors conclude that if "any inference can be drawn from these experiments, it may be that Mr. Knowles' effect operates upon the vasomotor system and relieves the local congestion concerned in a painful condition." Richmond proposes alternatively that healing may decrease muscle spasm.

Some investigations into psychic healing (*Journal of the American Society for Psychical Research***, 1954)—Frederick W. Knowles**
Psychic healing in organic disease. (*Journal of the American Society for Psychical Research***, 1956)—Frederick W. Knowles**
Experiments in the relief of pain. (*Journal of the Society for Psychical Research***, 1946)—Kenneth Richmond**

Though not using formal controls, Knowles and Richmond separated out some of the relevant and important from the superstitious and useless by serial additions or deletions in procedures. The length of follow-up time is unfortunately not specified in the Richmond series. Though hypothesizing that expectations are important on the part of healer and healee, Knowles does not speculate further on how these expectations may bring about the physical changes of healing.

Experiment with pain from experimental obstruction of circulation is unique in the healing literature. Drawing conclusions from these reports is difficult because of limited descriptive detail, inadequate controls, and in the artificial pain study, a lack of true need for healing.

The potential benefits of suggestion in addition to healing are not generally appreciated. It is not that either one or the other is effective, but that both are, and each may enhance the other. This has certainly been my own experience in my practice of psychotherapy combined with healing.

Again it is fascinating to note the spectrum of healing efficacy of Knowles, in contrast with that of the German healer, Trampler. Knowles seemed more effective with people who had observable, organic problems.

When doctors are comfortable with healing and use it in their clinical practice, it is immediately evident that there are many ways in which it can be helpful. I hope we will see more reports like the following one.

A Physician-Healer

Hans G. Engel

Engel is a physician who discovered he had healing abilities when his wife reported relief of a severe headache after he placed his hand on her forehead to soothe her.

Engel also had several experiences with self-healing. His glaucoma (elevated pressure in the eyeballs), for which he had taken eyedrops for several years, improved "along with other positive changes in my life."

Following the accidental death of one of his children and a painful divorce, he noticed enlargement of his lymph nodes. He suspected he had cancer and, in his depression, actually hoped for death. Eventually he went for a biopsy, then for removal of some of the nodes and a bone marrow biopsy. A malignant lymphoma was found, with several prestigious pathologists concurring on the diagnosis. He expected to live only a few months. For several weeks he took anticancer drugs but then stopped, explaining, "If I was fated to die I did not intend to interfere." He even published an article on his attitude towards his patients when he thought he had only a few months left to live. Then "somehow my outlook on life changed and I again considered the possibility of a personal future." Several months later his lymph nodes began to shrink and he has enjoyed excellent health ever since.[36]

Engel developed his healing abilities, including intuitive diagnosis. He routinely experienced sensations of cold as he passed his hands over diseased portions of his patients' bodies but occasionally felt tingling or something like a "'bulge' in the air above the skin surface overlying the painful site." His patients confirmed 80 to 90 percent of his impressions.

Engel shares observations on healing in 52 people with a variety of disorders, especially pain. Treatments in this series involved up to 50 or more weekly visits. Those unresponsive within four visits were dismissed from the program. Among other details, he notes that patients commonly felt he had touched them when he had only made passes near the body.

Engel cautions that healing should not be substituted for conventional therapy and should not be applied prior to obtaining a definitive medical diagnosis.

Energy Healing (*Research report, Ernest Holmes Research Foundation, 1978*)

Engel appears a well-qualified and careful physician, observer, and reporter. He is perhaps even too cautious and conservative in his report. For instance, in grading improvement he gives a zero to a person with a progressive neuromuscular paralysis called amyotrophic lateral sclerosis (also called Motor Neuron Disease, or Lou Gehrig's Disease) who claimed that he felt stronger and had greater muscular control after some treatments but showed no other significant response to his primary disorder. Had his research included greater numbers of patients and prospective rather than retrospective questionnaires, Engel might have gleaned even more information from his studies. He also finds that people who report psi experiences are less likely to have a positive response to healing. This finding is surprising and deserves further scrutiny.

Engel's observation that healees may report that they felt the hand of the healer touching them—while the healer definitely did not bring his or her hands closer than several inches to the body—has been noted by other healers. This belongs on the list of healing sensations along with heat, tingling, and vibration.[37][38]

Here are further reports on healing benefits for fractures, paralysis, and scleroderma.

Case Studies of Healing

John Hubacher, Jack Gray, Thelma Moss, and Frances Saba

This report describes in detail three cases of healings using "magnetic passes." These were the most successful of a series that dealt with 11 patients, of whom six showed sustained improvements; two had initial dramatic improvements but the original symptoms returned; and three did not respond.

Case 1: A 21-year-old man with severe multiple leg fractures was told by his physicians that repair was impossible and incessant pain inevitable unless the leg was amputated. Jack Gray, the healer, noted an exquisite sensitivity of the patient to his (the healer's) hands. When they were at a distance of one foot from this patient's body he complained of severe pain. Gray had to give healing from across the room.

Repeated, prolonged healing treatments with slow improvement were given over eight months, at which time X-rays demonstrated healing in the bones. After two years, the patient could walk, unaided by crutch or brace.

Case 2: A 42-year-old man had total paralysis of his right arm and hand following a bullet wound in his neck, which cut through a major artery and irreparably severed several nerves. A neurologist informed him that the arm would never move again. With three months' treatments ("primarily consisting of magnetic passes"), he regained the use of his arm and hand. Use of his thumb did not return until five months later. The neurologist could not explain this recovery. In fact, on his last medical visit, the patient was told there would be no charge because the neurologist had seen something he had not believed possible: movement not apparently prompted by neuronal connections.

Case 3: A 21-year-old woman suffered from advanced scleroderma (hardening of the skin)—barely able to walk and so limited in hand movements she could not even take care of her own toileting. Sporadic improvement was noted over ten months' treatment, with increased ability to care for herself, and decreased pain.

Patients experienced a deep altered state of consciousness during the "magnetic passes." Healer and patients reported intense sensations of heat and cold during treatments. Kirlian photography consistently demonstrated an increase in coronal flares and emanations from healees' fingers after treatments.[39]

A laboratory study of unorthodox healing (*Proceedings of the Second International Congress on Psychotronic Research,* 1975)

Such impressive results are found in only a small percent of healings. Unfortunately, descriptive details in this clinical summary are limited, and it is difficult to evaluate these reports. It would be helpful to know more about the "magnetic passes," the specifics of diagnoses, and the criteria for improvement. Direct reports from the examining physicians would also be useful.

The report of muscle function in an arm where nerves were apparently severed by a bullet, *if verified by assessments of nerve conduction*, would be a major finding, suggesting responses to healing that may confirm energy field activity.

Healing and Change in Healers and Healees
Francis Geddes

Geddes provides a history of healing in the church from biblical to modern times, pointing out that Christ used a variety of healing techniques and taught them to his disciples.

For his doctoral work, Geddes studied healers. In a five-day seminar, he trained groups from four congregations in LeShan techniques of healing. The groups met weekly for present and distant healings of 206 persons, and case records were obtained for 79 of the subjects. Of these, 13 reported dramatic acceleration in their rate of recovery from illness, ranging from minutes to two or three days; 31 reported some acceleration in the pace of recuperation within several days or weeks; and 35 reported no change in the recovery rate. Geddes speculates that the 127 who did not respond also experienced no change and were therefore unmotivated to report. Recovery ratings are based on healees' reports, since physicians treating them were uncooperative in providing records. Recovery included improvements in severe hepatitis, blindness, diabetes, and arthritis.

Geddes notes that the healers themselves experienced dramatic positive changes in well-being and sense of self as a result of their participation in the healing groups over the six months of the study. The author was surprised to discover the variety and depth of personal transformation and spiritual growth in the 28 healer subjects.

Healing Training in the Church (*doctoral dissertation, San Francisco Theological Seminary,* 1981)

The improvements probably represent impressive results of healing. However, the lack of medical inputs limits the value of such reports. Laypeople often misunderstand and therefore misrepresent their illnesses, as may lay experimenters.

Geddes's focus on the transformative nature of healing for healers is a helpful contribution to our appreciation of the effects of healing.

I have had similar experiences in giving and receiving healing treatment and have heard these echoed by other healers and healees. Spiritual awareness is one of the most profoundly helpful aspects of giving and receiving healing.[40]

The next study provides clinical observations on healing and adds an exploration of brainwaves with an electroencephalogram (EEG) during healing.

Therapeutic Touch
Dolores Krieger

Dolores Krieger has been a healer and has taught healing for many years. In this book she interlaces descriptions of clinical experiences, practical instructions in developing Therapeutic Touch (TT) skills, and comments from students and healers about their subjective sensations and inner experiences in developing as healers.

Krieger's book describes her experience of teaching more than 4,000 people over nine years. She feels that healers must want to heal, be motivated to help others, and be willing to introspect.

> The importance of helping the unconscious to emerge cannot be overemphasized. Whether as a nurse, physician, therapist or friend, helping or healing carries with it considerable responsibility, and under certain circumstances this may become a heavy load. The person playing the role of healer has need of a wealth of understanding coupled with a stable sanity. . . . (p.79)

She recommends TT for a wide range of conditions and knows of no illness unresponsive to TT in some degree. She observes that people practicing TT develop intuition and psi abilities along with healing skills. She also notes that cotton can both store and facilitate healing energy.[41]

She finds that belief in effectiveness of healing does not influence performance and that skeptics can be helped. "However, two personality variables—denial of illness and hostility—do have a negative effect on Therapeutic Touch, perhaps because they both may translate themselves graphically to the healer and inhibit the healer's efforts."

Researchers studied Krieger with EEG, electro-oculogram (EOG), and electrocardiogram (ECG) recordings during TT treatments on patients suffering from a variety of pains. Rapid synchronous beta activity was noted on the EEG when Krieger was in a sitting or standing position with eyes open or closed during TT treatments. The healees' EEG was unchanged during treatment.

The Therapeutic Touch: How to Use Your Hands to Help or Heal, 1979

This book presents excellent how-to exercises for learning healing and lovely descriptions, occasionally poetic, of the inner changes accompanying the development of healing skills. It has some of the best descriptions of how healers learn to heal.[42]

The EEG findings reported by Krieger during healing differ from those reported by other investigators.[43]

The EEG measures brainwaves in the cortex, the surface of the brain which lies just inside the skull. It records summaries of electrical activity in millions of cells that lie near electrodes placed on the scalp. When the body is given a repetitive stimulus such as touching the skin or shining light of a given intensity repeatedly, it is possible to record the evoked responses of the brain.

Here are studies from China on EEG recordings of healers and healees during healing. These are somewhat technical and readers without professional expertise may prefer to skip to the summaries.

EEG Recording and Qigong

Guolong Liu; Department of Physiology, Beijing College of Traditional Chinese Medicine, Beijing

Liu reports:

> The emitted qi also could alter functions of the nervous system, not only in human[s] but also in animal[s]. The activity of EEG was synchronized to the alpha rhythm and its power spectrum showed increases in certain frequencies . . . similar to the changes of EEG during the qigong meditation. . . . The emitted qi caused changes in auditory brainstem evoked responses (ABER) in anesthetized cats. In most of the cats, the ABER amplitude increased, particularly those components generated at the level of mesencephalon [deeper parts of the brain]. But in some animals, the ABER amplitude decreased.
> . . .The infrasonic radiation was measurable in the emitted qi. The dominant peak frequency of the infrasonic radiation was between 8.0 Hz and 12.5 Hz, overlapping with the frequency of the alpha waves in EEG. For the person receiving the emitted qi, the frequency of alpha wave often became synchronized to the infrasonic radiation. It is suggested that the infrasonic radiation in the emitted qi may be [the] cause [of] the observed changes in EEG.[44]

Effect of qigong state and emitted qi on the human nervous system (*Proceedings of the 1st International Congress of Qigong, UC Berkeley, California, 1990*—from qigong database of Sancier)

The Chinese have identified sound waves too low for the ear to perceive which are emitted by healers.

These are similar to the frequency of alpha waves in the brain, suggesting that these may be closely related. This is also in the range of the frequency of the standing electromagnetic wave that circles the earth. By mechanically replicating such sound waves they have produced healing responses.

The next study explores the effects of with infrasonic waves, stimulation along with the effects of emitted qi healing from a qigong master and of qigong meditation on the EEG. These translated reports are rather technical, but so fascinating I have included them here.

Qigong, Simulated Qigong, and the EEG

Guolong Liu

The effects of qigong meditation and emitted qi on the nervous system of humans and animals were measured by electroencephalography (EEG) and evoked potential (EP). Because of limitations of space, we outline only a few results of this multifaceted study:

> A study of the effects of qigong meditation was conducted on 14 subjects who had practiced qigong for one to three years. Compared with the control of 27 naive subjects who had never practiced qigong, qigong meditation led to a significant enhancement in the EEG frontal power spectrum, enhancement of EEG occipital power spectrum, and movement of the dominant alpha-wave frequencies from occipital to frontal lobes, i.e., reversal of frontal-occipital, enhancement of EEG power spectrum in all channels, and enhancement and synchronization of all alpha frequencies. The effects of emitted qi on the EEG and EP of four normal subjects produced much the same results as qigong meditation.
>
> A measurement was made of the intensity of the infrasonic energy emitted by 27 qigong "masters" who had practiced for 4 to 32 years. The intensity of this infrasonic energy ranged from 45db to 76db, with a background noise level of 40db. For six qigong masters, the infrasonic intensity was over 70db and the dominant peak frequencies were in the range of eight Hz to 12.5 Hz, which coincides with the frequencies of EEG alpha waves. In fact, the dominant alpha

frequency in the EEG power spectrum of the subjects tended to synchronize with that of the emitted qi. Imitation of the observable actions of qigong masters by 28 naive subjects produced effects similar to that of the control experiment.

In another experiment, an infrasonic generator that simulated emitted qi was found to produce effects on the EEG of 20 subjects similar to that of emitted qi. This result indicates that the effects of the infrasonic generator were not due to electromagnetic interferences from the generator.

To eliminate psychological influences of emitted qi, experiments were carried out on anesthetized cats by recording EP and on rabbits by recording EEG. Emitted qi from a qigong master changed both EP and EEG. For example in a study of 12 cats, emitted qi facilitated the Middle Latency Response (MLR) in six cases and inhibited it in six other cases. The MLR is the primary component of the auditory cortical evoked response and indicates activity of the cerebral cortex.

A study by EEG and evoked potential on humans and animals of the effects of emitted qi, qigong meditation, and infrasound from a qigong simulator (Beijing College of Traditional Chinese Medicine, China–abstract from Sancier, *American Journal of Acupuncture,* 1991; reprinted with permission).

These reports suggest that the nervous system of healees may be influenced by infrasonic waves from healers. It is frustrating that greater details are not provided.

Reports of infrasonic sound accompanying emitted qi healing are most interesting, particularly if synthetic infrasonic sound can duplicate healing effects on the EEG. Whether healing effects on physical conditions can be produced by infrasonic sound is the next step in research.[45]

Because the human brain and mind are so complex, it is difficult to sort out what is happening during spiritual healing. Studies of animals EEGs can be structured in a more controlled manner, allowing more precise clarifications of how the brain responds to healing.

Emitted Qi and Animal EEGs

Guolong Liu, Pei Wan, Xueyan Peng, and Xuelong Zhong; Beijing College of Traditional Chinese Medicine, Beijing, China

It is known that emitted qi alters the EEG and the cortical evoked potentials in man in our previous studies. In order to exclude the psychological influence when the emitted qi is applied to man, we carried out the experiment in . . . anesthetized cats. Distinct responses were noted in the brains of the cats in response to healing.

Influence of emitted qi on the auditory brainstem evoked responses (ABER) and auditory middle latency evoked responses (MLR) in cats (*Proccedings of the 1st World Conference for Academic Exchange of Medical Qigong, Beijing, 1988*—from qigong database of Sancier)

While the technical details of this study are daunting, its import is to suggest that healing can bring about measurable changes in the nervous system. This may be a mechanism whereby healing produces its effects, as the nervous system is a major regulator of the body.

Without more data and statistical analyses it is impossible to know whether the observed effects were significant.

The next report from China details a sophisticated study of the effects of healing on the microscopic structures of muscles.

Sports Medicine and Emitted Qi

Lin Jia, Jinding Jia, and Danyun Lu; National Research Institute of Sports Science, Beijing

It is the task of sports medicine to prevent and cure sport-related injuries. With increase in training intensity, muscle injuries occur frequently, directly affecting athletic careers. Progress in prevention and treatment are therefore of increasing concern in many countries.

In recent years, the research and application of the emitted qi is being developed in China. The emitted qi has been found to have physical and biological effects. Clinically, we have treated muscle soreness, scleroma in muscles, acute muscle sprain, muscle contusion and release of pain in athletes with the emitted qi and the result was satisfactory.

The purpose of this experiment was to investigate the preventive and therapeutic effect of the emitted qi on ultrastructural changes in the injured muscle caused by overstrain. Twelve healthy male rabbits . . . were divided into two groups, the control group and the emitted qi group. . . . It was found that the qualities and quantities of both fibrous and bony callus [in healing fractures] in the emitted qi group were superior to those in controls.

On the basis of the results we . . . consider . . . the emitted qi had a good therapeutic effect to promote healing of fractures.

Effects of emitted qi on ultrastructural changes of the overstrained muscle of rabbits (*Proceedings of the 1st World Conference for Academic Exchange of Medical Qigong, Beijing, 1988*—from qigong database of Sancier)

Healers universally report that healing can alleviate pains and hasten healing of soft tissue injuries. It is helpful to have objective confirmation of these effects.

I may have come across as unduly critical of medical researchers for not investing more interest in research. The same is true of healers. Few have bothered to record their observations in a systematic way that would advance our understanding of the mystery of healing. In their defense, it must be pointed out that few healers are trained in medical diagnosis or in the methodologies of research. It is also regrettable that very little funding has been available for healing research.

There are innumerable books on the experiences of healers. I have selected a few by very gifted healers who did a fair job of exploring how healing works.

Harry Edwards, one of England's great healers, was a keen observer and eager to experiment with various effects of healing.

Influenza and Healing

Harry Edwards

During a worldwide epidemic of Asian flu, the epidemiological progress of the disease was clear from country to country. It was calculated when the disease was likely to reach the United Kingdom and the public was warned.

Harry Edwards experimented on how to use healing as a preventive against contracting the virus.

> [W]e published . . . an invitation for our readers to join in this experiment. In addition, we enclosed in some twenty thousand letters sent out to the many who were at that time receiving absent healing a notice to the same effect.
>
> The notice said that we would be holding a mass absent healing intercession for all our patients and readers in order that they might be protected from the disease. We asked our patients and readers to inform us at once if they caught Asian flu, or had its symptoms.

Edwards estimated his experiment covered 40,000 people. The epidemic was severe in Britain, forcing many factories and schools to close and causing many deaths.

The result of our experiment was surprising. The number of letters we received telling us that our readers, patients, and their families had been infected was very few indeed—about a score. Considering the number of people involved in the experiment and that many of them lived in badly infected areas, by all normal reckoning we should have received reports from 500 to a 1,000 infected cases.

One school headmistress wrote to ask if we would place her school children within the protective influencing of spiritual healing. . . . The result was that while every other school in the area had to close down, this particular school had no need to, for the number of children who became ill was surprisingly few, and even those were very mild cases.

None of Edwards's staff contracted flu.

Thirty Years a Spiritual Healer, 1986

The Edwards experiment using healing as a preventive measure to protect against flu is an innovative application for healing. Unfortunately, because of the looseness of the study design, clear conclusions cannot be drawn from this experiment. For instance, patients may have neglected to advise the researchers that they had flu symptoms, consciously or unconsciously, out of loyalty to Harry Edwards. It may also be possible that some people did not respond because they died. A better arrangement would have been to take random samples of subjects and not to rely merely on the subjects' self-reporting.

If the results prove valid, it would be of interest to know whether the mass intercession involved single healers sending healing to large numbers of people simultaneously or whether a one-to-one distant healing was required in each case.[46]

Most healers find that although symptomatic relief may be obtained with healing for viral upper respiratory infections, it is rare to find cures of such illnesses with healing, once the symptoms have blossomed. Healers say they can eliminate viral infections when healing is given very early in the illness, but one is on shaky ground here without evidence from controlled studies.

Healing as a preventive to illness appears to have a vast, unexplored potential. This is probably the most neglected aspect of spiritual healing. It is a reflection on humanity's tendency to attend to problems only when they are troublesome rather than to anticipate them. Maimonides, a renowned doctor in the twelfth century, observed "The ability of a physician to prevent illness is a greater proof of his skill than his ability to cure someone who is already ill."

While I have generally included examples of the best in healing literature, I share with you here one of the less helpful ones, despite its being authored by the renowned Harry Edwards.

Harry Edwards on Healing
Harry Edwards

This is the sort of book that makes me want to cry. Edwards makes apologies for healers' not keeping records of healings, claiming it would take up too much time. He presents a book full of exceedingly brief excerpts of written testimonials from healees' reports of successful healings. He includes many conditions, such as cancer and other growths, surgery, tuberculosis, spinal diseases, disseminated sclerosis, paralysis, and others.

Though Edwards unquestionably was a powerful healer with a wealth of experience, he presented such brief excerpts in this book as to leave many possible alternative explanations for any of the cases he mentions. He claimed he engaged in spiritual healing, not faith healing. It is unfortunate that he forces the reviewer to rely only on faith for interpretation of this data.

This note is primarily to point out the benefits that might accrue with broader cooperation between healers and research oriented doctors.[47]
***The Evidence for Spiritual Healing*, 1953**

Benson Herbert[48] was a parapsychologist in England with an interest in healing. He made some simple observations on a healer with unusual abilities.

An Analysis of a Healer's Work
Benson Herbert

Herbert describes his personal success with spiritual healing for severe pains caused by a muscle sprain on his shoulder blade. He also discusses several of Suzanne Padfield's successful distant healings (without the healees' knowledge) and relates her procedures and specific visualizations in performing her healings. Such visualizations include:

- seeing the healee in perfect health;
- imagining oneself by the healee's bed, hearing her say she is getting well; and
- feeling as though one's self is being projected into the healee's mind.

Padfield tells of specific dangers to herself that she feels in doing her healing, including touching the patient or allowing herself to have images of illness—either of which she believes might make her ill.

Herbert measured Padfield's skin resistance, finding this to be about one-quarter of the mean of six other people. Her skin potentials fluctuated widely but were at least twice as wide as others in the group under similar conditions. He postulated that her low skin resistance would make her more sensitive to electromagnetic potentials in her environment. In this he was supported by Padfield's report that she is unusually sensitive to slight shocks from electrical appliances.

Near and distant healing (*International Journal of Paraphysics,* 1973)

Padfield's report of successful healings without healees' knowledge has been echoed by others. Herbert's cases are described in more detail and better documented than many other reports.

It is unclear whether Padfield's unusual bioelectrical activity is related specifically to her healing. A survey showed that 70 percent of people with unusual electrical experiences also had psi abilities (Shallis). Unusual electrical phenomena in healers have been detailed by others.[49]

It would be easy to determine if healers other than Padfield demonstrate unusually low skin resistance, as this is not difficult or expensive to measure. This appears well worth pursuing.

Looking at ever finer elements that might be affected by healing, there are reports from China of temperature changes with healing directed to the following:

- Saline, sugar, and chemical solutions (G. Meng et al. 1988a)
- DNA (G. Meng et al. 1988b)
- The protein tryptophan (G. Meng et al. 1988c)
- RNA (M. Sun et al.)
- Serum proteins (S. Li et al.)
- Enzymes (Y. Guo et al.)

In one study, the healing appeared to act through stainless steel (Y. Guo et al. 1988). These reports are too technical for inclusion here. In several of these studies distant healing was used.

These six studies from China suggest that RNA, proteins, and amino acids can be influenced in the laboratory from up to 2,000 miles away. It would appear likely that much of the human body, which consists of proteins, could also be *directly* influenced by healing. That is, the nervous system and conscious awareness of the person receiving healing may not have to be involved in order for healing to occur.

Studies of healing need not be technical. A healer who systematically records the results of treatments can contribute to our understanding of how healing works.

Gordon Turner was a rare healer who took the trouble to record and publish series of his observations and experiments. In the healing literature, the following reports are unique in their breadth and helpfulness in providing clues to some of the mysteries of this art.

Investigations by a Healer

Gordon Turner

Turner was a remarkably gifted natural healer in Britain. He returned to university studies as a mature student in order to better understand his healing. In three articles Turner discusses a number of his investigations into healing.

A survey involving 954 direct contact healing treatments on 353 people by 23 healers showed subjective sensations in touch healings: heat (mild to "burning"), a red weal appearing for several minutes, tingling, prickling like electricity, and coldness. Many also spoke spontaneously of a sense of peace.

Light-shielded photographic plates placed between healers' hands and healees' bodies were found to be exposed when they were developed, which Turner suggests is evidence of a healing energy transfer. Film exposures were produced only with sick plants and persons in need of treatment, not with healthy ones. "The best results were obtained with infrared film or X-ray plates."

Turner also describes why he used plants as experimental subjects: "Experiments take time. It was becoming difficult to find patients willing to put up with tedious research procedures. Volunteers were all too easily come by, but they seldom lasted more than one or two sessions."

He describes healing experiments in which cut flowers moved and seeds germinated in response to healing, as well as healing used to prevent foot-and-mouth disease in a herd of cows. Finally, he discusses studies of distant healing, in which groups of healers working together were more potent than single healers working alone.

What power is transmitted in treatment? *(Two Worlds,* July 1969a)

I Treated plants, not patients *(Two Worlds,* August 1969b)

I experiment in absent treatment *(Two Worlds,* September 1969c)

This is a fascinating series of studies with many helpful observations. Unfortunately, few details are provided regarding methods of healing or types of illnesses treated, and no rigorous controls were described.

I find the following specific observations of particular interest:

- Intense heat, cold, or electrical sensations felt by healees during contact healing appear from this study to predict a good prognosis. At the same time, a lack of any sensations felt by healer or healee does not necessarily indicate that no healing will take place.

- A healing energy is suggested by the photographic experiment, as in two other similar reports: Graham Watkins (1979) demonstrated exposure of film placed under anesthetized mice who were the subjects for healing, and Thelma Moss (1979) showed patterns on photographic film when the much-studied healer Olga Worrall held shielded film between her hands. It is difficult to differentiate whether this is an effect specifically of the healing or an exposure of film produced by direct action of thought.[50]

- Other healers have also caused plants to move during healings.[51]

- With widespread pollution caused by pesticides and chemical fertilizers, the potential contributions of preventive healing have much to offer, both in protecting crops and animals and enhancing their growth.

- Harry Edwards is the only other healer I have found who reports a preventive clinical use of healing, summarized earlier in this chapter. In a loose survey, he found that absent healing appeared to lessen the incidence of influenza during an epidemic. See also the Chinese reports of Lin Jia et al. on the preventive use of emitted qi on muscle strain in rabbits and Yuanfeng Chen on preventive treatment of cancer cells injected into mice—both earlier in this chapter.

- Turner reports sensations felt during distant healing. In support of that, we have Goodrich's controlled experiment, reviewed in Chapter 4. The timing of healing to coincide with healees' being in a receptive state appeared to produce more intense sensations in both these studies.

- It would seem likely that the effectiveness of healing may also be influenced by healees' being in a receptive state during the sending of healing, but this requires further study. Some healers believe healings take place irrespective of their timing or of healee synchronization with the healer. The beliefs of healers and healees may influence this factor. It may also not be an either/or situation but rather suggestion plus healing may be more effective than either alone.

- Groups of healers commonly send absent healing. Their rationale is that multiple healers add more cells to the battery and that ego involvement of individual healers is lessened because they don't feel individually responsible for the outcomes. I know of no other study which confirms healers' intuitive impressions that group healings are more potent than individual healings.

- Turner's mention of possible interference of thunderstorms with absent healing is also a unique report in the literature.

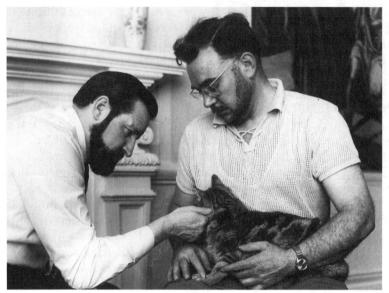

Figure 1-13. Gordon Turner was known for healing animals.
Photography by courtesy of Psychic News.

In asking our second question, "How does healing work?" we have many varied clues from these studies. It is sometimes challenging to know how much to believe these clues and which ones might be the invitations for a future Madame Curie.[52]

The following report examines healing from a completely different approach, using muscle testing. The Bidigital O-Ring Test (BDORT) tests the strength of grip between the thumb and first finger as an inner "truth meter." A strong grip is taken to indicate positive states of health or of mental state, while a weak grip indicates negatives.[53]

Qigong and the BDORT Test

Yoshiaki Omura

> The researcher used the Bidigital O-Ring Test [BDORT] to evaluate both the qigong master and subject being treated (Omura et al. 1989). During the qigong state, certain normal parts of the qigong master's body showed a minus response to the BDORT. The minus response corresponds to muscle strength weakening and usually appears only when an abnormality exists, with the exception of the thymus gland and strongly excited nerve fibres. Striking changes in the BDORT occurred at certain acupuncture points (CV-5, CV-6, CV-17, CV-22, Yintang [middle of forehead],

GV-20), meridians (entire Pericardium and Triple Burner) as well as the entire spinal cord, medulla oblongata, and various parts of the cerebral cortex. Similar changes occurred in the qigong master and patient while the qigong master was treating the patient.[54]

During the qigong treatment, the alpha wave in the EEG increased markedly in both the qigong master and patient. After discontinuing the qigong treatment, these changes disappeared completely. The researcher was able to reproduce these findings experimentally.

When areas of the body that are positive to the BDORT for bacteria or virus were treated with external qi, the BDORT response to specific bacteria or viruses often disappeared immediately. Similar changes occurred in in vitro experiments with bacterial cultures. . . .

The BDORT was also used to evaluate whether a qigong master is emitting positive or negative qi (Omura 1990a; Omura et al. 1989). This was accomplished by having the qigong master hold a paper, cloth or metal sheet between his two palms and then sending qi to his hands. If the qigong state was reached, the BDORT indicated that the paper developed two opposite polarities (positive or minus qi) which did not exist before and which lasted for an extended period of time (e.g. one year if it is not exposed to rapidly changing electric or magnetic fields) but disappeared rapidly when a rapidly changing electric or magnetic field was applied. Such positive qigongized paper has therapeutic value by giving relief or reduction of pain, reduction of spastic muscles, or improvement of circulatory disturbances by inducing a vasodilation effect by merely applying the qi-treated material to the area of circulatory disturbance for 20 to 30 seconds. However, negative qigongized material, which has the opposite effect of positive qigongized material, produces vasoconstriction.

Omura stored positive qi in various materials and drugs which were then used for improving circulation and inducing enhanced drug uptake in the abnormal area where the drug is to be delivered but cannot reach in sufficient therapeutic dosages. In his subsequent research (Omura 1990a; 1990b), he succeeded in creating pure positive or pure negative qigongized materials without any opposite polarity. By applying pure, positive qigongized materials he was able to treat some intractable pain and other intractable medical problems due to bacterial or viral infections, circulatory disturbances, and heavy metal deposits.

Simple method for evaluating the qigong state: transient changes in the qigong master and patient and the effects of qigong on blood circulation, bacteria, viruses, and the release of neurotransmitters and hormones at acupuncture points: A study using the Bidigital O-Ring Test imaging technique to evaluate the effects of qigong in the

qigong master and the patient (Heart Disease Research Foundation, New York; from Sancier, *American Journal of Acupuncture,* 1991; reprinted with permission)

This is an inadequately reported summary of studies from a researcher who appears to have a genius for exploring scientific frontiers. The use of inanimate materials as vehicles for healing is recommended by many healers.[55]

I have found muscle testing of the BDORT type described by Omura helpful in clinical practice. However, both in clinical practice and in an unpublished pilot study I did of the perception of biological energy fields, I have found it is subject to suggestion and very specific to the mental focus of the participants in its use. I would be most cautious in accepting any conclusions from a study without blinds for experimenter and subjects to eliminate expectancy effects.

Assuming that the observed effects are not due to suggestions or expectancies, this study suggests a quick and easy way for checking on the effects of healing. More on this in the next study.

Larissa Vilenskaya has been a researcher in parapsychology and healing for 30 years. She started this work in Russia, then emigrated to America. She continues to be a link between East and West.

Experiments in Healing

Larissa V. Vilenskaya[56]

Vilenskaya reports on several of her experiments that clarify the effects and possible mechanisms of healing. In one experiment, "Normal humans with no specific gifts" were taught to see auras generated by Vilenskaya "between two fingers of their hand."[57] In another, subjects were taught aura diagnosis of physical problems by touch.

In a third experiment, Vilenskaya used a sensitive astatic magnetometer to show that

> the magnetic field of the human hand varies with the physical and emotional state of the patient. . . . If the subject is prepared to perform healing, the intensity of the hand's magnetic field increases. At the same time, if a person just contracts the muscles of the arm, the intensity of the field decreases rapidly. . . . [D]uring an influence of a healer over a patient a decrease in the magnetic field of the latter was also detected.

In a fourth experiment, Vilenskaya investigated healing influence upon cucumber seeds showing that the optimal duration of the plant's exposure to bioenergetic influence was 10 to 15 minutes; "a longer duration of exposure resulted in a deterioration of growth and development of plants as compared with the results after the optimal exposure. . . ."

A second experimental series found that the optimal duration of the healing influence was about five to 10 minutes. "Comparison with the first series shows that the effect is very much dependent on the condition of the healer."

A scientific approach to some aspects of psychic healing (*International Journal of Paraphysics,* 1976)

Though interesting, the above results are reported with insufficient data for proper evaluation. In the first two, the aura experiments, no numbers are given; in the second two, conclusions are based on studies of only four subjects.

If valid, the observations concerning an optimal duration are of interest and concern for healing, suggesting that a potential for harm may exist as a result of healing being carried out beyond the optimal period. This is an important point, especially for student healers who may not have developed the often-reported sense that Vilenskaya also mentions of the point when a healing is completed.

I should add that reports of negative effects of healing, when positive effects are desired, have been found very rarely (in laboratory experiments with growth of bacteria and plants and with malaria in mice)[58] but not in clinical practice.

The controlled studies of healers' diagnostic abilities in Chapter 4 did not focus on their methods for arriving at intuitive impressions. One method that healers commonly report is the observation of colors in the aura, an apparent biological energy field around the body. There have been few studies of aura sensing such as the two that follow.

Diagnosis through Chakras and Auras

Shafika Karagulla and Dora van Gelder Kunz

Dora Kunz, a gifted clairvoyant healer, sat over several years with Shafika Karagulla, a neuropsychiatrist, to observe the auras and chakras of patients with various illnesses. Karagulla and Kunz report that the auras Kunz saw provided information that was highly correlated with the physical diagnoses Karagulla made. Occasionally Kunz was able to diagnose problems that had been unknown to the patients and doctors. Detailed descriptions of the patterns and colors reported by Kunz are reported, along with the medical diagnoses.

***The Chakras and the Human Energy Field,* 1989**

This method appears to offer a noninvasive and relatively inexpensive complement to conventional medical diagnostic tests.

Intuitive perceptions are a vital aspect of spiritual healing. They guide healers to know how and how long to give treatments. This is an area which has had little research.

No one had ever questioned whether various healers who see auras perceive the same thing or see things differently. While living in England, I set out to explore this question.

Auras and Intuitive Diagnosis

Daniel J. Benor

With the help of a general practitioner, Jean Galbraith,[59] we invited healers who see auras to simultaneously observe a series of patients with known diagnoses. In the first series we had eight healers. Each healer drew a picture of the colors they saw around each patient. They wrote down their interpretations of what they saw. Then we had each one read out their impressions. No one was more surprised than the healers to find that the divergences in aura observations and in their interpretations were far greater than the overlaps. It was like the blind men and the elephant. Each of the healers had previously believed they saw THE picture of what is going on inside their healees.

Next, we had each patient respond to their various aura readings. This was a second surprise. The patients resonated with most of the readings, different as they were. There was only one healer whose readings were consistently rejected by the patients.

It was apparent that each healer saw "a" picture rather than "THE" picture of the healee.

We repeated the procedure several months later with a more select group of four healers who had reputations amongst their colleagues for being very advanced in their aura perception abilities. These healers gave many more interpretations in the psycho-spiritual dimensions than the first group. We had the same results as before. The differences were far more prominent than the overlaps, and the patients resonated with aspects of each reading.

Intuitive diagnosis (*Subtle Energies*, 1992)

It appears that intuitive sensitives resonate with partial aspects of the people they observe. Each appears to look into the subject's inner dwelling place through a different window.

We must therefore be cautious, accepting any intuitive perceptions as only partly true. As I understand these findings, it appears that intuitive information is filtered through the deeper layers of the brain/mind in a manner very much similar to how dream materials bring information to the surface of our awareness from our unconscious mind. The various bits are clothed in garments cut out of our personal histories, fantasies, wishes, and anxieties. The end product is quite individual to each of us.

In this modest experiment is a world of information. I am reminded of the Japanese film, *Rashomon,* which tells the stories of four witnesses to a murder. Each account is so different that it almost seems they have seen four different murders. We have assumed that this is simply the psychological makeup of people that distorts their perceptions and memories of "objective" truth. If there were a film of the actual event, it would be possible to see what really happened. In the realms of subtle energies, it may be more difficult. Not only are there no films of events, but the perceptions of the events *and possibly even the events themselves* may be shaped by the beliefs and psychological awareness of the perceivers.

This is but the tip of a very large intuitive iceberg. Many sleuths will be needed to sort out this part of the mystery.[60]

Plants have been the subjects of many studies of healing. Plants are excellent subjects for research because they are inexpensive and demonstrate clearly measurable healing effects within a few days or weeks. They are far less complex than people to study. Here are some more studies that explore healing effects on plants.

Plant Growth and Prayer

Franklin Loehr

Loehr describes an extensive series of controlled experiments, ranging from very loose to carefully supervised. The basic design used several groups of seeds (usually corn or wheat) planted in identical pans. Earth was thoroughly mixed prior to filling the pans. Equal watering, light, and other conditions were carefully provided for the various pans. The experimenters then prayed over one pan for more rapid germination and growth of the seeds while ignoring the second pan. In many cases a third pan of seeds was included, over which they prayed for retardation of growth. In some cases prayer or healing was directed to the earth in the pans or the water used for watering the plants.

Results were in the desired directions about three times out of four (though not consistently). Seeds receiving positive prayer generally both germinated and grew more rapidly than control seeds. Negative prayer tended to retard germination and growth, frequently leaving seeds that did not sprout at all and sometimes plants that withered and died. The percent of spread between pans, in millimeters of growth, ranged from single digits to (frequently) 30 to 40 percent. Occasional spreads of 100-200 percent were obtained.

Similar results were obtained with ivy cuttings and silkworm eggs. The experimenters generally did not report blinds or statistical analyses.
The Power of Prayer on Plants, 1969

Though attempts were made to provide careful controls in some of the experiments, different experimenters participated and procedures are not sufficiently described to permit inclusion of these studies in the well-controlled category. More important, it is not clear if any of these experiments included proper blinds. Though it is impossible to accept the results at face value, this richly detailed and thoughtful book is most highly recommended.

> True science is in one sense the humblest and most reverent approach to truth. The scientific approach does not say to anything, "You must fit the ideas and requirements I have in mind for you." Rather, the scientist sits down before an object and says, "You tell me what you are. You don't need to learn my language to tell me. I'll learn yours so I can listen." This humility, this basic reverence, is an advantage of the objective approach of science over the doctrinaire approach of a dogmatic creed. (p. 94-95)

It is a puzzle to everyone involved with healing why some subjects respond to some healers some of the time but not all of the time. The next study examines one aspect of that question.

Gender and Healing

Enrique Novillo Pauli

Pauli, a Jesuit priest, reports on 20 experiments in which a variety of subjects, mostly school children, were requested to enhance the growth of Fescue Kentucky grass seeds planted in laboratory petri dishes. All dishes were watered equally from the same source; light and temperature were uniform; position of the dishes was rotated daily; and the experimenter and his assistants were blind as to experimental and control plant assignments. Experiments lasted 10 to 14 days. Growth was measured from the seedpod to the tip of the blade.

The whole group was given the task of influencing the entire batch of plants. Positive results were noted when male and female subjects had separate group targets. When male and female subjects were focusing on the same targets, the results were not significant. In one experiment, significant results were obtained when subjects and plants were separated by eight miles; in another when they were continents apart. In some experiments, males outperformed females; in another the reverse was true. "[The] magnitude of the effect seemed to be independent of the number of subjects participating."

PK on living targets as related to sex, distance and time (*Research in Parapsychology 1973*, 1974)

It would appear that distant healing was demonstrated and that the gender of healers may have been an influence in the group healings. One can only guess at the biases of the researcher and wonder whether this isn't an experimenter effect. Healers commonly gather in mixed groups for distant healings, and I have found no other reference to negative effects with mixed genders in healing.

These studies appear to have been performed with proper attention to rigorous procedures. Unfortunately, specific numbers and statistics are not given to support the claimed results.[61]

There are no studies as yet to indicate whether people who are good at encouraging plants to grow necessarily have healing abilities with animals and humans as well, but my own impression is that they do. In Russia and a few other Eastern European countries, prospective healers were screened through their abilities to enhance plant growth.[62]

The mental states conducive to healing may vary from healer to healer and from one time to another in the same healer. Only a few researchers have sought to clarify this important variable.

Healing and Seed Germination

Spindrift, Inc.

Spindrift is a Christian Science group that invested fifteen years in studying healing in various ways. They published summaries of their extensive work privately. Unfortunately, their two investigators were not fully familiar with rigorous research design and reporting. This makes it impossible to assess their work with any certainty. Several of their findings may lead to further productive investigation of healing effects on plants.

Spindrift's research was based on certain assumptions about the mental processes involved in healing.

Qualitative thought of a healer is described as not being goal-directed and having the capacity to return biological systems from physiological deviations towards more normative patterns. It may be expressed by a healer in some variation on the theme of "Thy will be done," or simply as a wish for the general well-being of the healee. *Nonqualitative thought* of a healer is goal directed and "pushes" a biological system towards a preconceived direction of change determined by the healer. It is commonly practiced by healers as mentally imaging the healee changing in whatever way is felt to be conducive to better health. For example, a healer might image that a healee sick with pneumonia is breathing freely and looking healthy.

A number of these Spindrift experiments have far-reaching implications. The experimenters set contingencies for choosing which of several series of plant batches were to receive healing. Healers and experimenters were blind to which were the chosen plants. Despite this, the chosen plants often germinated much faster than the controls. For instance,

> In our first experiment of this kind we used three cups of mung beans. We placed a penny in a closed box, thoroughly shook the box, and placed it aside until the experiment was over. The cups were labeled C (for control), H (for heads), and T (for tails).

> Treatment was given to the beans in the cup designated by the penny in the closed box. From . . . the results . . . it was concluded the penny was heads and when the box was opened this was the case.

In several repetitions of this design, the determining factor was varied to include a die in a closed box, decks of cards, and dollar bills of various currencies in sealed envelopes. Highly significant results were obtained, though statistical analyses are not reported as probabilities. The outcomes observed were in line with the contingencies (such as a coin being heads up) that were not consciously known to anyone until the end of the study.

Other experimentation looked at the question of whether or not faith can be measured in conjunction with qualitative thought. "Faith, or strong belief, comes in many forms: experimenter effect, faith healing, placebo effect and so on. It is present along with qualitative thought (either as belief in one's healing ability or as disbelief in one's healing ability) in every prayer."

***Prayer and Healing: Tests with Germinating Seeds,* 1991**

This is a most tantalizing, yet frustrating, set of studies. It closely parallels Solfvin's study of healing for malarial mice,[63] where it appears that *super-esp* was evident. That is, it seems possible that the participants in the Spindrift studies scanned the experimental elements with either telepathy, clairsentience, or precognition and then sent distant healing to the designated plants.[64]

Because of this possibility, it is impossible to support the contentions of the Spindrift group that distinctly different types of healing, such as qualitative and nonqualitative thought, were at play. The expectations of the experimenters may have not only set the stage for the experiment, but may also have directed the choreography of the results through psi powers. Their own results from the contingency experiments confirm this possibility.

The frustrating aspect of the Spindrift reports is that they do not separate speculations and beliefs from experimental hypotheses or presentations of the results. Individual experiments are not clearly delineated, so that it is impossible to know in many cases whether blinds were employed. Where blinds are mentioned, the methods for establishing and maintaining them are not described. These are some of the problems that make it extremely difficult to assess the results of these fascinating experiments.[65]

With much narrower focus, we have a study of healing on the growth of a single plant.

Prayer and a Single Blade of Grass
Robert N. Miller

Robert Miller reports a unique experiment in which he measured and recorded the growth rate of ordinary grass with exquisitely sensitive electronic equipment. "Under the constant conditions of lighting, temperature, and watering selected for the test," he reports, "the growth rate was approximately .006 inch per hour. At no time did the growth exceed .010 inch per hour in any of the preliminary experiments."

He then arranged for Olga and Ambrose Worrall, who were 600 miles away at the time, to "hold the seedlings in their thoughts at their usual 9:00 p.m. prayer time. One hour later they prayed for the plant by visualizing it as growing vigorously in a white light."

Before 9:00 p.m. the trace was a straight line with a slope representing a growth rate of .00625 inch per hour.

> At exactly 9:00 p.m. the trace began to deviate upward and by 8:00 a.m. the next morning the grass was growing .0525 inch per hour, a growth rate increase of 840%. (Instead of growing the expected 1/16 of an inch in a ten-hour period, the grass had sprouted more than 1/2 inch.) The recorder trace was continued for another 48 hours. During that time the growth rate decreased but did not fall back to the original rate.

The positive effect of prayer on plants *(Psychic,* 1972)

This is one of the few impressive direct effects of distant healing measured. Unfortunately, no independent controls were used to rule out other factors that might have affected the plant growth. It would also be useful to have an independent, mechanical measurement as a check on whether the healer might have been affecting the measuring instrument by psychokinesis rather than the plant. Worrall was not generally known for PK effects, but Miller himself noted that she could influence a cloud chamber.[66] Replication with other healers seems warranted and should be relatively simple.

As mentioned in Chapter 4, DNA is a protein, found in the chromosomes of cell nucleii, that controls heredity and cellular life in nearly all living organisms. The structure of this protein includes a pair of chains of nucleic acids (nucleotides), which are wound around each other in a double helix. The nucleotide chains are held together by hydrogen bonds between hydrogen atoms which form parts of the chain.

The Institute of HeartMath in California has developed a method of mental focus that brings about electrical coherence in heartbeats. The subjective awareness of people in this state is a deep feeling of love. People who achieve this ability are able to project healing energies, as demonstrated in the next study, through the alteration of conformance (winding) of DNA in the laboratory with mental intent.[67] Here are several studies addressing these effects.

Winding DNA through Healing Energies (I)
Glen Rein and Rolin McCraty

Doc Lew Childre, founder of the Institute of HeartMath, Leonard Laskow, M.D., and others trained in the methods of cardiac self-management were subjects of this study, along with people who had no such training, who served as controls. Electrocardiogram (ECG) recordings were made on all subjects to determine cardiac coherence. The coherence ratio was determined by the percent of coherent to noncoherent time segments during the entire two minutes of recording. About one minute after commencement of recordings, all subjects were given DNA samples to hold. They held these samples, which had been chemically treated to partially unwind, for two minutes while recordings continued. The amount of re-winding of the DNA (conformation) was measured through UV spectroscopy before and after exposure to the subjects.

The authors report:

> Individuals trained in generating focused feelings of deep love showed high coherence ratios in their ECG frequency spectra and all were able to intentionally cause a change in the conformation of the DNA. The DNA conformation was affected differently according to the specific intention. In some experiments, different intentions caused opposite effects on the DNA. Individuals who showed low coherence ratios, although in a calm state of mind, were unable to change the conformation of the DNA. . . . The UV spectra. . .indicates a very large increase in absorption (increased denaturation) of a DNA sample after being exposed to an individual generating a particularly high ECG coherence ratio. The observed changes reflected his intention to further denature the DNA. These changes were three-fold larger than those produced by maximal thermal and/or mechanical perturbation, well known to denature DNA.

Modulation of DNA by coherent heart frequencies (*Proceedings of the 3rd Annual Conference of the International Society for the Study of Subtle Energies and Energy Medicine,* 1993a)

A change in DNA was produced by a healer that is three-fold greater than could be produced by thermal or mechanical influences is impressive. However, it is difficult to assess this report because raw data are not provided and no statistical assessments are given to indicate whether the observed differences could have occurred by chance.

Healers' ability to influence DNA may be a most important clue in building an answer to our question, "How does spiritual healing work?" Numerous aspects of health and illness are related to protein synthesis, which is guided by information encoded within DNA chains in the nuclei of cells. If healers can influence DNA, they may be able to influence many of the metabolic, growth, immune, and repair processes within the body.

Intention as a factor in healing has been the subject of study of Rein and Spindrift.[68] It appears that healers' mental focus may play an important role in determining particular effects of healing.

Winding DNA through Healing Energies (II)
Glen Rein and Rollin McCraty

In a study similar to the previous one (with additional elements of distant healing),

> a continuous state of deeply focused love was generated by Doc Lew Childre and by ten other members of the Institute of HeartMath capable of mental and emotional self-management. In addition several gifted healers and five university student volunteers were also asked to focus on feeling love. . . .
>
> Individuals trained in generating feelings of deep love and appreciation showed high coherence ratios in their ECG frequency spectra . . . and all were able to intentionally cause a change in the conformation of the DNA. . . .
>
> The UV spectra . . . indicates a very large increase in absorption (denaturation) of DNA after being exposed to an individual generating a particularly high ECG coherence ratio which was sustained throughout the two minute exposure period. These changes were three-fold larger than those produced by maximal thermal and/or mechanical perturbation, well known to denature DNA. The effects observed here go well beyond simply causing the DNA to completely separate. . . .
>
> It was also of interest to determine whether coherent heart energy can influence DNA at a distance. . . . [I]n . . . one such experiment, where the individual generating coherent heart energy was approximately 0.5 miles from the DNA sample. . . . [t]he intention was to increase DNA winding. . . . In contrast to the

previous experiments in which the DNA conformation was measured immediately after being exposed to heart energy, these experiments examined the time course of the effects. The series of experiments indicate that different individuals and different intentions produce characteristic changes in the healing time course.

Local and non-local effects of coherent heart frequencies on conformational changes of DNA *(Proceedings of The Joint USPA/ IAPR Psychotronics Conference, Milwaukee, Wisconsin, 1993b)*

It is again impressive to see effects of intention on DNA, with a magnitude three times as high as with denaturation from heat or mechanical influences. The lack of raw data and statistical procedures leaves the validity of this series of studies in question.

Setting aside our questions on mechanisms of healing, let us now focus on some of the ways in which healing can be introduced in clinical settings.

Healing and psychotherapy are an excellent combination. The following study begins to explore the experiences of therapists in combining them.

Psychotherapy and Healing

William West

West surveyed psychotherapists who include spiritual healing in their therapy. He defined healing as a special atmosphere that seems to benefit clients, as well as spiritual healing as studied in *Healing Research*. His principal findings included:

- Respondents reported experiences of spirituality occurring more often when they participated in spiritual healing activities than in conventional religious practices. More than half of the respondents participated in such activities, including meditation and healing.
- Involvement in healing began most often through receiving healing or in mid-life crisis.
- Healing may be introduced deliberately by the therapist, or may occur spontaneously at particular moments during the therapy without the conscious initiation of the therapist.
- The most common spiritual healing experiences include awareness or activation of healing energies, awareness of being part of something which is greater than the client or oneself, and the deliberate engagement with healing by the laying-on of hands.

- Spiritual awarenesses are often linked with energetic interconnectedness.
- Creating an awareness of *spiritual space* invites the spiritual dimensions to be present in some manner.
- Labeling and describing the work of healing may be difficult for some therapists.
- It is difficult for many therapists to find supervision that allows for the inclusion of healing. To deal with this problem, West encouraged some of his respondents to come together in a support group, which they found to be highly satisfying and educational.

Counselors and psychotherapists who also heal *(Healing Review* 1995; *British Journal of Guidance and Counseling,* 1997)

Psychotherapists who integrate healing and spiritual awareness in their practices find it difficult to discuss the full scope of their work with most of their colleagues—who are entrenched in materialistic and reductionistic models of diagnosis and therapy. William West's work is a validation to those who use integrated care, confirming that there are others out there doing this and that there is a growing body of understanding about how to bring these methods into a harmonious clinical marriage.

I resonate very strongly with West's observations. In England and America I have brought together groups of psychotherapists who are also engaged in bodymind therapies, subtle energy work, integrative care, and spiritual healing. We meet periodically to share our views and experiences, learning from and with each other how to blend these modalities.

One would think that the psychological characteristics of healers would be a popular subject of research. Surprisingly, I have found only the following publication focusing on the subject.

Psychological Factors and Laying-on of Hands
Stephen A. Appelbaum

Applebaum regularly uses psychological tests in his private practice as a psychotherapist/psychoanalyst. He recruited 26 healers through recommendations of Norman Shealy[69] and others (15 men, 11 women, ages 24 to 70), considering these a representative sample of psychic healers. The study was conducted through informal interviews and psychological tests, including the Rorschach inkblot test (all 26 healers), Thematic Apperception Test (14 healers), an inventory and inquiry of the subjects' early memories (18 healers), and the Wechsler-Bellevue (1 healer). Appelbaum himself received healings and also explored giving laying-on of hands treatments. Though no formal control group was included, Applebaum felt his extensive clinical experience with these tests provided a comparison with findings that could be expected in comparable nonhealers. His primary measure was his subjective interpretation.

Not surprisingly, the healers were concerned whether Applebaum wanted to examine their sanity. In these anxieties they were similar to other people whom Applebaum researched.

Serious psychiatric disturbances were in fact suggested by the responses of three healers. About half the rest demonstrated sound reality testing. The remainder were somewhere between the disturbed and the sound ones. Applebaum writes at length about his observations of the healers, and includes comments from some of them.

The laying on of health: personality patterns of psychic healers (*Bulletin of the Menninger Clinic*, 1993)

While Appelbaum writes convincingly about aspects of healers' personalities, his observations are too narrow to capture the entirety of healing interactions. It would be helpful to have clearer descriptions of the healers, of their beliefs, and methods of healing.

Some of the characteristics that he identifies as outside the boundaries of the normal may relate to reliance of healers on intuitive and feeling perceptions. When these are assessed with the yardsticks of linear reality, they may well seem to be deviant.[70]

Though Applebaum cites single studies of healing on enzymes, plants, and mice, he makes no mention of the implications of these studies in suggesting far more complex mechanisms than he proposes for explaining healing.

Despite all these criticisms, I believe Applebaum has made a significant contribution to our appreciation of psychological factors relevant to healing. Some healers I have met appear to me to lack a grounding in everyday reality to a degree that leaves me uncomfortable, sometimes even concerned, about their abilities to counsel people with disease, dis-ease, and distress. I only hope that such studies can be replicated and extended so that we can learn to better appreciate the psychological strengths, weaknesses, and mechanisms of healers and healing interactions.

These studies about healers and healing have been reviewed with every effort to be objective and to avoid Type I research errors of accepting as true something which is not. In being as objective as possible, however, we stand to miss what healers and healees feel and say about their own experiences of healing—perhaps the most essential aspects of what we wish to study.[71]

The next series of studies explores *qualitative* aspects of the healing experience.

QUALITATIVE STUDIES OF HEALERS

In Western society, we so often view life as quantity and less often as quality. We see matter physically but neglect it philosophically. We opt for the linear blinders of objective science. The gaze grows straight and sharp and focused . . . and misses so much. . . .

—Katya Walter (p. 111)

Qualitative research explores the subjective experiences of healers and healees, in contrast with controlled studies of healing that establish whether or not healing effects can be identified. Though controlled studies are done with rigorous methodology, the very tightness of the methodology also introduces a narrowness of focus. The more certain the experimenter wants to be, the narrower the questions he or she can pose. We end up knowing more and more about less and less.

Qualitative research focuses in a systematic way on broader issues, such as the nature of the experiences of healers and healees during and after healings. The next group of studies make a good start in this direction.

I leave it to the reader to skim these studies, dipping into them as they appeal to you.

A Subjective Experience of Healing

Bryan Van Dragt

Van Dragt observes that explorations of healing have been marked by sensationalism, a lack of theory to explain the phenomenon, and serious difficulties in methodologies, particularly in experimental controls. His review of the literature showed that extraordinary effects of healing appeared to be related to specific interventions of the healers in humans and other living things. This study treats healing as a thing in itself so that research questions can be truly relevant to the phenomena.

Van Dragt focused on subjective experiences of 10 healers during healing. He conducted tape recorded interviews, using Rogerian-style (nondirective) approaches to explore the question, "What do you experience as you are engaged in healing?" Next, he analyzed the interview transcripts for major themes. Healers rated five out of the ten analyses for their completeness and accuracy.

Van Dragt then compiled a list of common denominators among the healers' experiences, producing a fundamental description, a unified account of the healer's experience. Analysis of the description produced a fundamental structure of healing.

Van Dragt concluded that healers perceive healing to take place in another reality: space and time, personal and physical boundaries, and boundaries between the individual and the transcendent are all permeable. Healers merged with their healees in the process of focusing on a caring intent to bring the healees into a state of wholeness and harmony. The vehicle for healing appeared to be the person and consciousness of the healer combined with a transcendent power. Healing appeared to add depth to the Rogerian principles of unconditional positive acceptance, congruence of healer and healee, and empathy.

Healers' interventions suggest that the boundaries of traditional psychotherapy can be transcended. The constructs of healers' realities suggest that it may be possible to bring to bear direct and effective participation of transcendent entities or forces in the therapeutic encounter and that spiritual elements may be vital to the healing process. The author points out that these beliefs have been promoted by the Christian church and suggests that psychotherapists would do well to consider the possible relevance of these dimensions in their practices.[72]

***Paranormal Healing: A Phenomenology of the Healer's Experience, Vols. I & II* (unpublished doctoral dissertation, Fuller Theological Seminary, School of Psychology, 1980)**[73]

A Profile of Christian Healing

James A. Tilley

Tilley extended the Van Dragt study on the basic qualities of healers' experiences. While Van Dragt studied healers from a variety of spiritual traditions, Tilley included only healers working within a Christian tradition. He chose 10 healers with established reputations, exploring their subjective experiences during healing. His aim was to determine a model of fundamental structure of Christian healing as it is experienced from the phenomenological (reported experience) standpoint of the healer. He extracted elements from the interviews that appeared to be common denominators, returning to validate these with the healers.

Tilley concluded that Christian healers attributed their healings primarily to God, not only as the facilitator of the healing, but also as the agent guiding them and using them as His instruments for healing. They viewed their own roles as being open, clear channels to allow the flow of the power of the Holy Spirit through themselves.

Tilley's healers were similar to those studied by Van Dragt in conceptualizing that they were channels for a transcendent power behind the healing. They differed in their views on the ultimate nature of the healing power. Van Dragt's healers more often viewed the transcendent healing power as being impersonal, and felt that healers and healees had to be congruent in order for healing to occur. Tilley's Christian healers usually perceived this to be a personal deity and felt that healers had to be congruent with God.

A Phenomenology of the Christian Healer's Experience (Faith Healing) **(doctoral dissertation, Fuller Theological Seminary, School of Psychology, 1989)**[73]

In combining spiritual healing with psychotherapy, I find that clients often feel this is a substantial help in dealing with their problems. Though I do not practice within a framework of organized religion, my experiences are similar to those described by Van Dragt and Tilley. It feels like I am a channel for a spiritual source of energy and a catalyst for healees to open into greater spiritual awareness.[74]

An Experience of Healing

Allan Cooperstein

Cooperstein, a clinical psychologist in Philadelphia, has made another start at systematic research of healers' beliefs. He explored the experiences and underlying psychological processes of healers as they engage in what he labels *transpersonal* healing.

He employed a heuristic approach in five stages. Starting with the writings of prominent healers, he distilled features of healing experiences and categorized them as best he could. Next, he analyzed the writings of three healer-researchers: Lawrence LeShan, Rebecca Beard, and Dolores Krieger. He then reorganized the combined materials through the systems approach to consciousness described by Charles Tart (1975), including transpersonal experiences. He devised a scoring protocol for systematizing and quantifying his data. The protocol was then applied to the writings of 10 healers and to interviews with 10 more healers, the latter selected on the basis of demonstrated healing abilities in research settings. The interview group ranked 14 areas of healing experience in order of importance in their individual practices.

Cooperstein describes a spectrum of healers' beliefs and states of consciousness.

Moving along the spectrum, he writes, "there is an increasing alteration of ordinary consciousness and adoption of (or absorption within) metaphorical beliefs that are increasingly remote from those applying to physical reality. . . ."

The Myths of Healing: A Descriptive Analysis of Transpersonal Healing **(doctoral dissertation, Saybrook Institute, California, 1990)**

Cooperstein begins sorting through a broader spectrum of healers' beliefs and practices. Much further research will be required to tease out the relevant factors in healings in general and even more work to elucidate critical factors in individual healings.

Impressions of Therapeutic Touch
Patricia Rose Heidt

Heidt interviewed seven nurses who had 3 to 11 years' experience in doing Therapeutic Touch healing, along with one healee recommended by each of these nurses. The seven healees, six women and one man, were 34 to 60 years old, selected for their willingness to be interviewed rather than for having particular symptoms. Prior to the interviews, patients had received 10 to 100 treatments (median 30) for a variety of conditions, including metastatic breast cancer, arthritis, severe asthma, and labor and delivery.

Confidentiality was assured for all participants. One healing session for each pair was observed, and then participants were individually interviewed. Interviews were tape recorded and transcribed. Heidt noted terms in the margin next to every line, summarizing what each expressed. These terms were condensed into such categories as "attuning," "affirming," and "unblocking," that summarized the entire experience.

Heidt provides examples of statements made under each category, including observations made about other nuances of their experiences. For instance:

> *Affirming*: "It's a gentle force and I allow this to work through me."
> "That feeling of not isolating the parts, not isolating my lungs from the rest of my body."
> *Quieting*: "Therapeutic Touch gives me a handle to be in control."
> "It's like taking a gray sky and putting some blue in. I can deal with more now."
> *Unblocking:* "There is usually this loose congestion, thickness, pressure, heat in the field, like moving clouds. I try to sweep that away. I do that before anything else, to clear everything loose out of there."
> "As the treatment was taking place, parts of my body were relaxing. My legs, which were drawn up, would straighten out. I literally felt that a physical thing was being drawn out of my body."

Openness—a qualitative analysis of nurses' and patients' experiences of Therapeutic Touch (*Image: Journal of Nursing Scholarship,* 1990)

The Experience of Therapeutic Touch
Nelda Samarel

In this qualitative study of healees' responses to Therapeutic Touch (TT), Samarel interviewed eight male and 12 female volunteers who were attending conferences of TT practitioners and patients. Subjects ranged in age from 30 to 68, with diagnoses including depression, osteoarthritis, multiple sclerosis, cancer, and HIV illness. Their experiences of receiving TT ranged from two days to seven years. Samarel identified her own conceptions of TT so that she could then suspend them in order to approach the healees' responses with as neutral an attitude as possible. Her view is that TT involves nurturing, caring, compassion, letting go, and energy.

Each subject was interviewed initially on the first or second conference day, with a focus on the question, "What is your experience of TT?" Follow-on questions clarified the subjects' responses. A second, clarifying interview was conducted two to four days later. Through summarizing and abstracting the interviews, Samarel identified focal elements that "were then synthesized to specify the meaning or meanings of the experience of TT from the perspective of each participant."

She describes a set of before-treatment physiological, emotional, and spiritual needs, and then lists physical and mental improvements, as well as heightened awareness of self, that occur as a result of the treatment.

She concludes that "TT promotes a dynamic process of growth and change in awareness, with increased fulfillment. It shifts focus from the physical to awareness of the mental and emotional and then to the spiritual aspects of being and becoming."

The experience of receiving Therapeutic Touch (*Journal of Advanced Nursing*, 1992)

Further qualitative analyses of healees' experiences of TT healing also provide helpful information on the commonalities between individuals. One study examines healing for pain and two for stress and anxiety.

Few studies have been done on benefits of healing for cancer. Kathy Moreland explored women's subjective experiences of Healing Touch when they were receiving chemotherapy for breast cancer.

Kathy Moreland

The Lived Experience of Receiving Healing Touch Therapy of Women with Breast Cancer Who are Receiving Chemotherapy: A Phenomenological Study, (*Healing Touch Newsletter* 1988)

Moreland explored the subjective experiences of 6 Canadian women with breast cancer to "the lived experience of receiving the chakra connection," a method of healing included in Healing Touch therapy. Treatments were given during the intravenous administration of chemotherapy. Two open ended interviews were conducted with the women at 3 and 7 days following their first and second courses of chemotherapy. Each subject was invited in a third session to assess the congruence of Moreland's summary to their personal experiences.

Three themes emerged from this investigation:

> The experience of receiving the chakra connection:
> **1.** is caring expressed as a partnership, a nurturing act and self care;
> **2.** creates altered consciousness of the passage of time, the surrounding environment, of thought and of the presence of the practitioner performing the care; and
> **3.** is a holistic experience, which involves physical, mental, emotional, and spiritual dimensions. (p.5)

The treatment gave these women a sense of being cared for, experiencing both physical and emotional warmth. An alteration of time perception was noted to be helpful in "getting through" the chemotherapy. The women suffered particularly from nausea and anxiety, the severity of which produced a variability in their responses to the healing treatments.

Moreland concludes that this treatment can help people to deal with the physical and emotional discomforts of cancer chemotherapy.

It is helpful to have this methodical study to confirm the numerous clinical reports on the helpfulness of healing as a complement to the routines of cancer chemotherapy.

I have seen only a brief summary of the next study, also on cancer.

Charlene Ann Christiano

The Lived Experience of Healing Touch with Cancer Patients,
(Miami: Florida Interantional University 1997)

Charlene Christiano explored the subjective responses of 3 women to Healing Touch. They reported a change in consciousness, experiencing a "oneness/ wholeness."

Post-Operative Pain and Therapeutic Touch
Rosze Barrington

Assuming that "[p]eople are irreducible unitary beings who are open vibrating energy fields extending beyond the skin and interacting totally and pan dimensionally with environmental energy fields through energy patterning," Barrington studied six people scheduled for coronary artery bypass surgery within 24 hours of her initial interview. Subjects were approached in the evening prior to their surgery and those who consented were interviewed in a semistructured format which was tape recorded. The concepts of energy patterns or transfers related to Therapeutic Touch (TT) were not discussed with participants.

In a process of interviews, Therapeutic Touch treatments, and evaluative tests, participants' experience of pain—and of TT—was recorded and subsequently analyzed.

Subjects reported sensations of warmth and comfort, as in the following:

> [I]t feels like a part was drawing energy or soreness out or something. Part of it felt like warmth, like I was holding my granddaughter . . . part of it felt like, at night, when I go to sleep and my back is aching and I try and force myself to relax . . . warm . . . soothing.

The experience of pain shifted after TT, with slower breathing, lowered pitch and intensity of voice, eyes dreamy and glazed and slowed answering to questions. Half of the participants had oral body temperature readings above 38.4 degrees C, lasting about four hours on the evening after their first TT session. No medical cause could be identified for this.

One participant withdrew from the study after the first TT treatment. He spontaneously raised the question of whether the researcher was implying energy transfers occurred between the TT practitioner and patient, saying that this was kooky.

A naturalistic inquiry of post-operative pain after Therapeutic Touch (In: Delores A. Gaut and Anne Boykin, *Caring as Healing*, 1994)

This is a useful qualitative summary of healees' responses to healing for pain. The information gleaned appears consistent with anecdotal reports.

What is most impressive is the positive note TT introduces into a pain treatment situation. Conventional pain relief therapy with pain medicines ordinarily involves only the lessening of the unpleasant experience of pain, often with side effects of drowsiness and blunted consciousness. Reports of strongly positive experiences following major surgery are highly unusual.

Adolescent Psychiatric Patients and Therapeutic Touch

Pamela Potter Hughes, Robin Meize-Grochowski, Catherine Neighbor, and Duncan Harris

Therapeutic Touch (TT) was studied qualitatively in an adolescent inpatient psychiatric unit where TT and other relaxation methods were already in regular use. Three nurses trained in Therapeutic Touch provided the treatments. Seven adolescents were chosen who were without overt psychoses, paranoia, or delusional ideation. There were four boys and three girls, ages 12 to 16, including Caucasian, Hispanic, American Indian, and African American ethnic groups. Duration of hospitalization ranged between 16 to 65 days, with an average of 35. Six were on standard "psychiatric medications, most likely antidepressants, ritalin, and possibly a neuroleptic."

TT was administered on a massage table in a room on the unit designated specifically for this purpose during the study. The adolescents were allowed to request appointments three times weekly over the two weeks of the study, each session lasting up to one hour.

Within one day of participants' first and last sessions, Hughes (the primary investigator) interviewed each one with a partially structured but open-ended series of questions. The focus was upon patients' perceptions of their hospitalization and relationships with the TT nurse; physical sensations experienced during TT; how safe patients felt in the treatment sessions; lessons learned about their bodies, minds and emotions; and any benefits they noted from treatments. Three adolescents participated in a group discussion. Transcriptions were subsequently coded and categorized.

Subjective statements included:

"I wasn't asleep but it felt good, like I was asleep but I wasn't asleep. It felt as good as sleeping."

"[I]t feels like you're in this shield and it takes you to a faraway place."

"It. . .it makes me feel safe and it makes me trust the nurses more and like I can communicate and deal with the nurses better. . . ."

"I've just been feeling in the ups ever since I've been doing this. . . I haven't been that depressed like I was before."

"[E]ver since. . . I started this program . . . when I'd come in here like if I was in a bad mood, it just changed my mood for the rest of the day."

Therapeutic Touch with adolescent psychiatric patients (*Journal of Holistic Nursing*, 1996)

Many may find that the subjective reports of healees speak more to them of the worth of healing than all the research evidence from controlled studies. I find that each approach adds in its own way to my understanding of healing.

It is fascinating to see the sifting and sorting of healing experiences through analyses of various investigators, and particularly helpful when they survey similar territories. If one takes the studies of Van Dragt and Tilley, and those of Heidt, Samarel, Barrington, and Hughes et al., one must wonder how much of the differences in these studies are real and how much they might be shaped by the beliefs of the investigators. For example, Van Dragt's healers viewed the healing as impersonal, while Tilley's healers felt a personal deity was involved. The particular adjectives chosen by each researcher under which she or he categorized responses must shape the analyses of the data.

It is very helpful to have Samarel's brief description of her own perspectives, providing the reader with some basis for understanding the mind behind the eyes and ears which perceived and analyzed the data presented by the healees.[75]

There is no such thing as an objective study. Every question we ask has to be based on certain assumptions. The best we can do is to gather as wide a spectrum of investigations as possible—as in this volume of *Healing Research*.

Therapeutic Touch practitioners may encourage healees and their families to develop their own healing gifts, to help themselves and each other.

Children's Observations of Healing
Nancy E.M. France

Nancy France explored with Therapeutic Touch (TT) children's experiences of perceiving the biological energy field. She videotaped four to six sessions of 20 to 40 minutes each with a convenience sample of 11 healthy children in Kentucky, aged three to nine years. The sessions continued until a child could feel the energy field of another person, ending with a debriefing session to help the children integrate their experiences.

The exploration looked at the child's perception of the TT experience, movements during treatment, perception of another's energy field, and the tendency of children to try to do TT on their own. Data included the children's drawings and parents' diaries.

The perceived experience of TT included such comments as "It felt weird . . . good . . . funny . . . like air . . . like I was static." "It felt like there was a force field around me and you couldn't touch me." Sensations of movement were common: "It felt like my energy was going outward . . . like something moving in my body." "It's like. . .taking out my energy. . . . When I feel hyper . . . I'm giving my energy away. So I'm not hyper."

France describes in some detail the children's reactions, and discusses structures of behavior that characterized all of the sessions.

The (child's perception of the human energy field) using Therapeutic Touch (*Journal of Holistic Nursing,* 1993)

One can only wish that every child might have the in-depth experiences that France describes.[76]

Here are several more qualitative studies, briefly summarized from abstracts.

Pamela Joan Peters
***The Lifestyle Changes of Selected Therapeutic Touch Practitioners: An Oral History (Alternative Medicine),* (dissertation), Walden University 1995**

Peters studied the effects of TT on the perspectives, health habits, lifestyles, interpersonal relationships, and spirituality of 12 TT practitioners. Healers had 4-15 years' practice. Open-ended, audiotaped interviews were used. All of the healers confirmed that they experienced lifestyle changes in all of the areas in question. Their personal lives and relationships also changed.

Lucila Levardo Cabico

A Phenomenological Study of the Experiences of Nurses Practicing Therapeutic Touch (master's thesis), Buffalo, NY: D'Youville College 1993

This study explored through semi structured interviews the experiences of five TT nurses. They reported that TT was a positive influence in their perspectives on being professional carers, despite the fact that they generally had to disguise the nature of their healing interventions in their work settings. In their personal lives they felt enhanced interpersonal sensitivity, inner calmness, strength, self-esteem, and spirituality.

Gwen Karilyn Hamilton-Wyatt

Therapeutic Touch: Promoting and Assessing Conceptual Change Among Health Care Professionals (dissertation) East Lansing: Michigan State University 1988

This dissertation focused on the changes brought about in 11 nurses by a two-day advanced TT workshop. Surveys, audiotaped interviews, and case studies showed some conceptual changes one week after the workshop, with loss of these gains after two months. Gains were greater for TT concepts than for holistic interventions. The concept of barriers to learning is explored.

Emily Joannides Markides

Complementary Energetic Practices: An Exploration Into the World of Maine Women Healers (Alternative Therapies, Healing), (dissertation) University of Maine 1996.

This study explored themes evolving in complementary medical practices. Two women practitioners each of the following types were interviewed: "acupuncture, craniosacral therapy, emotional cleansing work, direct energy work, homeopathy, osteopathic medicine, polarity therapy, Qigong, Reiki, therapeutic touch, and vibrational medicine... and two traditional medical doctors..."

Markides explored the wholistic nature of these practices, which focus more on caring than curing. She concludes that counselor education programs would be improved if they were to incorporate such methods and approaches.

Melanie Sue MacNeil

Therapeutic Touch and Tension Headaches: A Rogerian Study (master's thesis), D'Youville College 1995.

The pain experiences of 10 people with tension headaches were studied. Half were assigned to receive TT and half to receive mock-TT. The "Unitary Measurement Tool," a questionnaire developed by MacNeil, was given before and after interventions. A single TT treatrment reduced the pain in all who received it.

Jane S. Kiernan

The Experience of Therapeutic Touch in the Lives of Five Postpartal Women (Birth) (dissertation), New York, NY: New York University 1997.

Kiernan explored the qualitative experiences of five women after receiving TT 2-3 times weekly in their homes in the two months after their babies were born. They developed an openness, and felt safe and cared for by the healer. The shared, mutual experiences of healer and healees became a major focus of the study. There was a great development of intimacy and trust, which promoted self-disclosure.

Maureen Louise Doucette

Discovering the Individual's View of Receiving Therapeutic Touch: An Exploratory Descriptive Study (master's thesis), Canada: University of Alberta 1997.

Doucette identified four phases in the subjective experience of receiving TT: preparation, engagement with subtle energies, being immersed in the moment, and "moving beyond". A greater harmony of body, mind and spirit was felt. *Number of subjects is not stated in the abstract.

Ann M. Renard

The Experience of Healing from Deprivation of Bonding (Touch, Emotional Attachment), (dissertation) The Union Institute 1994.

Renard explored the influence of TT on 11 adult co-researchers who had experienced deprivation of bonding during childhood. Five aspects of the healing experience for this problem were identified: 1. unconscious bonding throughout life; 2. Life-hreatening crises requiring termination of relationships and seeking help; 3. bonding with compassionate people through new ideas; 4. self-bonding, particularly through the body; and 5. bonding with the "Essencel Source" and the integration of body, mind and spirit.

SURVEYS OF HEALEES

*In the modern world the intelligence of public opinion is the
one indispensable condition of social progress.*
  —Charles William Eliot (1869)

Surveys of healees have focused on subjective assessments of results and
satisfaction with treatment. I used to be concerned that these surveys could
reflect effects of suggestion more than of healing. Healees report subjective
relief from healing in almost every survey made. They have little appreciation for placebo effects and might as easily praise any nostrum whose effects
derive from suggestion rather than from any value inherent in the
treatment itself. They tend to Type I errors. My opinion has changed
because I realized that placebo reactions regularly produce improvements
in about a third of subjects, while healing is subjectively reported to be
effective in a much greater percent of cases. These surveys therefore indicate
overwhelming healee satisfaction with healing treatments.

Johannes Attevelt, as part of his doctoral dissertation at the State University
of Utrecht in the Netherlands, performed two studies of healees. Reports of
4,379 healees were gathered from treatment cards of 65 Dutch healers. The
first study surveyed healers' and healees' subjective assessments of effects of
healings immediately following the end of a period of treatment; the
second obtained healees' opinions on the efficacy of healings six months
following the termination of treatment.

The average age of healees was 47.5 years. The average duration of
illnesses for which they sought treatment was 7 years. Two-thirds were
women. The most frequent diseases for which healing was sought were
skeletal-locomotory (24 to 25 percent); neurological (20 to 21 percent);
heart and arterial (9 percent); respiratory and pulmonary (7 to 8 percent);
rheumatic (5 to 8 percent); and skin diseases (5 to 7 percent). A total of
4,656 complaints were listed, demonstrating that healees sometimes came
for more than one problem. Pain was a factor in 51 percent. Psychological
complaints totaled 1,397 cases, of which 50 percent were nervousness.

Healer and healee assessments correlated closely ($p < .001$). Their
opinions were that 42 percent were much improved; 24 percent rather
improved; 18 percent somewhat improved; 14 percent not improved; and
under 1 percent deteriorated. Combined "improved" groups total 84
percent. No correlation was found between improvement and age, sex or
duration of disease.

Repeated questioning of healees, at intervals of one and three months
following treatment, showed variability of responses ranging from slight to
50 percent changed. The presence of the healer during the interview led to
16 percent higher assessments of improvement by healees.

Attevelt also found that subjective healee assessments correlated well with objective measures of improvement, as reported in the last chapter.

David Harvey (1983) presents another thorough discussion on benefits derived from treatment, on circumstances under which these occurred and on healees' experiences during treatments. He states:

> Up until now, medicine has tended to regard the condition, rather than the patient, as the focal point of interest; but we are currently seeing a pendulum swing away from this extreme. . . .
>
> Quality of life, freedom from pain and related considerations cannot be weighted and calibrated, but they are probably the most important factors from the patient's point of view. . . .

Of 175 questionnaires mailed by Harvey, 151 responses were obtained (86 percent). An impressive number reported they felt significant improvement: complete recovery 30 percent; partial recovery 25 percent; and improved ability to cope with symptoms 24 percent. However, Harvey's selection was based on a request to nine healers to each choose 20 patients who had shown positive responses to healing. This does not leave us with a clear idea of the percent of people in general who might benefit from healing treatment. Harvey's survey is still recommended for its thorough, book-length discussion of numerous aspects of healees' subjective reports.

Louise Riscalla, for her doctoral dissertation, interviewed a series of people engaged in religious healing, "considered as healing of the whole person—body, mind, and spirit through the use of prayer, anointing with oil, and/or laying-on-of-hands." Her aim was to study "the motivations of individuals seeking religious healing and their perceptions of what happens as a result of the ministrations of a healer . . . ."

Riscalla selected churches at random near her home, and attended services without revealing that she was conducting a study. They included Episcopal, Presbyterian, Roman Catholic and nondenominational churches. She conducted open-ended interviews, recording information on types of problems to be healed and feelings experienced when seeking healing and (if any) with the process of healing.

Twenty-three people were interviewed (ages 9 to 65; 17 female; 17 married; 2 divorced). A range of occupational levels was represented. They sought help for physical and emotional problems, separately or in combination. These included cancer, blindness, deafness, colds, colitis, headaches, ulcers, alcoholism, feelings of resentment and hurt and "difficulties coping." When seeking healing, 65 percent were under the care of a physician.

"It appears that the service itself creates an atmosphere conducive to receptivity for healing . . . ." Of 17 experiencing touch healing, 82 percent reported the sensation of warmth during treatment; 6 percent experienced vibrations; 12 percent felt nothing. Riscalla reports 57 percent noted variation in emotional improvement and 28 percent in physical recovery, "which suggests that religious healing seems to focus on emotional conditions and on emotional aspects of physical illness which may, in many instances, be a major component." Greater improvement was reported from those attending less structured services.

Those reporting physical improvement were more likely to be older, under a physician's care and of lower occupational level. Those reporting emotional improvement were younger and had more emotion-related problems. Changes in emotional condition were only slightly related to physical improvement. Those who experienced improvement sometimes felt their lives had changed. Some attributed their improvements to powers of Jesus or God. Failure to recover was occasionally interpreted as insufficient faith or as God's will that they bear their illness.

Thirteen healers were interviewed (ages 28 to 62; 7 male; 85 percent married). All prayed for healing during the services. Of 11 who used the laying-on of hands method, two felt tingling, two experienced vibrations, two were aware of strength and power and two experienced the strength of God. Two reported they instantly knew when healing occurred, though they could not explain how they knew. Responsibility for healing was attributed to God. Everyone considered cooperation with physicians as important.

Katherine Boucher studied 11 healees for her doctoral dissertation. Nine (81 percent) showed varying degrees of benefit, with eight having marked physical improvement.

Patricia Westerbeke studied the belief systems and the healing process of people visiting Philippine healers (Westerbeke/Gover/Krippner). Of 85 approached, 62 completed a series of questionnaires before and during their visit to the healers. Only 11 returned one or both questionnaires mailed to them six and 12 months later.

> The data suggests that one's post-session confidence in psychic healing (as recorded on the second questionnaire) is positively correlated with several items on the first questionnaire: stated willingness to change one's way of life if it meant being healed . . . (p <.01), personal experience with psi phenomena . . . (p <.02), and one's pre-session confidence in psychic healing . . . (p < .01).
>
> The healee's post-session report on help obtained from the healer (on the second questionnaire) appears to be positively correlated with such items on the first questionnaire as pre-session confidence in psychic healing . . . (p < .01) and personal experience involving purported psi phenomena . . . (p < .02). In other words, a healee's confidence in psychic healing is, perhaps, preconditioned by experience with presumptively paranormal events.

Healees' long-term changes correlated significantly with these items in the questionnaires at the time of healing: confidence in healing before their treatments, beliefs they received help from the healer and perceived change in body energy (all p < .01) and with personal experience with purported psi phenomena (p < .02).

This study begins to explore which factors may predict positive outcomes. Its greatest flaw seems to be in the self-selection of 11 out of 85 healee respondents.

Stanley Krippner (1990) used the same questionnaire for a similar survey of experiential reactions of 10 (out of 16) healees to a Brazilian healer, Irmao (Brother) Macedo.

> [T]he individuals on this study tour were not seriously ill but joined it for other personal or professional reasons.
>
> These responses were significantly and positively related to professed improvement in one's spiritual viewpoint. . . .
>
> The perceived change in energy and vitality six months after the healing session was significantly related to a shift (at 12 months) toward a positive spiritual viewpoint. . . .

Erlender Haraldsson and Orn Olafsson randomly surveyed 1,000 persons from the National Registry in Iceland by questionnaire and telephone follow-up. The 902 responses indicated that 34 percent felt healing was very helpful; 57 percent somewhat beneficial (combined improvement: 91 percent); and 9 percent that it was of no use. There was some correlation with religiosity and positive response. No attempts were made to verify objectivity versus subjectivity of any changes brought about by the healings.

John Cohen is a general practitioner in London. At the request of a group of healers he referred 44 patients for healing from his National Health Service general practice of medicine in London. Of these, 17 had musculoskeletal pains and 11 had psychological problems.

> Of the 44 people who attended during the 20 weeks of the study, 31 (70%) were women and 13 (30%) were men. Ages ranged from 18 to 75 years (mean 45.5 years). The number of visits varied between one and 22 (mean 3.8); 16 (37%) came only once and six (14%) came more than eight times. The total number of healing sessions received was 167. . .
>
> . . .35 (80%) received counseling and support as well as healing when they attended while nine (20%) received healing alone; six (75%) of these attended for a booster session after previously successful healing. Improvement was rated by patients as: great deal better 12%; good deal better 36%; a little better 20%; a bit better 12%; no different 20%.

The combined improvement was 80 percent. Healers' expectations of improvement correlated closely with the observed healee reports.

Further analysis showed that:

- The greater the number of visits the greater the benefit.
- Those who did not feel they were going to respond visited only once.
- More women than men found the healing beneficial.

Dr. Cohen appears to believe that the benefits to his patients derived primarily from physical touch and compassionate attention.

In some instances, the point of view of healees may be radically different from that of investigators, as in the next survey.

E. Mansell Pattison et al. interviewed and also administered psychological tests to 43 fundamentalist Pentacostalists who received 71 faith healings. The researchers reported, "our psychological data demonstrate the extensive use of denial, externalization, and projection with . . . disregard of reality. . ." Pattison et al. suggest that the psychological beliefs and defense mechanisms of these subjects helped them adapt to their culture. The healings in this particular setting were not necessarily designed to decrease symptoms but seemed more oriented to reinforcing the religious community's belief systems. This points out the multiplicity of functions healing may serve.[77]

Most studies consider short-term effects of healing. The following is the only long-term assessment of healing benefits I have found.

Richard Wharton and George Lewith summarize 145 responses to a questionnaire received from 200 general practitioners in Avon, England, on their involvement with spiritual healing in 1986. The survey found that 6 percent believed it is very useful; 4 percent useful; 31 percent no opinion; 16 percent not useful; and 10 percent harmful. The number of practitioners involved confirms that healing is becoming an adjunct to conventional medical practice in the UK.

The greatest weaknesses of these surveys are that criteria for improvement are usually unspecified and that medical assessments to allow for comparison with populations of patients in other settings are not included. Still, the overall picture is that the majority of people are satisfied with healing treatments they receive in such settings.[78]

RISKS VS. BENEFITS OF HEALING

If a little knowledge is dangerous, where is the man who has
so much as to be out of danger?

—T. H. Huxley (1877)

We must be cautious with healing as with any other modality which is untested in conventional medical practice. Though no permanent negative effects of healing have been reported, there is certainly a possibility that it could be used injudiciously. For instance, it could be substituted for conventional therapies without, or against, medical advice. D. Coakley and G. W. McKenna give the instance of a woman who discontinued taking her thyroid hormone after attending a faith healing ceremony at her church. She had a recurrence of delusions, hallucinations and thought disorders which required psychiatric hospitalization. Return to hormone replacement produced a cure which had lasted six years.

In Britain, the Code of Conduct of the Confederation of Healing Organizations stipulates that healers must not diagnose and must not begin treatment without referring people first to their physician for evaluation of their problems. This is a wise precaution.

Another, temporary negative effect has been noted. Mild to moderate worsening of symptoms, especially pains, have been reported occasionally. These are usually transient. Some healees have discontinued treatments when this happened, and healers have not studied this systematically, making it impossible to be certain about the natural course of this development. Most healers report that improvements usually follow within days or weeks when healing is continued despite the initial increases in symptoms. Thus the temporary worsening of symptoms is viewed by many healers as a positive development, similar to other sensations perceived during healing, such as heat, cold, and tingling. This may also be similar to exacerbations of symptoms (*provocations*) which sometimes occur with homeopathic remedies and flower essences,[79] and to somato-emotional releases with bodymind therapies[80] before beneficial effects are seen.

Unexpected effects of healing were noted in some of the studies in Chapter 4.

In Wetzel's study of healing to increase hemoglobin, both increases and decreases were noted. It is of great interest that Straneva's study of red cell cultures also showed positive and negative effects of healing. There appears to be a repeated effect here with red blood cells which invites further exploration.

Hale's study of healing for anxiety showed significant reductions of anxiety in the C group but none in the E group. The brief abstract I have does not state whether the difference between E and C groups was significant. This apparent negative effects of healing on anxiety, if real, is a mild one. It could be explained by the personalities of the healer and mock healer or by a lack of effectiveness of the healers.

Snell (1980) reported that the growth of some cancer cell cultures that were meant to be inhibited were, in fact, enhanced. While at first reading this might appear a negative effect, it need not be the case. It might be that the healer had difficulty exerting a deliberately negative effect, which is what many healers report. The logical next question is, "If a healer enhances rather than inhibits the growth of cancer cells in vitro, could they not have the same effect on cancer cells in animals or humans?" Logic contradicts this suggestion. Healers focus on healing the animals or people with cancers, not on killing the cancer cells. The healing may act by enhancing the organisms' immune systems. Evidence from successful treatments of animals with cancers further supports this explanation and contradicts the suggestion that a healer might enhance *in-vivo* cancer growth.

If we use conventional medicine as a measure of the risks and benefits of spiritual healing, there is simply no question that healing is one of the safest interventions available. It is estimated that medical treatment is the fourth most common cause of death in the US. Negative drug reactions (side effects of properly prescribed medications) result in permanent disabilities and deaths. Combined with negligent medical treatment, this results in over 100,000 deaths annually. This number exceeds the annual fatalities from highway accidents, breast cancer, and AIDS. Perhaps as sobering, you are 9,000 times more likely to die under medical care than from firearms (Mercola). [81]

A measure of the risks of having healing is in the insurance record of healers. In Britain, where healing has been available in National Health Service hospitals for decades, malpractice insurance for a healer that offers virtually the same coverage provided for a family physician costs under ten pounds Sterling, compared to a cost of between 1,200 and 2,500 pounds (depending on the insurance company) for a general practitioner's annual coverage.

Considering the known risks and benefits, one can reasonably say that healing is one of the safest therapies available. [82]

We assume that Western medicine is at the leading edge of knowledge and skill about how to help people deal with their physical and psychological problems. We forget that the vast majority of people on this planet have very different views of how to conceptualize and address their health problems. In many of these cultures they are far wiser about spiritual healing than we are. The next section explores some of these healing traditions.

SHAMANISM

The notion that modern Europeans or Americans are essentially more rational than the members of non-literate societies must be classified as one of Western man's irrational assumptions.

—Victor Barnuow

A rich literature is available on healing in traditional, nonindustrial cultures, usually under the hands of shamans (medicine men).[83] Many of these articles and books, authored by Western academics, assume dismissive or even disparaging views of shamanic healings.

Kaja Finkler, for example, describes spiritualist healers in a Mexican temple. Many patients she queried reported that they experienced heat and tingling during spiritualistic treatments and that they considered these portions of the treatment to be the most important in the healing.

Finkler attributes little significance to this or to the one-third of the patients who responded positively to cleansing passes of the healers' hands around their bodies, and who identified these in particular with relief of symptoms. The healings seemed to increase tolerance for pain. She interprets these results as the products of suggestion, a response to cultural symbols employed by the temple healers. Her conclusions are that "the healing requisites of patients are rooted in cultural imperatives mediated symbolically by the curing act."

One must seriously question whether yardsticks for measuring medical and healing effectiveness in one culture are appropriate or sufficient for assessing it in another.

I learned a lesson on this theme in my clinical years in medical school. A man complained of a stomach ache with some weakness and generalized malaise. I was responsible as the examining student physician to ask the questions that would allow me to arrive at a correct diagnosis. Uneducated in medical syndromes, the patient did not know which of his bodily sensations or symptoms might be causing his illness and might not report vital information if I did not think to inquire about it. For example, if I hadn't asked about aches elsewhere I might have missed the fact that he had a lesser ache in his left jaw and that these symptoms all started when he was shoveling snow from his front walk. Without pointed questioning, based in a knowledge of medical syndromes, I could easily have construed his symptoms to be of gastric origin. Taking into consideration the information elicited by focused questions, the diagnosis of myocardial infarction (heart attack) was far more likely and indeed was confirmed by cardiogram. I had to think of this possible diagnosis in order to ask the questions which then confirmed it.

Similarly, a person unfamiliar with spiritual healing may see only the suggestion dimension of a healing interaction and may not know to ask about subtle energy interventions or spiritual awareness.

Had Finkler known something of spiritual healing, she might have asked other questions—for example, clarifying the subjective experiences of energy exchanges during healing—and might also have reached different conclusions.

Sidney Greenfield (1994), an anthropologist who has studied the Brazilian psychic healers, gives us the academic labels for this transcultural problem. The *emic* explanation "recognizes that peoples from other cultures who behave in ways that are unusual to us, as outsiders, often have their own ways to explain their behavior." The *etic* explanation "refers to the Western conviction that science should be able to provide 'objective' explanations for all phenomena."[84]

A few academics are more aware of healing and other psi capabilities of shamans.[85] Some of them not only observed shamanic practices but actually trained in their methods. These investigators were able to verify through personal experience much of what shamans report of their subjective states of consciousness. They were also able to effect healings. Harner now teaches these methods to interested Westerners; Villoldo has led groups of people to study under shamans; and Krippner has lectured and written voluminously on shamanism.

The most comprehensive discussion on shamanism and healing is by Krippner with Welch. They point out that although Western scientists have been eager to borrow herbal knowledge from shamans, they have ignored teachings in diagnosis and treatment for physical and psychological problems.

Shamans are

> tribally assigned magico-religious professionals who deliberately alter their consciousness in order to obtain information from the spirit world. They use this knowledge and power to help and to heal members of their tribe, as well as the tribe as a whole. (p. 27)
>
> From a psychological perspective, shamans are socially designated practitioners who purport to self-regulate their attention so as to gain access to information not ordinarily available to the members of the tribal group whose illnesses they are called upon to treat. . . . (p. 28)

Shamans are found in hunting, fishing and gathering tribes. They also serve as priests, magicians and story-tellers.

Sedentary tribes and societies

> institutionalized and dogmatized religion, taking the power away from the shaman and placing it in the temple, rituals and creeds. The shaman's duties were severely curtailed by priests and priest-

esses who assumed formal political status insofar as institutionalized religion was concerned. We use the term "shamanic healer" to describe practitioners who usually work part-time and whose political status is informal rather than formal. These shamanic healers still engage in disciplined alterations of consciousness that supposedly facilitate their access to the spirit world, especially to power animals. . . . (p. 39)

Many contemporary healers can be referred to as shamanistic rather than shamanic because their practices are only distantly related to shamanism. The practitioners falling into this category hold spiritual beliefs and engage in procedures that are based on assumptions about the human spirit. They frequently engage in rituals but rarely utilize deliberately-induced alterations in consciousness in their healing sessions. . . . (p. 81)

This presentation of Krippner and Welch is enormously helpful in adding to our appreciation of the spectrum of healing practices and beliefs around the world. I disagree with them, however, that only shamans alter consciousness. Though the altered states of Western healers may not be as dramatic as those of shamanic healers, they are nevertheless a distinct aspect of healing. They include at least a quieting of the mind or *centering*, and may extend to accessing various intuitive states of being, from clairsentience to precognition and channeling of spirits.

It is refreshing to see people trained in Western science accepting the wisdom of so-called primitives. These cultures may be less advanced than ours in technology but they are far more advanced in application of psi skills, especially intuitive awareness and healing. They are attuned to spiritual dimensions of awareness, which include the participation of all living things in the ecobiological system of our planet (commonly termed *Gaia*) and with the cosmos beyond. Their methods warrant careful scrutiny so that we may learn ways of healing to complement our modern medical methods. They, in turn, may learn to distinguish between the essential parts of their teachings and superstitious beliefs which may have little therapeutic benefit. Thus we may all gain insight into how healing works.

Shamanic medicine can clearly be of help to Western medicine. In 1993, people who were 20-40 years old started dying of an unidentified illness on Navajo reservations. They started with complaints of vague aches and fever, sore throats and bellies, and then developed difficulty breathing. Within a day they succumbed to an overwhelming pneumonia of unknown cause.

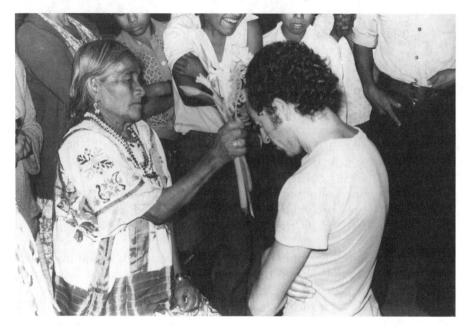

Figure 1-14. Maria Sabina, a Mexican shaman who uses hallucinogenic mushrooms, rituals and other methods of healing.

Photography by courtesy of Bonni Colodzin Moffet.

The Indian Health Service, New Mexico Department of Health, Los Alamos National Laboratory, Sandia National Laboratory, and the national Communicable Disease Center (CDC) were unable to identify an infectious organism or toxin which might be causing these rapid deaths. Theories ranged from AIDS to anthrax and even that radiation poisoning from a nuclear weapons storage site might be causing the deaths.

Ben Muneta, a Navajo medical doctor working for the CDC, asked the advice of a medicine man, Andy Natonabah.

"Natonabah told him the illness was caused by an excess of rainfall, which had caused the piñon trees to bear too much fruit." He showed Muneta "an old photograph of a sand painting with a mouse painted into it. . . ." Natonabah told him that many years ago such a sickness had occurred and that the sand painting had been used to treat it (Alvord/van Pelt, p. 120, 125).

"Look to the mouse," Ben Muneta was told. He took this information back to the CDC. Further investigations confirmed that a hantavirus caused these deaths. It is contracted from urine and droppings of deer mice who are infected with this virus. That year, the population of deer mice had swelled enormously because of an unusually heavy crop of piñon nuts.

Let me give another very speculative example of a lesson related to healing water from my own observations of archaeological excavations near the temple mount in Jerusalem. There is a mikve, or Jewish ritual bath, with a small adjacent reservoir (about 2 x 4 feet in area, and about 2.5 feet deep). The mikve and reservoir are connected by a hole about three inches in diameter that reportedly had been plugged with a bung. According to traditional explanations the reservoir used to be filled with rainwater and then blessed by the temple priests. Whenever the mikve bath water was drained and refilled with fresh water the new bath water was consecrated by opening up the bung to the reservoir, allowing a little of the consecrated water to flow in. Fresh rainwater was added to the reservoir as needed to prevent it from drying out. As long as the reservoir did not dry out, it was considered consecrated.

By conventional Western logic, the originally consecrated water in the reservoir would become diluted fairly quickly to the point that little of the original would remain. Any effects of the consecration would appear to have been purely symbolic, especially following many such serial dilutions over the period of a year between consecrations. Let us assume that the priests were aware of some healing effects of their blessings upon water. Recent research suggests that healing effects inherent in blessed water may be transmitted through vibrations or other energy phenomena that may not follow conventionally accepted Western laws of chemical dilutions. A small quantity of water treated by healing might, therefore, confer full healing potency to a bottle or to an entire reservoir of untreated water. This speculation of course must be properly tested in the laboratory. Homeopathy may have further observations to contribute on these matters.[86]

Much of the literature on shamanism and Eastern medicine (Kaptchuk for example) elaborates world views in which human beings constitute a small part of the cosmos, linked with nature via a vast web of psi and spiritual interactions. Descriptions of these interconnections vary widely and may seem to Western eyes so alien as to constitute mere superstitious beliefs. People in each culture believe wholeheartedly in their cosmologies and respond to elements within them.[87] A shaman draws upon imagery and beliefs from her or his culture in order to facilitate spiritual healings. In fact, it may be impossible for a healer from one culture to heal some patients from another because of dissimilar frames of reference.[88]

We may take simple lessons from cross-cultural studies which are relevant to our own medical care. If we allow that in various cultures healing may appear entirely different from healing in Western society, we might then be in a better position to re-examine the attitudes of patients in our own culture toward their healings. Western investigators have tended to discount patients' beliefs as unimportant or certainly inessential to the actual processes of healing. If we agree that alternative views may apply to healings in other cultures, should we not consider the perspectives of those undergoing healing treatment in our own culture as being relevant to their responses to healing, even if they differ from those of our scientist subculture?[89]

> *Traditional culture's healing education consists of three parts: enlargement of one's ability to see, destabilization of the body's habit of being bound to one plane of being, and the ability to voyage transdimensionally and return. Enlarging one's vision and abilities has nothing supernatural about it, rather it is "natural" to be a part of nature and to participate in a wider understanding of reality. Overcoming the fixity of the body is the hardest part of initiation.*
> —Patrice Malidoma Somè (p. 226)

Traditional, nonindustrialized cultures are universally more in tune with the environment than are the cultures of the industrialized world. A reverence for nature comes from many generations of experience in learning from and accommodating to nature—rather than dissecting, conquering and subjugating it. Shamanic practices of healing (McFadden) and trance states (Eliade; Harner 1980) bring about an awareness of one's relationship to the earth and everything on it. At this time, when excesses of materialism despoil resources and wanton pollution plagues and even threatens our existence, we have an urgent need to learn from nonindustrial societies how to heal ourselves and our planet.

Chief Seattle, a Native American, said to the president of the United States in 1854:

> Every part of this earth is sacred to my people. Every shining pine needle, every sandy shore, every mist in the dark woods, every clearing, and every humming insect is holy in the memory and experience of my people. The sap which courses through the trees carries the memories of the red man.
>
> The white man's dead forget the country of their birth when they go to walk among the stars. Our dead never forget this beautiful earth, for it is the mother of the red man. We are part of the earth and it is part of us. The perfumed flowers are our sisters; the deer, the horse, the great eagle, these are our brothers. The rocky crests, the juices in the meadows, the body heat of the pony, and man—all belong to the same family.

CONCLUSION

Our science is a drop; our ignorance a sea.
—William James

We have answered "Does healing work?" firmly in the affirmative. The research evidence adequately demonstrates that healing is an effective treatment and offers a potent complement to conventional therapies. We must get on with making it available to those in need.

We have barely begun to study the second question, "How does healing work?" The mystery called life challenges us to explore further. People suffering from illness and pain will benefit from this sleuthing and our world view will be broadened, to return us to awareness of our intimate interrelationship with nature.

Perhaps, at this stage of our explorations, we should be prepared to come up with more questions than answers.

Spiritual healing contradicts currently popular scientific paradigms. It challenges the prevalent Western world view, pointing out that it is apparently a limited case explanation for the cosmos. This closely parallels and in many ways overlaps the relationship of classical physics and modern physics. The natural laws which apply to the material world are accurate and helpful in understanding and manipulating that domain, but not appropriate for other dimensions of perception and interaction with non-material aspects of the world.

Healing strongly suggests that our bodies can be understood as energy in addition to understanding them as matter. Volume II of *Healing Research* explores this dimension.

Healing opens both healers and healees to spiritual awareness. Again this pushes the boundaries of materialistic beliefs. These dimensions are impossible to appreciate through words alone. When a traveler to a far land returns, she finds it difficult to describe the tastes of exotic fruit. We must taste of these dimensions in order to truly know them. However, as many Western people are quite new to learning about these dimensions, we may begin to study them through the research methodologies which guide the presentations in this series of *Healing Research*. Research evidence exists for survival of the spirit and for reincarnation. Volume III of *Healing Research* delves into these dimensions, bringing together studies from fields such as out-of-body and near-death experiences, channeling, apparitions, reincarnation, religious and mystical experiences.

Healing is not yet explained by existing theories. There are many clues and speculations at to what it is and how it happens. Volume IV of *Healing Research* organizes the clues so that patterns begin to emerge.

Each of us stands before the door to an understanding of healing. We have only to examine the world in new ways to find the keys. If we learn some of the methods of healing and psi we may not need material keys.

[T]he light the fire throws does not diminish the aboriginal mystery because of its power to illuminate some of the night. On the contrary, the mystery grows with the growth of consciousness.

—Laurens van der Post (1973)

Appendix A

Jesus of Nazareth was the most scientific man that ever trod the globe. He plunged beneath the material surface, and found the spiritual cause.

—Mary Baker Eddy (1875, p 16)

Healing in the Bible

Jesus' Individual healings	Healing type	Matthew	Mark	Luke	John
Simon's mother-in-law, fever	Touch; rebuked	8:14-15	1:29-31	4:38-39	
Leper	Touch	8:1-4	1:40-45	5:12-16	
Paralytic, carried by four	Sins forgiven	9:1-8	2:1-12	5:17-26	
Centurian's servant	Distant, synchronous	8:5-13		7:1-10	
Demonics at Gadara	Demons transferred to pigs	8:28-34	5:1-20	8:26-36	
Woman, bleeding	Touch-garment; faith	9:20-22	5:25-34	8:43-48	
Jairus' daughter raised	Belief; command	9:18-26	5:21-43	8:40-56	
Two blind men	Touch; faith	9:27-31		20:30-34	
Dumb, possessed (devil)	Drive out	9:32-34			
Withered hand	Command	12:9-14	3:1-6	6:6-11	
Man blind, deaf, possessed	(Drive out demon?)	12:22-30		11:14-26	
Daughter of Canaanite possessed (demon)	Distant, synchronous	15:22-28	7:24-30		
Epileptic boy	Prayer; exhortation	17:14-21	9:14-29	9:37-42	
Unclean spirit	Exhortation		1:21-28	4:31-37	
Deaf, speech impaired	Touch; spit; command		7:32-37		
Blind Bartemus	Faith		10:46-52	18:35-43	
Widow's son raised from dead	Touch of coffin; command			7:11-17	
Woman bent double by spirit	Touch			13:10-17	
Man with dropsy	Took hold			14:1-6	
Ten lepers	Suggestion; faith			17:11-19	
Nobleman's son	Distant, synchronous				4:46-54
Sick man at pool	Exhortation; caution: to stop sinning				5:2-18
Man blind from birth	Spit; mud; bathe in Siloam pool				9:1-15
Raising of Lazarus	Call; faith; precognition				11:1-14

Jesus heals many problems	Diseases and healing types	Matthew	Mark	Luke
Throughout Galilee	Every disease and sickness; demons; seizures; pain; paralytics	4:23-24		
At Simon's door	Touch; demons driven out 'with a word'	8:16	1:32-34	4:40-41
By Capernaum	Touch; people touching Jesus	12:15	3:7-12	6:17-19
Jesus tells of his healings	Blind see; lepers cured; lame walk; deaf hear; dead are raised; cures evil spirits, sicknesses	11:2-5		7:21-22
At Gennesaret	Touching him; edge of his cloak	14:35-36	6:55-56	
Before feeding 4,000	Lame, blind, mute, crippled healed	15:30-31		
In the temple	Blind and lame	21:14		
In home town, Nazareth	Touch; sick (miracles few, lacking faith)		6:5	

Jesus' healings of crowds	Diseases and healing types	Matthew	Mark	Luke
Before feeding 5,000		14:14		9:11
Beyond the Jordan		19:2		
In towns and villages	Every disease and sickness	9:35		

Jesus 'gives authority' to others to heal	Diseases and healing types	Matthew	Mark	Luke
Twelve Disciples	Heal sick; raise dead; cleanse leprosy; drive out demons	10:8		
Seventy-two believers	Heal sick; speak in tongues; pick up snakes; drink poison; touch-heal		16:17-18	10:1-9

Healings by Apostles	Diseases and healing types	Book, Chapter, Verses
Ananias	Paul regains sight bedridden eight years; exhorted	Acts 9:1-19; 22:6-13
Peter	Aeneas, paralytic	Acts 9:33-35
Peter	Dorcas raised by prayer; exhorted	Acts 9:36-41
Paul	Man lame from birth; faith; exhorted	Acts 14:8-10
Paul	Stops slave girl's precognition	Acts 16:16-19
Paul	Raises Eutychus who fell from third story	Acts 20:9-12
Paul	Resists poison snake	Acts 28:3-6

APOSTLES' HEALINGS OF CROWDS	DISEASES AND HEALING TYPES	BOOK, CHAPTER, VERSES
Philip	Paralytics, cripples; evil spirits came out in shrieks	Acts 8:6-7
Paul at Ephesus	Touch—handkerchiefs and aprons cured illnesses and evil spirits left	Acts 19:11-12
Paul at Melita Seven sons of Sceva evoking Jesus name	Sick Driving out spirits	Acts 28:9 Acts 19:13-16

OLD TESTAMENT HEALINGS	DISEASES AND HEALING TYPES	BOOK, CHAPTER, VERSES
Elisha and Shunamite's son	1. Staff on face (not done) 2. Touch-lying on boy	II Kings 4:18-27
Elisha and Naaman	Leprosy; washing seven times in Jordan	II Kings 5:1-19
Isaiah and King Hezekiah	Poultice of figs to boil when King was dying and prayed to God; (shadow goes back ten steps)	II Kings 20:1-11

Appendix I-B

Healing Organizations in the United States

Barbara Brennan School of Healing
Sciences
P.O. Box 2005
East Hampton, NY 11937
(516) 329-0951
Intensive, modular 4-year course

Society for Reiki Practioners and Teachers
Professional Membership Organization
USA and International
www.srpt.org

Consciousness Research and Training
Institute
Joyce Goodrich, PhD
325 W. 68 Street, Box 9G
New York, NY 10021
*Training in LeShan (distant) healing,
research, periodic newsletter*

Healing Touch
198 Union Boulevard, Suite 210
Lakewood, Colorado 80228
(303) 989-0581
Training, certification, referrals, research

Healing Touch Research
Cynthia Hutchinson
Htresearch@aol.com
*Clearinghouse for research - completed and
in progress*

International Center for Reiki Training
21421 Hilltop Street #28
Southfield, MI 48034
(800) 332-8112/248-948-8112
center@reiki.org web site: www.reiki.org
Training, newsletter, website

Nurse Healers-Professional Associates, Inc.
3760 S. Highland Drive #429
Salt Lake City, UT 84106
(801) 273-3399 Fax 273-3352
www.therapeutic-touch.org
NH-PA@therapeutic-touch.org
*Training, referrals, promotes wholistic
approaches and complementary
therapies, including Therapeutic Touch*

Qigong Database
The Qigong Institute
East-West Academy of Healing Arts
450 Sutter Street, Suite 2104
San Francisco, CA 94108
Tel/Fax (415) 323 1221 http://
www.healthy.net/qigonginstitute
*Outstanding collection of summaries of
Chinese research on qigong self-healing and
healer-healing (external qi/waiqi)*

American Polarity Therapy Association
P.O. Box 44-154
West Sommerville, MA 02144
(617) 776-6696
Referrals, training

International SHEN Therapy Association
3213 West Wheeler Street No. 202
Seattle, WA 98199 (206) 298-9468 FAX
283-1256

SHEN Therapy Centre
73 Claremont Park
Circular Road
Galway 091 25941 FAX 529807

SHEN Therapy Centre
26 Inverleith Row
Edinburgh EH3 5QH Tel/FAX 0131
551 5091
*Touch healing for emotional release of
tensions that may underlie physical
problems, including pain, musculoskeletal
problems, and many illnesses.*

Tai Chi
Wayfarer Publications
P.O. Box 26156
Los Angeles, CA 90026
Tel. (800) 888-9119 (213) 665-7773
Fax 665-1627
*Information on ancient Chinese exercises
which promote health and healing*

Upledger Institute
11211 Prosperity Farms Road
Palm Beach Gardens, FL 33410-3487
(407) 622-4706 (800) 233-5880
*Craniosacral therapy as a form of healing.
Cross-disciplinary courses for health
professionals, referrals*

Healing Organizations in England

All healers registered in these organizations abide
by a unified Code of Conduct.

Association for Professional Healers
92 Station Road
Bamber Bridge
Preston PR5 6QP
++ 44 1772 316726
*Promotes and supports healers practicing
in professional healthcare settings, training,
research*

Association for Therapeutic Healers
Elizabeth St. John
Neal's Yard Therapy Rooms
2 Neal's Yard
London WC2
++ 44 207 240-0176
*Focus on healing combined with
self-healing approaches, seminars,
workshops, newsletter, referrals (healers
are also trained in other CAM approaches)*

British Alliance of Healing
Associations
Mr. K. Baker
7 Ashcombe Drive
Edenbridge
Kent TN8 6JY
++ 44 1732 866832
*Umbrella for 30 healing associations,
training, referrals*

The College of Healing
Runnings Park
Croft Bank
West Malvern
Worcs. WR14 4BP
++ 44 1684 573868
Education and training

The College of Psychic Studies
16 Queensberry Place
London SW7 2EB
++ 44 207 589-3292
Promotes spiritual healing, courses, lectures

The Doctor-Healer Network
27 Montefiore Court
London N16
++ 44 208 800-3569
*Ongoing seminars for health care professionals and healers on
integrative care*

Fellowship of Erasmus
Moat House
Banyards Green
Laxfield
Woodbridge
Suffolk IP13 3ER
++ 44 1986 798682
*Treatment, channeled teachings, training in
color spectrum healing*

The Healing Foundation of the
R T Trust
Rowland Thomas House
Royal Shrewsbury Hospital South
Myron Oak Road
Shrewsbury
Shropshire SY3 8XF
++ 44 1743 231337
*Treatment, promotes wholistic
integrative care, referrals*

Maitreya School of Healing
1 Hillside
Highgate Road
London NW3
++ 44 207 482-3293
Color healing treatment, training, referrals

National Federation of Spiritual Healers
Old Manor Farm Studio
Church Street
Sunbury-on-Thames
Middlesex TW16 5RG
++ 44 1932 783164
Referrals ++ 44 1891 616080
*Treatment, training, magazine (largest UK
healing organization)*

Radionic Association
Baerlein House
Goose Green
Deddington

Banbury
Oxon Ox16 0SZ
++ 44 1869 338852
Training, referrals

Sufi Healing Order of Great Britain
91 Ashfield Street
Whitechapel
London E1 2HA
++ 44 207 377-5873
Treatment

White Eagle Lodge
Brewells Lane
Rake
Liss
Hants GU33 7HY
++ 44 1730 093300
Absent healing groups

Healing - Worldwide

Dachverband Geistiges Heilen e.V.
Haupt Str. 20
D-69117 Heidelberg
Germany
Tel. ++ 49 6221 169606 Fax 6221
169607

Europaische Aktion fur Therapiefreiheit
Recht auf Gesundheit
Vereinigung E:A:T:R:S
John Hart
Postbus 1489
NL-6201 BS Maastricht
The Netherlands
Tel. ++ 31 45 212076 Fax 4454 62273

Zu Luxemburg
Aulikki & Seppo Plaami
1 rue Pierre Dupong
L-7314 Heisdorf
Luxemburg
++ 352 37 7461

Zu Polen
Dr. phil. Jerzy Rejmer
Jochlerweg 2
CH-6240 Barr-Zug
Switzerland

Groupment National pour
L'Organisation de la Medecine Auxillaire
(GNOMA)
Michel Barthes (General secretary)
3 bis, rue Bleue
75009 Paris France

Det Norske Haelerforbundet
Else Egeland
Fanahammeren 9
Postboks 122
N-5047 Fana-Bergen
Norway
Tel/ Fax ++ 47 5 591 6015

Wholistic Approaches

American Holistic Medical Association
and American Holistic Nurses Association
4101 Lake Boone Trail, Suite 201
Raleigh, NC 27607
(800) 878-3373 or (919) 787-5146
Referrals, conferences, journals

American Preventive Medical Association
P.O. Box 458
Great Falls, VA 22066
(800) 230-2762 Fax (703) 759-6711
*Lobbies in government for legal acceptance
of complementary/ alternative therapies*

Canadian Complementary Medical
Association (CCMA)
(403) 229-0040

Moss, Ralph
*Alternative Medicine Online: A Guide to
Natural Remedies on the Internet*
Brooklyn, NY: Equinox 1997
Healing Choices Report Service
(718) 636-4433

American Association of Naturopathic
Physicians (AANP)
601 Valley Street, Suite 105
Seattle, WA 98109
(206) 328-8510 www.infinite.org/
Naturopathic.Physician
*Referrals, licensing information in a few
states*

Bastyr University
Natural Health Clinic
1307 North 45th Street, Suite 200
Seattle, WA 98103
(206) 632-0354
Postgraduate training in naturopathy

Canadian College of Naturopathic
Medicine
60 Berl Avenue
Etobicoke, Ontario M8Y 3CY
Canada
(416) 251-5261
*Diploma program equivalent to a degree in
the United States.*

The Institute for Naturopathic Medicine
66 1/2 North State Street
Concord, NH 03301-4330
(603) 225-8844
Public awareness

National College of Naturopathic
Medicine
11231 Southeast Market Street
Portland, Oregon 97216
(503) 255-4860
Referrals

Southwest College of Naturopathic
Medicine
6535 E. Osborn Road
Scottsdale, AZ 85251
(602) 990-7424
Naturopathic degree program

New Age, Healing Resources - Information, Conferences

Esalen Institute
Big Sur, CA 93920
(408) 667-3000
New Age conference center.

The John E. Fetzer Institute
1292 West KL Avenue
Kalamazoo, MI 49009
(616) 375-2000
Organizes seminars and conferences,
publishes Advances (focus on
psychoneuroimmunology and healing)

The Institute of Noetic Sciences
475 Gate 5 Road, Suite 300
Sausalito, CA 94965
(415) 331-5650
Large membership organization with
quarterly magazine
(Noetic Sciences Review), international
directory of New Age members. Annual
conference in summer.

The Intuition Network
475 Gate 5 Road, Suite 300
Sausalito, CA 94965
(415) 331-5650

Nursing

American Holistic Nurses' Association
4101 Lake Boone Trail, Suite 201
Raleigh, NC 27607
(800) 278-2462 http://ahna.org
Promotes wholistic approaches and
complementary therapies, including
Healing Touch. Certificate course in
Holistic Nursing. Quarterly journal

Nurse Healers-Professional Associates, Inc.
(See under Healing Organizations)
Promotes wholistic approaches and
complementary therapies, including
Therapeutic Touch Certification.

Certificate Program in Holistic Nursing
24 South Prospect Street
Amherst, MA 01002
(413) 253-0443 Fax 259-1034
cphn@cyberc.com

Institute of Rogerian Scholars
437 Twin Bay Drive
Pensacola, FL 32534
(800) 474-9793
Promoting theoretical and practical
approaches of Martha Rogers on
Therapeutic Touch

Orgone Therapy

American College of Orgonomy
PO Box 490,
Princeton, N.J. 08542.
Reichian therapies, Journal of Orgonomy

Qigong - See Healing

Research

International Society for the Study of
Subtle Energies and Energy Medicine
(ISSSEEM)
356 Goldco Circle
Golden, CO 80403-1347
303 425-4625 Fax 425-4685
74040.1273@compuserve.com web site:
vitalenergy.com/issseemf

National Center for Complementary and
Alternative Medicine (NCCAM)
P.O. Box 8218
Silver Spring, MD 20907-8218
(888) 644-6226 Fax (301) 499575-
http://nccam.nih.gov/nccam/
Studies and disseminates information on
alternative/complementary therapies,
funds research

Shamanism

Ruth Inge Heinze, PhD
Center for South and Southeast Asia
Studies
2321 Russell St. #3A
Berkeley, CA 94705
Annual conference, proceedings

The Foundation for Shamanic Studies
P.O. Box 670, Belden Station
Norwalk, CT 06852
(203) 454-2827

Endnote References

Introduction

[1] Reiki is a form of healing derived from a Japanese healer. More on this later in Vol. I Chapter 1. (Roman numerals indicate VOLUME number)

[2] Where names appear initially in quotes they are assumed names to protect the anonymity of the subjects.

[3] See a more detailed description of this healing encounter in the introduction to Volume IV.

[4] I have used *healee* in preference to *patient* because the latter is taken (in conventional Western medicine) to be a person who receives treatment from someone else for his ailments in a passive manner. The term healee indicates a person who shares in the responsibility for doing something about his condition, even though his participation may be unconscious, through various mind-body-spirit connections elucidated in this book. LeShan (1974a) was the first to use this term. Siegel (1990) suggests the term "respant," meaning responsible participant.

[5] In this revised edition I have applied more stringent criteria for including reports in the section on controlled studies than in the first edition. In this process I removed several dozen reports from the controlled studies section. Thus the absolute number of 198 controlled studies in the second edition appears to add only 43 studies to the series, when it actually adds about 60 studies.

[6] See Vol. II Chapter 1 on **psychoneuroimmunology (PNI)**

[7] See reviews of Capra, Dossey, Koestler, Zukav, and Benor (Vol. II Chapters 6 and 8) for a taste of **paradigm shifts**.

[8] Bensen; Evans/Richardson; Hutchings; Kolough; Pearson; Teitelbaum; Van Dyke; Wolfe; Wolfe/Millett

[9] I brought this research (which promises with simple techniques to reduce post-surgical pain, nausea, vomiting, urinary and bowel problems, and to shorten hospital stay) to the attention of numerous surgeons. It has been dismaying to hear most of them decline under various excuses (e.g. that they would be embarrassed to be seen speaking to their patients as they are coming out of anesthesia—and presumably therefore unable to respond to the surgeon's intervention). See Evans and Richardson 1988 for recent application of these methods.

[10] It took close to two years to find funds for a carefully designed controlled study of healing in surgical patients in 1982. Most foundations and other funding sources indicated that such research is outside their field of interest. I moved to live in England from 1987 to 1997 because I found the general practitioners (primary care physicians) there more open to collaborative research on healing and to integrating healing with conventional medicine.

[11] *The European Journal of Parapsychology; The Journal of the American Society for Psychical Research* (irregularly until 1957; regularly from 1970); *The Journal of Parapsychology; The Journal of the Society for Psychical Research; The Journal of Scientific Exploration;* and *Subtle Energies.*

Research in Parapsychology contains abstracts of presentations from the annual meeting of the Parapsychological Association without peer review, although papers are critiqued as they are presented and the authors have opportunity to revise the papers prior to publication.

[12] See detailed discussion of this study by Rosa, et al. in Vol. I Chapter 4.

[13] This incident is discussed in greater detail in Vol. II Chapter 2.

[14] See review of this study in Vol. I Chapter 4, section on healing for human physical problems.

[15] See review of this study in Vol. I Chapter 4, section on healing for plants.

[16] See summary of replicated studies at the end of Vol. I Chapter 4.

[17] See Volume II on **mechanisms for self healing** and on **energy medicine**; Vol IV Chapter 2 for theories of **spiritual healing**.

[18] See more on alternate ways of viewing the world in Vol. I Chapter 5 under **shamanism**; Vol. II Chapter 2 on **Chinese cosmology**; Vol. IV Chapter 2 on **theories explaining spiritual healing**; and Vol. IV Chapter 3 on **components of spiritual healing**.

[19] See the report of Michael Dixon in Vol. I Chapter 5. See also mention of cost-effectiveness studies of other complementary therapies in Vol. II Chapter 2.

[20] **This historical review** is taken from portions of Dossey 1982; Coddington; *H. Graham; Meek (chapter by Rindge); Pierrakos 1976; and Rose. Rose and Pierrakos has the best historical overviews and bibliographies. Dossey (1982) has the best discussion on **Cartesian influences on western medicine**. For discussions on **paradigm shifts** related to psi in general Kuhn is a must and Harman (1988) is highly recommended. See also Braude (1986); Collins/Pinch; and H. Evans (1982). Brested and Estes are interesting for **ancient Egyptian concepts of healing**. Krippner/ Welch provide an excellent discussion on shamans, medicine men, and spiritual dimensions in healing.

[21] I am indebted to Krippner/Welch for providing the basis of much of the discussion on shamanism.

[22] See Appendix A for a table of **Biblical references to healing**; also Cerutti and Meek for lists of Bible references to incidents involving psi as well as healing. See also Gardner (1986a; b) on healings of the Venerable Bede. Vol. III Chapters 8 and 11 discuss **religions and healing**. Bek/ Pullar; MacManaway; Rose.

[23] I am indebted to Louis Rose for providing much of the discussion on the history of Christian healing.

[24] See brief discussions of **placebos** in the introduction of Vol. I Chapter 4; also Vol. IV Chapter 3; and much more detailed consideration of placebo and suggestion effects in Vol. II Chapter 1.

[25] The **energy body** is discussed in Volume II. Research evidence for survival of the spirit is reviewed in Volume III.

[26] More on **mind-body** interactions in Volumes II and IV.

Endnotes Chapter 1 Healers

[1] **Factors influencing healing** are discussed in Vol. IV Chapter 3.

[2] More on **systems theory and healing** in Vol. II Chapter 1.

[3] More on **discomforts with healing and reasons healing has not been accepted** in Vol. IV Chapter 3.

[4] See research on **reincarnation** in Vol. III Chapter 3.

[5] See description of **Tapas Acupressure Technique** at the end of this chapter. EFT was developed by Gary Craig in the tradition of Roger Callahan's Thought Field Therapy. These and related approaches use acupressure points to clear emotional dross. These are briefly discussed in Vol. II Chapter 2

[6] See excerpts of **the views and theories of Edward Whitmont** in Vol. II Chapter 2; Vol. IV Chapter 2.

[7] More on **Jungian views and approaches** in Johnson; Sharp; von Franz; Chapter IV Chapter 3.

[8] On **Gaia** see Lovelock; Russell; Vol. IV Chapter 3.

[9] **Psychic and spiritual awarenesses** are discussed in detail, respectively, in Vol. I Chapter 3 and in Volumes III and IV of *Healing Research*.

[10] Herrigel; Persig; Tart

[11] See discussions of **near-death and mystical experiences** in Vol. III Chapters 2 and 9, respectively.

[12] Grad 1965/76; Grad et al. 1961; Smith 1972

[13] J. Smith; Grad 1965a/1976; Grad/Cadoret.

[14] See study of Estebany's use of cotton wool for healing mice (Grad 1965), reviewed in Vol. I Chapter 4; discussion in Vol. IV Chapter 3 under **storage and linger** effects.

[15] See research of Grad and Smith with Estabany reviewed in Vol. I Chapter 4.

[16] "Preliminary statement about the results of experimental work conducted by Evgenia Yuvashevna (Juna) Davitashvili at the Consultative and Diagnostics Center of . . . Moscow, affiliated with the City Polyclinic . . . during the period of November 17 through December 31, 1980."

[17] **Autogenic Training** is briefly discussed in Vol. II Chapter 2.

[18] B. Siegel 1986 reports he can stop operative bleeding by suggestions to the anesthetized patient. More on **suggestion and hypnosis** in Vol. II Chapter 1; on **Autogenic Training** and **Biofeedback** in Vol. II Chapter 2.

[19] See more on **Visualization** in Vol. I Chapter 3; Vol. II Chapter 2.

[20] An American method for psychic development.

[21] Ivanova 1978; 1980; 1983; 1986 adds further details on her theories and experiences. *Telesomatic reaction* is a term coined by B. Schwarz 1967.

[22] Green et al. 1991; reviewed in Vol. II Chapter 2 and Vol. IV Chapter 3.

[23] Fahrion, reviewed in Vol. I Chapter 5.

²⁴ **Kirlian photography** is discussed in Vol. II Chapter 3.

²⁵ More on **pendulums and dowsing** in Vol. II Chapter 4.

²⁶ "Margaret," described later in this chapter.

²⁷ See McRae for a detailed discussion on the **military potential of psychic weapons;** Targ/Harary for a more general discussion of East-West competition on the psi frontiers.

²⁸ **Homeopathy** is discussed in Vol. II Chapter 2.

²⁹ See more on Victor Krivorotov in Church/Sherr.

³⁰ **Chakras** are energy centers along the midline of the body. They are discussed in Vol. II Chapter 2.

³¹ See more on **photographic effects of healing** in Vol. IV Chapter 3.

³² See Vol. III Chapter 11 on spiritual and spirit healings.

³³ See Vol. II Chapter 1 on **mind-body interactions**.

³⁴ See Vol. III Chapter 3, 4, 5, and 11.

³⁵ For thorough discussions **of connections between emotions and physical symptoms** see Dethlefsen and Dahlke; Harrison; Hay; Rossi; Steadman.

³⁶ Louis Rose's observations are in Vol. I Chapter 5.

³⁷ Bloomfield 1990 also describes Linda Martel's healing, but is not as thorough as Graves.

³⁸ Estebany is described earlier in this chapter.

³⁹ See Appendix A for **Biblical references to healing**.

⁴⁰ More on **collective consciousness** in Vol. I Chapter 3 and Vol. IV Chapter 3.

⁴¹ Rindy Bakker is a Medical Doctor. In England doctors are given their title "Dr." before their name, rather than identified as "M.D." after their name. (We are, indeed, two nations divided by a language!)

⁴² After "Body-Mind Centering work" of Bonnie Bainbridge Cohen. See also tissue memories with organ transplants in Sylvia.

⁴³ See more on Motz's work with Dr. Mehmet Oz in Brown 1995; Motz 1998.

⁴⁴ Wirkus presents his views on healing earlier in this chapter.

⁴⁵ Many more details and more examples are provided in the original article.

⁴⁶ I look forward to launching an *International Journal of Healing and Caring*—on line in which such reports can be published, an upgrade from the *Doctor-Healer Network Newsletter*, when funding and/or support from a publisher can be found.

⁴⁷ Eisenberg's landmark articles in 1993 and 1998 document the growing use of complementary therapies in America. These articles have been highly influential in opening medical practitioners to learn more about integrated care.

⁴⁸ also spelled *chi* and *ki*

[49] See Guo and N. study in Vol. I Chapter 4.

[50] More on **Chinese medicine** in Vol. II Chapter 2.

[51] See TT studies reviewed in Vol. I Chapter 4.

[52] For further descriptions of **Therapeutic Touch** see Boguslaski 1980; Borelli/Heidt; Kunz 1995; Lionberger; MacRae; Melloy; Quinn 1979; 1988; 1989; Randolph 1984; Rowlands; Witt.

[53] On **Healing Touch** see Hover-Kramer. The principal group promoting and teaching Healing Touch is the American Holistic Nurses' Association (details in Appendix B).

[54] An assumed name to protect anonymity.

[55] **Kundalini energy** is described in Eastern meditative traditions, discussed in Vol. II Chapter 2 and Vol. IV Chapter 3. It is said to rise from the base of the spine, clearing away old energy blocks, opening a person to greater subtle energy and spiritual awarenesses. For discussion of **kundalini** phenomena see Greenwell; Sanella 1978. For photos of Cain at work see Harvey 1982.

[56] The use of **healee-held photographs for drawing healing to themselves** is also reported by Shubentsov; Tarpey (described in Volume II by Westlake).

[57] Arnold/Nevius; Rand; Ray.

[58] See Ray 1983 for discussion of theoretical bases for **Reiki**; F. Brown on Takata's teachings; Arnold/Nevius for practical descriptions of methods.

[59] See also Angelo; White and Swainson for other views of **spirit communication regarding healing**, and Beard on the general subject of spirit communication; **mediumistic experiences/channeling** in Vol. Chapter 5.

[60] See Green's study in Vol. I Chapter 5.

[61] Vogel, in public talks, seemed prone to exaggerations and Type I errors.

[62] See review of Sheely's study in Vol. I Chapter 4.

[63] For references to **shamanic practices** see Vol. I Chapter 5.

[64] For more on **psi phenomena** see Vol. I Chapter 3. For more on Huna healing see Pukui; S. King.

[65] In the Bhagavad Gita, especially the Judge translation; the Upanishads.

[66] Various **psychotherapeutic approaches** are discussed in Vol. II Chapter 1.

[67] See the views of Krivorotov earlier in this chapter.

[68] *Voodoo* is a term misused colloquially (especially in horror films) to designate deliberate, potently harmful cursing. Voodoo is actually a Haitian spiritistic religion.

[69] On **deliberate negative healing effects** see Eisenbud 1983; Dossey 1993; discussion in Vol. IV Chapter 3.

[70] Dorie D'Angelo, Charles Cassidy, Rosita Rodriguez, Harold Plume, Etel

deLoach, The Fullers, Bob Hoffman, Dorothy Vurnovas, Rev William Brown, Alberto Aquas, William McGarey (a physician who is exploring methods recommended by Edgar Cayce).

[71] See also Crenshaw; Fry; A. Taft; Valley Times for further details and Stemman 1983 for photographs of Willard Fuller.

[72] For detailed biographies of Cayce see Bolton; H. L. Cayce; Steam 1967; Sugrue. These are highly recommended for a view of the range of possibilities with applied psi. For Cayce remedies see W. McGarey; Karp.

[73] See more **intuitive diagnosis** in Vol. I Chapter 4

[74] See more on **psychokinesis (PK)** in Vol. I Chapter 3.

[75] Much more on **psychic surgery** in Vol. III Chapter 7.

[76] Numerous **shrines** around the world are alleged to promote healing. The most famous is the one at Lourdes, France. See Vol. I Chapter 5. It is unclear whether the cures should be attributed to the waters usually present at such shrines, to self-healing initiated by healee expectations, or to other causes. This report by Stelter provides the only reference I have found which suggests that human interventions may be causally connected with these cures as well. For a review of *Lourdes* and other shrine healings see review in Vol. I Chapter 5 and Vol. IV Chapter 2.

[77] **Theories for healing** are considered in Vol. IV Chapter 2.

[78] Much more on **mediumistic phenomena (channeling)** in Vol. III Chapter 5.

[79] Including: Josephina Sison, Rolling Thunder, Dona Pachita Olga Worrall, Hernani Andrade, Fausto Valle, and Josef Zezulka. Some of these healers are described in Vol. III Chapter 7.

[80] See **LeShan's theories** in Vol. IV Chapter 2.

[81] Formerly Rita Sewell

[82] See Vol. IV Chapter 2 for a discussion of theories of healing and IV-3 for topical discussions and analyses of aspects of healing.

[83] For resources related to the various healing methods see Appendix B.

[84] The healing systems are presented roughly in order of their seniority in numbers of years they have been taught.

[85] The possible benefits of blessed water, oil and of relics is supported by research showing that water can convey healing effects. See Vol. I Chapter 2, especially the Setzer study on water from a church sanctuary which was shown to be altered by spectrophotometry and which promoted plant growth; studies of plants which grow better when watered with healed water in Vol. I Chapter 4 and 5, cotton wool (see Grad"s study of mice on an iodine deficient diet, whose goiters were smaller when healed cotton wool was in their cages, in Vol. I Chapter 4; Estebany's report of various materials which seem to store healing, earlier in this chapter) can convey

healing; a summary of vehicles for healing in Vol. IV Chapter 3.

[86] More on **religions and spirituality** in Volume III.

[87] Some churches label complementary therapies and healing given outside their aegis as *New Age treatments*, which to them connotes a suspicion of potential involvement with evil.

[88] See Vol. III Chapter 6 on **spirit possession**.

[89] This is more often due to the poor judgement of self-styled exorcists than of the established ministries of deliverance, although the latter sometimes may also misdiagnose and treat inappropriately. Research on commonalities and differences in psychiatric and deliverance diagnoses and treatments is needed.

[90] More on **dowsing and radionics** in Vol. II Chapter 3.

[91] See **geopathic stress** in Vol. II Chapter 3.

[92] Benor 1992, discussed in Vol. II Chapter 2; IV-3.

[93] For instance, a dowser asked if a man was *allergic to milk*, receiving a "no" response. When the man related that he got indigestion with milk, the dowser asked *if milk was bad for this man*, receiving a "yes" response. Like many adults, this man lacked the enzyme necessary for digesting cow's milk but was not allergic to it.

[94] See **description of a pull-out** in Vol. IV Chapter 1.

[95] reviewed in Vol. I Chapter 4.

[96] reviewed in Vol. I Chapters 4 and 5.

[97] See discussion of craniosacral therapy in Vol. II Chapter 2.

[98] This is shifting gradually. See especially the writings of John Upledger, reviewed in Vol. II Chapter 2.

[99] See **craniosacral osteopathy**, and craniosacral therapy, including research, in Vol. II Chapter 2.

[100] Brennan 1987; 1993; Lowen; Pierrakos. **Bioenergetics** is discussed in Vol. II Chapter 1.

Endnotes Chapter 2 Measurements of Healers' Effects

[1] "Zena" is a composite of several nurse healers' reports.

[2] 4,500 gauss

[3] In the vicinity of 188.8 millimicrons.

[4] A multiple internal reflection (MIR) chamber, which is sensitive to wavelengths outside the normal laboratory range (Fenwick/ Hopkins).

[5] *Half-life* means the time it takes until half the strength of the effect is lost.

[6] This is a bi-refringent (a doubly refractive crystal) stage, which has not been previously reported and which, subsequently, Dean himself could not

reproduce (Dean 1987).

[7] See discussion on **non-hertzian fields** in Vol. IV Chapter 3.

[8] See discussions on these below and in Vol. IV Chapter 2 and 3. Schwartz et al. also found that this water had a specific peak at 1000 cm[-1] on Raman spectroscopy. Water treated with a caduceus coil or with a repetition rate of 30kHz produced changes in ultraviolet spectroscopy This effect was retained by the water over several months.

[9] Schwartz et al. used old equipment (the only equipment available to them) which did not have temperature controls for the samples being measured. This could have introduced variability in the measurements.

[10] Research of healing effects on DNA by the Institute of HeartMath is reviewed in Vol. I Chapters 4 and 5

[11] Two-tailed Wilcoxon test, z = -2.8 for statistical significance.

[12] One-tailed test.

[13] Patrovsky 1978; 1979; 1983b.

[14] See descriptions of **Picardi experiments on calcareous precipitates** in Gauquelin 1968, reviewed in Vol. II Chapter 4.

[15] by the editor of *Spiritual Frontiers,* 1980

[16] See more on variability with **geomagnetic and planetary influences** in Vol. I Chapter 3, Footnote 12, and in Vol. II Chapter 4.

[17] See also the recent studies of Radin on **group parapsychological effects** in Vol. I Chapter 3.

[18] Saklani did not use an MIR chamber in his measurements.. See studies of Saklani in Vol. I Chapter 4.

[19] See also Frydrychowski et al. on a study of **human serum photon emission**, reviewed in Vol. I Chapter 4.

[20] The studies of Watkins and colleagues are, reviewed in Vol. I Chapter 4. Influencing matter through intent is termed *psychokinesis* (PK). Healing is considered by some researchers to be *biological PK*. Their term for *healer* is *PK subject*. More on parapsychology in Vol. I Chapter 3

[21] More on **fields and energies associate with healing** in Vol. II Chapte 3; IV-2 and 3.

[22] Not to be confused with Herbert Benson of Harvard.

[23] See also Wilson and Barber for a discussion of **people who are gifted with psi, healing and visual imaging abilities**; Reviewed in Vol. II Chapter 1.

[24] See more on Rein's studies of Laskow in Vol. I Chapter 5.

[25] See Guogang Chen (listed in bibliography) for a Chinese study of external qigong on water, measured by Raman spectrometry.

[26] We must, of course, differentiate between magnetism as it is used here to

refer to EM fields surrounding an actual magnet and its use in the last century to describe hypnotic effects.

[27] **"Thoughtography"** is discussed in Vol. I Chapter 3.

[28] See Vol. II Chapter 3 and IV-3 on **Kirlian photography**.

[29] I am interested in developing surveys to explore which psychic and healing abilities cluster together.

Endnotes Chapter 3 Psi Phenomena

[1] Rhine 1961; 67; 78.

[2] Jahn & Dunne 1987; Puthoff & Targ; Schmidt; and others in Edge et al.

[3] The Biblical Matthew 25:31-33 appears to have been the source for these terms.

[4] Haraldsson; Hislop; Murphet 1972; 1978; Sandweiss.

[5] See also Pulos 1982 for further material on Thomas. McClure reports on a similar case of **light phenomena**. An excellent review of biological light phenomena is presented by Alvarado.

[6] Houck 1984b discusses electron microscopy of **metal bent by PK**. Hasted et al.; Isaacs 1985 discuss piezoelectric studies of PKMB. Kelly discusses **psychotronics**, the term used in (former) Eastern Block countries for mind-machine interactions. There are several early reports of bending of plastic cutlery in the same manner as metal is bent. As the molecular structure of plastic is very different from that of metals, this may add an important dimension to our clues regarding PK mechanisms. There are also some less well studied **related PK effects**, of plywood and of leather rings which have been joined by PK into chains, further broadening the PK horizons (Isaacs 1981). For discussions on paradigm shifts implied by macro-PK see Braude 1979a; b; 1986; Collins/Pinch.

[7] The originator of this approach is Jack Houck 1983; 1984a.

[8] More on **metal bending** in Eisenbud 1982; Franklin; Sasaki/Ochi; Shafer.

[9] See discussion in Vol. IV Chapter 3 on **reasons healing and psi have not been accepted**.

[10] On **thoughtography** see Eisenbud 1967; 1977; 1984; Eisenbud/Stillings; Fukurai; Ivanova 1978; Permutt; Rogo 1970; Ullman; Uphoff/Uphoff 1980

[11] For other good reviews of **poltergeist** material see Fodor 1958; Podmore; Thurston. Rogo 1974a discusses issues of the poltergeist and psychotherapy. Manning 1974 has a nice personal description of his experiences in producing poltergeist phenomena. Goss 1979 presents an annotated bibliography on poltergeists.

[12] For a comparison and contrast with **spirit phenomena** see Vol. III Chapters 4 and 5.

¹³ For more on **psi abilities in psychics and healers,** see Garrett 1949; Heywood; Karagulla; Kucharev/Vilenskaya; Manning; McCaffery; Murphet; Playfair 1975; L. Rhine 1970; Ullman 1974a; b; Uphoff 1987; Uphoff/Uphoff 1980a; b; Vasiliev 1963; 1965; Vitenskaya 1981a; b; **psi in animals** Rhine/Feather; Vilenskaya 1986. Interesting **reviews of psi** can be found in Edge et al. 1986 (excellent overall review); Fedor 1966; Haynes 1961; Inglis 1977; Moore 1976; Moss 1974; Murphy 1970 Nash 1978; 1986 (excellent overall reviews); Pratt 1973; Robinson 1981; Schmidt 1975; Sudre 1960 (translates much foreign language literature); Taylor 1975a; Ullman 1974; Watson 1979. Considerations of **aspects of research in psi** are provided by Ashby; Beloff 1974; 1977; Braude 1979a; b; Cadoret; Carington; Edge 1978a; Ehrenwald 1976a; Gauld 1976; Humphrey/Nicol; Irwin 1978; 1979; 1985; Jahn 1982; 1984; Jahn/ Dunne 1987; Kreitler/Kreitler; Marshall; Millar 1978; Nash 1978; 1986; Rao 1977; Rauscher 1983; Richards; Schmidt 1974; Stanford 1977; Tart 1963; 1972; 1975; Wolman 1977. On **psi, psychotherapy and psychopathology** see Benor 1986; Burg; Eilbert/Schmeidler; Krippner 1969; Mintz/Schmeidler; Pederson-Krag; Peterson 1975; 1987; Rogo 1974. On **hypnosis and psi** see LeCron; **other states of consciousness and psi** - Neppe; Osis/Bokert; Tart 1972. For discussions of **fears of psi** see Benor 1990 (also Volume IV-3, under 'Reasons healing has not been accepted'); Eisenbud 1983; Tart 1984; 1986a; Chapter III-13. Inglis 1986 discusses **retrocognitive dissonance,** whereby people seek to distort their memories of psi events to make them consonant **with** conventional reality. Bloch; Estes/Worth; Freud 1963 are of interest as **historical notes on psi. Psi in archaeology** is presented by S. Schwartz 1983; **military applications of psi** in Harary; McRae; Targ. On **conformance Theory** - Gruber; McCarthy et al. 1979; Brand 1980; Stanford/ Fox. On **physiological reactions to ESP** - Dean 1962; Lloyd 1973; Schouten 1976; Sieveking 1981; Targ/Puthoff 1974; Tart 1963. On **brain functions, hemispheric laterality and psi** - Brand 1975; Broughton; Ehrenwald; Lloyd. On the search for **electromagnetic fields to account for ESP** see Balanovski/Taylor. On **gravity and psi** see Gallimore; **geomagnetic influences on psi** - Persinger 1985; 1987; Rogo 1986a; Schaut/Persinger; Polyakov; Sergeyev; Tunyi. See Newton-Smith; Shallis for further discussion of **time,** and Barrington; Gribbin for discussion of apparent slips or warps in time. A movement among American **fundamentalists against "New Age" thought,** including psi and consciousness research, wholistic approaches, etc. is brewing, represented by J. Carr; Cumbey; Groothius. On **negative reactions by the science establishment to psi** see Mc Connell/Kuzman; Palmer, Honorton/Utts. On **fraudulent psychics**: Bishop; Keene; Randi.

¹⁴ Stanford 1974a; b; 1975; 1978.

¹⁵ Brand 1979; 1980; McCarthy 1979.

¹⁶ For more on **modern physics** see Vol. IV Chapter 2.

[17] On the **fallacy of trying to measure one science with the yardstick of another** see H. Smith; LeShan/Margenau 1980; 1982; Wilbur 1979.

[18] Braud 1994a; b; Utts.

[19] See Vol. II Chapter 4, for more **geobiogical effects**.

[20] Vol. IV Chapter 3 considers many such **factors relevant to healing**.

[21] Skeptics Alcock; Hansel; Neher and review by A. Hyman; skeptic Alcock reviewed by Morris; skeptics J. Booth; K. Frazier; M. Harris; P. Kurz and review by D. Stokes; skeptic Nolen criticized by Stelter; Randi reviewed by Benor 1989; U.S. National Academy of Sciences and McConnell/Kuzmen Clark. See also Dossey 1998b.

[22] See an example of this sort in Rosa et al. reviewed in Vol. I Chapter 4.

[23] See end of Vol. I Chapter 4 for a list of replicated studies.

[24] See research of Braud/Schlitz reviewed in Vol. I Chapter 4.

[25] See Vol. II Chapter 1; Naranjo/Ornstein on **right and left brain functions**.

[26] See Vol. III Chapter 7 on **psychic surgery**.

[27] See Vol. I Chapter 4 reviewing the Solvin 1982 experiment on malarial mice.

[28] See for instance the **joining techniques** of Neurolinguistic Programming through synchronizing breathing (Bandler/Grinder).

[29] See Vol. III Chapter 6 on mediumistic phenomena.

[30] See review of infrasonic sound research in Vol. I Chapter 4.

[31] J. Smith; G. Rein 1978; 1986; Muehsam reviewed in Vol. I Chapter 4.

Endnotes Chapter 4 Controlled Studies

[1] The only complementary therapies with more research are hypnosis (which has been studied over 200 years), acupuncture and psychoneuro-immunology, discussed in Vol. II Chapter 1.

[2] There are only two studies in this category. Sicher et al. report no checks to see that there weren't differences in treatments between the several centers where the patients with AIDS were treated. As there are no effective treatments for AIDS, any differences in treatments given at the verious centers are unlikely to have influenced the experimental or control group significantly. A brief report by Braud warrants credence, based on his overall meticulous work.

[3] There is evidence that randomization is actually impossible to achieve, due to super-psi. I have, however, acknowledged conventional wisdom by separating out those studies where randomization is by methods other than mechanically random procedures. More on randonization below.

[4] I offer consultation to researchers. See www.WholisticHealingResearch.com

[5] Randomization in the light of psi powers is problematic. Ramdomization by automated computer programs is considered the optimal approach in conventional science. Once we become aware of the PK effects on random number generators (RNGs), it seems possible that experiments could influence RNGs in line with their beliefs and through the agency of super-psi, to generate numbers which would assign subjects with appropriate characteristics to experimental or control groups in ways which could bias the results in the experimenters' preferred directions. In parapsychology this is called *intuituve data sorting*. See discussion of psi effects in Vol. I Chapter 3.

While it might seem far-fetched to suggest that psi powers could be used in such a complex way, research shows this is entirely possible. See for instance the study of Solfvin of malaria in mice in this chapter.

If this is the case, then there is really no way in which randomization can be achieved which is free of experimenter influence.

[6] See discussion on suggestion, placebo and experimenter effects in Vol. II Chapter 1.

[7] In tabulating the level of significance of results of studies, where more than one result is obtained and one result has a $p < .01$ or better, I have credited the study as demonstrating that level of significance—even though other findings in the study might not have reached that level of significance.

[8] See further discussions on **Type I and Type II research errors** in Vol. I Intro. and Vol. II Chapter 2.

[9] See the conclusion section at the end of Vol. I Chapters 4 and 5 in which the research is briefly summarized; and the discussion on **theories explaining healing** in Vol. IV Chapter 2.

[10] Excluded were: Patients admitted for cardiac transplant, where hospital stays were expected to be much longer than the general average on the CCU, and patients admitted for less than 24 hours because it could take longer than that to inform the intercessors to commence praying for them.

[11] This covered the CCU patients' entire hospitalization in 95 percent of the cases.

[12] Stage C-3, including CD4+ cell counts of less than 200 cells, a history of at least one AIDS-defining disease, and taking prophylactic treatment against Pneumococcus carinii.

[13] Improvements were noted on 4 out of 6 subscales, including depression, tension, confusion, and fatigue.

[14] Stage II HIV disease, when CD4 counts are less than 500/ cu mm (Center for Disease Control).

[15] This study follows Dixon's pilot exploration of healing reviewed in Vol. I Chapter 5. The findings on CD cells are important and therefore the study is inserted here. The statistically significant findings on anxiety and depression belong in a later section of this chapter, and are inserted in the table on healing for subjective experiences. In calculating the numbers of studies with significant results this study is counted only once.

[16] Dixon 1994; 1995, reviewed in Vol. I Chapter 5.

[17] Grad's research with plants is described later in this chapter.

[18] See description of **TT healing** in Vol. I Chapter 1.

[19] Wilson 1995 agrees that Krieger's work was methodologically weak and poorly reported.

[20] **Reiki healing** is discussed in Vol. I Chapter 1.

[21] See review of Snel/Hol later in this chapter.

[22] Straneva, reviewed later in this chapter.

[23] With or without salpingo-oophorectomy and/or appendectomy.

[24] Synchronistically, Zvi's father and my father were close friends in Israel for many years.

[25] This study is reviewed in greater detail below, along with other studies of healing for anxiety.

[26] Leb is reviewed later in this chapter under healing for subjective problems.

[27] **Need as a factor in healing** is discussed in Vol. IV Chapter 3.

[28] This study is reviewed from a brief Dissertation Abstract.

[29] Limited changes in sentence structure, without alteration in content, have been made to facilitate the flow of the presentations.

[30] No ratings of research rigor are given to translated studies.

[31] More on **Kirlian photography** in Vol. II Chapter 2.

[32] Reviewed in later reports.

[33] See furthur studies of external qi on EEGs; Z. Chen et al.; G. Liu et al.; and a study of infrasonic devices which simulate effects of external qi emissions: Z. Yuan.

[34] More on **neurohormonal and psychoneuroimmunological systems** in Vol. II Chapter 1.

[35] See more on biological **energies involved in healing** in Vol. IV Chapter 3.

[36] Further Chinese studies which clarify how infrasonic sound and healing are related. See G. Lin et al.; X. Peng et al.

[37] For further studies of external qi healing see: for diabetes (L. Feng et al.); hypertension with renal insufficiency (Pan/Zhang); pain (Houshen Lin; J. Zhang et al.); liver and gallstones (Jinzheng Li/Hekun Liu); cerebral atrophy (Guang Zhao/Qigang Xie); softening scars (Dingxing Ma); hypermetropia (far-sightedness) in children (L. Li et al.); food allergies (Chow Chu); putting people to sleep (Z. Zhong et al.); cardiac arrhythmias (C. Lo et al.); on skin blood flow (Xiu et al.); evoked EEG potentials (G. Liu et al.). These Chinese studies are referenced in the bibliography.

[38] More on **radionics devices** in Vol. II Chapter 4.

[39] Vol. II Chapter 1 addresses the issues of **placebo reactions and suggestion** in detail.

[40] See also Dixon, reviewed in Vol. I Chapter 5 on **cost effectiveness of healing**, including **savings on medication costs**

[41] Specific prodecures are not described in the study.

[42] This study is a late insertion which I was able to obtain only as a brief abstract from Slater.

[43] An account in the Supplement explores Bzdek's responses to these points.

[44] **Craniosacral osteopathy** is reviewed in Vol. II Chapter 2.

[45] On these and other **complementary therapies as energy medicine** see Vol. II Chapter 2. Network Chiropractic is an exception in its acknowledgment of energy aspects of its interventions.

(networkchiropractic.org)

[46] More on **Sensations during healing** in Vol. IV Chapter 3.

[47] More on **reasons healing has not been accepted** in Vol. IV Chapter 3.

[48] See descriptions of other **dynamic healers** in Vol. I Chapter 1.

[49] See author's experiences with healing in Vol. I Chapter 1

[50] Amended by Goodrich in personal communication 1997.

[51] See **LeShan** 1974a, reviewed in Vol. IV Chapter 2; **healer explanatory systems** of LeShan and Goodrich in Vol. I-Introduction.

[52] **Subjective sensations during healing** are also noted earlier in this chapter in the experiment with Reiki healers (Schlitz and Braud); with Aho in Sundblom et al; also in Turner 1969c, reviewed in Vol. I Chapter 5.

[53] Clark and Clark review some of the same **TT** material and conclude that there is insufficient evidence to support a belief in healing. I agree with Rogo 1986 that Clark and Clark take far too limited a look at the available evidence and, consequently, their conclusions are unwarranted. Meta-analyses by Abbot; Astin et al; Winsted-Fry/Kijek confirmed significant effects of TT in several series of studies.

[54] **Methods of learning healing** are reviewed in Vol. I Chapter 1.

[55] The few words of summary are taken from Slater, p. 133, Masters Abstracts International 1985, 42: 24(3). The volume for this year is 23 and no abstract is listed in the index under that name for this year.

[56] *SHEN healing therapists* in particular have reported good results with healing of people traumatized by terrorist activities. See description of SHEN healing in Vol. I Chapter 1.

[57] Because babies in hospitals haven't complained a lot, their emotional needs have been sorely neglected. In deeper psychotherapy, people may often bring up memories of traumatic events around the experience of being in utero, undergoing the trauma of birth and difficult experiences of early infancy. These traumas occur before babies are generally assumed by conventional psychologists to be able to absorb or recall them. Rebirthing,

LSD psychotherapy, and other forms of depth psychology are particularly likely to unearth such memories. More on some aspects of early memories in Vol. II Chapter 1 and Vol. III Chapter 3.

[58] Healing can be given through many modalities for various problems. Terry Woodford has developed audiotapes for babies with colic (and for the elderly) which, he reports, puts them to sleep within minutes (Audio Therapy Innovations, Inc., PO Box 550, Colorado Springs, CO 80901 719-473-0100).

[59] This is called the "file drawer effect," after the assumption that negative studies may be left, unpublished, in researchers' file drawers.

[60] See also study of Ogawa et al. on the effects of qigong healing on skin temperature of healers and healees.

[61] See also the study of Dixon, earlier in this chapter, on anxiety and depression. Dixon's findings are included in the table for anxiety and depression at the end of this section.

[62] See Vol. II Chapter 2 for a discussion of the **chakras,** the energy centers on the midline of the body.

[63] See also studies of Wright; Schwartz et al. on energy field assessment later in this chapter.

[64] See Vol. II Chapter 3 for more on **pendulums and dowsing** phenomena.

[65] Hodges; Lombardi; Lorusso/Glick; Mella; Oldfield/Coghill; Vogel See also discussion on the **use of crystals** in healing in Vol. IV Chapter 3.

[66] "a safe, low amperage (1-4) milliamps) stimulator which has been effective in relieving depression in some patients using it daily for two weeks" Shealy 1979; 1989.

[67] See description of **autogenic training**, a method of profound self-relaxation, in Vol. II Chapter 2.

[68] "90% of patients report feelings of deep relaxation within 10 minutes of photostimulation at 3 to 12 Hz." Shealy 1990.

[69] More on music and healing in Vol. II Chapter 2; IV-3.

[70] See discussions of **grief** as the highest-ranked item on the stress inventory and psychoneuroimmunology in Vol. II Chapter 1 and 2, respectively.

[71] See discussion of clairsentience in Vol. I Chapter 3..

[72] Particularly worth reading are Ivanova 1983; Ivanova with Mir; Krieger; Polyakov; Safonov; B. Schwarz; Vu; - regarding the learning and practice of methods of psi diagnosis. Many suggest that **a person may also diagnose his or her own illness**, such as with cancer, on an unconscious basis, including Dethlefson and Dahlke; Nash 1987. Art therapy and clinical use of drawings (e.g. Kubler Ross 1981; Siegel 1986) demonstrate a deep awareness of the unconscious mind regarding a person's own health status. Much of the latter is reviewed in Vol. II Chapter 1.

[73] See study of Turner in Vol. I Chapter 5; Study of Leb earlier in this chapter (without blinds).

[74] Dowsers (people who can identify water and other materials and information with the use of various devices) have been shown to respond to electromagnetic energy, as discussed in Vol. II Chapter 4.

[75] See discussion of Engel's findings in Vol. I Chapter 5, and of temperature and other healing sensations in Vol. IV Chapter 3.

[76] See a discussion of **dermal** optics in Vol. II Chapters 1 and 3, and IV-3.

[77] See a detailed discussion of **reasons healing and psi have not been accepted** in Vol. IV Chapter 3; earlier versions in Benor 1990; Dossey 1993.

[78] HEF = human energy field

[79] p. 1007, column 1, para 3.

[80] I must say that I am grateful to Rosa et al. for identifying a host of TT dissertations which I had not been aware of. Even with these references in hand, I was only been able to locate 3 of these in the hard copy of *Dissertation Abstracts International.* It was only on CD ROM disk that I was able to locate most of them.

[81] See discussion of **electrodermal responses** in Vol. II Chapter 1; studies of healing effects on electrodermal responses earlier in this chapter; Bagchi/Wenger.

[82] See discussion of **Kirlian photography** in Vol. II Chapter 3.

[83] See discussion on **sheep and goat effects** in Vol. I Chapter 3.

[84] See also the study of Leb, earlier in this chapter; and the pilot study of aura assessments by D. Benor in Vol. I Chapter 5

[85] This is a rather lengthy response to a very limited study. I feel it is warranted in view of the serious weight given to it by the editor of the prestigious journal in which it appeared.

[86] See also criticisms of Rosa et al. in Dossey 1998b; Leskowitz 1998.

[87] Experiment 2 is sketchily described in this article.

[88] See Vol. I Chapter 3 for more on **Stanford's conformance theory**. Braud (1993) points out that his own lability/inertia model (Braud 1981) and several quantum mechanical and noise-reorganization models of PK make similar predictions regarding the susceptibility of random systems to psi influence. See Rush 1976; Oteri 1975; Puharich 1979.

[89] I rate this study as II rather than III because Braud has published other, similar studies with sufficient detail for full assessment of the results and they are meticulously performed. In another experiment based on the **Conformance hypothesis**, using rye seeds and a random number generator, no statistically significant results were found (Munson - reviewed later in this chapter). See also Spindrift, in chapter 5.

[90] See also meta-analysis of Schlitz/Braud 1997.

[91] More on geo-biological effects in Vol. II Chapter 4.

[92] Braud (1993) points out that there are parallel studies in parapsychology where physiological measures were studied as indicators of psi responses: plethysmography— Dean 1962; EEG and GSR—Tart 1963; EEG—Lloyd 1973; Targ/Puthoff 1974. For reviews of these studies see Beloff 1974; Millar 1979; Morris 1977; Tart 1963.

[93] **Changes in electrical potentials in plants caused by mental influences** are reviewed in Ostrander/Schroeder; Vogel.

[94] See S. Yang et al. for a Chinese study of external qi on electromyographic measurements of muscle tension.

[95] See Ferguson, above, on the **SETTS test.**

[96] The reader might wish to explore this with the cooperation of another person. (Common sense cautions us not to strain weak or painful muscles in doing such exercises.) Hold your arm straight out to your side from your shoulder. Let your friend press down at the count of three on your wrist with two fingers of her or his hand to test your normal strength. Then think of some food which you have cravings for and let your friend test your strength again, noting any differences from your baseline strength.

The aim is not to push so hard that one completely overcomes their strength, but just to have a sense of how strong their hold is. You might also do this while thinking of something that makes you feel sad, or of anything else which may be a negative experience. When you have the image clear in your mind, again on the count of three let them press down on your arm. If the thing you image is a negative experience then your arm will usually be markedly weaker. Next, image to yourself that you are eating something which is healthy, engaged in an enjoyable experience, etc. Testing your arm this time should produce a stronger resistance. This allows you to explore your inner wisdom. It is of course, subject to distortions of anxieties, beliefs, and the like, but can still be a useful tool for inner explorations. More on **kinesiology** in Vol. II Chapter 2.

[97] Though this seems to be a biological energy phenomenon, it is not a spiritual healing effect. Therefore this study is not included in the research summary table.

[98] See more on **muscle testing for effects of qigong healing** in Omura, cited in Sancier 1991, reviewed in Vol. I Chapter 5.

[99] See Estebany's story in Vol. I Chapter 1.

[100] Summarizes Grad 1963; 1964; 1964b.

[101] See also the effects of qigong healing on enhancing recovery from bone fractures and brain injuries in animals, listed at the end of this section.

[102] More on **vehicles for healing** in Vol. IV Chapter 3; See also Estebany in Vol. I Chapter 1.

[103] Effects of **healer-treated water on plants** are described below.

[104] See Vol. II Chapter 1 for more on **experimenter effects**.

[105] **Sheep/goat effects** are discussed in Vol. I Chapter 3.

[106] See more on **vehicles for healing** in Vol. IV Chapter 3.

[107] **Time displacement of psi effects** is discussed in Vol. I Chapter 3.

[108] See also D. L. Zhang et al. for external qigong healing effects on immune system suppressed mice; R. Wu et al. for external qigong healing effects on subcellular elements in rats.

[109] It is unfortunate that the study of Collipp on healing for leukemia, reviewed earlier in this chapter, is such a poor one.

[110] See also light discussion of Knowles 1959 on possible healing influences on growth rates in rats.

[111] See the study of Collipp, earlier in this chapter, as an example of this problem.

[112] Translated abstract.

[113] See conference summaries of **qigong healing** in the Qigong Database of Sancier.

[114] **Psychoneuroimmunology (PNI) and other aspects of self-healing** are discussed in Vol. II Chapter 1.

[115] See also the studies of **action of healing on cells in the laboratory**, later in this chapter.

[116] Cesium emits radioactivity.

[117] Recently developed anesthetic agents allow people to waken very rapidly. This may lessen the need for healing in anesthesia.

[118] See full discussion on **negative effects of healing** in Vol. IV Chapter 3.

[119] See also Cahn and Muscle's experiment on an enzyme, described in a later section of this chapter, in which a linger effect was suggested.

[120] Watkins 1979 also describes **effects of healing on photographic film** placed under mice during the healing experiments with anesthesia. See discussion on photographic effects of healing; in Vol. I Chapter 3; Vol. II Chapter 3; Vol. IV Chapter 3.

[121] **Vehicles for healing** are reviewed in Vol. IV Chapter 3.

[122] See more **Chinese studies of healing for cancer in mice**: X. Chen et al.; L. Li et al.; Yang/Guan.

[123] See also the work of Julie Motz, on **healing given during surgery**, described in Vol. I Chapter 1. Healing given during surgery appears to open people to very deep awarenesses of old hurts which may be stored as memories in body tissues. See more on body-mind memories in Vol. II Chapters 1 and 2; Remarkable organ memories after transplant operation.

[124] Summarizes Grad 1963; 1964a; 1964b.

[125] Summarizes Grad 1964a; b; 1963; 1961.

[126] For more on **vehicles for healing** see Vol. I Chapter 3 and Vol. IV Chapter 3.

[127] **Dessication produced by healing** is reviewed in Vol. IV Chapter 3.

[128] See Vol. I Chapter 5 for a discussion on **shamanic practices**.

[129] See studies of Grad and of Wallack in this section.

[130] Sometimes also called "black thumb."

[131] See discussion on **dowsing and radionics** in Vol. II Chapter 4. Dowsing is the use of instruments such as rods or pendulums to find answers to questions which are held in focus in the dowser's mind. Classically, dowsers have helped to locate the best place for digging wells for water and oil. The dowsing instrument appears to work as a dial or feedback device for the unconscious mind of the dowser.

Dowsers in Britain may help public utilities companies to locate buried pipes and wires for which the maps are unavailable. Dowsing has also been used in wartime to locate landmines.

Vol. II Chapter 3 is devoted to dowsing and other subtle energy field phenomena.

[132] Studies of **healing action on enzymes** are described later in this chapter.

[133] K. Cohen; Kaptchuk; Thie.

[134] Shubentsov, reviewed in Vol. I Chapter 1.

[135] Luther Burbank—in Yogananda; Benor 1988; also on website www.WholisticHealingResearch.com. Dolin—in May/Vilenskaya; Edge 1976; Horowitz et al (negative findings); Kmetz; Ostrander/Schroeder; van Gelder (Kunz); Vogel 1974; Watson 1975.

[136] See discussion on **psychokinesis** in Vol. I Chapter 3.

[137] **Factors which may influence healing** are summarized and discussed in Vol. IV Chapter 3.

[138] Bechterev; Braud 1979; Duval; Etra; Gruber; Nash/Nash 1980; Osis 1952

[139] e.g. Turner Aug. 1969; 1970 (reviewed in Vol. Chapter 5); Shine

[140] Olga Worrall's healing is described in Vol. I Chapter 1.

[141] For more on bacterial mutation see also studies of Nash/ Nash, reviewed next; J. Gu et al.

[142] Microorganisms are used to manufacture antibiotics. Other studies showed effects of healing upon several such strains of bacteria: Z. Liu et al. 1993b.

[143] Stanford's conformance theory states that PK is more likely to be effective when acting upon a randomly distributed system. Healing would appear to be PK acting upon living systems, which have many physiological functions that are enormously complex or random (distribution of chemicals through the body; firing of nerve impulses, distribution of genes between chromosomes during cell division; and more). More on Conformance theory in Vol. I Chapter 3. Conformance theory was also relevant to the studies of Braud and colleagues on allobiofeedmack, discussed earlier in this chapter.

[144] On bacterial growth see also Nash/Nash, earlier in this chapter; Liu et

al; Gu/Wang/Wu et al. 1990 on bacterial mutation with qigong healing, reviewed later in this chapter; on fungal mutations Gu/Pan/Wu 1990.

[145] See review of Solfvin's study on malarial mice later this chapter

[146] **Proxy agents for healing** are discussed in Vol. IV Chapter 3.

[147] **Sheep/goat effects** are discussed in Vol. I Chapter 3.

[148] On **external qigong healing effects on fungal growth** see Gu/Pan/Wu; on mutations: Gu/Ding/Wu; Gu/Wang/Wu. For more on residual or linger effects of healing, see studies on anesthetized mice, reviewed above.

[149] See Grad, 1967 on the effects of saline held by depressed people on plant growth, reviewed above.

[150] The first two studies on Manning are also of interest in terms of telepathic controls over animal mobility though they are not directly relevant to healing.

[151] See also a similar experiment by Kmetz with Kraft, described in Vol. I Chapter 5.

[152] For studies of external qigong on **nasopharyngeal cancer cells and DNA**: X. Chen et al., L. Li et al.; on **erythrocytes and leukemia cells** Yang/Guan.

[153] Odd spontaneous effects such as the movement of objects without physical intervention of any agent are called random spontaneous psychokinesis (RSPK). These are discussed in Vol. I Chapter 3.

[154] For studies of external qigong on electrokinetic measurements in Raji cells: Mengdan Zhang et al.; and on nerve cells A. Liu et al 1990; G. Liu et al 1993. There are also studies showing effects of healing on EEGs.

[155] M. Green in this chapter; Strelkauskas/Quinn in Vol. Chapter 5.

[156] Other studies from China which explore parts of the immune system that may be influenced by healing; L. Feng 1988, 1990; L. Gu et al. 1988.

[157] 500 mg per ml. in .001 N HCI, pH3.

[158] As demonstrated by the studies of Wirth and Cram, reviewed earlier in this chapter.

[159] See Vol. IV Chapter 3 on **sensations during healing;** Turner in Vol. I Chapter 5; Clairsentient assessments earlier in this chapter.

[160] Except for some viruses, composed of RNA.

[161] Further studies on these methods are included in Vol. I Chapter 5.

[162] See other studies on **healing effects on water** in Vol. I Chapter 3.

[163] See summary of **vehicles for healing** in Vol. IV Chapter 3.

[164] See discussions on EM fields in Vol. II Chapters 3, Vol. IV Chapters 2 and 3.

[165] Solfvin 1984 mentions the following **unpublished manuscripts on healing research** which I have been unable to obtain: S. B. Harary; Heaton.

[166] Some studies I have placed in the "questionably acceptable" category may belong in the firmly convincing category, the deficiency being that I have not been able to obtain information to satisfy me of this. There are numbers of master's theses and doctoral dissertations that may belong in either of the above categories. I have simply not had the resources to purchase and review these.

The ranking and categorizing in this section may unfairly classify studies with excellent overall designs into a III or IV category, when their problems involved a single confounding variable (such as the failure to account for medications given to subjects in E and C groups). In a similar manner, studies of poorer quality may appear in III due to lack of information about them.

[167] Technical data not reported adequately or some other deficiency which leaves a question in an otherwise well designed study.

[168] This summary includes even studies with non-significant effects to round out the picture on replications. It is conservative in that translated studies have not been included in this summary, with the exception of Onetto/Elguin, which is a study done for professional degree at a university. Only single entries have been made for each report, even where more than one experiment has been reported within a study. The less rigorous studies have been included where the replications they present strengthen the possibility that further research in particular areas appears warranted. Greater details of studies can be found in the text and tables.

[169] Distant healing lends itself well to double-blind research design, because it makes it easy for researchers to assure that subjects do not know who received healing, while not requiring a mock treatment for the C group.

Endnotes Chapter 5 Further Clues

[1] This chapter is clearly open to **type I errors** (of accepting as true something which is false), but is meant to counterbalance Chapter 4, which is more prone to **type II errors** (of rejecting as false something which is true). See Tunnell for a discussion on the need for field research.

[2] For **anecdotal descriptions of healing** see Vol. I Chapter 1.

[3] Block: Dingwall; Playfair 1987.

[4] See also Vasiliev for a more recent report on telepathic hypnotic induction.

[5] See Vol. II Chapter 1 on **Hypnosis and Self-healing.**

[6] *Journal of the Statistical Society*, Vol. xxii, p. 355.

[7] There are very few studies of healing for infections. See C. Chou cited in the bibliography for a study of emitted qi on moniliasis (*candida* yeast infections)

[8] See discussion of hysterical (conversion) reactions in Vol. II Chapter 1.

[9] See reviews of **Lourdes and other shrine cases** also in Agnellet; Carrel; Fulda; Garner; F. Huxley; Lafitte; Lange; Larcher; Leuret/Bon; McClure; Myers/Myers; Sheldon; Swan; West 1948. See Thornton for Catholic shrines in the USA and Canada. For a further discussion of Lourdes cases, see Chapter III-8; Leuret/Bon; Fulda for a detailed description of a single case. For related cases at other shrines see Lange; McClure. Various *geographic locations are said to possess particular powers.* See for instance Westwood for a review of these; also Geobiological effects in Vol. II Chapter 4.

[10] These measurements show changes similar to those brought about in water by healers. Research on healing with water as a vehicle is summarized in Vol. I Chapters 2, 4 and 5.

[11] See discussions of psi effects transcending time and space in Vol. I Chapters 3, 4; Vol. IV Chapter 3.

[12] For **surveys of healees' assessments of their own healings** see reviews at the end of Vol. I Chapter 5.

[13] Strauch's paper is "based on a joint study undertaken in Germany by the Institute for Border Areas of Psychology and Mental Hygiene and the Medical Polyclinic, both affiliated with the University of Freiburg i. Br."

[14] A more detailed report on this project, by the same author, has appeared in German in two parts in the *Zeitschrift fur Parapsychologie und Grenzgebiete der Psychologie* ('Zur Frage der 'Geistigen Heilung,'' Vol. II, No. 1; Vol IV, No. 1).

[15] **Biofeedback** and **psychoneuroimmunology (PNI)** are discussed in Vol. II Chapter 1.

[16] See also examples of Eastern European healing in Vol. I Chapter 1 (Ivanova; Krivorotov; Shubentsov; Zezulka).

[17] This study reviewed from a brief abstract.

[18] See the study of Ferguson on the **SETTS test**, in Chapter 4.

[19] See more on **South American healers** in Vol. III Chapters 7 and 8.

[20] On **mediumistic channeling** see Vol. III Chapter 5.

[21] See report of this magnetic field observation in Vol. I Chapter 2.

[22] See Rein's **theoretical discussion on Non-Hertzian fields** as mediators for healing in Vol. IV Chapter 2.

[23] These states are described in detail in the supplement to Vol. I.

[24] **Spindrift**'s work with plants is summarized later in this chapter.

[25] See more on **vehicles for healing** in Vol. IV Chapter 3.

[26] On **geobiological effects on healing and biological energy phenomena** see Vol. II Chapter 4; Vol. IV Chapter 3.

[27] See discussion of **extraneous factors which may influence healing and psi effects** in Vol. IV Chapter 3 and Tables IV-9 and IV-10.

[28] Rose 1955 briefly outlines some of this same material.

[29] See examples of **Edward's** writing in this chapter and Vol. I Chapter 1.

[30] See discussion in Vol. IV Chapter 4 on **reasons healing has not been accepted**.

[31] See discussion on **spontaneous remissions** in Everson/Cole; O'Reagan/Hirschberg, reviewed in Vol. II Chapter 1.

[32] See also Everson and Cole in Vol. II Chapter 1 on spontaneous remissions.

[33] Schmeidler/Hess review Casdorph's work and add support to its credibility.

[34] **Psychic surgery** is described in Vol. III Chapter 7.

[35] Bartrop et al., Cyton; Schleifer et al.

[36] See discussion on **self healing** in Vol. II Chapter 1; Roud for a number of similar experiences; LeShan.

[37] The absence of skin temperature change despite strong sensations of heat during healing has been a consistent finding with most researchers.

[38] More on **sensations during healing** in Vol. IV Chapter 3.

[39] **Kirlian photography** is described in Vol. II Chapter 2.

[40] See much more on **spiritual awareness and spiritual healing** in Volume III.

[41] This observation is credited to the healer **Estebany**, who describes his work in Vol. I Chapter 1.

[42] For more on TT see also Boguswski; Borelli/Heidt; Krieger 1979b; Miller; Quinn 1988; 1989; Randolph 1984; Raucheisen; Rownds; Witt; Wright.

[43] e.g. Blundell; Cade/Coxhead, reviewed in Vol. IV Chapter 3.

[44] See Kashiwasake; Kawan et al. for further studies of emitted qi on electroencephalograms.

[45] See more on infrasonic sound effects on EEGs in the report of Peng and Liu in Vol. I Chapter 4.), and L. Guolong et al.

[46] See also the review of Turner's report of **preventive healing**, later in this chapter.

[47] In the Doctor-Healer Network in England there are regular meetings of healers, doctors, nurses, and other involved therapists, discussions focus on healees, methods and theoretical issues. For several years I published a

newsletter summarizing some of the observations which came from these meetings on integrated care. I am starting DHN groups now in the US.

[48] Not to be confused with Herbert Benson at Harvard.

[49] Agpaoa (in Stelter; Motoyama); Hochenegg (also in Playfair 1988); Kraft (also in MacDonald, et al.); Krivorotov (in Adamenko 1970). See discussions in Vol. I Chapter 3; II-3; IV-3.

[50] Eisenbud 1967; Eisenbud/Stillings; Fukurai. Thoughtography is discussed in Vol. I Chapter 3; Vol. IV Chapter 3.

[51] e.g. Hochenegg, in Playfair 1988. Hochenegg's attraction of plant leaves visually suggests an electrostatic effect, as when an electrostatically charged rod attracts bits of paper. Hochenegg is known for strong electrical effects, such as lighting fluorescent bulbs with his hands. This appears to be different from the effect on flowers described by Turner.

[52] See further descriptions of the work and views of **Gordon Turner** in Vol. I Chapter 1; (also brief mention in Vol. III Chapter 5)

[53] See more on **muscle testing** as a measure of states of physical and mental health under **Applied Kinesiology** in Vol. II Chapter 2.

[54] **Acupuncture** is discussed in Vol. II Chapter 2.

[55] See Estebany, Krieger, Vol. I Chapter 1; Grad, Saklani, Vol. IV Chapter 4, and detailed discussion in Vol. IV Chapter 3.

[56] American name: Laura V. Faith

[57] See also B. Brennan 1987; 1993; Pierrakos 1987 for similar methods of learning aura perception.

[58] See **risks vs. benefits of healing** in the end of this chapter; **negative effects of healing** Vol. IV Chapter 3; Dossey 1993.

[59] Then named Roberton.

[60] More on **aura diagnosis** in Vol. I Chapter 4 (hand perception) and Vol. II Chapter 2 (visable aura); on **biological energy fields** in Vol. II Chapter 3; Vol. IV Chapter 3; and on **the nature of reality and how we shape it** in Volumes III and IV.

[61] The reader might wish to do a simple experiment: Fill three pie tins or shallow bowls of equal size with equal amounts of potting soil from the same source. Number each one clearly with a label or marker. Sort out corn seeds of equal size from the same seed packet. Place an equal number of seeds in the soil of each container, being careful to position each seed with its pointy end down and flat end up, and to bury each to the same depth. Water each container with the same amount of water every one to three days, depending upon how fast they dry—being certain not to let the containers dry completely. See that each container gets an equal amount of light. Think positive, loving thoughts or project the wish to heal the first container. Ignore the second. Think angry or negative thoughts about the third. (Some prefer to omit the third.) If your healing ability with plants is

strong, you should see a noticeable difference between the speed at which seeds germinate and the amount of growth at the end of two weeks. Results may vary when you give healing at different times of day, and under different phases of the moon.

[62] e.g. Shubentsov in Vol. Chapter 1.

[63] Solfvin's study is reviewed in Vol. I Chapter 4.

[64] Super-ESP is discussed in Vol. I Chapter 3.

[65] It is a sad footnote to the Spindrift studies that its two investigators, both Christian Scientists, were ostracized from their church over differences in views over the conduct of research on spiritual matters. At the same time these healing researchers were terribly frustrated by the lack of interest shown in their work by the scientific community. In despair, they both suicided.

[66] **Worrall's cloud chamber study** is briefly described in Vol. I Chapter 3; Vol. IV Chapter 3.

[67] Further studies on these methods are included in Vol. I Chapter 4.

[68] **The Spindrift studies on intentionality in healing** are summarized earlier in this chapter.

[69] C. Norman Shealy, M.D. is a pioneer in wholistic medical treatments, including intuitive diagnosis and healing. See his studies in Vol. I Chapter 4; Foreword to Volume II.

[70] See discussions on **alternate realities** in LeShan 1974; 1976, reviewed in detail in Vol. IV Chapter 2.

[71] Further references which examine healing with some semblance of scientific approach include: Anonymous 1887; 1895; Davitashvili 1983; Dresser; Elliotson; Ferda; Goodrich 1976; Haynes 1977a; b; Herbert 1970 (too brief to be very helpful); 1979; Holzer 1974b; 1979; Ilieva-Even; Krippner 1973; MacRobert 1955; Rond; Vu. Some brief abstracts on healing: *Parapsychology Abstracts International* 1987, 5(2), nos. 2477-8; 2481-5 from the Polish *Psychotronika*

[72] Van Dragt's formulation of the healing process closely parallels that of LeShan (Goodrich 1973; LeShan 1974a), discussed in Vol. I Chapters 1; Vol. IV Chapters 2 and 3.

[73] Taken from abstract from University Microfilms International, printed in R. White 1991.

[74] See description and discussion of my work in Vol. Chapter I.

[75] Samarel's views are presented in I-supplment.

[76] Another qualitative study on TT may be of interest to readers (Nebauer). It is not summarized here because it explores the experiences of only one healer and one healee.

[77] This is an *etic* exploration of healing, contrasted with *emic* explorations

which accept the validity of traditional values in cultures other than those of the researchers. More on this under **Shamanism** later in this chapter.

[78] Millar/Snel review several Dutch surveys. I don't include these, as they are second-hand reports and I am unable to read the originals in Dutch.

[79] See discussions of **homeopathy** and **flower essences** in Vol. II Chapter 2.

[80] See discussions of **bodymind therapies** and **somatoemotional releases** in Vol. II Chapters 1 and 2.

[81] On medical errors see also Bates, et al; T. Brennan 2000, Brennan TA, et al; Kohn LT, et al; Leape; Milamed/ Hedley-Whyte; Momas EJ, et al; Peterson/ Brennan; Weiler, et al; and internet citation of J. M. Eisenberg.

[82] See more on risks and benefits of healing in Vol. IV Chapter 3.

[83] Technically, a medicine man is defined as a native healer. *Shamans* are *medicine men,* but not all medicine men are shamans. Shamans serve in many other capacities within their culture in addition to their duties as healers, such as in mediating disputes, officiating at religious holidays and rites of passage, etc.

References in related disciplines which deal with **shamanic healing,** and **healing in the context of Western sub-cultures and other cultures**: Achterberg 1985; Arvigo; Atkinson; Ayishi; R. J. Beck; Bhandari et al.; F. Bloomfield; Boshier; Boyd; Calderon; Constantinides; Dieckhofer; Dirksen; Dobkin de Rios 1972; 1984a; b; Eliade (a classic); Fabrega; Raquel Garcia; Raymond Garcia; Garrison; Geisler 1984; 1985; Glick; Golomb; Halifax; Hammerschlag; Harner (a classic); Heinze 1984; 1985 (excellent surveys); Helman; Hiatt; Hill; Hood; Hultkrantz; Humphrey; Joralemon; Kakar; Kaptchuk/Croucher; Kapur; Katz; Kerewsky-Halpern; S. King; Kleinman (essential to cross-cultural understanding of diagnosis and treatment); Kleinman/Sung; Koss; Krippner 1980b; Krippner/Villoldo; Kuang et al.; Landy; J. Long; M. Long 1976; 1978; Machover; McClain; McClenon; McGaa; McGuire; C. Miller; Morley/Wallis; Myerhoff; J. Nash; Orsi; Osumi/Ritchie; Oubre; Packer; Peters/Price-Williams; R. Prince 1972; Rauscher 1985; St. Clair 1970; 1974; Sandner; Scharfetter; P. Singer; Singer et al.; Sneck; Sobel; Swan 1986; Takaguchi; Torrey; Peters; Ullrich; Villoldo/Krippner; Webster; Winkelman; M. Young 1976; Zimmels.

Mexican: M. E. Brown; Rubel; Rubel et al.; J. C. Young.

Native American: Farrer; Hand; McGaa; W. Morgan; Morse et al.; Naranjo/ Swentzell; Powers; Reichard 1939; 1950; Topper; Yellowtail; M. Young.

Achterberg and Heinze focus most clearly on psi healing. For excellent discussions on factors in the healers' cultures which help to explain their effectiveness see: Gevitz; Harwood; Hufford; Kakar; Kleinman; Lanty; Romanucci-Ross et al.; R. H. Schneider; Servadio (reviewed in Chapter 4);

Terrell; Trotter; Unschuld.

[84] An example of etic explorations of healing is presented by Pattison et al., in the section on healee surveys earlier in this chapter.

[85] Achterberg 1985;. Harner 1980; Heinze; Krippner/Villoldo; Villoldo/Krippner are worthy of special mention.

[86] On healed water see: Dean 1985; Dean/Brame; Miller; Schwartz et al, See reviews in Vol. I Chapter 2. Dean 1985 observed, for instance, that the alterations in **UV spectrum produced by healers in water** was more pronounced when the water container had a greater air space in it. This may have been a fortuitous finding, but may possibly represent a further aspect of healing energy yet to be elucidated. See also Vol. II Chapter 2 on homeopathy.

[87] e.g. Chesi 1980; 1981; Finkler 1985

[88] Berman; Finkler 1985; Kiev 1964; 1968; Kleinman 1980; Phoenix; Servadio

[89] Berman is especially cogent in arguing these points.

GLOSSARY

±—When an average figure is given (e.g. for the systolic blood pressure of people in a study), a figure prefaced with a '±' may be added after the average to show the range that included about 2/3 of the population. This helps us to see how impressive the changes were that occurred as a result of treatment. For instance, if the average systolic blood pressure at the start of a study is 155±10 and after healing it is 147±9 then this is not a very impressive change, because the two averages overlap considerably. Despite this overlap, however, statistical analyses may show that the change is a significant one.

1 x 10³ — The little '3' in superscript following the '10' indicates that the number 10 is multiplied by itself 3 times - 10 x 10 x 10 = 1000. In other words, this is 1 x 1,000. This abbreviation is helpful when speaking of large numbers, saving the writing by the author and counting by the reader of the numbers of zeros in large numbers. Thus, 1 x 10⁹ is a 1 with 9 zeros after it, or one billion.

A—Ampere, a measure of electrical current; mA=milliampere, a thousandth of an ampere; A=micro-ampere,

Abreaction—Emotional release, often occurring in a psychotherapy setting as a part of the uncovering of hurts long-buried in the unconscious mind.

Affect—Emotions.

AK—See *applied kinesiology*.

Akasha—The cosmic light from which all consciousness is said (by Eastern mysticism) to derive. Some healers claim their diagnoses and prescriptions derive from "Akashic" records.

Aliquot—A portion of liquid taken from a sample for measure.

Allopathic— Conventional, Western medical practice.

Ambient—Present in the normal, everyday environment.

Apparition—Ghost; surviving aspect of a person that may be perceived by those still living.

Applied Kinesiology—See *kinesiolgy*.

ASC—Altered state of consciousness.

Ascitic fluid— Fluid that accumulates pathologically in the abdomen, often due to cancer.

ATP—Adenosine triphosphate, an important metabolic enzyme.

Auditory evoked response—EEG response to auditory stimuli.

Aura—Halo of color around objects, especially living things, perceived by psychics and correlated by them with physical, mental, emotional and spiritual states of the individual. It is possible that this perception does not occur through the ordinary visual processes, as some psychics report they can see auras with their eyes closed.

Bioplasma—Plasmas consist of subatomic particles, usually electrons with negative charges and nuclei with positive ones. If individual atoms are raised to very high temperatures they may become ionized. That is, their electrons may be forced away from their nuclei. Many plasmas exist only at high temperatures (e.g. a candle flame; ball lightning; the sun). Other plasmas exist at lower temperatures (e.g. the aurora borealis). *Bioplasma* is hypothesized as a fifth state of matter, consisting of a variety of particles such as free protons and electrons. These ions (charged particles) may coexist without assuming a particular molecular structure. Bioplasma may exist within and around living organisms. It is proposed that it does not require high temperatures as do many other plasmas because of the solid-state properties (e.g. semiconductance) of living organisms.

Blinds—experimental methods that leave the researchers and/or subjects being studied 'blind' to the conditions of the experiment so that they will not be biased in their expectations and thereby possibly influence the results. See Vol. I-Introduction and Vol. II Chapter 2 for full discussion on experimental methods.

BUN (Blood urea nitrogen)—A laboratory measure of kidney function.

Carcinoma—Cancer.

Cerebellum—Part of the brain at the base of the skull that smoothes and coordinates movements. (*Cerebellar* = in the cerebellum)

C group—Control, or comparison group in an experiment, contrasted with the E (experimental) group. (See also *controls*.)

Chakras—Energy centers identified originally by Eastern energy medicine practitioners, often helpful to healers in working on specific areas of healees' bodies. These centers influence the physical body organs adjacent to them.

Chromosomes—Units within genes that are inherited from generation to generation, controlling the growth, development, and ongoing life processes of each cell.

Chronic fatigue syndrome (CFS)—Chronic illness including fatigue, headaches, weakness, multiple allergies, foggy thinking, and other debilitating symptoms. The cause of CFS is unknown. Often associated with *fibromyalgia*.

Clairsentience—The knowing of information about an animate or inanimate object without sensory cues, perceived as visual, auditory, smell, taste, touch, or kinesthetic sensations. (See also *Psychometry*.)

Clairvoyance—The knowing of information about an animate or inanimate object without sensory cues, perceived as visual imagery. (See also *Clairsentience; Psychometry*.)

Colitis—inflammatory disease of the large bowel.

Colonoscopy—Examination of the colon through a long tube inserted in the rectum.

Confound—A factor (other than the factor or factors intended by the researchers to be the focus of a controlled study) that may have influenced the subjects of the study to produce the observed effects. For instance, researchers might be studying effects of a medication on anxiety, but *confounding* effects such as the attention given by the researcher might influence the subjects to relax—confusing or confounding the results.

Controls—In research: Comparison groups receiving either no treatment or a treatment of known effect that is used as a contrast with groups of patients receiving a new treatment of unknown effects, designated the "experimental" group. In mediumistic parlance: Spirit entities that speak through (control the mind of) the medium, usually in a trance state.

Cordotomy—Severing of pathways in the spinal cord, sometimes used to stop perception of chronic, severe pain.

Creatinine—Blood chemistry test reflecting kidney function.

Crohn's disease—ileitis; chronic inflammatory small bowel disease.

Cushing's disease—Obesity of the trunk of the body, hypertension, and other problems due to excessive activity of the adrenal gland.

Cushingoid—Having the appearance of Cushing's disease.

Cytofluorographic—Study of cells through special stains.

Cytoplasm—Contents of a cell around the nucleus.

Demography—Details that characterize a group of people, such as age, sex, etc.

Diastolic—The lower of the pair of numbers used to define blood pressure, reflecting arterial and coronary disease when permanently elevated.

Diastolic blood pressure—The lowest pressure measured for arterial blood.

Distal—Part of the body that is further away from the center of the body. (Opposite to *proximal*.)

DNA—Protein chains that encode genetic information in all living organisms.

Double Blind Study—Research in which neither the treating physician(s) nor the patients know who received active treatment and who received control (or placebo) treatment.

Dowsing—See Radiesthesia and Radionics.

Dysmenorrhea—Pains and other discomforts during menstrual periods.

Dyspenea—Shortness of breath.

E group—Experimental group, contrasted with the C (control) group in experiments.

ECG—Electrocardiogram; an electronic recording of voltages produced by contractions of the heart. (Also spelled EKG)

EDA—Electrodermal activity (see *GSR*).

EEG—See *electroencephalogram*.

Electroencephalogram (EEG)—an electronic recording of voltages between points on the scalp, reflecting in a very rough way some of the electrical activity of the brain, especially at the surface of the cortex. Various wave frequencies have been correlated with different states of consciousness.

EKG—See *ECG*.

EM—Electromagnetic.

Emetic—Drug that causes vomiting.

EMF—Electromagnetic field

EMG—Electromyogram, measuring muscle function, indicating whether certain muscular diseases are present.

Emic—Explanation that acknowledge that peoples from cultures other than our own, behaving in manners that are different from ours, usually have their own legitimate cultural explanations for their beliefs and behaviors. (Contrasted with *etic*)

Emitted qi—See external qi.

Enuresis—Lack of control of urination; at night this is *bedwetting*.

Enzyme—Biological chemical that facilitates and markedly accelerates biochemical reactions, enabling life processes as we know them to succeed.

EOG—Electro-oculogram, recording of eye movements.

Epithelialization—The filling in of a wound with normal tissues as the wound is repaired by the body.

Errors—see Research errors.

Erythema—Redness of skin, usually due to infection or injury.

Erythrocyte—Red blood cell (RBC).

ESPer—see *Sensitive*.

Etic—Explanations based on Western convictions that modern science can provide 'objective' explanations for every phenomena. (Contrasted with *emic)*

Experimenter effect (*Rosenthal effect*)—Subtle suggestion on the part of an experimenter (often unconsciously tendered) that leads the experimental subjects to demonstrate the behaviors the experimenter expects to find.

External qi—Qi (healing energy) emitted by a qigong master. (synonyms: *emitted qi; waiqi*)

Extra Sensory Perception (ESP)—The obtaining of information by telepathy, clairsentience, precognition and/or retrocognition, without cues from the "normal" senses (sight, sound, taste, smell, touch, or kinesthesia).

Faraday cage—Cage of wire mesh that excludes electromagnetic radiations.

Fascia—Connective tissues in the body.

Fibroblast—A cell that produces connective tissue for repairing wounds in the body.

Fibromyalgia—Painful muscles, cause unknown, that can be associated with chronic fatigue syndrome.

Frontalis muscle—Forehead muscle.

Ganzfeld—Standard bland visual and auditory stimuli that are commonly imposed on subjects in order to enhance the occurrence of psi phenomena.

Gastric—Stomach.

Gastroscopy—Examination of the stomach through a long tube that is swallowed and passed into the stomach.

Ghost—See *apparition.*

Goats—Non-believers in psi. (Contrasted with *sheep*).

General Practitioner (GP)—British equivalent of a primary care physician.

GSR—Galvanic skin response, an electric measure of resistance, correlating roughly with states of physical and emotional tension (See *EDA*).

Healing—Any systematic, purposeful intervention by a person purporting to help another living thing (person, animal, plant, or other living system or part thereof) to change via the sole process of focused intention or via hand contact or 'passes'. *Type 1 (distant, or absent healing)* is the projection of healing solely through efforts of the mind of the healer to the healee. *Type 2 (touch; near-the-body; or laying-on-of-hands healing)* is the projection of healing through the body of the healer to the healee. This may involve various movements of the hands of the healer around the body.

Hb—See *Hemoglobin*

Hemagglutinin—Antibody that causes clumping (agglutination) of blood cells.

Hematocrit—Numbers of red blood cells that are present in a person's blood stream.

Hemocytometer—instrument for counting cells, usually blood cells.

Hemoglobin—the oxygen-carrying protein in blood cells.

Hemolysis—Bursting of red blood cells, in some experiments induced by placing them in dilute saline solutions. This leads to water entering the cells to the point that they burst.

Hgb—See *hemoglobin*.

Histological/ Histopathologic—Studies of cells and tissues for abnormalities.

Hit—A successful attempt to produce psi effects. Term derived from visual *target* pictures for psi perception in the laboratory. Opposite to *miss*.

Holistic—See Wholistic

Homeostasis—The maintenance of normal, balanced functioning within a healthy range of processes, such as the body maintaining a balance of chemicals in the blood or of temperature that is conducive to normal functioning of the body.

Humerus—The arm bone between the shoulder and elbow.

Hypermetropia—Far-sightedness.

Hypotonic—More dilute than body fluids.

Iatrogenic—Caused by a medical intervention.

Idiopathic—Of unknown origins.

Infarction—Dying tissues due to blood clotting in the arteries that supply those tissues.

Infra-red (IR)—Shorter than red wavelengths, invisible to the naked eye but detectable by other animals and by instrumentation.

Infrasonic sound—Sound waves that are so low that they are inaudible to human ears.

Intraperitoneal—In the abdominal cavity.

Intuitive Data Sorting (IDS)—A person might use psi powers (clarsentience or precognition) in sorting subjects during the assignment of subjects to experimental and control groups, favoring one group with more robust or capable subjects and the other with more fragile, damaged, unskilled, or ill subjects. Thus a person wishing to see positive results who is sorting seeds into batches for healing and control conditions might pick seeds (consciously or unconsciously) that are less likely to germinate or to grow well for the control group and conversely for the healing group.

In vitro—In the laboratory.

In-vivo—In live organisms outside the laboratory.

Ion—Atom with a positive or negative electrical charge.

IR—See *infra-red*.

(Applied) Kinesiology (AK)—Testing of muscle strength to determine allergies and food/medicine sensitives, emotional states, etc.

Kirlian photography—Methods utilizing a small electrical charge (high voltage, low amperage) to produce photographs of objects with an aura of color around them. Used in Eastern European countries extensively for diagnosis of disease states in plants, animals, and humans.

KV—Kilovolt = 1,000 volts.

Laogong point—Acupuncture point on the palm of the hand.

Linger effect—Healing given to healees at a particular location appears sometimes to linger on, influencing beneficially others who are in the same location afterwards.

Lymphedema—Swelling in extremities due to impaired circulation, often following surgery such as radical mastectomy and radiotherapy for cancers.

Lymphocyte—White blood cell, part of the body's immune defense mechanism against disease.

Macrophages—White blood cells that engulf and destroy foreign materials (bacteria, destroyed cellular particles, etc.) in the body.

Manometer—Laboratory instrument for measuring the volume of gas.

Mantra—Words recited repetitively in meditation.

MAO—Monoamine oxidase, an enzyme in the nervous system that participates in communications between nerve cells and that appears to participate in shifts in moods.

Maxilla—The bone that houses the upper teeth.

Medium—Person who channels communications from spirits, often in trance. Some mediums can also produce PK effects and materialize physical likenesses of people who communicate through them.

Medulla oblongata—Deep portion of the brain.

Menière's disease—Attacks of dizziness, vertigo, nausea, and other symptoms of unknown origin, relating to disorders of the middle ear.

Meta-analysis—Statistical analysis of a series of studies in which statistical assessments were made on the results.

Metal bending—See *PKMB*.

Metastatic cancer—Cancer that has spread from its original site to one or more other sites in the body.

Middle Latency Response (MLR)—The primary component of the auditory cortical evoked response in the EEG, indicating activity of the cerebral cortex.

Mind Mirror—EEG with simultaneous displays of right and left cerebral hemisphere electrical activity.

Miss—A failed attempt to produce psi effects. Opposite to *hit*.

Mitochondria—Part of a cell where metabolic functions are regulated and processed.

Mitosis—Cell division. In cancers, mitosis is vastly increased and growth of the tumors is out of control of the body's regulatory mechanisms.

Mitral stenosis—Hardening of the mitral valve of the heart, with narrowing of the passage for blood through this valve.

mm Hg—Millimeters of mercury, units for measurements of blood pressure.

Morbidity—Illness or other negative effects upon health, as in the tiredness following anesthesia and surgery.

MV—Millivolt; thousandth of a volt.

NaCl—Chemical designation for table salt or saline, as in body fluids.

Naloxone—Chemical that neutralizes effects of opiates.

Natural Killer (NK) cells—White blood cells that attack invading organisms in the body.

Necrosis—Dying tissues, as in tumors that are being destroyed by healing or chemotherapy.

Neoplasm—Cancer.

Neurone—Nerve cell.

Neurotransmitter—Chemical that transmits a message between a nerve cell and other nerve cells or different cells.

nm—Nanometer, a billionth of a meter. A measure of the wavelength of light, used in spectrophotometers to identify the chemical composition of a substance.

Nocturia—Urination during sleep.

Noetic—Having properties that derive from inner experiences that are difficult to describe in the linear terms of everyday language.

Nucleus—Part of a cell that, like the brain in the body, regulates many of the functions of the cell.

OD value—Optical density value.

Obsession—Used interchangeably in mediumship with *possession*.

Oncology—The study and treatment of cancer.

Oscilloscope—Instrument displaying electromagnetic vibrational patterns on a screen.

Osmosis—The seepage or active transport of molecules across cell membranes.

Osmotic pressure—Fluid molecules press to enter a cell when there is a greater concentration of large molecules within the cell than in the surrounding fluid. The general tendency is for fluids to equalize their concentration on both sides of a permeable membrane like the cell wall. Fluid will thus pass from the less concentrated solution to the more concentrated one.

Osmotic stress—Cells placed in dilute saline solutions will swell as fluid enters the cell. (See *osmotic pressure*). If the saline solution is sufficiently weak, enough fluid will enter the cells to cause them to burst.

Osteoarthritis—Degenerative joint disease that includes pains, loss of cartilage, and limitations of range of motion.

Palliative care—Care provided for symptom relief, without intention or hope of cure.

Passes—Movements of the hands of a healer around the body of a healee, either following a prescribed or ritualistic pattern or dictated by the healer's psi or intuitive senses.

PBGM—Portable blood glucose meter.

Petri dishes—Flat, covered laboratory dishes used for cell cultures, sprouting seeds, etc.

Phantom limb—Sensations of a limb still being present after an amputation of that limb.

PK—See *psychokinesis*.

PKMB (*warm forming*)—Metal bending (or softening so that it can be bent) via psi effects.

Plumial—Leaflet emerging from seed.

Poltergeist effects—See *random spontaneous PK; RSPK*.

Possession—The alleged taking over of a person's behavior by a discarnate spirit.

***Post hoc* finding**—Experimental finding that was not predicted prior to the study but was noted after the experiment was performed. Such findings are considered suspect, as they might have occurred by chance, amongst many possible variables that are studied.

Potentize—To create a homeopathic solution of a remedy through serial dilutions. (See also *succussion*.)

Precognition—Knowing about a future event prior to its occurrence.

Prolapse—Tissues that protrude through an opening in the body, as when the lens of the eye protrudes through the iris after severe trauma to the eye, or the bladder of a woman protrudes into the vagina following trauma in giving birth.

Proxy—A person who is given healing instead of the person with the problem, used in cases where the healer cannot give healing directly. Proxy healing appears to be a variant of distant healing. It reaches the people in need regardless of their distance from the healer and proxy. The proxy seems to be a living *witness* (see definition).

Psi—Abbreviation for *parapsychological*, connoting ESP (telepathy, clairsentience, precognition, and retrocognition), and psychokinesis. Taken from the Greek letter Ψ

Psychokinesis (PK)—Moving or transforming an object without use of physical means, commonly referred to as *mind over matter*. (See also PKMB, RSPK, healing, and PS, which seem to be more specific forms of PK.)

Psychic surgery (PS)—Surgery performed with the hands or with a knife, in which very rapid healing occurs, often even instantaneously, usually without pain or excessive bleeding and with no subsequent infection (despite the fact that sterile techniques are not used).
     PS I: Healer manipulates aura.
     PS II: Healer manipulates physical body.
     PS III: A combination of I and II (Classification of Motoyama).

Psychometry—Clairsentience focused on a specific object. Psychics report that when people handle an object, especially over prolonged periods, they leave an impression upon that object that sensitives can pick up.

Rad—Measure of exposure to ionizing radiation.

Radicle—Root.

Radiesthesia (*Dowsing*)—The use of a device (e.g. pendulum, forked tree branch, etc.) to obtain clairsentient information.

Radionics—The use of more complex devices (usually calibrated, often with dials) to obtain clairsentient information and to project effects psychokinetically (e.g. healing).

Random spontaneous psychokinesis (RSPK)—Apparently random, spontaneous PK, usually associated with the presence of one particular individual who is presumed to be the unconscious agent producing these events.

RBC—Red blood cell.

Renal colic—Severe kidney pains.

Research errors—*Type 1*: Accepting as true something that is not. *Type 2*: Rejecting as invalid an effect that actually has some substance.

Respant—Responsible participant, a term coined by Bernie Siegel (1990).

Retrocognition—perceptions of events occurring prior to the time of their perception by the sensitive.

Ribosome—The site in a cell where protein synthesis takes place.

RNA—*Ribonucleic acid*, a protein involved in cell reproduction.

Rorschach Test—Inkblots that leave the viewer free to associate to any aspect of their form and/or color, thereby revealing the characteristic perceptions and interpretations of the viewer.

Rosenthal effect—See *Experimenter effect*.

RSPK—See *random spontaneous psychokinesis*.

Run—A group of individual trials within a research study.

Salpingo-oophorectomy—Surgical removal of the tubes of the uterus and ovaries.

Sciatica—Pain in the sciatic nerve, running from the lower back down the leg, often due to narrowing of the opening of the spinal cord.

Sedimentation rate (also *erythrocyte sedimentation rate*)—Rate at which red blood cells settle when a sample of blood is left to stand for a measured period of time, a very rough indicator of the presence of some infections and immunological problems.

Self—With small 's' designating an individual's personal sense of beingness; with capitalized 'S' designating a deeper or higher aspect of an individual that may include the unconscious mind, higher self, spirit, and/or soul.

Sensitive (*ESPer*)—Noun designating a person who has psi abilities.

Shadow—Unconscious, negative aspects of a person that often contribute to dis-ease and disease.

Sheep—Believer(s) in psi. (Contrasted with *goats*).

Sheep-goat effect—Believers (*sheep*) perform significantly better than chance, while disbelievers (*goats*) score significantly poorer than chance expectancy on psi tasks.

Sleight-of-hand—*Magic tricks*, i.e. clever deceptions that mislead the perceiver to believe that something paranormal might have occurred, when in fact it did not.

Soul—That eternal aspect of awareness that permeates all levels of self and Self, surviving physical death, learning and growing in its journey back to unity with the Creator.

Spectrophotometer (alt. *spectrograph*)—Scientific instrument that measures the wavelengths of light emitted by or transmitted through a given substance. Particular wavelengths identify specific substances.

Spirit—1. Synonym for *apparition* or *ghost*, the surviving aspect of self after death that may be perceived by the living; 2. A transcendent aspect of Self that connects the self to the eternal All.

Standard Deviation (S.D.)—The range within which about 66% of individuals will cluster around the average (mean) number in a randomly distributed sample. This provides a measure of how unusual a particular measurement may be. If the S.D. is, for instance 15 units, and a given measurement is 45, we know that this is well beyond the expected distribution for whatever is being studied. Statistical analyses can tell us precisely how unusual this is.

State-Trait Anxiety Inventory (STAI)—40 questions, 2 subscales, giving a measure of current, situational state of anxiety and long-term tendency to anxiety that can be pathological (Spielberger et al). Self-administered over 10-20 minutes. One of the most popular tests for anxiety, translated into 30 languages.

Stereotaxic—Measuring device that facilitates the precise location of a given organ (e.g. for the placement of electrodes in the brain).

Stigmata—Wounds appearing spontaneously, without cause for injury, often in the places Christ was wounded.

Stylopodium—Newt (salamander) equivalent of the human humerus arm bone.

Subcutaneous—Under the skin, as with injections given at this site.

Subject—Person studied in an experiment.

Succussion—Shaking a homeopathic remedy to enhance its potency.

Super-ESP—Using psi powers to scan the environment for meaningful information that then leads to PK influence over the environment to the benefit of the individual.

Synchronicity—A coincidence that is meaningful to a perceiver or participant in the component events.

Synesthesia—A crossed-sensory perception, such as hearing color, or feeling color through touch or by holding the hand above an object without touching it.

Systolic—The higher of the pair of numbers used to designate blood pressure, often rising transiently with states of anxiety.

Tachycardia—Excessively rapid heart rate.

Teleological—Assumption that there is an ultimate purpose and/or design in natural phenomena.

Telepathy—The transfer of thoughts, images, or commands from one living thing to another, without use of sensory cues.

Thaumaturgy—See *sleight-of-hand*.

Thematic Apperception Test (TAT)—Psychological test based on people's responses to photographs of people in ambiguous situations that allow the viewer to interpret them in many different ways.

Thoughtography—Production of photographic images by PK.

Tic doloreux—Severe pain in the face, of neurological origin.

Trigeminal neuralgia—Severe pain in the facial nerve, often of unknown origin.

Types I and II research errors—See *research errors*.

Ultra-violet—Longer than violet wavelengths, invisible to the naked eye but measurable by instruments.

UV—See *ultra-violet*.

V—See *volt*.

Vacuoles—Bubbles in cells.

VAS—See *visual analog scale*.

Ventricle—Chamber of the heart.

Villi—Pleural of *villus*, a peninsular projection from a cell wall. Villi in stomach and intestinal cells, for instance, protrude into the gut. They form a large surface area over which food molecules can be absorbed.

Visual Analog Scale (VAS)—Usually a 10 cm long line marked with *none* at one end and *worst possible* at the other end, used for subjective ratings of symptoms such as pain. The assessment is repeated over a period of time and changes in severity of symptoms are noted.

Volt—Measure of differences in electrical charge between two points.

Wholistic—This spelling is used rather than holistic because, rather than seeking to treat the whole person, the use of holistic has often been used to mean any kind of non-conventional treatment, such as acupuncture for back pain or herbal preparations for high cholesterol etc.

A wholistic approach to healing is based on the understanding that a person is not made of isolated parts; all the parts of an individual are interconnected. This includes the body, the emotions, the mind, the spirit, as well as the family, the social, and the work environments. When one aspect is under stress, all aspects can be adversely affected. Because of this, the cause of an illness, or ailment, may not be where the symptom manifests. For example: a stomach-ache may be caused by worry about one's marriage, a sore right foot could be the result of the fear of moving forward in one's career, or depression might be due to heavy metal intoxication.

With this in mind, when diagnosing a person's condition, all aspects of the individual need to be taken into consideration. Often the original cause is hidden behind the symptom. If a condition has existed for a long time, sub-conditions tend to develop that are covered up by the dominant symptom. When the dominant symptom is healed, a deeper layer of the condition can surface requiring attention. This process can continue until all the sub-layers are healed, including the original cause.

Wholistic diagnosis and treatment can make use of both conventional and alternative therapies. A course of treatment could involve a number of thera-pies: psychological exercises, bodywork, physical exercise, nutrition, acupunc-ture, affirmations, as well as drugs and surgery to name a few. A multi-skilled therapist able to work in a wide spectrum of therapies might administer a true wholistic treatment, or it could come from the coordinated effort of many therapists trained in different modalities.

The goal of wholistic healing is to help the individual return to wholeness wherein all aspects are healed and in harmony. With a deeper understanding it becomes apparent that everything is connected both within and without. This includes all people, all plants and animals, as well as the physical planet and the stars.

The field of wholistic healing is in its infancy. Even the best wholistic thera-pists use only a small portion of the skills and modalities available. One key factor is that the quality of healing the wholistic therapist is able to offer is influenced, to a great extent, by the degree that the therapist has achieved her own wholistic health.

> *William Rand*, publisher of Healing Research, distilled from discussions with *Dan Benor*

Witness—Object used by psychics, dowsers, and users of radionics devices to connect psychically with someone or something from a distance. For instance, in tracing a missing person, clothing belonging to this person helps the psy-chic to locate them. A blood of sputum sample may likewise help a dowser connect with a healee for diagnosis and treatment.

Xenoglossy—Speaking a language that was not learned by any known normal means, often presumed to be a manifestation of reincarnation memories.

BIBLIOGRAPHY

A

Abbot, Neil C, Healing as a therapy for human disease: a systematic review, *Journal of Alternative and Complementary Medicine* 2000, 6(2), 159-169.

Achterberg, Jeanne, *Imagery in Healing: Shamanism and Modern.*

Adamenko, Victor, Electrodynamic Systems, *J. of Paraphysics* 1970 (4) 113-121.

Adamenko, Victor, Living Detectors, *J. Paraphysics* 1972 (a), 6(1), 5-8.

Agnellet, M. *Accept These Facts. The Lourdes Cures Examined.* London 1958.

Alcock, James E., *Parapsychology: Science or Magic?*, New York: Pergamon 1981.

Alvord, Lori Arviso/ van Pelt, Elizabeth Cohen, *The Scalpel and the Silver Bear*, New York: Bantam 1999.

Alvarado, Carlos S. Observations of Luminous Phenomena Around the Human Body: A Review. *J. of the Society for Psychical Research* 1987, 54, 38-60.

American Psychiatric Association, *Diagnostic and Statistical Manual of Mental Disorders*, 4th ed., Washington: American Psychiatric Association 1994.

American Psychiatric Association, Practice guidelines for major depressive disorders in adults, *American J. of Psychiatry* 1993, 150(4) Suppl. 1-26.

Andrade, H.G. *A Corpuscular Theory of Spirit*, Sao Paulo: Privately published 1968.

Andus, L. G. Magnetropism: a new plant-growth response, *Nature* 1960, 185, 132.

Angelo, Jack, *The Healing Spirit: The Story of Dennis Barrett*, London: Rider 1990.

Annual-Science of Mind, The New Age of Healing, Los Angeles: *Science of Mind* 1979 (Briefs from conference).

Anonymous, A recent case of faith healing, J. of the Society for Psychical Research 1895 (Also in: *British Medical J.* Nov 16, 1895 From Corliss, W. R., The Unfathomed Mind: A Handbook of Unusual Mental Phenomena, Glen Arm, MD: The Sourebook Project 1982 (Case of follicular infection on beard responding to healing).

Appelbaum, Stephen A.: The laying on of health: personality patterns of psychic healers (Bulletin of the Menninger Clinic) 1993, 57(1), 33-40.

Arieti, S. *The Intra-psychic Self*, New York: Basic 1967.

Armstrong, O. K., Beware the commercialized faith healers, *Readers' Digest 1971* (Jun), 179-186.

Arnold, Larry E. and Nevius, Sandra K., *The Reiki Handbook*, Harrisburg, PA: ParaScience International (PSI) 1982.

Arvigo, Rosita, Sastun: My Apprenticeship with a Maya Healer, HarperCollins 1995.

Asano, M./ Stull, J.T. in Hidaka, H/ Hartshorne, D.J. (Eds), Myosin Phosphorylation in Calmodulin Antagonists and Cellular Physiology, Orlando, FL: Academic 1985, 225-260.

Ashby Robert H., *A Guidebook to the Study of Psychical Research*, New York: Weiser 1973.

Astin, John A/ Harkness, Elaine/ Ernst, Edzard, The efficacy of distant healing: a systematic review of randomized trials, *Annals of Internal Medicine* 2000, 132, 903-910.

Attevelt, J.T.M., *A Statistical Survey of the Patients of Paranormal Healers*, Amsterdam: Nederlands Federation for Paranormal and Naturopathic Healers 1981.

Attevelt, J.T.M., *Research into Paranormal Healing*, Doctoral Dissertation, State University of Utrecht, The Netherlands, 1988.

B

Backster, Cleve, Evidence of a primary perception in plant life, *International J. of Parapsychology* 1968, 10(6), 329-348.

Bacon, Mary Margarita, *The Effects of Therapeutic Touch on State Anxiety and Physiological Measurements in Preoperative Clients* (master's thesis, San Jose State University, 1997)

Bowers, D.P. *The Effects of Therapeutic Touch on State Anxiety and Physiological Measurements in Preoperative Clients* (Master's thesis), San Jose, CA: San Jose State University 1997.

Baer, Randal N. and Baer, Vicki, *The Crystal Connection: A Guidebook for Personal and Planetary Ascension*, San Francisco, Harper and Row, 1986.

Bagchi, B.K./ Wenger, M.A. Electrophysiological correlates of some yogi exercises, In: Kimaya, J. et al. (eds), *Biofeedback and Self Control*, Chicago: Aldine-Atherton 1971, 591-607.

Baginski, B., *Reiki: Universal Life Energy*, CA: Life Rhythms 1988.

Bailey, Alice A., *Esoteric Healing, V.VI*, New York: Lucis 1972.

Baker, A. T. (ed), *The Mahatma Letters of A.P. Sinnett, 2nd Ed.* (p.455 Letter No. CXXVII, 13 August 1882), London: Rider 1948 (orig. 1923).

Bakker, L.F., *Kwakzalverij en onbevoegd uitoefenen van de geneeskunst. [Quackery and unauthorized practising of medicine]*, Assen: Van Gorcum & Comp. 1969.

Balint, Michael, Notes on parapsychology and parapsychological healing, *International J. of Parapsychology* 1955, 36, 31-35.

Bandler, Richard and Grinder, John, *Frogs into Princes: Neurolinguistic Programming*, Moab, Utah: Real People 1979.

Baranger, P. and Filer, M. K., Amulets: The protective action of collars in avian malaria, *Mind and Matter*, Oxford, England: Radionics Centre 1967(Mar) [Excerpt from *Acta Tropica* 1953, 10(1)].

Barbanell, Maurice, *Harry Edwards and His Healing*, London: Psychic Book Club, 1953.

Barbanell, Maurice, *I Hear a Voice: A Biography of E. G. Fricker the Healer*, London: Spiritualist, 1962.

Barns, Echo Bodine, *Hands that Heal*, San Diego, CA: ACS 1985.

Barnuow, Victor, Paranormal phenomena and culture, *J. of the American Society for Psychical Research*, 1945, 40, 2-21.

Barrington, Mary Rose, A slip in time and place, *Fate*, 1985 (Oct), 88-94.

Barrington, Mary Rose, Bean growth promotion pilot experiment, *Proceedings of the Society for Psychical Research* 1982, 56, 302-304.

Barrington, Rosze: A naturalistic inquiry of post-operative pain after Therapeutic Touch (In: Delores A. Gaut and Anne Boykin, *Caring as Healing*, New York: National League for Nursing 1994).

Barros, Alberto et al., Methodology for research on psychokinetic influence over the growth of plants, *Psi Communicacion* 1977, 3(5/ 6), 9-30. (Summary, translated from Spanish, from: *Parapsychology Abstracts International* 1984, 1(2), 80, Abstr. No. 662).

Barry, J., General and comparative study of the psychokinetic effect on a fungus culture, *J. of Parapsychology* 1968, 32, 237-243.

Bartlett, J.G. *Recommendations for the medical care of persons with HIV infections*, Baltimore: Critical Care Amreica 1992.

Bartrop, R. et al., Depressed lymphocyte function after bereavement, *Lancet* 1977, 1, 834-836.

Batcheldor, K. J., Contribution to the theory of PK induction from sitter- group work, In: Roll, W. G.; Beloff, J. and White, R. (Eds), *Research in Parapsychology 1982*, Metuchen, NJ: Scarecrow 1983, 45-61. (Also in: *J. of the American Society for Psychical Research* 1984, 78(2), 105-132.)

Batcheldor, K. J., Report of a case of table levitation and associated phenomena , *J. of the Society for Psychical Research* 1966, 43(729), 339- 356.

Bates DW, et al, Incidence of adverse drug events and potential adverse drug events: implications for prevention, *Journal of the American Medical* 1995, 274:29-34.

Baumann, S.; Lagle, J. and Roll, W., Preliminary results from the use of two novel detectors for psychokinesis, In: Weiner, Debra H. and Radin, Dean I., (Eds) *Research in Parapsychology 1985*, Metuchen and London: Scarecrow 1986, 59-62.

Bayless, Raymond, *The Enigma of the Poltergeist*, NY: Ace 1967.

Beard, Rebecca, *Everyman's Search*, Chichester, England: Science of Thought Press 1951.

Beasley, Victor, *Subtle-Body Healing*, Boulder Creek, CA: University of the Trees 1979.

Bechterev, W., Direct influence of a person upon the behavior of animals, *J. of Parapsychology*, 1948, 13, 166-176.

Beck, A.T./ Steer, R.A. *Beck Deression Inventory Manual*, The Psychological Corporation, San Antonio, TX: Harcourt Brace Jovanovich 1987.

Beck, A.T./ Steer, R.A./ Carlson, M.G., Psychometric properties of the Beck Depression Inventory: twenty-five years of evaluation, *Clinical Psychology Review* 1988, 30, 77-100.

Beck, Rene and Peper, Eric, Healer-healee interactions and beliefs in therapeutic touch: Some observations and suggestions, In: Borelli, Marianne/ Heidt, Patricia, (Eds) *Therapeutic Touch*, New York: Springer 1981, 129-137.

Bek, Lilla/ Pullar, Philippa, *The Seven Levels of Healing*, London: Century 1986.

Beloff John, Psi phenomena: Causal versus acausal interpretation, *J. of the Society for Psychical Research*, 1977, 49(773), 573-582.

Beloff, John, *New Directions in Parapsychology*, London: Unwin/ Gresham 1974.

Benor, Daniel J. and Ditman, Keith S., Clinical psychopharmacological research: Problems, questions and some suggestions in analyzing reports, *J. of Clinical Pharmacology* 1967, 7, 63-76.

Benor, Daniel J., Psychic healing: research evidence and potential for improving medical care, In: Salmon, J. Warren, (Ed) *Alternative Medicines: Popular and Policy Perspectives*, London: Tavistock/ Methuen 1984(a).

Benor, Daniel J., Meta-awareness and meta-emotions as related to psychic healing, *Paper Presented at the Hopitality Suite Section of the American Psychological Association Meeting, Transpersonal Psychology Interest Group*, Toronto, 1984(b).

Benor, Daniel J., Believe it and you'll be it: visualization in psychic healing, *Psi Research*, 1985, 4(1), 21-56.

Benor, Daniel J., Lamarckian genetics: Theories from psi research and evidence from the work of Luther Burbank, *Research in Parapsychology 1987*, Metuchen, NJ: Scarecrow 1988.

Benor, Daniel J., Research in psychic healing, In: Shapin, Betty and Coly, Lisette, (Eds) Current trends in psi research, *Proceedings of an International Conference, New Orleans, LA, (Aug) 1984*, New York: Parapsychology Foundation 1986a.

Benor, Daniel J., The overlap of psychic 'readings' with psychotherapy, Psi Research, 1986b, 5(1,2), 56-78.

Benor, Daniel J., A psychiatrist examines fears of healing, *J. of the Society for Psychical Research* 1990, 56, 287-299.

Benor, Daniel J.: Intuitive Diagnosis, *Subtle Energies*, 1992, 3(2), 41-64.

Bensen, Vladimir B., One hundred cases of post-anesthetic suggestion in the recovery room, Presentation at 13th Annual Scientific Meeting of the American Society of Clinical Hypnosis, Miami Beach, FL 1970.

Berger, Ruth, *Medical Intuition: How to Combine Inner Resources with Modern Medicine*, York Beach, ME: Samuel Weiser 1995.

Berman, Morris, *The Reenchantment of the World*, NY: Bantam 1984.

Beutler, Jaap J: Attevelt, et al. Paranormal Healing and Hypertension, *British Medical J.* 1988, 296, 1491-1494.

Bibb, Benjamin O. and Weed, Joseph J., *Amazing Secrets of Psychic Healing*, West Nyack, NY: Parker 1976.

Bishop, George, *Faith Healing: God or Fraud?*, Los Angeles: Sherbourne 1967.

Bloch, M., *The Royal Touch: Sacred Monarchy and Scrofula in England and France* (Translated from French) London: Routledge and Kegan Paul; Montreal: McGill University 1973 (10 pp. refs.).

Bloomfield, Bob, *Linda Martel: Little Healer*, Tasburgh, England: Pelegrin Trust/ Pilgrim 1990.

Bloomfield, Bob, *The Mystique of Healing*, Edinburgh, England: Skilton and Shaw, 1984.

Bloomfield, Frena, Asking for rice: The way of the Chinese healer, *Shaman's Drum* 1985, 1, 33-36.

Boguslawski, M., The use of therapeutic touch in nursing *J. of Continuing Education in Nursing* 1979, 10(4), 9-15.

Boguslawski, Marie, Therapeutic Touch: A facilitator of pain relief, *Topics in Clinical Nursing* 1980, 2, 27-37.

Bolton, Brett, *Edgar Cayce Speaks*, New York: Avon 1969.

Boltwood, Geoff/ Courtenay, Anthea, *The Messenger: The Journey of a Spiritual Healer*, London: Piatkus 1994.

Bonnell, John Sutherland, *Do You Want to be Healed?*, New York: Harper and Row, 1968.

Bonny, Helen L and Savary, Louis M. *Music and Your Mind, Listening with a New Consciousness*. Port Townsend, WA: ICM 1983, Orig., New York: Collins Associates 1973.

Borelli, Marianne D. and Heidt, Patricia (Eds), *Therapeutic Touch: A Book of Readings*, New York: Springer 1981.

Borysenko, J., Healing motives: an interview with David C. McClelland, *Advances* 1985, 2(2), 29-41.

Bose, Jaqadis C., Awareness in plants, In: Muses, Charles and Young, Arthur M. (Eds), *Consciousness and Reality*, New York: Outerbridge and Lazard/ Dutton, 1972.

Boucher, Faith Katherine, *The Cadences of Healing: Perceived Benefits from Treatment Among the Clientele of Psychic Healers,* Doctoral dissertation, Univ. California, Davis 1980.

Bowers, Diane Patricia, *The Effects of Therapeutic Touch on State Anxiety and Physiological Measurements in Preoperative Clients* (Master's thesis), San Jose, CA: San Jose State University 1992.

Boyd, Doug, *Rolling Thunder,* New York: Delta/ Dell 1974.

Bramly, Serge, *Macumba: The Teachings of Maria Jose, Mother of the Gods,* New York: Avon 1979.

Braud, William G., The psi conducive syndrome: Free response gesp performance following evocation of 'left-hemispheric' vs. 'right-hemispheric' functioning, In: *Research in Parapsychology, 1974,* Metuchen, NJ: Scarecrow Press 1975, 17-20.

Braud, William G., Allobiofeedback: Immediate feedback for a psychokinetic influence upon another person's physiology, In: Roll, W. G (Ed), *Research in Parapsychology 1977,* Metuchen, NJ: Scarecrow Press 1978, 123-134.

Braud, William., Conformance behavior involving living systems, In: Roll, W.G., et al. (Eds), *Research in Parapsychology 1978,* Metuchen, NJ: Scarecrow Press, 1979, 111-115.

Braud, William G., Lability and inertia in conformance behavior, *J. of the American Society for Psychical Research* 1980, 74, 297-318.

Braud, William G. Lability and inertia in psychic functioning, In: Shapin, B./ Coly, L (eds), *Concepts and theories of parapsychology,* New York: Parapsychology Foundation 1981, 1-28.

Braud, William G., Distant mental influence of rate of hemolysis of human red blood cells, In: Henkel, Linda A./ Berger, Rich E. (Eds), *Research in Parapsychology 1988,* Metuchen, NJ/ London: Scarecrow 1989(a), 1-6.

Braud, William G., Using living targets in psi research, *Parapsychology Review* 1989(b), 20(6), 1-4.

Braud, William, On the use of living target systems in distant mental influence research, In: Shapin, Betty/ Coly, Lisette (Eds), *Psi Research Methodology: A Reexamination,* New York: Parapsychology Foundation 1990(a).

Braud, William G., Distant mental influence of rate of hemolysis of human red blood cells, *J. of the American Society for Psychical Research* 1990(b), 84.

Braud, William On the use of living target systems in distant mental influence research, In: Coly, L./ McMahon, Joanne D.S. (eds), *Psi Research Methodology: a Re-examination,* New York: Parapsychology Foundation 1993, 149-181.

Braud, William G.: Can our intentions interact directly with the physical world? *European J. of Parapsychology,* 1994(b), 10, 78-90.

Braud, William G.: The role of mind in the physical world: a psychologist's view, *European J. of Parapsychology,* 1994(a), 10, 66-77.

Braud, William; Davis, Gary/ Wood, Robert, Experiments with Matthew Manning, *J. of the Society for Psychical Research,* 1979, 50, 199-223.

Braud, William/ Schlitz, Marilyn, Psychokinetic influence on electrodermal activity, *J. of Parapsychology,* 1983, 47(2), 95-119.

Braud, William, et al., Further studies of the bio-PK effect: Feedback, blocking, specificity/ generality, *Presentation at Parapsychological Meeting,* 1984.

Braud, William/ Schlitz, Marilyn, Possible Role of Intuitive Data Sorting in Electrodermal Biological Psychokinesis (Bio-Pk), *Research in Parapsychology 1987,* 1988, 5-9.

Braud, William/ Schlitz, Marilyn. A Methodology for the Objective Study of Transpersonal Imagery, *Journal of Scientific Exploration* 1989, 3(1), 43-63.

Braud, William/ Schlitz, Marilyn: Consciousness interactions with remote biological systems: anomalous intentionality effects, *Subtle Energies* 1991, 2, 1-46.

Braud, William; Schlitz, Marilyn; Collins, John & Klitch, Helen, Further studies of the bio-PK effects: Feedback, blocking, specificity/ generality, *Presentation at Parapsychological Association Meeting 1984.*

Braude Stephen E., *ESP and Psychokinesis: A Philosophical Examination,* Philadelphia, PA: Temple University Press, Philosophical Monographs 1979(b).

Braude, Stephen E., The Observational theories in parapsychology: A Critique, *J. of the American Society for Psychical Research* 1979(a), 73, 349-366.

Breasted, J. H., *The Edwin Smith Surgical Papyrus,* Chicago: University of Chicago 1930.

Brennan, *Barbara, Hands of Light.* New York: Bantam 1987.

Brennan, Barbara, *Light Ascending*, New York: Bantam 1993.

Brennan, Troyen A. The institute of medicine report on medical errors — could it do harm? *New England Journal of Medicine* 2000, 342(15).

Brennan, T. A. et al, Incidence of adverse events and negligence in hospitalized patients: results of the Harvard Medical Practice Study I. *New England Journal of Medicine* 1991, 324, 370-376.

Brier R.; Savits, B./ Schmeidler, G. Tests of Silva mind control graduates, In: Roll, W.G.; Morris, R.L./ Morris, J.D. (Eds), *Research in Parapsychology 1973*, Metuchen, NJ: Scarecrow Press 1974, 13-15.

Brier, Robert, PK on a bio-electrical system, *J. of Parapsychology* 1969, 33, 187-205.

Brookes-Smith, C./ Hunt, D.W., Some experiments in psychokinesis, *J. of the Society for Psychical Research* 1970, 45, 265-280.

Broughton, R.S., Possible brain hemisphere laterality effects on ESP performance, *J. of the Society for Psychical Research* 1976, 48, 384-399.

Brown, C.C. et al. The EEG in meditation and Therapeutic Touch healing, J. of Altered States of Consciousness, 1977, 3, 169-180.

Brown, Chip, The experiments of Dr. Oz, *New York Times Magazine*, 1995, July 30.

Brown, Craig K. Spiritual healing in a general practice: using a quality-of-life questionnaire to measure outcome, *Complementary Therapies in Medicine* 1995, 3, 230-233.

Brown, Fran, *Living Reiki: Takata's Teachings*, Mendocino, CA: LifeRhythm 1992.

Brown, Patricia Ricciuti, The Effects of Therapeutic Touch on Chemotherapy-induced Nausea and Vomiting: A Pilot Study (Master's thesis), Reno: University of Nevada 1981.

Brown, William C., *A Treatise on Etheric Surgery*, Toccoa Falls, GA., Privately printed, nd, 16pp.

Bucholtz, Randi Anderson, *The use of Reiki therapy in the treatment of pain in rheumatoid arthritis*, M.S. in Nursing-Family Nurse Practitioner, University of Wisconsin-Oshkosh, 1996.

Burbank, Luther, Quote from Tompkins, Peter/ Bird, Christopher, *The Secret Life of Plants*, New York: Harper/ Row 1972, 134.

Burg, Bob, The puzzle of the psychic patient, *Human Behavior* Sep 1975, 25-30.

Burke, Abbot George, *Magnetic Therapy: Healing in Your Hands*, Oklahoma City: St. George 1980.

Burns, Jean, Consciousness and psi, *Psi Research* 1986, 5(1,2), 166-205.

Bush, A.M./ Geist, C.R. Testing electromagnetic explanations for a possible psychokinetic effect of Therapeutic Touch in germinating corn seed, Psycholog. Rep. 1992, 70, 891-896.

Bush, Anita M./ Geist, Charles R. Geophysical variables and behavior: LXX. Testing electromagnetic explanations for a possible psychokinetic effect of therapeutic touch on germinating corn seed, *Psychological Reports* 1992, 70, 891-896.

Butler, Patrick, *The Healing Hand Book: Training and Developing the Power to Heal*, London/ New York: Quantum 1990.

Byrd, Randolph C., Positive therapeutic effects of intercessory prayer in a coronary care population, *Southern Medical J.* 1988, 81(7), 826-829 (Quote reprinted by permission from *Southern Medical J.*).

C

Cabico, Lucila Levardo, *A Phenomenological Study of the Experiences of Nurses Practicing Therapeutic Touch* (Master's thesis), Buffalo, NY: D'Youville College 1993.

Cade, C. Maxwell/ Coxhead, N., *The Awakened Mind: Biofeedback and the Development of Higher States of Awareness*, New York: Delacorte Press/ Eleanor Friede 1978.

Cadoret, Remi J., The reliable application of ESP, *J. of Parapsychology* 1955, 19, 203-227.

Cahn, H./ Muscle, N., Towards standardization of "laying-on" of hands investigation, *Psychoenergetic Systems* 1976, 1, 115-118.

Cai, Fuchou/ Cai, Shangda/ Chen, Jion/ Zheng, Shusen/ Zhang, Jinmei/ Chen, Yienfen/ He, Jinhong – Sun Yat-Sen University of Medical Sciences, Guangzhou/ Qigong Society of Guangdong Province, Guangzhou, China –Influence of emitted qi on bioeffect of human fetal fibroblast with quantitative ultrastructure analysis *(3rd National Academic Conference on Qigong Science, Guangzhou, China. 1990* – from Qigong Database of Sancier).

Cai, Shangda/ Zeng, Guangyuan/ Lou, Shenhong/ Zhang, Jinmei/ Chen, Yienfeng/ He, Jinhong - Dept Biology, Sun Yat-Sen University of Medical Sciences, Guangzhou/ Dept Chemistry, South China Technical University, Guangzhou/ Dept Physiology, Sun Yat-Sen University of Medical Sciences, Guangzhou/ Qigong Society of Guangdong Province, China – Electron spin resonance (ESR) measurements of the effect of waiqi (emitted qi) on the free radical concentration in rat tissue *(3rd National Academic Conference on Qigong Science, Guangzhou, China. 1990* – from Qigong Database of Sancier).

Campbell, Anthony, 'Treatment' of Tumours by PK, *J. of the Society for Psychical Research* 1968, 44, 428. (Summary of Elguin, Gita H./ Onetto, Brenio, *Acta Psiquiat. Psicol. Amer. Lat.* 1968, 14, 47)

Cao, Qiyuan/ Li, Yongqion/ Cheng, Chenqing/ Liang, Jianxiong, Cancer Institute, Sun Yat-Sen University of Medical Sciences, Guangzhou 510060, China/ Dept Radiotherapy, Tumor Hospital, Guangzhou 510060, China, Inhibition of human nasopharyngeal carcinoma cells in vitro by emitted qi and gamma ray, *2nd World Conference for Academic Exchange of Medical Qigong, Beijing 1993.*

Cao, Xuetao/ Ye, Tainxing/ Gao, Yetao, Second Military Military Medical College, Shanghai, Effect of emitted qi in enhancing the induction in vitro of lymphokines in relation to antitumor mechanisms, *1st World Conference for Academic Exchange of Medical Qigong,* Beijing1988.

Cao, Xuetao/ Ye, Tainxing/ Gao, Yetao. Dept Microbiology & Immunology, Shanghai Hospital & Second Military Medical College, Shanghai, Antitumor metastases activity of emitted qi in tumor bearing mice, *1st World Conference for Academic Exchange of Medical Qigong, Beijing, 1988.*

Capra, Fritjof, *The Tao of Physics*, Boulder, CO: Shambala 1975.

Carington, Whately, *Telepathy*, London: Methuen 1946.

Carlson, Rick J. (Ed), *The Frontiers of Science and Medicine*, Chicago, IL: Henry Regnery 1975.

Carr, Joseph, *The Twisted Cross*, Shreveport, LA: Huntington House 1985.

Carrel, A., *Voyage to Lourdes*, New York 1950.

Carter, Mary E./ McGarey, William A., *Edgar Cayce on Healing*, Anderson, IN: Warner 1972.

Casdorph, H. Richard, *The Miracles*, Plainfield, N.J.: Logos International 1976.

Cassee, Th. P., Oubevoegde genezers en hun patienten: afwijkend gedrag in de gezinidheidszerg, *Sociologische Gids* 1970, 17, 399-410.

Cassee, Th.E., Onbevoegde genezers en hun patiänten, [Unauthorized healers and their patients: aberrant behavior in health care], *Sociologische Dids.* 1970, 17, 399.

Cassoli, Piero, *Il Guaritore* (Italian), Milan, Italy: Armenia 1979.

Cassoli, Piero, The healer: Problems, methods and results *European J. of Parapsychology* 1981, 4(1), 71-80.

Castronova, Jerri/ Oleson, Terri: A comparison of supportive psychotherapy and laying-on of hands healing for chronic back pain patients, *Alternative Medicine* 1991, 3(4), 217-226.

Cavallini, Giuliana, *Saint Martin de Porres*, Rockford, IL: Tan 1979.

Cayce, Hugh Lynn (Ed), *The Edgar Cayce Reader*, New York: Paperback Library, 1969.

Cayce, Hugh Lynn, *Gifts of Healing*, Virginia Beach, VA: Association for Research & Enlightenment, no date.

Cayce, Hugh Lynn, *The Edgar Cayce Reader #2*, New York: Paperback Library, 1969.

Centers for Disease Control, 1993 Revised classification system for HIV infection and expanded surveillance case definition for AIDS among adolescents and adults, *MMWR* 1992a Dec: 1 (RR-17): 1-19.

Cerutti, Edwina, *Mystic With the Healing Hands: The Life Story of Olga Worrall*, New York: Harper/ Row 1975.

Challoner, H. K., *The Path of Healing*, Wheaton, IL: Theosophical 1972.

Chapman, George (As told by Stemman, Roy), *Surgeon From Another World*, London: W. H. Allen 1978.

Chapman, George, *Extraordinary Encounters*, Aylesbury, Bucks, England: Lang 1973.

Chase, Edgar. *Personal Communications*, 1988.

Chen Guoguang: The curative effect observation of 24 cases under my 'outward qigong' treatment Proccedings of the 2nd International Conference on Qigong, Xian, China, September 1989.

Chen, Guoguang – Cadre Training College, Zhaotong Area, Yunnan Province – Material effect of mind and qi–research with the help of laser Raman spectrum analyzer (2nd World Conference for Academic Exchange of Medical Qigong. Beijing 1993–from Qigong Database of Sancier).

Chen, Xiaojun/ Gao, Qiynan/ Jao, Xianrong/ Zhang, Jinmei/ Huang, Canxin/ Fan, Xiuque–Cancer Institute, Sun Yat-Sen University of Medical Sciences, Guangzhou/ Dept Physiology, Sun Yat-Sen University of Medical Sciences, Guangzhou/ Qigong Association of Guangzhou, China–Effects of emitted qi on inhibition of human NPC cell line and DNA synthesis (3rd National Academic Conference on Qigong Science, Guangzhou, China. 1990–from Qigong Database of Sancier).

Chen, Xiaojun/ Yi, Qing/ Liu, Kela, Zhang, Jinmei/ Chen, Yusheng, Cancer Center, Sun Yat-sen University of Medical Sciences, Guangzhou 510060/ Dept Physiology, Sun Yat-sen University of Medical Sciences, Guangzhou 510060/ Qigong Association of Guangdong, China, Double-blind test of emitted qi on tumor formation of a nasopharyngeal carcinoma cell line in nude mice, *2nd World Conference for Academic Exchange of Medical Qigong, Beijing 1993*.

Chen, Yuanfeng, Shanghai Institute of Traditional Chinese Medical Science, Shanghai 200030, China, Analysis of effect of emitted qi on human hepatocarcinoma cell (BEL-7402) by using flow cytometry, *2nd World Conference for Academic Exchange of Medical Qigong. Beijing 1993*.

Chen, Yuanfeng, Shanghai Institute of Traditional Chinese Medical Science, Shanghai 200030, Effect of emitted qi on agglutinating reaction of human pulmonary adenocarcinoma cell (SPC-A1) mediated by ConA, *2nd World Conference for Academic Exchange of Medical Qigong, Beijing 1993*.

Chen, Zhaoxi [and others]—Dept Physiology, First Medical College of PLA, Guangzhou, China – Normal adult EEG can be changed by qigong waiqi (emitted qi) *(3rd National Academic Conference on Qigong Science, Guangzhou, China. 1990 – from Qigong Database of Sancier).*

Chesi, Gert. *Faith Healers in the Philippines*. Austria: Perlinger 1981.

Chesi, Gert. *Voodoo: Africa's Secret Power*, Translated by Klambauer, Ernst, Austria: Perlinger 1980.

China Sports Magazine, *The Wonders of Qigong: A Chinese Exercise for Fitness, Health and Longevity*, Los Angeles: Wayfarer 1985.

Chinese Academy of Sciences, Exceptional human body radiation, Trans. from Chinese: Paasche, J.H., *Psi Research* 1982, 1(2), 16-21.

Chopra, Deepak, *Quantum Healing: Exploring the Frontiers of Mind/ Body Medicine*, London/ New York: Bantam 1989.

Chou, Chu–Rehabilitation Hospital, Canada–Moniliasis treated by emitted qi and acupuncture therapy (2nd World Conference for Academic Exchange of Medical Qigong, Beijing 1993–from Qigong Database of Sancier).

Christie, Agatha, *The mysterious Affair at Styles*, 1920.

Chu, Chow–Canada Qigong Health Clinic–Use of emitted qi in qigong and acupuncture in the treatment of food allergies (*1st World Conference for Academic Exchange of Medical Qigong, Beijing 1988* - from Qigong Database of Sancier).

Church, Dawson/ Sherr, Alan, *The Heart of the Healer*, New York: Aslan 1987.

Clark, A.J./ Seifert, P. Client perceptions of Therapeutic Touch, Paper presented at Third Annual West Alabama Conference on Clinical Nursing Research 1992.

Clark, Philip E./ Clark, Mary Jo, Therapeutic Touch: Is there a scientific basis for the practice?, *Nursing Research* 1984, 33(1), 37-41.

Clayton, P. J., The sequelae and nonsequelae of conjugal bereavement, *American J. of Psychiatry* 1979, 1979, 136, 1530-1534.

Coakley D. McKenna G.W. Safety of Faith Healing, *Lancet* 1986, (8478), 444 Feb 22.

Coddington, Mary, *In Search of the Healing Energy*, New York: Warner/ Destiny 1978.

Cohen, J., *Statistical Power Analysis for the Behavioral Sciences* (2nd ed.), Hillsdale, NJ: Lawrence Erlbaum Associates 1988.

Cohen, John, Spiritual healing: a complementary role in general practice, *Modern Medicine* 1990 (Sep), 663-665.

Cohen, Kenneth S., *The Way of Qigong: The Art and Science of Chinese Energy Healing*, New York: Ballantine 1997.

Coker, Connie Lynn, *An Impact Evaluation of a Therapeutic Touch Continuing Education Activity* (Master's thesis), Toledo, OH: Medical College of Ohio 1987.

Colinon, M., *Les Guerisseurs*, Paris: Grosset 1957.

Collins, H. M., *Changing Order, Replication and Induction in Scientific Practice*, London: Sage 1985.

Collins, J. W., *The Effect of Non-contact Therapeutic Touch on the Relaxation Response*, Unpublished Master's Thesis, Vanderbilt University, Nashville, TN 1983.

Collip, P. J., The Efficacy of Prayer: A Triple Blind Study, *Medical Times* 1969, 97(5), 201-4.

Congressional Office of Technology Assessment, *Assessing the Efficacy and Safety of Medical Technologies,* Washington, D.C.: Congressional Office of Technology Assessment 1978.

Constantinides, P., Women Heal Women: Spirit Possession and Sexual Segregation in a Muslim Society. *Social Science in Medicine* 1985, 21 (6), 685-692.

Cooper, Ronda Evelyn, *The Effect of Theapeutic Touch on Irritable Bowel Syndrome* (Master's thesis), Clarkson College 1997.

Cooper, Wendy Ellen Copeland, Meanings of Intuition in Nurses' Work (Master's thesis), Canada: University of Victoria 1994.

Coopersmith, S. *Self-Esteem Inventories*, Palo Alto, CA: Consulting Psychologists Press 1981.

Cooperstein, Allan: The Myths of Healing: a summary of research into transpersonal healing experiences, *J. of the American Society for Psychical Research* 1992, 86, 99-133; *The Myths of Healing: A Descriptive Analysis of Transpersonal Healing*. Doctoral dissertation, Saybrook Institute, California 1990.

Cooperstem, M. Allan, *The Myths of Healing: A Descriptive Analysis and Taxonomy of Transpersonal Healing Experience*. Unpublished Doctoral Dissertation, Saybrook Institute, California 1990.

Cox, W. E., The influence of 'applied psi' upon the sex of offspring, *J. of the Society for Psychical Research* 1957, 39, 65-77.

Crenshaw, James, Reverend Fuller's Ministry of Healing, In: Fate Magazine, *Exploring the Healing Miracle*, Highland Park, IL: Clark 1983, 115-139 (Orig. In: Fate Magazine, Mar & Apr 1975).

Crisp, A.H./ Jones, M.G./ Slater, P., The Middlesex Hospital Questionnaire: a validation study, *Psychology*1978, 51, 269-180.

Croke, Piers, A Shower of Roses, *The Unexplained*, 1981, 3(36), 704-707.

Cuddon, Eric, The Relief of Pain by Laying on of Hands *International J. of Parapsychology* 1968, 10(1), 85-92 (Also In: Angoff, A (Ed), *The Psychic Force*. New York: Putnam's 1970).

Cuevedo, Oscar G., The Problem of healers: Part II, *Revista de Parapsychologia* (Portugese) 1973, 1(4), 4-

Cui, Rongqing; Zhao, Xiuquan; Yang, Jiafeng; Li, Hoengmin Dept Physiology, Beijing College of Traditional Chinese Medicine, Beijing 100029, China/ China-Japan Friendship Hospital, Beijing 100029, Effect of emitted qi to acupoints on somatosensory evoked potential recorded from the cortex following Zusanli (ST36) stimulation in cats, *2nd World Conference for Academic Exchange of Medical Qigong, Beijing 1993*.

Cui, Yuanhao/ Li, Shengping/ Meng, Guirong/ Sung, Mengyin/ Yan, Sixian/ Xin, Yan, Tsinghua University, Beijing/ Municipal Institute of Traditional Chinese Medicine of Chongqing, Sichuan Province, China, Effect of emitted qi on long-time tracking of UV spectroscopy on the fluorescence in dyestuff, *1st World Conference for Academic Exchange of Medical Qigong, Beijing 1988*.

Cumbey, Constance, *A Planned Deception*, East Detroit, MI: Pointe 1985.

Cumbey, Constance, *The Hidden Dangers of the Rainbow*, Shreveport, LA: Huntington House 1984.

D

Dallett, Jane O. *When the Spirits Come Back*, Toronto: Inner City 1988.

Darbonne, Madelyn M. et al., The effects of Healing Touch modalities on patients with chronic pain, (J. article in preparation).

Davis, Bruce/ Davis, Genny Wright, *The Heart of Healing*, Fairfax, CA: Inner Light, 1983.

Davis, Thomas N., III, Can Prayer Facilitate Healing and Growth?, *Southern Medical J.* 1986, 79(6), 733-735.

Davitashvili, Dzhuna, Verification of biotherapy by contemporary technology, *Proceedings 5th International Conference on Psychotronic Research* 1983, 2, 12- 19.

Davitashvili, Juna, Results in Healing, Selected Documents, In: Vilenskaya, Larissa (Translater and Editor), *Parapsychology in the USSR, Part III*, San Francisco: Washington Research Center 1981, 55-60.

de Carvalho, M. Margarida, An eclectic approach to group healing in Sao Paulo, Brazil: A pilot study (*J. of the Society for Psychical Research* 1996, 61(845), 243-249.

Dean, Douglas/ Brame, E., Physical Changes in Water by Laying-on-of-Hands, *Proceedings of the Second International Conference on Psychotronic Research, Monaco* 1975, 200-201.

Dean, Douglas, An examination of infra-red and ultra-violet techniques for changes in water following the laying-on of hands, *Unpublished Doctoral Dissertation, Saybrook Institute, CA* 1983.

Dean, Douglas, Personal Communication, 1985, 1987.

Dean, Douglas, Presentation at Scientific and Medical Network annual meeting, Dartington, 1989.

Dean, Douglas, Research in Healing: Effects on Water, Presentation at Workshop on Healing Research at the Combined 100th Society for Psychical Research and 25th Parapsychological Association Meeting, Cambridge, England Aug 1982.

Dean, Douglas, The Plethysmograph as an Indicator of ESP *J. of the American Society for Psychical Research* 1962, 41, 351-352.

Dean, E. D. The plethysmograph as an indicator of ESP, *J. of the Society for Psychical Research* 1962, 41, 351-353.

Dean, S. R./ Plyer, C. O., Jr./ Dean, M. L., Should Psychic Studies be Included in Psychiatric Education?, *American J. of Psychiatry* 1980, 137(10), 1247-1249.

Delsanto de Simic, Nelly, Microstructural Interactions of Biotherapist, *Proceedings of the 6thh International Conference on Psychotronics* 1986, 133- 134.

Derogatis, L. R., *SCL-90R administration, scoring and procedures manual*, Baltimore, MD: Clinical Psychometric Research 1977.

Dethlefsen, Thorwold/ Dahlke, Rudiger., *The Healing Power of Illness: the Meaning of Symptoms and How to Interpret Them.* Longmead, UK: Element 1990, (Original German 1983 Translation Peter Lerresurier).

Di Liscia, Julio C., Psychic healing: an attempted investigation, *Psi Comunicacion* 1977, 3(5/ 6), 101-110 (Abstract translated from Spanish, In: *Parapsychology Abstracts International) 1984*, 2(1), 82, Abstr. No. 669).

Dieckhofer, K., German Treatment of Epilepsy in the Middle Ages and by Paracelsus: On Hagiotherapy and Pharmacology in the 'Falling Disease', *Fortschrifft Medicine* 1986, 104(11), 232-235.

Ding-ming, Hsu, *The Chinese Psychic Healing* Taipei: Parapsychological Association 1984, 6.

Dingwall, Eric John, *Abnormal Hypnotic Phenomena: A survey of 19th Century Cases*, London: Churchill 1968.

Dirksen, Murl Owen, *Pentecostal Healing: A Facet of the Personalistic Health System In Pakal-Na, a Village in Southern Mexico.* Unpublished Doctoral Dissertation, University TN 1984.

Dixon, Michael, A healer in GP practice *The Doctor-Healer Network Newsletter 1994*, No. 7, 6-7.

Dixon, Michael, Does 'healing' benefit patients with chronic symptoms? A quasi-randomized trial in general practice, *J. of the Royal Society of Medicine* 1998, 91, 183-188.

Dobkin de Rios, Marlene., *Hallucinogens: Cross-Cultural Perspectives*, Albuguergue, NM: University of New Mexico 1984(a).

Dobkin de Rios, Marlene., The Vidente Phenomenon in Third Word Traditional Healing: An Amazonian Example, *Medical Anthropology* 1984, Winter , 60-70.

Dobkin de Rios, Marlene., *Visionary Vine: Hallucinogenic Healing in the Peruvian Amazon*, Prospect Heights, K: Waveland 1972.

Dollar, Carolyn Estelle, Effects of Therapeutic Touch on Perception of Pain and Physiological Measurements from Tension Headache in Adults: A Pilot Study (Master's thesis), Jackson: University of Mississippi Medical Center 1993.

Dong, Paul, *The Four Major Mysteries of Mainland China*, Englewood Cliffs, NJ: Prentice-Hall 1984.

Dossey, Larr., *Space, Time and Medicine*, Boulder, Colorado: Shambala 1982.

Dossey, Larry: Healing Words: The Power of Prayer and the Practice of Medicine, New York: Harper SanFrancisco 1993.

Dossey, Larry, Canceled funerals: a look at miracle cures, *Alternative Therapies* 1998a, 4(2), 10-18; 116-120.

Dossey, Larry, The right man syndrome: skepticism and alternative medicine, *Alternative Therapies* 1998b, 4(3), 12-19; 108-114 (91 refs).

Doucette, Maureen Louise, *Discovering the Individual's View of Receiving Therapeutic Touch: An Exploratory Descriptive Study* (Master's thesis), Canada: University of Alberta 1997.

Dowling, St. John., Lourdes Cures and Their Medical Assessment, *J. of the Royal Society of Medicine* 1984, 77, 634-638.

Dresser, Horatio (Ed.), *The Quimby Manuscripts*, New Hyde Park, New York: University Books 1969.

Dressler, David, Light Touch Manipulative Technique, *J. of Alternative and Complementary Medicine 1990.*

Dressler, David: Light Touch Menipulative Technique International J. of Alternative and Complementary Medicine (England) 1990, 8(4), 19-20.

Drury, Nevill, The Elements of Shamanism, Longmead, England: Element 1989.

Du, Luoyi - China Medical Qigong Society, Beijing - Effect of mind-control in qigong exercise investigated by an infrared thermovision imager (1st World Conference for Academic Exchange of Medical Qigong, Beijing 1988 - from Qigong Database of Sancier).

Duval, P., Exploratory Experiments with Ants (Abstract), *J. of Parapsychology*, 1971, 35, 58.

E
_____

Easton, Cassandra, *Psychic Families*, London/ New York: Foulshan 1995.

Eddy, Mary Baker, *Science and Health with Key to the Scriptures* 1875.

Edge, Hoyt L., A Philosophical Justification for the Conformance Behavioral Model, *J. of the American Society for Psychical Research* 1978(a), 72, 215-231.

Edge, Hoyt L. et al., *Foundations of Parapsychology: Exploring the Boundaries of Human Capability*, Boston & London: Routledge & Kegan Paul 1986.

Edge, Hoyt L, Plant PK on an RNG and the Experimenter Effect, In: Roll, W.G (Ed.), *Research in Parapschology 1977*, Metuchen, NJ: Scarecrow Press 1978(b), 169-174.

Edge, Hoyt, The Effect of Laying on of Hands on an Enzyme: An Attempted Replication, In:, *Research in Parapsychology, 1979*, Metuchen, NJ: Scarecrow 1980, 137-139.

Edwardes, Phil/ Mcconnell, James, *Healing for You: The Story of Phil Edwardes, a Healer with Remarkable Powers*, Wellingborough,

Northamptonshire, England: Thorsons, 1985.

Edwardes, Phil with De Saulles, Annette, *Touch them with Love*, Shaftesbury, England/ Rockport, MA: Element 1994.

Edwards, Harry, *The Evidence for Spirit Healing*, London: Spiritualist Press 1953.

Edwards, Harry, *Thirty Years a Spiritual Healer,* London: Herbert Jenkins, 1968.

Edwards, Harry., *The Science Of Spirit Healing*. London: Rider 1945.

Eeman, L. E., Co-Operative Healing: The Curative Properties of Human Radiations, London: Frederick Muller 1947.

Ehrenwald, Jan, Parapsychology and the Seven Dragons: A Neuropsychiatric Model of Psi Phenomena, In: Schmeidler, Gertrude (Ed.), *Parapsychology: Its Relation to Physics, Biology, Psychology and Physics*, Metuchen, NJ: Scarecrow Press 1976(a), 246-263.

Einstein, Albert, in Heisenberg, W., *Physics and Beyond*, New York: Harper & Row 1971, p. 63.

Eisenberg, David with Wright, Thomas Lee, *Encounters with Qi*, New York: W. W. Norton 1985.

Eisenberg, David et al. Unconventional medicine in the United States: Prevalence, costs and patterns of use, *New England J. of Medicine* 1993, 328, 246-252.

Eisenberg, H., *Inner Spaces: Parapsychological Explorations of the Mind*, Toronto: Musson Book Co. 1977.

Eisenberg, John M. (Director, Agency for Healthcare Research and Quality), *Statement on Medical Errors.* before the Senate Appropriations Subcommittee on Labor, Health and Human Services, and Education, December 13, 1999, Washington DC. Agency for Healthcare Research and Quality, Rockville, MD. http://www.ahrq.gov/news/stat1213.htm

Eisenbud, Jule/ Stillings, Dennis., Paranormal Film Forms and Paleolithic Rock Engravings, *Archaeus* 1984, 2(1), 9-18; 18-26.

Eisenbud, Jule., *Parasychology and the Unconscious*, North Atlantic Books 1983.

Eisenbud, Jule., *The World of Ted Serios*, New York; Pocket Books 1967.

Eisenbud, Jule/ Stillings, Dennis: Paranormal film forms and paleolithic rock engravings. *Archaeus* 1984, 2(1), 9-26.

Eisenbud, Jule: *The World of Ted Serios*. New York: Pocket Books 1967.

Eisenbud, Jule: Paranormal photography. In:

Wolman, Benjamin B. (Ed): *Handbook of Parapsychology,* New York: Van Nostrand Reinhold 1977, 414-432.

Eliade, Fagin, C., Stress: inplications for nursing research, *Image: J. of Nursing Scholarship* 1987, 19(1), 38-41.

Eliade, Mircea., *Shamanism: Archaic Techniques of Ecstasy,* Translator: W Trask, London: Routledge and Kegan Paul 1970.

Eliot, Charles William, Inagural address as president of Harvard 1869.

Eliot, George (Marian Evans Cross) *Stradivarius.*

Elliotson, J., Remarkable Cure of Intense Nervous Affections, Etc., *Zoist* 1847-1848, 234-253.

Elliott, G. Maurice, Spiritual Healing, *Parapsychology Foundation Newsletter* 1960 (Jul-Aug), 4-6.

Ellis, Esmé, *Pathway into Sunrise: Journey of a Wounded Healer,* Dorking, England: Blue Dragon 1997.

Engel, Hans G., Energy Healing, *Research Report* Los Angeles, CA: Ernest Holmes Research Foundation 1978, 1-15.

England, Ann (Ed.), *We Believe in Healing,* Crowborough, England: Highland 1986.

Estebany, Oszkar, *Personal Communication,* 1982.

Estlander, A.M./ Härkäpää, K. Presentation of a new attitude scale for patients with chronic pain, *Psychologia* 1985, 6, 428-432.

Evans, Carlton/ Richardson, Improved Recovery and Reduced Post Operative Stay After Therapeutic Suggestions During General Anaesthesia, *Lancet* 1988, 11, 491-493.

Evans, Hilary, *Spontaneous Sightings of Seemingly Autonomous Entities: A Comparative Study in the Light of Experimental and Contrived Entity Fabrications.*

F

Fabrega, Horacio Jr., The study of Medical Problems in Preliterate Settings, *Yale J. of Biology and Medicine* 43: 385-407, 1971.

Fabrega, Horacio, Jr., *Disease and Social Behaviour: An Elementary Exposition,* Cambridge, Massachussets: MIT 1974.

Fadiman, James, The Prime Cause of Healing: The Process of Exploring and Experiencing It, *J. for Holistic Health* 1977, p.11.

Fahrion, Steven, *Application of energetic therapy to basal cell carcinoma* (Pilot study, Topeka, Kansas, supported by the Office of Alternative Medicine, 1995, summary kindly provided by Fahrion).

Fedoruk, Rosalie Berner, *Transfer of the Relaxation Response: Therapeutic Touch as a Method for the Reduction of Stress in Premature Neonates,* Unpublished Doctoral Dissertation, University of Maryland 1984.

Feild, Reshad, *Here to Heal,* Shaftesbury, England: Element 1985.

Feng Lida/ Chen Shuying/ Wang Saixi/ Haixin, Chen – Navy General Hospital, China Immunology Research Center, Beijing – Effect of emitted qi on changes of rat T-cell subclasses in peripheral blood. (*3rd National Academy Conference on Qigong Science. Guangzhou, China 1990* – from Qigong database of Sancier).

Feng Lida/ Qian, Juqing/ Kang, Xiaoling - Chinese Immunology Research Center, Beijing - Effect of emitted qi on immune sticking function of red blood cells to tumor cells – (*2nd World Conferencefor Academic Exchangeof Medical Qigong, Beijing 1993* - from Qigong database of Sancier).

Feng Lida/ Wang, Yunsheng/ Chen, Shuying/ Chen, Haixing - Immunology Research Center, Beijing - Effect of emitted qi on the immune functions of mice (*1st World Conferencefor Academic Exchange of Medical Qigong, Beijing 1988* - from Qigong database of Sancier).

Feng, Lida/ Chen, Shuying/ Zhu, Lina/ Zhao, Xiuzhen/ Cui, Siqi, Chinese Immunology Research Center, Beijing, Effect of emitted qi on the growth of mice, (*2nd World Conference for Academic Exchange of Medical Qigong, Beijing 1993* – from Qigong Database of Sancier).

Feng, Lida/ Peng, Liaomin – Chinese Immunology Research Center, Beljing, – Effect of emitted qi on prevention and treatment of tumors in mice. (*2nd World Conference for Academic Exchange of Medical Qigong. Beijing 1993* – from Qigong Database of Sancier).

Feng, Lida/ Peng, Liaomin/ Qian, Juqing/ Cheng, Shuying - Chinese Immunology Research Center, Beijing 100037 – Effect of qigong information energy on diabetes mellitus (*4th International Conference on Qigong.*

Vancouver, British Columbia, Canada. 1995 – from Qigong Database of Sancier).

Feng, Lida/ Qian, Juqing/ Chen, Shugine – General Navy Hospital, Beijing – Research on reinforcing NK-cells to kill stomach carcinoma cells with waiqi (emitted qi) (*3rd National Academy Conference on Qigong Science, Guangzhou, China 1990* – from Qigong database of Sancier).

Feng, Lida/ Qian, Juqing/ Chen, Suqing [and others] – China Immunology Research Center, Beijing. Effect of emitted qi on human carcinoma cells – (*1st World Conference for Academic Exchangeof Medical Qigong, Beijing 1988* – from Qigong database of Sancier).

Feng, Lida/ Zhao, Xiuzhen – Immunology Research Center, Beijing - Effect of emitted qi on the L 1210 cells of leukemia in mice (*1st World Conference for Academic Exchange of Medical Qigong, Beijing 1988* – from Qigong database of Sancier).

Fenwick, Peter/ Hopkins, Roy, An Examination of the Effect of Healing on Water, *J. of the Society for Psychical Research* 1986, 53, 387-390.

Ferda, Frantisek., *J. Paraphysics* 1979, 13(5/6) 129, Abstract-Clairvoyant DX and Healing At Distance of 50 Km, Paper given at 4th International Congress on Psychotronic Research, 1979.

Ferguson, Cecilia Kinsel, *Subjective Experience of Therapeutic Touch (SETTS): Psychometric Examination of an Instrument,* Unpublished Doctoral Dissertation, University of Texas at Austin 1986.

Finkler, Kaja., *Spiritualist Healers in Mexico,* New York: Praeger 1985.

Flammonde, Paris, *The Mystic Healers,* New York: Stein and Day 1975.

Flaskerud, J.H. *AIDS/ HIV Infection: A reference for nursing professionals,* Philadelphia: W. B. Saunders 1989.

Fodor, Nandor, *Encyclopedia of Psychic Science,* USA: University Books, Inc. 1966 (large no. of people catalogued).

Fodor, Nandor, *On the Trail of the Poltergeist;* New York Citadel Press 1958.

France, Nancy E.M. The child's perception of the human energy field using therapeutic touch, *J. of Holistic Nursing* 1933, 11(4), 319-331.

Frazier, Kendrick, *Science Confronts the Paranormal,* Buffalo, NY: Promethius 1986.

Freud, Sigmund., *Studies in Parapsychology,* New York Collier 1963.

Fricker, E. G., *God is My Witness: The Story of the World-Famous Healer,* London: Eyre and Spottiswoode 1979.

Frost, Robert, *Dust in the Eyes* 1828.

Frost, Robert, quoted in Carlson/ Shield, p. 31.

Fry, Daniel W., *Can God Fill Teeth?*, Lakemont, GA: CSA Press 1970.

Frydrychowski, Andrzej F/ Przyjemska, Bozens;/ Orlowski, Tadeusz, An attempt to apply photon emission measurement in the selection of the most effective healer, *Psychotronika* 1985, 82-83. Abstract, translated from Polish by Alexander Imich, in *Parapsychology Abstracts International* 1987, 5(2), No. 2489.

Fukurai, T, *Clairvoyance and Thoughtography,* New York: Arno Press 1975.

Fukurai, T.: *Clairvoyance and Thoughtography.* New York: Arno 1975 (Orig. London: Rider 1931).

Fulda, Edeltraud, *And I Shall Be Healed: Autobiography of a Woman Miraculously Cured at Lourdes,* New York: Simon and Schuster, 1961.

Furlong, David, The Complete Healer: How to Awaken and Develop Your Healing Potential, London: Piatkus 1995.

G

Gagne, Deborah/ Toye Richard C., The effects of Therapeutic Touch and relaxation therapy in reducing anxiety (Archives of Psychiatric Nursing 1994, 8(3), 184-189.

Gagnon, T.A. & Rein, G, The biological significance of water structured with non-hertzian time-reversed waves, *J. of the US Psychotronics Association* 1990 4, 26-29.

Gaisson, Marie/ Bouchard, Louise, Effect of Therapeutic Touch on the well-being of person with terminal cancer, *J. of Holistic Nursing*, 1998, 16(3), 383-398.

Gallimore, J. G., *Relationship Between Parapsychology and Gravity, V. 3 of Handbook of Unusual Energies,* Mokelumne Hill, CA: Health Research, 1977.

Galton, F., Statistical Studies into the Efficacy of Prayer, *Fortnightly Review* 1872, 12, 125-135 (Reprinted in Roland, C.G., Does Prayer

Preserve?, *Archives of Internal Medicine* 1970, 125, 580-587).

Gao, Shufang/ Fan, Ronghao/ Yang, Guisheng/ Zhou, Yuqing – Dept Biology, Shandong University/ Research Academy of Qigong Science, Shandong/ Research Institute of Qigong and Parapsychology, Shandong University, China – Effect of qigong emanation (emitted qi) on physiology and biochemistry of cotton. *3rd National Academic Conference on Qigong Science, Guangzhou, China. 1990* - from Qigong Database of Sancier.

Gao, Zhenhua/ Zhang, Shiping/ Bi, Yongsheng – Shandon Traditional Chinese Medical College, Shandong, China – Effect of emitted qi acting on zasanli potnt of rabbits on myoelectric signals of Oddi's sphincter, *3rd National Academic Conference on Qigong Science, Guangzhou, China. 1990* – from Qigong Database of Sancier.

Garcia, Raquel, Healed by a Santera, In: Fate Magazine, <B>Exploring the Healing Miracle<B>, Highland Park, IL: Clark 1983, (Orig. Apr 1974).

Garcia, Raymond L., 'Witch Doctor?' A Hexing Case of Dermatitis, *Cutis* 1977, 19(1), 103-105.

Gardner, Nancy and Gardner, Esmond, *Five Great Healers Speak Here*, Wheaton, IL: Quest/ Theosophical 1982. (Reprinted by permission of The Theosophical Publishing House, Wheaton, IL, 1982; Copyright Nancy & Esmond Gardner).

Gardner, Rex, *Healing Miracles: A Doctor Investigates*, London: Barton, Longman and Todd 1986.

Gardner, Rex, Healing Miracles: A Doctor Investigates, London: Darton, Longman and Todd 1986.

Gardner, Rex, Miracles of Healing in Anglo-Celtic Northumbria as Recorded by the Venerable Bede and His Contemporaries: A Reappraisal in the Light of Twentieth Century Experience, *British Medical J.* 1983 (Dec 24-31), 287, 1927-1933. (Also reviewed in Rogo, D. Scott, The Power of Prayer, *Fate* 1986 (Aug), 43-50.

Garner, Jim, Spontaneous Regressions: Scientific Documentation as a Basis for the Declaration of Miracles, *Canadian Medical Association J.* 1974, 111, 1254-1264.

Garrard, Clare Thomasson, *The Effect of Therapeutic Touch on Stress Reduction and Immune Function in Persons with AIDS (Im-mune Deficiency)*, (dissertation) Birmingham: University of Alabama 1996.

Garrett, Eileen Jeanette, *Life is the Healer*, Philadelphia, PA: Dorrance, 1957.

Garrett, Eileen, *Adventures in the Supernormal: A Personal Memoir*, New York: Garrett Publications 1949.

Garrison, Vivian, Doctor, Espiritista or Psychiatrist? Health-Seeking Behavior in a Puerto Rican Neighborhood of New York City, *Medical Anthropology* 1977, 1, 65-180.

Garyaev, P.P./ Grigoriev, K.V./ Poponin, V.P. DNA solutions studied by Laser Correlation Spectroscopy: experimental evidence for spontaneous temporal self-organization, *Bulletin of Lebedev Physics Institute* 1992, 12.

Gauld, Alan, ESP and Attempts to Explain it, In: Thakur, S. (Ed), *Philosophy and Psychical Research*, London: Allan and Unwin 1976, 17-46.

Gauquelin, Michel, *The Scientific Basis of Astrology: Myth or Reality*, New York: Stein and Day 1969.

Geddes, F., *Healing Training in the Church*, Unpublished Ph.D. Dissertation, San Francisco Theological Seminary, 1981.

Geisler, Patrick V., Batcheldorian Psychodynamics in the Umbanda Ritual Trance Consultation, Part I, *Parapsychology Review* 1984, 15(6), 5-9.

Geisler, Patrick V., Batcheldorian Psychodynamics in the Umbanda Ritual Trance Consultation, Part II, *Parapsychology Review*, 1985(a), 16(1), 11-14.

Geisler, Patrick V., Parapsychological Anthropology II: A Multi-Method Study of Psi and Psi-Related Processes in the Umbanda Ritual Trance Consultation, *J. of the American Society for Psychical Research*, 1985(b), 79(2), 113-166.

Gerber, Richard, *Vibrational Medicine: New Choices for Healing Ourselves*, Santa Fe, NM: Bear & Co. 1988.

Giasson, Marie/ Bochard, Louise, Effect of Therapeutic Touch on the well-being of persons with terminal cancer, *J. of Holistic Nursing* 1998, 16(3), 383-398.

Gift, A. Visual analogue scales: measurement of subjective phenomena, *Nursing Research*, 1989, 38(5), 286-288. .

Glaser, B./ Strauss, A. *The Discovery of Grounded Theory*, Chicago: Aldine 1967.

Glass, G./ McGaw, B./ Smith, M., *Meta Analy-*

sis in Social Research, Beverly Hills, CA: Sage 1981.

Glick, Deborah Carrow, Psychosocial Wellness Among Spiritual Healing Participants, *Social Science Medicine* 1986, 22(5), 579-586.

Gmur, M. and Tschopp, A., Factors determining the success of nicotine withdrawal: 12-year follow-up of 532 smokers after suggestion therapy (by a faith healer), *International J. of the Addictions* 1987, 22(12), 1189- 1200.

Goddard, Henry H., The Effects of Mind on Body as Evidenced by Faith Cures, *American J. of Psychology* 1899, 10, 431-502.

Goldsmith, Joel S., *The Art of Spiritual Healing*, New York: Harper and Row 1959.

Goldstein, I. B., Reliability of stress profiling of selected muscle sites, In: Greenfield, N.S./ Sternbach, R.A. (eds), *Handbook of Psychophysiology*, New York: Holt, Reinhart, Winston 1972.

Golomb, L, Curing and Sociocultural Separatism in South Thailand, *Social Science in Medicine* 1985, 21(4), 463-468.

Goodrich, Joyce, Healing and meditation: Healing as a unitive experience. The LeShan work, *American Society for Psychical Research Newsletter* 1993, 18(2), 5.

Goodrich, Joyce, *Personal Communication*, 1982-1985.

Goodrich, Joyce, *Psychic Healing – A Pilot Study*, Doctoral Dissertation, Graduate School, Yellow Springs, Ohio 1974.

Goodrich, Joyce, Studies in Paranormal Healing , *New Horizons* 1976, 2, 21-24.

Goodrich, Joyce, The Psychic Healing Training and Research Project, In: Fosshage, James L. and Olsen, Paul, *Healing: Implications for Psychotherapy*, New York: Human Sciences 1978, 84-110.

Gordon, Andrea/ Merenstein, Joel H./ D'Amico, Frank/ Hudgens, David, The effects of Therapeutic Touch on patients with osteoarthritis of the knee, *J. of Family Practice* 1998, 47(4), 271-277.

Gordon, Richard., *Your Healing hands: The Polarity Experience*, Santa Cruz, California: Unity Press 1978.

Gordon, Thomas, *Parent Effectiveness Training*, New York: Plume/ Penguin 1970.

Goss, Michael., *Poltergeists: An Annotated Bibliography of Works in English, circa 1880-1975*, Metaden, NJ and London: Scarecrow 1979.

Gough, W, *Joint US-China experiment on the effect of external Qi on molecular structure using Raman spectroscopy,* Unpublished report, Foundation for Mind-Being, cited in Rein, 1992.

Grabiec, S.; Frydrychowski, A. F.; and Przyjemska, B., Photon Emission as an Indicator of the Degree of Activation by the 'Biofield,' *Psychotronika*, 1985, 80-82. (Translated from Polish by Alexander Imich.).

Gracely, R. H./ Kwilosz, D. M. The descriptor differential scale: applying psychophysical principles to clinical pain assessment, *Pain* 1988, 35, 279-288.

Grad, B., Cadoret, R. J. and Paul, G. I., The Influence of an Unorthodox, Method of Treatment on Wound Healing in Mice, *International J. of Parapsyhology* 1961, 3, 5-24.

Grad, B., A telekinetic effect on plant growth. I, *International J. of Parapsychology* 1963, 5(2), 117-134.

Grad, B., A telekinetic effect on plant growth II. Experiments Involving Treatment of Saline in Stoppered Bottles, *International J. of Parapsychology* 1964(a), 6, 473-498.

Grad, Bernard, A telekinetic effect on plant growth III. Stimulating and inhibiting effects, *Research Brief Presented to the Seventh Annual Convention of the Parapsychological Association, Oxford University*, Oxford, England Sep 1964(b).

Grad, Bernard R., Some biological effects of laying-on of hands: a review of experiments with animals and plants, *J. of the American Society for Psychical Research* 1965(a), 59, 95-127 (Also reproduced In: Schmeidler, Gertrude (Ed.) *Parapsychology: Its Relation to Physics, Biology, Psychology and Psychiatry*, Metuchen, NJ: Scarecrow 1976).

Grad, Bernard, PK effects of fermentation of yeast, *Proceedings of the Parapsychological Association* 1965(b), 2, 15-16.

Grad, Bernard, The 'laying on of hands:' implications for psychotherapy, gentling and the placebo effect, *J. of the Society for Psychical Research* 1967, 61(4), 286-305 (Also Reviewed In: Schmeidler, Gertrude (Ed.) *Parapsychology: Its Relation to Physics, Biology, Psychology and Psychiatry*, Metuchen, NJ: Scarecrow 1976).

Grad, Bernard, Personal communications 1987, 1992.

Graham, Helen, *Time, Energy and the Psychology of Healing*, London: Jessica Kingsley 1990.

Graves, Charles, *The Legend of Linda Martel*, London: Icon, 1968.

Gray, Isa, *From Materialization to Healing: Evidence of Both*, New York: Regency 1972.

Green, Elmer et al., Anomalous electrostatic phenomena in exceptional subjects, *Subtle Energies* 1991, 2(3), 69-94).

Green, M. Joanne, *Registered Nurses' Knowledge and Practice of Therapeutic Touch* (Master's thesis), Gonzaga University 1997.

Green, Peter, *Heal, My Son: The Amazing Story of John Cain*, Gerrards Cross, England: Van Duren 1985.

Green, William Michael, *The Therapeutic Effects of Distant Intercessory Prayer and Patients' Enhanced Positive Expectations on Recovery Rates and Anxiety Levels of Hospitalized Neurosurgical Pituitary Patients: A Double Blind Study* (dissertation), San Francisco: California Institute of Integral Studies 1993.

Greenfield, Sidney M. A model explaining Brazilian spiritist surgeries and other unusual, religious-based healings, *Subtle Energies* 1994, 5(2) 109-141.

Gregorczuk, Bozena, Combining Various Methods of Assistance in Biotherapy, *Proceedings of the 6th International Conference on Psychotronics* 1986, 135- 136.

Gresik, Vlademar, My Experience with Diagnostics, *Proceedings of the 6th International Conference on Psychotronics* 1986, 124.

Greyson, Bruce, Grossinger, Richard, *Planet Medicine: From Stone Age Shamanism to Post-Industrial Healing*, Boulder/ London: Shambhala 1982; Berkeley, CA: North Atlantic 1991.

Gribbin, John., *Time Warps*, New York: Delacorte/ Eleanor Friede 1979.

Groothuis, Douglas, *Unmasking the New Age*, Downers Grove, IL: Intervarsity.

Gruber, E. R., Conformance Behavior Involving Animal and Human Subjects, *European J. of Parapsychology* 1979, 3(1), 36-50.

Gu, Juefen/ Pan, Weixin/ Wu, Jun – China Pharmaceutical University Nanjing/ Jiangsu Qigong Sciences Society of Sports, Jiangsu, China – Effect of qigong emanation (emitted qi) on higher fungus flammulia velutipes sing (*3rd National Academic Conference on Qigong Science, Guangzhou, China. 1990b* – from Qigong Database of Sancier.

Gu, Juefen/ Wang, Yaowei/ Wu, Jun – China Pharmaceutical UniversityNanjing, Nanjing/ Jiangsu Qigong Sciences Society of Sports, Jiangsu, China – Effect of emitted qi on mutation to streptomyces mycarofarieus nov.sp.10204 (*3rd National Academic Conference on Qigong Science, Guangzhou, China. 1990a* – from Qigong Database of Sancier.

Gu, Ligang/ Yan, Xuanzuo/ Tao, Jundi/ Zhang, Li/ Xu, Yin/ Zhou, Yong/ Hai, Neihou/ Zhong, Xulong/ Lian, Shanhe, Institute of Qigong Science, Beijing College of Traditional Chinese Medicine, Beijing, China/ Tangshan Health Institute for Women and Children, Hebei Province, China, Effect of emitted qi on mouse spleen cells and tumor cells in vitro. *1st World Conf for Acad Exch of Medical Qigong, Beijing 1988*.

Guan, Haoben; Yang, Jainhong. Guangzhou College of Tradtional Chinese Medicine, Guangzhou – Effect of qigong waiqi (emitted qi) on IL-2 activity and multiplication action of spleen cells in mice *3rd National Academic Conference on Qigong Science, Guangzhou, China. 1990* – from Qigong Database of Sancier.

Guerrero, M.A. *The Effects of Therapeutic Touch on State-Trait Anxiety Level of Oncology Patients* (Master's thesis) Galveston: University of Texas 1985.

Gui, Yongfan/ Chen, Qi/ Li, Yinfa/ Jiang, Shan, Nanjing Aeronautical Institute, Nanjing, China, Physical characteristics of the emitted qi, *1st World Conference for Academic Exchange of Medical Qigong. Beijing 1988*.

Gulak, Jan, Lowering the Anxiety levels in Persons Undergoing Bioenergotherapy, *Psychotronika* 1985, 6-9. (Translated from Polish by Alexander Imich).

Guo and Ni, Studies of Qi Gong in Treatment of Myopia (Nearsightedness), Cited in: Eisenberg, David with Wright, Thomas Lee, Encounters with Qi, New York: W. W. Norton 1985, 202-203.

Guo, Yinglan; Geng, Xindu; Mi, Juanceng. Northwest University, Shanxi Province, China, Study of the mechanism of emitted qi. *1st World Conference for Academic Exchange of Medical Qigong. Beijing 1988*.

Guoguang, Chen, The curative effect observation of 24 cases under my 'outward qigong' treatment, *Proccedings of the 2nd International Conference on Qigong*, Xian, *China, September 1989* – from Qigong Database of Sancier.

H

Haberly, H. *Reiki: The Hawayo Takatas Story,* CA: Archedign 1990.

Haigler, Susan Lynne, *The Persuasive Implications of Therapeutic Touch in Doctor-Patient Relationships (Gender)* (dissertation), Seattle: University of Washington 1996 (touch for persuasion).

Hale, Elizabeth Habig, A study of the relationship between therapeutic touch and the anxiety levels of hospitalized adults, PhD Dissertation, College of Nursing,Texas Woman's University 1986.

Halifax, Joan., *Shaman: The Wounded Healer,* New York: Crossroads 1982.

Hamilton, M. A rating scale for depression, *J. of Neurology, Neurosurgery and Psychiatry* 1960, 23, 56.

Hamilton-Wyatt, Gwen Karilyn, *Therapeutic Touch: Promoting and Assessing Conceptual Change Among Health Care Professionals* (dissertation) East Lansing: Michigan State University 1988.

Hammerschlag, Carl A. The Dancing Healers: A Doctor's Journeyh of Healing with Native Americans, San Francisco: Harper & Row 1988.

Hammond, Sally, *We Are All Healers,* New York: Harper & Row 1973.

Hansel, C.E.M., *ESP: A Scientific Evaluation,* New York: Charles Scribner's Sons 1966.

Hansen, George., Deception by subjects in psi research, *J. of American Society for Psychical Research* 1990, 84(1), 25-80, 19pp. Refs.

Haraldsson, E., and Thorsteinsson, T., Psychokinetic effects on yeast: an exploratory experiment, In: W.C. Roll, R.L. Morris, and J.D. Morris, (Eds.), *Research in Parapsychology, 1972,* Metuchen, N.J.: Scarecrow Press 1973, 20-21.

Haraldsson, Erlendur, and Olafsson, Orn, A survey of psychic healing in Iceland, *Christian Parapsychologist* 1980, 3(8), 276-279.

Haraldsson, Erlunder, *Miracles are My Greeting Cards: an Investigative Report on the Psychic Phenomena Associated with Sathya Sai Baba,* London: Century 1987.

Harary, S. B., *A pilot study of the effects of psychically treated saline solution on the growth of seedlings,* Unpublished Manuscript, Psychical Research Foundation, 1975.

Harman, Willis, *Symposium on Consciousness,* New York: Penguin 1977.

Harman, Willis, *Global Mind Change,* Knowledge Systems 1988.

Harner, Michael., *The Way of the Shaman,* New York: Bantam/ Harper and Row 1980.

Harris, William S. et al, A randomized, controlled trial of the effects of remote, intercessory prayer on outcomes in patients admitted to the coronary care unit, *Annals of Internal Medicine* 1999, 159(19), 2273-2278.

Harrison, John., *Love Your Disease, It's Keeping You Healthy,* London: Angus and Robertson 1984.

Harvey, David, Healing at a stroke, *The Unexplained,* 1983, 13(153), 3046-3049.

Harvey, David, Taking the Cain cure, *The Unexplained,* 1982, 9(108), 2154-2157.

Harvey, David, *The Power to Heal: An Investigation of Healing and the Healing Experience,* Wellingborough, Northamptonshire, England: Aquarian 1983.

Harvey, Ruth S., Three healings to a gallon of tea, In: Fate Magazine, *Exploring the Healing Miracle* Highland Park, IL: Clark, 1983, (Orig. In: *Fate Magazine,* Nov 1978).

Hasted, John B.; Robertson, David and Arathoon, Peter, PKMB with Piezoelectric Sensors, In: Roll, William G.; Beloff, John and White, Rhea, *Research in Parapsychology 1982,* Metuchen, NJ and London: Scarecrow 1983, 39-42.

Hasted, John, *The Metal-Benders,* Boston: Routledge and Kegan Paul 1981.

Hastings, J. (editor), Ordeal In: *Encyclopedia of Religion and Ethics,* Vol IX: 507, Scribners': New York, 1955.

Haviland, Denis, Safety of Faith Healing, *Lancet* 1986 (Mar 22), 1(8482), 684.

Hay, Louise L., *You Can Heal Your Life,* Santa Monica, California: Hay House 1984.

Haynes, Renee, Faith Healing and Psychic Healing: Are They the Same?, *Parapsychology Review* 1977(a), 8(4), 10-13.

Haynes, Renee, Miraculous and Paranormal Healing, *Parapsychology Review* 1977(b), 8(5), 25-27.

Haynes, Renee, *The Hidden Springs: An En-*

quiry into Extrasensory Perception, London: Hollis and Carter 1961.

Heaton, E., *Mouse Healing Experiments*, Unpublished Manuscript, Foundation for Research on the Nature of Man, 1974.

Hebda, Hillard, *An Inquiry into Unorthodox Healing: Psychic Healing and Psychic Surgery*, M.A. Thesis, Governors State University (Human Learning and Development), 1975, (Abstract from *Parapsychology Abstracts International*, 1983, 1(2), No. 479, 58 Refs).

Heidt, Patricia Rose: Openness – A qualitative analysis of nurses' and patients' experiences of therapeutic touch (*Image: J. of Nursing Scholarship*, 1990, 22(3), 180-186 (Qotes by permission, copyright Sigma Theta Tau international).

Heidt, Patricia, *An Investigation of the Effect of Therapeutic Touch on the Anxiety of Hospitalized Patients*, New York University: Unpublished Ph.D. Dissertation 1979.

Heidt, Patricia, Effects of Therapeutic Touch on the Anxiety Level of Hospitalized Patient, *Nursing Research* 1981, 30, 30-37.

Heinze, Ruth-Inge (Ed), *Proceedings of the International Conference on Shamanism, St. Sabina Center, San Rafael, CA* , Berkeley, CA: Center for South and Southeast Asia Studies, University of California May 1984.

Heinze, Ruth-Inge, *Trance and Healing in Southeast Asia Today: Twenty-One Case Studies*, Berkeley, CA: University of California, 1983.

Heinze, Ruth-Inge, *Proceedings of the Second International Conference on the Study of Shamanism, San Rafael, CA 1985*, Berkeley, CA: Center for South and Southeast Asia Studies 1985.

Heisenberg, W. *Physics and Beyond*, New York: Harper & Row 1971.

Helman, Cecil G. *Culture, Health and Illness*, Oxford, England: Butterworth-Heinemann 1990.

Herbert, Benson, Alexi Krivorotov: Russian "Healer", *J. of Paraphysics* 1970, 4(4), 112 (poor, useless).

Herbert, Benson, Biogravitation: Experimental Evidence, *Proceedings of the 4th International Conference on Psychotronic Research*, Sao Paulo, Brazil 1979(b), 149-152.

Herbert, Benson, Near and Distant Healing, *J. of Paraphysics* 1973, 7(5), 213-218.

Herbert, Benson, Theory and practice of psy-chic healing, *Parapsychology Review* Nov Dec 1975, 6, 22-23.

Herrigel, E. *Zen in the Art of Archery*, New York: Pantheon 1953.

Herzberg, Eileen, *Spiritual Healing: A Patient's Guide*, Wellingborough, UK: Thorsons 1988.

Heywood, Rosalind, *ESP: A Personal Memoir*, New York: E.P. Dutton 1964.

Hiatt, J, Spirituality, Medicine and Healing , *South Medical J.* 1986, 79(6), 736-743.

Hill, Scott, Paranormal healing in Russia, *Fate* Aug 1981.

Hirschberg, Caryl/ Barasch, Marc Ian, *The Healing Path*, Honorton, Charles et al.: Psi communication in the ganzfeld: experiments with an automated testing system and a comparison with a meta-analysis of earlier studies, *J. of Parapsychology* 1990, 54, 99-139.

Hislop, John S., *My Baba and I* , San Diego: Birth Day 1985.

Holmes, A. Campbell, *The Facts of Psychic Science*, New Hyde Park, NY: University Books 1969.

Holzer, Hans, *Beyond Medicine: The Facts About Unorthodox, and Psychic Healing,* New York: Ballantine/ Random House 1974(b).

Holzer, Hans, *Psychic Healing: All the Facts About the Alternate Way to Good Health and Happiness*, New York: Manor 1979.

Honorton, Charles et al. Psi communication in the ganzfeld: eperiments with an automated testing system and a comparison with a met-analysis of earlier studies.

Honorton, Charles, Psi and Internal Attention States, In: Wolman, B. B. (Ed), *Handbook of Parapsychology*, New York: Van Nostrand Reinhold 1977, 435-472.

Honorton, Charles/ Ferrari, D.: Future telling?: a meta-analysis of forced-choice precognitive experiments, 1935-1987, *J. of Parapsychology*,1990, 53, 281-308 .

Hood, Mariya, *Magic Power to Heal*, Hicksville, NY: Exposition, 1976.

Horowitz, Kenneth A.; Lewis, Donald C. and Gasteiger, Edgar L., Plant "Primary Perception": Electrophysiological Unresponsiveness to Brine Shrimp Killing, *Science* 1975, 189, 478-480.

Horstmann, Lorna, *A Handbook of Healing*, Middlesex, England: National Federation of

Spiritual Healers, undated pamphlet, purchased 1985.

Horstmann, Lorna, *An Introduction to Spiritual Healing*, London: Rider and Co. 1964.

Houck, Jack, Conceptual Model of Paranormal Phenomena, *Archaeus* 1983, 1(1), 7-24.

Houck, Jack, PK Party History, *Psi Research* 1984(b), 3(1), 67-83.

Houck, Jack, Psychic Healing, *Archaeus Project Newsletter* 1984(a), 3(1), 13-14.

Houck, Jack, Surface Change During Warm-Forming, *Archaeus* 1984, 2(1), 27-50.

Hover-Kramer, D (ed), Healing Touch: A Resource for Health Care Professionals, Albany, NY: Delmar 1996.

Hu, Gang/ Fan, I. Ji/ Qiu, Yuzhen/ Chia, Jianyu – Laboratory of Catalysis, Shanghai Teacher's University, Shanghai/ Shanghai Qigong Institute – Biological effect of emitted qi with the blochronometer *3rd National Academic Conference on Qigong Science, Guangzhou, China. 1990* - from Qigong Database of Sancier.

Huang, Meiguang, General Hospital of PLA, Beijing, Effect of the emitted qi combined with self practice of qigong in treating paralysis, *1st World Conference for Academic Exchange of Medical Qigong, Beijing, 1988.*

Huang, Wengguo – Zhoushan Qigong Association, China – Prevention and cure of younster hyprometropla by qigong (*2nd World Conference for Academic Exchange of Medical Qigong. Beijing 1993* - from Qigong Database of Sancier.

Hubacher, John; Gray, Jack; Moss, Thelma and Saba, Frances, A Laboratory Study of Unorthodox, Healing, @U(Proceedings of the Second International Congress on Psychotronic Research, Monte Carlo) 1975, 440-44.

Hughes, Pamela Potter/ Meize-Grochowski, Robin/ Neighbor, Catherine/ Harris, Duncan, Therapeutic Touch with adolescent psychiatric patients, *J. of Holistic Nursing* 1996, 14(1), 6-23.

Hultkrantz, A., The shaman and the Medicine-Man, *Social Science Medicine* 1985, 20(5), 511-515.

Humphrey, B. M. and Nicol, J. F. The feeling of success in ESP, *J. of the American Society for Psychical Research* 1955, 49, 3-37.

Humphrey, Betty M., Paranormal Occurrences

Among Preliterate Peoples, *J. of Parapsychology* 1944, 8, 214-229.

Hunt, S.M. Measuring health status: a new tool for clinicians and epidemiologists, *J. of the Royal Society of General Practitioners* 1985, 35, 185-188.

Huo, Yuhua/ Zhao, Jing/ Zhan, Diankun/ Zhao, Xiaomei/ Yang, Guisheng, Nankai University, Tianjin, Beijing College of Acupuncture, Moxibustion, Traumotology, Tianjin Society of Somatic Science, China, Effect of emitted qi on higher temperature superconductors, *2nd World Conference for Academic Exchange of Medical Qigong, Beijing 1993.*

Hurley, Patricia, *The Effect of Trait Anxiety and Patient Expectation of Therapeutic Touch on the Reduction in State Anxiety in Preoperative Patients Who Receive Therapeutic Touch* (Dissertation), New York University 1993.

Hutchings, Donald D. The value of suggestion given under anesthesia: a report and evaluation of 200 consecutive cases, *American J. of Clinical Hypnosis* 1961, 4, 26-29.

Hutton, J. Bernard, *The Healing Power: The Extraordinary Spiritual Healing of Mrs. Leah Doctors and 'Dr. Chang,' Her Spirit Guide,* London: Leslie Frewin 1975.

Huxley, Francis, The Miraculous Virgin of Guadalupe, *International J. of Parapsychology* 1959, 1(1), 19-31.

Huxley, Thomas Henry, *On Elemental Instruction in Physiology* 1877.

I

Ikin, Alice Graham, *The Background of Spiritual Healing, Psychological and Religious,* London: Allen and Unwin, 1937.

Ilieva-Even, Yanina, A Case of Shamanistic Healing in Siberia, Translated by Vilenskaya, Larissa, *Parapsychology in the U.S.S.R. Part III,* San Francisco: Washington Research Center 1981, 63-64.

Inglis, Brian, *Retrocognitive Dissonance,* Theta 1986 13/ 14 (1), 4-9.

Inglis, Brian,, *Natural and Supernatural: A History of the Paranormal from Early Times,* England: Hodder and Stoughton 1977.

Irwin, H. J., *Psi and the Mind: An Information*

Processing Approach, Metuchen, NJ: Scarecrow 1979.

Irwin, H. J., Psi, attention and processing capacity, *J. of the American Society for Psychical Research* 1978, 72, 301-313.

Irwin, Harvey J., *Flight of Mind*, Metuchen, NJ: Scarecrow, 1985.

McNair, D.M. et al. *EdiTS Manual for the Profile of Mood States,* San Diego, CA: EdiTS 1992.

Isaacs, Julian D., Psychotherapeutic intervention in piezo-PK training studies, In: Weiner, Debra H. and Radin, Dean I., *Research in Parapsychology* 1985, Metuchen, NJ and London: Scarecrow 1986, 175-176.

Isaacs, Julian, A twelve session study of micro-PKMB training, In: Roll, William G.; Beloff, John and White, Rhea, *Research in Parapsychology 1982*, Metuchen, NJ and London: Scarecrow 1983, 31-35.

Isaacs, Julian, The Batcheldor Approach: Some Strengths and Weaknesses, *Presentation at the 25th Annual Convention of the Parapsychological Association/ 100th Annual Convention of the Society for Psychical Research* 1982.

Isaacs, Julian., The Batcheldor Approach: Some Strengths and Weaknesses, *J. of the American Society for Psychical Research* 1984, 78((2), 123-132.

Ivanova, Barbara, Incarnation-regressions: Informational, educational and healing effects, *Psi Research* 1986(b), 5(1,2), 16-28.

Ivanova, Barbara, Psycho- and auto-regulation , *International J. of Paraphysics* 1978, 12(1 & 2), 20-21.

Ivanova, Barbara, Reincarnation and healing, *Psi Research* 1986(c), 5(1,2), 28- 33.

Ivanova, Barbara, Some training experiments in clairvoyance, *Proceedings of the 5th International Conference on Psychotronic Research*, Bratislava 1983, 162-167.

Ivanova, Barbara, *The Golden Chalice*, (Mir, Maria and Vilenskaya, Larissa, Eds.), San Francisco, CA: H. S. Dakin 1986(a).

Ivanova, Barbara., Relation of Caraphenomena to Physical Fields, *International J. of Paraphysics* 1980, 14 (5 and 6), 110-112.

Ivanova, Barbara, Psychography in the USSR, *International J. of Paraphysics* 1978, 12(3 & 4), 81-84.

J

Jackson, Mary E. Mueller, The use of Therapeutic Touch in the nursing care of the terminally ill person, In: Borelli and Heidt, *Therapeutic Touch*, New York: Springer 1981.

Jacobson, Nils and Wiklund, Nils, Investigation of Claims of Diagnosing by means of ESP, In: *Research in Parapsychology 1975*, Metuchen, NJ: Scarecrow 1976, 74-76.

Jadad, A.R. et al, Assessing the quality of reports of randomized clinical trials: is blinding necessary? *Controlled Clinical Trials* 1996, 17, 1-12.

Jahn, Robert G. and Dunne, Brenda J., *On the Quantum Mechanics of Consciousness, with Application to Anomalous Phenomena*, Princeton, NJ: Princeton Engineering Anomalies Research Laboratory, School of Engineering/ Applied Science 1984.

Jahn, Robert G. and Dunne, Brenda J., *The Margins of Reality*, San Diego, CA and London: Harcourt, Brace Jovanovich 1987.

Jahn, Robert G., Out of this Aboriginal sensible muchness: consciousness, information, and human health, *J. of the American Society for Psychical Research* 1995, 89(4), 301-312.

Jahn, Robert G., The Persistent Paradox of Psychic Phenomena: An Engineering Perspective, *Proceedings of the IEEE* Feb 1982.

Jia, Lin/ Jia, Jinding. National Research Institute of Sports Science, Beijing, China [1], assignee. Effects of the emitted qi on healing of experimental fracture. 1st World Conference for Academic Exchange of Medical Qigong. Beijing, China, 1988.

Jia, Lin/ Jia, Jinding/ Lu, Danyun, National Research Institute of Sports Science, Beijing, Effects of emitted qi on ultrastructural changes of the overstrained muscle of rabbits, 1st World Conference for Academic Exchange of Medical Qigong. Beijing, China 1988.

Jobst, K. One man's meat is another man's poison: the challenge of psychic/intuitive diagnosis to the diagnostic paradigm of orthodox medical science, *Journal of Alternative and Complementary Medicine* 1997, 3(1), 1-3.

Johnson, P. Youlden, *Healing Fingers: The Power of Yoga Pranic Healing,* New York: Rider 1950.

Johnston, B. *New Age Healing*, England: Johnson 1975.

Joralemon, D., The Role of Hallucinogenic Drugs and Sensory Stimuli in Peruvian Ritual Healing, *Cultural Medicine and Psychiatry* 1984, 8, 399-430.

Joyce, C. R. B. and Welldon, R. M. C. The Objective Effcacy of Prayer: A Double-Blind Clinical Trial, *J. of Chronic Diseases* 1965, 18, 367-77.

Jung, Carl Gustav, *The Collected Works of C.G. Jung*, Adler, G./ Fordham, M./ Read, H. (eds), Translated by Hull, R. F. C., Bolligen Series XX, Princeton University.

Jurak, Alois, Curative Effects of Bioenergy, *Proceedings of the 6th International Conference on Psychotronic Research* 1986, 108-110.

K

Kakar, Sudhir, *Shamans, Mystics and Doctors: A Psychological Inquiry into India and its Healing Traditions*, Boston: Beacon, 1982.

Kanthamani, H. and Kelly, E. F., Awareness of success in an exceptional subject, *J. of Parapsychology* 1974, 38, 355-382.

Kaptchuk Ted , *The Web that Has No Weaver* NY: Congdon and Weed 1984.

Kaptchuk, Ted/ Croucher, Michael, *The Healing Arts: Exploring the Medical Ways of the World*, New York: Summit 1987.

Kapur, R. L., The role of traditional healers in mental health care in rural India, *Social Science and Medicine* 1979 (Jan), 138(1), 27-31.

Karagulla, Shafica, and Var Gelder Kunz, Dora, *The Chakras and the Human Energy Field*, Wheaton, IL, Quest/ Theosophical 1989.

Karagulla, Shafica, *Breakthrough to Creativity: Your Higher Sense Perception*, Santa Monica, CA: DeVorss 1967.

Karp, Reba Ann, *Edgar Cayce Encyclopedia of Healing*, New York: Warner 1986.

Kartsev, V. I., [Lethal gamma-irradiation and bioenergy therapy] *Parapsikhologiya i Psikhofizika* [*Parapsychology and Psychophysics*] Trans from Russian by May, Edwin C./ Vilenskaya Larissa, Mental influence on grey mice exposed to lethal doses of ionizing radiation, *Some Aspects of Parapsychological Research in the Former Soviet Union* 1994, 10-11.

Kashiwasake, Masaki: Double-blind tests of qi transmission from qi-gong masters to untrained volunteers (*J. of Mind-Body Science* 1993, 2(1), 81-87 (Japanese, with English summary).

Katz, Richard, *Boiling Energy: Community Healing Among the Kalahari Kung*, Cambridge, MA: Harvard University 1981.

Kawano, Kimiko/ Wang, Fengfong/ Duan Liye – Information Processing Center of Medical Sciences, Nippon Medical School – Double-blind tests of qi transmission from qigong masters to untrained volunteers: (2) changes in the brain waves of qi-receivers. Japanese Mind-Body Science. 1993, 2(1), 89-93 – from Qigong Database of Sancier.

Keane, P. and Wells, R., An examination of the menstrual cycle as a hormone related physiological concomitant of psi performance, *Paper Presented at Parapsychological Association Conference*, St. Louis 1978.

Keegan, Lynn, *The Nurse as Healer*, Albany, NY: Delmar 1994.

Keene, M. Lamar, as told to Spraggett, Allen, *The Psychic Mafia*, New York: Dell 1976.

Keller, Elizabeth and Bzdek, Virginia M., Effects of Therapeutic Touch on tension headache pain, *Nursing Research* 1986, 35, 101-104. (Unpublished M.A. Thesis, University of Missouri 1983).

Keller, Elizabeth Kolbet, Therapeutic Touch: A review of the literature and implications of a wholistic nursing modality, *J. of Holistic Nursing* 1984, 2(1), 24-29.

Kemp, Louise Marie, *The Effects of Therapeutic Touch on the Anxiety Level of Patients with Cancer Receiving Palliative Care* (Master's thesis), Canada: Dalhousie University 1994.

Keni, Ramakant, *Psychic Healing: My Personal Experiences*, Bombay: Somaiya 1981.

Kerewsky-Halpern, B., Trust, talk and touch in Balkan folk healing, *Social Science Medicine* 1985, 21(3), 319-325.

Kiecolt-Glaser, J. et al.., Chronic stress and immunity in family caregivers of Alzehimer's disease victims, Psychosomatic Medicine 1987, 49(2), 523-535.

Kief, Herman K. A method for measuring PK with enzymes, In: Roll, W. G.; Morris, R. L. and Morris, J. D. (Eds), *Research in Parapsychology 1972* Metuchen, NJ: Scarecrow 1973, 19-20.

Kiernan, Jane S. *The Experience of Therapeutic Touch in the Lives of Five Postpartal*

Women (Birth) (Dissertation), New York, NY: New York University 1997.

Kiev, Ari (Ed), *Magic, Faith and Healing: Studies in Primitive Psychiatry Today*, New York: Free Press/ Macmillan 1964.

Kiev, Ari, *Curanderismo: Mexican-American Folk Psychiatry*, New York: Free Press 1968.

King, George, *You Too Can Heal*, Los Angeles, CA: Aetherius, 1976.

King, Serge., *Kahuna Healing: Holistic Health and Healing Practices of Polynesia*, Wheaton, IL: Quest/ Theosophical 1983.

Kirkpatrick, Richard A. Witchcraft and lupus erythematosus, *J. of the American Medical Association* 1981, 245(9), 1937.

Kleinman, A. *Patients and Healers in the Context of Culture: an Exploration of the Borderland Between Anthropology, Medicine, and Psychiatry*, Berkeley University of California 1980.

Kleinman, A./ Sung, L. H. Why do indigenous practitioners succeessfully heal? *Social Science and Medicine* 1979, 13, 7-26.

Kleinman, Arthur M., Some issues for a comparative study of medical healing, *International J. of Social Psychiatry* 1973, 19(3/ 4), 160.

Kleinman, Arthur, *Patients and Healers in the Context of Culture: An Exploration of the Borderland Between Anthropology, Medicine, and Psychiatry*, Berkeley/ Los Angeles: University of California 1980.

Klos, Jethro, *Back to Eden*, Santa Barbara, CA: Woodbridge 1981.

Kmetz, John M., A study of primary perception in plant and animal life, *J. of the American Society for Psychical Research* 1977, 71, 157-168.

Kmetz, John M., An examination of primary perception in plants, *Parapsychology Review* 1975, 6(3), 21.

Knowles, F. W., My experience in psychic healing and parapsychology, *New Zealand Medical J.* 1971, 74, 328-331.

Knowles, F. W., Psychic healing in organic disease, *J. of the American Society for Psychical Research* 1956, 50(3), 110-117.

Knowles, F. W., Rat experiments and Mesmerism, *J. of the American Society for Psychical Research* 1959, 53, 62-65.

Knowles, F. W., Some investigations into psychic healing, *J. of the American Society for Psychical Research* 1954, 48(1), 21-26.

Ko, Wen-hsiung, Superstition or ancient wisdom?, *Fate* 1988 (Feb), 56-63.

Kobasa, S.C. et al., Personality and constitution as mediations in stress-illness behavior, J. of Health and Social Behavior 1980, 22(2), 368-378.

Koestler, Arthur, *The Case of the Midwife Toad*, New York: Random House 1971.

Kohn LT, et al (eds) To err is human: building a safer health system. Washington, D.C.: National Academy Press, 2000.

Kornfield, Jack, *A Path with Heart: A Guide through the Perils and Promises of Spiritual Life*, New York/ London Bantam 1993.

Korth, Leslie O., *Healing magnetism: The power behind contact therapy*, Wellingborough, Northants., England: Thorsons 1974.

Koss, J. D., Expectations and outcomes for patients given mental health care or spiritist healing in Puerto Rico, *American J. of Psychiatry* 1987, 144(1), 56-61.

Kowey, Peter R., Friehling, Ted D., and Marinchak, Roger A., Prayer meeting cardioversion, *Annals of Internal Medicine* 1986, 104(5), 727-728.

Kraft, Dean, *Portrait of a Psychic Healer*, New York: G.P. Putnams's Sons 1981 (Quotes reprinted by permission of author, copyright Dean Kraft).

Kramer, Nancy Ann, Comparison of Therapeutic Touch and casual touch in stress reduction of hospitalized children, *Pediatric Nursing* 1990, 16(5), 483-485.

Kreitler, Hans and Kreitler, Shulamith, Subliminal perception and extrasensory perception, *J. of Parapsychology* 1973, 37, 163-188.

Krieger, Dolores, *Foundations for Holistic Health Nursing Practices: The Renaissance Nurse*, Philadelphia: J.P. Lippincott 1981.

Krieger, Dolores, Healing by the 'laying-on' of hands as a facilitator of bioenergetic change: The response of in-vivo human hemoglobin, *Psychoenergetic Systems* 1976, 1, 121-129.

Krieger, Dolores, *Living the Therapeutic Touch*, New York: Dodd Mead 1987.

Krieger, Dolores, The relationship of touch, with intent to help or to heal, to subjects' in-vivo hemoglobin values, In: *American Nurses'*

Association 9th Nursing Research Conference, San Antonio, TX 1973 Kansas City, MO: American Nurses' Association 1974, 39-58.

Krieger, Dolores, *The Therapeutic Touch: How to Use Your Hands to Help or Heal*, Englewood Cliffs, NJ: Prentice-Hall 1979.

Krieger, Dolores, Therapeutic Touch during childbirth preparation by the Lamaze method and its relation to marital satisfaction and state anxiety of the married couple, In: Krieger, D. Living the Therapeutic Touch: Healing as a Lifestyle, New York: Dodd Mead 1987, 157-187.

Krieger, Dolores, *Therapeutic Touch Inner Workbook*, Santa Fe, NM: Bear & Co. 1997.

Krieger, Dolores, Therapeutic Touch: the imprimatur of nursing, *American J. of Nursing* 1975, 7, 784-787.

Krieger, Dolores, Peper, Eric, and Ancoli, Sonia, Therapeutic Touch, *American J. of Nursing,* April 1979, 660-665.

Krippner, Stanley and Solfvin, Gerald, Psychic healing: a research survey, 1984, 3(2), 16-28.

Krippner, Stanley and Villoldo, Alberto, Spirit healing in Brazil, *Fate*, Mar 1976.

Krippner, Stanley and Villoldo, Alberto, *The Realms of Healing*, Millbrae, CA: Celestial Arts 1976; 3rd. Ed. Rev. 1986.

Krippner, Stanley and Welch, Patrick, *Spiritual Dimensions of Healing: From Native Shamanism to Contemporary Health Care*, New York: Irvington 1992.

Krippner, Stanley, *A cross-cultural comparison of four healing models, Alternative Therapies in Health and Medicine* 1995, 1(1), 21-29.

Krippner, Stanley, A questionnaire study of experiential reactions to a Brazilian healer, *J. of the Society for Psychical Research* 1990, 56, 208- 215.

Krippner, Stanley, A suggested typology of folk healing and its relevance for parapsychological investigation, *J. of the Society for Psychical Research*, 1980(b), 50(786), 491-499.

Krippner, Stanley, Investigations of 'extrasensory' phenomena in dreams and other altered states of consciousness, *J. of the American Society of Psychosomatic Dentistry and Medicine* 1969, 16(1), 7-14.

Krippner, Stanley, Research in paranormal healing: Paradox and promise, *American Society for Psychical Research Newsletter* 1973, 19.

Krippner, Stanley/ Welch, Patrick, *Spiritual*

Dimensions of Healing: From Native Shamanism to Contemporary Health Care, New York: Irvington 1992 (22 pp refs).

Krivorotov, Victor K., Krivorotov, Alexei E., and Krivorotov, Vladimir K., Bioenergotherapy and healing, *Psychoenergetic Systems* 1974, 1, 27-30.

Krivorotov, Victor, Some issues of bioenergetic therapy, In: Vilenskaya, Larissa, Translator and Editor, *Parapsychology in the USSR, Part III.* San Francisco: Washington Research Center 1981, 30-41.

Kuang, Ankun et al., Long-term observation on Qigong in prevention of stroke - follow-up of 244 hypertensive patients for 18-22 years, *J. of Traditional Chinese Medicine* 1986, 6(4), 235-238. Also in: Kuang, A. K. et al., Comparative study of clinical effects and prognosis of 204 hypertensive patients treated with *Qigong) in 20 years of follow-up and its mechanisms,*

Kubler-Ross, Elizabeth, *Living with Death and Dying*, New York: Macmillan 1981; London: Souvenir 1982.

Kuhlman, Kathryn, *I Believe in Miracles*, New York: Pyramid 1969.

Kuhn, Thomas S, *The Structure of Scientific Revolutions*, The University of Chicago Press, Vol II , No.2, 1962, 1970.

Kunz, Dora, *Spiritual Healing: Doctors Examine Therapeutic Touch and Other Holistic Treatments*, Wheaton, IL: Quest 1995.

Kunz, Dora, *Healing seminar*, Pumpkin Hollow, 1982.

Kurtz, Paul., *The Transcendental Temptation: A Critique of Religion and the Paranormal*, Buffalo, New York: Promethius 1986.

L

Lacan, J., *Language of the Self*, Baltimore: Penguin 1965.

Lafitte, G., The Lourdes cures: Osteo-articular disorders, In: Flood (Ed), *New Problems in Medical Ethics*, Cork 1953 (from West, p.9; instantaneous cure).

Landy, David, *Culture, Disease and Healing: Studies in Medical Anthropology,* New York: Macmillan 1977.

Lange, Walter R., *Healing Miracles: The Story of the St. Rupertus Spring and its Miraculous, Health-Giving Water,* Brooklyn, NY: Walter R. Lange 1977.

Lansdowne, Z. F., *The Chakras and Esoteric Healing*, York Beach, MA: Samuel Weiser 1986.

Laotsu, *The Wisdom of Laotsu*, New York: Modern Library 1948.

Larcher, Hubert, Sacred places and paranormal cures, *Revue Metapsychique* 1981, 15(4), 19-28.

Larder, B.A. et al., HIV with reduced sensitivity to zidovudine (AZT) isolated during prolonged therapy, Science 1989, 243(3), 1297-1300.

Leape LL, Error in medicine, *Journal of the American Medical Association* 1994;272:1851-7.

Leb, Catherine, *The effects of Healing Touch on depression*, Master's Thesis, University of North Carolina 1996.

LeCron, Leslie, Hypnosis and ESP, *Psychic* Aug 1970.

Lee, Bonita, Vibrational essences – liquid consciousness? *Caduceus* 1996/ 7 Winter, No. 34, 41-45.

Lee, C., Qigong (Breath Exercise) and its major models, *Chinese Culture* 1983, 24(3), 71-79.

Lee, Richard H./ Wang, Xiaming, China Healthways Institute, 117 Granada, San Clemente, CA 92672, USA, Use of surface electromyogram to examine the effects of the infratonic QGM on electrical activity of muscles, a double-blind, placebo-controlled study, *2nd World Conference for Academic Exchangeof Medical Qigong*, Beijing 1993.

Leek, Sybil, *The Story of Faith Healing*, New York: Macmillan, 1973.

Leichtman, Robert R., Afterward to the Gift of Healing, *J. of Holistic Medicine* 1986, 8(1,2),67-78.

Leikam, W. C., *A Pilot Study on the Psychic Influence of E. Coli Bacteria*, Unpublished Manuscript, 1981.

Lenington, Sandra, Effects of holy water on the growth of radish plants, *Psychological Reports* 1979, 45, 381-382. (Abstract in *J. of Parapsychology*, 1980, 44, 386-7).

LeShan, Lawrence and Margenau, Henry, An approach to a science of psychical research, *J. of the Society for Psychical Research* 1980, 50, 273-283.

LeShan, Lawrence and Margenau, Henry, *Einstein's Space and Van Gogh's Sky*, New York: Macmillan 1982.

LeShan, Lawrence, *Alternate Realities*, New York: Ballantine 1976.

LeShan, Lawrence, *The Medium, The Mystic and The Physicist: Toward a General Theory of the Paranormal*, New York: Ballantine 1974(a); British edition – *Clairvoyant Reality*, Wellingborough, England: Thorsons. (Copyright 1966, 1973, 1974 by Lawrence LeShan. Quotations by permission of Viking Penguin, Inc.).

Leskowitz, Eric, Un-debunking therapeutic touch, *Alternative Therapies* 1998, 4(4), 101-102.

Leuret, Francois and Bon, Henri, *Modern Miraculous Cures: A Documented Account of Miracles and Medicine in the 20th Century*, New York: Farrar, Straus and Cudahy 1957.

Levesque, GV, *Miracle Cures for the Millions*, Bell Publishing Company, New York.

Lewicki, D. R./ Schaut, G.H./ Persinger, M.A. Geophysical variables and behavior: xliv days of subjective precognitive experiences and the days before the actual events display correlated geomagnetic activity, *Perceptual & Motor Skills* 1987, 65(1), 173-174.

Li, Caixi/ Jinlong/ Liu, Zhiyun/ Zhao, Guang/ Zhang, Yu/ Zhang, Guoxi, Xiyuan Hospital, China Academy of Traditional Chinese Medicine, Beijing – Effects of emitted qi on immune functions in animals *1st World Conf for Acad Exch of Medical Qigong, Beijing, China 1988*.

Li, Caixi/ Zhao, Tongjian/ Lu, Danyun/ Xu, Qingzhong – Xiyuan Hospital, China Academy of Chinese Traditional Medicine, China/ Xuanwu Hospital, Beijing/ Scientific Research Institute of National Physical Culture Commission, Xuanwu Hospital, Beijing – Effects of qigong waiqi (emitted qi) on immune functions of mice with tumors *3rd National Academic Conference on Qigong Science, Guangzhou, China. 1990* – from Qigong Database of Sancier.

Li, Desong/ Yang, Qinfei/ Li, Xiaoming/ Shi, Jiming, Institute Qigong Science, Beijing College of Traditional Chinese Medicine, Beijing 100029, Spectrum analysis effect of emitted qi on EEG on normal subjects, 2nd World Conference for Academic Exchange of Medical Qigong, Beijing 1993.

Li, Guowei/ Ding, Datong/ Zhou, Daming/ Zhao, Jing/ Wei, Tianbo/ Yang, Gueisheng/ Xie, Guoqang – Dept Biology, Nankai University, Tianjin/ Tianjin Physical Science Society, Tianjin, China – Chemical shift of ethanol (by NMR) elicited by qigong waiqi (emitted qi) *3rd National Academic Conference on Qigong Science, Guangzhou, China. 1990* – from Qigong Database of Sancier.

Li, Jinzheng/ Liu, Hekun – Beijing Institute of Traditional Chinese Medicine/ Shenyang Institute of Traditional Chinese Medicine, Shenyang, China – Clinical observation of liver and gallstones treated with qigong (*1st World Conference for Academic Exchange of Medical Qigong, Beijing 1988* – from Qigong Database of Sancier.

Li, Luying/ Xu, Hongwei/ Li, Xiaohui/ Wen, Qinfen/ Li, Jiamei/ Li – Shenzhuang Research Society of Human Body, Qigong Medical College, China – Effects of emitted qi and will on hyperchromic and hypochromic absorption spectra of DNA (*2nd World Conference for Academic Exchange of Medical Qigong. Beijing 1993* – from Qigong Database of Sancier.

Li, Shengping/ Meng, Guirong/ Cui, Yuanhao/ Sun, Mengyin/ Zhang, Fushi/ Tang, Yingwu/ Qiu, Yong/ Li, Jinghong/ Xin, Yan, Tsinghua University, Beijing/ Municipal Institute of Traditional Chinese Medicine of Chongqing, Sichuan Province, China, Effect of emitted qi on laser fluorescence and ultraviolet on the rhodamin dyestuff, (*1st World Conference for Academic Exchange of Medical Qigong, Beijing 1988*—from Qigong Database of Sancier.

Li, Shengping/ Su, Mengyin/ Meng, Guirong/ Cui, Yuanhao/ Xin, Yan, Tsinghua University, Beijing/ Municipal Institute of Traditional Chinese Medicine of Chongqing, Sichuan Province, China, Effect of emitted qi on bovine serum albumen by the ultraviolet and fluorescence spectrophotometer. (*1st World Conference for Academic Exchange of Medical Qigong, Beijing 1988* – from Qigong Database of Sancier.

Li, Shuzhun [and others] – Dept Immunology, Shandong Academy of Medical Sciences, Jinan, China – Effect of emitted qi on the immunoability of Immunosuppressed mice *3rd National Academic Conference on Qigong Science, Guangzhou, China. 1990* – from Qigong Database of Sancier.

Libchaber, Albert, Quoted in Gleick, James, Chaos, New York/ London: Viking/ Penguin 1987, p.195.

Li-Da, Fong, The effects of external Qi on bacterial growth patterns, *China Qi Gong Magazine* 1983, 1, 36 (Quoted in: Eisenberg, David with Wright, Thomas Lee, *Encounters with Qi,* New York: W. W. Norton 1985, 213.

Lin, Houshen – Shanghai Qigong Institute – Clinical and laboratory study of the effect of qigong anaesthesla on thyroldectomy (*1st World Conference for Academic Exchange of Medical Qigong, Beijing 1988* – from Qigong Database of Sancier.

Lin, Kuo., *A New Methodology of Qigong Applied in Cancer Treatment,* (Shanghai: The Scientific press, 1981), P.!.

Lin, Menxian/ Zhang, Jie/ Hu, Dongwe/ Ye, Zhumei – Fujina soul Skill Research Dept, Fu Zhou, China – Effect of qigong waiqi (emitted qi) on blood chemistry of mice radiated with x-rays *3rd National Academic Conference on Qigong Science, Guangzhou, China. 1990* – from Qigong Database of Sancier.

Lionberger, H., Dissertation Abstracts International 1985, 46, 2624B, University Microfilms No. 85-24-008.

Lionberger, Harriet Jacqueline, *An interpretive study of nurses practice of Therapeutic Touch,* Unpublished Doctoral Dissertation, University of California, San Francisco 1985.

Liu, Anxi/ Zhao, Jing/ Wang, Xishang/ Zhang, Jun – Dept Biology, Nankai University, China – Effect of waiqi (emitted qi) on singe sodium channel of cultured rate neurons *3rd National Academic Conference on Qigong Science, Guangzhou, China. 1990* – from Qigong Database of Sancier.

Liu, Anxi/ Zhao, Jing/ Zhao, Yong/ Du, Zhiqin, Dept Biology, Nankai University, Tainjin 300071, China, Modified effect of emitted qi on close-open kinetic process of sodium channels of rat cultural neuron cell, 2nd World Conference for Academic Exchange of Medical Qigong, Beijing 1993.

Liu, Guanquan/ Yang, Tsau/ Yao, Yuzhong/ Zhang, Jinmei/ Ming, Huasheng/ He, Jinhong – Dept Physiology, Sun Yat-Sen University of Medical Sciences, Guangzhou, China/ Guangdong Qigong Association, China – Effects of emitted qi on the characteristics of Interspike Interval of the cerebellar neurons of rats *3rd National Academic Conference on Qigong Science, Guangzhou, China. 1990* – from Qigong Database of Sancier.

Liu, Guolong, A study by EEG and evoked potential on humans and animals of the effects of emitted Qi, Qigong meditation, and infrasound from a Qigong simulator (Beijing College of Traditional Chinese Medicine, China – from Sancier 1991).

Liu, Guolong, Department of Physiology, Beijing College of Traditional Chinese Medicine, Beijing – Effect of qigong state and emitted qi on the human nervous system, 1st International Congress of Qigong, UC Berkeley, Calif, 1990

Liu, Guolong, Rongqing Cui, Xin Niu and Xueyan Peng – Beijing College of Traditional Chinese Medicine, Beijing – Nerval mechanisms of the qigong state and the effects of emitted qi, *1st World Conferencefor Academic Exchange of Medical Qigong, Beijing 1988.*

Liu, Guolong/ Cui, Rongqing/ Niu, Xin/ Peng, Xueyan – Beijing College of Traditional Chinese Medicine -*Nerval mechanisms of the qigong state and the effects of emitted qi* (1st World Conference for Academic Exchangeof Medical Qigong, Beijing 1988 – from Database of Sancier).

Liu, Guolong/ Wan, Pei/ Peng, Xueyan/ Zhong, Xuelong, Beijing College of Traditional Chinese Medicine, Beijing – Influence of emitted qi on the auditory brainstem evoked responses (ABER) and auditory middle latency evoked responses (MLR) in cats, *1st World Conference for AcademicExchange of Medical Qigong, Beijing 1988.*

Liu, Haitao [and others], Weifang Medical College, Shandong Province, China, Study of the inducing function of the emitted qi of qigong on the biological composition of a-amylase in wheat seeds. *1st World Conference for Academic Exchange of Medical Qigong, Beijing, 1988.*

Liu, Tehfu/ Wan, Minsheng/ Lu, Oulun – Shanghai Medical University – *Experiment of the emitted qi on animals* (*1st World Conference for Academic Exchange of Medical Qigong, Beijing 1988* - from Database of Sancier).

Liu, Yusheng et al. – Institute of Integration of Traditional and Western Medicine of PLA, First Medical College of PLA, Guangzhou, China – Study of the persistency of the effect of emitted qi on the biological effect on T cells in mice *3rd National Academic Conference on Qigong Science, Guangzhou, China. 1990* – from Qigong Database of Sancier.

Liu, Yusheng et al. Institute of Integration of Traditional and Western Medicine of PLA, First Medical College of PLA, Guangzhou – Effect of qigong waiqi (emitted qi) on the tumor killing activity of NK-cells in mice *3rd National Academic Conference on Qigong Science, Guangzhou, China. 1990* – from Qigong Database of Sancier.

Liu, Zirong/ Ren, Tao/ Ren, Jianping/ Zhang, Zhixiang, Dept Microorganism, Shandong University, China/ Yuan Study Research Institute, E. Zhou, Hubei Province, China, Comparative study of emitted qi and physical-chemical factors on the protoplasmic mutagenesis of micromonospora echinospord, *2nd World Conference for Academic Exchange of Medical Qigong, Beijing 1993.*

Liu, Zirong/ Wang, Jinshen/ Ren, Jianping/ Yuan, Hua, Microbiology Dept, Shandong University, Yuanji Study Research Institute, E. Zhou, Hubei Province, China, Study of the biological effect of emitted qi on microbes, *2nd World Conference for Academic Exchange of Medical Qigong, Beijing 1993.*

Lloyd, D. H. Objective events in the brain correlating with psychic phenomena, *New Horizons*, 1973, 1, 69-75 .

Lloyd, D. H., Objective events in the brain correlating with psychic phenomena, *New Horizon* 1973, 1, 69-75.

Lo, Chinhpaio/ He, Ahiqang/ Liu, Weimen/ Ge, Zuwen/ Zhou, Eaqiang/ Sun, Lifen/ Li Chunyan/ Xu Jianhao/ Wu, Yucan/ Ke, Heng/ Xu, Jianping – Jinan University, Guangzhou/ Guandong Institute of Material Medica, Guangzhou/ Quangdong Qigong Association, Guangzhou, China–Scanning electron microscopic observation on effects of qigong waiqi (emitted qi) on the membrane of mycardial cells in culture *3rd National Academic Conference on Qigong Science, Guangzhou, China. 1990* – from Qigong Database of Sancier.

Locker, Leonard, *Healing All and Everything*, Shaftesbury, England: Element 1985.

Loehr, Franklin, *The Power of Prayer on Plants*, New York: Signet 1969.

Lombardi, Ethel, *Personal Communication* 1981, 1984.

Long, Joseph K., *Extrasensory Ecology: Parapsychology and Anthropology*, Metuchen, NJ and London: Scarecrow 1977.

Long, Max Freedom, *Recovering the Ancient Magic*, Cape Girardeau, MO: Huna 1978 (Orig. 1936).

Long, Max Freedom, *The Secret Science Behind Miracles*, Marina del Rey, CA: DeVorss 1976 (Orig. 1948).

Lorr, M./ McNair, D.M., *Profile of Mood States (Bi-Polar Form)*, San Diego, CA: Educational and Industrial Testing Service 1988.

Lovelock, J.: *Gaia: A New Look at Life on Earth*. New York: Oxford University 1979.

Lu, Danyun/ Jia, Jingdin, National Research Institute of Sports Science, Beijing, China, Effect of emitted qi on the skeletal muscle of mice under the stress of ice-swimming – an electro-microscopic observation, *1st World Conf for Acad Exch of Medical Qigong. Beijing, China 1988.*

Lu, Guangjun/ Cai, Jun/ Chen, Xiaoye – Qigong Dept, Xiyuan Hospital, China/ institute of Basic Medical Sciences, China Academy of Traditional Medicine, Beijing – Pathological studies on treating rat gastric-ulcer treated with emitted qi *3rd National Academic Conference on Qigong Science, Guangzhou, China. 1990* – from Qigong Database of Sancier.

Lu, Huahao/ Wang, Lianfang/ Zhen, Jeiping/ Xie, Chunlin/ Chang, Jiaoying/ Luo, Jifeng/ Lin, Xiaoshang – 157 Central Hospital of PLA, Guangzhou – Effect of emitted qi on peripheral blood lymphocytes and subgroups in ICR mice *3rd National Academic Conference on Qigong Science, Guangzhou, China. 1990* – from Qigong Database of Sancier.

Lu, Huahao/ Zhen, Jieping/ Luo, Jifeng/ Wang, Lianfang/ Lin, Xiashang/ Liu, Jiang – Central Hospital of P.L.A., Guangzhou/ Dept Pharmacology, Chinese Medical College Guangzhou, Guangzhou, China – Effect of emitted qi on testosterone and estradiol in rats *3rd National Academic Conference on Qigong Science, Guangzhou, China. 1990* – from Qigong Database of Sancier.

Luo, Sen/ Chai, Shaoai/ Yi, Weiyuan/ Ren, Hetian/ Cao, Baozheng. Zhejiang Institute of Traditional Chinese Medicine, Zhejiang Province, China, Molecular biological effects of emitted qi on man, *1st World Conference for Academic Exchange of Medical Qigong, Beijing 1988.*

Luo, Xin; Zhu, Nianlin; Li, Liping; Liu, Fengzhen. Yunnan University, Kunming, China – Effect of qigong (emitted qi), PSI, and\bloradlatlon on some ultraviolet absorption spectra *3rd National Academic Conference on Qigong Science, Guangzhou, China. 1990* – from Qigong Database of Sancier.

Lynch-Sauer, J. using phenomenological research method to study nursing phenomena, In: Leininger, M.M. (ed), *Qualitative research methods in nursing*, Orlando, FL: Grune & Stratton 1985.

M

Ma, Dingxing – Stomatological Hospital, 4th Military Medical College, Xi'an, China – *Oral facial scar softened by qigong therapy (1st World Conference for Academic Exchange of Medical Qigong, Beijing 1988* – from Qigong Database of Sancier.

Macdonald, Michael Patrick , *Madness and Healing in Seventeenth Century England* (dissertation), Stanford, CA: Stanford University 1979.

MacDonald, R., Dakin, H. S., and Hickman, J. L., Preliminary studies with three alleged 'psychic healers,' In: Morris, J. D.; Roll, W. G. and Morris, R. L (Eds), *Research in Parapsychology 1976,* Metuchen, NJ and London: Scarecrow 1977.

MacManaway, Bruce with Turcan, Johanna, *Healing: The Energy That Can Restore Health*, Wellingsborough, England: Thorsons 1983.

MacNeil, Melanie Sue, *Therapeutic Touch and Tension Headaches: A Rogerian Study* (Master's thesis), D'Youville College 1995.

Macrae, J. Therapeutic Touch: a way of life, in Borelli/ Heidt.

MacRobert, R. G., When is healing "psychic?", *Tomorrow* 1955, 3(3), 47-55.

Madakasira, S./ O'Brien, K., Acute posttraumatic stress disorder in victims of a natural disaster, *J. of Nervous and Mental Disease* 1987, 175, 286-290. .

Magaray, Christopher., Healing and Meditation in Medical Practice, *Medical J. Australia* 1981, 1 , 338-341.

Manning, Matthew, *The Link*, New York: Holt, Rinehart and Winston, 1974.

Markides, Emily Joannides, *Complementary Energetic Practices: An Exploration Into the World of Maine Women Healers (Alternative Therapies, Healing),* (dissertation) University of Maine 1996.

Markides, Kyriacos C. *Fire in the Heart: Healers, Sages and Mystics*, London: Arkana/ Penguin 1991.

Markides, Kyriakos, *Homage to the Sun: The Wisdom of the Magus of Strovolos*, New York & London: Arkana 1987.

Markides, Kyriakos, *The Magus of Strovolos: The Extraordinary World of a Spiritual Healer*, London & Boston: Arkana 1985.

Matheny, K. et al., *Coping Resource Inven-*

tory for Sterss (CRIS), Atlanta: Health Prisms Inc. 1981.

Matthews, Caitlin, *Singing the Soul Back Home: Shamanism in Daily Life,* Shaftesbury, England/ Rockport, MA: element 1995.

May, Edwin C./ Vilenskaya, Larissa, 'Distant influence' on the eating behavior of white mice (*Some Aspects of Parapsychological Research in the Former Soviet Union* 1994, 9-10; *Subtle Energies* 1992, 3(3) 45-68.

McCaffery, John, *Tales of Padre Pio, The Friar of San Giovannni,* Garden City, NY: Image/ Doubleday 1981. (Orig. *The Friar of San Giovanni,* U.K.: Darton, Longman & Todd 1978.)

McCarthy, Donald; Keane, Patrice and Tremmel, Lawrence, Psi phenomena in low complexity systems: Conformance behavior using seeds, In: Roll, W. G (Ed)., *Research in Parapsychology 1978,* Metuchen, NJ and London: Scarecrow 1979, 82-84.

McClain, Carol Shepherd (ed), *Women as Healers: Cross-Cultural Perspectives,* New Brunswick, NJ: Rutgers University Press 1989, Abstract from White, Rhea A. *Exceptional Human Experience,* 1991, 9(2), 266.

McClure, Kevin, Miracles of the Virgin, *The Unexplained,* 1983, 11(131), 2614- 2617.

McConnell, Robert and Kuzmen Clark, Thelma, National Academy of Sciences Opinion on Parapsychology, *Presentation at 33rd Annual Meeting of the Parapsychological Association, Chevy Chase, MD* 1990.

McConnell, Robert and Kuzmen Clark, Thelma, The enemies of parapsychology, *Presentation at 33rd Annual Meeting of the Parapsychological Association,* Chevy Chase, MD 1990.

McCormack, H. M. et al.., Clinical applications of visual analogue scales: a critical review, *Psychological Medicine* 1968, 18, 1007.

McCullough, J., Plants and people, some exploratory experiments, *Parascience Proceedings* 1973, 39-42.

McDougall, W., Fourth report on a Lamarckian experiment, *British J. of Psychology* 1938, 28, 321-345.

McGaa, E. (Eagle Man). *Mother Earth Spirituality: Native American Paths to Healing Ourselves and Our World.* San Francisco: Harper & Row 1990.

McGarey, William A., *The Edgar Cayce Remedies,* New York: Bantam, 1983.

McGarey, William, *In Search of Healing: Wole-Body Healing through the Mind-Body-Spirit Connection,* New York: Perigee/ Berkeley 1996.

McGuire, Meredith B. with Kantor, Debra, *Ritual Healing in Suburban America,* New Brunswick, NJ: Rutgers University Press 1988, Abstract from White, Rhea A. *Exceptional Human Experience,* 1991, 9(2), 266.

McRae, Ron, *Mind Wars: The True Story of Secret Government Research into the Military Potential of Psychic Weapons,* New York: St. Martin's, 1984.

Medicine. Boston and London: New Science Library/ Shambala 1985.

Meehan , T.C. et al., The effect of Therapeutic Touch on postoperative pain, *Pain* 1990, Supplement p..149 (reprinted with kind permission of the publishers).

Meehan, T. C., *An Abstract of the Effect of Therapeutic Touch on the Experience of Acute Pain in Post-operative Patients,* Unpublished Doctoral Dissertation, New York University 1985.

Meehan, Thérèse Connell, Therapeutic Touch and postoperative pain: a Rogerian research study *Nursing Science Quarterly* 1993, 6(2), 69-78.

Meek, G. W., *Healers and the Healing Process,* Wheaton, IL: Theosophical Publishing House 1977. (Quotes reprinted by permission of publisher. Copyright George W. Meek, 1977.

Melzack, The McGill Pain Questionnaire: major properties and scoring methods, *Pain* 1975, 1, 277-299.

Meng, Guirong/ Li, Shengping/ Cui, Yuanhao/ Sun, Mengyin/ Zhu, Qunying/ Xin, Yan, Tsinghua University, Beijing, China/ Municipal Institute of Traditional Chinese Medicine of Chongqing, Sichuan Province, China, Effect of emitted qi the infrared thermal imaging system on temperature response of the samples, *1st World Conference for Academic Exchange of Medical Qigong, Beijing, 1988.*

Meng, Guirong/ Li, Shengping/ Sun, Mengyin/ Cui, Yuanhao/ Xin, Yan, Tsinghua University, Beijing/ Municipal Institute of Traditional Chinese Medicine of Chongqing, Sichuan Province, China, Effect of emitted qi on thymine by a recording spectrophotometer and a thermovision, *1st World Conference for Academic Exchange of Medical Qigong, Beijing 1988.*

550   *Bibliography*

Meng, Guirong/ Li, Shenping/ Sun, Mengyin/ Cui, Yuanhao/ Xin, Yan, Tsinghua University, Beijing/ Municipal Institute of Traditional Chinese Medicine of Chongqing, Sichuan Province, China, Effect of emitted qi on ultra-violet and infrared thermal imaging systems on L-trypotophan solution, *1st World Conference for Academic Exchange of Medical Qigong, Beijing 1988.*

Menvielle, M./ Bertheiler, A., The K-derived planetary indices: Description and availability, *Review of Geophysics* 1991, 29, 415-432.

Mercola, John, http://www.mercola.com/2000/may/14/doctor_accidents.htm

Mersmann, Cynthia A. *Therapeutic Touch and Milk Let Down in Mothers of Non-nursing Preterm Infants (dissertation)*, New York University 1993.

Mesmer, Franz Anton, *Mesmerism: A Translation of the Original Medical and Scientific Writings of F.A. Mesmer, M.D.*, (Trans. by Bloch, George J.), Los Altos, CA: William Kaufmann 1980.

Metta, Louis (Pseud.), Psychokinesis on Lepidoptera larvae, *J. of Parapsychology* 1972, 36, 213-221.

Mialowska, Zofia, Statistical assessment of Jerzy Rejmer's biotherapeuttical activity at an Izis Clinic in Warsaw, *Proceedings of the 6th International Conference on Psychotronic Research* 1986, 130-132.

Micozzi, Marc S., *Fundamentals of Complementary and Alternative Medicine*, New York/ London: Churchill Livingstone 1996.

Miettinen, M.A., Religious healing from a medical and psychological view, Dissertation, Tampere, Finland: Kirkon tutimeskeskus, Series A, No. 51, 1990.

Milamed DR/ Hedley-Whyte, J. Contributions of the surgical sciences to a reduction of the mortality rate in the United States for the period 1968 to 1988, *Annals of Surgery* 1994, 219, :94-102.

Millar, B., Physiological detectors of psi, *European J. of Parapsychology*, 1979, 2, 456-478 .

Millar, B., The observational theories: A primer, *European J. of Parapsychology* 1978, 2, 304-332.

Miller, Casper J., *Faith-Healers in the Himalayas*, Kathmandu, Nepal: Sahayogi 1979.

Miller, Lynn, An explanation of Therapeutic Touch using the science of unitary man, *Nursing Forum* 1979, 18(3), 278-287.

Miller, Paul, *Born to Heal: A Biography of Harry Edwards, the Spirit Healer*, London: Spiritualist Press 1969 (Orig. 1948).

Miller, Robert N., Paraelectricity, a primary energy, *Human Dimensions* (undated) V. 5(1 & 2), 22-26 (Also reported in: Miller, 1977).

Miller, Robert N., Study of remote mental healing, *Medical Hypotheses*, 1982, 8, 481-490. (Also reviewed briefly in: Maddock, Peter, International Parascience Institute: Toronto and London Conferences, 1981, *Parapsychology Review* 1982, 13(4), 7).

Miller, Robert N., The positive effect of prayer on plants, *Psychic* 1972, 3(5), 24-25.

Miller, Robert N., Reinhart, Philip B., and Kern, Anita, Scientists register thought energy, *Science of Mind* 1974, July, 12-16.

Miller, Robert, Methods of detecting and measuring healing energies, In: White, John and Krippner, Stanley, *Future Science*, Garden City, NY: Anchor/ Doubleday 1977.

Miller, Robert., *The Relationship Between the Energy State of Water and its Physical Properties*, Research paper, Ernest Holmes Research Foundation (undated).

Miller, Ronald, The Healing Magic of Crystals: An Interview with Marcel Vogel, *Science of Mind*, August 1984, 8-12.

Mills, Janet Melanie Ailsa (Pseudonym Challoner), *The Path of Healing*, Wheaton IL: Quest/ Theosophical, 1976.

Mintz, Elizabeth E., with Schmeidler, Gertrude R., *The Psychic Thread*, New York: Human Sciences 1983.

Mir, Maria and Vilenskaya, Larissa, *The Golden Chalice*, San Francisco, CA: H. S. Dakin.

Mircea, *Yoga: Immortality and Freedom*, New York: Princeton University 1958.

Mison, Karel, Statistical processing of diagnostics done by subject and by physician, *Proceedings of the 6th International Conference on Psychotronic Research* 1986, 137-138.

Misra, Margaret M. *The Effects of Therapeutic Touch on Menstruation* (Master's thesis), Long Beach: California State University 1994.

Momas EJ, et al, Incidence and types of adverse events and negligent care in Utah and Colorado, *Medical Care* 2000; 38:261-71.

Montagno, Elson de A., Clinical parapsychology: The spiritist model in Brazil, In: Weiner, Debra H. and Radin, Dean I. (Eds), *Research in Parapsychology 1985*, Metuchen, NJ and London: Scarecrow 1986, 171-172.

Montgomery, Ruth, *Born to Heal*, New York: Popular Library 1973.

Moore, Marcia, *Hypersentience*, New York: Bantam 1976.

Moore, Nancy G., The healing web: nursing borrows from Native American tradition to create a better approach to healing, *Alternative Therapies in Health and Medicine* 1996, 2(2) 30-31.

Kathy Moreland, The Lived Experience of Receiving Healing Touch Therapy of Women with Breast Cancer Who are Receiving Chemotherapy: A Phenomenological Study, *Healing Touch Newsletter* 1988, 8(3), 3;5.

Morley, Peter and Wallis, Roy (Eds), *Culture and Curing*, Pittsburgh, PA: University of Pittsburgh, 1978.

Morris, P.A. The effect of pilgrimage on anxiety, depression and religious attitude, Psychological Medicine 1982, 12, 291-294.

Morris, R. L. Parapsychology, biology, and anpsi, in Wolman, B.B. (ed), *Handbook of Parapsychology* 1977, 687-715 .

Morris, Robert L., Book review: Alcock, James E., Parapsychology: Science or Magic?, *J. of the American Society for Psychical Research* 1982, 76(2), 177-185.

Moss, Ralph, *Alternative Medicine Online: A Guide to Natural Remedies on the Internet*, Brooklyn, NY: Equinox 1997.

Moss, Richard, The mystery of wholeness, in: Carlson/ Shield, p. 35-41.

Moss, Richard., *The Black Butterfly: An Invitation to Radical Aliveness*, Berkeley, California: Celestial Arts 1986.

Moss, Thelma S., Photographic evidence of healing energy on plants and people, *Dimensions of Healing, Symposium of the Academy of Parapsychology and Medicine at Los Altos, CA* 1972, 121-131.

Moss, Thelma, *The Body Electric*, New York: St. Martin's 1979.

Moss, Thelma, *The Probability of the Impossible*, Bergenfield, NJ: New American Library 1974.

Moss, Vere, Non-physical factors in medical divination and treatment, *J. of the British Society of Dowsers* 1968, 20, 288-292.

Motoyama, Hiroshi., *Science and the Evolution of Consciousness, Ki and Psi*, Autumn Press 1978.

Motz, Julie, Energy work for breast cancer surgery patients, Unpublished report, 1996, presented at Annual Meeting of the American Holistic Medical Association, 1996. (PO Box 75, Lake Peekskill, NY 10537 hangels@pipeline.com)

Moy, Caryl Towsley, *Touch in the Therapeutic Relationship: An Exploratory Study with Therapists Who Touch* (Dissertation) Crbondale, IL: Southern Illinois University 1980.

Mueller Hinze, Maxine Louise *The Effects of Therapeutic Touch and Acupressure on Experimentally-Induced Pain* (dissertation), Austin, TX: University of Texas 1988.

Muehsam, David J., et al, Effects of qigong on cell-free myosin phosphorylation: preliminary experiments, Subtle Energies 1994, 5(1), 93-104.

Muktananda, S. *Guru Chitshaktivilas: The Play of Consciousness*, New York: Harper & Row 1971.

Muktananda, S. *Siddha Meditation: Commentaries on the Shiva Sutras and Other Sacred Texts*, Oakland, CA: S.Y.D.A. Foundation 1975.

Muller, F. M. (ed), *Sacred Books of the East: The Vedanta Sutras*, New Delhi, India: Motilal .

Munson, R. J., The effects of PK on rye seeds (Abstract), *J. of Parapsychology*, 1979, 43, 45.

Murphet, H., *Sai Baba, Avatar*, India: Macmillan 1978.

Murphet, H., *Sai Baba, Man of Miracles*, India: Macmillan 1972.

Murphy, Gardner, *Challenge of Psychical Research: A Primer of Parapsychology*, New York: Harper/ Colophon 1970.

Murphy, Joseph, *How to Use Your Healing Power*, San Gabriel, CA: Willing, 1957.

Myers, A. T. and Myers, F. W. H., Mind-cure, faith-cure and the miracles of Lourdes, *Proceedings of the Society for Psychical Research* 1894, 9, 160-209.

N

Nanko, Michael J., A report on the case investigation of Natuzza Evolo, *J. of the Southern California Society for Psychical Research*, 1985, 3, 6- 27.

Naranjo, Claudio, and Ornstein, Robert E, *On the Psychology of Meditaton*, New York: Penguin 1977.

Nash, C. B. and Nash, C. S., Psi-influenced movement of chicks and mice onto a visual cliff, In: Roll, W. G. and Beloff, J. (Eds), *Research in Parapsychology 1980*, Metuchen, NJ: Scarecrow, 1981, 109-110.

Nash, C. B. and Nash, C. S., The effect of paranormally conditioned solution on yeast fermentation, *J. of Parapsychology* 1967, 31, 314.

Nash, Carroll B., Medical parapsychology, In: White, R. A., *Surveys in Parapsychology*, Metuchen, NJ: Scarecrow 1976 (Orig. In: *Parapsychology Review*, 1972, 3, 13-18).

Nash, Carroll B., *Parapsychology: The Science of Psiology*, Springfield, IL: Charles C. Thomas 1986. (See also Nash, 1978).

Nash, Carroll B., Psychokinetic control of bacterial growth, *J. of the Society for Psychical Research* 1982, 51, 217-221.

Nash, Carroll B., *Science of Psi: ESP and PK*, Springfield, IL: C. C. Thomas 1978. (See also Nash, 1986).

Nash, Carroll B., Test of psychokinetic control of bacterial mutation, *J. of the American Society for Psychical Research*, 1984, 78(2), 145-152.

Nash, Carroll B., The possible detection of cervical cancer by ESP, *J. of the Society for Psychical Research* 1987, 54, 143-144.

Nash, June, The Logic of Behavior: Curing in a Maya Indian Town, *Human Organization* 1967, 26(3), 132-140.

Nebauer, Monica, Healing through Therapeutic Touch: one person's perspective, in: Gaut, D.A./ Boykin, A., *Caring as Healing*, New York: National League for Nursing 1994, 85-101.

Neher, Andrew., *The Psychology of Transcendence*, Englewood Ciffs, New Jersey: Spectrum/ Prentice Hall 1980.

Neppe, Vernon M., *The Psychology of Deja Vu: Have I Been Here Before?*, Johannesburg, South Africa: Witwatersrand University Press 1983.

Neppe, Vernon Michael., Anomalous Smells in the Subjective Paranormal Experiment, *Psychoenergetics* 1983, 5 , 11-28.

Nerem, Robert M., Levesque, H.E, Murina J., and Cornhill, J. Fedrick, Social Environment as a Factor in Diet-Induced Atherosclerosis, *Science* 1980-208, 1475-1476.

Newhan, Gayle, Therapeutic Touch for symptom control in people with AIDS, *Holistic Nursing Practice* 1989 (Aug), 45-51.

Newton-Smith, W. H., *The Structure of Time*, London: Routledge and Kegan Paul, 1984.

Nicholas, C., The effects of loving attention on plant growth, *New England J. of Parapsychology*, 1977, 1, 19-24.

Nichols, Beverley, *Powers that Be*, New York: St. Martin's, 1966.

Nin, Anaïs, *The Diary of Anaïs Nin* 1969, Fall 1943.

Niu, Xin/ Liu, Guolong/ Yu, Zhiming – Beijing College of Traditional Chinese Medicine – Measurement and analysis of the infrasonic waves from emitted qi (*1st World Conference for Academic Exchange of Medical Qigong, Beijing 1988* – from Qigong Database of Sancier.

Nixon, F., *Born to be Magnetic, Vol. 1*, Chemainus, British Columbia: Magnetic 1971 (poor).

Noble, Vicki, *Shakti woman: Feeling Our Fire, Healing Our World – The New Female shamanism*, New York: HarperCollins 1991.

Nolen, W. A., *Healing: A Doctor in Search of a Miracle*, New York: Random House 1974.

Nomura, Harehido (Electrotechnical Laboratory). Double-blind tests of qi transmittion from qigong masters to untrained volunteers: (3) analysis of qi emitted from the human body, Japanese Mind-Body Science 1993, 2(1), 95-111.

Null, Gary, Healers or hustlers? Part IV, *Self Help Update* Spring 1981, p. 18.

O

O'Regan, Brendan/ Hirshberg, Caryle: Spontaneous Remission: an Annotated Bibliography, Sausalito, CA: Institute of Noetic Sciences 1993.

Oakley, D. V. and MacKenna, G. W., Safety of faith healing, *Lancet* (Feb 22) 1986, 444.

Ogawa, Tokuo/ Hayashi, Shigemi/ Shinoda, Norihiko/ Ohnishi, Norkazu, Aichi Medical University, Japan/ Chinese-Japanese Institute of Qigong, Japan/ Shakti Acupuncture Clinic,

Japan/ Aichi Medical University, Japan, Changes of skin temperature during emission of qi, *1st World Conference for Academic Exchange of Medical Qigong, Beijing 1988.*

Olson, Melodie/ Sneed, Nancee/ LaqVia, Mariano/ Virella, Gabriel/ Bonadonna, Ramita, Stress-Induced Immunosuppression and Therapeutic Touch *Alternative Therapies* 1997, 3(2), 68-74.

Olson, Melodie/ Sneed, Nancee et al., Therapeutic Touch and post-Hurricane Hugo stress, *J. of Holistic Nursing* 1992, 10(2), 120-136.

Olson, Melodie/ Sneed, Nancee: Anxiety and Therapeutic Touch, *Issues in Mental Health Nursing* 1995, 16, 97-108.

Omananda, Swami, *The Boy and the Brothers*, New York: Doubleday, 1960.

Omura, Y. Connections found between each meridian (heart, stomach, triple burner, etc.) and organ representation area of corresponding internal organs in each side of the cerebral cortex; release of common neurotransmitters and hormones unique to each meridian and corresponding acupuncture point and internal organ after acupuncture, electrical stimulation, mechanical stimulation (including shiatsu), soft laser stimulation or Qigong, *Acupuncture Elec.* 1990(a), 14, 155-186.

Omura, Y. Storing of Qigong energy in various materials and drugs (Qigongization): its clinical application for treatment of pain, circulatory disturbances, bacterial or viral infections, heavy metal deposits, and related intractable medical problems by selectively enhancing circulation and drug uptake, *Acupuncture Elec.* 1990(b), 15, 137-157 .

Omura, Y. et al. Unique changes found on the Qigong (Chi Kung) master's and patient's body during Qigong treatment, their relationships to certain meridians and acupuncture points and the re-creation of therapeutic Qigong states by children and adults, *Acupuncture Elec.* 1989, 14(1), 61-89 .

Onetto, Brenio & Elguin, Gita H., *Psychokinesis in Experimental Tumorgenesis* (Abstract of dissertation in psychology, University of Chile 1964), *J. of Parapsychology* 1966, 30, 220. (Also in Spanish: *Acta Psiquiatrica Y Psicologia America Latina* 1968, 14, 47. See also brief comments of Campbell, Anthony in *J. of the Society for Psychical Research* 1968, 44, 428.

Orloff, Judith, Second Sight: The Personal Story of a Psychiatrist Clairvoyant, New York: Warner 1996.

Orsi, R. A., The cult of the saints and the reimagination of the space and time of sickness in twentieth-century American Catholicism, *Literature and Medicine* 1989, 8, 63-77.

Osis, Karlis and Bokert, Edwin, ESP and changed states of consciousness induced by meditation, *J. of the American Society for Psychical Research* 1971, 65, 17-65.

Osis, Karlis, A test of the occurrence of psi effect between man and cat, *J. of Parapsychology* 1952, 16, 233-256.

Ostrander, Sheila and Schroeder, Lynn, *Psychic Discoveries Behind the Iron Curtain*, New York: Bantam 1970.

Osumi, Ikuko and Ritchie, Malcolm, *The Shamanic Healer: The Healing World of Ikuko Osumi and the Traditional Art of Seiki-Jutsu,* London: Century 1987.

Oteri, L. (ed), *Quantum Physics and Parapsychology*, New York: Van Nostrand Reinhold 1975 .

Oubre, Alondra., Shamanic Trance and the Placebo Effect: The Case for a Study in Psychobiological Anthropology, *Psi Research* 1985, 5 (1/ 2),116-144.

Oursler, Will., *The Healing Power of Faith*, Hawthorn Books, New York 1957.

Owen, Iris M., with Sparrow, Margaret, *Conjuring Up Philip: An Adventure in Psychokinesis*, New York: Harper and Row 1976.

Oye, Robert, and Shapiro, Martin, Reporting Results from Chemotherapy Trials. *J. of the American Medical Association* 1984, 252, 2722-2725.

P

Packer, Rhonda, *Sorcerers, Medicine-Men and Curing Doctors: A Study of Myth and Symbol in North American Shamanism*, Unpublished Doctoral Dissertation, UCLA 1983.

Paddison, S. *The Hidden Power of the Heart*, Boulder Creek, CA: Planetary 1992.

Palmer, J., Scoring in ESP tests as a function of belief in ESP, Part I. The sheep-goat effect, *J. of the American Society for Psychical Research* 1971, 65, 373-408.

Palmer, John A.; Honorton, Charles, and Utts, Jessica, *Reply to the National Research Council Study on Parapsychology*, Research Triangle Park, NC: Parapsychological Association 1988.

Pan, L. B./ Zhang, Z. F. – Dept Nephrology, Nanfang Hospital, Guangzhou -Qigong treatment for hypertension caused by renal Insufficiency *3rd National Academic Conference on Qigong Science, Guangzhou, China. 1990* – from Qigong Database of Sancier.

Parapsychology Foundation, *Proceedings of Four Conferences of Parapsychological Studies*, New York: Parapsychology Foundation 1957, 43-65. (Includes brief discussions of Bender, H.; Booth, G.; Eisenbud, J.; Larcher, H.; Moser, U.; Saller, K.; Servadio, E.; Thouless, R. and Van Lennep, D. on the state of knowledge of healing at that date).

Parkes, Brenda Sue, *Therapeutic Touch as an Intervention to Reduce Anxiety in Elderly Hospitalized Patients*, Unpublished Doctoral Dissertation, University of Texas at Autstin 1985.

Patrovsky, V., Effect of some force field on physical properties of water and some salt solutions, *Proceedings of the 5th International Conference on Psychotronic Research*, Bratislava 1983, 88-95.

Patrovsky, V., Healers, water and force fields, *Proceedings of the 4th International Conference on Psychotronic Research*, Sao Paulo, Brazil 1979, 42- 43.

Patrovsky, V., On the bioactivation of water, *International J. of Paraphysics* 1978, 12(5 & 6), 130-132.

Pattison, E. Mansell et al., Faith healing, *J. of Nervous and Mental Diseases* 1973, 156, 397-409.

Pauli, Enrique Novillo, PK on living targets as related to sex, distance and time, In: Roll, W. G.; Morris, R. L. and Morris, J. D (Eds), *Research in Parapsychology* Metuchen, NJ: Scarecrow 1973, 68-70.

Pavek, Richard, 325 Years of Healing in England, Ireland and Scotland, Part 1, *Caduceus* Issue no. 29, 32-34; Part 2, Issue no. 30, 36-38.

Pavlov, Ivan. *Conditioned Reflexes and Psychiatry*, New York: International Publishers 1941.

Pearson, Robert E. Response to suggestion given under general anesthesia, *American J. of Clinical Hypnosis* 1961, 4, 106-114.

Peck, Susan D. (Eckes), *The Effectiveness of Therapeutic Touch for Decreasing Pain and Improving Functional Ability in Elders with Arthritis* (Dissertation), University of Minnesota 1996.

Pederson-Krag Geraldine, Telepathy and Repression, *Psychoanalytic Quarterly* 1947, 16, 61-68.

Peltham, Elizabeth, Therapeutic Touch and massage, *Nursing Standard*, 1991, 5(45), 26-28.

Peng, Xueyan/ Liu, Guolong. Beijing College of Traditional Chinese Medicine, Beijing, China, Effect of emitted qi and infrasonic sound on somatosensory evoked potential (SEP) and slow vertex response (SVR), *1st World Conference for Academic Exchange of Medical Qigong. Beijing 1988*.

Permutt, Cyril, *Beyond the Spectrum: A Survey of Supernormal Photography*. Cambridge, England: Patrick Stephens 1983.

Persig, Robert M. *Zen and the Art of Motorcycle Maintenance*, New York/ London: Bantam 1979.

Persinger, M. A., Geophysical variables and behavior: xxx, intense paranormal experiences occur during days of quiet, global, geomagnetic activity, *Perceptrual & Motor Skills* 1985, 61, 320-322.

Persinger, M. A./ Schaut, G. B., Geomagnetic factors in subjective telepathic, precognitive and postmortem experiences, *J. of the American Society for Psychical Research* 1988, 82, 217-235.

Persinger, Michael A., Spontaneous telepathic experiences from *Phantasms of the Living* and low global geomagnetic activity, *J. of the American Society for Psychical Research* 1987, 81(1), 23-36.

Persinger, Michael A., Subjective telepathic experiences: geomagnetic activitity and the ELF hypothesis, Part II. Stimulus features and neural detection, *Psi Research* 1985, 4(2), 4-23.

Peters, Larry and Price-Williams, Towards an Experiential Analysis of Shamanism, *American Ethnologist* 1980, 7 (3), 379-413.

Peters, Larry., *Ecstasy and Healing in Nepal,* Malibu, California: Undena 1981.

Peters, Pamela Joan, *The Lifestyle Changes of Selected Therapeutic Touch Practitioners: An Oral History (Alternative Medicine),* (dissertation), Walden University 1995.

Peterson, James W., *The Secret Life of Kids: An Exporation into Their Psychic Senses,* Wheaton, IL: Quest/ Theosophical 1987.

Peterson, James, Extrasensory abilities of children: An ignored reality?, *Learning* 1975 (Dec), 10-14.

Peterson LM/ Brennan TA, Medical ethics and medical injuries: taking our duties seriously. *J Clin Ethics* 1990, 1, 207-11.

Pfeiffer, Tomas, *Personal Communication about J. Zezulka* 1991.

Philpy, Sylvia/ Hutchinson, Cynthia Poznanski, *HEALTH Tool for HT Research (for healers and healees)*, Healing Touch International, 2002 Linden Dr., Boulder, CO 80304, HTResearch@aol.com.

Phoenix, (New Directions in the Study of Man), *J. of the Association for Transpersonal Anthropology*.

Piaget, J. *The Essential Piaget*, Gruer, H./ Voneche, J. (eds) New York: Basic 1977.

Pierrakos, John C., *Core Energetics: Developing the Capacity to Love and Heal*, Mandocino, California: LifeRhythm 1987.

Pierrakos, John C., *Human Energy Systems Theory: History and New Growth Perspectives*, New York: Institute For the New Age of Man 1976.

Pilla, A. A. et al., Pulse burst electric fields significantly accelerate bone repair in an animal model, *Proceedings, 14th Annual International Conference of the IEEE Engineering in Medicine and Biology Society*, Piscataway, NJ, 1992, 283.

Pitot, H.C. et al., Hepatomas in tissue culture compared with adapting liver in vivo, *National Cancer Institute Monographs* 1964, 13, 229.

Playfair, G. L, *The Unknown Power*, New York: Pocket 1975.

Playfair, Guy Lyon, Austria's medical shocker, *Fate* 1988 (Sep), 41(9), 42-48.

Playfair, Guy Lyon, *If This Be Magic*, London: Jonathan Cape 1985b.

Playfair, Guy Lyon, *Medicine, Mind and Magic: The Power of the Mind-Body Connection in Hypnotism and Healing*, Wellingborough, Northants, England: Aquarian/ Thorsons 1987.

Playfair, Guy Lyon, Twenty years among the tables, *Psi Research*, 1985a, 4(1), 96-107.

Pleass, C. M. and Dey, D. N., Using the doppler effect to study behavioral responses of motile algae to psi stimulus, In: Radin, D. I. (Ed), *Proceedings of Presented Papers: Parapsychological Association 28th Annual Convention*, Alexandria, VA: Parapsychological Association 1985, 373-405.

Pleass, C. M. and Dey, Dean, Conditions that appear to favor extrasensory interactions between homo sapiens and microbes, *J. of*

Scientific Exploration 1990, 4(2) 213-231.

Podmore, Frank, Poltergeists, <B>Proceedings of the Society for Psychical Research<B> 1896, 12, 45-115.

Polk, S.H. Client's Perceptions of Experiences Following the Intervention Modality of Therapeutic Touch (Master's thesis) Tempe: Arizona State University 1985.

Pollack, Jack Harrison, *Croiset: The Clairvoyant*, Garden City, NY: Doubleday 1964.

Polyakov, Vadim, *Extrasensory Praxis*, Translation of Russian booklets on work in St Petersburg – seeking publisher – and *Personal communication* 1992.

Ponder, Catherine, *The Dynamic Laws of Healing*, Marina Del Rey, CA: De Vorss 1966.

Post, Laurens van der, *The Voice of the Thunder*, New York/ London: Penguin 1994.

Post, Nancy Whelan, *The Effects of Therapeutic Touch on Muscle Tone* (masters thesis) San Jose, CA: San Jose State University 1990.

Poulton, Kay, *Harvest of Light: A Pilgrimage of Healing*, London: Regency 1968.

Pratt, Gaither J, *ESP Research Today: A Study of Developments in Parapsychology Since 1960*, Metuchen, NJ: Scarecrow 1973.

Presentation at the 25th Annual Convention of the Parapsychological Association/ 100th Convention of the Society for Psychical Research at Cambridge, 1982.

Prince, Raymond., Fundamental Differences of Psychoanalysis and Faith Healing, *International J. of Psychiatry* 1972, 10(1), 125-128.

Puharich, A. (ed), *The Iceland Papers*, Amherst, WI: Essentia Research Associates 1979 .

Puharich, Andrija., Pachita: Instant Surgeon, *The Unexplained* 1983, 13 (154), 3074-3077.

Pulos, Lee., Evidence of Macro-Psychokinetic Effects Produced by Thomas of Brazil, *Psi Research* 1982, 1(3),27-40.

Purska-Rowinska, Ewa and Rejmer, Jerzy, The effect of bio-energotherapy upon EEG tracings and on the clinical picture of epileptics, *Psychotronika* 1985, 10-12 (Translated from Polish by Alexander Imich.).

Puthoff, H. E. and Targ, R. A., A perceptual channel for information transfer over kilometer distances: Historical perspective and recent research, *Proceedings of the IEEE* 1976, 64, 329-354 (Cited in Schaut and Persinger).

Puthoff, Harold and Targ, Russell, PK experiments with Uri Geller and Ingo Swann, In:

Roll, W. G.; Morris, R. L. and Morris, J. D. (Eds), *Research in Parapsychology 1973* Metuchen, NJ: Scarecrow 1974, 125-128.

Q

Qian, Shusen/ Gou, Shangtong/ Shen, Hongxun – Institute of Basic Medical Sciences, Chinese Academy of Medical Sciences, Beijing/ International Institute of 'Taiji Wuxigong', Gent, Belgium – Preliminary experimental research on the curative effect of waiqi (emitted qi) of qigong on tumors (in mice) *3rd National Academic Conference on Qigong Science, Guangzhou, China. 1990* – from Qigong Database of Sancier.

Qian, Shusen/ Shen, Hongxun, Tumor Lab of Radiation and Nuclear Medicine, Medical School of Chent University, Belgium, Curative effect of emitted qi on mice with MO4 tumors, *2nd World Conference for Academic Exchange of Medical Qigong, Beijing 1993.*

Qian, Shusen/ Sun, Wei/ Liu, Qing/ Wan, Yi/ Shi, Xiaodong, China Rehabilitation Research Center, Beijing 100077, Influence of emitted qi on cancer growth, metastasis and survival time of the host *2nd World Conference for Academic Exchange of Medical Qigong, Beijing 1993.*

Quinn, Janet F., One nurse's evolution as a healer, *American J. of Nursing* (Apr) 1979, 662-665.

Quinn, Janet F., Building a body of knowledge: research on Therapeutic Touch 1974-1986, *J. of Holistic Nursing* 1988, 6(1), 37-45.

Quinn, Janet F., Future directions for Therapeutic Touch research, *J. of Holistic Nursing* 1989(b), 7(1), 19-25.

Quinn, Janet F., Therapeutic Touch as energy exchange: Replication and extansion, *Nursing Science Quarterly* 1989(a), 2(2), 79-87.

Quinn, Janet F./ Strelkauskas, Anthony J., Psychoimmunologic effects of Therapeutic Touch on practitioners and recently bereaved recipients: A pilot study, *Advances in Nursing Science,* June 1993, 13-26.

Quinn, Janet, *An Investigation of the Effect of Therapeutic Touch Without Physical Contact on State Anxiety of Hospitalized Cardiovascular Patients,* Unpublished Ph.D. Thesis, New York University 1982.

R

Radin, D. et al., Remote mental influence of human electrodermal activity, *European J. Parapsychology* 1995, 11, 19-34.

Radin, D./ Ferrari, D.: Effects of consciousness on the fall of dice: a meta-analysis, *J. of Scientific Exploration* 1991, 5, 61-83 .

Radin, D.I./ Nelson, Roger D., Evidence for consciousness-related anomalies in random physical systems, *Foundations of Physics* 1989, 20,.

Rama, S., *Path of Fire and Light: Advanced Practices of Yoga,* Honesdale, PA: Himalayan International Institute 1986.

Rama, S., *Perennial Psychology of the Bhagavad Gita,* Honesdale, PA: Himalayan International Institute 1985.

Rama, S., *Wisdom of the Ancient Sages: Mundaka Upanishad,* Honesdale, PA: Himalayan International Institute 1990.

Randall, J. L., An attempt to detect psi effects with protozoa, *J. of the Society for Psychical Research* 1970, 45, 294-296.

Randi, James, "Be healed in the name of God!" An Expose of the Reverend W. V. Grant, *Free Inquiry* 1986 (Spring), 8-19.

Randi, James, *The Faith Healers,* Buffalo, NY: Promethius 1987.

Randolph, Gretchen Lay, *The Differences in Psychological Response of Female College Students Exposed to Stressful Stimulus, When Simultaneously Treated by Either Therapeutic Touch or Casual Touch*, Unpublished doctoral dissertation, New York University 1979.

Randolph, Gretchen Lay, Therapeutic and physical touch: physiological response to stressful stimuli, *Nursing Research* 1984, 33(1), 33-36.

Randolph, Gretchen Lay, Therapeutic Touch and physical touch: physiological response to stressful stimuli, *Nursing Research* 1984, 33(1), 33-36.

Rao, Kanthamani and Puri, I. Subsensory perception (SSP), extrasensory perception (ESP) and meditation In:, *Research in Parapsychology 1976*, Metuchen, NJ: Scarecrow 1977, p. 77-79.

Rao, Ramakrishna, On the nature of psi: An examination of some attempts to explain ESP and PK, *J. of Parapsychology* 1977, 41, 294-351.

Raphaell , Katrina., *Crystal Healing* Volume II, New York: Aurora 1987.

Rattemeyer, M./ Popp, F.A./ Nagl, W., Evidence of photon emission from DNA in living systems, *Naturwissen* 1981, 68, 572.

Raucheisen, Mary L., Therapeutic Touch: Maybe there's something to it after all, *RN* 1984, 47(12) 49-51.

Rauscher, Elizabeth A. and Rubik, Beverly A., Human volitional effects on a model bacterial system, *Psi Research* 1983, 2(1), 38-48.

Rauscher, Elizabeth A. and Rubik, Beverly, A., Effects on motility behavior and growth of salmonella typhimurium in the presence of a psychic subject, In:, *Research in Parapsychology 1979*, Metuchen, NJ: Scarecrow 1980.

Rauscher, Elizabeth A., The physics of psi phenomena in space and time, Part I. Major principles of physics, psychic phenomena and some physical models, *Psi Research* 1983, 2(2), 64-87; Part II. Multidimensional geometric models, *Psi Research* 1983, 2(3), 93-120.

Rauscher, Elizabeth, Psi applications: alternative healing techniques in Brazil, *Psi Research* 1985, 4(1), 57-65.

Rawnsley, Marilyn M., H-E-A-L-T-H: A Rogerian perspective, *J. of Holistic Nursing* 1985, 2, 25-29.

Ray, Barbara Weber, *The Reiki Factor*, Smithtown, N.Y.: Exposition 1983.

Rebman, Janine M./ Wezelman, Rens/ Radin, Dean I. et al., Remote influence of human physiology by a ritual healing technique, *Subtle Energies* 1995, 6(2), 111-134.

Redner, Robin/ Briner, Barbara/ Snellman, Lynn, Effects of a bioenergy healing technique on chronic pain, *Subtle Energies* 1991, 2(3), 43-68.

Regan, Georgina and Shapiro, Debbie, *The Healer's Handbook: A Step by Step Guide to Developing Your Latent Healing Abilities*, Dorset, England: Element 1988.

Regush, Nicholas M. (Ed*)*, *Frontiers of Healing: New Dimensions in Parapsychology*, New York: Avon 1977.

Rehder, H., Wanderheilungen, ein Experiment (German) *Hippocrates* 1, 26, 577- 580, (Quoted in: Frank, J. *Persuasion and Healing*, New York: Schocken 1961).

Reilly, Harold J. and Brod, Ruth Hagy, *The Edgar Cayce Handbook for Health Through Drugless Therapy*, New York: Jove 1979.

Rein, Glen/ McCraty, Rollin: DNA as a detector of subtle energies *Proceedings of the 4th Annual Conference of the International Society for the Study of Subtle Energy and Energy Medicine*, Boulder, CO 1994.

Rein, Glen/ McCraty, Rollin: Local and non-local effects of coherent heart frequencies on conformational changes of DNA *Proceedings of The Joint USPA/ IAPR Psychotronics Conference*, Milwaukee, WI 1993(b).

Rein, Glen, A psychokinetic effect of neurotransmitter metabolism: Alterations in the degradative enzyme monoamine oxidase, In: Weiner, Debra H. and Radin, Dean (Eds), *Research in Parapsychology 1985*, Metuchen, NJ and London: Scarecrow 1986, 77-80.

Rein, Glen, An exosomatic effect on neurotransmitter metabolism in mice: A pilot study, *Second International Society for Parapsychological Research Conference*, Cambridge, England 1978.

Rein, Glen, Biological interactions with scalar energy: Cellular mechanisms of action. *Proceedings of the 7th International Association for Psychotronics Research*, Georgia 1988.

Rein, Glen, Effect of non-hertzian scalar waves on the immune system. *J. of the U.S. Psychotronics Association* 1989, 15-17.

Rein, Glen, *Quantum Biology: Healing with Subtle Energy*, Quantum Biology Research Labs, P.O. Box 60653, Palo Alto, CA 94306 1992 (a).

Rein, Glen, Role of consciousness on holoenergetic healing: a new experimental approach. Boulder, CO: *Proceedings of International Society for the Study of Subtle Energies and Energy Medicine, Second Annual Conference*, June 1992 (b).

Rein, Glen, Utilization of a cell culture bioassay for measuring quantum fields generated from a modified caduceus coil, *Proceedings of the 26th International Energy Conversion Engineering Conference*, Boston, MA 1991.

Rein, Glen/ McCraty, Rollin: Structural changes in water and DNA associated with new physiologically measurable states, *J. of Scientific Exploration* 1995, 8(3), 438-439 (reprinted with permission of the publishers, ERL 306, Stanford University, Stanford, CA 94305-4055, FAX 415 595 4466.

Rein, Glen/ McCraty, Rolin: Modulation of DNA by coherent heart frequencies, *Procedings of the 3rd Annual Conference of the International Society for the Study of Subtle Energies and Energy Medicine*, Monterey, CA 1993(a).

Reinharz, S. Phenomenology as a dynamic process, *Phenomenology and Pedagogy*, 1983, 1, 77-79 .

Rejmer, Jerzy, A Test to measure bioenergetic influence with the aid of spectrometry by nuclear magnetic resonance, *Proceedings of the 6th International Conference on Psychotronic Research* 1986, 25.

Rejmer, Jerzy, An attempt to measure the bioenergetic effect by nuclear magnetic resonance spectrometry, *Psychotronika* 1985, 86. (Translated from Polish by Alexander Imich).

Renard, Ann M., *The Experience of Healing from Deprivation of Bonding (Touch, Emotional Attachment),* (dissertation) The Union Institute 1994.

Retallack, Dorothy, *The Sound of Music and Plants*, Santa Monica, CA: DeVorss 1973.

Rhine, J. B. and Feather, S. R., The study of cases of 'psi-trailing' in animals, *J. of Parapsychology* 1962, 26, 1-22.

Rhine, J. B., *Extrasensory Perception*, Boston: Branden 1964.

Rhine, Louisa E., *ESP in Life and Lab: Tracing Hidden Channels*, New York: MacMillan 1967.

Rhine, Louisa E., *Hidden Channels of the Mind*, New York: William Morrow 1961.

Rhine, Louisa E., *Mind Over Matter*, New York: Collier 1970.

Richards, John Thomas, *SORRAT: A History of the Neihardt Experiments in Rapport and Telekinesis (1961-1981)*, N.J.: Scarecrow 1982.

Richmond, Kenneth, Experiments in the relief of pain, *J. of the Society for Psychical Research* 1946, 33, 194-200.

Richmond, Nigel, Two series of PK tests on paramecia, *J. of the Society for Psychical Research* 1952, 36, 577-578.

Rindge, Jeane Pontius (Ed) Quote from *Human Dimensions* 1977, 5(1,2).

Riscalla, Louise Mead, A study of religious healers and healees, *J. of the American Society for Psychosomatic Dentistry and Medicine* 1982, 29(3), 97- 103.

Roberton, Jean, Spiritual healing in general practice, *J. of Alternative and Complementary Medicine* 1991 (Apr), 9(4), 11-13; Part II: (May), 9(5), 21- 23.

Roberts, C. A., *Vic Coburn: Man with the Healing Touch*, New York: Thomas Nelson 1975.

Roberts, Estelle, *Fifty Years a Medium*, London: Corgi/ Transworld, 1969.

Roberts, Ursula, *Health, Healing and You*, London: Max Parrish, 1964.

Robertson et al., Inhibition and recovery of growth processes in roots of *Pisum sativum L.* exposed to 60-Hz electric fields, *Bioelectromagnetics* 1981, 2, 239.

Robinson, Diana, *To Stretch a Plank: A Survey of Psychokinesis*, Chicago, IL: Nelson-Hall 1981.

Robinson, Diana, *To Stretch a Plank: A Survey of Psychokinesis*, Chicago, IL: Nelson-Hall 1981.

Robinson, Loretta Sue, *The Effects of Therapeutic Touch on the Grief Experience,* (dissertation) Birmingham: University of Alabama 1996.

Rogers, Martha E., Nursing: A science of unitary man, In: Riehl, J. P. and Roy, C. (Eds), *Conceptual Models for Nursing Practice*, 2nd Ed., New York: Appleton-Century-Crofts 1984, 329-337.

Rogers, Martha E., *The Theoretical Basis of Nursing*, Philadelphia, PA: F. A.Davis 1970.

Rogo, D. S., Psychotherapy and the poltergeist, *J. of the Society for Psychical Research* 1974, 47, 433-447.

Rogo, D. Scott, Can weather make you psychic?, *Fate* (Jan) 1986(a), 39(1), 65-69.

Rogo, D. Scott, In pursuit of the healing force, In: Fate Magazine, *Exploring the Healing Miracle*, Highland Park, IL: Clark 1983(a) (Orig. *Fate Magazine* Mar 1983).

Rogo, D. Scott, Psi and shamanism: A reconsideration, *Parapsychology Review* 1983(b), 14(6), 5-9.

Rogo, D. Scott, Science debates therapeutic touch, *Fate* 1986(c), 39(12), 70-77.

Rogo, D. Scott, The power of prayer, *Fate* (Aug) 1986(b), 43-50.

Rogo, D. Scott: Photographs by the mind. *Psychic* April 1970(a).

Roland, C. G., Does prayer preserve?, *Archives of Internal Medicine* 1970, 125, 580-587, (Reprinted from Galton, F., Statistical Studies into the Efficacy of Prayer, *Fortnightly Review* 1872, 12, 125-135).

Rolf, Ida, *Rolfing: The Integration of Human Structures*, Santa Monica, CA: Dennis-Landman 1977.

Roll, Wiliam , *The Poltergeist*, Garden City, New York: Nelson Doubleday 1972.

Roll, William; Montagno, Elson; Pulos, Lee and Giovetti, Paola, *Physical Mediumship: Some Recent Claims*, Presentation at 100th Society for Psychical Research and 25th Parapsychological Association Conference, Aug 1982.

Romanucci-Ross, L.; Moerman, D. E. and Taneredi, L. R. (Eds), *The Anthropology of Medicine: From Culture to Method*, South Hadley, MA: Bergin & Garvey 1983.

Roosevelt, Franklin Delano, Speech accepting Democratic nomination for presidency, Chicago, July 2, 1932.

Rosa, Linda et al., A close look at Therapeutic Touch, *J. of the American Medical Association* 1998, 279(13), 1005-1010.

Rose, Louis, *Faith Healing*, London: Penguin 1971.

Rose, Louis, Some aspects of paranormal healing, *J. of the Society for Psychical Research* 1955, 38, 105-120.

Rosenstiel, A./ Keefe, F.J., The use of coping strategies in chronic low back pain patients: relationship to patient characteristics and current adjustment, *Pain* 1983, 17, 33-44..

Rosenthal, R. *Meta-Analytic Procedures for Social Research*, Beverly Hills, CA: Sage 1984.

Rossi, Ernest L., *The Psychobiology of Mind-Body Healing: New Concepts of Therapeutic Hypnosis*, New York, London: WW Norton 1986.

Roth, Suselma D. *Effect of Therapeutic Touch Concepts on the Anxiety Levels of Nursing Students in a Psychiatric Seting* (Master's thesis), Bellarmine College 1995.

Roud, Paul C., *Making Miracles: An Exploration Into the Dynamics of Self-Healing*, Wellingborough, England: Thorsons 1990.

Rowlands, D., Therapeutic Touch: Its effects on the depressed elderly, *Australia Nurses J.* 1984, 13(11), 45-46, 52.

Rubik, B. and Rauscher, E., Effects on motility behavior and growth rate of *salmonella typhimurium* in the presence of Olga Worrall, In: Roll, W. G. (Ed), *Research in Parapsychology 1979*, Metuchen, NJ: Scarecrow 1980.

Rush, J., Physical aspects of psi phenomena, In Schmeidler, G. (ed), *Parapsychology, Its Relation to Physics, Biology, Psychology and Psychiatry*, Metuchen, NJ: Scarecrow 1976, 6-39 .

Rush, James E., *Toward a General Theory of Healing*, Washington, D.C.: University Press of America 1981.

Russell ,Edward., *Report On Radionics: Science of the Future, The Science Which Can Cure Where Orthodox Medicine Fails*, Suffolk, England: Neville Spearman 1973.

Russell, Edward, *Design for Destiny*, London: Neville Spearman 1971.

Russell, Peter, *The Global Brain: Speculations on the Evolutionary Leap to Planetary Consciousness*. Los Angeles: Tarcher 1983.

S

Safonov, Vladimir, Personal experience in psychic diagnostics and healing, In: Vilenskaya, Larissa, *Parapsychology in the USSR, Part III*, San Francisco: Washington Research Center 1981, 42-45.

Saklani, Alok, Preliminary tests for psi-ability in shamans of Garhwal Himalaya, *J. of the Society for Psychical Research* 1988, 55(81), 60-70.

Saklani, Alok, Psychokinetic effects on plant growth: further studies, In: Henkel, Linda A. and Palmer, John, *Research in Parapsychology 1989*, 1990, 37- 41.

Salmon, E. H., *He Heals Today, of a Healer's Case-Book*, Worcs., England: Arthur James 1951 (cases, very brief).

Salmon, J. Warren (Ed), *Alternative Medicines: Popular and Policy Perspectives*, New York: Methuen/ London: Tavistock 1984.

Samarel, Nelda, The experience of receiving Therapeutic Touch, *J. of Advanced Nursing* 1992, 17,651-657.

Sancier, Kenneth M., Medical applications of Qigong and emitted Qi on humans, animals, cell cultures, and plants: review of selected scientific research, *American J. of Acupuncture* 1991, 19(4), 367-377.

Sancier, Kenneth M./ Chow, Effie Poy Yew, Effects of external and internal Qi as measured experimentally by muscle testing; also in: Healing with Qigong and quantitative effects of Qigong, *J. of the American College of Traditional Chinese Medicine* 1989, 7(3), 13-19.

Sandner, Donald, Navaho symbolic healing, *Shaman's Drum* 1985, 1, 25-30.

Sandroff, Ronni, A skeptic's guide to Therapeutic Touch, *R.N.* (Jan) 1980, 25-30.

Sandweiss, Samuel H., *Spirit and the Mind*, San Diego, CA: Birth Day 1985.

Sanford, Agnes, *The Healing Light*, St. Paul, MN: Macalester Park 1949.

Sasaki, K. Shigami/ Ochi, Yasuo, Observation of the deformation of pure aluminum plates by psychokinesis, *J. of the Psi Science Institute of Japan* 1982, 7(1), 7-13.

Sauvin, Pierre Paul., In: Tompkins and Bird.

Scharfetter, C., The shaman: Witness of an old culture — Is it revivable?, *Schweiz. Arch. Neurol. Psychiatr.* 1985, 136(3), 81-95. (German with English abstract).

Schaut, George B. and Persinger, Michael A., Subjective telepathic experiences, geomagnetic activity and the ELF hypothesis, Part I: Data analysis, *Psi Research* 1985, 4(1), 4-20.

Schechter, E.: Hypnotic induction vs control conditions: illustrating an approach to the evaluation of replicability in parapsychological data, *J. of the American Society for Psychical Research* 1984, 78, 1-27 .

Scheel, Nancy R. *The Development and Initial Testing of an Instrument to Assess Advanced Practice Nursing Graduate Students' Knowledge and Attitudes Toward Healing Touch*, Master's Thesis, Mankato, MN: Mankato State University 1997.

Schiegl, Heinz, *Healing Magnetism: the Transference of vital Force*, York Beach, ME: Weiser 1987 (Orig. German 1983).

Schleifer, S. J. et al.., Suppression of lymphocyte stimulation following bereavement, *J. of the American Medical Association* 1983, 250(3), 374-377.

Schlitz, Marilyn J. and Braud, William G., Reiki plus natural healing: An ethnographic/ experimental study, *Psi Research* 1985, 4(3/ 4), 100-123 (Also in: Weiner, Debra and Radin, Dean (Eds), *Research in Parapsychology 1985*, Metuchen, NJ and London: Scarecrow 1986, 17-18).

Schlitz, Marilyn PK on living systems: further studies with anesthetized mice, Presentation at Southeastern Regional Parapsychological Association 1982, (Reviewed in: Weiner, Debra H., Southeastern Regional Parapsychological Association Conference, *J. of Parapsychology,* 1982, 46, 51-53; also, more briefly, in Weiner, Debra H., Report of the 1982 SERPA Conference, *Parapsychology Review*, 1982, 13(4), 13).

Schlitz, Marilyn, PK on living systems: further studies with anesthetized mice,

Presentation at Southeastern Regional Parapsychological Association, 1982, (Reviewed in: Weiner, Debra H., Report of the 1982 SERPA Conference, *Parapsychology Review*, 1982, 13(4), 13).

Schlotfeldt, Rozella M., *Critique of the Relationship of Touch, with Intent to Help or Heal to Subjects' In-vivo Hemoglobin Values: A Study in Personalized Interaction*, Paper at American Nurses' Association 9th Nursing Research Conference, San Antonio, TX 1973.

Schmeidler, Gertrude R. and Hess, Leslie B., Review of Casdorph, H. Richard, *The Miracles*, In: *J. of Parapsychology* 1986, 50(1), 75-79.

Schmeidler, Gertrude, *Personal communication* 1987.

Schmeidler, Gertrude., The Relation Between Psychology and Parapsychology in: Schmeidler, Gertrude R., *Parapsychology: Its Relation to Physics, Biology, Psychology and Psychiatry*, Metuchen , New Jersey: Scarecrow 1976.

Schmidt, Helmut, A logically consistent model of a world with psi interactions, In: Oteri, L. (Ed), *Quantum Physics and Parapsychology*, New York: Parapsychology Foundation 1975. 205-228.

Schmidt, Helmut, Comparison of PK action on two different random number generators, *J. of Parapsychology* 1974, 38, 47-55.

Schmidt, Helmut, PK effect on pre-recorded targets, *J. of the American Society for Psychical Research* 1976, 70, 267-291.

Schmidt, Helmut, PK effect on pre-recorded targets, *J. of the American Society for Psychical Research* 1976, 70, 267-291.

Schmitt, M, Stanford, R, Free Response ESP During Ganzfield Stimulation , The Possible Influence of the Menstrual Cycle Phase,, *J. of the American Society of Psychical Research* 1978, 72, 177.

Schouten, S. A., Autonomic psychophysiological reactions to sensory and emotive stimuli in a psi experiment, *European J. of Parapsychology* 1976, 1, 57-71.

Schul, Bill, *The Psychic Frontiers of Medicine*, Greenwich, CT: Fawcett 1977.

Schuller, Donna Elizabeth, *Therapeutic Touch and Complementary Therapies: A Public Policy Paper* (Master's thesis), New York Medical College 1997 (not research).

Schuller, Donna Elizabeth, *Therapeutic Touch and Complementary Therapies: A Public Policy Paper* (Master's thesis), New York Medical College 1997 (not research).

Schutze, Barbara, Group counseling, with and without the addition of intercessory prayer, as a factor in self esteem, *Proceedings of the 4th International Conference on Psychotronic Research*, Sao Paulo, Brazil 1979, 330-331.

Schwartz, Gary E./ Russek, Linda G./ Beltran, Justin, Interpersonal hand-energy registration: evidence for implicit performance and perception, *Subtle Energies* 1995, 6(3), 183-200.

Schwartz, Gary E. R./ Nelson, Lonnie/ Russek, Linda G. S./ Allen, John J. B. Electrostatic body-motion registration and the human antenna-receiver effect: a new method for investigating interpersonal dynamical energy system interactions, *Subtle Energies* 1996, 7(2), 149-184.

Schwartz, Stephan A., *The Alexandria Project*, New York: Delta/ Eleanor Fried/ Dell 1983.

Schwartz, Stephen, *Infrared spectra alteration in water proximate to the palms of therapeutic practitioners*, Preliminary paper presented at 29th Annual Parapsychological Association Meeting, Aug 1986; full paper: Los Angeles, CA: Mobius Society. Published in: *Subtle Energies* 1990, 1(1), 43-72.

Schwarz, Berthold E., Possible telesomatic reactions, *J. of the Medical Society of New Jersey*, 1967, 64, 600-603.

Schweitzer, Susan Fredricka, *The Effects of Therapeutic Touch on Short-Term Memory Recall in the Aging Populatio: A Pilot Study* (Master's thesis), Reno: University of Nevada 1980.

Scofield, A. M. and Hodges, R. D., Demonstration of a healing effect in the laboratory using a simple plant model, *J. of the Society for Psychical Research* 1991, 57, 321-343.

Seiki, Nakasato/ Machi, Yoshio, Japanese Qigong Institute, Tokyo Denki University, Tokyo, Japan, Activation of seed germination and growth with emitted qi, *2nd World Conference for Academic Exchange of Medical Qigong, Beijing 1993*.

Sergeyev, Gennady, Biorrhythms and the biosphere, Translated from Russian, *Psi Research* 1982, 1(2), 29-31.

Servadio, E., Unconscious and Paranormal Factors in Healing and Recovery, *15th Fredric WH Myers Memorial Lecture,* London: Society for Psychical Research 1963.

Setzer, J. Schoneberg, The God of Ambrose Worrall, *Spiritual Frontiers* 1983, 15(2), 15-22.

Shafer, Mark G., PK metal bending in a semiformal group, In: *Research in Parapsychology 1980*, Metuchen, NJ: Scarecrow 1981. 33-35.

Shallis, Michael, *On Time*, New York: Schocken, 1983.

Shallis, Michael, *The Electric Shock Book*, London: Souvenir 1988.

Shao, Xiangmin/ Liu, Guanchan/ Zhou, Qijing/ Yu, Fanger/ Xu, Hefen/ Xue, Huiling/ Zhang, Changming/ Wu, Kang – Dept Pathology, Naval Medical College, Nanjing/ Jiangsu Provincial Research Institute of Traditional Chinese Medicine, Nanjing/ Chassis Plant, Nanjing Automobile Factory, China – Effect of qigong waiqi (emitted qi) on the growth and differentiation of implanted tumor cells in mice *3rd National Academic Conference on Qigong Science, Guangzhou, China. 1990* – from Qigong Database of Sancier.

Shapiro, A.K./ Morris, L.A., The placebo effect in medical and psychological therapies, In: Bergin, Allen E./ Garfield, Sol L. (Eds), *Handbook of Psychotherapy and Behavior Change*, New York: Wiley 1971. 369-410 (9 pp refs)..

Shapiro, Francine, *Eye Movement Desensitization and Reprocessing*, New York/ London: Guildford 1995.

Sharp, Daryl*: Personality Types: Jung's Model of Typology,* Toronto: Inner City 1987.

Shealy, C. Norman, Effects of Transcranial Neurostimulation upon mood and serotonin production: a preliminary report, *Il Dolore* 1979, 1(1), 13-16.

Shealy, C. Norman, Relaxation with synchronous photo-stimulation: the Shealy RelaxMate™. Presented at the meeting of American Academy of Neurological and Orthopedic Surgery, December 1990.

Shealy, C. Norman, Cady, R.K., Wilkie, R.G., et al., Depression: A diagnostic, neurochemical profile and therapy with Cranial Electrical Stimulation (CES), *The J. of Neurological and Orthopaedic Medicine and Surgery* 1989, 10(4), 319-321.

Shealy, C. Norman with Freese, Arthur S., *Occult Medicine Can Save Your Life*, New York: Bantam 1977.

Shealy, C. Norman et al.. Non-pharmaceutical treatment of depression using a multimodal approach (*Subtle Energies* 1993, 4(2), 125-134.

Shealy, Norman and Myss, Caroline, *AIDS: Passageway to Transformation*, Walpole, NH: Stillpoint 1987.

Shealy, Norman, Clairvoyant diagnosis, In: Srinivasan, T. M., *Energy Medicine Around the World*, Phoenix, AZ: Gabriel 1988, 291-303.

Shealy, Norman, The role of psychics in medical diagnosis, In: Carlson, Rick (Ed), *Frontiers of Science and Medicine*, Chicago, IL: Contemporary 1975.

Sheldon, Michael, How Joan was cured at Lourdes, In: Fate Magazine, *Exploring the Healing Miracle,* Highland Park, IL: Clark 1983 (Orig. *Fate Magazine* Feb. 1955).

Sheldrake, Rupert, *Seven Experiments That Could Change the World,* London: Fourth Estate 1994.

Shen, George J., Study of mind-body effects and Qigong in China, *Advances* 1986, 3(4), 134-142.

Shen, Jiaqi et al. Shanghai Qigong Institute, Shanghai – Physlcal and biomedical effects of emitted qi. *3rd National Academic Conference on Qigong Science, Guangzhou, China. 1990* – from Qigong Database of Sancier.

Shepard, Stephen Paul, *Healing Energies*, Provo, UT: Hawthorne, 1981.

Sheppard, J.M., D'Angelo...Italy's great healer, In: Fate Magazine, *Exploring the Healing Miracle*, Highland Park, IL: Clark 1193 (Orig. *Fate Magazine* Jul. 1953).

Sherman, Harold, *Your Power to Heal*, New York: Harper and Row 1972.

Shine, Betty, *Mind to Mind: The Secrets of Your Mind Energy Revealed*, London and New York: Bantam 1989.

Shubentsov, Yefim, Healing Seminar, Philadelphia, July 1982.

Shuzman, Ellen The Effect of Trait Anxiety and Patient Expectation of Therapeutic Touch on the Reduction in State Anxiety in Preoperative Patients Who Receive Therapeutic Touch (dissertation) New York: New York University 1993.

Sicher, Fred; Targ, Elisabeth; Moore, Dan; and Smith, Helene S., A randomized, double-blind study of the effects of distant healing in a population with advanced AIDS, Western J. of Medicine 1998,.169(6), 356-363].

Siegel, Bernard., *Peace, Love and Healing*, London:Ryder 1990.

Siegel, Bernie S., *Love, Medicine and Miracles:* *Lessons Learned About Self-Healing From a Surgeon's Experience with Exceptional Patients*, New York: Harper and Row 1986.

Sies, M. M., An Exploratory Study of Relaxation Response in Nurses Who Utilize Therapeutic Touch (Master's thesis) Tucson: University of Arizona 1987.

Sies, M. M., An Exploratory Study of Relaxation Response in Nurses Who Utilize Therapeutic Touch (Master's thesis) Tucson: University of Arizona 1987.

Sieveking, Paul., The Strange World of Twins, *The Unexplained* 1981, 5(57), 1121-1125.

Silbey, Uma., *The Complete Crystal Guidebook: A Practical Guide to Self Development, Empowerment and Healing*, San Francisco: U-Read 1986.

Simington, Jane A./ Laing, Gail P. Effects of Therapeutic Touch on anxiety in the institutionalized elderly, Clinical Nursing Research 1993, 2(4), 438-450.

Singer, M. et al., Indigenous treatment for alcoholism: the case of Puerto Rican spiritism, *Medical Anthropology* 1984, 8(4), 246-273.

Singer, Philip (Ed), *Traditional healing: New science or new colonialism?*, Buffalo, NY: Conch Magazine, 1977.

Dressen, Linda J./ Singg, Sangeeta, Effects of Reiki on pain and selected affective and personality variables of chronically ill patients, *Subtle Energies* 1998, 9(1), 51-82

Skinner, B.F. *Science and Human Behaviour*, New York: Macmillan 1953.

Slater, Victoria E. The safety, elements, and effects of Healing Touch on chronic non-malignant abdominal pain, University of Tennessee, Knoxville, College of Nursing, 1996.

Slater, Victoria E., Healing Touch, In: Micozzi, p.121-136.

Slomoff, Daniel A. Traditional African medicine: voodoo healing, In: Heinze, Ruth-Inge, *Proceedings of the 2nd International Conference on the Study of Shamanism*, San Rafael, CA: Independent Scholars of Asia, Inc. 1985, 56-57.

Slomoff, Danny, Ecstatic spirits: A West African healer at work, *Shaman's Drum* 1986(b), 5, 27-31.

Smith, Cyril. W and Best, Simon., *Electromagnetic Man: Health and Hazard in the Electrical Environment*, London: J.M. Pent and Sons 1989.

Smith, D. M., Safety of faith healing, *Lancet* (Mar 15) 1986, 1(8481), 621.

Smith, Fritz Frederick, *Inner Bridges: A Guide to Energy Movement and Body Structure*, Atlanta, GA: Humanics New Age 1986.

Smith, Huston, *Forgotten Truth: The Primordial Tradition*, New York: Harper/ Colophon 1977.

Smith, Justa, Paranormal effects on enzyme activity, *Human Dimensions* 1972, 1, 15-19.

Smith, Richard, Where is the wisdom...? *British Medical J.* 1991, 303, 798-799.

Smith, Warren, *Strange and Miraculous Cures*, New York: Ace 1969.

Sneck, William Joseph, *Charismatic Spiritual Gifts: A Phenomenological Analysis*, Washington, D.C.: University Press of America 1981.

Snedegor, George W. *Statistical Methods*, Ames, Iowa: Iowa State College, 4th Edition, 1948, 447.

Snel, F. and Millar, B., *PK with the enzyme trypsin*, Unpublished Manuscript, 1982.

Snel, F. W. J. J./ van der Sijde, P. C., The effect of retro-active distance healing on babesia rodhani (rodent malaria) in rats, *European J. of Parapsychology*, 1990-1991, 8, 123-130.

Snel, Frans and Hol, P. R., Psychokinesis experiments in casein induced amyloidosis of the hamster, *European J. of Parapsychology* 1983, 5(1), 51-76.

Snel, Frans and Millar, Brian, The elements of so called 'paranormal healing:' Can these be identified from modern medical practice? *Nederlande Tydschrift voos Integrale Geneeskunde* 1984, 1(3), 15-19.

Snel, Frans W. J. J., PK influence on malignant cell growth, *Research Letter of the University of Utrecht* 1980, 10, 19-27.

Snel. Frans W. J. J./ van der Sijde, Peter C. The effect of paranormal healing on tumor growth, *J. of Scientific Exploration* 1995, 9(2), 209-211.

Sodergren, Kathleen Anne, *The Effect of Absorption and Social Closeness on Responses to Educational and Relaxation Therapies in Patients with Anticipatory Nausea and Vomiting During Cancer Chemotherapy* (Master's thesis) Minneapolis: University of Minnesota 1994.(Rosa 1993).

Solfvin, G. F., Studies of the effects of mental healing and expectations on the growth of corn seedlings, *European J. of Parapsychology* 1982(a), 4(3), 287-323.

Solfvin, Gerald F., Psi expectancy effects in psychic healing studies with malarial mice, *European J. of Parapsychology* 1982(b), 4(2), 160-197.

Solfvin, Gerald, Towards a model for mental healing studies in real life settings, In: Roll, W.G.; Beloff, J. and White, R.A. (Eds), *Research in Parapsychology 1982*, Metuchen, NJ: Scarecrow 1983, 210-214.

Solfvin, Jerry, Mental healing, In: Krippner, Stanley (Ed), *Advances in Parapsychological Research 4* Jefferson, NC: McFarland 1984, 31-63. (Reviews sketchily most of the studies in this bibliography, plus several unpublished studies not covered here, including studies of telepathic control over movements of animals).

Somé, Malidoma Patrice, *Of Water and the Spirit: Ritual, Magic, and Initiation in the Life of an African Shaman*, New York: Tarcher/ Putnam 1994.

Southwood, Malcolm S. *The Healing Experience: Remarkable Cases from a Professional Healer*, London: Piatkus 1994.

Spielberger, C.D. et al. *Manual for the State-Trait Anxiety Inventory (Form Y)*, Palo Alto, CA: Consulting Psychologists Press 1991.

Spiritual Frontiers Editor, Research report: Setzer's sanctuary effect, *Spiritual Frontiers* 1980, 12(1), 20-23.

Spiritual Scientist, New Spiritual Science Foundation, Street Farmhouse, Scole, Diss, Norfolk IP21 4DR, England.

Spottiswoode, S. J. P. Geomagnetic activity and anomalous cognition: a preliminary report of new evidence, *Subtle Energies* 1990, 1(1), 65-77.

Spraggett, Allen, *Kathryn Kuhlman: The Woman who Believed in Miracles*, New York: World 1970.

St. Clair, David, *Psychic Healers*, New York: Bantam/ Doubleday 1979 (Excerpts reprinted by permission of Doubleday & Co., Inc. Copyright David St. Clair 1974, 1976).

St. Clair, David, Spiritism in Brazil, *Psychic* (Dec) 1970, 2(3), 8-14.

Stanford, R. G. and Fox, C. An effect of release of effort in a psychokinetic task, In: Morris, J. D.; Roll, W. G. and Morris, R. L. (Eds), *Research in Parapsychology 1974*, Metuchen, NJ: Scarecrow 1975. 61-63.

Stanford, R. G. et al.., Psychokinesis as psi-mediated instrumental response, *J. of the*

American Society for Psychical Research 1975, 69, 127-133.

Stanford, R. G., Towards reinterpreting psi events, *J. of the American Society for Psychical Research* 1978, 72, 197-214.

Stanford, Rex G., An experimentally testable model for spontaneous psi events. I. Extrasensory events, *(J. of the American Society for Psychical Research* 1974(a), 68(1), 34-57.

Stanford, Rex G., An experimentally testable model for spontaneous psi events, II. Psychokinetic events, *J. of the American Society for Psychical Research* 1974(b), 68(4), 321-356.

Stanford, Rex G., The application of learning theory to ESP performance: A review of Dr. C. T. Tart's monograph, *J. of the American Society for Psychical Research* 1977, 71, 55-80.

Steadman, Alice, *Who's the Matter With Me*, Marina del Rey, CA: DeVorss 1969.

Stearn, Jess, *Edgar Cayce: The Sleeping Prophet*, New York: Bantam 1967.

Stein, Diane, *Reiki: A Complete Guide to Ancient Healing Arts*, Freedom, CA: Crossing 1996.

Stelter, Alfred, *Psi-Healing*, New York: Bantam 1976.

Stemman, Roy. New Teeth for Old, *The Unexplained* 1983, 12 (139), 2770-2773.

Stemman, Roy. Surgeon from the Other Side, *The Unexplained* 1983, 12(142), 2838-2840.

Stewart, Ian/ Joines, Vann, *TA Today: A New Introduction to Transactional Analysis*, Nottingham: Lifespace 1987.

Stokes, Douglas M., Promethian fire: The view from the other side, *J. of Parapsychology* 1987, 51(3), 249-270.

Straneva, Jo A. Eckstein, *Therapeutic Touch and In Vitro Erythropoiesis* (dissertation) Indiana University School of Nursing 1993.

Strauch, Inge, A contribution to the problem of "spiritual healing," Part II (German) Abstract, *Zeitschrift fur Parapsychologie und Grenzgebiete der Psychologie* 1960, 4(1), 24-55 (Abstract translated in *Parapsychology Abstracts International* 1983, 1(2), No. 363).

Strauch, Inge, Medical aspects of "mental" healing, *International J. of Parapsychology* 1963, 5(2), 135-165. (Quotes with permission of Parapsychology Foundation, Inc.).

Strauss, Anselm/ Corbin, Juliet, *Basics of Qualitative Research: Grounded Theory Procedures and Techniques*, Newbury Park, CA/ London: Sage 1990.

Sudre, Rene, *Treatise on Parapsychology*, Winchester, MA: Allen and Unwin 1960.

Sugrue, Thomas, *There is a River*, New York: Dell 1970.

Sullivan, H. S., *The Interpersonal Theory of Psychiatry*, New York: Norton 1953.

Sun, Jiwang/ Yuan, Rui/ Yang, Cuifeng – Gansu, China – Analysis of 51 cases with coronary heart disease treated by qigong (*1st World Conference for Academic Exchange of Medical Qigong, Beijing 1988* – from Qigong Database of Sancier.

Sun, Mengyin/ Li, Shengping/ Meng, Guirong/ Cui, Yanghao/ Xin, Yan, Tsinghua University, Beijing/ Municipal Institute of Traditional Chinese Medicine of Chongqing, Sichuan Province, China, Effect of emitted qi on ultraviolet spectrum of a yeast RNA solution. *1st World Conference for Academic Exchange of Medical Qigong, Beijing 1988(c)*.

Sun, Mengyin/ Li, Shengping/ Meng, Guirong/ Cui, Yuanhao/ Sun, Mengyin/ Guo, Jinliang/ Sha, Jinguan/ Yan, Sixian/ Xin, Yan, Tsinghua University, Beijing/ Municipal Institute of Traditional Chinese Medicine of Chongqing, Sichuan Province, Effect of emitted qi on AgBr dyestuff by electric paramagnetic resonance spectrometer, *1st World Conference for Academic Exchange of Medical Qigong, Beijing 1988(a)*.

Sun, Mengyin/ Li, Shengping/ Meng, Guirong/ Cui, Yuanhao/ Xin, Yan, Tsinghua University, Beijing, China/ Municipal Institute of Traditional Chinese Medicine of Chongqing, Sichuan Province, China, Effect of emitted qi on long-time tracking of UV spectroscopy on the solution of potassium dichromate, *1st World Conference for Academic Exchange of Medical Qigong, Beijing 1988(b)*.

Sun, Mengyin/ Li, Shenping/ Meng, Guirong/ Cui, Yuanhao/ Xin, Yan, Tsinghua University, Beijing/ Municipal Institute of Traditional Chinese Medicine of Chongqing, Sichuan Province, China, Effect of emitted qi on trace examination of UV spectroscopy on the DNA solution of fish sperm. *1st World Conference for Academic Exchange of Medical Qigong, Beijing 1988(d)*.

Sun, Silu/ Tao, Chun, Weifang Medical College, Shandong Province, China, Biological effect of emitted qi with tradescantic paludosa micronuclear technique, *1st World Conference* for Academic Exchange of Medical Qigong, Beijing 1988.

Sundblom, D. Markus, Haikonen, Sari et al.: The effect of spiritual healing on chronic idiopathic pain – A medical and biological study, *Clinical J. of Pain* 1994, 10, 286-302.

Swan, Jim, When paranormal is normal: Psi in native american culture, *Psi Research* 1986, 5(1,2), 79-105.

Sykes, Pat, *You Don't Know John Cain?*, Gerrard's Cross, England: Van Duren 1979.

Szantyr-Powolny, Stefania, Notes from a doctor-healer in Warsaw, *Doctor-Healer Network Newsletter* 1993, No.4, 4-5.

Szymanski, Jan A., Application of electric field measurements in research of bioenergotherapeutic phenomena, *Proceedings of the 6th International Conference on Psychotronics* 1986(b), 68-71.

Szymanski, Jan A., Research on changes in the crystallization of copper chhloride under the influence of bioenergotherapeutic interaction, *Proceedings of the 6th International Conference on Psychotronics* 1986(a), 145.

T

Taft, Adon (Religious Ed.), *Miami Herald* May 4 1968.

Takaguchi, Naoko, *Miyako Shamanism: Shamans, Clients and Their Interactions*, Unpublished Doctoral Dissertation, UCLA 1984.

Takahashi, Masaru and Brown, Stephen, *Qigong for Health: Chinese Traditional Exercise for Cure and Prevention*, New York: Japan 1986.

Tang, Yipeng/ Sun, Chenglin/ Hong, Qingtao/ Liu, Chunmei/ Li, Liaoming, Institute of Qigong Science, Beijing College of Traditional Chinese Medicine, Beijing 100029, Protective effect of emitted qi on the primary culture of neurocytes in vitro against free radical damage, *2nd World Conference for Academic Exchange of Medical Qigong, Beijing, 1993*.

Targ, R./ Puthoff, H. Information transmission under conditions of sensory shielding, *Nature* 1974, 252, 602-607 .

Targ, Russell and Harary, Keith, *The Mind Race: Understanding and Using Psychic Abilities*, New York: Villard 1984.

Targ, Russell and Puthoff, H., Information Transmission Under Conditions of Sensory Shielding, *Nature* 1974, 251, 602-607.

Targ, Russell and Tart, Charles T., Pure clairvoyance and the necessity of feedback, *J. of the Society for Psychical Research* 1985, 79, 485-492.

Tart, Charles T., Physiological correlates of psi cognition, *International J. of Parapsychology*, 1963, 5, 375-386.

Tart, Charles T., The application of learning theory to ESP performance, *Parapsychological Monographs*, New York: Parapsychology Foundation 1975, 15.

Tart, Charles T.: *Transpersonal Psychologies*. New York: Harper and Row 1975(a).

Tart, Charles, Acknowledging and dealing with the fear of psi, *J. of the American Society for Psychical Research* 1984, 78(2), 133-143.

Tart, Charles, Possible physiological correlates of psi cognition, *International J. of Parapsychology* 1963, 5, 375-386 .

Tart, Charles, Psychics' fears of psychic powers, *J. of the American Society for Psychical Research* 1986a, 80(3), 279-292.

Tart, Charles, States of consciousness and state-specific sciences, *Science* 1972, 176, 1203-1210.

Tart, Charles, *Waking Up*, Boston: New Science/ Shambhala 1986b.

Tart, Charles: States of consciousness and state-specific sciences. *Science* 1972, 176, 1203-1210.

Tatum, J. Clinical intuition and energy field resonance, In: Leskowitz, E. (ed), *Transpersonal Hypnosis*, New York: Irvington (1998).

Taylor, Allegra, *I Fly Out with Bright Feathers: The Quest of a Novice Healer*, London: Fontana/ Collins 1987.

Taylor, J., G and Balanovski, E., Is There Any Scientific Explanation For the Paranormal?, *Nature* 1979, 279, 631-633.

Taylor, John, *Superminds: An Investigation into the Supernatural*, London: Picador/ Pan/ Macmillan 1975.

Tebecis, Andris K., *Mahikari: Thank God for the Answers at Last*, Tokyo, Japan: L. H. Yoko Shuppan 1982.

Tedder, W. and Monty, M., Exploration of long-distance PK: A conceptual replication of the influence on a biological system, In: Roll,

W.G. et al. (Eds), *Research in Parapsychology 1980*, Metuchen, NJ: Scarecrow 1981. 90-93.

Teschler, Wilfried, *The Polarity Healing Handbook: A Practical Introduction to the Healing Therapy of Energy Balancing*, San Leandro, CA: Interbook 1986.

Tester, M. H., *The Healing Touch*, London: Psychic 1982 (Orig. 1970).

Tharnstrom, Cchristine Ann Louise, *The effects of Non-contact Therapeutic Touch on Parasympathetic Nervous System as Evidenced by Superficial Skin Temperature and Perceived Stress* (Master's thesis) San Jose, CA: San Jose State University 1993.

The Medical Group, *The Mystery of Healing*, Wheaton, IL: Theosophical 1958 (Republished under authorship of the Theosophical Society 1983.)

Theosophical Research Center, *The Mystery of Healing*, Wheaton, IL: Theosophical 1980 (also published under the authorship of 'The Medical Group').

Thie, John F., *Touch for Health*, Marina del Rey, CA: DeVorss 1979.

Thomas-Beckett, Julie Gwen, *Attitudes Toward Therapeutic Touch: A Pilot Study of Women with Breast Cancer* (Master's thesis) East Lansing: Michigan State University 1991.

Thompson, C. J. S., *Magic and Healing*, London: Rider, 1946.

Thorley, Kevan, Disappearing gallstones, *Lancet* (Jun 2) 1984, 1(8388), 1247- 1248.

Thornton, Francis Beauchesne, *Catholic Shrines in the United States and Canada*, New York: Wilfred Funk 1954.

Thunberg, Ursula, Crossing the rim into healing consciousness, *Bridges, Magazine of the International Society for the Study of Subtle Energies and Energy Medicine* 1997, 7(4), 7; 17-20.

Thurston, Herbert., *Ghosts and Poltergeists*, Chicago: Henry Regnery, 1954.

Thurston, Herbert., *The Physical Phenomena of Mysticism*, London: Burns Oates 1952.

Tian, Laike/ Zhang, Jiyue/ Zhang, Yuanming – Dept Physics, Northwestern University, Chengdu, China/ Commercial Bureau, Wenjiang Country, Sichuan Province, China – Effect of emitted qi on making laser holographic grating. *3rd National Academic*

Conference on Qigong Science, Guangzhou, China. *1990* - from Qigong Database of Sancier.

Tilley, James A. *A Phenomenology of the Christian Healer's Experience (Faith Healing)*, Unpublished doctoral dissertaion, Fuller Theological Seminary, Schol of Psychology, 1989, Abstract from University Microfilms International, printed in White, Rhea A. *Exceptional Human Experience*, 1991, 9(2), 265-266.

Timosenko, Alexander, Contributions to the investigation of the "Backster effect," *Proceedings of the 6th International Conference on Psychotronics* 1986, 160-163.

Tinworth, Jane, Dynamic healing, *Caduceus* 1989 (No. 7), 10-11.

Torrey, E. Fuller, *The Mind Game: Witchdoctors and Psychiatrists*, New York: Bantam 1972.

Torwesten, H., *Vedanta: Heart of Hinduism*, New York: Grove Wdidenfeld 1985.

Truman, Harry S. in: Miller, Merle, *Plain Speaking: An Oral Biography of Harry S. Truman* 1974.

Tunnell, Gilbert B., Three dimensions of naturalness: An expanded definition of field research, *Psychological Bulletin* 1977, 84(3), 426-437.

Tunyi, I. et al., The influence of geomagnetic activity upon the psychotronical diagnosis and therapy, *Proceedings of the 6th International Conference on Psychotronic Research* 1986, 118-119.

Turner, Gordon, *A Time to Heal: The Autobiography of an Extraordinary Healer*, London: Talmy, Franklin 1974.

Turner, Gordon, *An Outline of Spiritual Healing*, London: Psychic Press 1970.

Turner, Gordon, I experiment in absent treatment (Part 3 of 4-Part Series), *Two Worlds* (Sep) 1969, 281-283.

Turner, Gordon, I treated plants, not patients (Part 2 of 4-Part Series), *Two Worlds* (Aug) 1969, 232-234.

Turner, Gordon, Psychic energy is the power of life (Part 4 of 4-Part Series), *Two Worlds* (Oct) 1969, 302-303.

Turner, Gordon, What power is transmitted in treatment? (Part 1 of 4-Part Series), *Two Worlds* (Jul) 1969, 199-201.

U

U.S. Department of Health, Education and Welfare, *Guide for the clinical evaluation of Analgesic Drugs*, Washington, D.C.: U.S. Government Printing Office.

Ullman, Montague, Parapsychology and Psychiatry Chapter 52.2a In: Freedman, A.; Kaplan, H. and Saddock, B. (Eds), *Comprehensive Textbook of Psychiatry*, 2nd Ed., Baltimore: Williams and Wilkins 1974(b), p. 2552-2561.

Ullman, Montague, Symposium: Psychokinesis on stable systems: Work in progress In: Roll, W.G., Morris, R.L. and Morris, J.D. (Eds), *Research in Parapsychology 1973*, Metuchen, NJ: Scarecrow 1974(a), 120-125.

Ullman, Montague, The Bindelof Story, Part II, *Exceptional Human Experiences* 1994, 12(1), 25-31.

Ullrich, Ann Christine, Traditional healing in the Third World, *J. of Holistic Medicine* 1984, 6(2), 200-212.

Uphoff, Walter and Uphoff, Mary Jo, *Mind over Matter: Implications of Masuaki Kiyota's PK Feats with Metal and Film for: Healing, Physics, Psychiatry, War and Peace, Et Cetera*, Oregon, WI: New Frontiers Center 1980.

Uphoff, Walter and Uphoff, Mary Jo, *New Psychic Frontiers: Your Key to New Worlds*, Gerards Cross, England: Colin Smythe 1980.

Uphoff, Walter, H., Uri Geller, *New Frontiers* 1987, Nos. 22/ 23, 8-9.

Uphoff, Walter/ Uphoff, Mary Jo, *New Psychic Frontiers: Your Key to New Worlds*. Gerards Cross, England: Colin Smythe 1980.

Upledger, John and Vredevoogd, Jon D, *Craniosacral Therapy;* Chicago: Eastland 1983.

Utts, Jessica: Replication and meta-analysis in parapsychology, *Statistical Science* 1991, 6(4) 363-403.

V

van der Post, Laurens., *The Lost World of the Kalahari*, Aylesbury, England: Hazell, Watson and Viney 1973.

Van Dragt, Ryan *Paranormal Healing: A Phenomenology of the Healer's Experience*, Vols. I & II. Unpublished doctoral dissertation, Fuller Theological Seminary, School of Psychology 1980, Abstract from University Microfilms International, printed in White, Rhea A. *Exceptional Human Experience*, 1991, 9(1), 117-118.

Vasiliev, L. L., *Experiments in Distant Influence: Discoveries by Russia's Foremost Parapsychologist*, New York: Dutton 1976. Previously published as *Experiments in Mental Suggestion (Rev. Ed.)* Hampshire, England: Gally Hill Press/ Institute for the Study of Mental Images 1963. (See also review of the latter by Rush, J.H.).

Vasiliev, Leonid L., *Mysterious Phenomena of the Human Psyche* (Translated from Russian), New Hyde Park, NY: University Books 1965.

Vaughan, A., Investigation of Silva Mind Control claims, In: *Research in Parapsychology 1973*, Metuchen, NJ: Scarecrow 1974, 51.

Vilenskaya, Larissa (Ed), Soviet "accumulators" of healing energies, *Psi Research* 1985(b), 4(1), 68-78.

Vilenskaya, Larissa V., Optimal period for biofield activity, *International J. of Paraphysics*, 1976(a), 19(1 & 2), 9-12.

Vilenskaya, Larissa, "Extraordinary" Israelis, *Psi Research* 1985(d), 4(3/ 4), 148-163.

Vilenskaya, Larissa, A scientific approach to some aspects of psychic healing, *International J. of Paraphysics* 1976(b), 10(3), 74-79.

Vilenskaya, Larissa, around Italy in search of "miracles:" The healers who work with animals, *Psi Research* 1985(e), 4(3/ 4), 164-180.

Vilenskaya, Larissa, Bioelectronics in Leningrad and Alma-Ata, *Psi Research* 1982, 1(4), 27-35.

Vilenskaya, Larissa, Development of abilities of remote diagnostics and psychic healing (of Barbara Ivanova), In: Vilenskaya, Larissa (Translater and Editor), *Parapsychology in the USSR, Part III*, San Francisco: Washington Research Center 1981, 46-51.

Vilenskaya, Larissa, Firewalking and beyond, *Psi Research* 1985f, 4(2), 89-109.

Vilenskaya, Larissa, On PK and related subjects' research in the USSR, In: Uphoff, Walter and Uphoff, Mary Jo, *Mind over Matter*, Oregon, WI: New Frontiers Center 1980.

Vilenskaya, Larissa, Psi and Qigong in China: Interview with Paul Dong, *Psi Research* 1985(a), 4(1), 81-95.

Vilenskaya, Larissa, Psychoregualtion and psychic healing, *Parapsychology in the USSR, Part I,* San Francisco: Washington Research Center 1981, 26-33.

Vilenskaya, Larissa, Qigong, psi, healing and human potential in the People's Republic of China, *Psi Research* 1985(c), 4(3/ 4), 124-133.

Vilenskaya, Larissa, Understanding and healing animals: Interview with Penelope Smith, animal consultant, *Psi Research* 1986, 5(1,2), 208-213.

Villoldo, Alberto and Krippner, Stanley, *Healing States: A Journey into the World of Spiritual Healing and Shamanism,* New York: Fireside/ Simon and Schuster 1987.

Vishnu-devananda, S., *Hatha Yoga Pradipika,* New York: Om Lotus 1987.

Vogel, M., Man-plant communication, In: Mitchell, E.D. and White, J., (Eds) *Psychic Exploration,* New York: G.P. Putnam's Sons 1974.

Von Franz, Marie-Louise/ Hillman, James: *Jung's Typology.* Zurich: Spring 1971.

Vu, Alexander, Determining blood pressure at a distance, In: Vilenskaya, Larissa (Translator and Editor), *Parapsychology in the USSR, Part III,* San Francisco: Washington Research Center 1981, 61-62.

W

Walker, Scott et al., Intercessory prayer in the treatment of alcohol abuse and dependence: a pilot investigation, *Alternative Therapies* 1997, 3(6), 79-86.

Wallace, Amy and Henkin, Bill, *The Psychic Healing Book,* New York: Delacorte 1978.

Wallack, Joseph Michael, Testing for the psychokinetic effect on plants: effect of a 'laying on' of hands on germinating corn seed, M.S. Thesis, West Georgia College 1982, Summarized in *Psychological Reports* 1984, 55, 15-18.

Walsh, Roger N., *The Spirit of Shamanism,* New York: Tarcher/ Putnam 1990.

Walsh, Roger, Phenomenological mapping: a method for describing and comparing states of consciousness, *J. of Transpersonal Psychology* 1995, 27(1), 25-56 (5pp refs).

Wan, Sujian/ He, Yuzhu/ Hao, Shuping/ Liu, Yuding/ Yu, Chuan, Qigong Institute, Beijing Military Region, Beijing/ Hebei Langfarg People's Hospital, Beijing Agricultural University, Beijing, Repeated experiments by using emitted qi in treatment of spinal cord injury, *2nd World Conference for Academic Exchange of Medical Qigong, Beijing 1993.*

Wang, Jisheng. Institute of Psychology, Chinese Academy of Sciences, Beijing, Role of qigong on mental health *2nd World Conference for Academic Exchange of Medical Qigong, Beijing 1993.*

Wang, Yonghuai/ Zhou, Lei/ Xu, Dong/ Huang, Junjie/ Li, Yan/ Ge, Zheng, Quantitative survey of systematic deviations in Brownian movement experiment affected by qi, *1st World Conference for Academic Exchange of Medical Qigong. Beijing, 1988.*

Wang, Zhengchang/ Huang, Jain/ Wu, Zijuan – Shanghai Qigong Institute – *Prellminary study of the relationship between qigong and energy metabollem; the changes in blood ATP content (1st World Conference for Academic Exchange of Medical Qigong, Beijing 1988 –* from Database of Sancier).

Wang, Zhengchang/ Shan, Genxing/ Zang, Wenyi – Shanghai Qigong Institute/ Shanghai Institute of Radiation Medicine/ Shanghai Academy of Qigong Research – Preliminary observation on the effect of walql (emitted qi) on the function of making blood *3rd National Academic Conference on Qigong Science, Guangzhou, China. 1990* – from Qigong Database of Sancier.

Watkins, G. K. and Watkins, A. M.. Possible PK influence on the resuscitation of anesthetized mice, *J. of Parapsychology* 1971, 35(4), 257-272.

Watkins, G. K., Watkins, A. M., and Wells, R. A., Further studies on the resuscetation of anesthetized mice, In: Roll, W. G.; Morris, R. L. and Morris, J. D. (Eds), *Research in Parapsychology 1972,* Metuchen, NJ: Scarecrow 1973, 157-159.

Watkins, Graham K. and Watkins, Anita, Apparent psychokinesis on static objects by a 'gifted' subject: A laboratory demonstration, In; Roll, W. G. et al. (Eds), *Research in Parapsychology 1973,* Metuchen, NJ: Scarecrow 1974.

Watkins, Graham K., Psychic healing: The experimental viewpoint, In: Roll, W. G. (Ed),

Research in Parapsychology 1978, Metuchen, NJ: Scarecrow 1979, 21-23.

Watson, Lyall, *Lifetide*, New York: Bantam 1979.

Watson, Lyall., *The Romeo Error*, Garden City, New York: Anchor/ Doubleday 1975.

Webster, H., *Taboo, A Sociological Study*, Stanford, California; Stanford University Press 1942.

Weiler PC, et al, *A measure of malpractice: medical injury, malpractice litigation, and patient compensation*, Cambridge, MA: Harvard University 1993.

Wells, Roger and Klein, Judith, A replication of a "psychic healing" paradigm, *J. of Parapsychology* 1972, 36, 144-147.

Wells, Roger and Watkins, Graham, Linger effects in several PK experiments, In: Morris, J. D.; Roll, W. G. and Morris, R. L., (Eds) *Research in Parapsychology 1974*, Metuchen, NJ: Scarecrow 1975, 143-147.

Wendt, Sharon J. *The Radiant Heart: Healing the Heart, Healing the Soul*, Munster, IN: Radiant Heart Press (520 Ridge Road, Munster, IN 46321) 1995.

West, D. J., *Eleven Lourdes Miracles*, London: Helix 1957.

West, D. J., The investigation of spontaneous cases, *Proceedings of the Society for Psychical Research* 1948(b), 264-300.

West, William, Counsellors and psychotherapists who also heal, *British J. of Guidance and Counselling* 1997, 25(2)

Westerbeke, Patricia; Gover, John and Krippner, Stanley, Subjective reactions to the Phillipino "healers:" A questionnaire study, In: Morris, J. D.; Roll, W. G. and Morris, R. L. (Eds), *Research in Parapsychology 1976*, Metuchen, NJ: Scarecrow 1977, 70-71.

Westlake, A., *The Pattern of Health: A Search for a Greater Understanding of the Life Force in Health and Disease*, Berkeley, California: Shambala 1973.

Westlake, Aubrey T., *The Pattern of Health: A Search For a Greater Understanding of the Life Force In Health and Disease*, New York: Devin-Adair 1961.

Wetzel, Wendy S. Healing touch as a nursing intervention: wound infection following caesarian birth—an anecdotal case study, *J. of Holistic Nursing* 1993, 11(3), 277-285.

Wetzel, Wendy S., Reiki healing: a physi-ologic perspective, *J. of Holistic Nursing* 1989, 7(1), 47-54.

Wharton, Richard and Lewith, George., Complementary Medicine and the General Whitaker, Kay Cordell, *The Reluctant Shaman*, HarperSanFrancisco 1991.

White, John and Krippner, Stanley (Eds), *Future Science*, Garden City, NY: Anchor/ Doubleday 1977.

White, Rhea, A comparison of old and new methods of response to targets in ESP experiments, *J. of the Society for Psychical Research* 1964, 58(1), 21-56.

White, Ruth and Swainson, Mary, *The Healing Spectrum*, Suffolk, England: Neville Spearman, 1979.

Whitmont, Edward C., *The Alchemy of Healing: Psyche and Soma*, Berkeley, CA: Homeopathic Education Services and North Atlantic Books 1993.

Wilbur, Ken., *Eye to Eye, Science and Transpersonal Psychology*, Revision, 1979, 2(1).

Wilkinson, H. P./ Gauld, A. Geomagnetism and anomalous experiences 1868-1980. *Proceedings of the Society for Psychical Research* 1993, 57, 275-310.

Wilson, Colin, The horrors of healing, *The Unexplained* 1983, 12(137), 2734-2737.

Wilson, D. F. Therapeutic touch: Foundations and current knowledge, *Alternative Health Practitioner* 1995, 1(1), 55-66.

Wilson, Sheryl C. and Barber, Theodore X., The fantasy-prone personality: Implications for understanding imagery, hypnosis and parapsychological phenomena, *Psi Research* 1982, 1(3), 94-116.

Winkelman, Michael James, *A Cross-cultural Study of Magico-Religious Practitioners*, Unpublished Doctoral Dissertation, University of CA Irvine 1984.

Winkelman, Michael, A cross-cultural study of shamanistic healers, *J. of Psychoactive Drugs* 1989 (Jan/ Mar), 2(1), 17-24 (from *Exceptional Human Experiences* 1991, 9(2), 265, excerpt #04876).

Winn, Godfrey, *The Quest for Healing*, London: Frederick Muller 1956.

Winstead-Fry, Patricia/ Kijek, Jean, An integrative review and meta-analysis of Therapeutic Touch research, *Alternative Therapies* 1999, 5(6) 59-67.

Winston, Shirley, *Research in Psychic Healing: A Multivariate Experiment*, Unpublished Doctoral Dissertation, Union Graduate School, Yellow Springs, OH 1975.

Wirkus, Mieczyslaw, *Personal Communications* 1987, 1-2-1.

Wirth, Daniel P./ Cram, Jeffery R., Multi-site electromyographic analysis of non-contact therapeutic touch, *International J. of Psychosomatics* 1993, 40(1-4), 47-55.

Wirth, Daniel P./ Cram, Jeffrey R., The psychophysiology of nontraditional prayer, *International J. of Psychosomatics* 1994, 41(1-4), 68-75.

Wirth, Daniel P./ Cram, Jeffrey R./ Chang, Richard J., Multisite electromyographic analysis of Therapeutic Touch and qigong therapy, *Journal of Alternative and Complementary Medicine* 1997, 3(2), 109-118.

Witmer, J./ Zimmerman, M. Intercessory prayer as medical treatment, *Skeptical Inquirer* 1991, 15, 177-180.

Witt, J., Relieving Chronic Pain, *Nurse Pract* 1984, 9(1), 36-38.

Wolfe, L. S. Hopnosis in anesthesiology, in: LeCron, L. M. (Ed), *Techniques of Hypnotherapy*, New York: Julian 1961, 188-212.

Wolfe, L. S./ Millet, J.B. Control of post-operative pain by suggestion under general anesthesia, *American J. of Clinical Hypnosis* 1960, 3, 109-112.

Wolman, Benjamin B. (Ed), *Handbook of Parapsychology*, New York: Van Nostrand 1977, 547-556.

Wolpe, J., *Psychotherapy By Reciprocal Inhibition*, Palo Alto, California: Stanford University Press 1958.

Wooding, Valerie, *John Cain Healing Guide*, England: Van Duren 1980.

Woods, D.L. The Effect of Therapeutic Touch on Disruptive Behaviors of Individuals with Dementia of the Alzheimer Type (Master's thesis), Seattle: University of Washington 1993.

Worrall, Ambrose A. and Worrall, Olga N. with Oursler, Will, *Explore Your Psychic World*, New York: Harper and Row 1970 (Quotes reprinted by permission of the publishers.)

Worrall, Ambrose A. and Worrall, Olga N., *The Gift of Healing*, New York: Harper and Row 1965.

Worrall, Ambrose A., A philosophy of spiritual healing, *Spiritual Frontiers* 1983, 15(2), 23.

Worrall, Olga, *Personal communication* 1982.

Worrall, Olga, *Presentation at Healing in Our Time Conference, Washington, D.C.,* Nov 1981.

Wright, Susan M., The use of therapeutic touch in the management of pain, *Nursing Clinics of North America* 1987, 22(3), 705-714.

Wright, Susan Marie, *Development and Construct Validity of the Energy Field Assessment Form* (Dissertation), Rush University College of Nursing 1988.

Wu, Banghui/ Wu, Ruixian/ Kaiying, Du/ Shiying, Wu/ Jumu, Zhu/ Kongzhi, Song/ Xianggao Li,/ Rongliang, Lan/ Liangzhong Zhaou, Sichuan University, Sichuan Province, China/ Institute of Space Medical Engineering, China, Effects of emitted qi on silicon's crystalline state, *1st World Conference for Academic Exchange of Medical Qigong, Beijing 1988.*

Wu, Rongqing/ Xi, Xiaoming/ Chen, Ling/ Qi, Songping – Beijing College of Traditional Chinese Medicine – *Investigation of the biological effect of emitted qi with fluorescence probes (1st World Conference for Academic Exchange of Medical Qigong, Beijing 1988* – from Database of Sancier).

Wu, Zudao/ Yang, Guisheng – Dept Microbiology, Shandong University/ Qigong Science Research Society, Shandong, China – Effect of emitted qi on molecular conformation of cellulase *3rd National Academic Conference on Qigong Science, Guangzhou, China. 1990* – from Qigong Database of Sancier.

X

Xiu, Ruijuan/ Ying, Xiaoyou/ Cheng, Jun/ Duan, Chouggao/ Tang, Tao – Institute of Microcirculation, CAMS, Beijing – Studies of qigong effect on the human body [via] macro and micro-circulatory parameters measurement. *1st World Conference for Academic Exchange of Medical Qigong, Beijing 1988.*

Xu, Hefan/ Xue, Huiling/ Zhang, Chenging/ Shao, Xiangming/ Liu, Guanchan/ Zhou,

Qijing/ Yu, Fanger/ Wu, Kang – Jiangsu Provincial Research Institute of Traditional Chinese Medicine, China/ Dept Pathology, Naval Medical College, China/ Chassis Plant, Nanjing Automobile Factory, Nanjing, China – Study of the effects and mechanism of qigong waiqi (emitted qi) on implanted tumors in mice *3rd National Academic Conference on Qigong Science, Guangzhou, China. 1990* – from Qigong Database of Sancier.

Y

Yan, Naihau, Sensational Qigong feats, *China Reconstructs* 1985 (Jul) 34(7), 60-61.

Yan, Xin/ Lu, Zuyin/ Yan, Sixian/ Li, Shengping, Municipal Institute of Traditional Chinese Medicine of Chongqing, Sichuan Province, China/ Institute of High Energy Physics, Academia Sinica, Beijing/ Tsinghua University, Beijing, Effect of emitted qi on the polarized plane of a laser beam, *1st World Conference for Academic Exchange of Medical Qigong, Beijing 1988.*

Yan, Xuanzuo [and others] – Dept Immunology, Biejing College of Traditional Chinese Medicine, Beijing – Effects of qigong waiqi (emitted qi) on Immune function of immunosuppressed mice *3rd National Academic Conference on Qigong Science, Guangzhou, China. 1990* – from Qigong Database of Sancier.

Yang, Jinhong/ Guan, Haoben – Guangzhou College of Traditional Chinese Medicine, Guangzhou – Effect of emitted qi on human lymphocytes and tumor cells in vitro *3rd National Academic Conference on Qigong Science, Guangzhou, China. 1990 – from Qigong Database of Sancier).*

Yang, Kongshun/ Guo, Zhongliang/ Xu, Hong/ Lin, Housheng/ Zhao, Bangzu/ Zhou, Daohong, Guiyang College of Traditional Chinese Medicine, Guizhou Province/ Shanghai Qigong Institute/ Guiyang College of Traditional Chinese Medicine, Guizhou Province, China, Influence of electrical lesion of the periaqueductal gray (PAG) on the analgesic effect of emitted qi in rats, *1st World Conference for Academic Exchange of Medical Qigong, Beijing 1988.*

Yang, Kongshun/ Xu, Hong/ Guo, Zhongliang/ Zhao, Bangzu/ Li, Zhaohuei, Guiyang College

of Traditional Chinese Medicine, Guizhou Province, China, Analgesic effect of emitted qi on white rats. *1st World Conference for Academic Exchange of Medical Qigong, Beijing 1988.*

Yang, Sihuan/ Shi, Jiming/ Yang, Qifei/ Zheng, Ziliang – Institute of Qigong Sciences, Beijing College of Traditional Chinese Medicine/ Medical University of Shandong, China – Experlmental research on the braking phenomenon of the upper limbs evoked by qigong waiqi (emitted qi) (*3rd National Academic Conference on Qigong Science, Guangzhou, China. 1990*– from Qigong Database of Sancier.

Yao, Yuzhong/ Zhang, Jinmei/ Liu, Gangquan/ Wang, Liwei. Sun Yat-Sen Univeristy of Medical Sciences, Guangzhou, China, Effects of emitted qi on the spontaneous discharges of cerebellar neurons in rats, *1st World Conference for Academic Exchange of Medical Qigong, Beijing 1988.*

Ye, Fanyang/ Chen, Tainyou/ Zhang,Wengong, Qigong Clinic, Fuzhou Hospital of Traditional Chinese Medicine, Fuzhou, China, IR study of heavy water treated by emitted qi, *2nd World Conference for Academic Exchange of Medical Qigong, Beijing 1993.*

Ye, Ming/ Shen, Jiaqi/ Yang, Yuanjin/ Fan, Juefen/ Liu, Guizheng/ Wu, Xiaohong – Qigong Institute, Shanghai Academy of Traditional Chinese Medicine – Observatlon of In vitro effect of emitted qi on human peripheral blood lymphocytes (*1st World Conference for Academic Exchange of Medical Qigong, Beijing 1988 -* from Database of Sancier).

Yogananda, P., *Autobiography of a Yogi*, Los Angeles: Self-Realization Fellowship 1946.

Yogananda, P., *Scientific Healing Affirmations: Theory and Practice of Concentration*, Los Angeles: Self-Realization Fellowship 1962.

Yongjie, Zhao/ Hongzhang, Xu, EHBF Radiation: Special features of the time response, *Psi Research* 1982, 1(4), 20-22.

Young, Alan, Some implications of medical beliefs and practices for social anthropology, *American Anthropologist* 1976, 78(1), 5-24.

Young, Alan, *Spiritual Healing: Miracle or Mirage*, Marina del Rey, CA: DeVorss 1981.

Young, D./ Aung, S. An experimental test of psychic diagnosis of disease, *Journal of Alternative and Complementary Medicine* 1997, 3(1), 39-53.

Yuan, Zhifu – Family Acupuncture Center, San Clemente, CA 92672, USA – Survey of 100 doctors using simulated qigong In the USA (*2nd World Conference for Academic Exchange of Medical Qigong. Beijing 1993* – from Qigong Database of Sancier.

Z

Zambetis, Donna Blanche, *Attitudes of Women with Breast Cancer Toward Therapeutic Touch* (Master's thesis), Michigan State University 1996.

Zeng, Qingnan, Qigong - ancient way to good health, *China Reconstructs* 1985, 34(7), 56-57 (Cited in *Psi Research* 1985, 4(3/ 4), 139).

Zezulka, J., Biotronic Healing, *Psychoenergetic Systems* 1976, 1, 145-147.

Zezulka, J., One healer's views *Proceedings of the Second International Congress on Psychotronic Research*, Paris: Institut Metaphysique International 1975.

Zhang, Ciling/ Chen, Fakai/ Zhang, Jinmei/ Wang, Ping - Sun Yat-Sen University of Medical Sciences, Guangzhou/ Association of Natural Gong of Shen Xuan Sen Jiao, China - Preliminary studies of effects of emitted qi on pneumocystis carinii In Infected rats (AIDS related) *3rd National Academic Conference on Qigong Science, Guangzhou, China. 1990* - from Qigong Database of Sancier.

Zhang, Fengde/ Zhao, Jing/ Yue, Huiqin/ Liu, Guiqin/ Liu, Anxi – Dept Biology, Nankai University, Tianjin, China – Study of molecular biology of functional mechanism of emitted qi on proteins *3rd National Academic Conference on Qigong Science, Guangzhou, China. 1990* – from Qigong Database of Sancier.

Zhang, Fengde/ Zhao, Jing/ Yue, Huiqin/ Liu, Guiqin/ Zhao, Xiaomei, Dept Biology, Nakai University, Tianji, Beijing College of Acupuncture, Moxibustion, Traumotology, China, Effect of emitted qi on the reaction of malate dehyrogenase. *2nd World Conference for Academic Exchange of Medical Qigong, Beijing 1993*.

Zhang, Jiang [and others] – China – Influence of qigong waiqi (emitted qi) on volume of blood flow to visceral organs In rabbits under normal and hemorrhagic shock conditions. *3rd National Academic Conference on Qigong Science, Guangzhou, China. 1990* – from Qigong Database of Sancier.

Zhang, Jie/ Hu, Dongwu/ Ye, Zhumei – Fuzhou General Hospital, Nanjing Command PLA, Fuzhou – Effect of waiqi (emitted qi) on experimental bone fracture in mice *3rd National Academic Conference on Qigong Science, Guangzhou, China. 1990* – from Qigong Database of Sancier.

Zhang, Jinmei/ Chen, Yanfeng/ He, Jinhong/ Xian, Tian/ Yi Yuan - Dept Physiology, Sun Yat-Sen University of Medical Sciences, Guangzhou, China/ Xian Tian Yi Yuan Qigong, Guangdon Qigong Association, China - Analgeslc effect of emitted qi and the preliminary study of its mechanism *3rd National Academic Conference on Qigong Science, Guangzhou, China. 1990* – from Qigong Database of Sancier.

Zhang, Jinmei/ Liu, Ganquan/ Yao, Yuzhong/ Ming, Huasheng/ Zhou, Donglin/ Zheng, Fankai – Dept Physiology, Sun Yat-Sen University of Medical Sciences, Guangzhou/ Yi Ji Chan of Internal Power of Shaoling Qigong, China – Antagonism of bicuculline on the Inhibitory effect of emitted qi on spontaneous unit activites of cerebellar neurons *3rd National Academic Conference on Qigong Science, Guangzhou, China. 1990* – from Qigong Database of Sancier.

Zhang, Jinmei/ Zhang, Ciling/ Chen, Fakai, Sun Yat-Sen University of Medical Sciences, Guangzhou 510060, China, Preliminary study of the effect of emitted qi on experimental animals infected by pneumocysitis carinii, *2nd World Conference for Academic Exchange of Medical Qigong, Beijing 1993*.

Zhang, Li/ Wang, Li/ Yan, Yuanzuo/ Ge, Dongyu/ Zhou, Yong, Institute of Qigong Science, Beijing College of Traditional Chinese Medicine, Beijing 100029, Adjusting effect of emitted qi on the immune function of cold-stressed mice, *2nd World Conference for Academic Exchange of Medical Qigong, Beijing 1993*.

Zhang, Li/ Yan, Xuanzuo/ Wang, Shuhua/ Tao, Jundi/ Gu, Ligan/ Xu, Yin/ Zhou, Young/ Liu, Dong – Institute of Qigong Science, Beijing College of Traditional Chinese Medicine – *Immune regulation effect of emitted qi on Immunosuppressed animal model* (1st World Conference for Academic Exchangeof Medical Qigong, Beijing 1988 – from Database of Sancier).

Zhang, Meigui/ Ye, Zhengzhong/ Feng, Wanling/ Lai, Ronghong – Central Laboratory, Guanzhou Medical College, Guanzhou/ Dept Anatomy, Guangzhou Medical College, Guanzhou, China – Experimental study on the bioeffect of qigong waiqi (emitted qi) on propagation of diploid fibroblast *3rd National Academic Conference on Qigong Science, Guangzhou, China. 1990* – from Qigong Database of Sancier.

Zhang, Mengdan/ Zhu, Fangzhou/ Tan, Ming/ Li, Jiansong/ Duan, Weicai – Zhongshan University, Guangzhou/ Guangdong Qigong Science Association, Guangzhou, China – Effect of qigong emanation (emitted qi) on surface structure and electrokinetic behaviour of Rap cells *3rd National Academic Conference on Qigong Science, Guangzhou, China. 1990* – from Qigong Database of Sancier.

Zhang, Yuanming/ Tian, Laike/ Yan, Wenhong – Dept Physics, Northwestern University, Chengdu, China – Impact of qigong telecontrol experiment (emitted qi) on structure of matter *3rd National Academic Conference on Qigong Science, Guangzhou, China. 1990* – from Qigong Database of Sancier.

Zhang, Zuqi/ Pei, Zhaohua/ Huang, Yilian/ Huang, Pingfang – South China Normal University, Guangzhou/ Guangzhou Bao Lin Qigong School, Guangzhou, China – Waiqi (emitted qi) accelerates resuscitation of frozen tilapia and its mechanism *3rd National Academic Conference on Qigong Science, Guangzhou, China. 1990* – from Qigong Database of Sancier.

Zhao, Guang/ Xie, Qigang – Xiyuan Hospital, China Academy of Tradtional Chinese Medicine, Beijing and Beijing Normal University – A case of cerebral atrophy cured by qigong (*1st World Conference for Academic Exchange of Medical Qigong, Beijing 1988* – from Qigong Database of Sancier.

Zhao, Jing/ Zhan, Diankun/ Zhao, Xiaomei/ Yang, Guisheng, Nankai University, Tianjin, Beijing College of Acupuncture, Moxibustion, Traumotology, Tianjin Society of Somatic Science, China, Effect of emitted qi on the chemical shift of active proton, *2nd World Conference for Academic Exchange of Medical Qigong, Beijing 1993.*

Zhao, Tongjian/ Li, Caixi/ Lu, Danyun/ Xu, Qinahong - XuanWu Hospital China Academy of Chinese Traditional Medicine, Beijing/ China Academy of Chinese Traditional Chinese Medicine/ Scientific Research Institute of the National Medicine, Beijing – Investigation of effects of external energy waiqi (emitted qi) on gilomas of mice *3rd National Academic Conference on Qigong Science, Guangzhou, China. 1990* – from Qigong Database of Sancier.

Zhong, Ziliang/ Yu, Bingzhen/ Wang, Jianmin – Teacher's Office of Biological Medical Engineering of Shandong Medical University, Shandong/ Animal's Experimental Center, Physiological Teacher's Office of Shandong Medical University, Shangdong, China – Utilizing qigong (emitted qi) to make people sleep and wake up *3rd National Academic Conference on Qigong Science, Guangzhou, China. 1990* - from Qigong Database of Sancier.

Zhou, Lidong [and others] – First Medical College of PLA, Guangzhou – Mechanisms of the anti-tumor effect of qigong waiqi (emitted qi) *3rd National Academic Conference on Qigong Science, Guangzhou, China. 1990* – from Qigong Database of Sancier.

Zhou, Yong [and others] – Institute of Qigong Science, Beijing College of Traditional Chinese Medicine – Marvellous phenomenon of human peculiar function – disappearance of hundreds millions of bacteria from tube (destruction of E. coli by emitted qi) *3rd National Academic Conference on Qigong Science, Guangzhou, China. 1990* – from Qigong Database of Sancier.

Zhou, Yong/ Yan, Xuanzuo/ Zhang, Li, Qigong Institute, Beijing College of Traditional Chinese Medicine, Beijing 100029, Effect of emitted qi on the change of antibody dependence cell-mediated cytotoxicity (ADCC) of K cell o mice caused by injury of left and right brain cortex, *2nd World Conference for Academic Exchange of Medical Qigong, Beijing 1993.*

Zhukoborsky, Savely, An experimental approach to the study of psychic healing In: Vilenskaya, Larissa, Translator and Editor, *Parapsychology in the USSR, Part III*, San Francisco: Washington Research Center 1981, 52-54.

Zigmond, A.S./ Snaith, R.P. The hospital anxiety and depression scale, *Acta Psychaitrica Scandinavia* 1983, 67, 361-370 .

Zimmels, H. J. *Magicians, Theologians and Doctors*, London: Edward Goldston and Sons 1952.

Zukav, Gary, *The Dancing Wu Li Masters*, New York: William Morrow 1979.

NAME INDEX

SUBJECT INDEX

Healing Research

These additional volumes by Dr. Benor will be released in 2002-2003.

Vol. II: *Consciousness, Bioenergy and Healing* presents complementary therapies as energy medicine - placing mind/body medicine and spiritual healing as common denominators among all therapies. It also explores psychological self-healing, demonstrating how the mind and the emotions can have profound effects on the body.

Vol. III: *Science, Spirit and the Eternal Soul* reviews fascinating scientific research which supports many of the reports of healers and mystics, including: out-of-body experiences, near-death and pre-death experiences, apparitions, channeling, reincarnation, spiritual aspects of health, and survival of the spirit and soul after death. Studies confirm many of these experiences. This research, along with mystical experiences and anecdotal reports of ghost, spirits, nature spirits and angels, form a coherent pattern of worlds beyond our own.

Vol. IV: *Theory and Practice of Spiritual Healing* is a definitive discussion of healing research and practice. A spectrum of theories explain spiritual healing, supporting biological energy medicine and non-local consciousness as new paradigms. This volume includes a comprehensive, topical summary of the previous volumes. Dr. Benor's personal experiences as a practicing psychiatric psychotherapist and healer are also shared.

Daniel J. Benor, M.D. is a practicing wholistic psychiatrist. As author of the Healing Research series, he is an internationally recognized authority on the scientific study of spiritual healing. He is a Founding Diplomate of the American Board of Holistic Medicine and on the advisory board of the journals, Alternative Therapies in Health and Medicine, Subtle Energies (ISSSEEM), and Frontier Sciences. He is on the Board of Directors of ISSSEEM, a member of the Advisory Council of the Association for Comprehensive Energy Psychotherapy (ACEP), and on the Advisory Board of the Research Council for Complementary Medicine (UK). He is the editor and publisher of the newly launched International Journal of Healing and Caring - On Line. He can be contacted through his web site at www.WholisticHealingResearch.com.